T0123883

THE LIFE OF OUR LORD JESUS CHRIST IN MEDITATIONS

VOLUME II

THE LIFE OF OUR LORD JESUS CHRIST

IN MEDITATIONS

BY

MAURICE MESCHLER, S.J.

TRANSLATED BY SISTER MARY MARGARET, O.S.B.

VOLUME II

B. HERDER BOOK CO.
15 & 17 SOUTH BROADWAY, ST. LOUIS 2, MO.
AND
33 QUEEN SQUARE, LONDON, W. C.
1953

Printed in U.S.A.

NIHIL OBSTAT

Rt. Rev. Wm. Fischer, S.T.D.

Censor Librorum

IMPRIMATUR

✠ *Joseph E. Ritter*

Archiepiscopus

Sti. Ludovici, die 23 Nov. 1949

Tenth Printing

Library of Congress Catalog Card Number: 50-1304

Vail-Ballou Press, Inc., Binghamton and New York

CONTENTS

II

THE TEMPORAL LIFE OF JESUS

II. THE PUBLIC LIFE OF JESUS

E. THE PUBLIC LIFE OF JESUS FROM THE FEAST OF TABERNACLES TO THE FEAST OF THE DEDICATION OF THE TEMPLE

(continued.)

PAGE

The Blind and Dumb Demoniac 1
The Woman Who Called Our Lady Blessed 6
The Sign of Jonas 9
Our Lord's Censure of the Pharisees 13
Open, Fearless Confession 17
Warning Against Covetousness 21
Excess of Temporal Cares 24
Apostolic Poverty 27
The Office of Superior 30
Decision for or against the Kingdom of Christ 33
The Parable of the Fig-tree 37
The Healing of the Crippled Woman 41
The Parable of the Grain of Mustard-seed 44
The Parable of the Leaven 46
The Parable of the Seed 47

F. THE PUBLIC LIFE OF JESUS FROM THE FEAST OF THE DEDICATION OF THE TEMPLE UNTIL THE PASSION

The Feast of the Dedication 49
The Number of the Elect, and the Rejection of Israel 54
Attempt of Herod and the Pharisees to Intimidate Our Lord 57
The Dinner in the Pharisee's House. First Part: the Dropsical Man . . . 61
Second Part: Parable of the Order of Rank at a Marriage-feast . . 63
Third Part: Advice to the Host 65
Fourth Part: The Parable of the Great Supper 67
Renunciation and Hatred of Self, the Indispensable Condition of the Following of Christ 71
The Parable of the Lost Sheep and the Lost Groat 76
The Parable of the Prodigal Son 80
The Parable of the Unjust Steward 84
The Parable of the Rich Man and Lazarus 88
Three Apostolic Virtues 92
The Raising of Lazarus 94

PAGE
The Decision to Put Our Saviour to Death 105
The Ten Lepers 110
The Coming of the Kingdom of God 113
The Parable of the Unjust Judge 116
The Parable of the Pharisee and the Publican 118
Indissolubility of Marriage. Virginity 121
Our Saviour and the Children 125
The Rich Young Man 129
Lesson upon Riches and Voluntary Poverty 134
The Laborers in the Vineyard 139
Prediction of the Passion 143
The Sons of Zebedee 145
The Blind Man of Jericho 149
Zacheus 152
The Parable of the Ten Pounds 156
The Meal at Bethania 159
The Entry into Jerusalem 164
The Fig-tree 170
The Purification of the Temple 173
The Parable of the Husbandmen 179
The Parable of the Marriage-feast 182
The Coin of Tribute 186
Repulse of the Sadducees 190
Last Repulse of the Pharisees 193
The Censure of the Pharisees 197
The Widow's Mite 202
The Gentiles and the Vow of Sacrifice 204
The Discourse on Mount Olivet. First and Second Part. Prediction of Persecutions, of the Chastisement to Overtake the City, and of the Tokens of the Last Judgment 208
The Discourse on Mount Olivet. Third Part. The Last Judgment 215
Preparation for Our Lord's Advent. Parables of the Porter, the Virgins, and the Talents 223

G. RETROSPECT OF THE PUBLIC LIFE OF JESUS

The Teaching of Our Lord 228
The Miracles of Our Lord 233
The Example of Virtue Set by Jesus 238
Our Saviour's Example of Virtue in Relation to God 238
Our Saviour's Example of Virtue in Relation to His Neighbor . . . 245
Our Saviour's Example of Virtue in Relation to Himself 249
Concluding Meditation upon the Active Life of Jesus. Results of His Teaching and Miracles 254

III. THE LIFE OF THE PASSION, AND THE DEATH OF JESUS

Prediction of the Passion. Introduction to the Meditations upon the Passion 258
Judas Betrays Our Lord for Money 262
Preparation of the Paschal Lamb 267
The Legal Paschal Meal. First Part of the Last Supper 271
Christ Washes His Disciples' Feet. Second Part of the Last Supper . . . 277
The Institution of the Holy Eucharist. Third Part of the Last Supper . . 281
The Farewell Discourse. Fourth Part of the Last Supper. Introduction to the Farewell Discourse 288

PAGE

The Farewell Discourse. First Part: The Last Charge 292
The Farewell Discourse. Second Part: The Last Words of Comfort . . 298
Christ's Prayer for His Disciples 308
The Walk to the Mount of Olives 316
The Agony on Mount Olivet 320
The Arrest of Jesus 329
The First Judicial Sitting in Caiphas' House 335
Peter's Denial of Jesus 341
The Rest of the Night of the Passion, in Caiphas' House 346
Final Sentence of the Great Council 348
The End of Judas 352
First Hearing before Pilate 355
Jesus before Herod 361
Second Appearance before Pilate. Barabbas. Pilate Washes His Hands . . 364
The Scourging 370
Our Lord Is Mocked and Crowned with Thorns 373
Last Stage of the Proceedings under Pilate 377
Condemnation of Jesus 381
The Carrying of the Cross 385
The Escort of Our Cross-bearing Saviour 389
The Crucifixion 393
The Title over the Cross 397
The Division of our Saviour's Garments 399
Jesus Is Mocked on the Cross 401
The Good Thief 403
The Mother of Jesus and His Friends and Relatives beneath the Cross . . 405
The Eclipse of the Sun 408
The Desolation of Jesus on the Cross 410
The Thirst of Jesus on the Cross 414
The Death of Jesus on the Cross 416
The Opening of Jesus' Side 423
The Descent from the Cross 427
The Burial of Jesus 431
The Great Sabbath 434

III

THE GLORIOUS LIFE OF JESUS

1. THE GLORIOUS LIFE OF JESUS ON EARTH

The Resurrection of Christ 439
The Glorious Life from the Resurrection to the Ascension. Aim and Signification of This Life 445
The Revelation of the Resurrection to Christ's Enemies 446
Christ Appears to His Blessed Mother 449
The Holy Women at the Sepulcher 451
Peter and John at the Sepulcher. Our Lord Appears to Peter 455
St. Mary Magdalen 458
The Disciples on the Way to Emmaus 462
Christ's Manifestation of Himself to the Apostles in the Cœnaculum . . 466
Our Lord Appears to St. Thomas 469
The Apparition at the Lake of Genesareth 472

PAGE
The Apparition on the Mountain 476
Retrospect of the Glorious Life on Earth 479

2. THE GLORIOUS LIFE OF JESUS IN HEAVEN

The Ascension 482
Christ's Sitting at the Right Hand of God 486
The Days Preceding the Descent of the Holy Ghost 489
The Descent of the Holy Ghost 493

IV

MYSTICAL LIFE OF JESUS IN THE CHURCH

The Life of Jesus in the Holy Eucharist 501
Christ in the Church 508
Christ Continues to Live in the Christian People 514
Christ and the Religious State 519
Christ and the Hierarchy 524
Christ and the Saints of the Church 529
Christ and the World 533
Concluding Meditation 538
The Gospels for Sundays and Feast-days 553
Index 555

Maps

1. Plan of Jerusalem.
2. Sketch of the Temple.

II

THE TEMPORAL LIFE OF JESUS

II. THE PUBLIC LIFE OF JESUS

E. The Public Life of Jesus from the Feast of Tabernacles to the Feast of the Dedication of the Temple (continued).

The Blind and Dumb Demoniac

Luke 11:14. And he was casting out a devil, and the same was dumb. And when he had cast out the devil, the dumb spoke; and the multitudes were in admiration at it.—15. But some of them said: "He casteth out devils by Beelzebub, the prince of devils."—16. And others tempting, asked of him a sign from heaven.—17. But he seeing their thoughts, said to them: "Every kingdom divided against itself shall be brought to desolation, and house upon house shall fall.—18. And if Satan also be divided against himself, how shall his kingdom stand? Because you say that through Beelzebub I cast out devils.—19. Now if I cast out devils by Beelzebub, by whom do your children cast them out? Therefore they shall be your judges.—20. But if I by the finger of God cast out devils, doubtless the kingdom of God is come upon you.—21. When a strong man armed keepeth his court, those things are in peace which he possesseth.—22. But if a stronger than he come upon him and overcome him, he will take away all his armor wherein he trusted, and will distribute his spoils.—23. He that is not with me, is against me; and he that gathereth not with me, scattereth.—24. When the unclean spirit is gone out of a man, he walketh through places without water, seeking rest; and not finding, he saith: I will return into my house whence I came out.—25. And when he is come, he findeth it swept and garnished.—26. Then he goeth and taketh with him seven other spirits more wicked than himself, and entering in they dwell there. And the last state of that man becomes worse than the first."

Matt. 12:22. Then was offered to him one possessed with a devil, blind and dumb; and he healed him, so that he spoke and saw.—23. And all the multitudes were amazed, and said: "Is not this the Son of David?"—24. But the Pharisees hearing it, said: "This man casteth not out devils but by Beelzebub the prince of the devils."—25. And Jesus knowing their thoughts, said to them: "Every kingdom divided against itself shall be made desolate; and every city or house divided against itself shall not stand.—26. And if Satan cast out Satan, he is divided against himself; how then shall his kingdom stand?—27. And if I by Beelzebub cast out devils, by whom do your children cast them out? Therefore they shall be your judges.—28. But if I by the Spirit of God cast out devils, then is the kingdom of God come upon you.—29. Or how can anyone enter into the house of the strong, and rifle his goods, unless he first bind the strong? And then he will rifle his house.—30. He that is not with me, is against me; and he that gathereth not with me, scattereth.—31. Therefore I say to you: Every sin and blasphemy shall be forgiven men, but the blasphemy of the Spirit shall not be forgiven.—32. And whosoever shall speak a word against the Son of Man, it shall be forgiven him; but he that shall speak against the Holy Ghost, it shall not be forgiven him, neither in this world nor in the world to come.—33. Either make the tree good, and its fruit good; or make the tree evil, and its fruit evil; for by the fruit the tree is known.—34. O generation of vipers, how can you speak good things, whereas you are evil? For out of the abundance of the heart the mouth speaketh.—35. A good man out of a good treasure bringeth forth good things; and an evil man out of an evil treasure bringeth forth evil things.—36. But I say unto you, that every idle word that men shall speak, they shall render an account for it in the day of judgment.—37. For by thy words thou shalt be justified, and by thy words though shalt be condemned. . . .—43. And when an unclean spirit is gone out of a man, he walketh through dry places seeking rest, and findeth none.—44. Then he saith: I will return into my house from whence I came out. And coming he findeth it empty, swept, and garnished.—45. Then he goeth, and taketh with him seven other spirits more wicked than himself, and they enter in and dwell there; and the last state of that man is made worse than the first. So shall it be also to this wicked generation."

MARK 3:22. And the scribes who were come down from Jerusalem said: "He hath Beelzebub, and by the prince of devils he casteth out devils."—23. And after he had called them together, he said to them in parables: "How can Satan cast out Satan?—24. And if a kingdom be divided against itself, that kingdom cannot stand.—25. And if a house be divided against itself, that house cannot stand.—26. And if Satan be risen up against himself, he is divided, and cannot stand, but hath an end.—27. No man can enter into the house of a strong man and rob him of his goods, unless he first bind the strong man, and then shall he plunder his house.—28. Amen I say to you, that all sins shall be forgiven unto the sons of men, and the blasphemies wherewith they shall blaspheme;—29. But he that shall blaspheme against the Holy Ghost, shall never have forgiveness, but shall be guilty of an everlasting sin."—30. Because they said: "He hath an unclean spirit."

We are not told where the cure of the blind and dumb demoniac was wrought; probably it was in Judaea. Judaea seems also to have been the scene of the following mysteries, up to the Feast of the Dedication. According to St. Mark's statement (3:22) this miracle at all events took place in the lowlands.

1. OUR SAVIOUR HEALS A BLIND AND DUMB DEMONIAC

The miracle was as follows: A demoniac who was both blind and dumb was brought to our Saviour (Matt. 12:22). According to St. Luke the blindness and dumbness would seem to have been the effect of possession, for this devil was dumb, and as soon as he was cast out the dumb man spoke (Luke 11:14). According to St. Matthew's version the miracle may have been threefold; cure of dumbness, cure of blindness, and expulsion of the devil. In any case it was an extraordinary and palpable miracle, and yet wrought in such a simple manner.

The effect it produced upon the people was therefore also extraordinary. All were astonished and cried out: "Is not this the Son of David?" (i.e. the Messias.) Probably this cry had never hitherto been so loud and universal.

2. THE PHARISEES TAKE OCCASION FROM THE MIRACLE TO BLASPHEME AGAINST OUR LORD

This great miracle and the serious effect produced by it upon the people irritated the Pharisees and their adherents to the highest pitch, and they spread abroad amongst the people (yet so as not to be heard by our Saviour) the rumor that He Himself was possessed by Beelzebub (Mark 3:22), and that He only cast out devils through him, the prince of the devils (Matt. 12:24; Luke 11:15).

This was a terrible outbreak of unbelief, blasphemy, and scorn. Beelzebub was the idol of the Accaronites (IV Kings 1:3), the god of flies and insects, probably because he was supposed to protect the country against the plague of flies. He was called the prince of the devils, because they are the principle of destruction, death and decay, and flies are the symbol of decay; for this reason he is called by St. Mark an "unclean spirit" (3:30). The Pharisees spread this report amongst the people, and perhaps there may have been many who agreed with them (Luke 11:15).

3. OUR SAVIOUR REPUDIATES THE BLASPHEMY

But our Saviour was not ignorant of what had been said (Luke 11:17; Matt. 12:25). He therefore called the people together, and gave His answer partly openly, partly in a parable (Mark 3:23). This answer was threefold.

Our Saviour first points out the folly and absurdity of the blasphemy, and this in two ways. "How," He says, "can Satan cast out Satan? Then he is divided against himself, and his kingdom cannot stand" (Mark 3:23–26; Matt. 12:25, 26; Luke 11:17, 18), any more than any other kingdom, or the Israelite nation itself, in which the kingdoms of Israel and Juda made war upon each other. Further, if it be true that I cast out devils through the devil, what follows from this, but that your sons, i.e. the Apostles or your own exorcists (Acts 19:13), are also possessed?

You surely do not mean to imply that (Luke 11:19; Matt. 12:27).

Secondly, our Saviour draws from the point gained a very important positive conclusion. If, then, I do not cast out devils through the devil, I do it through the finger of God (Luke 11:20; Matt. 12:28; Ex. 8:19), i.e. through the Holy Ghost (Matt. 12:28), and then there is One stronger than the devil in the world; then the kingdom of God is come upon you (Matt. 12:28; Luke 11:20). A strong man is overcome, disarmed, and robbed of his possessions only by one stronger than himself (Matt. 12:29; Mark 3:27; Luke 11:21, 22). The Messias and Satan were both known by the appellation of "the Strong One" (Isa. 11:2–4; Soph. 1:14). In every case of expulsion of devils the power of the Stronger is most palpably shown, and to a still greater degree in the redemption of the entire human race from the power of the prince of the world (John 12:31; I John 3:8). And our Saviour seals this truth with the inference that there is no middle position and no temporizing in the battle between the Strong One and the Stronger. "He that is not with Me, is against Me; and he that gathereth not with Me, scattereth" (Matt. 11:30; Luke 11:23). This applies to all, and the last words especially to the leaders and pastors of Israel, whose task it was to "gather," in accordance with the example and task of the Messias (Matt. 23:27; John 11:52; Ps. 105:47; Ez. 36:24). Whoever resists the Messias gives up the task of the Israelite nation, falls away from truth and morality, and is a hireling and destroyer (John 10:12).

Thirdly, our Saviour answers by a condemnation and a threat of punishment. First, He designates their conduct as the most terrible sin, viz. blasphemy and sin against the Holy Ghost. He shows the heinousness of this sin by its essential characteristics. It consists in ascribing to the devil, out of malice and obduracy of heart, miracles wrought by the Holy Ghost for the confirmation of faith and the conversion of sinners (Mark 3:30). It is therefore a sin of the hardened, obdurate will, a sin of malice, not of weakness such as may be the case with blasphemies against the Son of Man, in Whom the Godhead is not so apparent as in the aforesaid miracles, which are convincing proofs of the divine truth. Secondly, our Saviour shows the awfulness of this sin from its punishment. It obtains no forgiveness; not because it cannot be forgiven, but because our Lord foresees that as a matter of fact such blasphemers will not repent, or that God has decided not to give them those special graces which lead to conversion, on account of their wickedness and hardness of heart (Mark 3:28–30; Matt. 12:31, 32). This wickedness, says our Saviour further, exists in the Pharisees. For if it is true that a good tree brings forth good fruit, and that good words proceed from a good heart; and if the contrary also is true; what a viper-brood of wickedness, unbelief and malice you must be, who utter such blasphemies! (Matt. 12:33, 34.) Therefore the judgment awaits you. For if even an idle word is judged and punished, how much more then such blasphemy! (Matt. 12:36, 37.) Lastly, our Saviour casts the blasphemy concerning possession back upon the Pharisees themselves, by applying to all the people (or at any rate to the pharisaically-minded among them) the similitude of the devil who, when he has been driven out of a soul, returns with a reinforcement of other devils and takes possession of it anew, and with worse consequences. Formerly the nation had been possessed by the "unclean spirit" of idolatry; freed from this after the Babylonian captivity, it fell a prey to the spirits of unbelief in Sadduceeism and of incarnate pride in Pharisaism; and thus the "last things" were and were still becoming really "worse," since they rejected the Messias, blasphemed the Holy Ghost, raged against the Church, and lastly, like a host of raving madmen and demoniacs, perished with their city and Temple (Matt. 12:43–45; Luke 11:24–26). That was also an expulsion of devils, but a fatal one, and a terrible judgment upon their sins against the Holy Ghost.

This mystery is full of significance from many points of view. In the first place, it shows the growing opposition and hostility to our Saviour on the part of the Pharisees and their party, and the progress of their perversity and unbelief. They already go farther in their malice and fury than on the Feast of Tabernacles (John 7:20; 8:48). Our Saviour also pronounces the sentence of their rejection more plainly and emphatically (John 8:44), calling them (as John the Baptist had formerly done) a generation of vipers, and declaring them all to be possessed by the devil. Thus the position becomes more and more strained. Secondly, as regards our Saviour, we see His glorious intellect revealed here, as well as His moderation and patience in the face of these frightful and revolting blasphemies; His beautiful and fertile mind is seen in His choice of such telling similitudes and His harmonious development of them (as, for example, that of the strong man whom the enemy overcomes, and that of the restless nature of the unclean spirits); then the acuteness and readiness with which He immediately repudiates the blasphemy; lastly, the majesty and modesty with which He speaks of Himself (indeed, only alludes to Himself) as the "Strong One," i.e. the Messias and God, and gives to the Holy Ghost greater honor than to His own Humanity. Thirdly, the mystery is important on account of the utterances on various points of faith, such as the Divinity of the Holy Ghost, the nature of sins against the Holy Ghost, and the existence of a Purgatory or place of purification in the next world (Matt. 12:32). Equally plain is our Saviour's statement with regard to the real advent of the kingdom of God or of the Messias (Matt. 12:28). Fourthly, the mystery casts flashes of light upon the kingdom and the doings of the evil spirits. Their restlessness and homelessness, their preference for what is physically wild and terrible, their love of spying and also their combined attacks upon souls and upon Christ's kingdom are briefly and strikingly depicted, no mere ornament of speech (Tob. 8:3; Bar. 4:35; Luke 8:2, 29).

The Woman Who Called Our Lady Blessed

Luke 11:27. And it came to pass, as he spoke these things, a certain woman from the crowd lifting up her voice said to him: "Blessed is the womb that bore thee, and the paps that gave thee suck."—28. But he said: "Yea rather, blessed are they who hear the word of God and keep it."

In the midst of the grave discussion with the Pharisees, a woman among the people broke forth into praise of the Mother of our Lord.

1. The Praise of Mary out of the Mouth of this Woman

The occasion of this sudden praise was probably the great miracle of the expulsion of the evil spirit, and the marvelous and majestic manner in which our Saviour repulsed His enemies; as St. Luke seems to indicate by the words: "As He spoke these things, a certain woman from the crowd lifting up her voice said" etc. (Luke 11:27). That is to say then, the power, majesty and charm of the words of Jesus, in which it was so evident that a far superior and more sublime Being spoke, were the first occasion of the praise. Another cause was doubtless the insolent unbelief, depravity, and vulgar mockery of the Pharisees and their adherents, who, instead of accepting our Lord's miracles and putting faith in His words, turned away in their wickedness and insulted and blasphemed the Most Holy in the most outrageous manner. Every good and noble heart must perforce turn from them in horror and indignation. The woman's praise, then, was a sudden and loud protest against such outrageous behavior.

The praise itself is not addressed, as might have been expected, directly to our Saviour. The woman does not exclaim: Blessed is the heart in which such wisdom dwells; blessed are the gracious lips which pour forth such sweet words; blessed is the hand which performs miracles. She says nothing of all this. Her thoughts turn instinctively to the Mother of Jesus. Perhaps she was a mother herself, and thought of the privileges and rights which a mother has over her child. She envied the Mother who possessed such a Son; she envied her the happiness of being near Him, waiting upon Him, commanding Him, and having the right to a special place in His Heart; she too would like to be near Him, yes, very near, in contrast to His enemies, who turn away from Him in unbelief and hate. Thus she also acknowledges by this praise all the glorious qualities of our Saviour Himself; indeed her words are the expression of faith, admiration, love, and heartfelt attachment to our Lord. And she proclaims this praise loudly, before all the people, for she "lifted up her voice from the crowd," quite unconcerned about the enemies of Jesus, who reviled and blasphemed Him. Her testimony was undoubtedly pleasing to our Divine Saviour.

2. OUR SAVIOUR'S ANSWER TO THE PRAISE

In His answer our Saviour does three things.

First, He does not deny the high privilege of His holy Mother. On the contrary, He confirms it and also the woman's acknowledgment of her. "Yea," she is indeed blessed, He answers (Luke 11:28). He Himself also calls her blessed, adding in the following words a new motive for doing so; namely, not only on account of her blood-relationship to Himself is she blessed, but also on account of her faith and holiness. By the words: "Who hear the word of God, and keep it" (Luke 11:28), one is involuntarily reminded of what is written of Mary, that she "kept all those words in her heart" (Luke 2:51), and of the praise by Elizabeth: "Blessed art thou that has believed" (Luke 1:45). If a correction lies in the answer, then it applies not to His Mother, but to the woman and all who might perhaps have only the corporal relationship in view, and who did not sufficiently esteem the spiritual.

Secondly, by His answer He comforts the woman and all of us, by drawing attention to another basis of connection with Him, which all may share if they choose; namely, the acceptance and preservation of the faith. Our Saviour is a heaven-sent Teacher, the Redeemer of all, the Way and the Door of salvation for all; and by faith we have part in Him. For this reason He draws the attention of His hearers to that which concerns them all, and which is more necessary for salvation and participation in Him than anything else. Without faith even the dignity of divine motherhood would have been useless.

Thirdly, our Saviour hereby gives His enemies also a new exhortation to accept the faith, because faith is the first condition of belonging to Him.

3. IMPORTANCE OF THIS INCIDENT

In the first place, the utterance of this woman of the people is the bright and consoling side of this diabolical scene, a bright ray of light, as it were, in the midst of the darkness of unbelief, blasphemy and hatred which surrounds our Saviour, and which reminds one involuntarily of hell. God has His own souls everywhere, and they stand out in strong relief, lighting up the horrible night of error and malice. These words of the woman, so full of faith, must have been a real refreshment and comfort to our Saviour.

Secondly, the occurrence is important on account of the deep stress laid upon faith. This mystery is an earnest exhortation to faith, and to a life of faith. Faith is of far more importance than all other conceivable privileges. These words of our Lord concerning faith are a great comfort for all of us, for we all, with the grace of God, can believe and gain a part in Christ; the example of this woman proves it.

Thirdly, our Saviour's words are an earnest warning. The same miracle and the same teaching of our Lord produce in the hearts of the Pharisees poison, gall, and corruption of the worst kind, and in the poor woman heavenly enlightenment and enthusiastic love; the former become devils in malice, the latter an apostle and confessor of the truth.

Lastly, the mystery is a true prelude to the veneration of the Blessed Virgin in the Church, and this in three respects: in the devotion itself, in the grounds on which it is based, and in the practice of the devotion. This devotion began at the foundation of Christ's kingdom, with Gabriel and Elizabeth; with the extension of the kingdom this veneration increased, as we see in the case of Simeon in the Temple; and now it makes its way among the people also. The Author of this devotion is the Holy Ghost, who has promised through Mary herself that all generations shall call her blessed (Luke 1:48). Two reasons are given in this mystery for the veneration of Mary. The first of these is her position with regard to Christ through blood-relationship and maternal dignity, which is so naturally and vividly expressed by the woman. Mary is the true Mother of Christ, and if we honor Him we must also honor His Mother. The second motive is touched upon by Christ Himself, when He calls His Mother blessed on account not only of her maternal dignity, but also of her faith and holiness. These are the same motives as Elizabeth had already mentioned (Luke 1:42–45). They are throughout all ages the valid and determining motives of the veneration of Mary. But we also see here illustrated the practice of this veneration of the Mother of God. It consists in boundless reverence, respect and love, which are expressed in word and deed. Under the present circumstances, the words of this woman are an act of courage and hardihood. She is the type of the Christian people of all ages, who, regardless of the spirit of the times and all the unbelief and mockery of the world, march openly and freely through town and country, the rosary in their hands and the praise of Mary on their lips.

The Sign of Jonas

Luke 11:16. And others tempting, asked of him a sign from heaven.—. . . 29. And the multitudes running together, he began to say: "This generation is a wicked generation; it asketh a sign, and a sign shall not be given it, but the sign of Jonas the prophet.—30. For as Jonas was a sign to the Ninivites, so shall the Son of Man also be to this generation.—31. The queen of the south shall rise in the judgment with the men of this generation, and shall condemn them; because she came from the ends of the earth to hear the wisdom of Solomon; and behold more than Solomon here.—32. The men of Ninive shall rise in the judgment with this generation, and shall condemn it; because they did penance at the preaching of Jonas; and behold more than Jonas here.—33. No man lighteth a candle, and putteth it in a hidden place, nor under a bushel; but upon a candlestick, that they that come in may see the light.—34. The light of thy body is thy eye. If thy eye be single, thy whole body will be lightsome; but if it be evil, thy body also will be darksome.—35. Take heed therefore that the light which is in thee be not darkness.—36. If then thy whole body be lightsome, having no part of darkness; the whole shall be lightsome, and as a bright lamp shall enlighten thee."

MATT. 12:38. Then some of the scribes and Pharisees answered him, saying: "Master, we would see a sign from thee."—39. Who answering said to them: "An evil and adulterous generation seeketh a sign; and a sign shall not be given it, but the sign of Jonas the prophet.—40. For as Jonas was in the whale's belly three days and three nights; so shall the Son of Man be in the heart of the earth three days and three nights.—41. The men of Ninive shall rise in judgment with this generation, and shall condemn it; because they did penance at the preaching of Jonas. And behold a greater than Jonas here.—42. The queen of the south shall rise in judgment with this generation, and shall condemn it; because she came from the ends of the earth to hear the wisdom of Solomon, and behold a greater than Solomon here."

On the same occasion some of those present asked our Saviour for a sign from heaven in ratification of His mission. This demand had already been made on a former occasion (Mark 8:11; Matt. 16:1), and this mystery is in many respects similar to that. According to St. Matthew the demand was made by Pharisees and scribes (Matt. 12:38); according to St. Luke, by "others" among "the multitudes" (Luke 11:14–16); but in any case they were Pharisees in sentiment, though not so malicious as those who ascribed the miraculous power of Jesus to the devil. They wished to avoid the duty of believing, by requiring extraordinary signs. What they demand is, as in the former case, "a sign from heaven," which was quite superfluous and useless, because our Saviour had worked miracles enough since then (and indeed immediately before this), and because this request was promoted by the same bad intention as the former had been. Perhaps it was made by the same persons as on the former occasion, and very likely just because they had then met with a refusal; they hoped to expose Him again, to excuse themselves and to palliate their unbelief by His rejection of their demand. It was probably for this reason that they made it before all the people. Our Saviour designates the reason which prompted it, in this case as in the former, as bad and blameworthy, as unbelief in short, saying that only "an evil and adulterous generation seeketh a sign" (Matt. 12:39; Luke 11:29), i.e. a generation which has fallen away from God and lost the faith. We will here speak only of what is new in this reply of our Saviour.

1. OUR SAVIOUR PROMISES THE SIGN OF JONAS

On the first occasion our Saviour had simply refused to give a sign (Mark 8:12). Now He promises one, and a very great and glorious one, too; namely, the sign of Jonas (Luke 11:29, 30; Matt. 12:39, 40). Jonas was in several respects a type of our Saviour, especially by his prophetic office; but also by his being cast into the sea to propitiate God and save the crew, and lastly by his marvelous deliverance out of the body of the fish. Our Saviour lays especial stress upon this last resemblance, thus indicating His glorious Resurrection from the dead as the miracle which was to become the principal sign of His divine mission. In truth, the Resurrection is a far greater miracle than the deliverance of Jonas; it is not merely "a sign from heaven," but to heaven, the sign of signs and the seal of all miracles.

2. OUR SAVIOUR PREDICTS THE JUDGMENT OF UNBELIEF

By the miracle of Jonas our Saviour predicts His own Death and Resurrection. By both He will become a sign to the Jews, as Jonas was a sign to the Ninivites by his apparent death and deliverance (Luke 11:30); but with this difference, that the Ninivites believed, but the Jews do not and will not believe. Our Lord therefore announces to them the judgment and their own rejection, whilst the Gentiles will be received into the kingdom of God.

Our Saviour bases this judgment upon two reasons. First, upon the depravity and wickedness of the Jews. By His reference to Jonas, He indicates one of the worst—perhaps *the* worst of all—periods before the double captivity, namely that of Elias and Eliseus. Corruption was almost universal, in spite of the miracles wrought by these two prophets. It had for its consequence the Assyrian captivity (Eccli. 48:13-16). The Israelites were worse than the Gentiles, among whom the prophets Elias, Eliseus, and Jonas found credence. Our Saviour also cites the example of the Queen of Saba (III Kings 10:1), who, induced by the fame of Solomon's wisdom, came from a great distance with presents in order to do him homage and to learn from him to know the true God. Thus the heathens—the Ninivites and the Queen of Saba—will rise up in the judgment against the Jews, accuse them, confound and convict them by the example of their desire for truth, their penance and high esteem of God's grace (Luke 11:31, 32; Matt. 12:41, 42). The rejection of Israel and the reception of the Gentiles into the kingdom of God is hereby sufficiently expressed. But the thought was intolerable to the Jews, that the Gentiles should have even equal rank and equal rights with themselves in the kingdom of God. Secondly, our Saviour bases the sentence of condemnation, pronounced upon Israel, upon the greatness of the marks of grace which it had despised, by saying with reference to Himself: "Behold more than Solomon . . . more than Jonas here" (Matt. 12:41, 42; Luke 11:31, 32). Jonas, with his gift of prophecy, his apparent death and deliverance, was indeed only a faint image of our Saviour; as was Solomon also, with all his royalty, wisdom, riches and power. By the allusion to Solomon our Saviour reminds the Jews of the most glorious period of the kingdom of Israel; and yet its splendor vanishes before what Israel now experiences, sees and hears. The Head of all the prophets and kings is now there, the true "first-born, high above the kings of the earth" (Ps. 88:28). All the more therefore do the Jews deserve condemnation for their indifference, unbelief, and resistance of such graces. This resistance is strikingly emphasized by the threefold contrast, which gradually rises to a climax: a heathen woman and the Jews; the "ends of the earth" and "here"; Solomon, Jonas, and the Son of Man.

3. OUR SAVIOUR EXPOSES THE CAUSE OF THEIR UNBELIEF

With the intention of exposing the cause of their unbelief, our Saviour makes use of a parable. The master of a house places a candle upon a high candlestick, that it may give light. But the eyes of those for whom it is to shine must also be clear, if they are to see. If this is the case, then their whole body, so to speak, sees and becomes light; if not the entire man will be in darkness, in spite of the light set up. All then depends upon our own eyes, and therefore our Saviour admonishes us: "Take heed therefore that the light," i.e. the organ and source of light and vision, the eye, "which is in thee, be not darkness" (Luke 11:33–36; Matt. 5:15; 6:22).

The same thing is true of the interior eye, the eye of the soul, i.e. the power of discerning and receiving supernatural truth. It is not enough that the truth gives us light; the eye of the mind must be clear and untroubled, in order to recognize this truth where its light shines out. Then it will enlighten the entire man, and he will be able to comprehend all the strength and beauty of the heavenly light, as a ray of eternal truth. But if the mind is dull and clouded it does not see the truth, and the entire man remains in darkness. This interior darkness comes from the will, the irregular passions, and wickedness, which do not allow reason and grace to have their due. The light is set up; it shines with a bright radiance, and yet the blind do not see it. But the cause of their not seeing it does not lie in the light, but in the interior blindness of men.

The most important thing in this mystery is the public and solemn announcement of the Death and Resurrection of Jesus as the principal proof of His divine mission and doctrine, though this announcement is somewhat obscure as yet and given under the shadowy figure of the typical Jonas. By this as well as by the allusion to Solomon the typical character of the Old Testament is again acknowledged and declared, and a splendid light is thrown upon our Saviour, Who unites in His own Person all the splendor of the world of types, and eclipses it. The relation of the will and the passions to faith is also of great importance. Faith presupposes the good will to believe, and this is very clearly and strikingly taught in this short parable.

Our Lord's Censure of the Pharisees

Luke 11:37. And as he was speaking, a certain Pharisee prayed him that he would dine with him. And he going in, sat down to eat.—38. And the Pharisee began to say, thinking within himself, why he was not washed before dinner.—39. And the Lord said to him: "Now you Pharisees make clean the outside of the cup and of the platter; but your inside is full of rapine and iniquity.—40. Ye fools, did not he that made that which is without, make also that which is within?—41. But yet that which remaineth, give alms; and behold all things are clean unto you.—42. But woe to you Pharisees, because you tithe mint and rue and every herb, and pass over judgment and the charity of God. Now these things you ought to have done, and not to leave the other undone.—43. Woe to you Pharisees, because you love the uppermost seats in the synagogues, and salutations in the market-place.—44. Woe to you, because you are as sepulchers that appear not, and men that walk over are not aware."—45. And one of the lawyers answering, saith to him: "Master, in saying these things, thou reproachest us also."—46. But he said: "Woe to you lawyers also; because you load men with burdens which they cannot bear, and you yourselves touch not the packs with one of your fingers.—47. Woe to you who build the monuments of the prophets; and your fathers killed them.—48. Truly you bear witness that you consent to the doings of your fathers; for they indeed killed them, and you build their sepulchers.—49. For this cause also the wisdom of God said: I will send to them prophets and apostles, and some of them they will kill and persecute.—50. That the blood of all the prophets which was shed from the foundation of the world, may be required of this generation,—51. From the blood of Abel unto the blood of Zacharias, who was slain between the altar and the temple. Yea I say to you, it shall be required of this generation.—52. Woe to you lawyers, for you have taken away the key of knowledge; you yourselves have not entered in, and those that were entering in you have hindered."—53. And as he was saying these things to them, the Pharisees and the lawyers began vehemently to urge him, and to oppress his mouth about many things,—54. Lying in wait for him, and seeking to catch something from his mouth, that they might accuse him.

1. OCCASION OF THE CENSURE

The occasion of the reprimand was the Pharisee's invitation to dine (Luke 11:37). The remarkable manner in which it was given, during our Lord's discourse, would almost lead one to suspect that the motives which prompted it were none of the best. Probably it proceeded either from outward politeness (since it was the custom to show hospitality to teachers of the law), or from a mere wish to appear courteous before the people (from pharisaical ostentation), or from the malicious desire of laying a trap for our Saviour. However, since the Evangelist makes no further remark about it, it is possible that the Pharisee's intention may have been a good one. A further occasion was given by his suspicious and wicked thoughts, upon seeing that our Lord did not wash before sitting down to table (Luke 11:38). We see here the old narrow-mindedness, intolerance, pride and injustice of his caste.

On our Saviour's side the first circumstance was His acceptance of the invitation. He accepted it through politeness. Indeed, He never shuns unpleasant occurrences, for He can thus impart good whilst receiving evil. Another circumstance was His omission to wash. He was not at all bound to do so, because there was no law which enjoined washing on such an occasion; and by neglecting the ceremony He by no means wished to give scandal, but to impart instruction.

2. THE CENSURE

In response to the wicked thoughts of the Pharisee our Lord now gave the following reprimand. It has two parts, the first of which concerns the Pharisees, the second the scribes.

Our Saviour first reproaches the Pharisees with hypocrisy, and in a very energetic manner, beginning: "Now you Pharisees make clean the outside of the cup and of the platter, but your inside is full of rapine and iniquity." He makes use of this similitude of the cup and the platter to show their hypocrisy, because there were many such utensils on the table, which the Pharisees scrupulously examined and cleansed, whilst allowing their hearts to remain full of theft and wickedness (Luke 11:39). This wickedness consisted in defrauding widows, using bribery in the courts of justice, and oppressing the poor, as may be gathered from our Lord's teaching on other occasions (Matt. 23:14, 23, 25; Luke 16:14). He shows the perversity of this behavior by His reference to God (Luke 11:40), Who had given the laws of exterior separation and purification only as a means to interior purity (Lev. 19:2), and Whose honor required inward cleanliness quite as much as outward, and indeed far more. Further, our Saviour gives the Pharisees a means to free themselves from the impurity of their hearts, viz. almsgiving—bestowing the contents of their cups and platters upon the poor; for almsgiving combined with contrition and a purpose of amendment justifies, and almsgiving even without these often obtains the grace of conversion and removes the primary evil of hard-heartedness and covetousness. Secondly our Lord reproaches the Pharisees with folly, calling them "fools" (Luke 11:40), who observe with exaggerated care little things that are not required by the law, such as tithes of the smaller garden produce (e.g. mint and rue), and at the same time make nothing of violating the great commandments of justice and charity (Luke 11:42). Thirdly He upbraids them with their pride and vanity, as shown in their preference for the first and most conspicuous seats in the synagogue, and in their love of being respectfully saluted in the market-place; and this not merely as a mark of distinction paid to their rank, but as an acknowledgment of their intellectual and spiritual superiority and holiness (Luke 11:43). He emphasizes and illustrates the reproach by likening them to hidden, unrecognizable graves in the open field, which are not avoided by the passers-by, simply because they do not perceive them, and so walk over and touch them without knowing what filth and decay are contained therein, and with what corruption they come into contact. By touching a grave, the Jews incurred uncleanness according to the law (Num. 19:16); and for this reason the graves were annually whitewashed to render them easily distinguishable. Our Saviour here alludes to the manner in which the Pharisees deceive and contaminate the people, by veiling their true character, which is nothing but corruption.

The second part of the reprimand concerns the scribes or lawyers. It was occasioned by a lawyer himself, who protested against the accusation of the Pharisees, on the ground that it struck at the prestige of the scribes as well, because the whole pharisaical code was based upon the principles laid down by them, and the two sects made common cause (Luke 11:45). The scribes and lawyers were an official caste, and were intended to be the spiritual guides of the people. Our Lord reproaches them first with the unjust imposition of intolerable burdens (Luke 11:46). The law itself was already hard enough, with its regulations concerning Levitical uncleanness, the celebration of the Sabbath, the restrictions with regard to food and intercourse with the Gentiles; and to this the scribes added the far harder yoke of the "precepts of men" (Mark 7:7). These consisted of regulations for the purification of clothing, of the body, and of vessels for food and drink, and included also the Sabbath observances; and they imposed all this as a binding law, without any distinction and with inexorable strictness. Secondly, our Lord reproaches them with their insincerity. Whilst they themselves did not keep the laws, but violated them in secret, they punished every transgression of them by others, regardless of circumstances. Further, they rebuilt the sepulchers of the murdered prophets, and made other pretences of thus condemning the evil deeds committed against them by their forefathers, whilst entertaining the same dispositions and committing the same outrages upon the Apostles whom our Lord was now about to send them. They (the scribes) will act with regard to these Apostles just as the Wisdom of God has recorded of the times of Zacharias (II Par. 24:19), and will incur the same punishment (II Par. 24:22, 23). Abel is the first martyr mentioned in the Old Testament, and Zacharias, the son of Joiada (Barachias), the last (Luke 11:49–51). Lastly, our Saviour censures the scribes for their infidelity to their vocation, which was to lead the people to Christ; for He is the end of the law (Gal. 3:24). The knowledge of Christ is a true treasure-house, a sanctuary, to which the scribes had the key in the law and the Scriptures. But they made no use of it either for themselves or for the people, but on the contrary took it away from the latter; for the law as they interpreted it did not lead *to* Christ, but from Him (Luke 11:52).

3. EFFECT OF THE REPRIMAND

The scribes and Pharisees, instead of being struck to the heart, became only more exasperated than ever against their formidable censor, and more confirmed in their resistance and hatred towards Him; they organized a scheme of fiercest enmity, and laid snares for Him by continually asking questions, in order to extract something from His answers which could be turned into an accusation against Him (Luke 11:53, 54). A fresh increase of hatred (which now proceeds to open attack) is here plainly to be observed.

With a view to delineating the character of Jesus, we may here particularly notice how compliant He is, and how He accommodates Himself to circumstances; and on the other hand how resolute and frank, indeed uncompromisingly severe when dealing with dishonesty, hypocrisy, selfishness and folly. It is the first time that He warns the Pharisees with His stern, judicial "woe." Nothing is so repugnant to Him as the character of the Pharisees and scribes, precisely because it is the sharp and complete antithesis of His own spirit, which knows only sincerity, good sense, humility, simplicitiy, and fidelity to duty.

Open, Fearless Confession

Luke 12:1. And when great multitudes stood about him, so that they trod one upon another, he began to say to his disciples: "Beware ye of the leaven of the Pharisees, which is hypocrisy.—2. For there is nothing covered, that shall not be revealed; nor hidden, that shall not be known.—3. For whatsoever things you have spoken in darkness, shall be published in the light; and that which you have spoken in the ear in the chambers, shall be preached on the house-tops.—4. And I say to you, my friends: Be not afraid of them who kill the body, and after that have no more that they can do.—5. But I will show you whom ye shall fear: fear ye him, who after he hath killed, hath power to cast into hell. Yea, I say to you, fear him.—6. Are not five sparrows sold for two farthings, and not one of them is forgotten before God?—7. Yea, the very hairs of your head are all numbered. Fear not therefore; you are of more value than many sparrows.—8. And I say to you: Whosoever shall confess me before men, him shall the Son of Man also confess before the angels of God;—9. But he that shall deny me before men, shall be denied before the angels of God.—10. And whosoever speaketh a word against the Son of Man, it shall be forgiven him; but to him that shall blaspheme against the Holy Ghost, it shall not be forgiven.—11. And when they shall bring you into the synagogues, and to magistrates and powers, be not solicitous how or what you shall answer, or what you shall say.—12. For the Holy Ghost shall teach you in the same hour what you must say."

Matt. 10:17. "But beware of men. For they will deliver you up in councils, and they will scourge you in their synagogues;—18. And you shall be brought before governors, and before kings for my sake, for a testimony to them and to the Gentiles.—19. But when they shall deliver you up, take no thought how or what to speak; for it shall be given to you in that hour what to speak.—20. For it is not you that speak, but the Spirit of your Father that speaketh in you. . . .—24. The disciple is not above the master, nor the servant above his lord.—25. It is enough for the disciple that he be as his master; and the servant as his lord. If they have called the master of the house Beelzebub, how much more them of his household?—26. Therefore fear them not. For nothing is covered that shall not be revealed; nor hid, that shall not be known.—27. That which I tell you in the dark, speak ye in the light; and that which you hear in the ear, preach ye upon the house-tops.—28. And fear ye not them that kill the body, and are not able to kill the soul; but rather fear him that can destroy both soul and body in hell.—29. Are not two sparrows sold for a farthing? And not one of them shall fall on the ground without your Father.—30. But the very hairs of your head are all numbered.—31. Fear not therefore; better are you than many sparrows.—32. Everyone therefore that shall confess me before men, I will also confess him before my Father who is in heaven;—33. But he that shall deny me before men, I will also deny him before my Father who is in heaven."

1. CIRCUMSTANCES OF THE DISCOURSE

The circumstances which led up to this discourse were as follows.

First, as regards time, it was delivered after the meal in the Pharisee's house, where our Saviour had unmasked and unsparingly exposed the wickedness of the scribes and Pharisees.

Secondly, the latter were infuriated at this, consulted together and formed a plot against our Saviour, which they at once proceeded to execute (Luke 11:54). It was about this time, either immediately after the above-mentioned meal or perhaps a few days later, that our Lord delivered this discourse.

Thirdly, it was naturally to be feared that the Apostles, the disciples and people might be intimidated by the threats and proceedings of the Pharisees. A word of encouragement was therefore opportune, and so our Saviour profited by the occasion to deliver this encouraging address, whilst an innumerable multitude were gathered round Him, thronging and pushing each other (Luke 12:1).

2. THE DISCOURSE

The discourse consists of two parts.

The first part contains the precept and enunciates the truth which our Saviour wishes to inculcate upon His hearers. The precept is a double one. He first warns them all not to hold with the Pharisees, not to belong to their party nor follow their teaching. "Beware ye of the leaven of the Pharisees" (Luke 12:1). Secondly, they should on the contrary hold fast to His doctrine, and not be afraid to confess it publicly, regardless of the persecution of the Pharisees. This precept is contained in the words: "There is nothing . . . hidden that shall not be known; for whatsoever things you have spoken in darkness, shall be published in the light" (Luke 12:2, 3), or as it is rendered in the corresponding passage of St. Matthew's Gospel: "That which I tell you in the dark, speak ye in the light; and that which you hear in the ear, preach ye upon the house-tops" (Matt. 10:27). This is a proverb, and alludes, as has already been observed, to the custom in the East of making proclamations to the people from the low, flat roofs of the houses.

The second part contains motives for both precepts. One motive to induce us to beware of the doctrine of the Pharisees is that their character and doctrine are but "leaven" (Luke 12:1), and bad leaven too, an infectious and morally corrupt compound of malice and wickedness; because it is hypocrisy, giving out human precepts for divine commands, and base passions for virtue. Our Saviour does not then retract the words He had spoken against the Pharisees at the banquet. On the contrary, He confirms them in a few words. He says no more just now, before the people, out of considerations of prudence. A second motive is that the hypocrisy of the Pharisees will and must be unmasked before the whole world, and this precisely through the preaching of the Apostles (Luke 12:2, 3; Matt. 10:27), by their public proclamation of the truth which He now imparts to them in private, and through which they will expose and confound this hypocrisy.

With regard to fearless confession of His doctrine in spite of all persecutions, our Saviour adduces very strong motives. They are four in number. In the first place, if anyone is to be feared, it is certainly God, and not men. Men can at most kill the body, nothing more. But God cannot only kill the body, but also cast both body and soul into hell (Luke 12:4, 5; Matt. 10:28). The second motive is the protection and providence of God, without which nothing takes place, and which will assist the confessors of the faith in bodily as well as spiritual needs. As regards the body, nothing will happen without God's permission. Our Saviour illustrates this truth very strikingly by God's care for creatures of far less value than men, such as the sparrows, an apparently worthless species of bird at the mercy of chance and wanton cruelty. Yet they are under God's especial protection, not only as a class, but as regards the life and death of each individual bird; and the same thing is true of every single hair of our head. Who knows or concerns himself as to whether there is a sparrow less in the world, or whether a hair has fallen from his head? And yet it does not take place without the knowledge and permission of God (Luke 12:6, 7; Matt. 10:29–31). The Holy Ghost renders a similar but still more positive assistance to confessors of the faith when they stand before courts of law. They are not to be anxious about their answers; He will inspire them with what they are to say (Matt. 10:18–20; Luke 12:11, 12). The third motive is taken from the relation of the Apostles and disciples to our Saviour. They are His servants, His disciples, and the members of His household. His lot will therefore be theirs also. Looked at from this point of view, the motives for suffering seem very natural, self-evident, honorable and desirable (Matt. 10:24, 25; cf. Rom. 5:3; I Peter 4:14). The fourth motive for fearlessness is the reward promised to a fearless confession, and the punishment of the denial of Christ's doctrine. The reward is strongly emphasized by the antithesis in both clauses of the text: Who confesses? You and I, the Son of Man. And before whom? Before men, and before the Heavenly Father and the holy angels (Luke 12:8, 9; Matt. 10:32, 33). Testimony is rewarded by testimony, the human by the divine, the earthly by the heavenly. What an honor and what a reward for "faithful witnesses," to be led before the Heavenly Father by our Saviour! But on the contrary what disgrace and punishment follow from the same contrast (as emphasized by Mark 7:38), and especially if the denial is a positive blasphemy against the Holy Ghost, as had just been the case in the preceding mystery on the part of the Pharisees, as a warning to whom our Lord once more declares this sin to be unpardonable (Luke 12:10)! There is no assistance of the Holy Ghost in a denial of the faith, and especially in such a one. On the contrary, another spirit exerts his influence here; the spirit of lying, hatred and blasphemy.

3. CONCLUSION

One cannot read or meditate upon this discourse without receiving the vivid impression that the situation becomes henceforth serious and critical. Our Saviour had never before spoken of testimony rendered before judgment-seats at the cost of life. He thereby indicates that His disciples must be prepared for everything, even the very worst. He opens out a distant view of the future of the Church, which passes through bloody and bloodless persecutions, cowardly denial and courageous confession, until the end of time; and which finds its close in the corresponding reward and punishment at the great Judgment Day. He unfolds this vista before all the people, because confession of the faith is binding upon all, and because the number of faithful witnesses will be made up of all races and ages.

As opposed to this grave prospect, our Saviour brings forward the most solid and encouraging motives of the fear of God, trust in His protection, and joyful anticipation of the glorious reward to come. These are the very motives and thoughts which have strengthened the martyrs of all ages and made them invincible in all temptations and sufferings. The promised protection of God has never failed them. The whole history of the bloody and the bloodless witness of the Church is a confirmation of the predictions and promises of this discourse.

Here again we have an example of the way in which our Saviour supports the force of His eloquence by powerful motives and beautiful development of them.

Warning against Covetousness

Luke 12:13. And one of the multitude said to him: "Master, speak to my brother that he divide the inheritance with me."—14. But he said to him: "Man, who hath appointed me judge or divider over you?"—15. And he said to them: "Take heed and beware of all covetousness; for a man's life doth not consist in the abundance of things which he possesseth."—16. And he spoke a similitude to them, saying: "The land of a certain rich man brought forth plenty of fruits.—17. And he thought within himself, saying: What shall I do, because I have no room where to bestow my fruits?—18. And he said: This will I do: I will pull down my barns, and will build greater; and into them will I gather all things that are grown to me, and my goods.—19. And I will say to my soul: Soul, thou hast much goods laid up for many years; take thy rest, eat, drink, make good cheer.—20. But God said to him: Thou fool, this night do they require thy soul of thee; and whose shall those things be which thou hast provided?—21. So is he that layeth up treasure for himself, and is not rich towards God."

1. Occasion of the Warning

The occasion was given by a man among the people, who interrupted our Lord's address by requesting Him to induce his brother to divide his inheritance with him (Luke 12:13). According to the law the first-born son received twice as much as any of the others (Deut. 21:17), because he had also to provide for the mother and unmarried sisters. The younger sons received a sum of money, which often led to disputes.

From the warning with which our Saviour responds, it would seem that it was covetousness on the part of the man or his brother that induced him to make the request. In order to obtain his end he wished to make use of our Lord's influence against his brother, who was possibly also present at the discourse. Such is the fruit that men derive from the divine teaching of the Saviour! Whilst He was speaking in such an inspiring and impressive manner of confession of the faith, even to the sacrifice of all temporal things and of life itself, this man was occupied only with earthly thoughts and desires.

2. Our Divine Saviour's Answer

In His answer our Saviour does two things. He first refuses the man's request, and then gives a warning against covetousness.

He refuses the request by asking who had appointed Him to be a judge between the man and his brother (Luke 12:14). He does not mean by this that He has no right to give decisions of this kind. He had the right, but it was not a part of His immediate duty to make use of it. He was come not to judge, but to redeem; not on account of temporal affairs, but for the sake of souls; and it would have been only a hindrance to this spiritual object to have mixed Himself up with worldly business. He would thus have confirmed men in their solicitude for temporal goods by His own example, would have made enemies of all those against whom He gave His decision, have been pestered with applicants, and have lost precious time. There are plenty of other judges for such matters. Lastly, it would have been a degradation for our Saviour to occupy Himself with such things. He is the End of all created things, and not the means. This is the meaning of His refusal (cf. John 8:3; Luke 20:22).

Secondly, our Saviour profits by the opportunity to warn us against covetousness. He enlarges upon three points with regard to this. First, He shows us in what covetousness really consists. It does not consist in the simple care for temporal necessaries, but in solicitude for the superfluous and unnecessary. Covetousness is not attached to temporal possessions because they are necessary, and inasmuch as they are necessary, but sets its heart upon possessions as such, and can therefore never have enough of them. For this reason our Saviour says that superfluity is not necessary to life (Luke 12:15). Secondly, He gives us motives against covetousness in the form of a parable, in which He shows in the life and principles of a covetous man the detriments of covetousness (Luke 12:16). The first detriment is the torturing anxiety, not to expend well what one has acquired, but to keep and possess it. The harvest is so great that the man does not know where to put it. He must build new barns (Luke 12:17). The second detriment is godlessness. He speaks of the "things that are grown to him," of "his goods," not of God's gifts (Luke 12:18). He does not think of thanking God, any more than of giving something to the poor. The third disadvantage is the degradation which ensues from it. He calls upon his soul to eat and drink, as if it were no more than a brute beast (Luke 12:19). The fourth is false confidence. He promises himself many years of enjoyment, and the very same night the "fool" is summoned away by death. And what becomes of all his property? (Luke 12:20.) Thirdly and lastly, our Saviour points out the remedy against covetousness, viz. the opposite kind of zeal, to become "rich towards God" (Luke 12:21) by virtue and good works.

3. LESSONS TO BE DRAWN FROM THE INCIDENT

In the first place we may learn the folly and unhappiness of covetousness or the passion for temporal goods and possessions. It is folly to try to satisfy our poor soul and make it happy with money and goods; folly, to fancy oneself secure in the possession of temporal things; folly, to strive immoderately after things that will certainly forsake us some day, of which we may be bereft at any moment, and of which absolutely nothing, not even a trace, remains. The unhappiness of covetousness consists in its power of degrading us, in its unfruitfulness for time and eternity, and in the responsibility and punishment incurred thereby (Eccl. 5:19; 11:19; Job 27:16). Why are all things temporal given to us, if not that by means of them we may become "rich towards God" in virtue and good works? But that is not the spirit of the world. On the contrary, its spirit is shown exactly in the "man of the multitude." He and many others of our Saviour's time lived only for temporal things, and expected only a rich Messias. Even the most sublime and inspiring teaching of our Saviour was not able to lift from their hearts the dead-weight of earthly and covetous thoughts and wishes. Far from it; this man sees in the influence of the popular and eloquent master only a tool to serve his covetous desires.

On the other hand we see the spirit of Jesus. Our Saviour must assuredly have been angered by the unworthiness of sentiment and speech with which the man interrupted his discourse. But He appears to have manifested His displeasure only in the word "Man," with which He begins His answer; then He passes on to an objective reply. He, who was so ready to grant any petition, rejects with decision this covetous request; for it He has no word of countenance, only earnest admonition. In doing this He has traced out the line of conduct for the Church and apostolic men. They should never allow themselves to be made the servants and tools of worldly concerns, for the reasons already mentioned. He recognizes in His answer the right of the State in the sphere of worldly affairs (Luke 12:14), but yet does not yield His supreme right (and that of the Church) to take exterior and temporal matters into His own hands, when it is necessary for the welfare of souls. The answer is no basis for the so-called separation of Church and State, but confirms their mutual relations and preserves to each its own vocation.

Excess of Temporal Cares

Luke 12:22. And he said to his disciples: "Therefore I say to you, be not solicitous for your life, what you shall eat; nor for your body, what you shall put on.—23. The life is more than the meat, and the body is more than the raiment.—24. Consider the ravens, for they sow not, neither do they reap, neither have they store-house nor barn, and God feedeth them. How much are you more valuable than they?—25. And which of you by taking thought can add to his stature one cubit?—26. If then you be not able to do so much as the least thing, why are you solicitous for the rest?—27. Consider the lilies how they grow; they labor not, neither do they spin; but I say to you, not even Solomon in all his glory was clothed like one of these.—28. Now if God clothe in this manner the grass that is today in the field, and tomorrow is cast into the oven; how much more you, O ye of little faith?—29. And seek not you what you shall eat, or what you shall drink; and be not lifted up on high.—30. For all these things do the nations of the world seek. But your Father knoweth that you have need of these things.—31. But seek ye first the kingdom of God and his justice; and all these things shall be added unto you."

Matt. 6:25. "Therefore I say to you, be not solicitous for your life, what you shall eat, nor for your body, what you shall put on. Is not the life more than the meat, and the body more than the raiment?—26. Behold the birds of the air, for they neither sow, nor do they reap, nor gather into barns; and your heavenly Father feedeth them. Are not you of much more value than they?—27. And which of you by taking thought can add to his stature one cubit?—28. And for raiment why are you solicitous? Consider the lilies of the field how they grow; they labor not, neither do they spin.—29. But I say to you, that not even Solomon in all his glory was arrayed as one of these.—30. And if the grass of the field, which is today, and tomorrow is cast into the oven, God doth so clothe; how much more you, O ye of little faith?—31. Be not solicitous therefore, saying: What shall we eat, or what shall we drink, or wherewith shall we be clothed?—32. For after all these things do the heathens seek. For your Father knoweth that you have need of all these things.—33. Seek ye therefore first the kingdom of God, and his justice; and all these things shall be added unto you.—34. Be not therefore solicitous for tomorrow. For the morrow will be solicitous for itself; sufficient for the day is the evil thereof."

Our Lord immediately turns away from the covetous man to His disciples (and probably also to the people), and passes on from the warning against covetousness to another against excessive solicitude for temporal necessities. It is now no longer a question of the passion for superfluities, but of the immoderate care for daily wants, for life, food, and clothing (Luke 12:22; Matt. 6:25).

1. WHEREIN THE EXCESS OF THESE CARES CONSISTS

The irregularity of this solicitude may lie in its object; namely, when this object is not in our power and does not depend upon us, such as future events, which we must leave to God (Matt. 6:27, 31, 34). The disorder may further consist in the manner in which we strive after the necessaries of life; namely, when we put this solicitude for temporal things in the first place, and make them as it were our object in life, or when we pursue these cares without faith or trust, as though no Divine Providence existed and we must be our own providence. Our Saviour calls this a heathen, godless existence, such as was really led by many of the Jews (Luke 12:30; Matt. 6:30, 32). Many heathens thought that God does not know our wants nor trouble Himself about us. Lastly, the irregularity of this kind of solicitude consists in that disquietude whereby through sheer anxiety we become distracted and lose our self-possession. This is the meaning of the words "*in sublime tolli*" (Luke 12:29). Our Saviour warns His hearers against all this.

2. WHY THIS EXAGGERATED ANXIETY MUST BE AVOIDED

Our Saviour gives us two classes of motives.

The first class relates to God. God is wise and gracious. He has bestowed upon us great and precious gifts, the body and life; how much more then will He give us food and clothing, which are necessary for this body and life, and yet not of such value as the body and life themselves (Luke 12:23; Matt. 6:25)! Further, God provides not only necessaries, but even superfluities for many less noble creatures, such as ravens and sparrows. They neither sow nor reap, and have no barns nor store-houses, as do men. God Himself feeds them from His Hand (Luke 12:24; Matt. 6:26). So it is also with the lilies and the grass. They neither labor nor spin, and yet they flourish. God does not clothe them poorly and scantily, but in a beautiful and radiant vesture, so that even Solomon in all his glory, clad in his garments of white, purple, gold and azure-blue, was not thus arrayed. And yet what are they? Nothing but grass, which today flourishes and tomorrow is used for fuel. How much more then will God provide for you! This conclusion is twice repeated by our Saviour (Matt. 6:26, 30; Luke 12:24, 28). In short, an omniscient, faithful, gracious and fatherly Providence exists. This truth is shortly and touchingly summed up in the sentence: "Your Father knoweth that you have need of all these things" (Matt. 6:32; Luke 12:30). Not to believe and trust in this Providence, therefore, is heathenism (Luke 12:30; Matt. 6:32).

The other motives are taken from the characteristics of this immoderate solicitude. It is useless. With all our care we cannot lengthen our life one instant. We cannot even increase our own stature; how much less power then have we over what is above and outside of us! (Luke 12:25, 26; Matt. 6:27.) Further, it is unwise to make the burden of our daily cares heavier by anxiety for the future; God wisely distributes these cares over days and years, so that we can bear them easily. It is therefore unwise to try to bear the burden of a life's cares all at once, because this is impossible (Matt. 6:34).

3. WHAT MEANS OUR SAVIOUR GIVES US FOR AVOIDING THIS EXCESSIVE CARE

Our Saviour indicates as the best means to draw down upon ourselves the fatherly care of Divine Providence, solicitude and labor for the kingdom of God and its justice (Matt. 6:33; Luke 12:31). And what is to be understood by this kingdom of God and its justice? The kingdom of God is heaven and all that leads to it, the whole economy of grace, or in other words the salvation of our soul. To this economy of salvation belong also prayer (cf. the Our Father), labor, and well-regulated care. The "seeking the kingdom of heaven and its justice" may also be understood in a far higher sense, as signifying the apostolic activity conformable to one's state of life, or work for the propagation of the Church and the welfare of souls. Our Saviour may probably have had this also in view.

If we thus "seek the kingdom of God" for ourselves and others, we may hope that God will add all temporal necessaries as a free gift. As a merchant often throws something into the bargain when dealing with good customers, or a prince rewards great merits by material gifts as well as by honors, so our good God treats those who labor for His kingdom. In comparison with the eternal reward, temporal prosperity is no more than an extra gift thrown in (Ps. 36:25; 54:23; I Peter 5:7). On the other hand, God often deprives us of temporal blessings on account of our want of solicitude for His kingdom.

What a true and lofty view of life our Divine Saviour unfolds here! What a magnificent intellect, which sees so clearly into the relations of the visible world with the higher sphere of Christian truth, and lays it before us in such beautiful, touching figures and comparisons! The Heart of God, our Saviour's own Heart, is here portrayed in Its sublime sentiments and loving care for creatures. One cannot hear and reflect upon these beautiful words without being stimulated to heartfelt piety and childlike trust in the fatherly care of God. This childlike trust and freedom from care and this lofty disinterestedness are of great importance for the kingdom of Christ, and especially for His servants and apostles.

Apostolic Poverty

Luke 12:32. "Fear not, little flock, for it hath pleased your Father to give you a kingdom.—33. Sell what you possess and give alms. Make to yourselves bags which grow not old, a treasure in heaven which faileth not; where no thief approacheth, nor moth corrupteth.—34. For where your treasure is, there will your heart be also.—35. Let your loins be girt, and lamps burning in your hands,—36. And you yourselves like to men who wait for their lord, when he shall return from the wedding; that when he cometh and knocketh, they may open to him immediately.—37. Blessed are those servants, whom the Lord when he cometh shall find watching. Amen I say to you, that he will gird himself, and make them sit down to meat, and passing will minister unto them.—38. And if he shall come in the second watch, or come in the third watch, and find them so, blessed are those servants.—39. But this know ye, that if the householder did know at what hour the thief would come, he would surely watch, and would not suffer his house to be broken open.—40. Be you then also ready; for at what hour you think not, the Son of Man will come."

Matt. 6:19. "Lay not up to yourselves treasures on earth; where the rust and moth consume, and where thieves break through and steal.—20. But lay up to yourselves treasures in heaven; where neither the rust nor moth doth consume, and where thieves do not break through, nor steal.—21. For where thy treasure is, there is thy heart also.—22. The light of thy body is thy eye. If thy eye be single, thy whole body shall be lightsome.—23. But if thy eye be evil, thy whole body shall be darksome. If then the light that is in thee, be darkness; the darkness itself how great shall it be?—24. No man can serve two masters. For either he will hate the one, and love the other; or he will sustain the one, and despise the other. You cannot serve God and mammon."

Matt. 24:42. "Watch ye, therefore, because ye know not what hour your Lord will come.—43. But this know ye, that if the goodman of the house knew at what hour the thief would come, he would certainly watch, and would not suffer his house to be broken open.—44. Wherefore be you also ready; because at what hour you know not, the Son of Man will come."

The above lesson is certainly intended for the Apostles and their successors in office (Luke 12:41). Our Lord requires of them not merely avoidance of covetousness, but all immoderate solicitude for temporal things.

1. WHEREIN APOSTOLIC POVERTY CONSISTS

Our Lord tells us wherein it consists. "Sell what you possess, and give alms" (Luke 12:33); "sell whatsoever thou hast, and give to the poor, and thou shalt have treasure in heaven" (Mark 10:21). The Apostles are to part with all their property, without any intention or prospect of recovery or compensation here below. And they are to do this to promote good works, and for the sake of their own perfection, in order to become "rich towards God" (Luke 12:21); for the sake of Christ's kingdom (Luke 12:31) and the sure reward in heaven (Luke 12:33). This is an enthusiastic contempt of earthly things, and the perfection of evangelical poverty (Matt. 19:21; Ps. 111:9). This perfection involves no less than a complete renunciation of all temporal means of support and defence in the pursuit of their apostolic aim and mission, in a world full of powerful enemies who are equipped with all temporal aids. For this reason our Saviour calls His little band of Apostles a "little flock" (Luke 12:32), despised and destitute, in the midst of cunning and ferocious wolves, without any natural means of defence and attack (Matt. 10:16). This is great perfection, and the complete death of the natural desire for assistance, power, and protection.

2. HOW OUR SAVIOUR ENCOURAGES THE APOSTLES TO THIS POVERTY

Our Saviour gives three motives for this poverty.

The first motive is the certainty of success, in spite of the natural insufficiency of the means employed. "Fear not" amid your natural poverty and destitution, for according to the gracious dispensation of "your Father," the "kingdom" (i.e. heaven) is yours, and therefore whatever leads to it—life, stability, the victory of the Church—will never be lacking to you here below (Luke 12:32). This promise and this conviction give confidence, courage, and independence of all the powerful aids of the world.

The second motive is the Apostles' own spiritual advantage. Instead of earthly, uncertain possessions they gain eternal ones. All earthly possessions are exposed to vicissitudes; certain metals to rust, silk and purple to moths, and everything to thieves, or at any rate to the great thief, Death, who takes from everyone all he has. Earthly possessions blind and seduce the heart and the mind (Matt. 6:21–23), and draw them away from God and His service (Matt. 6:24); whereas the heavenly possessions which they gain (i.e. merit and souls saved) are "bags which grow not old," "treasures which fail not," "treasures in heaven" (Luke 12:33; Matt. 6:20). And therefore the Apostles will not fall into forgetfulness of God here below, for "where your treasure is, there will your heart be also," with its thoughts, wishes, and affection (Luke 12:34).

The third motive for the practice of this poverty is that it produces activity and assiduity in the service of God and the Gospel. Activity is absolutely necessary for this service, and our Lord demands it (Luke 12:35). He describes very clearly and powerfully in what is consists. The Apostles are to be "girt, and lamps burning in their hands," and thus to wait perseveringly from one night-watch to another, the whole night through, so prompt and ready for service that they do not let their lord wait when he comes, not even as long as is necessary to gird themselves and light the lamp (Luke 12:36, 38). Nothing is to be too much for them, nothing too long or too arduous. But they are not to do this without reason. Our Lord adds beautiful motives for this faithful service. First, the uncertainty and yet certainty of the master's coming. He will assuredly come, but it is uncertain whether at the first, second, or third watch of the night (Luke 12:38). The Jews divided the night into three or four watches, from 6 to 9, from 9 to 12, from 12 to 3, and from 3 to 6 (cf. Matt. 25:5, 19). Our Lord emphasizes and illustrates this uncertainty by another similitude, viz. the behavior of a householder, who would certainly watch, did he know that a thief was going to break in (Luke 12:39, 40). Our Lord will come therefore and take us by surprise like a thief. The second motive is the reward, which is beautiful and touching, as suits such a touchingly zealous service (Luke 12:37, 38). Our Lord twice calls such servants blessed. They are blessed in the approbation and praise of their master, and blessed in the service he renders them in return. Our Saviour celebrates His wedding-feast with His Father in heaven. He comes as a bridegroom, to fetch His servant home as a bride. Therefore He bids him sit down and serves him like an equal, as He did at the Last Supper, full of graciousness and condescension. By this "sitting down" and being served is indicated the delightful rest as well as the joy and honor of heaven; rest in return for the long watching and waiting, honor for the attendance and humble service.

3. IN WHAT THE IMPORTANCE OF THESE INSTRUCTIONS FOR THE APOSTOLIC LIFE CONSISTS

Our Saviour here depicts in broad, bold outlines three very important qualities of the apostolic laborer.

The first quality is trust in God, which does not expect the victory of His cause and the success of apostolic activity from the power of natural, human means, such as influence, riches, influential friends, or talent; but solely from God and His grace, as the Apostle St. Paul so often and so emphatically says (I Cor. 2:5; I Thess. 1:5; II Cor. 6, 7). The apostolic laborer therefore readily forgoes human aids, or at least does not expect to derive his success from them. This is true spirituality, and it rests upon the words of our Saviour: "It hath pleased your Father to give you a kingdom," i.e. the mastery and victory.

The second quality is this elevation of the mind to God, which seeks no earthly advantages, but wishes only to become "rich towards God" by rendering service to the Church and saving souls. These are the "bags which grow not old," which Death cannot seize.

The third quality is indefatigable and persevering zeal in the service of God, the Church and souls, as our Saviour describes it in the faithful and assiduous servant; a truly touching and heroic willingness, a real exuberance of joy in serving, watching, and holding oneself in readiness, such as we see in the Saints. This readiness for service is the martyrdom of the holy confessors, truly worthy of their beautiful reward.

But all this is impossible without the spirit of poverty, freedom from the burden of temporal things, the spirit of detachment. This spirit alone overcomes indolence, throws away the crutches of temporal make-shifts, and supports itself upon the strength of the Living God. This is the powerful spirit of evangelical poverty, which fears nothing and overcomes everything. Our Saviour here depicts the new corps of picked men, the new people which He calls into existence for the kingdom of God. It is small and helpless as regards outward appearance, but powerful and invincible in its interior spirit.

The Office of Superior

Luke 12:41. And Peter said to him: "Lord, dost thou speak this parable to us, or likewise to all?"—42. And the Lord said: "Who (thinkest thou) is the faithful and wise steward, whom his lord setteth over his family, to give them their measure of wheat in due season?—43. Blessed is that servant, whom when his lord shall come he shall find so doing.—44. Verily I say to you, he will set him over all that he possesseth.—45. But if that servant shall say in his heart: My lord is long a-coming; and shall begin to strike the men-servants and maid-servants, and to eat and to drink, and be drunk;—46. The lord of that servant will come in the day that he hopeth not, and at the hour that he knoweth not, and shall separate him, and shall appoint him his portion with unbelievers.—47. And that servant who knew the will of his lord, and prepared not himself, and did not according to his will, shall be beaten with many stripes.—48. But he that knew not, and did things worthy of stripes, shall be beaten with few stripes. And unto whomsoever much is given, of him much shall be required; and to whom they have committed much, of him they will demand the more."

MATT. 24:45. "Who, thinkest thou, is a faithful and wise servant, whom his lord hath appointed over his family, to give them meat in season?—46. Blessed is that servant, whom when his lord shall come he shall find so doing.—47. Amen I say to you, he shall place him over all his goods.—48. But if that evil servant should say in his heart: My lord is long a-coming;—49. And shall begin to strike his fellow-servants, and shall eat and drink with drunkards;—50. The lord of that servant shall come in a day that he hopeth not, and at an hour that he knoweth not;—51. And shall separate him, and appoint his portion with the hypocrites; there shall be weeping and gnashing of teeth."

It might certainly be doubted whether our Saviour had given this model of perfect readiness for all, or for the Apostles alone. St. Peter therefore inquires His meaning (Luke 12:41).

1. OUR SAVIOUR INTENDS THIS IDEAL OF READINESS TO SERVE FOR THE APOSTLES AND ALSO FOR OTHER SUPERIORS

The wealthy Israelite households were presided over, as regards the distribution of food etc., by a slave who acted as house-steward (Gen. 24:2; 39:4). Peter now asks in his own name and in that of all his fellow-Apostles (that is to say, in the name of the future teaching Church), who is to be understood by the "householder" of the parable (Luke 12:41). Our Saviour leaves this particular question unanswered, and addresses His reply to all who occupy the post of superior (Luke 12:42). There is therefore no doubt that He here had in view, first, the Apostles and bishops, as superiors of the different Churches, and St. Peter as the head of the whole Church; and secondly, all who occupy the position of superior.

2. WHAT QUALITIES OUR LORD REQUIRES OF THE APOSTLES AND OF SUPERIORS IN GENERAL

Our Saviour specifies four qualifications for the office of an Apostle and superior.

First, fidelity. He names this first (Luke 12:42). The superior must take care of his lord's interests as if they were his own, and not seek his personal advantage at his master's expense.

Secondly, prudence (Luke 12:42). Prudence is the virtue of superiors; without this the end for which they have been appointed is not attained, and everything gets into disorder.

The third quality of a superior is justice towards his lord and his inferiors (Luke 12:45). He is to give the latter their portion at the proper time (Luke 12:42). Slaves formerly received their reward in kind. Doctrine and the Sacraments are not the property of ecclesiastical superiors, who are only stewards (or "dispensers," I Cor. 4:1), and must administer them according to the demands of justice (I Cor. 5:12) and circumstances (I Tim. 5:1).

The fourth quality is mildness and kindness, no harshness nor tyranny (Luke 12:45; Matt. 24:49). Nothing would be less advantageous to our Lord's interests than a want of kindness.

3. WHAT MOTIVES OUR LORD ADDUCES FOR GOOD ADMINISTRATION OF AN OFFICE

Our Lord expressly mentions the reward as one motive. Because the administration is comprehensive, anxious and arduous, and therefore also meritorious, the lord sets the servant over all his goods (Luke 12:44; Matt. 24:47). The reward is proportionate to the office and work. This assurance of reward has something very cordial in it; it is like an expression of personal gratitude for great services, which have likewise been rendered out of personal affection.

There are also other motives suggested by the office itself, namely, the honor and eminence of the function of representing our Lord and undertaking the administration in His stead; then the confidence which He places in a superior, entrusting to him all His temporal goods, souls, and the property of the Church; lastly, the love which our Lord must bear towards those who represent Him. They have a special place in His Heart.

The last motive mentioned is the punishment which follows upon bad administration. The lord will certainly call the unfaithful steward to account, and will surprise him in his disorderly behavior (Luke 12:46; Matt. 24:48, 50). He will then depose ("separate") him from his office, cause him to be put to death by a most terrible punishment, viz. that of being cut asunder and hewn in pieces (Hebr. 11:37; I Kings 15:33; Dan. 13:55, 59), and "appoint him his portion with unbelievers" (Luke 12:46), or "hypocrites" (Matt. 24:51). This "portion" will be proportionate to his knowledge, which in this case is complete with regard to his office and duties, since the administrator belongs to the teaching Church. If even simple disobedience is severely punished, how much more conduct which is openly and consciously opposed to position, knowledge, and duty (Luke 12:47, 48; Matt. 24:51; James 3:1; Wisd. 6:7)! The severity of the punishment is justified by the infidelity, folly, wontonness and injustice shown by such behavior. This disgraceful conduct and neglect of duty show further how right our Saviour is in ascribing fidelity and assiduity in the performance of duty to the spirit of detachment and the absence of self-seeking (Luke 12:35).

Decision for or against the Kingdom of Christ

Luke 12:49. "I am come to cast fire on the earth; and what will I but that it be kindled?—50. And I have a baptism, wherewith I am to be baptized; and how am I straitened until it be accomplished?—51. Think ye that I am come to give peace on earth? I tell you no, but separation.—52. For there shall be from henceforth five in one house divided; three against two, and two against three.—53. The father shall be divided against the son, and the son against his father, the mother against the daughter, and the daughter against the mother, the mother-in-law against her daughter-in-law, and the daughter-in-law against her mother-in-law."—54. And he said also to the multitudes: "When you see a cloud rising from the west, presently you say: A shower is coming; and so it happeneth.—55. And when ye see the south wind blow, you say: There will be heat; and it cometh to pass.—56. You hypocrites, you know how to discern the face of the heaven and of the earth; but how is it that you do not discern this time?—57. And why even of yourselves do you not judge that which is just?—58. And when thou goest with thy adversary to the prince, whilst thou art in the way, endeavor to be delivered from him; lest perhaps he draw thee to the judge, and the judge deliver thee to the exactor, and the exactor cast thee into prison.—59. I say to thee, thou shalt not go out thence, until thou pay the very last mite."

Matt. 10:34. "Do not think that I came to send peace upon earth; I came not to send peace, but the sword.—35. For I came to set a man at variance against his father, and the daughter against her mother, and the daughter-in-law against her mother-in-law;—36. And a man's enemies shall be they of his own household."

1. THIS ADDRESS IS A SUMMONS TO DECIDE FOR THE KINGDOM OF CHRIST

This address is nothing but the resumption, continuation and conclusion of the summons to decide for Christ's kingdom, which had begun with the words: "Fear not" (Matt. 10:26; Luke 12:4). This subject had been interrupted by the petty incident of the man who sought to obtain a verdict against his brother (Luke 12:13). In connection with this our Saviour gives instructions concerning covetousness and excess of temporal cares, ending with the spirit of apostolic poverty, which fits a man for the perfect discharge of the duties of a pastor and superior. With the concluding thought of the punishment which will follow upon the neglect of these pastoral cares and duties, He reverts to the resolute and self-sacrificing adoption of the cause of the Gospel, which by its very nature requires a firm bearing, even in the face of the greatest difficulties and sacrifices. Such is the purpose and signification of this address. St. Matthew (10:34) also connects the thoughts in this manner.

2. MOTIVES FOR THIS DECISION

Our Saviour shows the necessity of this self-sacrificing resolution and determination in three figures, in which He explains to us the nature of His kingdom. All three urge us to show this resolution in spite of sacrifices and adversities. The first figure is contained in the words: "I am come to cast fire upon the earth, and what will I but that it be kindled?" (Luke 12:49.) Christianity then is a fire, by its very nature and also by its doctrines of faith and morals. They shine clearly and brightly into the mind and heart of every man; and as fire seizes and purifies all metals, so they seize upon all that is false, selfish, dark and sinful in man, and effect in him the painful process of purification (often outwardly even, since the profession of the Christian religion may involve suffering and death). Christ has brought this fire in the shape of His law, and He casts it on the earth among men that it may do its work, enlighten and consume. The Holy Spirit is also meant by this fire, because it was upon His coming that the flame of Christianity began to give out light and heat; outwardly by preaching, inwardly by the cleansing process wrought in the hearts of men. He was to "convince the world of sin, and of justice, and of judgment" (John 16:8; Luke 3:16).

The second figure is contained in the words: "I have a baptism wherewith I am to be baptized" (Luke 12:50). Our Saviour evidently speaks here of His future Passion under the figure of a baptism (Mark 10:38). It is a baptism in the waters of tribulation (Ps. 68:2, 15; 143:7), which overwhelm and engulf Him; indeed, it is a baptism of blood. But it is a baptism, a religious consecration, a sacrifice which propitiates God and atones for sin. The baptismal font of Christ's Passion becomes the font of the whole world (Rom. 6:3). This baptism of suffering undergone by Him is now a model for all Christians. For through baptism we enter the Church and become Christians; it is the death and burial of the old sinful man, and obliges us all even to endure martyrdom, under certain circumstances. All who receive baptism must be prepared for the waters of tribulation. Our Saviour likewise shows us what must be our dispositions with regard to baptism, in the words: "And how am I straitened until it be accomplished" (Luke 12:50). Since this baptism, though propitiatory and well-pleasing to God, is very painful, He fears it, although in another sense He also desires it. Thus the Heart of the Redeemer is agitated by natural anxiety and fear on the one hand, and by reverence, love and desire on the other (cf. John 11:27). These may and must be the sentiments of all who embrace Christianity.

The third figure of Christianity and Christ's kingdom shows us that it is in nature and effect a combat, a separation and painful division. "Think ye that I am come to give peace on earth? I tell you no, but separation" (Luke 12:51) and "the sword" (Matt. 10:34). The aim of Christ's kingdom is peace (Luke 2:14; 10:5; John 14:27; 20:19; I Cor. 7:15), but sinfulness and enmity to God reign in us and around us, and therefore peace can only be obtained through war and strife within and without. Wherever nature opposes the supernatural and becomes a hindrance and an enemy, be it within a man or in his surroundings, there the hindrance must be cut asunder with the sword of mortification. Our Saviour describes to us very vividly the division and separation which the Gospel will bring into families (Luke 12:52, 53; Matt. 10:35, 36). Thus does Christianity appear everywhere in history, from the time of the Apostles and Martyrs until the present day; it may call from unbelief or heresy to the true faith, or (amongst Catholics) from an ordinary life to perfection.

This, then, is the idea of Christianity and the kingdom of Christ; it is a fire, a baptism of suffering and blood, a sword that brings division and separation even into a man's heart and home, as the Apostle says: "The word of God is living and effectual, and more piercing than any two-edged sword, and reaching unto the division of the soul and the spirit, of the joints also and the marrow; and is a discerner of the thoughts and intents of the heart" (Heb. 4:12). Whoever is not prepared for this cannot be a disciple of Jesus. We must be able to bear being burned and cut asunder, and whoever cannot endure and overcome the dread and bitter plunge into the waters of tribulation and humiliation is not worthy of our Saviour.

3. URGENCY OF THE DECISION

The kingdom of Christ by its very nature requires this firmness and determination, and that without delay; for the kingdom is there, and everyone is called upon to make his decision, and must make it, if he does not wish to incur judgment.

That the Messias and the kingdom of God are there, and that the Jews may know this and as a matter of fact do know it, our Saviour shows by a telling personal proof which He has already employed once before (Matt. 16:2). You understand the signs of the weather so well, that you would be ashamed if what you had predicted with regard to it did not come true. But the signs of the coming of the Messias, His kingdom and dispensation, in which "that which is just" (Luke 12:57) prevails, are much surer and more important, so that you are "hypocrites" (Luke 12:56) if you say that this is not the case; and all the more so because you might discern it of yourselves (Luke 12:57). By "hypocrites" our Lord designates the pharisaically-minded portion of His hearers.

He speaks of their judgment and punishment in a kind of parable or similitude, in which He warns us to come to terms with an adversary, lest he deliver us up to the judge, the jailer, and the prison, out of which there is no deliverance until the last farthing is paid (Luke 12:58, 59). The adversary here signifies conscience, the jailer death, and the prison hell.

This address is of great importance; first on account of the revelation with regard to the true character of Christianity, essential elements of which, if it is to save man, must be mortification and the spirit of sacrifice, on account of the Fall and the consequent degeneracy of our nature. Secondly, the mystery teaches us what sentiments we must entertain with respect to the claims of our religion. The dispositions which our Saviour requires of us are resolution and readiness for any sacrifices, if we do not wish to get into conflict with our conscience. Thirdly, the address is important on account of the prediction of the Passion, in the beautiful and profound figure of baptism; and also on account of the disclosure of our Saviour's feelings and dispositions with regard to His Passion. His words again afford us a glimpse of the divinely-human emotions of His Sacred Heart. Fear and reverence, dread and desire agitate it, when He permits the thought of His Passion, which is now ever drawing nearer, to work upon His mind. We feel the approach of the decisive moment in the gravity and agitated tone of His words.

The Parable of the Fig-tree

Luke 13:1. And there were present at that very time some that told him of the Galileans, whose blood Pilate had mingled with their sacrifices.—2. And he answering said to them: "Think you that these Galileans were sinners above all the men of Galilee, because they suffered such things?—3. No, I say to you; but unless you shall do penance, you shall all likewise perish.—4. Or those eighteen upon whom the tower fell in Siloe, and slew them; think you that they also were debtors above all the men that dwelt in Jerusalem?—5. No, I say to you; but except you do penance, you shall all likewise perish."—6. He spoke also this parable: "A certain man had a fig-tree planted in his vineyard, and he came seeking fruit on it, and found none.—7. And he said to the dresser of the vineyard: Behold for these three years I come seeking fruit on this fig-tree, and I find none. Cut it down therefore; why cumbereth it the ground?—8. But he answering said to him: Lord, let it alone this year also, until I dig about it, and dung it;—9. And if happily it bear fruit; but if not, then after that thou shalt cut it down."

The news came that Pilate had caused a number of Galileans to be massacred whilst offering sacrifice in the Temple. Our Saviour was evidently not in Jerusalem at the time, and probably not in Galilee either, but somewhere in Judaea (Luke 13:2). Pilate's act of violence may probably have taken place in one of the three festival weeks after the Feast of Tabernacles. At all events it was on an occasion when strangers had made a pilgrimage to Jerusalem for some feast.

1. THE ACCOUNT OF THE MURDER OF THE GALILEANS

The narrators were perhaps pilgrims who had just returned from Jerusalem, and had there been witnesses of the bloody deed. One can easily picture to oneself the account accompanied by thoughts, feelings and expressions of national, political and religious indignation at the horrible crime, and at the intolerable oppression and cruelty of the foreign rulers. One feels as it were this indignation in the words that the blood of the Galileans had been "mingled with their sacrifices" (Luke 13:1), which imply an abominable deed and a terrible profanation of the Temple. It may be seen from the context that the narration was accompanied by expressions of suspicion that the death of these unfortunate people at a religious solemnity was a result of exceptionally great crimes on their part. We have already met with this prejudice once before (John 9:2). In this case it was justified, as it were, by the solemn prayer of consecration made at the Dedication of the Temple (III Kings 8:28 seq.). The narrators and other bystanders might expect an answer from our Saviour upon both points, the more so as those who had fallen were his fellow-countrymen.

The narration shows so exactly the state of the unhappy nation and the barbarous and reckless violence of the governor, who never let it have any rest, with his renewed encroachments and ill-treatment. Pilate had seized the Temple treasure for the construction of an aqueduct; hence the tumult. From the fortress of Antonia the Romans commanded the whole Temple, and could forcibly interfere at any moment. On the other hand there is also expressed here the mingling of political and religious pride so characteristic of the nation, which fancied that God could not forsake it unless in consequence of non-observance of the law. It was not conscious of any such infidelity, and no one could convince it of this. Hence the excitement of the people and their wonder that God could allow their Temple and sacrifices to be thus desecrated and trodden under foot by heathens. They could find no other explanation but that secret crimes of the fallen men must have been the cause of this outrage.

2. OUR SAVIOUR'S ANSWER, AND HIS ADMONITION TO DO PENANCE

For the national and political irritation our Saviour has not a word. He surely pitied the oppressed people with His whole heart; but He will not add fuel to the fire of their excitement. This did not answer His purpose.

On the other hand, He turns His attention to the spirtual pride of the people, and exhorts them to do penance and in this way turn the occurrence to their own good. It was by no means to be assumed that the victims had been especially wicked, more so than any other Galileans; any more than that the eighteen inhabitants of Jerusalem, who had been killed shortly before at the pool of Siloe by the fall of one of the towers of the city-wall, had been worse than their fellow-citizens. The depravity of the inhabitants of Galilee and Jerusalem was great enough for all to be in need of penance (Luke 13:2, 4). Our Saviour here alludes to an incident which must have occurred recently and was still fresh in the memory of all. The pool of Siloe lay under the high towers of the city-wall (cf. Introd., p. 5). It is not known what had occasioned the fall of this tower.

If they did not all do penance, similar ruin would befall them also (Luke 13:3, 5). Their imaginary piety, their sacrifices and their Temple would no more protect them from destruction than the Temple and the sacrifice had shielded the Galileans and the men of Jerusalem at the pool of Siloe, to which special power and divine protection were ascribed, because it was the symbol of the House of David and of the Messias (John 9:7). These words, although no one at this time understood their meaning, were a true and striking prophecy, which was fulfilled in the destruction of the city and Temple. Some of the people were killed on the Temple hill, in the subterranean passages of which they had taken refuge, and were buried beneath the ruins. Thus the blood of the Galileans around the altar of sacrifice and the falling tower of Siloe were truly prophetic.

3. OUR SAVIOUR SHOWS IN A PARABLE THE FOUNDATION FOR HIS EXHORTATION TO DO PENANCE

Our Saviour propounds the parable of the unfruitful fig-tree in order to show the grounds for His exhortation to penance. There are three points of especial importance in this parable.

First, the unfruitfulness of the fig-tree, which stands in a vineyard. The fig-tree signifies the Israelite nation. The comparison is well chosen. The vine and the fig-tree are among the most ordinary agricultural products of Palestine, and are proverbial as denoting the blessing upon the land (Deut. 8:8; III Kings 4:25; Mich. 4:4). Israel had already been repeatedly compared to the fig-tree and its fruit (Jer. 24:1; Osee 9:10). As a type of the future Church it is still oftener compared to a vine (Ps. 79:9; Isa. 5). But here it is represented as an unfruitful fig-tree in the midst of a flourishing vineyard; perhaps in contrast to the young Church, which bears and will continue to bear fruit, whilst the fig-tree had borne none (although three years had already elapsed since fruit might have been expected from it), but had frustrated all hopes and efforts (Luke 13:6).

The second point is the desire and the patience of the owner of the vineyard, and the pity, care, and intercession of the vine-dresser. The owner of the vineyard is the Heavenly Father, and the vine-dresser represents all the prophets and finally our Divine Saviour. For nearly three years He has now been tending His vineyard (and in particular the "fig-tree," Israel) with all possible industry, by His teaching, example and miracles; He intercedes for it (Luke 13:8), and will finally water it not only with His sweat, but even with His Blood.

The third point is the threat to cut down the tree if it does not bear fruit (Luke 13:7). The menace is justified, since the tree only takes up room and injures other fruit-bearing trees. Even the vine-dresser agrees with this (Luke 13:9). This is only a repetition of the threat uttered just before, that they would all perish (Luke 13:3, 5). We see how ingenious is our Lord's comparison of Israel to the fig-tree in the vineyard. The Church is a new and larger plantation. Israel is only a fig-tree, and finds its place therein. But if it remains unfruitful and only injures the vineyard, then it will be cast out of God's plantation as a useless tree. By this parable, then, our Lord does but announce in another form God's judgment and punishment, and gives the reasons for it in His touching care for Israel on the one hand, and its persistent unfruitfulness, uselessness and harmfulness on the other, all under the figure of the fig-tree.

In this parable the beautiful intellect of our Saviour is again displayed. We see how ingeniously He explains invisible things by similes taken from visible nature, and how exactly He keeps to the manners and customs of the country in the development and application of these similes. The borders of the vineyards in Palestine are mostly planted with almond, peach and fig-trees. But of still more importance is the openness and straightforwardness with which He can speak earnest truths even to His fellow-countrymen and friends. He does not except the Galileans in speaking of depravity and need of penance. On the contrary, He even hints that the Galileans who had been slain had incurred destruction by their own fault, though not by special crimes. Further, our Saviour here shows true apostolic tact, by not entering into considerations and claims of national spirit and the national temporal interests. He has not so much as a word for them. On the contrary, He refers all events to the welfare of souls. He takes occasion from the doom of the Galileans and the unfortunate citizens of Jerusalem to exhort the people to penance, and to threaten them with a similar punishment in case of their perversity. He certainly best promotes even the temporal interests of the nation in this way. Our Saviour here gives us all the lesson that, before God, only innocence or penance can give confidence and security.

The Healing of the Crippled Woman

Luke 13:10. And he was teaching in their synagogue on the Sabbaths.—11. And behold there was a woman who had a spirit of infirmity eighteen years; and she was bowed together, neither could she look upwards at all.—12. Whom when Jesus saw, he called her unto him, and said to her: "Woman, thou art delivered from thy infirmity."—13. And he laid his hands upon her, and immediately she was made straight, and glorified God.—14. And the ruler of the synagogue (being angry that Jesus had healed on the Sabbath) answering, said to the multitude: "Six days there are wherein you ought to work; in them therefore come and be healed, and not on the Sabbath-day."—15. And the Lord answering him, said: "Ye hypocrites, doth not everyone of you on the Sabbath-day loose his ox or his ass from the manger, and lead them to water?—16. And ought not this daughter of Abraham, whom Satan hath bound, lo, these eighteen years, be loosed from this bond on the Sabbath-day?"—17. And when he said these things, all his adversaries were ashamed; and all the people rejoiced for all the things that were gloriously done by him.

1. The Healing

With regard to the time and place of the miracle, the circumstances are as follows: it was on a Sabbath-day and in a synagogue, where our Lord was teaching the people (Luke 13:10). Whether it was some weeks or only a few days after the preceding mystery, cannot be ascertained.

The motive for working this miracle on the Sabbath and in presence of the people was certainly not any intention of annoying or irritating the Pharisees. From St. Luke's words (13:11, 12) we should say that our Lord had seen the woman in the crowd by chance, especially as her condition made her sufficiently conspicuous. The motive, then, was pity and compassion for the miserable condition of the woman. She had been for eighteen years quite crippled and bent, so that she could neither stand upright nor look upwards. Her condition was made worse by the additional fact that the deformity was the effect of possession. The Evangelist calls the disease "a spirit of infirmity" (Luke 13:11), and our Saviour says that the devil had thus bound and fettered her, the daughter of Abraham (Luke 13:16). Hence His compassion, and such active and kindly compassion. He sees her, and calls her to Him quite unasked; expels the devil with the simple words: "Woman, thou art delivered from thy infirmity"; and then lays His hands upon her, as if in sign of taking possession of her, confirming her recovery and strengthening her health, and also as an assurance of His protection (Luke 13:12, 13), for the imposition of hands signifies all this.

2. REPROOF FROM THE RULER OF THE SYNAGOGUE

The ruler of the synagogue seems to have been a thorough Pharisee. He could not master his annoyance and anger at seeing this miracle wrought on the Sabbath, and burst forth into words of reproach. Our Saviour calls his behavior and words "hypocrisy" (Luke 13:15) and insincerity. And so it was, in three respects.

First, the ruler is angry with our Saviour for having healed on the Sabbath; yet he does not attack Him, but the people, as though they had taken the initiative and occasioned the miracle by their requests. He knows quite well that this is not the case, but he pretends to think so. He means our Saviour, but finds fault with the people; probably because he did not wish to appear to proceed against our Lord, or because he feared to get the worst of it if he addressed himself directly to Him, whilst the people did not dare to make any reply.

Secondly, he passes off his annoyance as zeal for the law of Sabbath observance (Luke 13:14), whereas it was in reality only hatred of our Saviour and eccentricity and perversity in the interpretation of this law. The regulations of the Pharisees were innumerable with regard to what was permitted on the Sabbath in the way of remedies and medical aid. In the scrupulous observance of these regulations they quite overlooked the essential object of the Sabbath, viz. the performance of works of piety. This very man had just been praying aloud for the advent of the Messias, and had either read or heard the Scriptures, every page of which speaks of mercy and good deeds.

Thirdly, the ruler of the synagogue puts an extremely odious construction upon the conduct of our Saviour and the people, though under the pretence of great moderation. "Six days there are wherein you ought to work; in them therefore come and be healed, and not on the Sabbath-day" (Luke 13:14), as though the people had only come thither in order to be healed, and our Saviour were a traveling quack who exercised his healing art on the Sabbath particularly. The ruler designates even the mere imposition of hands as "work."

3. OUR SAVIOUR'S REPLY

The reply, like the miracle, was (as the people said) "glorious" (Luke 13:17). It was glorious especially by the fearlessness, plain-speaking and energy with which our Lord exposes the covert hypocrisy of the man. Perhaps he was rich and influential, and might revenge himself. But all this has no weight with our Saviour. He calls him and all who are of the same persuasion simply "hypocrites" (Luke 13:15).

Further, the reply was "glorious" in its acuteness and unanswerable conclusiveness. What was done for an animal without violation of the law, our Lord thinks, might surely be done for a human being also (Luke 13:15, 16). He carries out this thought in very ingenious contrasts. To the "ox" and "ass" He opposes the "daughter of Abraham," to the "loosing from the manger" the "loosing from the bonds of Satan," to the "leading to water" the imposition of hands, and to the twenty-four hours of a Sabbath the eighteen years of possession by the devil. Our Saviour makes use of the same similitude elsewhere, but in a different manner (Matt. 12:12). The act of freeing from the sad slavery of Satan is surely a work of piety quite in keeping with the spirit of the Sabbath, and it typifies the eternal rest of God and of the Saints in heaven. The point of the answer lies in the contrast between the ease with which the Pharisees dispensed themselves from the Sabbath observance when it was a question of their own petty interests, and their excessive rigor when much higher interests of their fellow-men were at stake.

Our Saviour's enemies could oppose nothing to His severe and conclusive reply. They were silenced and abashed, but yet did not amend. The people on the other hand were full of joy at all the glorious words and deeds of our Lord (Luke 13:17).

In this mystery the nature of the evil spirits is again very clearly manifested. Malicious and full of hatred towards God, they also persecute His image, His human child adopted in grace, and torment and humiliate it. As animals are tied up, fastened to the manger, and led about by the bridle, so Satan treats humanity, represented in this woman; and unhappily often with the cognizance and consent of men, who allow themselves to be guided by the Evil One through their evil passions as by reins. On the other hand, our Saviour appears as the destroyer of the works of Satan (I John 3:8). He immediately recognizes the enemy, and by expelling him removes the cause of the infirmity also, as He elsewhere first pardons sin and then heals the disease which is the result of it (Matt. 9:2).

The Parable of the Grain of Mustard-seed

Luke 13:18. He said therefore: "To what is the kingdom of God like, and whereunto shall I resemble it?—19. It is like to a grain of mustard-seed, which a man took and cast into his garden, and it grew, and became a great tree; and the birds of the air lodged in the branches thereof."

Matt. 13:31. Another parable he proposed unto them, saying: "The kingdom of heaven is like to a grain of mustard-seed, which a man took and sowed in his field;—32. Which is the least indeed of all seeds; but when it is grown up, it is greater than all herbs, and becometh a tree, so that the birds of the air come and dwell in the branches thereof."

Mark 4:30. And he said: "To what shall we liken the kingdom of God? Or to what parable shall we compare it?—31. It is as a grain of mustard-seed, which when it is sown in the earth, is less than all the seeds that are in the earth;—32. And when it is sown, it shooteth up, and becometh greater than all herbs, and shooteth out great branches, so that the birds of the air may dwell under the shadow thereof."

Our Saviour probably propounded this parable and the following one for the second time, and most likely on His way to Jerusalem (Luke 13:22) to the Feast of the Dedication. St. Matthew and St. Mark place it at an earlier period. A repetition was quite in keeping here, because our Saviour was nearing the accomplishment of His life's task (Luke 9:51), and the disciples were expecting the speedy commencement of His kingdom (Luke 19:11). On account of the similarity of the matter contained, the parable of the seed is also added here.

1. Object of the Parable

The reason of the parable is evidently that our Lord wishes to instruct His disciples concerning the manner in which His kingdom will begin and develop upon earth. It will grow from an insignificant and humble beginning to great strength and exterior power for good, quite contrary to the Jewish opinion and expectations, which are purely natural and human.

2. Judicious Selection of the Parable

And why, then, does our Saviour choose the figure of a mustard-tree, and not (for example) of a cedar, like Ezechiel? (Ez. 17:22.) Perhaps there was such a mustard-tree growing within sight of our Saviour and His hearers. At all events the figure chosen was very familiar and very appropriate as regards the points of comparison, indeed more so than that of a cedar, and of more practical utility.

The points of comparison are two in number: the insignificance of the beginning, and the importance and greatness of the intrinsic power, utility, and exterior development. The mustard-tree answers to all this. Its seed is one of the smallest seeds used in the agriculture of the East; indeed, its diminutive size seems to have been proverbial (Luke 17:6). Its pungency and utility in domestic economy is well known. On account of this pungent and refreshing sharpness it is a common article of food and medicine, especially in the East. And as regards its exterior appearance, the tiny grain develops and grows to the size of a small figtree. The birds are fond of its shade.

3. VERIFICATION AND FULFILMENT OF THE PARABLE

What our Saviour said of His Church in a similitude has become a universal law.

It has become a law, first, in our Saviour Himself, the Model of the Church and of all the elect. How inconsiderable, how insignificant was His appearance, to the sensual eyes of the Jews! In His Passion and Death He seemed to be completely vanquished, but now all power and strength belong to Him (Apoc. 5:13; 7:12).

Secondly, it has become a law in the Church. Everywhere arising from a small beginning, she gathers strength and increases in extent and power, by virtue of her catholicity; and in interior power and efficacy by her doctrine and Sacraments, faith and grace (Dan. 2:34, 35, 44). There is nothing great in ideas, truths, or high aims that is not to be found in the Church. Nations and great minds seek her and find an abode in her, as the birds are attracted to the mustard-tree and alight on its branches. With sectarians, on the contrary, doctrine is without sap and strength; it is what our Lord has called salt without savor.

Thirdly, the parable is fulfilled in each individual. He also must begin with humility and self-abasement and become small in order to enter the Church. The more he penetrates into the spirit of the Church, the smaller he must grow. But at the same time he becomes imbued with the strength and efficacy of the divine "grain of mustard-seed," and becomes a powerful instrument in the hand of God.

The Parable of the Leaven

Luke 13:21. "The kingdom of God is like to leaven, which a woman took and hid in three measures of meal, till the whole was leavened."

Matt. 13:33. Another parable he spoke to them: "The kingdom of heaven is like to leaven, which a woman took and hid in three measures of meal, until the whole was leavened."

1. OBJECT OF THE PARABLE

The object of this parable is similar to that of the preceding one. This also is a prediction of how the kingdom of God, the Church, will thrive and expand, but here more with regard to interior progress and the manner in which it takes place, viz. by a constant, quiet increase through its own innate and invincible power; whilst the former parable takes more into consideration the diminutive proportions of the beginning on the one hand, and the greatness of the development on the other. The Jews expected that the kingdom of God would come into existence suddenly and by forcible means, and that it would be only for their nation, not for the whole mass of mankind. Both parables are therefore a kind of program of the development of God's kingdom—certainly a strange contrast to what the Jews pictured to themselves.

2. DEVELOPMENT OF THE PARABLE

Our Saviour again chooses for His purpose a figure taken from domestic life and familiar to all; viz. the use of leaven. In the East the women make the bread. Three measures of flour seems to have been the usual quantity for one baking (Gen. 18:6; I Kings 1:24).

The leaven is put into the mass of dough and works inwardly, not quickly, violently, or only upon one part, but slowly and quietly, through its own power and heat, and upon the whole mass. It makes the dough light and spongy, raises it, and makes it wholesome and fit for food. The flour and water without leaven would be a heavy and unwholesome mass.

3. APPLICATION OF THE PARABLE

The parable has been verified in the Church, the kingdom of the Messias. She did not become what she is abruptly, by a sudden, decisive act. Christ placed within her the leaven, the power of life, increase and spiritualization, by the Holy Ghost, the word of faith and the grace of the Sacraments; and through her He communicated these gifts to the entire human race. Thus she now works by means of this power bestowed upon her, interiorly, slowly, from one end to another. We must have patience and wait and hope. But the leaven is beginning to work everywhere; it rises and spreads throughout the whole mass of humanity. What would mankind be without this vivifying leaven? The Church is in every respect a contrast to Judaism and to the sects, which have no inward germ of vital power, but grow by outward means or through the leaven of false doctrine and teaching.

The parable is also fulfilled in the spiritual life of every individual. In the spiritual life things do not go on by fits and starts, but quietly, and imperceptibly. Faith and grace work upon the intellect, the intellect informs the will, the will makes decisions affecting the principles, thoughts, words, actions, and finally upon the whole life and the interior man.

The Parable of the Seed

Mark 4:26. And he said: "So is the kingdom of God, as if a man should cast seed into the earth,—27. And should sleep and rise, night and day, and the seed should spring and grow up whilst he knoweth not.—28. For the earth of itself bringeth forth fruit, first the blade, then the ear, afterwards the full corn in the ear.—29. And when the fruit is brought forth, immediately he putteth in the sickle, because the harvest is come."

1. SIGNIFICATION OF THE PARABLE

Our Saviour evidently treats in this parable of the nature and essential character of the kingdom of God, the Church (Mark 4:26, 30). He has here a different intention from that of the two preceding parables, in which He holds up to view the wonderful exterior propagation of the Church on the one hand, and its quiet interior action on the other. In this parable our Lord depicts in a few touches, under the figure of the process undergone by seed, the course and various stages of the development of the Church. He says that it is with the kingdom of God as with seed sown in the earth by a man, who then lies down to rest and next day pursues other occupations (Mark 4:27). In the meantime the earth does its work upon the seed, without any further assistance on the man's part. It makes the seed spring up; first the blade appears, then the ear, and finally the grain (Mark 4:27, 28). Then the man takes the sickle and gathers in his harvest (Mark 4:29). In the sowing, maturing, and reaping of the seed are delineated in a few strokes the foundation, development, and final state of the Church of Christ. Between these two extreme points of the visible intervention of Christ lies the time of development, which He, having ascended into heaven, does not execute visibly, but invisibly, through the mysterious virtue which He has deposited in the Church and which works within her unerringly, until He comes again to judgment (Apoc. 14:15; Joel 3:13). These are the great stages of the development of the Church upon earth.

2. CONCLUSIONS

In the first place, our Saviour appears in this parable in all the power and glory of His influence upon the Church. He is her Author and Perfecter, and bestows upon her from His throne in heaven every blessing and increase. The mysterious virtue latent in the Church works only under the influence of His grace, like the earth under the influence of the sun and the rain. He, as the Head, never forsakes the Church, His Body (Matt. 28:20); He gives the increase (I Cor. 3:6) and is all in all to her. We have here also a charming example of how gracefully our Lord speaks. He does not scorn to ornament and develop the figures of which He makes use in His instructions (Mark 4:28).

The successors of the Apostles are the bishops, who, as preachers of the Word, may be regarded as being in a subordinate manner sowers, who sow the seed during Christ's absence in heaven and thus supplement, promote and continue His work here below. For preachers a double admonition may be drawn from this parable: first, that it is not they who bring about the increase, but the grace of Christ (I Cor. 3:7), and they must therefore keep themselves humble; secondly, that they must not be discouraged if the seed takes time to ripen into fruit in souls, like seed in the plowed field. After all, the fruit of souls is so precious that no length of time should be considered too long to wait.

Lastly, the parable finds its counterpart in the soul of every Christian in whom the seed, once sown, springs up under the influence of grace; first in the blade of good desires, then in the ear of execution, and finally in the fruit of merit for eternity.

F. The Public Life of Jesus from the Feast of the Dedication of the Temple until the Passion

This period is of the highest importance, containing as it does the address on the Feast of the Dedication, the miracle of the raising of Lazarus from the dead, and the solemn entrance into the city on Palm Sunday. These three events form the culminating point of our Lord's revelation of Himself by teaching and miracles. In return the unbelief of the Jews leads to another attempt upon the life of our Saviour, unpremeditated in the first instance, but followed by the formal, official decision of the Great Council to put Him to death. In consequence of this decision they seek to entrap Him, by captious disputes, into saying something which could be turned into a legal basis for His condemnation. Our Saviour frustrates all these snares, and His endeavors to induce the people to believe, by ever plainer threats of judgment and punishment, become henceforth more marked. The scene of this period of His life is partly Judaea, but chiefly Peraea.

The Feast of the Dedication

John 10:22. And it was the Feast of the Dedication at Jerusalem; and it was winter.—23. And Jesus walked in the temple in Solomon's porch.—24. The Jews therefore came round about him, and said to him: "How long dost thou hold our souls in suspense? If thou be the Christ, tell us plainly."—25. Jesus answered them: "I speak to you, and you believe not; the works that I do in the name of my Father, they give testimony of me.—26. But you do not believe, because you are not of my sheep.—27. My sheep hear my voice; and I know them, and they follow me.—28. And I give them life everlasting; and they shall not perish for ever, and no man shall pluck them out of my hand.—29. That which my Father hath given me is greater than all; and no man can snatch them out of the hand of my Father.—30. I and my Father are one."—31. The Jews then took up stones, to stone him.—32. Jesus answered them: "Many good works I have shown you from my Father; for which of those works do you stone me?"—33. The Jews answered him: "For a good work we stone thee not, but for blasphemy; and because that thou being a man, makest thyself God."—34. Jesus answered them: "Is it not written in your law: I said, you are gods?—35. If he called them gods, to whom the word of God was spoken, and the Scripture cannot be broken;—36. Do you say of him, whom the Father hath sanctified and sent into the world: Thou blasphemest; because I said, I am the Son of God?—37. If I do not the works of my Father, believe me not.—38. But if I do; although you will not believe me, believe the works, that you may know and believe that the Father is in me, and I in the Father."—39. They sought therefore to take him, and he escaped out of their hands.—40. And he went again beyond the Jordan into that place where John was baptizing first; and there he abode.—41. And many resorted to him, and they said: "John indeed did no sign,—42. But all things, whatsoever John said of this man, were true." And many believed in him.

On the Feast of the Dedication our Saviour again appeared in Jerusalem.

1. THE JEWS DEMAND OF OUR SAVIOUR AN OPEN DECLARATION OF HIS RANK AS THE MESSIAS

The circumstances of this public and stern demand were as follows:

The Dedication was a feast that had been kept for 200 years, in remembrance of and in thanksgiving for the purification of the Temple from the abominations of the heathen worship which King Antiochus had forcibly introduced but which Judas Machabeus had abolished after his conquest of the city (I Mach. 4:52, 59; II Mach. 10:5–8). The feast was celebrated with great solemnity, a special feature of it being the kindling of lights in the houses, for which reason it was also called the Feast of Lights, or the Feast of Tabernacles of the month of Casleu (December). Everything connected with it was calculated to arouse in the people sentiments of gratitude towards God (John 10:22). The scene of the demand was the Temple, which had always been regarded as the seat of revelation of the Messias, and the occurrence took place in that part of the Temple known as Solomon's porch, which formed the eastern enclosure of the Temple court. This was the sole remnant of the colossal foundations of Solomon's Temple, upon which a magnificent porch had now again been erected. Here our Saviour taught, walking up and down, probably because He could not well address the people in the fore-courts, in the open air, on account of the frequent winter rains (John 10:22, 23).

The demand itself comes from the Jews, i.e. the pharisaically-minded party inimical to our Saviour; and it is made in a most striking, earnest, and almost threatening manner. They surround Him in Solomon's porch and ask Him how long he means to keep them in suspense and agitation; if He is the Christ, He should say so plainly and unequivocally (John 10:24). One sees from these words what a burning question this was among the people. The demand was not made from any good motive. Our Saviour had already spoken about Himself and His Nature plainly enough for those who were well-disposed (John 5:26; 6:35; 7:38; 8:12, 18, 58; 5:25). But such was their contrary spirit that, if He spoke, they desired signs (John 2:18; 6:30); if He performed signs, they wanted speeches; if He bore witness to Himself, they repudiated His words as evidence given of Himself (John 8:13); if He appealed to the signs and the testimony of His Father, they demanded a confession from His own lips (Schanz). The demand was most likely made with the intention of getting some clear statement from Him which would afford a pretext for taking proceedings against Him, either before the Sanhedrim or before the Roman authorities; for according to the conception of the Jews the Messias was a half-spiritual and half-secular ruler. It was therefore not readiness to believe that prompted the inquiry, but fresh malice.

2. OUR SAVIOUR TESTIFIES THAT HE IS TRULY GOD

In His answer our Saviour does three things.

First, He avoids giving a direct answer to the question whether He is the Messias.[1] And why? In the first place, because He could not answer it directly. He could not exactly reply in the affirmative, because He was not the Messias according to their conception of Him; nor in the negative, because He was the true Messias. In the second place, it was not necessary; for, as He Himself says, He had borne sufficient testimony to Himself, and even proved His identity by miracles (John 10:25). Lastly, it was quite useless; for they did not and would not believe Him. He tells them too, as He had often done already, the reason of their unbelief (John 10:26; 6:44); that they are not His sheep, who follow Him and hear His voice (John 10:26, 27). On the contrary, they do not merely persist in their unbelief, but even persecute Him and His sheep, by laying them under the ban of the synagogue (John 9:22). In this evasive answer our Saviour gives no less than four reasons for believing in Him. First, He briefly recapitulates here all the proofs He has already given of His Divinity: the testimony of His miracles, the testimony of His Father, and His own testimony (John 10:25); secondly, He calls the Jews' attention to the incredulous dispositions which they oppose to all this (John 10:25, 26); thirdly, He holds up to their view the happy lot of His sheep who believe in Him, viz. security and eternal happiness (John 10:27, 28); fourthly, He points out to them the fatal results of their unbelief, and the futility of their enmity against Him and His sheep (John 10:26, 28).

Secondly, our Saviour takes occasion from these last words to bear witness to His true Divinity and personal Sonship. In spite of your unbelief (He continues), I shall gather My sheep together and lead them to their destination, and no one will be able to

[1] In the Greek version the text is: "I *have* told you."

pluck them out of My hand (John 10:28). He gives as a reason for this that "what My Father hath given Me (i.e. divine power) is greater than all," or according to another reading: The Father, Who is greater than all, has given Me the sheep, and when they are in My hand, they are also in His, "and no one can snatch them out of the hand of My Father" (John 10:29). "I and the Father are one" (John 10:30), not only by conformity of will, but by unity and identity of power, and therefore also of nature and substance. Our Saviour demonstrates here His true Divinity and consubstantiality with the Father, by the unity and identity of their power. They are two Persons, but one in nature. And so the Jews quite correctly understood it; for they say that He is blaspheming, making Himself God, whereas He is only a man (John 10:33), and therefore they wish to stone Him (John 10:31). Thus our Lord tells the Jews more than they had asked; indeed, this is the clearest and plainest testimony of His Divinity that He had as yet given, although He merely calls Himself "the Son of God," not directly "God," probably in order not to shock His hearers.

Thirdly, our Lord confirms this testimony of His Divinity. As the Jews wish to stone Him on account of this statement, He not only does not retract it, but even insists upon it and gives a fresh proof of it. At first, indeed, He checks their uproar and fury by quite unexpectedly reminding them of the benefits He had conferred upon them, in return for which they now wish to stone Him; and also by calling their attention to the fact that there is no reason for being scandalized at His calling Himself the Son of God, since God's messengers, kings, prophets, and even godless judges are called in the Scriptures "sons of God" (Ex. 7:1; 22:28; Ps. 81:6). By this adroit turn of the phrase He restrains the fury of the crowd and compels them to resume the conversation. But He draws from this very turn of phrase, which seems at the outset like a concession, a new proof of His statement. If, He says, even the prophets may be called the sons of God without doing violence to the Scriptures, how much more He whom the Father has sanctified (consecrated, anointed; I Kings 7:1; Jer. 1:5; Ex. 13:2) by the communication of the Divine Nature, and sent into the world (John 10:34, 35, 36). All the prophets and kings were only shadows and types; He is the actual Son of God. Our Saviour further calls their attention to the miracles which the Father works through Him; these are a sufficient proof that the Father is in Him and He in the Father, which is the same thing as saying that He and the Father are one (John 10:37, 38). Thus He not only does not retract His testimony of His Divinity, on their threatening to stone Him, but repeats and solemnly confirms it.

3. OUR SAVIOUR ESCAPES FROM THE POWER OF THE JEWS AND GOES INTO PERAEA

The Jews responded by attempting to seize our Lord, in order either to stone Him or to take Him prisoner. "But He escaped out of their hands" (John 10:39). From this it would seem that they had already laid hold of Him, and so it was either His awe-inspiring appearance or some other miracle that frustrated the plan of His enemies.

From Jerusalem our Lord went to the Jordan and crossed over to Peraea, to the district where John had first baptized and He Himself had commenced His ministry. There He continued to work (John 10:40), and with better results than in Judaea. There the great Baptist and his ministry and especially his testimony of Jesus were still fresh in the memory of the people. Now our Lord Himself came, and this testimony of John's, together with the great and numerous miracles wrought by our Saviour (for John had worked none), enabled them to recognize Him as the same of whom the Forerunner had borne witness; thus many believed in Him (John 10:41, 42). They formed a correct conception of John's relation to Jesus. He was inferior to our Lord, and his own significance and importance consisted precisely in the witness he bore to Him. As John had formerly paved the way for our Saviour's appearance by his testimony, so now, though already dead, he did not cease to bear witness to Him. On the other hand our Saviour verified the testimony of His faithful disciple before all who were of good will.

This Feast of the Dedication confirms the ancient truth that Jerusalem and its Temple are the seat of revelation and of the glory of the Messias; here the knot of His destiny and that of the nation is tied. The appearance of Jesus causes great excitement in the Jewish world; He is the vital question that chiefly agitates the people. Our Saviour replies to the stormy, impatient questions as to whether He is the Messias or not, by the clearest and most glorious revelation of His Divinity and Divine Sonship. This statement of His has always been regarded as one of the most important of His own testimonies to His Divinity. The character of our Lord is also here revealed; we see the majesty of His superhuman calmness and freedom, in the midst of the tumult of contradiction and mortal hatred, and we notice especially the marvelous wisdom and adroitness with which He checks and restrains the murderous onset of the infuriated mob by bringing forward two striking thoughts. But Jerusalem and the Temple, although the seat of revelation, are also the center of contradiction and unbelief. In face of this revelation of the truth and in presence of this manifestation of God opposition becomes still more hardened in unbelief and obstinacy. Our Lord can no longer show Himself amongst His own people without danger of meeting His death at their hands. Things have gone so far that they are ready to stone the Messias in His own Temple, and with the very stones of His Temple. This would indeed have been a "dedication" of the Temple, and the true abomination of desolation in the holy place. Who can fail to see the justice of the retribution for this act, when the people themselves later on meet their destruction and are buried under the stones of their Temple? Yet the dark and stormy day of the Feast of the Dedication closes with a bright, calm evening, in the believing reception of our Lord by the people beyond the Jordan. Towards evening, when the sun is sinking and the shades have already fallen upon the heights of Jerusalem, the mountains beyond the Jordan are still bright with the rainbow tints cast by the luminous orb.

The Number of the Elect, and the Rejection of Israel

Luke 13:23. And a certain man said to him: "Lord, are they few that are saved?" But he said to them:—24. "Strive to enter by the narrow gate; for many, I say to you, shall seek to enter, and shall not be able.—25. But when the master of the house shall be gone in, and shall shut the door, you shall begin to stand without, and knock at the door, saying: Lord, open to us; and he answering shall say to you: I know you not whence you are.—26. Then you shall begin to say: We have eaten and drunk in thy presence, and thou hast taught in our streets.—27. And he shall say to you: I know you not whence you are; depart from me, all ye workers of iniquity.—28. There shall be weeping and gnashing of teeth, when you shall see Abraham and Isaac and Jacob, and all the prophets in the kingdom of God, and you yourselves thrust out.—29. And there shall come from the east and the west and the north and the south, and shall sit down in the kingdom of God.—30. And behold, they are last that shall be first, and they are first that shall be last."

1. THE QUESTION ABOUT THE NUMBER OF THE ELECT

The circumstances of this mystery were as follows:

The scene was some place in Peraea. There, very likely in connection with an address or a conversation held on the way (Luke 13:22), our Saviour was asked if only few would be saved (Luke 13:23).

The questioner may have been a disciple or someone among the people. From the context one might be led to think that he held the Jewish idea that Israel could not be rejected, because it had Abraham for its father (John 8:33, 39; Matt. 3:9). At all events the question was put with Israel alone in view.

The inquiry as to whether only few would be saved was a very useless one; it shows curiosity, childish fear, and spiritual idleness. Of what use would it be to us to know whether many or few will be saved? The only effect would be either to discourage us or to lead us into presumption and sloth.

2. OUR SAVIOUR'S ANSWER

Our Saviour in His love and wisdom knows how to turn even this useless question to some account in His answer, which contains three points.

First, He does not give a direct answer to the question whether "few" would be saved, and this for the above reason. He merely says that "many" would fail to attain salvation, and through their own fault (Luke 13:24).

Secondly, He lays greater stress upon the causes why many do not attain salvation, thus giving at the same time the means which help us to gain it. These causes and means are two in number. The first cause of damnation is that many do not take any trouble to enter by the narrow gate which alone leads to salvation (Matt. 7:14). This "narrow gate" is the mortification of the passions by observance of the commandments and counsels. The former at least must be obeyed (Luke 13:24). The second cause is neglect to take advantage of the time of God's grace and long-suffering. Our Saviour illustrates this by a very clear and pertinent figure taken from daily life in a family, where the master of the house awaits the return of his guests and the members of his household, and at length, tired of waiting, rises, shuts up the house, and inexorably turns them away from the door as "strangers" (Luke 13:25) and "workers of iniquity" (Luke 13:27).

Thirdly, our Saviour gives a very powerful description of this punishment of exclusion and rejection (which takes place at the Last Judgment), as a motive for making good use of the time of grace. In the first place, the punishment is inexorable; all lamentations and representations about family ties and former friendly relations to the master of the house are useless (Luke 13:25–27). Further, it is very bitter, on account of the pain of loss of the Messianic kingdom, which is typified by a palace in which a large company is assembled at a splendid banquet (Luke 13:28). The loss is portrayed in the torments of conscience and the pains of the senses indicated by "weeping and gnashing of teeth," the expression of rage and despair. Lastly, the punishment is hard on account of the humiliation felt by the members of the household at seeing themselves shut out and standing outside the door, whilst strangers and people whom they had despised take their places (Luke 13:29), and thus the first become last and the last first (Luke 13:30).

3. SIGNIFICATION OF THE ANSWER

The chief signification of this answer is that it is a public and solemn prediction and justification of the rejection of Israel and call of the Gentile nations. It is quite evident that the Jews are meant by those who are shut out. Our Saviour expressly says that they will be "thrust out" (Luke 13:28), and the description of the heavenly kingdom, with Abraham and the prophets as the chief partakers of the banquet, agrees with this. The Israelites were really members of God's household (Isa. 63:16), His children even, by His continual dwelling and journeying with them, by the intercourse of sacrifice and the communication of the revelation, and lastly by their blood-relationship to the Messias (Hebr. 2:14). They were not a little proud of this, considered themselves superior to all other races (Luke 13:30), and thought that God could not forsake them, on account of the Temple. And God had dealt with Israel just as the master of the house in the parable did with his family. It had grown late now; with the Messias the last respite of grace had come for them, and they despised it. Therefore the punishment of rejection is sure, hard and unrelenting, and the bitterest drop in the cup is the thought that the heathen would take the places which had been destined for them, the "children of the kingdom." It is the first plain and public announcement made by our Saviour of the rejection of

Israel and the election of the Gentiles, and is quite in accordance with the great prophecies (Gen. 18:18; 22:18; Isa. 60:3). Even the fact that only a remnant of Israel would be saved had already been prophesied (Isa. 10:19 seq.).

The mystery has also a general signification. It teaches us that we should not trouble ourselves about idle, sophistical questions of the spiritual life, such for example as the present one concerning the small number of the elect. Our Saviour's treatment of it shows us the practical way to take them. Instead of discussing it, He shows us how to grasp and use the means that lead us surely and safely to heaven. With regard to these He does not leave us in uncertainty. It is certainly useless to try to investigate whether many or few will be saved; but it is of infinite importance for us to know whether we shall be saved or not, and if possible we should strain every nerve to acquire the certainty of our being on the right road to eternal happiness. Our Saviour gives us sure information about it; viz. the signs of "striving" and the "narrow gate." If we do not give way to our passions, but do violence to them, even when it is very hard for us, then we are on the right way. The pains we take in God's service are a pledge of eternal blessedness. The "shutting of the door," for the human race in general, is the Last Judgment; and for each individual, the moment of death.

Attempt of Herod and the Pharisees to Intimidate Our Lord

Luke 13:31. The same day there came some of the Pharisees, saying to him: "Depart and get thee hence, for Herod hath a mind to kill thee."—32. And he said to them: "Go and tell that fox: Behold I cast out devils, and do cures today and tomorrow, and the third day I am consummated.—33. Nevertheless I must walk today and tomorrow and the day following; because it cannot be that a prophet perish out of Jerusalem.—34. Jerusalem, Jerusalem, that killest the prophets, and stonest them that are sent to thee, how often would I have gathered thy children as the bird doth her brood under her wings, and thou wouldst not?—35. Behold your house shall be left to you desolate. And I say to you, that you shall not see me till the time come, when you shall say: Blessed is he that cometh in the name of the Lord."

During our Saviour's ministry in Peraea the Pharisees came one day and warned Him against Herod, advising Him to leave the province because, as they declared, this prince intended to kill Him (Luke 13:31). Peraea belonged to Herod's territory (cf. Introd., p. 2).

1. THE ATTEMPT AT INTIMIDATION

It seems beyond doubt that Herod really had some share in the news brought to our Saviour by the Pharisees. If the information that he intended to kill Him had been only an invention of theirs, it is hard to see why our Lord, Who knew everything, should have sent a message to him. This would have been exposing Himself to their ridicule. Herod must therefore have had some part in the proceeding.

But it is uncertain what was the precise part that he took in the affair. It may easily be conceived that Herod, who may have happened to be in Peraea at that time, was disturbed at the news of our Saviour's arrival and deeds, as he had formerly been in Galilee, after the murder of John the Baptist (Luke 9:7–9). He wished to get Him out of his territory, partly on account of his own uneasy conscience, partly out of consideration for the Jews, who could not endure that a man so hated by them should find protection and freedom in his dominions. Herod might undoubtedly have put our Lord to death; but the murder of John had already caused him sufficient pangs of conscience, and he seems, too, as a pleasure-loving man of the world, to have been averse to violent measures. Besides this he had to take into account the people, who honored our Lord very highly. He may for this reason have tried to find a way out of the dilemma by sending a threat to Him through the Pharisees, in order to make Him leave Peraea. This seems to be most in accordance with the wording of our Lord's message to him.

But it is also possible that the whole affair was a disgraceful plot of the Pharisees. Perhaps they importuned Herod to put our Lord to death; in that way they would get rid of their much-feared opponent without running any risk of getting into trouble with the people. But if Herod, for the above reasons, could not make up his mind to use violence with our Lord, they could suggest to him at least to frighten Him by a threat of capital punishment and thus induce Him to leave the province. Thus (they may have thought) our Lord would be compelled to go back into Judaea, where He could not escape their snares. So they probably offered to convey the threat to Him in Herod's name. This assumption is confirmed by those words of our Lord's answer which concerned the Pharisees. So much at any rate is certain, that they did not bring the message out of friendship for Him. It was a base trick, in the contrivance of which the Pharisees and the Herodians had again made common cause.

2. OUR SAVIOUR'S ANSWER

In His answer our Lord shows that He sees through the whole plot. The answer itself has two parts, addressed respectively to the different authors of the menace.

The first part is the answer to Herod. Our Lord calls him a "fox," and thus describes not only the part that he plays in this trick, but his entire character. It was a compound of egotism, craft and intrigue, rather than of energy, courage or violence. Our Saviour sends him word that He will take no notice of the threat, but will continue to teach and to work the miracles that seemed to frighten Herod so much, just as He had done before. This is the meaning of "today and tomorrow and the day following" (cf. Osee 6:3). And then He would "be consummated," i.e. He would stop, or put the crowning touch to His work by death (Luke 13:32).

The Pharisees wished to kill our Lord at any price, either through Herod or by causing Him to quit Peraea and return to Judaea, where death awaited Him. His answer to them was to the effect that, although He would not comply with their wish just at present, still He would sooner or later leave Peraea. He had another journey of definite duration in view; by which, probably, He means His last excursions from this moment onwards, including the one undertaken for the purpose of restoring Lazarus to life, and others to Ephrem, to Samaria, and to Jericho (Luke 13:22; 17:11; 18:31). This journey would take Him to Jerusalem and to death, as they wished; for it was impossible that a prophet should perish out of Jerusalem (Luke 13:33). He hereby designates Jerusalem as the real hot-bed of all the conspiracy and enmity against Him. It is not Herod He has to fear, but Judaea and Jerusalem.

Our Lord is deeply moved in pronouncing the name of Jerusalem, and breaks into a thrilling apostrophe of that city, as the head and representative of the whole nation. In this apostrophe He does three things. First, He draws a grand and touching picture of the grace and mercy shown by God to Jerusalem, from the beginning up to the present hour, through all the prophets, down to Christ. He depicts this divine love and mercy under the touching simile of a bird's care for her brood, watching over them, gathering them under her wings and protecting them (Luke 13:34). He seems here to be alluding to the beautiful metaphor of the Divine Eagle, Who bore the people out of Egypt through the desert and sheltered them under His wings, as it were, from His throne of grace in Jerusalem (Deut. 32:11; Isa. 31:5). Secondly, our Saviour upbraids the city with her ingratitude, callousness, cruelty and hardness of heart, as seen in her stoning and killing the prophets and messengers of God, one after another, and now threatening even the Messias with the same fate. The history of Israel is a history of waste of God's graces and tokens of divine love (Luke 13:34). How powerfully this resistance of human wickedness to God's greatest graces and favors is expressed in the words: "I would . . . and thou wouldst not"! Finally, our Lord predicts the punishment about to befall the unhappy city. He will forsake her and the Temple in which He had dwelt for centuries; He will withdraw His protection from the latter and abandon it to desolation and devastation, until they cry: "Blessed is he that cometh in the name of the Lord," i.e. until the day when Israel will be converted to Him (Rom. 15:26) at the end of the world.

3. CONCLUSIONS

We are moved to compassion when we consider in what a net of mean, malevolent plots our Lord is entangled, how all are conspiring against Him, and the snares are closing round Him. No district can offer Him security any longer; cunning and threats are employed against Him.

In the midst of all this our Lord retains full consciousness of His office and its issue. He sees through all the plots and watches with unshaken calmness their development and completion. He does not retire before them. He has His definite plan and follows it out, and no threat can move Him from it. On the contrary, it is really He who threatens. It is, unhappily, the only resource that the unbelief and obduracy of the Jews have left Him. Again and again He openly and solemnly announces the impending judgment, but always with renewed proofs and offers of mercy. He is the "father of the family," who waits on until late in the night, expecting his tardy children. Like a mother-bird, He cries out again and again and spreads out His wings to cherish and protect His brood. It is the last effort of the Good Shepherd to save His flock from the destruction to which it is doomed (Zach. 11:4). There is something heart-rending in the tone of His plaints, and even in His grave irony (Luke 13:33).

The Dinner in the Pharisee's House
First Part: The Dropsical Man

Luke 14:1. And it came to pass when Jesus went into the house of one of the chief of the Pharisees on the Sabbath-day to eat bread, that they watched him.—2. And behold there was a certain man before him that had the dropsy.—3. And Jesus answering, spoke to the lawyers and Pharisees, saying: "Is it lawful to heal on the Sabbath-day?"—4. But they held their peace. But he taking him, healed him and sent him away.—5. And answering them, he said: "Which of you shall have an ass or an ox fall into a pit, and will not immediately draw him out on the Sabbath-day?"—6. And they could not answer him to these things.

Probably the scene of this mystery also was in Peraea, but possibly further inland. A great part of the population of Peraea was composed of Jews, and the province kept up much intercourse with Judaea. The position of the various parties was much the same. Here also there were many Pharisees and scribes to be found, as may be surmised from the preceding mystery (Luke 13:31).

1. THE TEMPTATION

One Sabbath-day our Lord entered the house of one of the chief of the Pharisees in order to dine there, probably in response to an invitation from the master of the house. The latter's intention in giving this invitation may not have been exactly a bad one, but still he was not well disposed towards our Saviour. The company at table was composed of the most uncompromising Pharisees and scribes (Luke 14:3), who were hostile as regards both actions and dispositions, as may be seen in the course of the mystery. For this reason we are expressly told that they "watched Him," to see if He would venture to do anything opposed to their views and customs. Derogatory as this was to our Lord's dignity, He nevertheless accepted the invitation in this as in other cases, thus exercising His benevolence and unselfishness for the good of souls.

A second circumstance fraught with danger for our Lord was the appearance, apparently quite at the beginning of the meal, of a poor dropsical man. It is probable that the sufferer, urged by his distress and full of confidence in our Lord, had come uninvited through the open doors into the guest-room (Luke 14:2). He seems to have said nothing, perhaps for fear of the Pharisees, because it was a Sabbath-day. It certainly does great honor to our Saviour thus always to be surrounded by the distressed and unfortunate, like a shepherd by his sheep. Thus the whole banquet was full of temptations and snares for Him.

2. THE TRIAL TO WHICH OUR LORD SUBJECTS THE PHARISEES

The Pharisees were on the watch for any word or deed that would serve as an occasion for an accusation against our Lord. He does not overlook the sufferer, His compassion urges Him to heal him.

On the other hand He knows very well how the Pharisees are watching Him, and how often they have already accused Him of profaning the Sabbath, on account of the cures He has wrought on that day. What does He do? He simply asks the Pharisees and lawyers if it is permissible to heal on the Sabbath-day (Luke 14:3), and He does this for the following reasons: to make them consider the matter from the stand-point of reason and conscience; to test whether they are seeking the truth in simplicity and sincerity, and whether they have profited by His instructions; and lastly to elicit their approval of the cure He is about to perform, in order that they may not be able to accuse Him. He thus places them in a very awkward dilemma.

How do the Pharisees stand the test? According to the conviction which they always expressed, they ought to have answered that it was not permissible. But they do not say this, because they fear to meet with a cutting refutation. Neither do they say that it *is* permissible, because they do not wish to contradict and expose themselves or to bear testimony to the truth. They do not answer therefore, but remain silent (Luke 14:4). If they were honest, they would have answered; this very insincerity and dishonesty finally ended in their ruin.

3. THE DECISION

Our Divine Saviour now made the decision and gave the answer to the question Himself, and this in two ways.

First, in deed, by touching the sick man, healing and dismissing him (Luke 14:4). Thus He gave not only a new proof of His power and goodness, but also a new divine confirmation of His doctrine concerning the sanctification of the Sabbath.

The second part of His answer was the question put by Him to the Pharisees: whether one of them, if his ox or ass were to fall into a pit on the Sabbath-day, would leave it lying there or pull it out. The comparison was practical and to the point, so that no one could refute it. So they were silent again (Luke 14:6). The first-named mode of action would be unreasonable, and no one pursued it, in spite of the strictness of the law of the Sabbath; so that it could not be against the law to take the second course. Reason and revelation do not oppose each other in this case. But they do so just as little with regard to the healing of the sick. Our Saviour had made use of the same comparison on a former occasion, at the healing of the infirm woman (Luke 13:15); but here He employs it again in another form. The similitude between an animal falling into the water and a man dying of dropsy is remarkably good and aptly chosen. Though our Saviour says the same thing a second time, yet He says it in a different wav

The Dinner in the Pharisee's House
Second Part: Parable of the Order of Rank at a Marriage-feast

Luke 14:7. And he spoke a parable also to them that were invited, marking how they chose the first seats at the table, saying to them:—8. "When thou art invited to a wedding, sit not down in the first place, lest perhaps one more honorable than thou be invited by him,—9. And he that invited thee and him, come and say to thee: Give this man place; and then thou begin with shame to take the lowest place.—10. But when thou art invited, go, sit down in the lowest place; that when he who invited thee cometh, he may say to thee: Friend, go up higher. Then shalt thou have glory before them that sit at table with thee.—11. Because every one that exalteth himself, shall be humbled; and he that humbleth himself, shall be exalted."

The healing of the dropsical man was, as it were, the introduction to the dinner. Immediately afterwards our Lord propounded the parable of the order of precedence at a marriage-feast.

1. Circumstances of the Parable

The first circumstance which led to the parable was the pride, arrogance, and lack of all modesty displayed by the Pharisees invited to the dinner in taking their places. Our Saviour noticed that they did not merely cherish a secret wish for the first seats, but even openly pushed their way to them (Luke 14:7). Even in this they showed their pride and self-esteem, as He elsewhere points out. Not even the presence of an eminent guest and a stranger restrained them from this arrogant and unbecoming conduct. And this was only one side of their pride. They had the same high opinion of themselves in spiritual matters, and thought that the first places in God's kingdom also belonged to them by right. Thus they were true Pharisees that our Lord had before Him here.

The second cause was His beautiful habit of doing good everywhere, by word and deed. This custom of His proceeded from His ardent zeal for souls and His wish to be of use to everyone. He is not merely a fellow-guest and a good companion, but also a benefactor and physician, not only of the body (as is seen in the case of the dropsical man), but also of the soul. His fellow-guests were all very infirm of soul, far more infirm than the dropsical man. Their hearts swelled with egotism and prejudice, and were almost bursting with pride.

The third reason (or rather the necessary condition) of the parable was our Lord's undaunted courage. He censures evil, wherever and however He finds it; and if it ventures to show itself exteriorly and thus gives scandal, then He does so publicly.

2. THE PARABLE AND ITS SIGNIFICATION

Our Saviour begins by saying that, if anyone is invited to a banquet, he should not at once, of his own accord, take the first place; in that case he would run the risk of being put in the last and humiliated before everyone. On the contrary, he should choose the last place, and then he may possibly be invited to take the seat of honor (Luke 14:8–10). Although the application is obvious, still our Saviour speaks in a very considerate and general way, and it was quite the custom with the scribes and Pharisees to propound and discuss moral maxims when at table.

As regards its signification, the parable has every appearance of being a purely natural piece of good advice, viz. to be modest and not arrogant, because arrogance often leads to humiliation, but modesty to honor. We see here that our Saviour does not scorn natural motives, but gives nature her due honor, and establishes His doctrine by its conformity with her. Nature and the supernatural do not contradict each other; indeed, nature is the handmaid of the supernatural. Still this does not alter the fact that we may and should rise from natural motives to supernatural ones.

But the parable may, in the opinion of some, be taken in a still deeper sense. It is surely not without intention that our Saviour makes use of the word "wedding" instead of "banquet"

(Luke 14:8). He thus gives the parable a deeper and supernatural meaning. In the views and phraseology of Jewish theologians the joys of heaven and of the reign of the Messias were often typified under the figure of a wedding. The expression was quite a familiar one (Matt. 8:11; 10:15; Luke 22:30; Apoc. 19:7). Thus the order of precedence among a company at table might be regarded as a symbol of their rank in heaven. It is certain that the very Pharisees who here claimed for themselves the first places at table, also considered themselves entitled to make the same demand with respect to the wedding-feast of heaven. Thus it was an earnest admonition that our Lord here addressed to them, to lay aside their arrogance and pride, for these were not the means by which to attain to the first places in the kingdom of the Messias and of heaven.

3. THE CONCLUSION AND MORAL OF THE PARABLE

Our Saviour expressly adds the lesson and moral of the parable: "Everyone that exalteth himself, shall be humbled; and he that humbleth himself, shall be exalted" (Luke 14:11). That is not always true of the order of things in this world, but it is the law of divine justice. These words, then, also set forth the law of admission to the kingdom of God, and of the order of precedence therein, as well for the Jews of that age as for the Christians of this. No one can claim the kingdom of heaven as a thing to which he has a right; for eternal life is a grace (Rom. 6:23), and if it can be merited or earned in any way, it is only by humility. It is quite certain that no one can enter either the Church or heaven without a certain degree of humility and submission to the divine economy of salvation; and the humbler we are here below, the greater will be our share in the honors of heaven.

THE DINNER IN THE PHARISEE'S HOUSE
THIRD PART: ADVICE TO THE HOST

LUKE 14:12. And he said to him also that had invited him: "When thou makest a dinner or a supper, call not thy friends, nor thy brethren, nor thy kinsmen, nor thy neighbors who are rich; lest perhaps they also invite thee again, and a recompense be made to thee:—13. But when thou makest a feast, call the poor, the maimed, the lame, and the blind;—14. And thou shalt be blessed, because they have not wherewith to make thee recompense; for recompense shall be made thee at the resurrection of the just."

1. WHAT LED OUR LORD TO GIVE THIS ADVICE TO THE HOST

Upon sitting down to table our Lord seems to have cast a glance over the company assembled. Probably the host had only invited men of his own clique and opinions, and most likely only rich men, relatives, and neighbors (Luke 14:12). He had not given a thought to the poor of the neighborhood, many of whom were perhaps (as was usually the case at such houses and on such occasions) standing round about the house. Not even the man who had been healed had found a place at the table (Luke 14:4). This spirit of caste, so characteristic of the nation, which contemptuously abandoned everything and everyone who was not its equal or ally, such as the poor, the despised, public sinners and Gentiles; this egotistical spirit, which only confers benefits with a view to its own profit, displayed itself here in the host, as the other side of the pharisaical character (viz. intolerable arrogance) had just been manifested by the guests. So our Saviour wished by these words also to reprove the pharisaical spirit; and as He had just been of service to the guests, so He now wishes to do good to the host by giving him this lesson.

2. THE ADVICE GIVEN TO THE HOST

The advice of our Lord is directly opposed to the host's pharisaical conduct. He tells him that, when he gives a feast, he should not invite friends, relatives, and rich men, but strangers, poor, maimed, lame and blind; and that he should invite them with the intention, not of receiving an invitation from them in return, but of obtaining eternal life and being recompensed at the resurrection of the just (Luke 14:12, 13, 14). Every word here is worthy of note, especially the intention. We ought by preference to forego every temporal recompense, to be glad when we do not receive any, and to console ourselves with the prospect of a reward in heaven.

3. WHY OUR SAVIOUR GAVE THIS ADVICE

In the first place, He wishes here to give a thoroughly supernatural principle, which is evidently opposed to the natural, egotistical spirit; and by this means to reveal His own spirit, which is nothing but the noblest unselfishness and purest piety. To do good, not from natural motives and for the sake of temporal advantages, but solely for the sake of God and heaven, that is the true mark of the spirit of faith and unselfishness, the spirit of Jesus. Our Saviour does not forbid us to invite those whom we love; but still there is something better to be done, in so far as the obtaining of eternal life is our object. We see this exemplified in the lives of the Saints. If the Pharisee had acted upon this principle, it would have made a Saint even of him.

But besides this our Saviour also wishes to indicate the principles which regulate participation in the feast at the resurrection of the just (Luke 14:15), which is to compensate us for all. Evidently the proud are excluded, and in their stead the poor and despised (who here represent the Gentiles, those who answered the call into the Church; Luke 14:21, 23), are admitted. The selfish are also excluded; and the unselfish of heart, who thought it more blessed to give than to receive, find admittance. Whoever therefore wishes to have part in Christ must love the poor. Hence that supernatural respect and preference for the poor and sick which is to be found in the Church and whenever the spirit of Christ reigns. On this account they were called in the Middle Ages, so characterized by the spirit of faith, "our dear masters, the poor"; on this account so many charitable institutions and establishments were erected, where the destitute could lead a peaceful life; and often when the rich gave feasts and merry-makings, the poor man had his share. Here our Saviour is evidently preparing the way for the following parable.

The Dinner in the Pharisee's House
Fourth Part: The Parable of the Great Supper

Luke 14:15. When one of them that sat at table with him had heard these things, he said to him: "Blessed is he that shall eat bread in the kingdom of God."—16. But he said to him: "A certain man made a great supper, and invited many.—17. And he sent his servant at the hour of supper to say to them that were invited, that they should come, for now all things are ready.—18. And they began all at once to make excuse. The first said to him: I have bought a farm, and I must needs go out and see it; I pray thee, hold me excused.—19. And another said: I have bought five yoke of oxen, and I go to try them; I pray thee, hold me excused.—20. And another said: I have married a wife, and therefore I cannot come.—21. And the servant returning told these things to his lord. Then the master of the house being angry, said to his servant: Go out quickly into the streets and lanes of the city; and bring in hither the poor and the feeble and the blind and the lame.—22. And the servant said: Lord, it is done as thou hast commanded, and yet there is room.—23. And the lord said to the servant: Go out into the highways and hedges, and compel them to come in, that my house may be filled.—24. But I say unto you, that none of those men that were invited shall taste of my supper."

On the same occasion our Saviour also propounded the parable of the Great Supper.

1. CIRCUMSTANCES UNDER WHICH THE PARABLE WAS SPOKEN: ITS AIM

The immediate occasion of the parable was the exclamation of one of the guests, probably a Pharisee, who, at the mention of the resurrection and the recompense of the just, which he pictured to himself in the customary manner under the figure of a banquet, broke out into the words: "Blessed is he that shall eat bread in the kingdom of God" (Luke 14:15). The grave tone of the parable leads one to surmise that these words were inspired not only by a desire for sensual gratification, but also by the proud assurance of the Pharisee. In all probability the speaker was one of those to whom the parable applied, and in no flattering sense.

Our Saviour's answer is the parable itself, and His intention in propounding it is to teach the Pharisees and the whole Israelite nation that a mere wish does not suffice to ensure participation in the heavenly Supper, and still less proud assurance, if one neglects to fulfil the conditions and accept the invitation of the Master of the feast, in other words, if one allows the time of grace to expire without profiting by it. In this case it is shown that the scorners would be justly excluded and the grace of the invitation given to others. So will it be in the kingdom of heaven. Thus the parable is not merely a repetition of this gracious invitation, but also the prediction and establishment of the truth that Israel will be excluded from the kingdom of God and the Gentiles called and received into it.

2. DEVELOPMENT AND APPLICATION OF THE PARABLE

The parable has three parts.

The first part contains the gracious invitation to the supper. The host is rich and powerful, he prepares a great supper for many (Luke 14:16); he has a large house, in which there is still room, although great numbers have already entered (Luke 14:22). He is kind, too, for he wishes to benefit many, indeed everyone without distinction (Luke 14:21); he wishes to have his house full, and therefore invites very courteously (Luke 14:17), and as it were compels the guests to come (Luke 14:21, 23). But he is also just, and full of noble self-respect (Luke 14:21, 24); he does not throw away his honors and benefits. This Master of the feast is no other than God, the Heavenly Father, Who has been represented in a recent parable as the "Master of the house" (Luke 13:25). The servants who give the invitation in His Name are Christ and the Apostles who go in Christ's Name first to the Jews, then to the Gentiles (Acts 13:46). The Great Supper to which the invitation is issued is the kingdom of the Messias, God's kingdom, and here in the first instance the Church, which is the Messianic kingdom in its preparation on earth. It is therefore of vital importance to accept the first invitation to enter the Church, because otherwise no second one, to heaven, will be issued. The Church upon earth is the great house in which "many," indeed all, may find room, and where the "great supper" is held. But this "supper" also signifies heaven, the consummation of the earthly Church. Heaven is indeed the "great supper" or evening meal. First with regard to time, viz. at the end of the world and its work; secondly as regards repose, enjoyment, honor and joy, viz. in the superabundance of divine blessings; lastly, on account of the vastness of the assemblage. Blessed in very truth is he who shall obtain a place at this banquet (Luke 14:15). Both these significations of the "great supper" are combined in the great Eucharistic Feast, which is the center and focus of the Church on earth, and at the same time the type, preparation and foretaste of heaven by the possession and enjoyment of Christ, God Himself. Our Lord completes His covenant by the institution of this banquet and by His sacrificial Death; then the hour for the feast has come, and servants are sent forth bearing the invitations (Luke 14:17). The Church herself ratifies this interpretation of the parable, by choosing this portion of Holy Scripture as the Gospel for the Sunday within the octave of Corpus Christi.

The second part of the parable is concerned with the dispositions and conduct of those invited to the feast. None of them will come; all reject the invitation. Their excuses are stated. With one it is his temporal possessions; he has bought a farm, and wishes to go and inspect it (Luke 14:18). Another is engrossed in the pursuit of his business; he has bought some oxen on approval and is just about to try them (Luke 14:19). The third has taken a wife, and she is more to him than all the honors and joys of the banquet (Luke 14:20). Thus one and all refuse the invitation and do not come. These guests represent the Pharisees and others not a few, who oppose and despise the new salvation offered to them by Christ. All these allow the time of grace to elapse without taking advantage of it.

The third part of the parable treats of the punishment of these scorners of Christ's grace and favor. It is twofold. First, they will never gain admission to the banquet, nor share in it in any way. They will be excluded from the kingdom of God and the Messias in its full signification. Since they will have nothing to do with the Church, neither will they be admitted into heaven (Luke 14:24). The punishment is well deserved. Their contempt of the invitation, which has been issued in the name of the master of the feast and conveyed to them with every mark of honor by his authorized servants, is tantamount to contempt of the master himself. To say the least, the reasons they urge in excuse for declining it are by no means flattering, nay are rather a positive insult to him. Besides, his pleasure in the feast is spoilt and unnecessary expense occasioned. He has therefore a right to be angry (Luke 14:21), and he breaks with them for ever. This applies to the greater part of the Pharisees and rulers (John 7:48, 49). The second punishment is that the invitation is now passed on to others, who accept it and take the places intended for those to whom it had first been issued (Luke 14:22). But this is a great humiliation for the latter, for these new guests are precisely the people whom they have been accustomed to despise and regard as unworthy even of a glance. There are two classes of these: first, those who dwell in the town and are therefore fellow-citizens of the rejected guests: the poor, the feeble, the blind, and the lame (Luke 14:21); and secondly, homeless strangers who lingered about the roads and hedges outside the town (Luke 14:23). Who does not recognize in the former the publicans and sinners, and in the latter the Gentiles? Both these classes of men were regarded by the Pharisees as unworthy of the kingdom of God, and now the good master has them brought in as it were by force (Luke 14:21, 23); i.e. they are induced to follow Christ by special interior and exterior graces. These are now the happy heirs of the kingdom of God and the Messias.

3. CONCLUDING REFLECTIONS

This parable reveals the character of our Saviour under many aspects. As He describes Himself therein under the figure of the master of the feast, He is rich, kind and just. He knows how to show mercy and bestow grace, but conciliation has its limit; when this is reached punishment ensues, and He proclaims it in the most fearless manner. It needed courage to behave, under such circumstances, as our Saviour did at this dinner. They were watching Him in order to find something of which to accuse Him. And He takes the whole distinguished company to task, one after another; censures all their pharisaical vices and misdeeds; and finally proclaims their punishment, though only mildly at first, and in the form of a parable. Here we have another instance of His use of a parable to bring home disagreeable and dangerous truths. It is also worthy of note how repeatedly our Saviour publicly predicts the exclusion of Israel from the kingdom of the Messias, just at this time and here in Peraea. Here, in the district beyond the Jordan, in the midst of green fields almost like gardens, stands Mount Nebo, where Moses had his view of the Promised Land and then died without setting foot upon it, as a punishment for his doubt (Num. 20:12; Deut. 34:1–6). It is very fitting therefore that our Lord should here proclaim the exclusion of Israel from the Messianic kingdom, of which the Promised Land was a type and pledge. But when He threatens punishment, He never omits to point out the evils which will lead to it, and to lift a warning voice against them. These evils are enumerated in the insincerity, pride, hardness of heart, and worldly aims and pursuits which serve as an excuse for the guests first invited.

But the punishment is not unfruitful. It benefits others, by conferring upon them what it takes away from Israel. We are the descendants of those poor, homeless strangers whom our Lord so graciously sent His servants to seek out in highway and hedgerow and lead to the banquet of His kingdom. For centuries they have been flocking into the Church and into heaven, and the "children of the kingdom" stand outside in much the same homeless condition in which He found us.

Finally, the parable contains an earnest exhortation to us all to make good use of the time of God's gracious invitation, and not to fritter it away in worldly pursuits.

Renunciation and Hatred of Self, the Indispensable Condition of the Following of Christ

Luke 14:25. And there went great multitudes with him; and turning, he said to them:—26. "If any man come to me, and hate not his father, and mother, and wife, and children, and brethren, and sisters, yea and his own life also, he cannot be my disciple.—27. And whosoever doth not carry his cross and come after me cannot be my disciple.—28. For which of you having a mind to build a tower, doth not first sit down and reckon the charges that are necessary, whether he have wherewithal to finish it,—29. Lest after he hath laid the foundation, and is not able to finish it, all that see it begin to mock him,—30. Saying: This man began to build, and was not able to finish.—31. Or what king about to go to make war against another king, doth not first sit down and think whether he be able with ten thousand to meet him that with twenty thousand cometh against him?—32. Or else whilst the other is yet afar off, sending an embassy, he desireth conditions of peace.—33. So likewise everyone of you that doth not renounce all that he possesseth, cannot be my disciple.—34. Salt is good. But if the salt shall lose its savor, wherewith shall it be seasoned?—35. It is neither profitable for the land, nor for the dunghill, but shall be cast out. He that hath ears to hear, let him hear."

MATT. 10:37. "He that loveth father or mother more than me, is not worthy of me; and he that loveth son or daughter more than me, is not worthy of me.—38. And he that taketh not up his cross and followeth me, is not worthy of me.—39. He that findeth his life, shall lose it: and he that shall lose his life for me, shall find it."

1. INTRODUCTORY CIRCUMSTANCES

Our Saviour was walking along the road, perhaps immediately after the dinner in the Pharisee's house. At any rate it was not long after, and probably whilst He was still in Peraea.

He was accompanied by great multitudes of people (Luke 14:25); indeed, He seems to have found much sympathy and faith in Peraea (John 10:42). Thus there may have been many who, attracted by the wondrous charm of His personality as well as of His words, counted it a joy and an honor to see our Lord in their vicinity and publicly escort Him on His way, in spite of the Pharisees' hostility, or even on that very account. They probably felt quite at home with Him already, and reckoned themselves among His disciples.

But it was not a triumphal march that our Lord was taking. The days of His Assumption were drawing nearer and nearer (Luke 9:51). Since His departure from Galilee He had been advancing by a circuitous route towards Jerusalem, the place of its completion. His Passion and the Cross were growing ever more clearly present to His mind, and casting their shadow over His thoughts, emotions (Luke 12:50; 13:32), and words. It was therefore time to state in clear and definite terms the conditions and essential character of the service and imitation of Him, in order that no one might be in doubt about them. So, turning to the people, He propounds to them the sole conditions upon which they could become His disciples (Luke 14:25).

2. THE DOCTRINE OF RENUNCIATION

The doctrine now propounded by our Saviour is that of renunciation. He first says that, in order to be His disciples, it is not enough to come to Him (Luke 14:26), i.e. simply to believe in and accompany Him, as these people did, but that they must make up their minds to complete renunciation and detachment.

Next He goes on to explain wherein this self-renunciation consists. He terms it "hating" one's parents and relatives, oneself, and even one's life (Luke 14:26). By this "hating" He means that one must not put one's relatives nor even one's life before higher things, before the Will of God; but put them in the second place, renounce them, treat them as enemies, as soon and inasmuch as they prove to be a hindrance to the Will of God and to our duty towards Him (Matt. 10:37). Our Lord calls this renunciation "carrying the cross and following" Him, through all that may befall us in life (Luke 14:27; Matt. 10:38). But the cross is the very synonym of all pain, shame, and every temporal evil, even of death. Thus these two expressions "hating" and "carrying the cross" comprise all sacrifices, negative and positive, from forsaking and renouncing one's possessions to sacrificing life itself; in short, everything that a human heart can be called upon to endure. Whoever then wishes to be a true disciple of Jesus must make up his mind to this from the very outset. This is the condition.

And it is worthy of note how our Saviour expresses this condition. In the first place, very forcibly and impressively. He makes use of a negative form of expression: "He cannot be My disciple," and repeats it several times (Luke 14:26, 27, 33), in order that no one may fail to hear or understand it. Secondly, He says it to everyone, not only to the Apostles but also to the people who were with Him at the time and wished to remain with Him; for we are told that He turned to them and addressed them (Luke 14:25). This self-renunciation, then, is a necessary condition not merely of the apostolic life, but even of ordinary Christian life. Everyone who becomes a Christian must be ready and willing to make these sacrifices, if circumstances require them of him. The self-renunciation here spoken of is nothing but Christian self-denial or mortification (Matt. 16:24; Mark 8:34; Luke 9:23).

3. RATIONALE OF THIS DOCTRINE

It follows from the very nature of the self-denial which is the necessary condition of the following of Christ, that this following of Him is a difficult undertaking which costs a great deal, and that we must therefore first provide ourselves with sufficient means for it. These means are the firm resolution and determination to do all that such self-denial may require of us.

Our Saviour illustrates the necessity of this determination by three figures, of which the first two should be taken together, because they very much resemble each other. He compares His followers to men about to build a tower or wage war against an enemy. Both these undertakings are very laborious and costly, and we must prudently weigh them beforehand, and consider whether we have sufficient money to meet the cost of building, or sufficient troops to contend with the enemy's forces, as the case may be; otherwise the end will be defeat and disgrace, or at best ignominious conditions of peace. So it is with the imitation of Christ. It entails many sacrifices, and therefore resolution and the spirit of sacrifice are absolutely necessary. This determination—to overcome oneself, to practice renunciation and self-denial, and to carry the cross—is the money and the troops that we need. Without them we shall not succeed in our undertaking (Luke 14:28–32). If this "following" after Christ and being His disciples refers to the apostolic life, then the consideration whether to undertake the building or not and the request for peace are to be taken in the literal sense; for the apostolic life is not a matter of obligation, but optional and of supererogation. But if the simple Christian life is meant here, these words cannot mean that we are to consider whether we will follow Christ or not; that is not a matter of choice, for them to "make peace" would be to enter into a compact with the world and with Satan. They can therefore only mean that we should, from the very outset, get a clear idea of what the following of Christ involves, and arm ourselves with readiness for sacrifice. We must not imitate the multitude in this case, who became His adherents exteriorly, and thought that nothing more remained to be done. We must not take the beginning for the end, or else disappointment and surrender will be the result.

Further our Saviour illustrates the necessity of this readiness for sacrifices of all kinds by the comparison of the salt (Luke 14:34, 35). Salt is good, but if it loses its savor it is good for nothing. The Apostles and Christians in general are to preserve themselves and others from the corruption of the world; that is to say, they are to season and purify it (Matt. 5:13). But for this the pungency of salt is necessary. This pungency and strength consists in the will and determination to deny and mortify oneself. Whoever has allowed this salt within him to become insipid has reason to fear the threat of our Lord, that he will not only accomplish nothing good, be "unprofitable," but will even degenerate and bring disgrace upon himself (Luke 14:35). And our Lord adds: "He that hath ears to hear, let him hear." This is a sign that what He has just said is something of great importance. The exhortation applies to all Christians, but was especially addressed to the Israelites of that period, whose subsequent fate was for the most part actually that of the insipid salt to which our Saviour compares them. According to these words of His, the want of abnegation and determination is followed by a threefold punishment of progressive severity: mockery, loss of freedom, and the infamy of being useless and worthless.

With regard to the character of Jesus we may here note the beautiful sincerity with which He so frankly and openly tells us all that we have to expect if we mean to follow Him. He is sincerity itself. He has no other standard for Himself; He follows the same way of self-abnegation and sacrifice which He proposes to us.

But the most important thing here is the fundamental law and condition of the following of Christ, the great law of self-denial and its bearing not only upon the apostolate but also upon Christianity in general. Neither the one nor the other is possible or imaginable without this resolution of practising self-denial. This spirit of abnegation is the money with which the tower of salvation and of Christian and apostolic perfection is built from the very foundation, solid and firm. It is the army which must be maintained and sent into the field against the enemies of God and of our salvation, which are no others than the Evil One, the world in league with him, and the legion of our own passions and temptations. We see, too, in the figures and ideas by which our Lord describes self-denial to us, the qualities which this self-denial must have. In the first place, it must proceed from principle. Self-denial must be our principle and our law, and must be practised on principle from the very beginning. Evil and hostility to God, whether within or without us, is also a principle, a law and a standing power, which can only be overcome by an opposite principle, law and power. Further, our self-denial must be universal, extending over all our passions. No sacrifice, not even that of life itself, must be excepted. Every passion that we do not overcome is a hostile army and a fortress in our rear. Lastly, self-denial must be constant and continual. Only thus can it be a law and a standing power. Thus practised, it brings safety, comfort and merit for ourselves, edification for the world, honor and joy for the Church, the Gospel and Christ; but the contrary course is productive of nothing but dishonor, shame, and injury for us and for His cause.

The Parable of the Lost Sheep and the Lost Groat

Luke 15:1. Now the publicans and sinners drew near unto him to hear him.—2. And the Pharisees and scribes murmured, saying: "This man receiveth sinners and eateth with them."—3. And he spoke to them this parable, saying:—4. "What man of you that hath an hundred sheep, and if he shall lose one of them, doth he not leave the ninety-nine in the desert, and go after that which was lost, until he find it?—5. And when he hath found it, lay it upon his shoulders rejoicing;—6. And coming home call together his friends and neighbors, saying to them: Rejoice with me, because I have found my sheep that was lost?—7. I say unto you, that even so there shall be joy in heaven upon one sinner that doth penance, more than upon ninety-nine just who need not penance.—8. Or what woman having ten groats, if she lose one groat, doth not light a candle and sweep the house, and seek diligently until she find it?—9. And when she hath found it, call together her friends and neighbors, saying: Rejoice with me, because I have found the groat which I had lost?—10. So I say to you, there shall be joy before the angels of God upon one sinner doing penance."

The scene of this and the following parable seems still to have been in the province of Peraea.

1. Circumstances and Aim of the Parable

With regard to the circumstances, we are told that publicans and public sinners came to our Saviour and listened to His discourses (Luke 15:5), and came in great numbers. They were attracted, as those in Galilee had been, by the mildness, moderation and wisdom of His doctrine, and also by His affability and benevolence. We may imagine how confident and how eager for salvation they showed themselves, as soon as they found a heart full of pity and sympathy for them.

But the Pharisees and scribes came also, not for the sake of their own souls' welfare, but to watch; not rejoicing at the conversion of the publicans, that lost contingent of the flock of Israel, but full of vexation and displeasure. They even gave loud vent to this annoyance. They "murmured" at our Lord's receiving sinners and eating with them (Luke 15:2). Here we see again the true pharisaical spirit, the narrow-mindedness, the irritated pride which caused them to regard themselves alone as just and holy, whilst in reality they were far worse than the public sinners on account of their uncharitableness and conscious resistance to recognized truth. We are not told by Scripture that our Lord ate with sinners on this occasion. He had done so once, in Galilee; and possibly this may have been for them sufficient ground to accuse Him of doing so now. If so, it is an example of the power of ingrained prejudice and idle tattle.

Under these circumstances it was our Saviour's intention not only to attract the publicans and encourage them to true conversion, but also to give a lesson to the Pharisees. For this reason He preaches on mercy, sketching a magnificent picture of its nature, motives, and methods; and on the other hand He shows how sinful man must act in order to become partaker of it. He delineates the spirit that profits by the Redemption, and also the spirit upon which it is thrown away. These circumstances and this intention of our Saviour's are of great importance in connection with the two following chapters, which draw from them their aim and their uniformity.

2. THE PARABLE

The persons spoken of in this parable are a shepherd (or an owner of a flock) who loses a sheep, and a woman who loses a groat. The lost object is an outward, material possession. The owner's loving anxiety to recover it is here very beautifully delineated in three respects.

First, in the esteem for the object lost. The sheep and the groat belong to the shepherd and the woman as their own property. The sheep is his, and the groat is hers. On this account they are dear to them, however insignificant their actual value may be. For a man who has only a hundred sheep, even one is of importance; and a groat (about five cents) is of importance to a poor woman. It is the earnings of a hard day's work (Matt. 20:2). In their sorrow over their loss they scarcely heed what they still possess (Luke 14:4, 8).

Secondly, the loving anxiety of the owners is displayed in the trouble they take to recover the lost objects. The shepherd forsakes the ninety-nine sheep, is not deterred by the long distance, searches and calls through the vast, pathless and gloomy desert until he finds the sheep. Indeed, a poor lost sheep is a most pitiable animal. It has neither instinct to find the way back, nor means to defend itself. So the shepherd has compassion on it, does not abuse or punish it when he finds it, but entices it back to him, lays it on his shoulders rejoicing, and carries it back to the fold (Luke 15:4, 5). The woman lights a candle (which in ancient times was a somewhat troublesome thing to do), searches and sweeps every corner of the house (poor dwellings were only lighted from the door-way), and thus burns almost more candle and takes more trouble than the groat is really worth.

Thirdly, their affectionate solicitude is seen in their joy at recovering the lost objects. It is a great joy. Proceeding from the finder, it is communicated by word of mouth to sympathetic neighbors and friends, and finds an echo in their hearts (Luke 15:6, 9).

3. APPLICATION OF THE PARABLE

The application, a very obvious one, is briefly expressed in the words: "There shall be joy in heaven upon one sinner that doth penance, more than upon ninety-nine just who need not penance" (Luke 15:7, 10). It is the divine mercy which is described in the parable, as seen under the three traits of esteem, solicitude for the sinner, and triumph at his salvation.

First, we see God's esteem for us. He sees in us His property and His own image, just as the sovereign of a country sees his image upon a groat or other coin. The Heavenly Father sees in us His creatures, the children of His eternal decrees; He embraces in us His own Son, to Whom He has given us as companions. And the Son sees and loves in us the gracious Will and decree of the Father (John 6:37, 39; 10:15, 28, 29). Hence their esteem and love for us (Wisd. 15:2).

Secondly, God's mercy is seen in the great solicitude with which He seeks sinners, especially in the abundant means of grace appointed by Him for Israel, for the whole human race, and for each individual. This mercy appeared in bodily form in Christ, the Good Shepherd, Who in order to hasten after the "lost sheep," the human race, became Man, and still continues to pursue poor sinners by interior, preventing graces, carrying them back upon His shoulders in the Holy Sacraments and by the zealous efforts of His priests. By the light that Eternal Wisdom has caused to shine upon this world through the Incarnation, even the "lost groat" is found amid the dust of this earth, and is placed, after having regained its brightness, in the royal treasury.

Lastly, God's mercy shows itself in the joy spoken of in this parable. It is a great and extraordinary joy that He takes in the pardon and conversion of a sinner, because goodness and mercy are His sweet attributes (Ps. 108:21), and nowhere do they shine with more glorious brightness than in the forgiveness of sins. It is a universal joy. Because God rejoices, therefore all who are near and dear to Him rejoice also; and the nearer they are to Him, the more they rejoice. The angels especially rejoice, those "friends and neighbors" of God. They rejoice for God's sake and also for our sake. They are our noble, faithful friends in heaven, devoid of all envy.

Our Saviour evidently had a twofold end in view in giving this clear and touching lesson upon the mercy of God. First, He wished to attract, comfort, and encourage poor sinners by pointing out to them this divine mercy, its nature and effects; He wished to draw them to penance and conversion, by holding out to them the prospect of an exceedingly kind reception from God, and by showing them how much He desires their conversion and how they can thus cause Him and the whole heavenly host to rejoice. Could there be more beautiful and touching motives for penance? Secondly, He also wished to work upon the Pharisees by this parable. He wished to bring them to other views and sentiments with regard to poor sinners, by showing them how very different God's thoughts and treatment of such were from theirs. They (the Pharisees) despised and avoided sinners, excluded them altogether from the kingdom of God, and did not rejoice at their efforts at amendment and the responses made to the same by others; but God esteems them, loves them, seeks them with great persistence, receives them kindly, and rejoices with all the heavenly court at their return. Does He not show them, by the significant contrast between their "murmuring" and the great "joy in heaven and with the angels" (Luke 15:7, 10), how repugnant to God their dispositions are, and how they must give them up and acquire God-like ones in their place, if they wish to be His "friends and neighbors"? Perhaps, too, there may have been in the "ninety-nine just who need not penance" a gentle, but earnest thrust at their fancied justice and holiness. At all events the figure of the shepherd is well-chosen. It shows our Saviour as the Good Shepherd, the Pharisees as bad shepherds or pastors of the people

(Ezech. 34:1, 4, 16). The parable should incite us all to admire and praise the mercy of God, and to thank Him for thus extending it to all men. It should further urge us to acquire these dispositions of love and kindness towards all our erring fellow-men. The parable applies especially to such of us as have embraced the apostolic vocation, but it may well be taken to heart by all earnest Christians.

The Parable of the Prodigal Son

Luke 15:11. And he said: "A certain man had two sons;—12. And the younger of them said to his father: Father, give me the portion of substance that falleth to me. And he divided unto them his substance.—13. And not many days after, the younger son gathering all together went abroad into a far country, and there wasted his substance living riotously.—14. And after he had spent all, there came a mighty famine in that country, and he began to be in want.—15. And he went and cleaved to one of the citizens of that country. And he sent him into his farm to feed swine.—16. And he would fain have filled his belly with the husks the swine did eat; and no man gave unto him.—17. And returning to himself, he said: How many hired servants in my father's house abound with bread, and I here perish with hunger?—18. I will arise, and will go to my father, and say to him: Father, I have sinned against heaven and before thee;—19. I am not now worthy to be called thy son: make me as one of thy hired servants.—20. And rising up he came to his father. And when he was yet a great way off, his father saw him, and was moved with compassion, and running to him fell upon his neck and kissed him.—21. And the son said to him: Father, I have sinned against heaven and before thee, I am not now worthy to be called thy son.—22. And the father said to his servants: Bring forth quickly the first robe and put it on him, and put a ring on his hand and shoes on his feet;—23. And bring hither the fatted calf and kill it, and let us eat and make merry;—24. Because this my son was dead, and is come to life again; was lost, and is found. And they began to be merry.—25. Now his elder son was in the field, and when he came and drew nigh to the house, he heard music and dancing;—26. And he called one of the servants, and asked what these things meant.—27. And he said to him: Thy brother is come, and thy father hath killed the fatted calf, because he hath received him safe.—28. And he was angry, and would not go in. His father therefore coming out, began to entreat him.—29. And he answering said to his father: Behold, for so many years do I serve thee, and I have never transgressed thy commandment, and yet thou hast never given me a kid to make merry with my friends:—30. But as soon as this thy son is come, who hath devoured his substance with harlots, thou hast killed for him the fatted calf.—31. But he said to him: Son, thou art always with me, and all I have is thine;—32. But it was fit that we should make merry and be glad, for this thy brother was dead, and is come to life again; he was lost, and is found."

This parable follows immediately upon the preceding one. It has the same object in view; but it pursues it more urgently and in greater detail. It contains three points, corresponding to the three chief persons in the parable: the prodigal son, the father, and the elder son.

1. THE PRODIGAL SON

Here the object lost is not a material thing, no part of exterior property, but a son, a being gifted with reason, beloved by his father and as it were one with him. This is the real position of man to God, according to the Divine Will. Man is a child of God, favored, tenderly loved, and raised to a high dignity and union with Him (Luke 15:11).

From this ensues a second amplification of the preceding parable, namely, the greatness of the error and misfortune when such a being separates himself from God and is lost. The error is powerfully delineated in the younger son in his insolent and inconsiderate demand for his inheritance, which he receives in money, since the first-born usually inherited the real estates (Luke 15:12); and further in his forsaking father and home and wasting his property by a life of dissipation (Luke 15:13). Youthful levity (he was the younger son), love of freedom, and prospect of being unhappy with his father, lead him to this step. His state is sketched in masterly outlines, in the inward abandonment and outward poverty which ensue from the abuse of freedom (Luke 15:14); in the state of dependence and servitude into which the erring one falls; and lastly in the deep degradation so tellingly expressed in the occupation of tending swine, the very synonym of utter depravity for a Jew (Luke 15:15). In fact the wretched man was worse off than the swine even, and envied the animals the fruit of the locust-tree, with which they were abundantly provided, whilst his own food was scanty on account of the dearth (Luke 15:16). This is a masterly picture of the state of every sinner, of the "public sinners" as well, and especially of the Gentiles, with whom the publicans had considerable intercourse and with whom they were commonly linked in the language of the day (Matt. 18:17). Heathenism was indeed a state of the most terrible poverty, in consequence of the waste of natural and supernatural blessings; a state of the most shameful slavery to Satan and the passions, and of terrible desolation.

The third amplification arises from the plight of the lost and fallen one; it treats of his conscious, voluntary penance and reparation. This also is described with inimitable beauty. The prodigal son in his misery begins to reflect. He compares his present state with his former one, and remembers how kind his father is even to hired laborers. He hopes to obtain pardon, resolves to return and make amends, and starts off at once on his journey. On meeting his father he acts up to his resolution (Matt. 17:21). It is the very picture of perfect penance and conversion.

In the errors and conversion of the prodigal son lies, first, encouragement to the publicans to do penance and be converted. They see therein their own misery and the way to escape it. Secondly, there is encouragement for the Pharisees also, to show compassion and mercy towards the publicans. This is to be found not only in the greatness of the misery described, but also in the courage and nobility of mind with which the prodigal makes amends for his transgressions.

2. THE FATHER

The father's excessive goodness and mercy are shown, first, in his respect for his son's freedom, in allowing him to depart with his inheritance. God acts in like manner. He guides us with great indulgence (Wisd. 12:18), and knows how to turn even a wrong line of action to good, preferring to bring good out of evil rather than to permit no evil at all.

There is no direct mention here of any search for the lost one, by which feature mercy was so beautifully displayed in the preceding parable; the only thing of the kind we are told is that the father saw him afar (Luke 15:20). Nevertheless it is indirectly contained in the fact of the preventing grace conferred by God, by which He, as it were, seeks the sinner and effects his conversion.

His mercy is all the more touchingly revealed, first, in the tenderness of His reception, in the immediate forgiveness granted at the first word; for we see the father stifling the self-accusation upon the lips of the son with his kiss of pardon, so that the latter did not finish what he had intended to say (Luke 15:21). Secondly, it is seen in the restoration of the former condition: of riches, by the "first robe"; of equality of rank, by the ring, the pledge of love (Gen. 41:42; Jer. 22:24); of freedom and noble estate, by the shoes, marking the contrast between the son and the slave who went unshod. All this symbolizes the state of grace in which the sinner is placed by justification (Luke 15:22).

Finally, the love and goodness of the father are also displayed in the heartfelt joy he shows at the banquet, for which the best calf is fetched and killed, and music and dancing are ordered (Luke 15:25); in the joy so touchingly expressed in his own words: "Let us eat and make merry, because this my son was dead, and is come to life again; was lost, and is found" (Luke 15:24); and lastly, in the words he addresses to his elder son in excuse of the prodigal returned (Luke 15:28, 31, 32). In all this there is a wonderful outpouring of love and mercy, the more so as the son's ingratitude to his father has been so great. And yet it is but a symbol and a shadow of the mercy of God towards the penitent sinner. How beautiful and impressive a lesson was this for the sinners and Pharisees who were listening!

3. THE ELDER SON

Many regard the elder son as a type of the Pharisees, and probably they are right. In the preceding parables our Saviour had only given the Pharisees a hint of the merciful dispositions which they ought to entertain for the publicans, but He had not touched upon their hardness of heart. In this parable He speaks to them more plainly.

First, He depicts their spirit in the odious behavior of the elder son. This son represents the hardness and one-sidedness of their sect; the field he has been cultivating is Jewish righteousness (exterior works only), and he has just returned from it, puffed up with pride in his possessions (Luke 15:25, 28). He knows nothing of God's merciful dealings with sinners (Luke 15:26), and does not understand them. He meets them with proud envy and exasperation (Luke 15:28); for his father he has only sullen insolence (Luke 15:29) and for his brother contempt, calling him not his brother, but the son of his father (Luke 15:30), and making bitter remarks upon his misfortunes. Here we have the pharisaical spirit depicted feature by feature. It was more or less characteristic of the entire Jewish nation. Even the Apostles needed a special divine command in order to induce them to turn their attention to the Gentiles (Acts 10:28).

Secondly, our Saviour gives the Pharisees motives for abandoning their hard-hearted dispositions. One motive lies in the behavior of the father, who comes out himself to persuade his son to take part in the general rejoicing (Luke 15:28). Another is expressed in his touching arguments, in which he lays stress upon the happiness which the elder son has enjoyed with him, and on the other hand upon the pitiable misery of the younger son, whose amendment and return certainly ought to be the subject of rejoicing (Luke 15:31, 32).

Thus the parable of the prodigal son is really the continuation and climax of the preceding one, and aims at the same twofold end, only more powerfully and impressively. In truth, in this inimitably beautiful parable there is a loftiness of sentiment and a power of persuasion calculated not only to induce sinners to amend their ways (for which they find a type and motive in the prodigal son), but also to instil into the Pharisees the merciful dispositions with which God treats sinners. The same motives which are to lead the latter to penance are held up to the Pharisees to fill them with kindness of heart towards their erring brethren. Our Saviour does not say whether the elder son accepted the invitation and went in, or not. It is for the Pharisees themselves to decide. As a matter of fact the greater part of Israel did not go in, but remained outside in its anger, pride, and envy. They would not tolerate sinners and ancient heathendom, or share the Father's house with these, in spite of His endeavors to persuade them; but preferred to abandon it. It is their own choice. Mercy becomes their accuser and judge, God's mercy, of which our Saviour here sketches such a beautiful and touching picture, and in which He so gloriously reveals His own Heart.

The Parable of the Unjust Steward

Luke 16:1. And he said also to his disciples: "There was a certain rich man who had a steward; and the same was accused unto him, that he had wasted his goods.—2. And he called him, and said to him: How is it that I hear this of thee? Give an account of thy stewardship; for now thou canst be steward no longer.—3. And the steward said with himself: What shall I do, because my lord taketh away from me the stewardship? To dig I am not able; to beg I am ashamed.—4. I know what I will do, that when I shall be removed from the stewardship, they may receive me into their houses.—5. Therefore calling together everyone of his lord's debtors, he said unto the first: How much dost thou owe my lord?—6. But he said: An hundred barrels of oil. And he said to him: Take thy bill and sit down quickly, and write fifty.—7. Then he said to another: And how much dost thou owe? Who said: An hundred quarters of wheat. He said to him: Take thy bill, and write eighty.—8. And the lord commended the unjust steward, forasmuch as he had done wisely; for the children of this world are wiser in their generation than the children of light.—9. And I say to you: Make unto you friends of the mammon of iniquity; that when you shall fail, they may receive you into everlasting dwellings.—10. He that is faithful in that which is least, is faithful also in that which is greater; and he that is unjust in that which is little, is unjust also in that which is greater.—11. If then you have not been faithful in the unjust mammon; who will trust you with that which is the true?—12. And if you have not been faithful in that which is another's; who will give you that which is your own?—13. No servant can serve two masters; for either he will hate the one, and love the other, or he will hold to the one, and despise the other; you cannot serve God and mammon."—14. Now the Pharisees, who were covetous, heard all these things; and they derided him.—15. And he said to them: "You are they who justify yourselves before men; but God knoweth your hearts; for that which is high to men, is an abomination before God.—16. The law and the prophets were until John; from that time the kingdom of God is preached, and everyone useth violence towards it.—17. And it is easier for heaven and earth to pass, than one tittle of the law to fall.—18. Everyone that putteth away his wife and marrieth another, committeth adultery; and he that marrieth her that is put away from her husband, committeth adultery."

This parable appears to have followed immediately upon the preceding ones.

1. BEFORE WHOM AND FOR WHOM OUR LORD PROPOUNDED THE PARABLE

Our Lord's auditors were first the disciples (Luke 16:1), i.e. the twelve Apostles and also His other followers; secondly, the Pharisees, for we are told that they "derided Him" (Luke 16:14); and lastly, in all probability, the publicans (Luke 15:1). So it was much the same audience as had been present at the preceding parables; at all events, the object and tenor of this parable are suited to these different classes.

2. OUR LORD'S AIM IN PROPOUNDING THIS PARABLE

In pursuit of the same aim as in the preceding parable, our Lord teaches us here an indirect way to salvation. The straight and right road, after we have fallen into sin, is penance; and this road He had shown us in the preceding parable of the prodigal son. But there is also an indirect road to salvation, and that is the good use of temporal riches, in order thereby to obtain the grace of reconciliation with God. This is what our Saviour teaches us in this parable. This lesson was especially adapted for the publicans among the audience. They were to ensure conversion or perseverance by employing their money in works of charity. Perhaps the parable was simply an actual occurrence, drawn from the proceedings of the officials of the Roman fiscal administration. The "rich man," in that case, represents the Emperor (Luke 3:12, 13; 19:8). It was also suited to the Pharisees, for whom this means might serve as an indirect way to salvation, since they did not see the necessity of penance. Our Saviour had already recommended it to them once before (Luke 11:41). It is the last and easiest way to heaven. And it was also suited to the disciples and all the faithful. The employment of temporal goods in works of charity is the way to heaven for countless numbers of people. The intention is clearly expressed in the words: "Make to yourselves friends of the mammon of iniquity, that when you shall fail, they may receive you into everlasting dwellings" (Luke 16:9).

3. HOW OUR SAVIOUR TRIES TO ATTAIN THIS END

Our Lord tries to attain this end in three ways: first, by the parable; secondly, by other motives which He adduces for all in general; lastly, by special motives for the Pharisees.

The parable contains many motives directed to the above-named end. The rich man, who appears to be the owner of vast estates (Luke 16:5–7), is good and benevolent; but still he watches over his revenues, requires an account of them (Luke 16:2), and inflicts punishment, such punishment as is inflicted on a gentleman, viz. deprivation of office and dignity (Luke 16:2). This rich man is God, in His goodness, wisdom, and justice. The steward is wasteful (Luke 16:1), idle (Luke 16:3), and dishonest, but sharp and prudent enough in his way (Luke 16:3–7). He represents the human race and the use and abuse made by it of the many temporal goods entrusted to it by God. Men also have recourse to prudent stratagem when they perform works of charity, making of the poor friends who obtain for them by their prayers the grace of conversion and thus provide for their future. The debtors, then, are the poor, and indeed all to whom as friends and children of God we do good. They provide for their rich benefactors, so to speak, by praying for them; God regards the good works performed for love of Him as a kind of debt that He owes to the rich, and He gives them the grace of conversion as interest and part-payment. The debtors are the only people whose favor the steward can gain by means of his official authority, and without harming himself. The rich man praises the prudence and craftiness with which the steward provides for his future, not his dishonesty. Indeed, one cannot help applauding his cunning as such. The motives given here for imitating this proceeding of the steward are: first, the certainty of being called to account for the stewardship; secondly, the punishment; thirdly, the facility with which one can provide for oneself in this way; and lastly, the Master's willingness to take such prudence into account. He positively encourages us to practise this holy cunning, by pointing to the example of the "children of the world," who "are wiser in their generation (i.e. in their business transactions) than the children of light" (Luke 16:8), i.e. of God. He expressly applies the parable to works of justice and charity, and shows how we can employ for good works and the profit of our soul even the "mammon of iniquity" (Luke 16:9), whether He terms it iniquitous on account of the manner in which it is often acquired, or on account of its misuse for sinful purposes. This cunning, then, is innocent, not sinful, but a good work, and productive of good.

Secondly, our Saviour adds other general motives to ensure the same end; these apply to all, but perhaps bear an especial reference to the publicans. He first says that, by making a good use of money and other temporal goods, which in themselves are "the least" of blessings (Luke 16:10), very often "unjust," dangerous and vain (Luke 16:11), and not the real good of our soul, but alien to it ("another's," Luke 16:12), we learn how to make a good use of what is "greater," "true," and "our own" (i.e. grace and the means of salvation); according to the common proverb, that he who is faithful in little things will also be faithful in greater ones. Further, our Saviour adds that one cannot serve two masters if they are opposed to each other (as God and love of riches are), but only if one is subordinate to the other. We must therefore "serve" (i.e. employ) our money in such a manner that it does not injure our soul's welfare, but even promotes it (Luke 16:13).

Thirdly, our Saviour gives other motives directed to the same end, with particular application to the Pharisees. The Pharisees themselves led up to them by mocking at His advice (Luke 16:14). They based their mockery upon their own riches, which they regarded as a divine reward for their punctilious observance of the law, and therefore considered it quite possible to combine the service of these "two masters," contrary to our Saviour's words (Luke 16:13). But in their observance of the law there was nothing but interior corruption and wickedness. This wickedness consisted in their covetousness and avarice (Luke 16:13), and in their presumption in ascribing to themselves a sanctity which needed no penance, nor purification by almsgiving. Our Saviour now enlarges upon this latter point, saying that their self-righteousness and apparent sanctity might certainly pass as such before men, but was an "abomination before God" (Luke 16:15). He gives two proofs of this. First, the prophets and the Old Law served only as a preparation for the New down to the time of John the Baptist. Now the Messianic kingdom had appeared, and they opposed the Gospel with violence and deprived the people of it (Luke 16:16). Secondly, they fashioned and explained the moral law to suit their own vile passions: e.g. the law of divorce, which, according to their conception and teaching of it, simply furthered and protected adultery. But the law, as God's eternal decree, could not be altered one tittle, and would therefore judge and condemn them as corruptors of it (Luke 16:17, 18). For all these reasons they stood in great need of penance, or at least of the practice of almsgiving; indeed their need was greater than that of others.

This lesson of our Saviour's is of very great and practical importance, because it gives us a true idea of temporal things and teaches us the right use of them, thus opening out to us an indirect road to salvation. What countless numbers of rich people, who would otherwise have perished through the dangers of riches, have found the way to heaven by following this counsel! Almsdeeds and works of charity are a sure way, because our Saviour grants us the grace of conversion and even promises heaven as a reward for them (Tob. 4:11; 12:9). And they are not merely a sure way, but also a pleasant one; God blesses those who practise them with consolation, gentleness of heart, and new pleasure in doing good, and then it is easy to gain heaven (Isa. 58:7 seq.). How thankful we must be to our Lord for His goodness, which makes use of every possible way to lead us to heaven! But it is also clear how deserving of condemnation were the Pharisees in their pride and wickedness, since they scorned even this path. It is worthy of note how expressly our Saviour reproaches them with their covetousness and immorality.

The Parable of the Rich Man and Lazarus

Luke 16:19. There was a certain rich man who was clothed in purple and fine linen and feasted sumptuously every day.—20. And there was a certain beggar named Lazarus, who lay at his gate full of sores,—21. Desiring to be filled with the crumbs that fell from the rich man's table, and no one did give him; moreover the dogs came and licked his sores.—22. And it came to pass that the beggar died, and was carried by the angels into Abraham's bosom. And the rich man also died; and he was buried in hell.—23. And lifting up his eyes, when he was in torments, he saw Abraham afar off, and Lazarus in his bosom;—24. And he cried and said: Father Abraham, have mercy on me, and send Lazarus that he may dip the tip of his finger in water, to cool my tongue, for I am tormented in this flame.—25. And Abraham said to him: Son, remember that thou didst receive good things in thy life-time, and likewise Lazarus evil things; but now he is comforted, and thou art tormented.—26. And besides all this, between us and you there is fixed a great chaos; so that they who would pass from hence to you, cannot, nor from thence come hither.—27. And he said: Then, father, I beseech thee, that thou wouldst send him to my father's house;—28. For I have five brethren; that he may testify unto them, lest they also come into this place of torments.—29. And Abraham said to him: They have Moses and the prophets; let them hear them.—30. But he said: No, father Abraham; but if one went to them from the dead, they will do penance.—31. And he said to him: If they hear not Moses and the prophets, neither will they believe if one rise again from the dead

This parable of the rich man and Lazaraus appears to have followed immediately upon the preceding one.

1. OBJECT OF THE PARABLE

This parable is the impressive conclusion of the two preceding ones, and especially of the last point of the second of these, on the unjust steward. Our Saviour had recommended in this the practice of almsgiving as a means of salvation, first to all in general, and then to the Pharisees in particular, because they mocked at His counsel. He had brought forward reasons to warn them not to rely upon their pretended justice. He now adds to these one last thrilling appeal, viz. the description of the terrible punishment which awaits them if they do not lay aside their hardness of heart, immorality and unbelief, and obtain for themselves the grace of conversion by corporal works of mercy. The punishment of the impenitence of the Pharisees is the chief subject of the parable.

2. DEVELOPMENT OF THE PARABLE

The development of the parable is partly concerned with the rich man, partly with Lazarus. The rich man typifies the Pharisees; Lazarus, in contrast to him, is the type of the poor (including sinners and Gentiles), who are all contemptuously set aside by the Pharisees and regarded as unworthy of the kingdom of God.

The rich man typifies the Pharisees in two respects. First, in his punishment. This punishment, as here described, is twofold. Its negative side consists in exclusion from "Abraham's bosom," the Paradise of eternal bliss. Paradise, or heaven, is especially connected with Abraham, who is the father of the faithful and the depositary of the promises for all his descendants (Matt. 8:11; Luke 13:28; Gen. 12:3; Rom. 5:17, 18). The rich man is buried in hell (Luke 16:22), and only beholds Paradise from "afar off" (Luke 16:23), for it is a long distance from hell (Luke 16:26). The positive part of his punishment consists in pains and suffering of body as well as of soul. He is "buried in hell" (Luke 16:22); he is "in torments" (Luke 16:23), in flames (Luke

16:24); it is a "place of torments" in which he lies (Luke 16:28). The soul is also tortured by the knowledge and remembrance of heaven (Luke 16:23). All these punishments are very great, so great and intolerable that the hard, proud man beseeches, entreats, even implores Lazarus to bring him some alleviation (Luke 16:24); but he finds no mitigation of his pain (Luke 16:25), it is unchangeable, eternal (Luke 16:26), and just. Everyone receives a definite portion of joy, either in this life or in the next. He can choose which he pleases; and what he chooses, that he receives (Luke 16:25). In short, the rich man's damnation is such a great misery that the greatest temporal wretchedness endured by Lazarus here below cannot be compared to it.

The rich man again typifies pharisaic Judaism on account of the reason assigned for his punishment. This reason is also twofold. In the first place it is his misuse of temporal things, his gluttony, luxury (Luke 16:19), and hard-heartedness towards the poor, not even giving the crumbs from his table to poor, despised Lazarus (Luke 16:21). The reason of his damnation, then, is his neglect of the advice which our Saviour had just given in the parable of the unjust steward. The second reason is his unbelief (even with regard to the Mosaic revelation), which veils itself in an arbitrary desire for miracles (Luke 16:30). The condemned man virtually declares his unbelief as well as that of his brethren, i.e. of the entire pharisaic party in Israel; and Abraham confirms the admission (Luke 16:31). It was the last reason for the rejection of the people. They disbelieved not merely our Saviour but Moses also, and this disbelief in Moses had as a natural sequel their failure to believe in the miracles or even in the Resurrection of Christ.

Lazarus, the other character in the parable, is the type of the poor and forsaken, i.e. the sinners and heathens, whom the Pharisees treated with great haughtiness and contempt. Lazarus typifies these unfortunates in three respects. First, in his temporal condition of destitution, poverty and humiliation. He lies in the fore-court of the rich man's house, he is full of sores and starving with hunger, in the company of dogs, those animals so despised in the East; he dies in misery and of misery (Luke 16:20, 21). Thus the poor, sinners and heathens were regarded by the Pharisees. Secondly, Lazarus is the type of patience, humility, and faith. In all these virtues the publicans and heathens of the Gospel compare favorably with the Pharisees, as we have often opportunity to observe (Matt. 8:8; Mark 7:28). In consequence of these virtues Lazarus is the type of the poor in his admission to Paradise, into which he is carried by the angels (Luke 16:22), whilst the rich man, the type of unbelieving Israel, is cast out. Thus the poor and the heathens become the possessors and inheritors of all the consolations and blessings promised by God, whereas faithless Israel loses any right to this inheritance (Luke 16:24).

3. SIGNIFICATION AND IMPORTANCE OF THE PARABLE

On looking closely into the parable we find that our Saviour here does two things.

First, He threatens the unbelieving Jews and tells them what their punishment will be, if they do not repent, do penance, and believe. And it is surprising to see what a clear and comprehensive description our Saviour gives here of the punishments of hell. Taking for granted the doctrine of faith regarding these punishments, we find everything that we know about this unhappy state confirmed in this parable: the punishment of loss, positive pain of soul and body, and the unchangeableness, eternity, and justice of these punishments, all is depicted here in weighty and significant words.

Secondly, our Saviour declares (though gently and without emphasis) the certainty that, on account of its unbelief in spite of His many miracles, Israel will not escape this unhappy fate. It is most significant that, in response to the lost man's entreaty that Lazarus might be sent "from the dead" to bear testimony to his brethren of the dreadfulness of hell's punishments, He makes Abraham say that they had Moses and the prophets, and that if they did not believe these, they would not heed even the admonition of one who had risen from the dead (Luke 16:31). Probably our Saviour is here alluding to the impending restoration to life of Lazarus, and also to His own Resurrection and that of many just men of the Old Covenant after His Death; for it is surely not without design that He calls the poor mendicant Lazarus and speaks of the "rising from the dead" (Luke 16:31). But neither the one nor the other of these miracles sufficed to inspire the Jews with faith. Our Saviour here hints at this sad fact and prepares their minds for these extraordinary miracles, in order that, on the fulfilment of His words, they might remember them and believe.

Three Apostolic Virtues

Luke 17:1. And he said to his disciples: "It is impossible that scandals should not come; but woe to him through whom they come.—2. It were better for him that a mill-stone were hanged about his neck, and he cast into the sea, than that he should scandalize one of these little ones.—3. Take heed to yourselves. If thy brother sin against thee, reprove him; and if he do penance, forgive him.—4. And if he sin against thee seven times in a day, and seven times in a day be converted unto thee, saying: I repent; forgive him."—5. And the apostles said to the Lord: "Increase our faith."—6. And the Lord said: "If you had faith like to a grain of mustard-seed, you might say to this mulberry-tree: Be thou rooted up, and be thou transplanted into the sea; and it would obey you.—7. But which of you having a servant plowing or feeding cattle, will say to him when he is come from the field: Immediately go, sit down to meat;—8. And will not rather say to him: Make ready my supper, and gird thyself and serve me whilst I eat and drink, and afterwards thou shalt eat and drink?—9. Doth he thank that servant for doing the things which he commanded him?—10. I think not. So you also, when you shall have done all these things that are commanded you, say: We are unprofitable servants; we have done that which we ought to do."

This apostolic instruction may also very probably have been given in Peraea; at all events it took place before the restoration of Lazarus to life and our Lord's last journey to Jerusalem, because the latter is only mentioned after this instruction (Luke 17:11). The three virtues that our Lord especially recommends to the Apostles are fraternal correction and readiness to forgive, strong faith, and lastly humility.

1. FRATERNAL CORRECTION AND FORGIVENESS

Our Saviour gave this admonition in connection with a repetition of one of His former lessons concerning scandal, its existence in the world (Luke 17:1), and the serious evil which it causes (Luke 17:1, 2). He says here much the same as He had done on the former occasion, before His journey to Jerusalem for the Feast of Tabernacles (Matt. 18:7 seq.; Mark 9:41–49), and then continues: "Take heed to yourselves," i.e. lest you also should have a share in this scandal by neglecting the duty of reproof and correction. Perhaps our Saviour had in view especially the scandals which would arise for His disciples during His Passion and Death: the betrayal of Judas, the fall of Peter, the growing hatred of the Jews for Himself, and their bloody persecution of Him. Probably He wished to prepare the disciples now for these future occurrences.

Our Saviour mentions here (Luke 17:3) as on the former occasion fraternal correction as the first means of combating the scandal and occasion of sin given to others. Besides the motives He had formerly urged, namely the importance of the act (because it is a means of stemming and removing the evil of sin) and its sublimity (since it is an act of charity and mercy), He seems here to lay especial stress upon the obligation of performing it, for He beings His admonition with the words: "Take heed to yourselves" (Luke 17:3). The reason of this is that the Apostles, by virtue of their position, could perform this correction more easily and successfully than anyone else. As a second means our Lord mentions magnanimous forgiveness; presupposing, however, that the offender recognizes his fault and repents of it (Luke 17:3). In this case we must always pardon, either officially by absolution, or by personal forgiveness. By "seven" our Saviour indicates an indefinite number; the meaning is that we must forgive as often as our neighbor comes to us repentant (Luke 14:4). As motives we may take, first, the fact that our Saviour exhorts us to do this; secondly, that forgiveness is the best means of putting an end to sin, otherwise we perpetuate it; finally, that we ourselves so often come to God with the petition for forgiveness of our sins.

2. STRONG FAITH

The second virtue here recommended by our Lord to His Apostles is faith, and an especially strong and sublime faith.

The reason of this exhortation was the disciples' petition for an increase of faith (Luke 17:5). This petition may perhaps have been prompted by the prediction of future scandals (Luke 17:1), or by observing how constantly our Saviour urges the necessity of faith, ascribes everything to it, and by it makes all things possible (Matt. 17:19; Mark 9:22). By faith, they rightly thought, they would acquire strength for their vocation in all its magnitude, strength to overcome all obstacles and also to fulfil the precept, not always easy to be obeyed, which He had just given them.

Our Saviour's answer confirms this view of faith taken by the Apostles, and says that even miracles are not impossible to it; by means of it they would even be able to remove a mulberry-tree with a word (cf. Matt. 21:21). Perhaps there may have been a tree of this kind standing before our Lord (Luke 17:6). It was not necessary to have an extraordinarily high degree of faith in order to do this; even the lowest degree of miraculous faith (*fides miraculorum*) would suffice. For this reason our Saviour employs the expression "like to a grain of mustard-seed." He seems to hold out to the Apostles the prospect of obtaining this faith, and even to promise it to them; at least such is the implication of the Greek text. They actually received it at the descent of the Holy Ghost.

3. HUMILITY

Our Saviour then adds a similitude in which He inculcates humility, and humility of a touching kind. A master has a servant who acts in the double capacity of plowman and cook. When he comes home in the evening from his work in the field, the master does not tell him to rest and eat, but bids him prepare his (the master's) supper first, and then attend to his own wants. And the servant has no particular thanks to expect for doing this (Luke 17:7–9).

The reason why our Saviour adds this similitude is evidently the possibility, and even danger, that a man who possessed this strong faith might grow vain of the glorious deeds he performed by it, and think he had a claim to special gratitude and reward from God.

Our Lord therefore applies the similitude to the Apostles in particular. It applies to them exactly. They are the servants, the shepherds, vine-dressers and domestics of Christ. The apostolic ministry is manifold, and occupies the whole man, all his strength and all his time; but still it does not give him a right to any special recompense or privilege. Sublime and manifold as it is, and carefully as its holders may acquit themselves of it, they have no claim to any special rights. Whatever our Lord gives them in that way is of His pure grace and condescension (Luke 12:37; John 13:13–15). Even the capability to serve is a grace. For this reason He rightly says: "When you shall have done all these things that are commanded you, say: We are unprofitable servants; we have done that which we ought to do" (Luke 17:10). This applies not only to the Apostles' endowments, but to everyone's gifts. Our Saviour here describes in general the relation of the creature to the Creator.

The Raising of Lazarus

John 11:1. Now there was a certain man sick, named Lazarus, of Bethania, of the town of Mary and of Martha her sister.—2. (And Mary was she that anointed the Lord with ointment and wiped his feet with her hair; whose brother Lazarus was sick.)—3. His sisters therefore sent to him saying: "Lord, behold, he whom thou lovest is sick."—4. And Jesus hearing it, said to them: "This sickness is not unto death, but for the glory of God, that the Son of God may be glorified by it."—5. Now Jesus loved Martha, and her sister Mary, and Lazarus.—6. When he had heard therefore that he was sick, he still remained in the same place two days;—7. Then after that he said to his disciples: "Let us go into Judaea again."—8. The disciples say to him: "Rabbi, the Jews but now sought to stone thee, and goest thou thither again?"—9. Jesus answered: "Are there not twelve hours of the day? If a man walk in the day, he stumbleth not, because he seeth the light of this world;—10. But if he walk in the night, he stumbleth, because the light is not in him."—11. These things he said, and after that he said to them: "Lazarus our friend sleepeth; but I go that I may awake him out of sleep."—12. His disciples therefore said: "Lord, if he sleep, he shall do well."—13. But Jesus spoke of his death; and they thought that he spoke of the repose of sleep.—14. Then therefore Jesus said to them plainly: "Lazarus is dead;—15. And I am glad for your sakes that I was not there, that you may believe; but let us go to him."—16. Thomas, therefore, who is called Didymus, said to his fellow-disciples: "Let us also go, that we may die with him."—17. Jesus therefore came, and found that he had been four days already in the grave.—18. (Now Bethania was near Jerusalem, about fifteen furlongs off.)—19. And many of the Jews were come to Martha and Mary, to comfort them concerning their brother.—20. Martha therefore as soon as she heard that Jesus was come, went to meet him; but Mary sat at home.—21. Martha therefore said to Jesus: "Lord, if thou hadst been here, my brother had not died;—22. But now also I know that whatsoever thou wilt ask of God, God will give it thee."—23. Jesus saith to her: "Thy brother shall rise again."—24. Martha saith to him: "I know that he shall rise again in the resurrection at the Last Day."—25. Jesus said to her: "I am the resurrection and the life; he that believeth in me, although he be dead, shall live:—26. And everyone that liveth and believeth in me, shall not die for ever. Believest thou this?"—27. She saith to him: "Yea, Lord, I have believed that thou art Christ, the Son of the living God, who art come into this world."—28. And when she had said these things, she went, and called her sister Mary secretly, saying: "The master is come and calleth for thee."—29. She, as soon as she heard this, riseth quickly and cometh to him;—30. For Jesus was not yet come into the town; but he was still in that place where Martha had met him.—31. The Jews therefore, who were with her in the house and comforted her, when they saw Mary, that she rose up speedily and went out, followed her, saying: "She goeth to the grave, to weep there."—32. When Mary therefore was come where Jesus was, seeing him, she fell down at his feet, and saith to him: "Lord, if thou hadst been here, my brother had not died."—33. Jesus therefore, when he saw her weeping, and the Jews that were come with her weeping, groaned in the spirit, and troubled himself,—34. And said: "Where have you laid him?" They say to him: "Lord, come and see."—35. And Jesus wept.—36. The Jews therefore said: "Behold how he loved him."—37. But some of them said: "Could not he, that opened the eyes of the man born blind, have caused that this man should not die?"—38. Jesus therefore again groaning in himself, cometh to the sepulcher; now it was a cave; and a stone was laid over it.—39. Jesus saith: "Take away the stone." Martha, the sister of him that was dead, saith to him: "Lord, by this time he stinketh, for he is now of four days."—40. Jesus saith to her: "Did not I say to thee, that if thou believe, thou shalt see the glory of God?"—41. They took therefore the stone away; and Jesus lifting up his eyes said: "Father, I give thee thanks that thou hast heard me;—42. And I knew that thou hearest me always, but because of the people who stand about, have I said it; that they may believe that thou hast sent me."—43. When he had said these things, he cried with a loud voice: "Lazarus, come forth."—44. And presently he that had been dead came forth, bound feet and hands with winding-bands, and his face was bound about with a napkin. Jesus said to them: "Loose him and let him go."—45. Many therefore of the Jews who were come to Mary and Martha, and had seen the things that Jesus did, believed in him.—46. But some of them went to the Pharisees, and told them the things that Jesus had done.

The great miracle of the raising of Lazarus now follows. In order to work it our Saviour quitted the district east of the Jordan, and came to Bethania in Judaea.

1. EVENTS IN THE EAST-JORDAN DISTRICT

The events in the East-Jordan district which are connected with this mystery may be classified under two headings: the message of the sisters of Lazarus, and our Saviour's behavior with regard to it.

Whilst our Saviour was still working in the East-Jordan district there came a message from the sisters of Lazarus, saying that their brother was seriously ill. Lazarus' family, consisting of himself and his two sisters, Martha and Mary (John 11:1), appears to have been greatly and widely esteemed (John 11:19). They dwelt in Bethania, not quite two miles from Jerusalem (John 11:18); they were very pious and devoted to our Lord (John 11:2; Luke 10:38), and were loved by Him in return (John 11:3, 5). This family had now a hard trial to bear, namely the mortal sickness of the brother, its head (John 11:3). So the sisters sent to our Lord a message full of faith, humility, modesty, and touching confidence (John 11:3). They simply mention the sickness, and leave all the rest to Him.

And how does our Saviour behave towards the family? He loves them (John 11:5). This may be seen from the fact that He repeatedly speaks of Lazarus, is evidently with him in spirit, and follows the course of the sickness (John 11:7, 11, 14). For this reason He first comforts the sisters with the mysterious words that the sickness is not unto death, but for the glory of God and His own honor (John 11:4). Nevertheless He remains two days longer at the place where He had received the message, although He knew that Lazarus died on the same day that it had reached Him. Why does He delay so long, whilst in other cases He shows Himself so ready to come and help? (Matt. 8:7; 9:19.) The reason may probably have been that our Lord would not interrupt His apostolic labors on account of private affairs. Besides, He knew that the glory of God would be promoted by the death of Lazarus; and He did not show any the less love to him and his family in putting off His journey and permitting His friend to die than He would have done by merely curing his sickness, for this death afforded both Lazarus and his sisters an opportunity of practising many virtues: patience, fraternal affection, humility, and trust in God. Our Lord wished to confer a greater benefit upon Lazarus, by raising him from the dead. At length He starts for Judaea (John 11:11, 15, 17), and herein lies a new and great proof of His love for Lazarus and his sisters. Upon our Saviour's naming Judaea as His destination, the disciples were startled and remonstrated with Him, reminding Him how the Jews had wished to stone Him on the Feast of the Dedication (John 11:8). He calmed their fears by a simile. As a pedestrian is in no danger as long as the daylight lasts, so it was with Him; His working-day was not yet over, the night of His Passion was not yet at hand; the pedestrian had not in his own power the light of day and life, but He Himself had (John 11:9, 10). Nevertheless it was the way to death upon which they now entered, as St. Thomas said in his words of exhortation to his fellow-Apostles (John 11:16). This very miracle was the proximate cause of the Death of Jesus. Our Saviour knew this well, and yet He went thither to work it (John 11:17).

These events beyond the Jordan are the remote preparation for the miracle. They are, as it were, the first act of the great drama, in which the whole play, with its actuating, impelling forces and motives and the circumstances of time and place, is introduced, its threads gathered, the plot unfolded, and a glimpse of the momentous issue given. The significance and importance of the miracle are indicated, as regards time, place, and circumstances. It is to be performed in the vicinity of Jerusalem, almost before the gates of the city, upon a man of high standing and influence, belonging to a rich and respected family. This man must die and be buried, in order to make the miracle more striking and irrefutable. And in order that Lazarus may die, our Lord delays His departure; thus the plot thickens. The various aims of the miracle are also laid bare. God is to be glorified thereby, our Saviour proved to be the Messias, and the faith of the disciples strengthened. As proximate and impelling cause is specified our Saviour's love of His friends, and this love is displayed in the most striking way. Even the connection of the miracle with the great impending Passion is indicated, in the words: "Let us also go that we may die with Him" (John 11:16); faintly and mysteriously, indeed, but still one feels it. The whole atmosphere into which this introductory scene leads us is so close, sultry and ominous, that one already seems to see the flash of the spark which will be followed by the discharge.

2. EVENTS IN BETHANIA IMMEDIATELY BEFORE THE MIRACLE

The events beyond the Jordan form the remote introduction to the miracle. The events in Bethania which immediately precede the miracle derive their significance from the fact that they are the last and immediate preparation made by our Lord for working it. By them, first, the actual fact of the miracle is to be so palpably established that no one can deny that it is a victory over death and decay. Secondly, its aim and significance are to be made clear, inasmuch as it is a proof and effect of the love of Jesus, and also a proof of His Godhead and divine mission. Everything is arranged with a view to these two ends.

Upon the arrival of Jesus in Bethania He is told that Lazarus has been buried four days already (John 11:17). The grave is closed (John 11:38, 41), and when our Saviour commands them to open it, Martha says that decay must have set in already (John 11:39). Besides this our Lord finds on His arrival a large number of Jews, who had come from Jerusalem to pay a visit of condolence to the sisters (John 11:19). These are all proofs of the fact of Lazarus' death. Further, the Jews accompany Mary to Jesus (John 11:31), go with Him to the grave (John 11:42), and are thus obliged to witness in person the restoration to life. Probably people would have denied the fact, if only the disciples and the sisters had seen it. Thus the material fact of the miracle is established by the care of our Lord.

The inward significance of the miracle, as an act of His love, now remains to be established. This takes place in the beautiful scene when Mary comes and casts herself weeping at Jesus' feet, as Martha had probably done (John 11:32); when the Jews who accompany her (John 11:33) stand round, dissolved in tears, and all in their helplessness look to our Lord as their sole helper; and when He Himself repeatedly begins to weep through deep emotion, yet, commanding Himself with an effort, asks: "Where have you laid him?" (John 11:33, 35, 38.) This is a deep mystery of the interior, emotional life of Jesus. Commentators make a distinction between His "groaning" and "troubling Himself," and see therein two separate meanings. The expression "groaning" indicates the violent emotion of repugnance, reluctance, and anger. This perturbation of mind felt by our Lord may be thus explained. He is on the point of working this extraordinary miracle; He is urged to it on all sides, by those whom He dearly loves as well as by His own Heart. But at the same instant His mind sees the whole bearing of the miracle. It was the deciding cause—the introduction, as it were—of His own Passion and Death. He saw how this miracle, the most glorious proof of His love and divine power, would be for His enemies a signal of attack; He saw before His very eyes some who would hurry away from the place, from the thrilling impression of the divine deed, to lay the snares in which He was to be entrapped (John 11:46). He saw, too, in the death and burial of His friend Lazarus, His own Death, so full of shame and pain, the most terrible mystery of wickedness; He saw, in the sorrow and tears of the sisters and friends of Lazarus, the sorrow and inconsolable grief of His holy Mother and His friends at His own Death and Burial. The whole dark mystery of the "hour of darkness" rose before His mind, and His soul was suddenly plunged into the bitterness and horror of death. It was like a foreboding cloud of the stormy night of Gethsemani, and He allowed His Soul to struggle in this anguish of repugnance, sorrow and oppression. How natural that His Soul should resist, and shudder at performing the fatal miracle! (Keppler.) These emotions had made themselves felt before this, though not without His own Will (Luke 12:50).

Our Saviour "troubled Himself," wept (John 11:35). What was the reason of His grief and tears? Evidently not, or at least not directly, the death of His friend; for though this might cause the sisters and friends of the deceased man to shed tears, on account of the temporal separation and bereavement, it could not cause our Lord to do so, since He was just about to restore him to life. Neither was it, we may be sure, the state of Lazarus' soul in the next world, for Lazarus was a Saint, and had died in the love and grace of Jesus. What, then, was the reason? We can scarcely imagine any other than that heartfelt compassion for the grief of Lazarus' sisters and friends, which we call sympathy. When a good man sees a friend in deep grief and well-founded sorrow, the mere sight of this is enough to move him to shed tears also. One string set in motion makes another of equal pitch vibrate. We have here therefore a true and touching proof not only of the true human nature of Jesus, which includes a temperament with all its faculties and emotions, but also a proof how human, kind, tender, and full of feeling this temperament of our Lord's was. And these tears grow still more precious to us, when we reflect how our Saviour weeps. These emotions and tears are not under our control; they come and go, whether we will or not, and for this reason they are not always of much value in our case. With our Saviour they were quite voluntary, and subject to His Will as regards both origin and intensity. Nothing found access to His holy Soul, and no emotion made itself felt there, but what He wished and as He wished. In this case, then, He saw that the pain of the sisters and friends of Lazarus was justified, well-governed, and holy; and therefore He permitted this realization to have its full influence upon His feelings, and to work upon them so powerfully that they found vent in tears. Our Saviour was not ashamed of this emotion and these tears. He did not turn away to hide them, as men of kindly disposition often do, who are easily touched but ashamed to show it. He stands amid the weeping group and weeps with them, and the tears roll gently down His beautiful, manly cheeks, so that all can see them. O beautiful tears, precious tears, precious not only for Lazarus and his family, but for all of us! Our Lord sheds them not only on account of our sins, but even over our temporal distress. What a kind heart, and what a tender, human, sympathetic love this presupposes! Truly "the Word is made flesh." Tears are the blood of the heart and of love; indeed, they prove more sympathetic love than even blood does. One can give one's life for another from a mere sense of duty, but if we weep for someone, he has certainly won our heart and affection. The Jews understood this signification of our Lord's tears at once, and said: One can see how He loved Lazarus; how was it then that He allowed him to die, since He was able even to give sight to the blind man? (John 11:36, 37.) Such is the mystery of the grief and tears of Jesus. At the grave itself, at the moment when He was about to perform the miracle, He once more permitted this emotion—whether of fear or of sorrow—to pass over His Soul (John 11:38). But it was not His custom to take even one step backward or hesitate a moment to fulfil the Will of His Heavenly Father, and so He goes forward to the work, resolute and ready for death. By this act He Himself reveals to us His love of God and of Lazarus, as the cause of the miracle.

But the significance of the miracle as a proof of our Saviour's

Godhead and divine mission had also to be shown. This He does, first, at His meeting with Martha. She, as the prudent housewife and eager disciple of Jesus, comes to meet Him, alone (John 11:20); a little later she calls Mary aside to tell her of His arrival (John 11:29), in order not to bring our Saviour into contact with the uncongenial Jewish company. She is full of faith and trust in the love and power of Jesus (John 11:21), which can still help even now, at all events by the power of His intercession with God (John 11:22). But that is not enough for our Lord. She must rise still higher in her faith. She must not only believe that her brother will rise again at the general resurrection (John 11:23, 24), or merely through the intercession of Jesus with the Father; she must believe that He, Who stands before her, has in Himself the truly Divine Life, that He is true God, and that as such He can restore life by His own power and whenever He pleases. That is "the glory of God" which is to be made manifest through this miracle (John 11:4, 40), and that is the meaning of the beautiful words: "I am the resurrection and the life." Our Saviour adds in explanation: "He that believeth in Me, although he be dead (in the body), shall live (by the resurrection); and everyone that liveth and believeth in Me (although he may die the death of the body), shall not die for ever," i.e. on account of the life of the spirit and the immortality of the resurrection. This explains and substantiates both the terms "resurrection" and "life." Our Saviour exacts this faith as a condition of the miracle: "Believest thou this?" (John 11:25, 26.) And later on, at the grave, as Martha seems to waver a little, fearing the effects of decay, He again reminds her of this condition (John 11:40) and of the glorious profession of faith that she had already made: "Yea, Lord, I have believed that Thou art Christ, the Son of the Living God, Who art come into this world," i.e. that Thou art the Messias, and that Thou canst do all that Thou testifiest of Thyself (John 11:27). This faith, this view of the miracle, was what our Saviour wished. Mary seems to have been in complete possession of it already, and therefore He requires of her no further preparation or disposition of mind (John 11:32). By this preparation the sisters were to cooperate in the miracle and to deserve it.

But far more powerfully and solemnly still does our Lord reveal this signification of the miracle to the Jews, for whom chiefly He wrought it. He had so disposed matters that a great number of Jews from Jerusalem (of the upper classes, some friendly, others disaffected) should be witnesses of this miracle. There they gathered around our divine Saviour and the sisters. It was to be made clear and brought home to them what the signification, the efficient cause, and the object of the miracle were, and how they ought all to look upon this deed as a divine sign, and turn it to advantage to attain to faith in the divine mission of Jesus. With this intention, then, our Saviour makes His solemn prayer to His Heavenly Father before the sepulcher. In this prayer He lays stress upon two points. He first thanks the Father for having heard Him (John 11:41). This "hearing" is not to be understood as though our Saviour did not work the miracle of His own power, but merely through His intercession, as the Saints did; for He says immediately after that He knows that the Father always hears Him (John 11:42), which is tantamount to saying that He possesses the gift of miracles as His own peculiar and innate power. But He thanks the Father rather for having given Him the opportunity of performing such a glorious deed for His glory and the good of the Jews, to which His (Christ's) own prayer could assuredly contribute. He thanks Him also, because He must perform it at His risk and at the sacrifice of His own life; He thanks Him as God-Man, with reference to His human nature, which has received everything from the Father and is subject to Him; He thanks Him, finally, and ascribes to Him the working of the miracle, on account of the Jews, who did not regard Him as the Son of God, nor even as a man of God, but as the tool of the devil (Matt. 9:34; 12:24). In order to bring home to them that He did not (as they thought) work the miracle of His own (human) power, but in the Name and power of God—that is to say, that the miracle was really a divine sign—He ascribes it to the Father. This is only another way of expressing the thought that He has so often set before the Jews already (John 5:19, 30; 8:28, 29; 10:25). In conformity with this our Saviour further mentions the object of the miracle, viz. that the "people who stand about" may believe that God has sent Him (John 11:42). He works this miracle, then, for the express purpose of proving His divine mission. For this reason He says the prayer aloud, so that all could and should hear it. Never yet had He so expressly appealed to His miraculous power in any single case, in order to prove His rank as the Messias, and thus to challenge faith or unbelief. Everything was now at stake; the preparations were made.

3. MIRACLE

And now followed the miracle, so great in itself and in its effects.

The miracle is remarkable in its very nature. It is a restoration to life of a dead person, and proves the independent power of the Son of God over life and death. It was different from the other miracles of this kind wrought by our Lord, as it took place after decay had already set in. As one of the holy Fathers says, our Saviour snatched the little daughter of Jairus from the hands, the youth of Naim from the jaws, but Lazarus from the very bowels of Death. As regards the circumstances of the miracle, it is divine, like all the miracles of Jesus, but yet unique in the simplicity of its efficient cause and in the completeness and extraordinary suddenness of the effect. Our Saviour does not enter the sepulcher, but remains outside, and merely calls with a loud and powerful voice: "Lazarus, come forth!" (John 11:43.) He does this in order to show that His call is the concrete instrument of His divine power. And another most extraordinary circumstance, which seems almost like a second miracle, is that Lazarus not merely comes to life again, but rises, comes forth, and suddenly stands before our Saviour in the midst of the bystanders, although all his limbs (according to the Jewish custom of burial) were bound and wrapped in linen bands, and his head covered with a cloth, so that in the natural course of things he could neither walk nor stand (John 11:44) until our Saviour commanded his bonds to be loosened.

Holy Scripture does not record any of the immediate effects of the miracle. But one may imagine what feelings of fear and awe, joy and gratitude must have passed through the hearts of those present; how Lazarus and the sisters adored and thanked our Saviour, and rejoiced with the Apostles in His glory; how the Jews, paralyzed with fear and terror, saw the reanimated corpse suddenly approach them, stand amongst them, and emerge to the daylight from under the grave-clothes. It was not Jesus of Nazareth, not the mighty teacher of the law, not one of the old prophets, nor yet a spirit from the other world who worked this miracle in their midst. It was the Living God Himself. One word from Him rings through the abysses of eternity and brings the soul back from the ends of the world beyond; a flash of lightning pierces the darkness of the grave, and rekindles in the dead bones the spark of life. Life Eternal, the Judge of the living and the dead, stands among them in bodily form. The judgment is passed immediately. Many of the Jews around, overpowered by the power of the divine testimony, believe (John 11:45; 12:11); but others depart with all speed, hasten to the Pharisees, inform them (whether with good or bad intent) of the miracle (John 11:46), and thus pave the way for the ensuing results.

Such is the raising of Lazarus. The great significance of the mystery is derived from the fact that it is the culminating point of Christ's revelation of Himself by means of miracles. With the exception of His own Resurrection it is the greatest miracle that He wrought. It is great not only in its nature but also in is circumstances, which our Saviour Himself, as is very evident, makes use of in order to excite the suspense of the people to the highest pitch possible. In no other case does He so appeal to His Godhead and challenge faith or unbelief. Lastly, the miracle is great in its effects. The threads of the past and the future here unite. The preceding miracles, even that wrought upon the man born blind (John 11:37), are merely the ground-work, so to speak, for this one, and serve to support and enhance it. The future, with both glory and death, develops from it. The glorious entry into Jerusalem on Palm Sunday is only a recognition and homage paid to Jesus by the people in consequence of this miracle (John 12:17); and the rage of His enemies (who now have recourse to the most extreme measures), His Passion and Death are its natural result. It was altogether too much for unbelief, to call Lazarus back from eternity and set him up at the very gates of Jerusalem as one risen from the dead. He was henceforth the living evidence of the truth of the words which our Lord had once spoken to the Jews in the Temple: "As the Father raiseth up the dead, and giveth life; so the Son also giveth life to whom He will" (John 5:21). "Amen I say unto you, that the hour cometh, and now is, when the dead shall hear the voice of the Son of God; and they that hear, shall live. For as the Father hath life in Himself, so He hath given to the Son also to have life in Himself" (John 5:25, 26). Lazarus has now, as our Saviour said in the parable, really returned to bear witness to his brethren (Luke 16:31); yet they do not believe, but decide to put to death both Lazarus and Him Who raised him to life (John 12:10). This is the sad and affecting side of the miracle, and we understand now that our Saviour, to Whose mind this prospect lay open, experienced a natural hesitation and reluctance to give this signal for His own Death.

But this is also a manifestation of the love of our Divine Saviour for His own. There is scarcely any mystery in which this love is so plainly revealed in all its qualities. It is an omniscient love, from which nothing is concealed, and which always bears us in mind and occupies itself with us; and it is surely a great comfort to know that He, Who loves us, also sees us. It is a wise and fatherly love, which may permit hard things to befall us, but only for our good. It is a self-sacrificing love, which has devoted itself for all of us, as well as for Lazarus; a tender love, which even sheds tears for our sufferings and distresses. Finally, it is an omnipotent love, which can do everything, can help us even where no one else is able to help, and whose word of command has authority even beyond the grave. And this love, this Heart is not dead; it lives on in heaven and here amongst us in the Blessed Sacrament, and feels for us just as tenderly and lovingly as of yore. What a happiness to have Him for our faithful friend, Who does not forsake us even when all others depart! How much to be envied was the family of Lazarus, of which it is recorded that Jesus loved it, and what ought we not to do, in order to gain for ourselves this love and friendship! Lazarus and his sisters teach us how we can win the Heart of Jesus, viz. by faith in Him, by heartfelt attachment and devotion to Him, and lastly by gratitude and firm confidence, no matter what may happen. What new love and gratitude Lazarus must have felt for our Lord! Our Lord will one day perform upon us all the miracle He wrought upon Lazarus. His voice will arouse us all to the life of glory, and in our glorified bodies we shall all be witnesses to His love and power for all eternity.

The Decision to Put Our Saviour to Death

John 11:45. Many therefore of the Jews who were come to Mary and Martha and had seen the things that Jesus did, believed in him.—46. But some of them went to the Pharisees, and told them the things that Jesus had done.—47. The chief priests therefore and the Pharisees gathered a council, and said: "What do we, for this man doth many miracles?—48. If we let him alone so, all will believe in him; and the Romans will come and take away our place and nation."—49. But one of them named Caiphas, being the high priest that year, saith to them: "You know nothing,—50. Neither do you consider that it is expedient for you that one man should die for the people, and that the whole nation perish not."—

51. And this he spoke not of himself; but being the high priest of that year, he prophesied that Jesus should die for the nation,—52. And not only for the nation, but to gather together in one the children of God that were dispersed.—53. From that day therefore they devised to put him to death.—54. Wherefore Jesus walked no more openly among the Jews, but he went into a country near the desert, unto a city that is called Ephrem, and there he abode with his disciples.—55. And the Pasch of the Jews was at hand; and many from the country went up to Jerusalem before the Pasch, to purify themselves.—56. They sought therefore for Jesus; and they discoursed one with another, standing in the temple: "What think you, that he is not come to the festival day?" And the chief priests and the Pharisees had given a commandment, that if any man knew where he was, he should tell, that they might apprehend him.

1. OCCASION OF THE DECISION

The circumstance which indirectly led to the decision was the hatred and envy entertained by the ruling party towards Jesus, and their fear of Him. But the direct cause was the news of the great miracle He had wrought in the raising of Lazarus. Some of the Jews who had witnessed it brought them the first tidings (John 11:46), perhaps in order to shield themselves from the unpleasant consequences which their presence at the miracle might have brought upon them. The news spread on the wings of the wind, and must have set the whole town in commotion. To deny the miracle was impossible, and so it was high time to come to some decision, if any measures were to be taken against our Saviour. "We must act now or never," His enemies seem to have said, as we see from their deliberations (John 11:48); and so the Great Council was called.

2. THE DELIBERATIONS

The originators of the deliberations were the Pharisees and the chief priests; either Caiphas, the acting High Priest, or Annas (who had been deposed by the Romans, but still possessed great influence), or the heads of the principal priestly families. The summons was an official one, and therefore the entire Great Council assembled (John 11:47).

These official assemblies were held either in a room in the southern side-buildings of the priests' court of the Temple, called Gazith or stone-room, or (according to another tradition) in a country-house of the High Priest's, on the so-called "Hill of the Wicked Council."

The question under deliberation concerned the measures which were to be taken against Jesus; matters could not remain as they were (John 11:47, 48). The president (probably Caiphas), together with his colleagues who were of the same mind, explained the reasons of this. In the first place, Jesus worked many miracles (John 11:47). They do not deny our Lord's miracles, therefore, but acknowledge them; indeed, they say He "doth many miracles." Secondly, if things went on like this, everyone would believe in Him as the Messias; there would be public disturbances leading to the complete overthrow of the existing order (John 11:48). Thirdly, this would give the Romans a pretext for coming and taking the city and Temple and for depriving the nation of all the rights and privileges it had hitherto enjoyed (John 11:48). They ascribe to our Saviour their own ideas of the Messianic kingdom, and pretend solicitude for their nation. This was nothing but hypocrisy. If our Lord had held with them and there had been a chance of success, they would have sided with Him against the Romans, regardless of the welfare of the nation.

This, then, was the question proposed, and now they probably deliberated what was to be done, whether to arrest Him, kill Him, or otherwise put it out of His power to do them any harm. It would seem that opinions were divided; at least it is probable that the more sensible members and the friends of Jesus, such as Nicodemus and Joseph of Arimathea, called attention to the absurdity and insufficiency of the grounds for proceeding against Jesus. It is really no crime, to work miracles. On the contrary, they should have believed in these miracles, or at least have inquired into them. The real motive which actuated them was the fear lest they might be obliged to acknowledge Him and so lose their own position. There was no mention whatever made of blasphemy or profanation of the Sabbath, of which they had so often accused Him.

3. THE DECISION

At last Caiphas put an end to the matter (John 18:14). He did this, first, with great irritation and want of consideration for the other councilors, probably on account of their opposition and their doubts. "You know nothing, neither do you consider" (John 11:49), are the words he casts in their teeth. Secondly, he brought about the decision in a most unscrupulous manner, supporting his proposal to kill Jesus by the false assumption that His influence was dangerous to the state; and thirdly and lastly, with great injustice, saying that it was better that one man should die than that the whole nation should perish. This was certainly a lesser evil in itself, but still it was neither just nor permissible to put a man to death without cause. He made the end justify the means.

In spite of all this, Caiphas succeeded in bringing about the wished-for decision. The council gave way, and agreed that Jesus should be put to death. There had been deliberations upon the matter before this, but not official ones, or when they were official (e.g. John 7:30, 32, 45) the decision had not been in favor of capital punishment. But now the die was cast. On this occasion the Great Council seems to have decided also upon the measures to be taken against our Divine Saviour, particularly upon the edict that anyone who knew His whereabouts was to inform the authorities, in order that He might be arrested (John 11:56). The whole assembly as well as the decision was a wretched mixture of insincerity, hypocrisy, lying, malice, and injustice. A true *concilium malignantium*, or "Wicked Council," as it is usually called.

Nevertheless the decision found ratification, as regards its matter and wording, in the counsels of the Most Holy Trinity. There too it was decided that it was better for "one man" to die than for the whole nation to perish. And this decree was a work of justice; it was just and right that the sin of the world should be expiated by the death of one; for God, against Whom the offence was committed, has the right to determine the measure of satisfaction. It was likewise a work of mercy, that only one should die for all, and a work of wisdom, that this death of one should become the foundation of the union and unity of all, by breaking down the barriers between nations and establishing the one great universal Church (John 11:52; 10:16). The Heavenly Father ratified the founding of this universal Church upon the basis of our Lord's Death; and thus He showed His love for us men, by giving His own Son for us and establishing a common home for us through His Death. And in order to reveal His decree of justice, mercy, and wisdom, God in wondrous manner made use of this very counsel of iniquity, the hatred and false wisdom of Caiphas. What seemed best to Caiphas in his diabolical malice was confirmed as the best by God, in His holy and merciful designs. Caiphas prophesied, as St. John observes, because he was High Priest for that year (John 11:51); but he did so unconsciously, in another sense and with quite an opposite intention. Caiphas understood by "the people" the Jewish nation alone, but God the whole human race. This is certainly a touching mark of God's fidelity to the ancient priesthood, to whom He had accorded the high distinction of proclaiming His Will to the people (Num. 27:21; Deut. 17:8, 9). As Caiphas did not consult the Lord, he was quite unconscious of uttering His Will; but in bringing forward the plan originated by malice he was fully aware of what he was doing, and thus he brought ruin upon his people instead of being of use to them. With the Death of Jesus the ancient priesthood ceased, and thus its last prophecy was a prediction concerning the new High Priest.

But in the counsels of the Most Holy Trinity as well as at the meeting of the Great Council there was One present, Who also took part in the deliberations and their ratification. This was our Divine Saviour Himself. He knew everything, heard everything, and ratified the decree of Caiphas, according to the plan of His Heavenly Father, with great humility, love and devotion. He offered Himself for us with infinite love. But when His friends in the Council brought Him word of what had been decided, He quitted the neighborhood of Jerusalem, and went northeastwards to the little town of Ephrem, high above the sea-level, on the outskirts of the desert of Jericho (cf. Introd., p. 5). Probably His road led through Anathoth, the birth-place of the prophet Jeremias, who is a living type of the suffering Messias. He retired before His enemies, not in order to escape death, but to wait for the time appointed by God and to put His disciples out of danger. This may probably have taken place in January, according to our reckoning, about six weeks before the last Feast of the Pasch and our Saviour's Death.

This resolution of the Great Council, therefore, was the answer to the great miracle of the raising of Lazarus. This answer was an official one, given by the heads and representatives of the whole nation, prompted by the High Priest, and resolved upon in the Temple, in the shadow of the Holy of Holies. It was the answer of unbelief, obduracy, insincerity, and mortal hatred, to the highest act of love and mercy, and therefore it was fatal. The pretext brought forward was the welfare of the nation, but it was the ruin of the nation that it accelerated and sealed. Nothing but faith in the Messias could save them. Nevertheless God made use of the answer of this wicked High Priest to proclaim to the world the deepest mystery of His mercy. The High Priest was to do this, and in words which expressed in the best and most complete manner the eternal decree of the Redemption. This chosen prophet proclaimed the salvation of the whole world and the ruin of his own people, and thus became a Balaam in a contrary sense from his prototype.

The Ten Lepers

Luke 17:11. And it came to pass, as he was going to Jerusalem, he passed through the midst of Samaria and Galilee.—12. And as he entered into a certain town, there met him ten men that were lepers, who stood afar off;—13. And lifted up their voice, saying: "Jesus, Master, have mercy on us."—14. Whom when he saw he said: "Go, show yourselves to the priests." And it came to pass, as they went, they were made clean.—15. And one of them, when he saw that he was made clean, went back, with a loud voice glorifying God,—16. And he fell on his face before his feet, giving thanks; and this was a Samaritan.—17. And Jesus answering, said: "Were not ten made clean? And where are the nine?—18. There is no one found to return and give glory to God, but this stranger."—19. And he said to him: "Arise, go thy way; for thy faith hath made thee whole."

Our Saviour now set forth on His last journey. From Ephrem He went through Samaria and Galilee to the Jordan; then along the eastern bank of the river, through Peraea and Galaad, to Jericho, Bethania and Jerusalem. Of His ministry in Samaria and Galilee at this time little is known, with the exception of the cure of the ten lepers. This mystery has a threefold meaning.

1. Historical Signification of the Mystery

Several points in this mystery correspond with our Lord's former cure of a leper (Matt. 8:2; Mark 1:40; Luke 5:12), but others differ from it. Among these latter there are three points of special importance.

With regard to the circumstances, there are here ten lepers, not merely one. One at least is a Samaritan. Our Saviour has already left Ephrem and is journeying northwards through Samaria and Galilee, on His way to the Jordan. It is probable that the scene of the event was some place in Galilee; tradition says Ginaea, the Djennin of today. Lepers were allowed to approach one another, and even to live together. Thus we find here a whole party of poor lepers in company. Their common misfortune overcame the antipathy of nationality and religion. The lepers seem to have met our Saviour by chance, but had probably already heard of His presence in the country and His wonderful deeds. They remained standing at a distance, and begged Him to heal them (Luke 17:11–13).

The miracle itself was worked in consideration of their misery, faith and confidence. Their very cry: "Master, have mercy on us," is full of reverence, desire and trust. But their faith is especially shown in the circumstance that they all immediately obeyed our Lord's direction to show themselves to the priests, and started off even before they were healed (Luke 17:14). The cure took place only on the way. As at the cure of the first leper, our Saviour keeps strictly to the regulations of the law, and tests the faith of the ten men by sending them to the priests, although they were not yet healed. In this case our Lord did not touch the lepers, nor did He bid them keep the miracle a secret.

With regard to the effects of the miracle there is a difference between the lepers. In misfortune, in faith and confidence, and in their cure they had been united; but not so in the test of gratitude. They had evidently not gone far when they saw themselves healed. Perhaps they had only to go into the town, for Ginaea (Ain Gannim or Engannim) was a Levite city (Jos. 19:21; 21:29). But only the Samaritan came back to thank our Lord, as soon as he perceived himself to be cured. He fell at His feet and thanked Him (Luke 17:15, 16). None of the others appeared; they all remained away, either from insensibility and want of humility, or because the priests themselves or the fear of offending them restrained them from coming. At all events it was something blameworthy that kept them away, for our Saviour evidently complains of "the nine," whilst praising the faith, confidence, and gratitude of "the stranger," and ascribing his cure to his faith (Luke 17:19). He then dismisses him with new graces, perhaps even with the belief in His Divinity.

2. FIGURATIVE MEANING OF THE MYSTERY

We evidently have in the Samaritan and the nine (who were probably Jews) all of whom were lepers and whom our Saviour healed, a threefold type of heathenism and Judaism.

First, in their common misery, viz. sin. Leprosy is always regarded as a type of sin, and is treated accordingly. "God hath concluded all in unbelief, that he may have mercy on all" (Rom. 11:32). "All have sinned and do need the glory of God" (Rom. 3:23).

Secondly, the lepers are a type of heathenism and Judaism in that they have a common Deliverer. All are led to our Saviour and healed by Him, because in Him alone is salvation for all (Acts 4:12).

Thirdly, they typify heathenism and Judaism in their behavior towards our Lord. The Jews accept our Saviour's benefits, but only appreciate temporal mercies; they do not arrive at true faith, because they have no humility. They regard all His benefits as a matter of course, and receive them without thanks. They prefer their ceremonies even to the natural duty of gratitude, they remain with their priests, those tyrants and faithless shepherds of souls, and perish with them. But the Gentiles, the "strangers," are full of humility and gratitude, and thus obtain faith and reception into the Church.

3. MORAL SIGNIFICATION OF THE MYSTERY

Our Saviour here recommends above all the virtue of gratitude. We may mention three reasons for this.

First, one feels from our Saviour's words that the ingratitude of the "nine" pains Him sensibly. He asks if ten have not been healed, and where the nine are (Luke 17:17). On the other hand, He is visibly pleased at the gratitude of the one, and the more so since he is a Samaritan. Greater benefits have been vouchsafed to the Jews, and therefore they ought to have a better comprehension of the supernatural and of their duties toward God. Vocation and special preference are no reason to be less grateful to Him, but quite the contrary.

Secondly, gratitude is an act of justice, as well as of good manners. We should either not accept benefits, or, if we do accept them, we should take upon ourselves the obligation of gratitude. Gratitude is a virtue, and not merely a mark of good breeding; ingratitude is a vice, and not merely bad manners.

Lastly, gratitude makes us noble-minded and humble, awakens friendship and kindness, and is thus the source of new favors, whilst ingratitude chokes the source of benefits. God is our greatest Benefactor, and therefore we must be grateful not only to men, but above all to Him; we must not forget His benefits, but make Him at least the return of gratitude.

The Coming of the Kingdom of God

Luke 17:20. And being asked by the Pharisees when the kingdom of God should come, he answered them and said: "The kingdom of God cometh not with observation;—21. Neither shall they say: Behold here, or behold there. For lo, the kingdom of God is within you."—22. And he said to his disciples: "The days will come when you shall desire to see one day of the Son of man, and you shall not see it.—23. And they will say to you: See here, and see there. Go ye not after, nor follow them;—24. For as the lightning that lighteneth from under heaven, shineth unto the parts that are under heaven; so shall the Son of Man be in his day.—25. But first he must suffer many things and be rejected by this generation.—26. And as it came to pass in the days of Noe, so shall it be also in the days of the Son of Man.—27. They did eat and drink; they married wives and were given in marriage, until the day that Noe entered into the ark; and the flood came, and destroyed them all.—28. Likewise as it came to pass in the days of Lot; they did eat and drink, they bought and sold, they planted and built;—29. And in the day that Lot went out of Sodom, it rained fire and brimstone from heaven, and destroyed them all.—30. Even thus shall it be in the day when the Son of Man shall be revealed.—31. In that hour he that shall be on the house-top, and his goods in the house, let him not go down to take them away; and he that shall be in the field, in like manner let him not return back.—32. Remember Lot's wife.—33. Whosoever shall seek to save his life, shall lose it; and whosoever shall lose it, shall preserve it.—34. I say to you: In that night there shall be two men in one bed; the one shall be taken, and the other shall be left.—35. Two women shall be grinding together; the one shall be taken, and the other shall be left. Two men shall be in the field; the one shall be taken, and the other shall be left."—36. They answering say to him: "Where, Lord?"—37. Who said to them: "Wheresoever the body be, thither will the eagles also be gathered together."

Our Saviour seems to have been still on this side of the Jordan when the question concerning the coming of the kingdom of God was put to Him.

1. THE QUESTION

The subject of the question was, when (and probably also how) the kingdom of God would come (Luke 17:20). By the "kingdom of God" is understood the Messianic kingdom (Acts 1:6; Dan. 2:44).

The question was occasioned partly by our Saviour's proclamation of the kingdom, partly by the general expectation of it, and partly by the intrinsic importance of the question, which was a vital point of Jewish theology.

The intention which prompted it was not necessarily a bad one; the questioners may have wished to hear what the great Master thought of this cardinal point of the Jewish faith, what was His teaching with regard to it, and whether He called Himself the Messias.

The questioners are Pharisees, according to whose ideas the Messias and His kingdom must be revealed with great ostentation, vanity and worldly pomp, and with a great display of power and glory.

2. THE ANSWER

Our Saviour's answer, which is addressed to His disciples as well as to the Pharisees, is a double one. He distinguishes a twofold advent of His kingdom.

He likewise makes two statements with regard to the first advent; the first concerning the manner of His appearance, the second concerning the time. As regards the manner, He informs the Pharisees (to whom the answer is directly addressed) that the kingdom of the Messias would not come in a very conspicuous way, as they expected, but without "observation" (i.e. ostentation), viz. in poverty and humility. At all events there would be no such outward pomp that one would be able to say with certainty: "Behold, it is here, or there" (Luke 17:20). And as regards the time, He says that the kingdom is already amongst them, in their very midst (Luke 17:21; cf. John 1:26; Matt. 12:28; Luke 11:20).

This statement concerning the first advent is immediately followed by another concerning the second, and this latter is especially for the disciples (Luke 17:22). By this second advent our Lord means the Last Judgment. With regard to the time when this will take place, He first mentions His Passion and Death, which are to precede it (Luke 17:25). Secondly, He says that the disciples will suffer great tribulation, so that they will long for but one single day of the human life of our Lord (i.e. for His glorious coming to Judgment); but they will not obtain it, and their tribulation will continue (Luke 17:22). Thirdly, immorality and impiety will have reached the highest pitch, as in the days of Noe and Lot (Luke 17:26–30). The manner of this coming will be conspicuous and so brilliant that there is nothing to which it can be compared, not even to the flash of lightning. It will be as extraordinarily sudden and universally observed as were the flood and the rain of fire and brimstone upon Sodom (Luke 17:27, 29, 30). To the disciples' question, where this would occur, our Saviour returns the mysterious answer: "Wheresoever the body shall be, thither will the eagles also be gathered together" (Luke 17:36, 37); i.e. the Judgment will take place there, where our

Saviour is, and thither the elect will hasten to assemble around Him (cf. Matt. 24:28; Job 29:30). Our Lord follows up this announcement of the Judgment by the following exhortations: First, not to let themselves be seduced by the false Messiases (Luke 17:23) who will arise. Secondly, to sacrifice all temporal goods (Luke 17:31, 32), even life itself, rather than yield to this danger, for all these things will be restored to them (Luke 17:33). Thirdly, to be prepared, because the Judgment will come upon them unawares, tearing away one from the side of his bed-fellow, another from her companion at the grinding-mill (Luke 17:34, 35). In Palestine the corn is ground by two women who work the hand-mill together.

3. IMPORTANCE OF THE ANSWER

The importance of the answer arises from the fact that it clears up the confused ideas about the coming and the nature of the Messianic kingdom, by this plain distinction of a twofold advent —one in poverty and humility, the other in power and glory— and thus characterizes the nature of the kingdom present and to come. Our Saviour withdraws the thoughts of His hearers from expectations of outward pomp, and brings before them the essential character of the present kingdom, which consists in peace and humility and is above all things interior.

Secondly, the answer is important because it states that the kingdom of God is not a thing of the future, but is already present among them, in their midst; whether in His own Person, or in the hearts of the Apostles and the faithful. This meaning, though veiled, certainly lies in the answer.

Thirdly, it is most significant that our Saviour announces His second Advent as being the Last Judgment. Henceforth He will speak more and more plainly of the divine chastisements. He likewise takes advantage of this opportunity to remind His disciples once more of His impending Passion.

Lastly, our Saviour's answer has a general signification, inasmuch as His statements concerning the Last Judgment are also applicable to the death of each individual. Death is the coming of the Son of God for each one in particular, and it will be attended by similar circumstances.

The Parable of the Unjust Judge

Luke 18:1. And he spoke also a parable to them, that we ought always to pray, and not to faint,—2. Saying: "There was a certain judge in a certain city, who feared not God, nor regarded man.—3. And there was a certain widow in that city, and she came to him, saying: Avenge me of my adversary.—4. And he would not for a long time. But afterwards he said within himself: Although I fear not God, nor regard man;—5. Yet because this widow is troublesome to me, I will avenge her, lest continually coming she at last weary me."—6. And the Lord said: "Hear what the unjust judge saith.—7. And will not God revenge his elect who cry to him day and night, and will he have patience in their regard?—8. I say to you that he will quickly revenge them. But yet the Son of Man, when he cometh, shall he find, think you, faith on earth?"

The events just recorded were immediately followed by the parable of the unjust judge.

1. Object of the Parable, Prayer in Affliction

The words: "He (our Lord) spoke also a parable to them, that we ought always to pray, and not to faint" (Luke 18:1), show that this parable is directly connected with the preceding discourse. Our Saviour had just spoken of the afflictions which even the Apostles would suffer at His coming to judgment (Luke 17:22). He now indicates prayer as a remedy for these, and encourages them to practise it.

2. Motives for Prayer

The motives are contained partly in the parable itself, partly in the application that our Saviour makes of it.

The parable itself contains beautiful motives for fervent and untiring prayer in the time of affliction and oppression. These motives are drawn from the conduct of the judge as well as from that of the oppressed widow. First, the judge (as is so often the case in the East) is a wicked, unjust, unscrupulous man, who fears neither God nor man; yet the untiring importunity of the widow makes him yield, and he helps her to her rights at last, that she may not weary him longer (Luke 18:4, 5). To this judge our Lord opposes His Heavenly Father, Who must help the oppressed to their rights. But God is more than the opposite of the unjust judge. He is justice itself and infinite goodness. It is His interest to hold fervent prayer in honor, for He has pledged Himself, His goodness and His justice to hear it, by His own promise. Secondly, the widow also affords us beautiful motives for prayer.

On the one hand, she is a stranger to the judge; but on the other, she lives in the same town and has a right to his help. Further, she is unprotected and at the mercy of her adversary; she has no resources to fall back upon but prayers and entreaties. But she makes use of this means untiringly and victoriously (Luke 18:3, 5). What a striking picture this is of the Church! First, in her dependence upon God, Whose city and kingdom she is here below; secondly, in her unprotected state, having no weapon to employ against her oppressors except patience; and lastly, in her wise policy, not holding arguments with them, but going straight to God for help, to Him Who holds in His Hands the hearts of men and the ends of the earth. From Him she obtains her end by unceasing prayer. God will not resist persevering prayer. The words of the godless judge sound much like those of God to Moses, when he interceded for the people (Deut. 9:14). Prayer is the only power that God heeds (so to speak), though only because it is His Will to be moved by it.

In the application which our Saviour Himself makes of this parable, He gives us a new motive for prayer in tribulation, by promising to hear this prayer. This "hearing" consists in the aid of the law, i.e. in compensation for injuries and losses suffered, as well as in the punishment of the oppressors. This is why our Saviour says: "Will not God revenge His elect . . . and will He have patience in their regard?" (Luke 18:7.) No, He will avenge them quickly and unexpectedly, as is described in the preceding discourse. The persecutors of the Church are often overtaken by a sudden and quite unexpected chastisement (Luke 18:8). And at the worst, even the longest time of trial is short, compared with the time of reward.

3. QUALITY OF PRAYER

Our Saviour also indicates in His application a necessary quality of prayer and a condition of its being heard: viz. prayer must be continual, persevering, and unwearying, "day and night" (Luke 18:7). "We ought always to pray" (Luke 18:1), i.e. much and often, and not to desist from disgust, pusillanimity, or despair. One does "always" what one does much and often, and never ceases to do. As may be seen from the parable, perseverance has a special power of obtaining what is asked, because this perseverance presupposes humility, earnest will, and ardent desire (Luke 11:8). But, our Lord concludes, will the Son of Man, when He cometh to judgment, find faith upon earth, either in the world or among His own, that faith which is strong and persevering enough in prayer to bear the distresses and dangers of the coming judgment? (Luke 18:8.) It is a plaintive cry that is wrung from His Heart, when He sees on the one hand how much He does to plant faith firmly in the hearts of men, and on the other hand the terrible misery into which they will fall on account of their unbelief, and into which His own Israel is about to fall so soon.

In this parable we have another example of the variety of shapes and forms which our Saviour can give to the same material. The importance of perseverance in prayer is pointed out by Him elsewhere in the parable of the friend who comes at night to ask for bread, and whose petition is granted on account of his importunity (Luke 11:8). What a touching mark of His kindness of heart it is, that He thus points out to us the power of prayer especially in great affliction, encourages us to practise it, and shows us the Heart of God and the power and magnificence of prayer so clearly and adequately.

The Parable of the Pharisee and the Publican

Luke 18:9. And to some who trusted in themselves as just and despised others, he spoke also this parable:—10. "Two men went up into the temple to pray; the one a Pharisee, and the other a publican.—11. The Pharisee standing prayed thus with himself: O God, I give thee thanks that I am not as the rest of men, extortioners, unjust, adulterers; as also is this publican.—12. I fast twice in a week; I give tithes of all that I possess.—13. And the publican standing afar off would not so much as lift up his eyes towards heaven, but struck his breast, saying: O God, be merciful to me a sinner.—14. I say to you this man went down into his house justified rather than the other; because every one that exalteth himself, shall be humbled; and he that humbleth himself, shall be exalted."

This parable is intimately connected with the preceding one as regards matter, if not as regards time. In the preceding parable and at His prediction of His advent (Luke 17:23–37) our Saviour had recommended watchfulness, penance, good works, and prayer. But all this must be animated by sentiments of humility. For this reason He here recommends humility and warns against pride in good works. He had no need to go far for living pictures to illustrate His meaning. He had usually Pharisees among His hearers, veritable personifications of self-confidence and contempt of other men (Luke 18:9). But those whom they chiefly despised were the poor publicans. The parable turns upon these two points, the poles, as it were, of the Jewish school of thought. It applies to the Pharisees, but also to the Apostles and to us all. Our Saviour selected the subject of public prayer in the Temple (Luke 18:10), because He wished to recommend humility in prayer, and because it is just in this important matter that a man shows his inward spirit and what religious training has done for him.

1. THE PHARISEE

The Pharisee is the very picture of pride and self-righteousness, even in prayer.

This is seen at once in his outward demeanor, his position and gestures. He went into the Temple and stood there (Luke 18:11). It was not exactly the standing posture that betrayed pride, for the Jews prayed sometimes standing (III Kings 8:22), sometimes kneeling (Dan. 6:10; Acts 7:59; 9:40; 21:5), sometimes lying prostrate (II Kings 12:16; I Mach. 4:40; Eccli. 1:10), sometimes sitting (II Kings 7:18; III Kings 19:4). But this "standing" has a special sense; he planted himself there, so to speak, in an ostentatious and insolent manner, like a praying statue, as though he came into God's house as a creditor (Matt. 6:5).

But his wretched pride is manifested still more plainly in his prayer, which so exactly expresses his thoughts and sentiments. It has a positive and a negative side. It begins with praise and thanksgiving (Luke 18:11), but soon veers round into self-praise. Praise of God is to the Pharisee only a pretext and an opportunity for praising himself. Instead of remembering his sins, he considers his virtues and merits, and makes a display of them. But they are all exterior acts that he reckons upon. Instead of fasting only once a year, he does so twice a week; he gives tithes of everything; not simply of his general income, but even of cummin, fruits, and vegetables (Luke 11:42; 18:12; Matt. 23:23). This man has nothing to pray for; he has everything. He has nothing to ask pardon for; he is holy, and only needs to give thanks, and even his thanksgiving reminds him of his virtues, just as everything around him does of his superiority to other men. Compared to him, they are only thieves, dishonest men, adulterers. Probably he turned round to see if there was anyone to see and hear him, and thus his glance fell upon the publican, whom he immediately condemned (Luke 18:11). This is indeed terrible pride, to think that one has no faults, nothing but virtues, and all the virtues too, and to boast of them before God and accuse and condemn everyone else. There is no greatness before God; but here we find its semblance. The

Pharisees must have been like this in reality. Our Saviour probably drew the picture from life. These were the flower of the nation! One can only wonder how a man could ever rise to such a pitch of pride. But it was the result of their tradition and exclusiveness.

2. THE PUBLICAN

The publican, on the contrary, is the picture of interior and exterior humility. He is of the lowest and most abject class of the people, and feels himself to be really guilty and sinful. He has no confidence in his own righteousness, but only in God's mercy.

His outward demeanor corresponds to these interior sentiments of humility. He does not push his way offensively into the Temple; nay, he rather considers himself unworthy to approach it, and remains standing at the door, "afar off" (Luke 18:13). In contrast to the Pharisee, he does not even dare to look up for very shame. He strikes his breast in sign of contrition and penance, and says: "O God, be merciful to me a sinner." He openly acknowledges his guilt and asks pardon for it. This is true humility.

3. GOD'S JUDGMENT

Our Saviour pronounces judgment upon the two men in the words: "I say to you, this man (the publican) went down into his house justified, rather than the other (the Pharisee)" (Luke 18:14). This wording and the context show that the publican alone was justified, and the Pharisee condemned; for our Lord immediately continues: "Every one that exalteth himself shall be humbled, and he that humbleth himself shall be exalted"; and it is quite certain that one can only be justified on the ground of humility. At all events the Pharisee's behavior is anything but a good preparation for justification. Our Saviour's mode of expression is the customary though mild way of saying that he was not justified, but condemned by God (Matt. 5:19; 21:31). And this was the just punishment for his having declared himself just and condemned everyone else, the publican in particular. God's judgment is quite the contrary of his own.

Our Saviour evidently wishes here to teach us humility, especially in our intercourse with God. True humility of heart and consciousness of our sinfulness is the most natural and seemly behavior before Him. We get on best with these virtues. God bends in condescension to the humble, whereas He resists the proud and drives them far from Him, with a curse instead of a blessing. Further, our Lord intended to stigmatize and censure the intolerable pride of the Pharisees, and to pronounce judgment upon them. Their character is an abomination before God, as He had told them once before (Luke 16:15), and they will be expelled from the Temple, while the humble publicans and the Gentiles enter in.

Indissolubility of Marriage. Virginity

Matt. 19:1. And it came to pass, when Jesus had ended these words, he departed from Galilee, and came into the coasts of Judaea beyond Jordan,—2. And great multitudes followed him, and he healed them there.—3. And there came to him the Pharisees tempting him, and saying: "Is it lawful for a man to put away his wife for every cause?"—4. Who answering, said to them: "Have ye not read that he who made man from the beginning, made them male and female?" And he said:—5. "For this cause shall a man leave father and mother, and shall cleave to his wife, and they two shall be in one flesh;—6. Therefore now they are not two, but one flesh. What therefore God hath joined together, let no man put asunder."—7. They say to him: "Why then did Moses command to give a bill of divorce, and to put away?"—8. He saith to them: "Because Moses by reason of the hardness of your heart permitted you to put away your wives; but from the beginning it was not so.—9. And I say to you, that whosoever shall put away his wife, except it be for fornication, and shall marry another, committeth adultery; and he that shall marry her that is put away, committeth adultery."—10. His disciples say unto him: "If the case of a man with his wife be so, it is not expedient to marry."—11. Who said to them: "All men take not this word, but they to whom it is given.—12. For there are eunuchs, who were born so from their mother's womb; and there are eunuchs, who were made so by men; and there are eunuchs, who have made themselves eunuchs for the kingdom of heaven. He that can take, let him take it."—5:31. "And it hath been said: Whosoever shall put away his wife, let him give her a bill of divorce.—32. But I say to you, that whosoever shall put away his wife, excepting the cause of fornication, maketh her to commit adultery; and he that shall marry her that is put away, committeth adultery."

Mark 10:1. And rising up from thence, he cometh into the coasts of Judaea beyond the Jordan; and the multitudes flock to him again; and as he was accustomed, he taught them again.—2. And the Pharisees coming to him asked him: "Is it lawful for a man to put away his wife?" tempting him.—3. But he answering, saith to them: "What did Moses command you?"—4. Who said: "Moses permitted to write a bill of divorce and to put her away."—5. To whom Jesus answering, said: "Because of the hardness of your heart he wrote you that precept; —6. But from the beginning of the creation God made them male and female.—7. For this cause a man shall leave his father and mother, and shall cleave to his wife;—8. And they two shall be in one flesh. Therefore now they are not two, but one flesh.—9. What therefore God hath joined together, let not man put asunder."—10. And in the house again his disciples asked him concerning the same thing.—11. And he saith to them: "Whosoever shall put away his wife and marry another, committeth adultery against her.—12. And if the wife shall put away her husband, and be married to another, she committeth adultery."

Our Saviour had left Galilee and Samaria, and had gone across the Jordan to Peraea (Matt. 19:1; Mark 10:1). Here the Pharisees came to Him one day with a question concerning the dissolubility of marriage.

1. THE QUESTION

As regards the attendant circumstances of this question, our Saviour was surrounded by great throngs of people, whom He taught and healed (Matt. 19:2; Mark 10:1).

The subject of the question was whether a man could put away his wife, i.e. completely dissolve the marriage-bond, "for every cause" (Matt. 19:3; Mark 10:2). The questioners were Pharisees, whose opinions were much divided concerning this matter. Some (the disciples of Shammai) allowed divorce only in cases of adultery, others (disciples of Hillel) for any cause the parties were pleased to urge; whilst, as a matter of fact, the law required for divorce a reason which made living together painful and repugnant (Deut. 24:1). It is a well-known fact that a sad state of things prevailed with regard to this matter, not only among the Gentiles, but also with the Jews; and this was chiefly in consequence of the Pharisees' lax interpretation of the law.

The question may therefore have been principally occasioned by the fact that the subject was much discussed, and perhaps also by the fact that our Saviour had shortly before (in Peraea) blamed the Pharisees for their unjustifiable tenets regarding this point, with which tenets, of course, their practice corresponded (Luke 16:18).

The intention of the questioners was by no means a good one. They only wished to tempt our Lord (Matt. 19:3; Mark 10:2). The temptation consisted in bringing Him into conflict, according to the turn taken by His answer, either with the law, with His own teaching, with the one or the other school of thought, with the prevailing custom, or even with Herod himself, within whose dominion the question was put.

2. OUR SAVIOUR'S ANSWER IN PRESENCE OF THE PEOPLE

Our Saviour's answer in presence of the people may be divided into three parts.

First, He very wisely frustrates their hopes of bringing Him into conflict with the law, by citing the original law itself. After a preliminary question as to what Moses had commanded for such cases, He asks if they have not read how God Himself had originally instituted matrimony and also decreed its unity and indissolubility. Although God had created man male and female (Gen. 1:27), we find nevertheless a threefold unity: first, the unity of origin, Eve from Adam (Gen. 2:21, 23); secondly, the unity in the marriage-bond, for the purpose of propagation (Gen. 2:22); lastly, the unity of the natural impulse, which is more powerful than all other natural impulses, and which Adam himself testifies to be the Will of God (Gen. 2:24). Thus God had united man and wife by a triple bond; marriage had made them two in one flesh, and thence our Saviour deduces its indissolubility: "What God hath joined together, let not man put assunder" (Mark 10:6–9; Matt. 19:4–6), any more than he would part the members of his own body, because he is not lord of the natural law.

Secondly, our Saviour explains the meaning of the bill of divorce. The Pharisees had immediately retorted by asking why then had Moses commanded a bill of divorce to be given (Matt. 19:7; Mark 10:3, 4). Our Lord answers that the bill of divorce was not the real law, but an exemption from the law, a permission, which God had granted under definite conditions—namely a valid reason and the delivery of a document—on account of their hardness of heart and want of charity and in order to avoid worse evils (Matt. 19:8; Mark 10:5). He had tolerated similar exemptions and mitigations of the law in other respects also, e.g. polygamy, vengeance of blood etc.

Thirdly, our Saviour gives the decision. He restores the original institution of matrimony, abolishes the exemption, the permission of a bill of divorce, and declares that the marriage-bond itself can never be dissolved; only a separation (in the sense of living apart) can be permitted in the case of adultery on the part of one. This is the sense of the passage in St. Matthew's Gospel (5:32 and here 19:9). Thus the first part of the ninth verse agrees with the other verses, and also with other passages of Scripture (Mark 10:11, 12; Luke 16:8; I Cor. 17:10) and with the interpretation of the Church (Trid. Sess. 24, can. 7). The Apostles themselves seem to have understood our Saviour's words in this sense, since they immediately afterwards say to Him, if that is the case with matrimony, then it is better not to marry (Matt. 19:10). This, then, was the answer that our Saviour gave the Pharisees.

3. DEVELOPMENT OF THE ANSWER IN PRESENCE OF THE DISCIPLES

On arriving home the disciples again brought up the same topic (Mark 10:10), expressing the opinicn that, if there could in no case be any real dissolution of the marriage-bond, it was better not to marry (Matt. 19:10).

In His answer our Saviour does two things.

He first confirms the answer He had given to the people and the Pharisees, aboslutely denying the possibility of any dissolution of matrimony, and admitting of no exception (Mark 10:11, 12). According to the law, the right of giving a bill of divorce belonged to the man alone. But the women seem to have made use of it also, e.g. Herod's sister Salome, and Herodias (Mark 10:12).

Secondly, our Lord responds with regard to the celibacy proposed by the disciples as advisable under the circumstances. He gives here a beautiful instruction concerning the state of virginity embraced from supernatural motives, for the sake of the kingdom of heaven. In the first place, He says, a special grace of enlightenment and strength is requisite for this state of life. "All men take not this word, but they to whom it is given" (Matt. 19:11). "He that can take, let him take it" (Matt. 19:12). The natural impulse is the most powerful (Matt. 19:5; Mark 10:7), and therefore special grace is needed. From this it follows, secondly, that this state is a free one, which cannot be imposed upon anyone, but must be voluntarily chosen and embraced; it does not suffice to be driven to it by natural necessity or outward force. For this reason our Saviour speaks of eunuchs by nature, eunuchs by compulsion, and eunuchs of free will (Matt. 19:12). Thirdly, even free choice is not sufficient without a supernatural motive: "for the kingdom of heaven" (Matt. 19:12) and for the service of the Church and the Gospel. Thence it follows, lastly, that this state of life is lofty and sublime, and at the same time possible and even easy, because it is the result of freedom and of grace. Under the influence of grace an impulse is developed, far more powerful than the strongest natural instinct, namely to adhere to God and serve His kingdom, and to obtain His glory.

The question which had occasioned this discussion proceeded from the depths of human insincerity and disgraceful sensual errors; and now our Saviour, in His teaching, soars upwards to the proclamation of world-renewing thoughts, institutions, and laws, and to the revelation of what is most glorious and beautiful in all Christianity, namely the restitution of marriage to its original form, and the institution of celibacy, the state of virginity. Herein lies the importance of this mystery. In the luminous development of our Lord's thoughts we have the three different forms which have been assumed by matrimony. The first is the ideal traced by God in our first parents; and, after this, the alliance of the Jewish nation with God was also an indissoluble marriage-bond (Isa. 55:3). The second is the obscuring of this ideal by the bill of divorce and by polygamy. The third is Christian marriage, which in its indissolubility is the restoration of the first ideal, and in its sacramental character the amplification and perfection of the same. It is this sanctified marriage, with its indissolubility and its sacramental blessing, which forms the dispositions for the celibate and virginal state in the Church. Grace finds in Christian matrimony a well-prepared soil. There will always be souls who cannot make up their minds to the indissoluble bonds of matrimony, who wish to be free and to strive after the crown of the angels already in this mortal life; souls who turn to the ideal and celestial, and who wish to be generous in their service of God. The state of celibacy, of virginity devoted to the service of God, is reserved for these. It is of this that our Saviour is speaking. His words ring like a prophecy, a prediction of the Apocalyptic vision of the bright and chosen throng who accompany the Lamb, the virginal souls who follow Him wherever He goes (Apoc. 14:4). How gloriously these innumerable choirs shine out against the somber darkness of the world! Even Judaism could show but a few isolated examples of this heavenly state.

Our Saviour and the Children

Luke 18:15. And they brought unto him also infants, that he might touch them. Which when the disciples saw, they rebuked them.—16. But Jesus calling them together said: "Suffer children to come to me and forbid them not; for of such is the kingdom of God.—17. Amen I say to you: Whosoever shall not receive the kingdom of God as a child, shall not enter into it."

Mark 10:13. And they brought to him young children, that he might touch them. And the disciples rebuked those that brought them.—14. Whom when Jesus saw, he was much displeased, and saith to them: "Suffer the little children to come unto me, and forbid them not; for of such is the kingdom of God.—15. Amen I say to you, whosoever shall not receive the kingdom of God as a little child, shall not enter into it."—16. And embracing them, and laying his hands upon them, he blessed them.

Matt. 19:13. Then were little children presented to him, that he should impose hands upon them and pray. And the disciples rebuked them.—14. But Jesus said to them: "Suffer the little children, and forbid them not to come to me; for the kingdom of heaven is for such."—15. And when he had imposed hands upon them, he departed from thence.

This beautiful incident likewise occurred in Peraea.

1. LITTLE CHILDREN ARE BROUGHT TO OUR SAVIOUR

Probably it was the mothers who wished to present their little children to our Saviour (Mark 10:13; Luke 18:15).

What was the intention of these mothers? They wished our Saviour to pray over their children (Matt. 19:13), to touch them (Mark 10:13; Luke 18:15), or lay His hands upon them and bless them (Matt. 19:13). The children seem to have been quite little; possibly there were even infants among them. They could not therefore receive the benefit of instruction or any similar favor, but the mothers wished to procure for them at least the benefit of a blessing. Among all religious nations, and especially among God's chosen people, great value was always set upon a blessing. The power to bless, i.e. to confer spiritual and temporal advantages, is peculiar to God and to those who represent Him in some way or other, especially fathers, priests, men of God and teachers of His law, participators in His holiness and authority. Thus we see in the history of the chosen nation that God blesses first of all (Gen. 1:22), then the patriarchs (Gen. 27:4, 33; 48:14; 49:28), priests, and divine messengers (Deut. 33:1). The blessing itself was always regarded as a pledge of divine protection against all evil, and of the complacency and favor of God, which was to make the person blessed himself a vessel and an instrument of grace and blessing. The blessing of the partriarchs had the peculiar virtue of conferring the great grace and honor of being a progenitor of the Messias and a link in the chain of His descent from Adam. The mothers, then, intended to obtain for their children the manifold benefits of a blessing.

And why did they seek this benefit for their children especially at our Saviour's hands? They must surely have been induced to do this by the high opinion they had of His holiness, goodness, and power. They certainly regarded Him as a man of God; indeed, their action seems almost like a confession of His Divinity. At all events they sought to procure spiritual or temporal advantages for their children by our Saviour's blessing. Possibly the children themselves, if they were old enough, may have eagerly pushed their way up to Him, attracted by His friendliness; at any rate they did not run away from Him (Matt. 18:2), but felt quite at home by His side.

2. THE DISCIPLES WILL NOT MAKE WAY FOR THE CHILDREN

Our Saviour seems to have been in some house when the mothers came to Him with their children (Mark 10:17); at any rate they could not reach Him directly, and were obliged to apply to His followers, the Apostles, in order to gain admittance. But the disciples would not consent, and repulsed them (Matt. 19:13; Mark 10:13; Luke 18:15).

What was the reason of this behavior on the part of the disciples? Perhaps our Saviour was tired and in need of rest, and they wished to spare Him this fresh exertion. Or perhaps there were too many children, and they knew that He Himself could refuse nothing, and did everything thoroughly. And very likely they did not consider the matter worth so much labor and exertion. The children were very young, and it was only a question of His blessing. There may however have been a little pharisaical strictness in this. In this incident we see that the disciples had not yet learned the value that our Lord placed on the traits characteristic of childhood, traits that must be cultivated for admission to heaven.

3. HOW OUR SAVIOUR RECEIVES THE CHILDREN

Our Saviour's attention being attracted in some way to the matter—perhaps by the loud altercation between the disciples and the mothers, who were not easy to put off—He blamed the behavior of the Apostles and had the children brought to Him. Here we see above all the goodness of our Lord. He rejects no means of doing good and making people happy; He is even displeased with the Apostles (Mark 10:14) for so misunderstanding their office and His spirit, and spends Himself in acts of love and kindness to the little ones. He embraces them, lays His hands upon them, and blesses them (Mark 10:16; Matt. 10:15); and doubtless He did this to all the children, however many they were, so that it took Him a long time.

Secondly, we see here the loving kindness of our Saviour. It is always a kind and gracious act, when a priest blesses a child. But when our Saviour, the great Prophet and Lawgiver, God in the form of a Man, devotes Himself so willingly to little children and takes so much trouble with them, it shows indeed most wonderful kindness of heart.

Lastly, our Saviour reveals His great wisdom in His own conduct and in the answer with which He blames the conduct of the Apostles. This answer tells us that a child is by no means unimportant, but on the contrary of great importance and significance: "The kingdom of heaven is for such" (Matt. 19:14; Mark 10:14; Luke 18:16). What He came to found, to conquer, and to bestow upon men at the price of His labor, Passion, and Death, the children are to receive. They are to be princes of heaven, children of God, children of His Father, and His own little brethren. All the great and glorious plans of God, the success of all His institutions are to repose and slumber in these childish hearts, one day to be manifested as a glorious reality. Besides, their qualities make them ready recipients of these favors.

Yes, our Saviour even holds up these little ones to the Apostles and to us all as models, to teach us how we are to push on to this glorious goal and receive the kingdom of heaven in our hearts. "Amen I say to you, whosoever shall not receive the kingdom of God as a little child, shall not enter into it" (Mark 10:15; Luke 18:17). Innocence, humility, obedience, docility, and simplicity are the beautiful and striking characteristics of childhood. These are precisely the qualities with which we must receive God's kingdom, and without which no one will have a share in the kingdom of heaven. A child, then, is something great, important, and holy, and well worthy of every attention and care, of love and labor; all the more so because it is so weak and in such need of help, and because the world and the hellish foe press round it with all their force and cunning, in order to ensure their future victory by corrupting it now. Perhaps, too, these little ones reminded our Saviour of His own childhood days, and made Him think of the persecution of His Infancy, and how a father and a Mother had protected and saved Him. At any rate He saw in the child the secret of heaven and the desire of His Father and the holy angels; He saw the dark plots of hell and the world against childhood, and how many of these poor little ones would be lost in spite of all the titles He had established for them to a great and glorious future in the Church and in heaven, through guilty neglect of duty on the part of their parents and of priests, their natural guardians and masters. This was what our Saviour saw in the children, and what made Him so full of condescension and loving sympathy; and this was why He thought He could not do too much for them.

This is a very important mystery; partly because it shows us our Saviour in His eminent wisdom and lovable, touching goodness, refusing nothing and thinking no trouble too great, and partly on account of the important conclusions we may draw from it with regard to ourselves. We learn from it to be kind to everyone, and not to reject as insignificant anything that can tend to promote the welfare of souls. Further, it teaches us not to be guilty of any negligence with regard to the training and education of childhood and youth. How much these words and this example of Christ's have wrought in the Church! How many, how countless are the sacrifices to which souls have been led by them! How many institutions for the training and education of youth have originated therefrom! How many Orders have been founded, and what blessings the young have derived from them! We have here another striking example of how truly the words and deeds of Jesus are words of life and blessing, concealing within themselves the germs and vital strength of world-renewing thoughts, establishments and institutions. Finally, we have here an exhortation to become as children ourselves, for the sake of the kingdom of God. It is difficult, but sublime, and well worth striving for.

The Rich Young Man

Luke 18:18. And a certain ruler asked him, saying: "Good Master, what shall I do to possess everlasting life?"—19. And Jesus said to him: "Why dost thou call me good? None is good but God alone.—20. Thou knowest the commandments: Thou shalt not kill; Thou shalt not commit adultery; Thou shalt not steal; Thou shalt not bear false witness; Honor thy father and mother."—21. Who said: "All these things have I kept from my youth."—22. Which when Jesus had heard, he said to him: "Yet one thing is wanting to thee; sell all whatever thou hast, and give to the poor, and thou shalt have treasure in heaven; and come, follow me."—23. He having heard these things, became sorrowful; for he was very rich.

Mark 10:17. And when he was gone forth into the way, a certain man came running up, and kneeling before him, asked him: "Good Master, what shall I do that I may receive life everlasting?"—18. And Jesus said to him: "Why callest thou me good? None is good but one, that is God.—19. Thou knowest the commandments: Do not commit adultery; Do not kill; Do not steal; Bear not false witness; Do no fraud; Honor thy father and mother."—20. But he answering said to him: "Master, all these things I have observed from my youth."—21. And Jesus looking on him, loved him, and said to him: "One thing is wanting unto thee: go, sell whatsoever thou hast, and give to the poor, and thou shalt have treasure in heaven; and come, follow me."—22. Who being struck sad at that saying, went away sorrowful; for he had great possessions.

MATT. 19:16. And behold one came and said to him: "Good Master, what good shall I do that I may have life everlasting?"—17. Who said to him: "Why askest thou me concerning good? One is good, God. But if thou wilt enter into life, keep the commandments."—18. He said to him: "Which?" And Jesus said: "Thou shalt do no murder; Thou shalt not commit adultery; Thou shalt not steal; Thou shalt not bear false witness;—19. Honor thy father and thy mother; and, Thou shalt love thy neighbor as thyself."—20. The young man saith to him: "All these have I kept from my youth; what is yet wanting to me?"—21. Jesus saith to him: "If thou wilt be perfect, go, sell what thou hast, and give to the poor, and thou shalt have treasure in heaven; and come, follow me."—22. And when the young man had heard this word, he went away sad; for he had great possessions.

This mystery seems to have followed immediately upon the preceding one. As soon as our Saviour had come out of the house in which He had blessed the children, the young man came towards Him (Mark 10:17).

1. THE QUESTION ASKED BY THE YOUNG MAN

The questioner is a young man (Matt. 19:20), rich (Mark 10:22) and respected, a "ruler" (Luke 18:18), perhaps of a synagogue. He is noble and respectful in his demeanor, words and gestures, for he greets our Saviour very reverently (Mark 10:17); lastly, he is sincere, pure in morals, full of appreciation and capacity for a higher life of virtue. This is shown by his questions, as well as by the fact that our Saviour loved him (Mark 10:21).

The first question the youth addresses to our Saviour is twofold. He inquires first about the way of salvation, and then about that of perfection (Matt. 19:16, 20; Mark 10:17; Luke 18:18). Thus his question does not concern useless, frivolous matters (Matt. 12:38; 22:24), nor temporal goods, such as health or money (Matt. 9:18; Luke 12:13), nor yet spiritual things broached only from motives of curiosity and with bad intent (Matt. 22:36). He is noble-minded, and strives truly after morality, even the highest and best. He seems, then, to have had all the good qualities requisite for a candidate for the apostolic vocation, and therefore our Saviour received him with joy and cordiality. He looked at him, and loved him (Mark 10:21). Only there seems to have been something strange, impulsive, excitable and overemotional in the manner in which the youth approached our Lord and presented his request. He ran up to Him, immediately cast himself at His Feet, and broke out impulsively into the words: "Good Master, what shall I do?" (Mark 10:17.)

It would seem from this that, with all his good qualities, he allowed himself to be too much carried away by his feelings, and possessed little strength of will, decision, or stability. He apparently belonged to that class of men with whom the Word of God falls upon stony, shallow ground (Matt. 13:20 seq.; Mark 4:16; Luke 8:13). Such a disposition might be dangerous for his good purposes.

2. OUR SAVIOUR'S ANSWER

Our Saviour's answer was exactly suited to the way in which the question was introduced and put.

The somewhat remarkable manner of address, remarkable both in words and gestures, with which the youth approaches Him, is met by our Saviour with the rather surprising words: "Why callest thou Me good? And why askest thou Me concerning good? None is good but God alone" (Mark 10:18; Matt. 19:17; Luke 18:19). What is the meaning of these words? They are first a beautiful proof of our Saviour's modesty, showing how He referred all praise to God. But they have in all probability a deeper motive. He saw the emotion and imagination, the rashness and mobility in the character of the youth, and may have wished by this cool answer to set bounds to his enthusiasm and restrain it. Such impulsive persons easily allow themselves to be captivated and influenced by exterior, non-essential things, and attach themselves to outward appearances and natural gifts. Thus this youth too might perhaps, though unconsciously and doubtless with good intentions, be filled with enthusiasm for the Sacred Humanity of our Saviour, without being sensible of the final aim of his endeavors, God alone. Our Saviour wished to purify his intention, to direct it towards God and thus elevate, strengthen and confirm his resolution. Lastly, one cannot help admitting that there is a want of harmony between the youth's outward demeanor, the subject of his request, and his form of address: "Good Master"; indeed, it shows want of faith. After his humble genuflection and request for instruction concerning the way of salvation, and after what he had heard, seen, and perhaps guessed of our Saviour, one would have expected him to take Him for something more than a good teacher of the law; he might be expected simply to acknowledge Him as Messias and God. Perhaps this is what our Saviour wishes to help him to do. In His reply: "God alone is good," He almost puts into his mouth the confession: "But Thou art God." God alone can teach the way of salvation and perfection. Our Saviour is evidently longing to raise the youth to the level of faith, that he may be enabled to accept His invitation to the apostolic life. In this reply, then, He gives him a little reproof for his defective faith, and holds out a friendly hand to help him to perfect it.

Secondly, in answer to the question regarding the way of salvation and eternal life, our Saviour simply refers him to the commandments (Luke 18:20; Mark 10:19; Matt. 19:17–19). These are the simple, straightforward direction, the open high-road to heaven. Our Lord only mentions those of the second table, because these presuppose the ones contained in the first.

Since the youth has already observed all this, feels drawn to still better things, and asks if there is nothing higher for him to strive after (Matt. 19:20), our Saviour's third answer reveals to him the evangelical counsels or means of perfection: "Go, sell what thou hast, and give to the poor, and thou shalt have treasure in heaven; and come, follow Me" (Matt. 19:21; Mark 10:22; Luke 18:22).

These answers of our Saviour manifest first His wisdom and prudence. They are suited to the questioner's power of comprehension and desire; otherwise they would be useless and would only do harm. Secondly, they manifest His sincerity and decision. He fully satisfies an honest desire. His response is complete and exhaustive, and suffices for the will in every respect. Lastly, these answers also manifest the goodness of our Saviour. He knows how to take hold of a man and elevate his ideas in the most powerful, wonderful and attractive manner; and when He demands a sacrifice, He also holds out the prospect of a reward. In return for the sacrifice of his family and property, the youth was to gain the privilege of being a member of Jesus' household and to receive a high place in heaven.

3. THE RESULT OF THE ANSWER

Unfortunately the answer had no good results. The youth, taken aback at our Saviour's reply and the sacrifices He demanded, became sorrowful and went away (Luke 18:23; Mark 10:22; Matt. 19:22). He gave up striving after perfection, gave up the idea of becoming a disciple of Jesus, and seems never to have returned to Him. No wonder our Saviour grew sad as He looked after him. The youth had thrown away a great vocation. It is folly, certainly, to push one's way into a vocation against God's Will, but none the less deplorable is the decision which defeats His intentions when He invites us to enter upon a high vocation.

And what was the reason of this? The young man became sorrowful. Sadness, despondency, want of joyousness and resolute will were the first cause. The second was his irregular attachment to riches. He was very wealthy, and his heart cleaved to his wealth. His houses, his gardens and vineyards, the loved inheritance of his parents: to renounce all these, to forsake them, nay, even to sell them and give the proceeds to the poor? That was too much to ask. He had expected easy means of perfection, and now the actual requirements appeared cruel to him. The last cause was want of trust in God. Distrust and despair are always the consequences of such attachments. The more one leans upon this world's goods for support, the less reliance one has upon God and oneself, and one can but fall with these feeble supports. Why could he not do as he was told, trusting in God Who had called him and drawn him to Himself, as so many others did? What might he not have become, after such a good beginning, and what did he become? Must not the sorrowful parting look that our Saviour cast upon him as he went have hung like a dark cloud over his whole life? Such was the effect of sadness, irregular attachment, and want of trust in God.

The importance of this mystery lies first in the fact that our Saviour here laid the foundation and drew the plan for the division of His Church, His earthly kingdom, into two important states of life, viz. the secular and the religious, with their exact differences and characteristics. The essential thing in the secular state is the observance of God's commandments, and heaven is promised in reward for this. The religious state is one of free choice. Our Saviour says "If thou wilt" (Matt. 19:21), because the very essence of this state of life is the observance of the counsels, which are nothing else than special means to perfection, not ordered nor prescribed by Christ, but merely set before us as highly pleasing to God, and left to our free choice. The counsels also are practically enumerated here. Poverty is first mentioned expressly, and chastity and obedience are implied in the single life and intimate companionship of our Saviour. The aim of the religious state is likewise specified, viz. perfection, special service of God and the Church, and a privileged place in the kingdom of heaven, where all that we forsake here below is put out to interest and promised to us as a future reward, under the figure of a great and royal treasure. Thus is sketched for us in a few words the plan of the religious state, which has drawn innumerable souls from the pursuits of the world and won for them perfection and heaven, and which is ever supplying the Church with skilled armies for her missions and works of charity, and realizing and continuing the Life of Jesus here below. In this case again the words of our Lord have sown a seed of wondrous, eternal life.

Lesson upon Riches and Voluntary Poverty

Luke 18:24. And Jesus seeing him become sorrowful, said: "How hardly shall they that have riches enter into the kingdom of God!—25. For it is easier for a camel to pass through the eye of a needle, than for a rich man to enter into the kingdom of God."—26. And they that heard it said: "Who then can be saved?" —27. He said to them: "The things that are impossible with men, are possible with God."—28. Then Peter said: "Behold, we have left all things, and have followed thee."—29. Who said to them: "Amen I say to you, there is no man that hath left house, or parents, or brethren, or wife, or children for the kingdom of God's sake,—30. Who shall not receive much more in this present time, and in the world to come life everlasting."

Mark 10:23. And Jesus looking round about, saith to his disciples: "How hardly shall they that have riches enter into the kingdom of God!"—24. And the disciples were astonished at his words. But Jesus again answering, saith to them: "Children, how hard is it for them that trust in riches, to enter into the kingdom of God!—25. It is easier for a camel to pass through the eye of a needle, than for a rich man to enter into the kingdom of God."—26. Who wondered the more, saying among themselves: "Who then can be saved?"—27. And Jesus looking on them, saith: "With men it is impossible, but not with God; for all things are possible with God."—28. And Peter began to say unto him: "Behold, we have left all things, and have followed thee."—29. Jesus answering, said: "Amen I say to you, there is no man, who hath left house, or brethren, or sisters, or father, or mother, or children, or lands for my sake and for the Gospel.—30. Who shall not receive an hundred times as much, now in this time; houses, and brethren, and sisters, and mothers, and children, and lands, with persecutions, and in the world to come life everlasting.—31. But many that are first, shall be last, and the last, first."

Matt. 19:23. Then Jesus said to his disciples: "Amen I say to you, that a rich man shall hardly enter into the kingdom of heaven.—24. And again I say to you: It is easier for a camel to pass through the eye of a needle, than for a rich man to enter into the kingdom of heaven."—25. And when they had heard this, the disciples wondered very much, saying: "Who then can be saved?"—26. And Jesus beholding said to them: "With men this is impossible; but with God all things are possible."—27. Then Peter answering, said to him: "Behold we have left all things, and have followed thee; what therefore shall we have?"—28. And Jesus said to them: "Amen I say to you, that you who have followed me, in the regeneration, when the Son of Man shall sit on the seat of his majesty, you also shall sit on twelve seats, judging the twelve tribes of Israel.—29. And everyone that hath left house, or brethren, or sisters, or father, or mother, or wife, or children, or lands for my name's sake, shall receive an hundredfold, and shall possess life everlasting. —30. And many that are first, shall be last, and the last shall be first."

Our Lord's meeting with the rich youth is immediately followed by His lesson concerning voluntary poverty and the dangers of riches.

1. OCCASION OF THE INSTRUCTION

The lesson consists of two parts, one concerning riches and the other concerning voluntary poverty. The case of the youth who would not renounce his riches, but went away sorrowful, gave rise to the first part. Our Saviour looked at him (Luke 18:24), and then cast a significant glance at the bystanders (Mark 10:23), and this glance was the introduction to His lesson concerning riches.

The second part of this discourse, viz. that concerning voluntary poverty, was occasioned by St. Peter's question as to how matters stood with them (the disciples), and what reward they would receive, who had left all and followed Christ (Matt. 19:27; Luke 18:28; Mark 10:28).

2. THE LESSON ITSELF

The incident with the youth in question affords our Saviour an opportunity of speaking of the danger of riches. In what does this danger consist? In this: that one not only fails to strive after perfection and attain to it, but fails even in saving one's soul, in gaining heaven. Our Saviour expressly says so: "How hardly shall they that have riches enter into the kingdom of God!" (Mark 10:23; Matt. 19:23; Luke 18:24.) And the Apostles understood it so, too, for they wondered (Mark 10:26; Matt. 19:25), were astonished (Mark 10:24), and said: "Who then can be saved?" (Mark 10:26; Matt. 15:25; Luke 18:26.)

Our Saviour also gives proofs of the reality and truth of this danger. His express assertion is an extrinsic confirmation of it. He repeats this assertion three times, emphasizes it with the words: "Amen I say to you" (Matt. 19:23), and confirms it by a comparison, saying that it is, naturally speaking, just as impossible for a rich man to enter heaven as for a camel to go through the eye of a needle (Luke 18:25; Mark 10:25; Matt. 19:24); it can only be accomplished by the grace of God, because nothing is impossible to grace (Matt. 19:26; Mark 10:27; Luke 18:27). And He maintains this point, in spite of all the wonder and astonishment of His disciples. Our Saviour also gives an intrinsic proof of the proposition. Riches lead us to place our hopes in them (Mark

10:24); they distract us, draw away our hearts from God and heavenly things, and offer every means of satisfying the passions; and what is worse than all, we make an earthly paradise of them, and will have nothing more to do with a heavenly and supernatural one. Thus a man relies upon himself and thinks God is not necessary to his happiness. This danger can only be overcome by the grace of God. In another passage of Holy Writ a rich man who is without sin and does not trust in money is called a wonder (Eccli. 31:9).

Upon hearing this most earnest teaching upon the danger of riches, St. Peter asks what then is in store for those who have left all and followed our Lord. In His answer our Saviour holds out the prospect of a glorious reward, and then adds the condition for its attainment.

The first condition is to forsake everything, just as He had required the rich youth to do. This was what Peter and the other Apostles had understood and already complied with: "We have left all things" (Matt. 19:27; Mark 10:28; Luke 18:28). And this was how our Saviour meant it to be understood, for He says that one must forsake houses, and lands, and family (Matt. 19:29; Mark 10:29; Luke 18:29). Secondly, one must forsake these temporal things for our Saviour (Mark 10:29), for His Name's sake (Matt. 19:29); and also with apostolic aims in view, in order to follow Him and share His labors for the kingdom of God and the Gospel (Luke 18:29; Mark 10:29). It is thus that poverty becomes truly apostolic, practised for the sake of evangelical perfection, which consists in caring not merely for one's own salvation and perfection, but also for that of one's fellow-men.

The reward is a double one; for this life as well as for the world to come. The earthly recompense is expressed by our Lord in the terms: "much more in this present time" (Luke 18:30), "an hundredfold" (Matt. 19:29), "houses, and brethren, and sisters, and mothers, and children, and lands" (Mark 10:30). This "hundredfold" certainly means in the first instance spiritual blessings, viz. freedom, immunity from cares, joy, childlike disposition, heartfelt prayer, trust in God, aptness for work, and incalculable supernatural merit. And our Saviour promises not only spiritual but also temporal blessings. By being associated to the apostolic life and becoming a member of the household of Christ, the Apostle enters another and a larger family, and participates in its temporal blessings: comfort, guidance, protection, and the joys of a life in common. This is that temporal happiness in life which is so great in the apostolic imitation of Christ. And this "with persecutions" (Mark 10:30), i.e. in spite of persecutions, in spite of the interior and exterior sacrifices which will never be lacking in the Church Militant, and especially in the apostolic life. It seems as though our Saviour had here seen in spirit the marvelous fertility and blessing of the Church and her Orders, which, like the people of God in the wilderness, march along hard pressed by enemies on every side, yet strong and courageous; without abundant temporal goods, but strengthened by a wondrous food and refreshed by miraculous waters. The eternal reward is likewise a double one. It consists first in the certainty of eternal life and heaven. Our Saviour pledges His word for it (Matt. 19:28; Mark 10:29; Luke 18:29). There is scarcely any other promise so clear and direct. Secondly, the reward consists in a special degree of glory, honor, power and joy in heaven; and our Lord holds out the prospect of this. "In the regeneration," i.e. in the perfection, reconstitution and final accomplishment of the kingdom of God, "when the Son of Man shall sit on the seat of His majesty," they will sit by His side "on twelve seats, judging the twelve tribes of Israel" (Matt. 19:28). So they are to be the dignitaries, the nobility of Christ's kingdom, and to take a special part in the Last Judgment as His assessors. The reason is that for the office of judge great wisdom and nobility of mind are requisite, and they have given proof of these qualifications by despising and renouncing all earthly things for the sake of Christ's kingdom. Further, they have already taken part in His regal state and judicial office in the Church here below; they have defended, elevated and extended His kingdom by their labors and sacrifices; and so it is just that they should be acknowledged and rewarded as high dignitaries and promoters of it in heaven also, especially since the future judgment is only a ratification of what they have bound and loosed here on earth. This double recompense of the Apostles in heaven will also, proportionately, fall to the lot of all who have forsaken everything for Christ's sake, because they have manifested the same wisdom and greatness of soul. By the twelve tribes we understand not merely the Israelite nation, but the entire human race (Matt. 19:29; Mark 10:29; Luke 18:29); indeed, according to St. Paul (I Cor. 6:3) they will judge the fallen angels also. Thus the whole course of affairs, the entire appearance of this new order of things will be unexpected and quite different from what it is in this world. A surprising transposition will take place; many a one who was poor, weak, and despised here below will there be the possessor of power, honors, and joys. For this reason our Saviour adds: "Many that are first shall be last, and the last shall be first" (Matt. 19:30; Mark 10:31).

3. CONCLUSION AND SIGNIFICATION

In the first place, our Saviour pronounces for all (the Jewish nation included, although He does not expressly mention it) this truth that, in the kingdom of glory, there will not be found the order of rank that the Jews and the worldly-minded imagine. Abraham and the patriarchs of the nation will not be the first, but the Apostles (Matt. 19:28, 30). As the government of the Church here below has been changed (Matt. 18:18), so also will the order in heaven be changed. Indeed, our Lord even hints that many who now hold a high position in the Jewish Church will not enter heaven at all (Luke 13:28). The Apostles are really the last in the estimation of the leading Pharisees, and yet they will be the first.

But the instruction has also a far more general signification than this. Our Saviour here develops the relation between poverty and evangelical and apostolic perfection, and shows for what reason poverty is made the first condition and laid down as the first counsel. The counsels are the chief means to perfection, i.e. to perfect love and the special service of God; and their importance consists in removing the principal hindrances to love of Him. But riches are the first and most universal hindrance, on account of their great danger even to salvation. This hindrance must first be removed; and it is effected by poverty. Thus, in His teaching concerning temporal riches, our Saviour has shown the necessity of poverty, as the first motive for choosing it; and in the second part of the instruction He enlarges upon its advantages, as a second motive, making magnificent promises for this life and the next. This address, then, is merely the foundation and illustration of the apparently hard demand made of the youth, and an earnest and touching exhortation to embrace apostolic poverty. The young man should have waited for these words and taken them to heart. They are the glorious legacy of holy poverty. Nothing deeper, more comprehensive or more beautiful could have been said. It is poverty which gives birth to the religious, nourishes him corporally and spiritually, forms and educates him for glorious work in the Church, and finally makes a magnificent provision for him in heaven. For this reason some holy founders have called poverty a mother, and commanded their sons to honor and love her as such.

The Laborers in the Vineyard

Matt. 20:1. "The kingdom of heaven is like to an householder who went out early in the morning to hire laborers into his vineyard.—2. And having agreed with the laborers for a penny a day, he sent them into his vineyard.—3. And going out about the third hour, he saw others standing in the market-place idle,—4. And he said to them: Go you also into my vineyard, and I will give you what shall be just.—5. And they went their way. And again he went out about the sixth and the ninth hour; and did in like manner.—6. But about the eleventh hour he went out and found others standing, and he saith to them: Why stand you here all the day idle?—7. They say to him: Because no man hath hired us. He saith to them: Go you also into my vineyard.—8. And when evening was come, the lord of the vineyard saith to his steward: Call the laborers and pay them their hire, beginning from the last even to the first.—9. When therefore they were come that came about the eleventh hour, they received every man a penny.—10. But when the first also came, they thought that they should receive more; and they also received every man a penny.—11. And receiving it they murmured against the master of the house,—12. Saying: These last have worked but one hour, and thou hast made them equal to us, that have borne the burden of the day and the heats.—13. But he answering said to one of them: Friend, I do thee no wrong; didst thou not agree with me for a penny?—14. Take what is thine, and go thy way; I will also give to this last even as to thee.—15. Or is it not lawful for me to do what I will? Is thy eye evil, because I am good?—16. So shall the last be first, and the first, last; for many are called, but few chosen."

This parable also follows immediately upon the preceding discourse, and is particularly connected with the words: "Many that are first shall be last, and the last shall be first" (Matt. 19:30).

1. CONNECTION OF THE PARABLE WITH THE PRECEDING DISCOURSE, AND ITS PRINCIPAL AIM

The substance of the preceding address is this: The Apostles, and not the dignitaries of the Church of the Old Covenant, not even the holiest and most pre-eminent among them (Matt. 19:28), will be the first in the heavenly kingdom of the Messias; and in this consists, among other things, the great change and transposition of which our Saviour had spoken (Matt. 19:30).

This statement might have two effects upon the Apostles. First, they might grow presumptuous at the prospect of such dignities; and secondly, it might seem to them, as to the Jews in general, inexplicable and unjust that they, the Apostles, devoid as they were of all the requisite qualifications, should be preferred to so many great men, prophets, and saints of the Old Testament.

In answer to the thoughts that they might presumably entertain, our Saviour now explains in the parable that this decree of predestination to the first places in the kingdom of heaven ought not to excite anyone to presumption or discontent, because it is a decree of God's goodness and justice. This is the real, immediate end of the parable, and the principal lesson to be derived from it.

2. DEVELOPMENT OF THE PRINCIPAL AIM OF THE PARABLE

It is a very happy choice, and well suited to the circumstances of time and country, that this aim should be expressed by means of the parable of the laborers in the vineyard. It was spring-time, and work was in full progress in the fields, gardens, and vineyards. Our Saviour could see how the day-laborers betook themselves every morning to the market-places in the towns, and were hired by the employers for one day, as is customary in the East. He now draws from these circumstances the figure for His parable. The vineyard signifies religion, the Church; the master of the vineyard, God; the steward is Christ, and the laborers are the human race. The day signifies the duration of each individual life, and also of that of the entire human race; the penny is eternal life, heaven. But in heaven there are, as had been shown in the preceding instruction, privileged beings, distinguished above others ("first," "chosen"), and these are represented here in the parable by the laborers who come last, and yet receive the same reward as the first. They are thus really the "first" and "chosen" ones with respect to the reward.

In pursuit of this principal aim our Saviour makes two points clear in this parable. First, He repeats in the most decisive manner that the aforesaid great change of positions will take place; and secondly, He justifies this divine decree, so that no one can take offence at it.

First, then, He again confirms the statement He had made in the preceding address, that in the glory of the Messianic kingdom quite another order of things will prevail with regard to distinctions and first places. With this intent He repeats the closing words of the said address: "The last shall be first, and the first, last" (Matt. 19:30; 20:16). And He explains this decree by the words with which He concludes the parable: "Many are called, but few chosen" (Matt. 20:16). This sentence comprises the great law by which the whole question of predestination is governed, both in the case when the vocation has met with a response and when it has not. It has a bearing on election to glory pure and simple, as well as on special degrees and distinctions of glory. It states that predestination is a thing that cannot be merited, solely a gift of the freest and purest love of God, and that in spite of all the cooperation required on the part of man and in spite of the fact that glory is bestowed as a reward for this cooperation, divine love has perfect freedom of choice and preference. If even election and effectual vocation to glory is a pure gift of grace, how much more then predestination to preference in the degree of glory. And it is a question of this preference here; not of glory itself, but of distinctions in glory. For all the laborers receive the penny, which is the symbol of glory, but the last receive a relatively greater reward. In this sense we must here understand the words of our Saviour: "Many are called, but few are chosen." Elsewhere (Matt. 22:14) they signify election simply to glory.

Secondly, our Saviour justifies this divine decree by showing that it is on the one hand a work of God's goodness, and on the other a work of His justice; and therefore no one has any reason to be puffed up on account of being chosen for distinction in glory, and no one has any right to complain if he sees himself excluded from these distinctions. Election to marks of distinction is a work of God's goodness. The parable proves this in words and facts. It is surely pure goodness, when the last arrivals receive as much as the first, the whole penny; and the Master of the vineyard lays stress on this, too. "I will also give to this last even as to thee. Or is it not lawful for me to do what I will? Is thy eye evil, because I am good?" (Matt. 20:14, 15.) Indeed, one can see from the whole behavior of the master to the different laborers that goodness, and not necessity, is what leads him to hire them. He wishes to confer a benefit upon them, by giving them the penny. So the Apostles have no reason at all to exalt themselves unduly. It is pure goodness that they, and not others, are chosen for the first places. The choice of some for the first places in the new kingdom of God is likewise a work of His justice, so that no one has a right to complain of exclusion from these distinctions. Evidently the Pharisees and their views are meant here; they were annoyed not only that others and not themselves were to have the first places in the Messianic kingdom, but even that any others

(Gentiles especially) should gain admittance to it at all. Our Saviour exactly describes them in the behavior of the laborers who were first called. They hoped to receive more than the last comers (Matt. 20:10), and murmured (Matt. 20:11), laying stress upon the time, the "burden and heat" they have borne in the master's service (Matt. 20:12). But the latter repeatedly insists that he does them no injustice: "I do thee no wrong; didst thou not agree with me for a penny? Take what is thine, and go thy way" (Matt. 20:13, 14). He terms their behavior ignoble envy: "Is thy eye evil, because I am good?" (Matt. 20:15.) Thus all the thoughts which bring out the aim of the parable are thrown by the facts and words into strong relief.

3. OTHER INCIDENTAL LESSONS OF THE PARABLE

Besides this special aim of enlightening the Apostles with respect to the privileges which were to fall to their lot, there are various other general lessons in the parable well worth taking to heart.

First, all men are called to salvation, to heaven. This truth is very clearly expressed in the parable, when the lord of the vineyard enters the market and looks round for laborers at almost every time of the day, at the third, sixth, ninth, and eleventh hours. He invites all whom he finds into his vineyard, nay, he presses them to come. "Why stand you here all the day idle?" (Matt. 20:6.) This lesson is based upon the truth that God wills the salvation of all men, and has therefore appointed means of salvation for all times, from that of the patriarchs and prophets down to Christ and our own day. He likewise invites men at all ages of life. The Jews are the first invited. God wishes to make men happy, and therefore He forces Himself, so to speak, upon them.

Secondly, the parable likewise contains the lesson that all must follow the call, labor and persevere to the end, even though it be only for a moment, in order to merit eternal bliss as a reward. Heaven is only given as reward, and though it—the "penny"—is given to all who work, still it falls to the lot of no one who does not obey and work. Whoever does not follow the call, but remains standing idle in the market-place, is a sluggard, remains a beggar, and offends by the very fact of his idleness and waste of time.

Thirdly, there are various degrees of glory. The reward is not equal in every case. Some have privileges and distinctions. But the distinctions are the work of God's free goodness and mercy; and just as no one may be puffed up on account of them, so no one may be angry if they do not fall to his lot. God can, by an unusual measure of His free preventing grace, cause a man to gain a much greater reward of glory than one would expect from the duration of his labor. Thus the greater degree of glory is at once reward and grace, and not a subject either for self-exaltation or for justifiable censure.

Prediction of the Passion

Luke 18:31. Then Jesus took unto him the twelve and said to them: "Behold, we go up to Jerusalem, and all things shall be accomplished which were written by the prophets concerning the Son of Man;—32. For he shall be delivered to the Gentiles, and shall be mocked, and scourged, and spit upon;—33. And after they have scourged him, they will put him to death, and the third day he shall rise again."—34. And they understood none of these things, and this word was hid from them, and they understood not the things that were said.

Mark 10:32. And they were in the way going up to Jerusalem; and Jesus went before them, and they were astonished; and following were afraid. And taking again the twelve, he began to tell them the things that should befall him,—33. Saying: "Behold, we go up to Jerusalem, and the Son of Man shall be betrayed to the chief priests, and to the scribes and ancients, and they shall condemn him to death, and shall deliver him to the Gentiles;—34. And they shall mock him, and spit on him, and scourge him, and kill him; and the third day he shall rise again."

Matt. 20:17. And Jesus going up to Jerusalem, took the twelve disciples apart, and said to them:—18. "Behold, we go up to Jerusalem, and the Son of Man shall be betrayed to the chief priests and the scribes, and they shall condemn him to death,—19. And shall deliver him to the Gentiles to be mocked, and scourged, and crucified, and the third day he shall rise again."

1. CIRCUMSTANCES OF THE PREDICTION

Our Saviour had already re-entered Judaea (following the Jordan eastwards) in the neighborhood of Jericho; for all the Evangelists remark that "they" (i.e. He and the Apostles) were "going up to Jerusalem" (Luke 18:31; Mark 10:32, 33; Matt. 20:17). These were now the last days before the week of the Pasch, and the last miles of the road that separated Him from the city and from His Passion. On the hills and heights fires already burned, announcing the new moon and inviting the people to join in the festal pilgrimage to Jerusalem, which awakened a holy joy throughout the entire country. All preparations were being made for the feast, and processions of pilgrims were being formed one after another and were setting out on their march. The spring had begun, and heaven and earth seemed to be preparing for the feast. Under such circumstances our Saviour journeyed along with His disciples and once again predicted His Passion.

2. THE PREDICTION

This prediction has the peculiarity of giving in detail, as no other does (cf. Matt. 16:21; 17:21, 22), the principal circumstances of the Passion. It states that our Saviour would be betrayed to the chief priests and scribes, mocked, scourged, spat upon, condemned, delivered over to the Gentiles, killed, crucified (Matt. 20:19); and that He would then rise again (Luke 18:32, 33; Mark 10:33, 34; Matt. 20:18, 19). It is a complete picture of His Passion and shameful Death.

What was our Saviour's intention in making this prediction? In the first place, He wished to prepare the Apostles for the terrible blow which was about to fall upon them within such a short time, and to comfort and strengthen them for it. For this reason He added that this had been predicted of the Son of Man by the prophets (Luke 18:31). Further, He wished to lead them thereby to take a right view of His Passion, to see that it was not a failure of His plans and an unforeseen fatality, but a divine and eternal plan, and that everything must happen according to this. Lastly, He wished thereby to demonstrate His prophetic spirit and sincerity. Nothing is to happen to the disciples of which He has not told them beforehand.

How does our Saviour make known this prediction? With regard to exterior circumstances, He revealed His Passion to the Apostles in private, not before the people (Matt. 20:17; Mark 10:32; Luke 18:31), because there was no object in doing this. They would not have understood Him if He had told them of it. On the contrary, such a public communication would only have created surprise, scandal, and excitement. He would do nothing to hinder His Passion. Further, He showed great courage and resolution. He led the way; the disciples only followed Him hesitatingly and with trepidation, because He was leading them back to Jerusalem, and they were astonished at His firmness (Mark 10:32). But as regards His interior sentiments, His anxiety and apprehension must have been increasing with every step. Every hour was bringing Him nearer to His fate. Whilst nature all around was budding into new life, all hearts joyfully anticipating the Feast of the Pasch, and the pilgrim processions passing Him with their festive chants, He was thinking of His Death, and everything around Him was an earnest preparation for His great Sacrifice.

3. EFFECT OF THE PREDICTION UPON THE DISCIPLES

The impression made upon the disciples by the prediction and its attendant circumstances was threefold.

First, they were astonished (Mark 10:32) that He could speak of His Death and specify Jerusalem so positively as the scene of it, and yet approach ever nearer to the city, unhesitatingly and full of resolution.

Secondly, the disciples were afraid (Mark 10:32). Even without our Saviour's clear and definite prediction, a new journey to Jerusalem must have filled their hearts with earnest forebodings and misgivings (John 11:16); how much more so now that He Himself had spoken such ominous words! Nevertheless they kept faithfully by His side (Mark 10:32).

Thirdly, the Apostles did not understand our Lord's prediction (Luke 18:34), and could make nothing of His words. In the first place, they loved Him so heartily and were so much attached to Him, that they could not possibly imagine Him a prey to such sufferings, or to death. Further, they had seen so many proofs of His Divinity that such a death, indeed any death at all, seemed to them a simple impossibility for Him. Lastly, they had not yet grasped the mystery of the Cross at all, and our Lord had already said so many mysterious things, that they could not comprehend the real sense of His words. The Cross *is* a mystery, and this mystery only became clear to them through the descent of the Holy Ghost.

The Sons of Zebedee

Mark 10:35. And James and John, the sons of Zebedee, come to him saying: "Master, we desire that whatsoever we shall ask, thou wouldst do it for us."—36. But he said to them: "What would you that I should do for you?"—37. And they said: "Grant to us that we may sit one on thy right hand, and the other on thy left hand, in thy glory."—38. And Jesus said to them: "You know not what you ask. Can you drink of the chalice that I drink of; or be baptized with the baptism wherewith I am baptized?"—39. But they said to him: "We can." And Jesus saith to them: "You shall indeed drink of the chalice that I drink of; and with the baptism wherewith I am baptized, you shall be baptized;—40. But to sit on my right hand, or on my left, is not mine to give to you, but to them for whom it is prepared."—41. And the ten hearing it, began to be much displeased at James and John.—42. But Jesus calling them, saith to them: "You know that they who seem to rule over the Gentiles, lord it over them; and their princes have power over them.—43. But it is not so among you, but whosoever will be greater, shall be your minister;—44. And whosoever will be first among you, shall be the servant of all.—45. For the Son of Man also is not come to be ministered unto, but to minister, and to give his life a redemption for many."

MATT. 20:20. Then came to him the mother of the sons of Zebedee with her sons, adoring and asking something of him.—21. Who said to her: "What wilt thou?" She saith to him: "Say that these my two sons may sit, the one on thy right hand, and the other on thy left, in thy kingdom."—22. And Jesus answering, said: "You know not what you ask. Can you drink the chalice that I shall drink?" They say to him: "We can."—23. He saith to them: "My chalice indeed you shall drink; but to sit on my right or left hand is not mine to give to you, but to them for whom it is prepared by my Father."—24. And the ten hearing it, were moved with indignation against the two brethren.—25. But Jesus called them to him, and said: "You know that the princes of the Gentiles lord it over them; and they that are the greater exercise power upon them.—26. It shall not be so among you; but whosoever will be the greater among you, let him be your minister;—27. And he that will be first among you, shall be your servant;—28. Even as the Son of Man is not come to be ministered unto, but to minister, and to give his life a redemption for many."

At about the same time Salome and her two sons, James and John, approached to make a request of our Saviour (Matt. 20:20; Mark 10:35).

1. THE PETITION

The twofold prediction concerning the special distinction of the Apostles in the glory of the Messianic kingdom (Matt. 19:28) and the Death and Resurrection of our Lord Himself may probably have given rise to this petition. This much they could gather from our Saviour's words, that the decisive time was approaching and the kingdom of God about to be established. Probably the two Apostles had spoken of these predictions to their mother, who had very likely halted on her pilgrimage to the feast in Jerusalem in order to pay them a visit, and she thought she had better make use of the opportunity to provide for her sons.

The petition itself, that they might sit one on our Lord's right hand and the other on His left—in other words, that they might occupy the first places in His kingdom (Matt. 20:21; Mark 10:37)—was partly good and admissible, but partly also inadmissible. It was good and commendable inasmuch as it was prompted by a lively faith in our Saviour, His Divinity, and His unlimited power, and secondly by love for her sons, for whom she could wish nothing better than to be in close proximity to our Lord; lastly, because it was made with touching simplicity and familiarity, for she told our Lord that He must grant beforehand what they asked (Mark 10:35). Besides this, Salome was one of the holy women who had specially attached themselves to our Lord and rendered Him many services; perhaps, too, she may have been already a widow, and she had generously made Him the sacrifice of both her sons. So she deserved consideration. The two sons themselves belonged, by virtue of their devotion and resolute character, to the first among the Apostles. What was less good, indeed, quite inadmissible, in the petition was, that it arose from the false supposition that the Messianic kingdom would be a temporal one; secondly, that the matter asked for was a special distinction, and our Saviour had just said (in the parable of the laborers in the vineyard) that such distinctions depend entirely upon God; and lastly, that they wished to obtain this distinction merely by asking for it. They desired our Lord to give them the first places in the Messianic kingdom simply on the ground of their asking (III Kings 2:19; Ps. 109:1; Mark 26:64). Zebedee's sons probably felt themselves that their petition was not a fitting one; for this reason they wished our Saviour to pledge His word beforehand, and for this reason also, perhaps, they came to our Lord secretly to make the request (Matt. 20:24; Mark 10:41; cf. III Kings 2:20).

2. THE ANSWER

Our Saviour's answer contains three points of excellence.

First, He shows (humanly speaking) great caution, greater than Solomon had once done (III Kings 2:20). He does not let Himself be bound beforehand, nor pledge His word until He has heard the request. He asks: "What would you that I should do for you?" (Mark 10:36.)

Secondly, He shows extraordinary wisdom and kindness in the manner in which He refuses the request of His intimate friends. He shows them gently and lovingly that it is thoughtless and inadmissible, saying: "You know not what you ask" (Matt. 20:22; Mark 10:38). He also gives reasons for His refusal, viz. that the attainment of this high aim does not depend upon simple requests, but upon other conditions. The first condition is contained in His question: "Can you drink of the chalice that I drink of, or be baptized with the baptism wherewith I am baptized," this chalice and baptism that await Me before I enter upon My kingdom? (Mark 10:38; Matt. 20:22.) Our Saviour here alluded to His Passion (Luke 12:50; Matt. 26:39; John 18:11; Jer. 25:15) and to the share they must take in it before they could enter into His kingdom. They answer boldly in the affirmative (Matt. 20:22; Mark 10:39), and our Saviour, well pleased, prophetically replies that they will drink of His chalice (Mark 10:39; Matt. 20:23). The second condition consists in God's predestination. Such distinctions cannot be merited, even by death, if they have not been bestowed upon us by the predestination of the Father (Matt. 20:23; Mark 10:40); and therefore we should not ask for them. Works of power and providence, predestination therefore included, are ascribed to God the Father. At all events our Saviour cannot grant them out of pure friendship. This is a very decided rebuff, but given very gently and quietly. This calmness and gentleness are rendered all the more admirable by the fact that our Saviour was not thinking of His glorious kingdom at this moment, but was on the contrary full of solemn, somber pictures of His Passion, and under such circumstances such a discordant note must have been most painful to Him.

Lastly, He displays in this answer admirable sincerity and uprightness. He promises nothing and refuses nothing. His answer is so worded that the other Apostles also can hear it without offence.

3. RESULTS OF THE PETITION

This step of Zebedee's sons had two results: great displeasure on the part of the Apostles, and an excellent lesson as a reproof of this displeasure on the part of our Saviour.

When the other ten Apostles heard of this secret proceeding of Zebedee's family, they became indignant (Mark 10:41; Matt. 20:24). It is not clear how the secret became public; perhaps by imprudence on the part of the two Apostles themselves or of their mother, or by secret inquiries on the part of the others, possibly of Judas. At all events the cause of their displeasure was not virtue, but envy and ambition. So they themselves were afflicted with the very vice which scandalized them in the other two.

Our Saviour now made use of this disposition of the Apostles to give them an earnest lesson, in order to deter them from ambition and striving after rank and dignities. He called them all together (Matt. 20:25; Mark 10:42), instructed them first concerning the nature of Christian and ecclesiastical government, and then gave them a beautiful motive for taking the lesson to heart and acting in accordance with it. The essence of Christian and ecclesiastical government does not consist in simply being superior or first, nor yet in commanding, ruling, and exercising power over others, especially not when this is done arbitrarily and with selfish aims and intentions; but in serving the public weal and the welfare of each individual, even to the complete sacrifice of oneself. One must regard oneself as the last and the servant of all (Matt. 20:26, 27; Mark 10:43, 44). And whoever wishes to obtain the first place, let him be the last and the servant of all. Our Saviour illustrates this truth by its opposite in secular, heathen government, which reversed the right order of things and thus degenerated into tyranny and despotism (Matt. 20:25; Mark 10:42). As a first motive He seems to indicate the unhappiness of the nations under their heathen rulers, saying: "You know," i.e. you can see it in Herod and the Roman governors and Gentile princes in the vicinity. As a second motive He adduces His own example; He had come not to be served, but to serve, and to give His life for all (Mark 10:45; Matt. 20:28).

This mystery throws fresh light upon the character of our Divine Saviour. He knows how to give even His favorite disciples a decided refusal, but with such calmness and consideration, such delicacy and amiability, that no one can take it amiss; and by His answer He leads them ever deeper into His own spirit. We have here, too, an example of how He lets no imperfection on the part of His disciples pass unreproved; but the reproof is contained in an instruction calculated to elevate their character. Above all, He tolerates no ambition in His Apostles, because nothing is more repugnant to the character of the Apostolate. Lastly, the instruction concerning the nature of ecclesiastical government is an original and magnificent specimen of His spirit, and is thence of infinite importance and extent. How marvelously beautiful, how divine is the Christian rule based upon these principles, of which our Saviour is the very life and example! This mystery is nothing else than a practical confirmation of the principal lesson in the parable of the laborers in the vineyard.

The Blind Man of Jericho

Luke 18:35. Now it came to pass, when he drew nigh to Jericho, that a certain blind man sat by the wayside, begging.—36. And when he heard the multitude passing by, he asked what this meant.—37. And they told him that Jesus of Nazareth was passing by.—38. And he cried out, saying: "Jesus, Son of David, have mercy on me."—39. And they that went before, rebuked him, that he should hold his peace. But he cried out much more: "Son of David, have mercy on me." —40. And Jesus standing commanded him to be brought unto him. And when he was come near, he asked him,—41. Saying: "What wilt thou that I do to thee?" But he said: "Lord, that I may see."—42. And Jesus said to him: "Receive thy sight, thy faith hath made thee whole."—43. And immediately he saw, and followed him, glorifying God. And all the people when they saw it, gave praise to God.

MARK 10:46. And they come to Jericho; and as he went out of Jericho with his disciples and a very great multitude, Bar-Timeus the blind man, the son of Timeus, sat by the wayside begging.—47. Who when he had heard that it was Jesus of Nazareth, began to cry out, and to say: "Jesus, Son of David, have mercy on me." —48. And many rebuked him, that he might hold his peace. But he cried a great deal the more: "Son of David, have mercy on me."—49. And Jesus standing still commanded him to be called. And they call the blind man, saying to him: "Be of better comfort; arise, he calleth thee."—50. Who casting off his garment leaped up, and came to him.—51. And Jesus answering, said to him: "What wilt thou that I should do to thee?" And the blind man said to him: "Rabboni, that I may see."—52. And Jesus said to him: "Go thy way, thy faith hath made thee whole." And immediately he saw, and followed him in the way.

MATT. 20:29. And when they went out from Jericho, a great multitude followed him.—30. And behold two blind men sitting by the wayside heard that Jesus passed by, and they cried out, saying: "O Lord, thou Son of David, have mercy on us."—31. And the multitude rebuked them that they should hold their peace. But they cried out the more, saying: "O Lord, thou Son of David, have mercy on us."—32. And Jesus stood, and called them, and said: "What will ye that I do to you?"—33. They say to him: "Lord, that our eyes be opened."—34. And Jesus having compassion on them, touched their eyes. And immediately they saw, and followed him.

Our Saviour now came with His companions to Jericho (Mark 10:46). St. Luke relates that a blind man was healed on His entrance into the town (Luke 18:35). According to St. Matthew's account, He healed two blind men on leaving Jericho, whilst St. Mark only speaks of one, whom he calls Bartimeus (Mark 10:46; Matt. 20:29, 30). Probably some circumstance had made the disciples already acquainted with him, or else he received this name in the Church later on, as a disciple of our Lord. In order to reconcile the different accounts, we must assume that two distinct cures were wrought by our Lord, and that St. Matthew has put the two together. On account of the similarity of their attendant circumstances, the two cures have not been separated in this meditation; and since the healing of the two blind men in Capharnaum (Matt. 9:27) likewise presents several similar details, we shall consider here only those which are different and peculiar to this miracle.

1. OUR SAVIOUR'S ESCORT

Three Evangelists remark that our Saviour was conducted through Jericho by a large company of people. "A great multitude followed Him" (Matt. 20:29; Mark 10:46); the attention of the blind men was attracted by "the multitude passing by," some in advance, some behind (Luke 18:36, 39). Our Saviour was at that time in the districts of Peraea, at the very height of His influence and power, on account of His doctrine and miracles; and all the people were on their way to the Paschal Feast. The crowds considered it a happiness and an honor to be in the company of Jesus.

Here, too, we see distinctly the character of the nation. Upon the blind men's question as to who was passing by with such a large escort, the people told them that it was Jesus of Nazareth (Luke 18:37; Mark 10:47; Matt. 20:30). When the former began to cry out loudly and call Him the Son of David, they grew angry and bade them be silent (Luke 18:39; Mark 10:48; Matt. 20:31). Perhaps they were vexed at such unbecoming behavior; or probably many of them did not like to hear our Saviour thus entitled, for fear of the Pharisees. Or they may have wished to spare Him the annoyance of a delay, out of consideration for our Saviour Himself. But as He inquired for the blind men, the people (or at any rate the more mildly disposed among them) turned to them and exhorted them to take courage, for He was calling them (Mark 10:49). Such is the nature of a crowd, subject to every varying mood or emotion. The people, here and on later occasions, form with their loud expressions of gratitude a kind of choir, which gives expression to the emotions aroused by and corresponding to our Saviour's actions.

2. DISPOSITIONS OF THE BLIND MEN

We must not be surprised at finding so many blind men here. Jericho is a town on the principal high-road; now, at the time of the Pasch, it was thronged with pilgrims on their way to the feast, and many poor, blind, and infirm people gathered together in order to collect alms from them. For this reason we find it related of all the blind men healed here that they had taken up their post by the wayside to beg (Matt. 20:30; Mark 10:46; Luke 18:35).

The dispositions of the blind men, too, are quite in accordance with the benefit which fell to their lot. In the first place they give vent to their great desire of being healed, by their loud and vehement calling after our Saviour, as soon as they have once heard that it is He Who is passing by. All reproof, all rebuke of their unmannerly conduct does not deter them from it; on the contrary, it stimulates them to cry out still more loudly and urgently (Luke 18:38, 39; Mark 10:47, 48; Matt. 20:30, 31). It was the decisive moment, now or never. Further, their desire finds expression in their haste to go to our Lord as soon as they hear that He is willing for them to come, and in the touching eagerness with which they reply to His question as to what they desired: "Lord, that our eyes be opened" (Matt. 20:33; Mark 10:51; Luke 18:41). Bartimeus even jumped up and threw away his mantle, in his joy and eagerness to get to our Lord as quickly as possible (Mark 10:50). Their faith and confidence is no less vigorous. All that they do and say shows great reverence and an exalted idea of our Saviour. They call Him "Lord" (Matt. 20:33; Luke 18:41), "Rabboni" (Mark 10:51), and confess Him publicly before all the people as the Son of David, the Messias (Luke 18:38, 39; Mark 10:47, 48; Matt. 20:30). Our Saviour ascribes the miracle to their faith (Mark 10:52; Luke 18:42).

3. THE CURE

As a rule our Saviour made use of certain ceremonies when healing the blind. Here He merely touched the eyes of the two whom He healed on leaving Jericho (Matt. 20:34). The first one, outside the town, seems to have been cured by the simple words: "Receive thy sight" (Luke 18:42).

In this we see our Lord's goodness, no less than His power. As soon as He hears the blind men call, He stands still and has them summoned to Him (Luke 18:40; Mark 10:49; Matt. 20:32), asks them sympathetically and with kingly graciousness and generosity what they wish Him to do to them (Matt. 20:32; Mark 10:51; Luke 18:41), and has compassion on their miserable state (Matt. 20:34).

So many miracles in such quick succession must necessarily cause the people to break out in words of admiration and praise of God (Luke 18:43). The blind men, full of gratitude and praise, followed our Lord on His pilgrimage to Jerusalem.

Zacheus

Luke 19:1. And entering in, He walked through Jericho.—2. And behold there was a man named Zacheus, who was the chief of the publicans; and he was rich.—3. And he sought to see Jesus who he was; and he could not for the crowd, because he was low of stature.—4. And running before, he climbed up into a sycamore tree that he might see him; for he was to pass that way.—5. And when Jesus was come to the place, looking up, he saw him, and said to him: "Zacheus, make haste and come down; for this day I must abide in thy house."—6. And he made haste and came down, and received him with joy.—7. And when all saw it, they murmured, saying that he was gone to be a guest with a man that was a sinner.—8. But Zacheus standing said to the Lord: "Behold, Lord, the half of my goods I give to the poor; and if I have wronged any man of anything, I restore him fourfold."—9. Jesus said to him: "This day is salvation come to this house; because he also is a son of Abraham.—10. For the Son of Man is come to seek and to save that which was lost."

Our Saviour does not seem to have stayed or done any other works in beautiful Jericho, the city of priests, so rich in gardens and palms, the seat of great commerce and one of the principal places of custom. The mystery in which Zacheus plays a part took place just as He was leaving the town (Luke 19:1).

1. ZACHEUS

Zacheus is depicted to us in very different lights. He is introduced as "the chief of the publicans" (Luke 19:2). He seems therefore to have been the first customs-officer and tax-gatherer of the district, subordinate only to the deputy of the chief Roman tax-gatherer of the province. He is further represented as a rich man (Luke 19:2). This must have been the case, for otherwise he could not have been chief customs-official, on account of the security he had to give; besides, the customs-district of Jericho probably offered great advantages in this respect, owing to the fertility of the soil and the importance of its position as chief center of the inland trade. From the offer Zacheus makes (Luke 19:8) it is plain enough that he must have been rich. From the very fact of his being tax-gatherer in chief, it is easy to understand that he stood in ill repute with the Jews, that they regarded him as one of the very worst sinners, and abhorred him as such (Luke 19:7).

But Zacheus is also shown in another light. He had most likely heard of Jesus' wisdom, goodness and miraculous power before this, for our Saviour repeatedly had to traverse this district. So he had a high opinion of Him, which must have been enhanced by the miracles that had just taken place. As he now heard that Jesus was passing through the town, he felt an ardent desire to see Him and make His acquaintance (Luke 19:3), but in his humility did not think himself worthy to do so. Nevertheless he could not resist the desire at least to see Jesus; and therefore, since on account of his small stature he could not get a sight of

Him among the crowd, he took the childlike resolve of hurrying on in front and climbing up one of the sycamore trees outside the town (as perhaps some people of the lower classes or the youthful inhabitants may have done), in order to look down at our Saviour as He passed by (Luke 19:4). The roads and approaches to the towns are often planted with these sycamores, because they have tall, knotted trunks with wide-spreading branches covered with foliage, and thus afford shade to the passers-by. Since they have branches low down, they are easy to climb. Thus Zacheus waited in this hiding-place to catch sight of our Lord. This is indeed a sign of a simple, humble heart. But his humility and childlike simplicity are still more strikingly displayed when our Lord invites Himself to his house, and the bystanders express their surprise and displeasure that a sinner should have the honor of entertaining Him (Luke 19:7). Zacheus does not take this amiss. On the contrary, he comes and stands before our Lord (either directly here under the tree or before leading Him into his house), and with outstretched arms promises in the excess of his happiness and in thanksgiving for this visit to give the half of his fortune to the poor, and to restore fourfold whatever he may have extorted from anyone unjustly (Luke 19:8). His words certainly seem to imply that he cannot call to mind any particular injustice; nevertheless, if he should have injured anyone, he is ready to make ample amends. Besides this he is willing to give immediately as alms the half of his fortune, which was assuredly not a small one. And this is the great sinner! Could there be a better or nobler heart? Was he not a hundred times better than the avaricious, hard-hearted Pharisees? Though of course grace had worked powerfully upon his heart at this moment, still the fact throws a very favorable light upon the man and his life.

2. OUR SAVIOUR

Our Saviour shows Himself not less amiable and generous, and in three respects.

First, He knows well the dispositions and desire of Zacheus; He sees every step he takes, and especially the desperate attempt he makes to behold Him. For this reason our Lord now halts just under the tree, and looks up at the very spot where Zacheus is watching from his hiding-place (Luke 19:5).

Secondly, our Saviour not only grants Zacheus' desire; He even anticipates and goes beyond it. Zacheus had only hoped to see

Him and make His acquaintance, and lo, He calls him down, invites Himself to his house and becomes his Guest, so that he can see Him, speak to Him, and learn to know Him, as much as he likes. That is certainly a great honor and a great happiness, infinitely more than Zacheus had dared to hope.

Thirdly, our Lord rewards Zacheus with inestimable graces of justification and bliss, and perhaps even with an apostolic vocation; for he is said to have become Bishop of Caesarea later on. Our Lord sums up all this in the beautiful words: "This day is salvation come to this house . . . for the Son of Man is come to seek and to save that which was lost" (Luke 19:9, 10). What more could Zacheus have wished?

3. THE PEOPLE

By the people we must understand all who accompanied our Lord and witnessed the incident with Zacheus (Luke 19:7); a gathering of people of all dispositions and shades of thought, probably intermingled with Pharisees and perhaps with priests and scribes. Instead of rejoicing and praising God that "salvation had come" to Zacheus, they murmured and even gave loud vent to their displeasure that our Lord had "gone to be a guest with a man that was a sinner" (Luke 19:7). They had just seen Him work two or more miracles, and had praised God and acknowledged the divine mission and holiness of our Saviour. One would think these glorious miracles would surely have been enough to convince them that He could not immediately afterwards do a thing contrary to justice and right. But it was not the case. Zacheus was a public sinner, and thereupon the old prejudice awoke at once and they turned away with disapproval.

Our Saviour maintains His line of action, and excuses and justifies it by pointing out that Zacheus also was by birth and descent a son of Abraham, and that it was His mission to save all the lost sheep of Israel, without excluding anyone (Luke 19:9). He had given the very same answer before, on similar occasions (Matt. 9:13; 15:24; 18:11; Luke 5:32).

This mystery is of importance with regard to the character of Jesus, inasmuch as it gives us, first, a beautiful insight into His goodness. He rewards good wherever He finds it. He only waits for our good will, and comes forward to meet it. Zacheus has only gone a few steps out of the town and climbed a tree to see our Saviour pass by, and how he is rewarded! What graces are bestowed on him! Further, this mystery shows us our Lord's liberty of spirit, which never suffers Him to be guided or influenced by ancient prejudices. He looks into the heart of the matter, not at the exterior. How mean and narrow-minded all the Israelite dignitaries are beside Him! Lastly, this mystery also proves the great courage of our Saviour. It was no slight matter to oppose by word and deed such a universal, fixed and deep-rooted prejudice, and publicly to call Zacheus, the sinner of sinners, a son of Abraham. These words are a condemnation of the Synagogue, which wished to appropriate to itself, so to speak, the salvation of the world, and to shut others out from it.

The Parable of the Ten Pounds

Luke 19:11. As they were hearing these things, he added and spoke a parable, because he was nigh to Jerusalem; and because they thought that the kingdom of God should immediately be manifested.—12. He said therefore: "A certain nobleman went into a far country to receive for himself a kingdom, and to return.—13. And calling his ten servants, he gave them ten pounds, and said to them: Trade till I come.—14. But his citizens hated him; and they sent an embassage after him, saying: We will not have this man to reign over us.—15. And it came to pass that he returned, having received the kingdom; and he commanded his servants to be called, to whom he had given the money, that he might know how much every man had gained by trading.—16. And the first came, saying: Lord, thy pound hath gained ten pounds.—17. And he said to him: Well done, thou good servant, because thou hast been faithful in a little, thou shalt have power over ten cities.—18. And the second came, saying: Lord, thy pound hath gained five pounds.—19. And he said to him: Be thou also over five cities.—20. And another came, saying: Lord, behold here is thy pound, which I have kept laid up in a napkin;—21. For I feared thee, because thou art an austere man; thou takest up what thou didst not lay down, and thou reapest that which thou didst not sow.—22. He saith to him: Out of thy own mouth I judge thee, thou wicked servant: thou knewest that I was an austere man, taking up what I laid not down, and reaping that which I did not sow;—23. And why then didst thou not give my money into the bank, that at my coming I might have exacted it with usury?—24. And he said to them that stood by: Take the pound away from him, and give it to him that hath the ten pounds.—25. And they said to him: Lord, he hath ten pounds.—26. But I say to you, that to everyone that hath shall be given, and he shall abound; and from him that hath not, even that which he hath shall be taken from him.—27. But as for those my enemies, who would not have me reign over them, bring them hither, and kill them before me."—28. And having said these things, he went before, going up to Jerusalem.

As they continued their journey, Jesus propounded the parable of the ten pounds (Luke 19:11).

1. Circumstances of the Parable

The circumstances which led to the parable are very plainly stated (Luke 19:11). The universal opinion among the disciples as well as among the people was, that our Saviour would now enter Jerusalem in His rank as "Son of David" (i.e. Messias), and begin his reign. Many recognized Him as Son of David, and He was on the way to Jerusalem. Perhaps, too, they had interpreted His words about regaining "what was lost" in a sense partly political, partly religious, in connection with the independence of Israel. At all events He had stated often enough that His mission was about to be accomplished in Jerusalem. This general opinion gave rise to the parable.

2. AIM OF THE PARABLE

In opposition to this opinion our Saviour now wishes to teach them, first, that He will indeed enter into His kingdom; but secondly, that this will not be now, but that He will only return to begin His reign after a long absence; thirdly, that His adherents are to endeavor in the meantime to prepare for the opening of His kingdom, by making a good use of the time and means given them. It is not of importance to know the time of His coming, but to make a good preparation for His arrival; the "how," not the "when" is the thing to be considered.

3. DEVELOPMENT OF THE PARABLE

Our Saviour probably drew the figure in which He expressed these thoughts from the political situation of the Jewish land at that time. The princes went to Rome to get their position sanctioned. The accession of King Archelaus, in particular, was attended by circumstances very similar to the details of the parable. Archelaus, a son of Herod the Great, went to Rome to have his claim to the crown ratified. The Jews sent ambassadors after him to thwart his plans and dissuade the emperor. But Archelaus carried his point by bribery, and had then as king an opportunity of taking revenge on his enemies and rewarding his faithful friends, who had had much to suffer in the meantime.

The nobleman in the parable is our Saviour Himself, truly of noble origin by His descent from David, His virginal Birth, and especially by His true Divinity. He "goes away" by His Passion and Death, in order to receive from His Father's hands the glory of His kingdom; and then returns again, whether in the special judgment at the death of each individual or in the universal Judgment, but at an unspecified time. He will surely come, will royally reward His true and zealous servants and punish according to their deserts the negligent among them, as well as the enemies who hate Him (Luke 19:12, 15, 22, 27).

There are three classes among His subjects. First, there are His faithful, zealous, and prudent servants. He entrusts money to them to trade with (Luke 19:13). They manage it so well, that at His return He finds it increased fivefold, or at least doubled. Their master rewards them in proportion to their zeal and prudence by setting them over cities and lands (Luke 19:16–19). The trust-money, ten pounds (about $150 of our money), is little; probably because it is out of the nobleman's private income, or because our Saviour wishes to veil the political foundation of the parable, or to teach us that one can merit a great deal in the spiritual life by very little things. It is especially worthy of note that the reward is taken from the state property, and therefore brings in incomparably more possessions and honors; five cities for five pounds, and a territory with ten cities for ten pounds. The reward is proportioned to the good qualities of the servants, their prudence, skill, zeal and humility, which last is so beautifully shown in their answer (Luke 19:16, 18), as also to the goodness and royal munificence of their master.

The second class of servants merely keep what is entrusted to them and give it back again, but take no pains to increase it (Luke 19:20). Their dispositions are clearly depicted in the answer of the third servant (Luke 19:21), and in the reproach made to him by his lord (Luke 19:22, 23). They are: fear, idleness, insolence and injustice. What less could be asked of a man than to put the money out to interest? And he does not even do that. For this reason his lord calls him a wicked and slothful servant. The reproach made by the servant himself is not at all applicable to our Saviour. He is not severe, but just, and this very fact ought to urge His servants to zeal and carefulness. As a punishment, the money is taken away from the idle servant and given to one of the better and more zealous ones (Luke 19:24–26). This is also the case in everyday life (Matt. 13:12). The rich man can easily increase his riches; the poor man can easily lose all that he has. And in the spiritual life also one can forfeit grace by negligence and obtain greater graces by zeal.

The third class consists of other subjects of the king, but yet his enemies, who hate him and do not wish him to rule over them (Luke 19:14). Their punishment is as strikingly set forth as the reward of the others. His enemies cannot escape it; they are simply cut down by the companions and satellites of the king, by his own order (Luke 19:27). Thus it was at the destruction of Jerusalem, and thus it will be at the Last Judgment, of which the judgment upon Jerusalem is a type.

After our Lord had concluded the parable He proceeded on His way up to Jerusalem (Luke 19:28); and in this also He is truly a nobleman, a king, in His courage and majestic firmness on the way to suffering, death and victory.

Here we see the glorious character of our Saviour shine forth with new luster. He gradually reveals more and more of His royalty. Here He fitly calls Himself merely a nobleman, an aspirant to the crown, because He will only receive His exterior kingdom from the hand of His Father. He is truly a king; first, in the clear consciousness of His royal dignity and self-respect, which is shown in the chastisement He inflicts upon His enemies and negligent vassals. It is the first time that our Saviour speaks of a bloody retribution upon His enemies. Secondly, He is a king in the great liberality with which He divides His kingdom among His faithful adherents, and rewards even their smallest services. His lofty, practical wisdom and prudence are also shown by the way in which He is able to propound solemn and bitter truths under the figure of well-known facts and events, and to turn attention from the useless guessing and conjecturing about the coming of His kingdom to what prepares for and promotes it, viz. the good use of time and grace. He insists upon this very strongly.

The Meal at Bethania

John 11:55. And the Pasch of the Jews was at hand; and many from the country went up to Jerusalem, before the Pasch, to purify themselves.—56. They sought therefore for Jesus; and they discoursed one with another, standing in the temple: "What think you, that he is not come to the festival day?" And the chief priests and the Pharisees had given a commandment, that if any man knew where he was, he should tell, that they might apprehend him.—12:1. Jesus therefore six days before the Pasch came to Bethania, where Lazarus had been dead, whom Jesus raised to life.—2. And they made him a supper there; and Martha served, but Lazarus was one of them that were at table with him.—3. Mary therefore took a pound of ointment of right spikenard, of great price, and anointed the feet of Jesus and wiped his feet with her hair; and the house was filled with the odor of the ointment.—4. Then one of his disciples, Judas Iscariot, he that was about to betray him, said:—5. "Why was not this ointment sold for three hundred pence, and given to the poor?"—6. Now he said this, not because he cared for the poor, but because he was a thief, and having the purse, carried the things that were put therein.—7. Jesus therefore said: "Let her alone, that she may keep it against the day of my burial;—8. For the poor you have always with you; but me you have not always."—9. A great multitude therefore of the Jews knew that he was there; and they came not for Jesus' sake only, but that they might see Lazarus, whom he had raised from the dead.—10. But the chief priests thought to kill Lazarus also;—11. Because many of the Jews by reason of him went away, and believed in Jesus.

MARK 14:3. And when he was in Bethania in the house of Simon the leper, and was at meat; there came a woman having an alabaster box of ointment of precious spikenard, and breaking the alabaster box she poured it out upon his head.—4. Now there were some that had indignation within themselves, and said: "Why was this waste of the ointment made?—5. For this ointment might have been sold for more than three hundred pence, and given to the poor." And they murmured against her.—6. But Jesus said: "Let her alone, why do you molest her? She hath wrought a good work upon me;—7. For the poor you have always with you, and whensoever you will, you may do them good; but me you have not always.—8. She hath done what she could; she is come beforehand to anoint my body for the burial.—9. Amen I say to you: wheresoever this Gospel shall be preached in the whole world, that also which she hath done shall be told for a memorial of her."

MATT. 26:6. And when Jesus was in Bethania in the house of Simon the leper,—7. There came to him a woman having an alabaster box of precious ointment, and poured it on his head as he was at table.—8. And the disciples seeing it, had indignation, saying: "To what purpose is this waste?—9. For this might have been sold for much, and given to the poor."—10. And Jesus knowing it, said to them: "Why do you trouble this woman? For she hath wrought a good work upon me;—11. For the poor you have always with you; but me you have not always.—12. For she in pouring this ointment upon my body hath done it for my burial.—13. Amen I say to you, wheresoever this gospel shall be preached in the whole world, that also which she hath done shall be told for a memory of her."

1. STATE OF AFFAIRS AT OUR LORD'S ARRIVAL IN BETHANIA

St. John gives us the circumstances in detail. The feast of the Pasch was at hand, and all the roads were thronged with pilgrims on their way to the city. Many had already arrived there, in order to prepare for the feast by making sacrifices of atonement for personal transgressions of the law. Later on the sacrifices would be entirely taken up with the feast (John 11:55). Many of these pilgrims from the neighboring districts, such as Galilee, Peraea, and Judaea, might probably have met our Saviour or heard of Him before, and so there was much talk and inquiry about Him already, and even search for Him, before His arrival in Bethania, especially on the part of the ill-disposed. The disturbance was increased by the chief priests' secret order that whoever became acquainted with the whereabouts of Jesus was to give them information of it, in order that they might arrest Him. The Pharisees probably took care to make known this measure taken by the authorities (John 11:56). Thus all preparations were made and the snares set. His obedience to the law was to lead Him into the trap.

In spite of all these circumstances, so menacing and full of ill omen, our Saviour came to Bethania six days before the Feast of the Pasch, that is to say, on the Friday before His Passion (John 12:1). St. Matthew (26:6) and St. Mark (14:3) only casually relate His sojourn at Bethania and the meal in question, without any precise determination of the time. They bring it in here, in order that it may serve as a basis and introduction to the betrayal by Judas.

2. THE MEAL AT BETHANIA

Probably our Saviour went to stay with Lazarus (John 12:1) and spent the Sabbath there. On this Sabbath, however, He received an invitation to dine at the house of Simon the leper (Matt. 26:6; Mark 14:3), who was probably a friend and neighbor of Lazarus' family and a disciple of our Saviour's. It was there, then, that the banquet was held. Lazarus was also among the guests, and his two sisters and their domestics undertook the service (John 12:2). There are three important points about this meal: the beautiful deed of Mary, the disgraceful conduct of Judas, and our Lord's behavior to them both.

In Mary three qualities of especial beauty are delineated. First, her generosity. She had reserved for herself the privilege of performing the ceremony of honor towards the honored Guest, and had bought for this purpose a pound of the purest and most costly spikenard "in an alabaster box," for 300 pence (about $50), as Judas estimated. These boxes, or rather vases, were generally made with a long, slender neck, sealed up, which had to be broken off when the ointment was going to be used. So Mary broke the vase, anointed the Feet of Jesus with the spikenard (John 12:3), and poured the remainder over His Head (Matt. 26:7; Mark 14:3). Thus she really did all that generosity could do (Mark 14:8). Secondly, she reveals in this ceremony her great humility. She wiped our Lord's Feet with her hair (John 12:3). Lastly, she displays in all this not only her humility, generosity, gratitude and reverence, but also her faith and religious veneration for Jesus. One does not treat a mere man in this manner, but God alone. It was an act of homage shown by her to Him as God, and who can fathom the fervor, love and devotion with which she did it? "The house was filled with the odor of the ointment" (John 12:3).

The behavior of Judas forms an unworthy, nay a disgraceful

contrast to hers. We are told, it is true, that "some" of the disciples took note of this liberality of Mary's, and expressed their disapproval of it (Matt. 26:8; Mark 14:4). St. John mentions Judas only (John 12:4). If there were others besides, then at all events their disapproval was not prompted by the same intention as his nor did it proceed from such dispositions. Perhaps they may have considered Mary's act as a pious extravagance, which they thought even our Saviour Himself would not approve of, owing to His simplicity and humility, especially as He so often recommended works of mercy to the poor. But Judas' words were prompted by a low, mean disposition, indifference, unbelief and aversion to our Saviour; he murmurs, reproves, and calls it senseless waste (Matt. 26:8; Mark 14:4). The religious veneration shown to Jesus annoys him; he considers it unfounded and excessive. It is nothing but hypocrisy when he says that the ointment would have procured alms for the poor (Matt. 26:9; Mark 14:5). It was pure covetousness and a desire of theft on his part. He kept the money given to our Saviour and His disciples for the poor, and stole from the bag; and he only wished Mary had given the price of the ointment, because he might then have kept a part or the whole of it for himself (John 12:5, 6).

Our Saviour first takes Mary's part against him: "Let her alone, why do you molest her?" (Mark 14:6; Matt. 26:10; John 12:7.) Secondly, He expressly declares that she has wrought a good work upon Him (Matt. 26:10; Mark 14:6), and proves it by first refuting the objection made on behalf of the poor. He is poor too, and stands far above all other poor; indeed, it is only for His sake that people do good to them, and now is the very time to perform good works for Him, since He is about to go away, whilst the poor never leave us (Matt. 26:11; Mark 14:7). From this last thought He develops a very touching motive to account for Mary's action in His regard. She has anointed Him for His burial, as St. Matthew (26:12) and St. Mark (14:8) plainly tell us. St. John writes somewhat mysteriously: "Let her alone, that she may keep it against the day of my burial" (12:7); she is now using it for this purpose. It is not clear whether Mary knew the deep meaning of this anointing beforehand. It may be that this very knowledge had called forth such generosity. At all events her loving heart in this matter obeyed the inspiration of Providence. On the evening after our Lord's Death it will not be vouchsafed to her to do this. Thirdly, our Saviour rewards Mary for her good work by promising that it will be constantly remembered in the Church throughout all ages (Matt. 26:13; Mark 14:9), as indeed has been the case. Thus the odor of her balsam still fills "the whole house" of the Church.

3. CONSEQUENCES OF THE SOJOURN AT BETHANIA

The importance of this sojourn of Jesus in Bethania is derived from the fact that the threads of the plot begun by the miracle of the raising of Lazarus are taken up and continued, and new ones interwoven.

In the first place, it was soon rumored abroad in the city that Jesus was in Bethania, and in the course of these days many Jews came out to see Him and Lazarus. Many of them believed in our Lord and became His disciples (John 12:9, 11).

In consequence of this the chief priests agreed together to make away with Lazarus as well, because his presence was a living witness to the mission of Jesus and told against themselves (John 12:10).

The pomp of our Lord's entry into the city on the following day will be a third result (John 12:12, 17, 18).

At last a fact comes to light which had hitherto been concealed, but which was to be of the greatest importance in connection with the following events. The sad disposition of Judas, the unhappy disciple who was to bring about the fatal end, is revealed at this meal, when Mary anoints Jesus. Perhaps this very anointing may have helped to make him decide to betray our Lord. At all events it unveils his heart and the passions by which Satan and the wicked world took possession of him and drew him down to perdition. The manner in which Mary and Judas are represented affords us matter for earnest reflection and deep thought. How different, how entirely opposite are the paths they tread! Where did they both begin, and where do they end? Judas, the Apostle, now an unbeliever and a thief, who even uses for his own ruin the means entrusted to him for works of charity, which might have saved him; and Magdalen, a poor sinner notorious for her evil life, now the generous disciple of Jesus, glowing with love for Him! Whilst some rise from the lowest depth to holiness and heaven, others fall from heaven to hell. How admirable is the calmness and moderation with which our Saviour defends His own cause and Mary's against this base man and his reproach! What did not Judas deserve, and yet how quietly and touchingly our Saviour speaks! How well-pleasing Mary's generosity must have been to Him, and how plainly His words show us the thoughts and feelings that already filled His Heart! The Cross and the Sepulcher are ever present to Him, and yet how patient, how loving, and how large-hearted He is in His instructions!

The Entry into Jerusalem

Mark 11:1. And when they were drawing near to Jerusalem and to Bethania at the Mount of Olives he sendeth two of his disciples,—2. And saith to them: "Go into the village that is over against you, and immediately at your coming in thither, you shall find a colt tied, upon which no man yet hath sat; loose him and bring him.—3. And if any man shall say to you: What are you doing? Say ye that the Lord hath need of him; and immediately he will let him come hither."—4. And going their way, they found the colt tied before the gate without in the meeting of two ways; and they loose him.—5. And some of them that stood there said to them: "What do you, loosing the colt?"—6. Who said to them as Jesus had commanded them, and they let him go with them.—7. And they brought the colt to Jesus; and they lay their garments on him, and he sat upon him.—8. And many spread their garments in the way; and others cut down boughs from the trees, and strewed them in the way.—9. And they that went before and they that followed cried, saying: "Hosanna:—10. Blessed is he that cometh in the name of the Lord; Blessed be the kingdom of our father David that cometh; Hosanna in the highest."—11. And he entered into Jerusalem, into the temple; and having viewed all things round about, when now the eventide was come, he went out to Bethania with the twelve.

Luke 19:29. And it came to pass when he was come nigh to Bethphage and Bethania unto the Mount called Olivet, he sent two of his disciples,—30. Saying: "Go into the town which is over against you; at your entering into which, you shall find the colt of an ass tied, on which no man ever hath sitten; loose him and bring him hither.—31. And if any man shall ask you: Why do you loose him? You shall say thus unto him: Because the Lord hath need of his service."—32. And they that were sent went their way, and found the colt standing, as he had said unto them.—33. And as they were loosing the colt, the owners thereof said to them: "Why loose you the colt?"—34. But they said: "Because the Lord hath need of him."—35. And they brought him to Jesus. And casting their garments on the colt, they set Jesus thereon.—36. And as he went, they spread their clothes underneath in the way.—37. And when he was now coming near the descent of Mount Olivet, the whole multitude of his disciples began with joy to praise God with a loud voice for all the mighty works they had seen,—38. Saying: "Blessed be the king who cometh in the name of the Lord, peace in heaven, and glory on high."—39. And some of the Pharisees from amongst the multitude said to him: "Master, rebuke thy disciples."—40. To whom he said: "I say to you, that if these shall hold their peace, the stones will cry out."—41. And when he drew near, seeing the city, he wept over it, saying:—42. "If thou also hast known, and that in this thy day, the things that are to thy peace, but now they are hidden from thy eyes.—43. For the days shall come upon thee; and the enemies shall cast a trench about thee, and compass thee round, and straiten thee on every side;—44. And beat thee flat to the ground, and thy children who are in thee, and they shall not leave in thee a stone upon a stone; because thou hast not known the time of thy visitation."

Matt. 21:1. And when they drew nigh to Jerusalem, and were come to Bethphage, unto Mount Olivet; then Jesus sent two disciples,—2. Saying to them:

"Go ye into the village that is over against you, and immediately you shall find an ass tied, and a colt with her; loose them and bring them to me.—3. And if any man shall say anything to you, say ye, that the Lord hath need of them; and forthwith he will let them go."—4. Now all this was done that it might be fulfilled which was spoken by the prophet, saying:—5. "Tell ye the daughter of Sion: Behold thy king cometh to thee, meek, and sitting upon an ass and a colt the foal of her that is used to the yoke."—6. And the disciples going did as Jesus commanded them.—7 And they brought the ass and the colt; and laid their garments upon them, and made him sit thereon.—8. And a very great multitude spread their garments in the way; and others cut boughs from the trees, and strewed them in the way;—9. And the multitudes that went before, and that followed, cried, saying: "Hosanna to the Son of David; Blessed is he that cometh in the name of the Lord; Hosanna in the highest."—10. And when he was come into Jerusalem, the whole city was moved, saying: "Who is this?"—11. And the people said: "This is Jesus the prophet, from Nazareth of Galilee." . . .—14. And there came to him the blind and the lame in the temple; and he healed them.—15. And the chief priests and scribes seeing the wonderful things that he did, and the children crying in the temple, and saying: "Hosanna to the Son of David," were moved with indignation,—16. And said to him: "Hearest thou what these say?" And Jesus said to them: "Yea; have you never read: Out of the mouth of infants and of sucklings thou hast perfected praise?"—17. And leaving them, he went out of the city into Bethania, and remained there.

John 12:12. And on the next day a great multitude, that was come to the festival day, when they had heard that Jesus was coming to Jerusalem,—13. Took branches of palm-trees, and went forth to meet him, and cried: "Hosanna, blessed is he that cometh in the name of the Lord, the king of Israel."—14. And Jesus found a young ass, and sat upon it, as it is written:—15. "Fear not, daughter of Sion; behold, thy king cometh sitting on an ass's colt."—16. These things his disciples did not know at the first; but when Jesus was glorified, then they remembered that these things were written of him; and that they had done these things to him.—17. The multitude therefore gave testimony, which was with him when he called Lazarus out of the grave, and raised him from the dead.—18. For which reason also the people came to meet him; because they heard that he had done this miracle.—19. The Pharisees therefore said among themselves: "Do you see that we prevail nothing? Behold, the whole world is gone after him."

On the day following the Sabbath our Saviour and His disciples left Bethania, and went to Jerusalem. This walk ended by becoming a most glorious entry into the city, a real triumphal procession. This fact is of the greatest importance, and this day is certainly the most glorious one in the mortal life of Jesus.

1. OUR SAVIOUR MANIFESTS HIS POWER AND GLORY IN THIS TRIUMPHAL ENTRY

Our Saviour is determined to show His power today, and for once to take His place as Lord and Master. This power and glory are especially shown in three points.

First, in the outward display of pomp and power. He has started on the road to Jerusalem with His disciples. But today He will not go on foot, as His poverty usually obliges Him to do. As soon as

He is a little way out of Bethania, He commands two of His disciples to go on ahead as far as Bethphage and bring Him an ass that was tied up there with her foal. If the owner made any objection, they were to say: "The Lord hath need of them." This was done (Matt. 21:23; Mark 11:1–6; Luke 19:29–34). In place of a horse-cloth and saddle the disciples threw their garments over the animals' backs, and Jesus mounted the foal and had the ass led riderless by His side (Matt. 21:7; Mark 11:7; Luke 19:35). Probably the disciples walked in procession with Jesus in their midst, and the people in the vicinity followed. In their enthusiasm they spread their garments as a carpet on the road (an act always considered a great mark of devotion and veneration; cf. IV Kings 9:13), and also cut boughs from the trees and strewed them in the way (Matt. 21:8; Mark 11:8). As they all descended the Mount of Olives together, the disciples and the people in front and in the rear broke out with one accord into the enthusiastic cry: "Hosanna to the Son of David! Blessed be the king who cometh in the name of the Lord, and blessed be the kingdom of our father David that cometh! Peace in heaven, and glory on high! Hosanna!" (Matt. 21:9; Mark 11:9, 10; Luke 19:37, 38.) As soon as the pilgrims encamped around Jerusalem saw the procession and heard the song of praise, they caught up the enthusiasm, went in crowds to meet our Lord, broke boughs from the palm-trees, and joined in the cry: "Hosanna, blessed is he that cometh in the name of the Lord, the king of Israel!" (John 12:13.) Thus a procession of almost interminable length approached the city in a state of indescribable enthusiasm, and entered, as it seems, not by the nearest (the Golden) gate, but by some other, so as to traverse the whole city. This created great excitement, and everyone began to ask who it was that was entering in this way. They were told in reply that it was "Jesus the prophet, from Nazareth in Galilee" (Matt. 21:10, 11). Our Lord now entered the Temple and healed blind and lame people, whilst children (whether those in the service of the Temple or others is not recorded) broke out afresh into the cry: "Hosanna to the Son of David" (Matt. 21:14, 15). Then He "viewed all things round about" the Temple, not as a pilgrim come to the feast, but as a son surveying his father's house (Matt. 11:11).

Even as regards the exterior His entry was a glorious one; but it acquires still greater importance when we come to consider its signification. It was not a mere political demonstration, but a religious one. It was a real pilgrimage, a procession, a solemn recognition of the miracles of Jesus, His proclamation as King and Messias, and the solemn act by which He took possession of the city and Temple. This was especially indicated by the carrying and waving of palms, olive and myrtle boughs (I Mach. 13:51; II Mach. 10:7), and by the singing of the solemn responses: "Hosanna! Blessed is he that cometh in the name of the Lord!" (Ps. 117:26.) These songs and ceremonies were a part of the Feast of Tabernacles, which was entirely a Messianic feast, and they expressed the formal acclamation and greeting of the longed-for heir of David's throne. For this reason the Evangelists tell us that the disciples broke into loud praise of God for all the miracles they had seen (Luke 19:37), and that the people gave Him this testimony because they heard that He had wrought the miracle of the raising of Lazarus (John 12:17, 18). This triumphal procession was the literal fulfilment of the great prophecy of Zacharias, that the Messias would come to Sion "poor, and riding upon an ass and upon a colt the foal of an ass" (Zach. 9:9). This beast of burden had not carried anyone before, because it was to do a sacred service (Num. 19:2; Deut. 21:3; I Kings 6:7). The holy Fathers also regard this circumstance as indicative of the rule of the Messias over the Gentile world. The foal that carries Him is the symbol of heathendom, whilst the old ass represents Judaism. Our holy Church says on Palm Sunday that these palms and olives also signified the victory of the Redeemer over the prince of death. The great significance of this procession was not to dawn upon the Apostles until later (John 12:16).

Lastly, the glory of this triumph is enhanced by the cause which brought it about. It is no other than our Saviour Himself, His Person, and the power of His grace and Godhead, that have been so gloriously manifested in miraculous works. He comes without an army, without treasures, without armor or war-horse. But with Him comes the Holy Ghost with His inspirations of grace, and today His sway is undisputed. The enthusiasm passes on from the disciples to the people, and no one interferes. Even Pilate and his double garrison, usually so mistrustful of every public demonstration on the Feast of the Pasch, do not stir. The Pharisees cannot prevent it. In vain do they come up to our Saviour at the foot of the Mount of Olives, and, annoyed at the cries of "Hosanna," demand of Him to forbid His disciples to continue; in vain do the chief priests and scribes rebuke Him for permitting the unseemly cries of the children in the Temple; He merely replies: "If these (the disciples and the children) shall hold their peace, the stones will cry out" (Luke 19:39, 40), and reminds them of the prophecy: "Out of the mouth of infants and sucklings Thou hast perfected praise" (Matt. 21:16). They themselves are forced to acknowledge that nothing is of any use, "the whole world is gone after Him" (John 12:9). This triumphal procession intimidated His enemies and made them desist from their plan of seizing Jesus during the days of the feast (Matt. 26:5). It was certainly a glorious day. Never yet had High Priest or king had such a triumph, and the glory of the day was entirely our Lord's own work.

2. WHY OUR SAVIOUR CELEBRATES THIS TRIUMPH

The reasons why our Saviour celebrates this triumph are as follows.

First, it had been prophesied that the Messias would take possession of the city and Temple in this manner (Zach. 9:9). Indeed, Jerusalem and its Temple are always the scene of the Messianic revelations, and for this reason all the Evangelists give such a detailed and full account of this incident.

Secondly, our Saviour wished to deprive His enemies of their last pretext for unbelief. They were always expecting a Messias to come with power and glory, and could not imagine Him otherwise. Now they had Him thus. He also wished to frighten them from carrying out their murderous plans. He had told them Himself that they would not see Him in Jerusalem again until people cried to Him: "Blessed is he that cometh in the name of the Lord!" (Luke 13:35.) This triumphal entry was a great grace for them, and their last visitation; in very truth a blessed day, their day, as our Saviour Himself says (Luke 19:42).

Thirdly, He intended to prove that His future Passion and Death were voluntary and of His own free choice. A man who held such sway over the minds of the people could also hold his own against his enemies. This entry was His answer to the question whether He would appear at the feast and to the order to give information of His whereabouts, that He might be arrested (John 11:56), and also to their determination to kill Him (John 11:53). The tables were turned, and today their lives were in His hands.

Lastly, our Saviour wished to add to the disgrace of His Death by the contrast with the glory of this triumph, and therefore He chose for the scene of His Passion Jerusalem, and for the time the Paschal Feast, thus bringing His shameful Death into close proximity, as regards both time and place, to the splendor of this triumphal procession. In the same city, and by the same people who were now the witnesses and instruments of His exaltation, it was His will to suffer and die. The great and wonderful spirit of Jesus makes shame His glory and glory His shame. He takes possession of the city, that He may be crucified in it and by its people.

3. HOW OUR SAVIOUR CELEBRATES THIS TRIUMPH

Outwardly our Saviour celebrates this triumph with great modesty, humility and amiability. He comes, as had been prophesied of Him, without any vain, warlike pomp, simple, gentle, riding upon an ass; He comes as beseems His character of Prince of Peace and King of God's priestly people, who are "not to put their trust in horses and chariots, but in the Name of God"; He comes as all the prophets and priests and kings of good times had come; He comes as Priest, to found His kingdom of peace by the arts of peace and not of war, by humility, meekness and poverty. Not even the animal He rides nor the outward equipment of the procession is His own property. But what He wills is given Him; the love of His subjects provides Him with everything.

Interiorly also our Saviour celebrates this triumph very humbly. He knows the nothingness of all temporal greatness and glory. Over these very palms that are now trampled under foot by the ass He rides, He will soon be dragged from one judge to another, and finally to the place of crucifixion. The same people who now cry "Hosanna" will shout a few days later: "Away with Him! crucify Him!" He saw quite plainly, too, how everything proceeded from Himself and His grace, and therefore He did not take pride in the homage and honor paid to Him. Further, He celebrated His triumph with great compassion for the unhappy city and its inhabitants, so that He began to weep, lamenting their blindness and the punishment that was soon to overtake them. He described this punishment in brief but striking words (Luke 19:41–44). From the Mount of Olives He could see the city and Temple glittering in all their glory in the rays of the morning sun, and in spirit He saw vividly how those walls would be blackened, broken, and leveled to the ground; He saw the pretty, fresh-cheeked children who now ran singing by His side, lying bleeding, charred, and multilated corpses in the streets of the stormed city; He saw the magnificent sanctuary reduced by flames to a heap of débris. From the very place where He now was, Titus led the siege and sent his legions to storm the city. Our Lord saw all this, and His grief and compassion forced tears and sighs from Him even in the midst of the honors and joys of the triumphal procession. Lastly, He celebrated His triumph with a keen anguish, caused by the thought of His approaching Passion and Death. Everything reminded Him of it: the places by which the procession passed—Gethsemani, Cedron, the streets and palaces where His enemies lurked, nurturing their hate; the participators in His triumph—the people, the disciples, and especially Judas, who was walking beside Him. The procession was a fuel to the fire of the hatred of many, and signs of this were not lacking, e.g. the equivocal question of the citizens, as to who was entering thus (Matt. 21:10), and the open demand of the Pharisees that our Lord should bid the exulting disciples and children be silent (Luke 19:39, 40; Matt. 21:16). It was really for Him more like a funeral procession than a triumph. He suffers Himself to be adorned and led to sacrifice. It was the very day upon which it was customary to take the Paschal lamb from the flock and bring it into the house, decked out with flowers and ribbons.

Such was the day of His entry into Jerusalem. It is a grand reflection of the Passion, life, and destiny of the God-Man. Glory and death, honor and shame, wealth and poverty, joy and an abyss of anguish are interwoven in wondrous contrasts and sharp lines; to some He is light and salvation, to others blindness and perdition. The whole forms a brilliant and glorious introduction to the Passion. Late in the evening our Lord quitted the Temple with the Apostles, and went out to Bethania again (Matt. 21:17; Mark 11:11).

The Fig-tree

Mark 11:12. And the next day when they came out from Bethania, he was hungry.—13. And when he had seen afar off a fig-tree having leaves, he came, if perhaps he might find anything on it; and when he was come to it, he found nothing but leaves; for it was not the time for figs.—14. And answering, he said to it: "May no man hereafter eat fruit of thee any more for ever." And his disciples heard it. . . .—20. And when they passed by in the morning, they saw the fig-tree dried up from the roots.—21. And Peter remembering, said to him: "Rabbi, behold the fig-tree, which thou didst curse, is withered away."—22. And Jesus answering, said to them: "Have the faith of God.—23. Amen I say to you, that whosoever shall say to this mountain: Be thou removed and be cast into the sea, and shall not stagger in his heart, but believe that whatsoever he saith shall be done, it shall be done unto him.—24. Therefore I say unto you, all things, whatsoever you ask when ye pray, believe that you shall receive, and they shall come unto you.—25. And when you shall stand to pray, forgive, if you have aught against any man; that your Father also, who is in heaven, may forgive you your sins.—26. But if you will not forgive, neither will your Father, that is in heaven, forgive you your sins."

MATT. 21:18. And in the morning returning into the city, he was hungry.—19. And seeing a certain fig-tree by the wayside, he came to it; and found nothing on it but leaves only, and said to it: "May no fruit grow on thee henceforward for ever"; and immediately the fig-tree withered away.—20. And the disciples seeing it wondered, saying: "How is it presently withered away?"—21. And Jesus answering said to them: "Amen I say to you, if you shall have faith, and stagger not, not only this of the fig-tree shalt thou do, but also if you shall say to this mountain, Take up and cast thyself into the sea, it shall be done.—22. And all things whatsoever you shall ask in prayer believing, you shall receive." . . .—6:14. "For if you will forgive men their offences; your heavenly Father will forgive you also your offences.—15. But if you will not forgive men; neither will your Father forgive you your offences."

1. CAUSE OF THE CURSE

Early on Monday morning our Lord went with the disciples from Bethania to Jerusalem, and on the way began to feel hungry (Mark 11:12; Matt. 21:18). Seeing a fig-tree by the roadside a little distance off, He went towards it, in order to gather fruit and satisfy His hunger. But He found nothing but leaves, and therefore cursed the tree (Mark 11:13; Matt. 21:19).

The immediate cause was therefore the barrenness of the tree, together with our Lord's hunger. But this hunger is evidently of two kinds. First, the real, actual, bodily hunger, in the usual sense of the word. From this we may see that He did not think much about His bodily wants. There seems to have been no banquet on the preceding day, Jerusalem had prepared none for Him; He had very likely passed the night in prayer, and now, the first thing in the morning, He is on His way to the Temple, fasting, without having satisfied His need of nourishment. But His hunger is also a mystical one; He hungers for the conversion and salvation of the Israelite nation and the entire human race. Without this interpretation it is impossible to explain the miracle. We are told that it was not the time for figs (Mark 11:13). As a matter of fact they ripen in June and again in August, and sometimes the fruit remains on the tree till winter. But now, in March or at the beginning of April, it was certainly not the season for figs, and our Lord knew well that there were none. And in any case, why should He make the tree wither away, simply because it bore no fruit? He wished to set up at the very gate of the city a warning, that the people might see how unfruitful they were, and what a punishment awaited them. Probably the tree never bore any fruit at all, for on good fig-trees one can usually see the fruit before the leaves, and the contrary is a sign that they are growing wild. So the tree stood by the roadside, pretending to bear fruit and yet bearing nothing but leaves, a true picture of Israel, which, though it stood on the path of God's mercies and institutions of grace, and had been tended by our Lord Himself for three years with much labor and trouble, yet bore nothing but the leaves of a mere outward observance of the law. On the strength of this it was puffed up with immoderate pride, and pushed away the healing hand of God. Israel is often represented in Scripture by the symbol of a fig-tree (Isa. 6:13; Ez. 19:10; Osee 10:1; Mich. 7:1).

2. THE MIRACULOUS CURSE

The miraculous anathema was simply as follows: Our Saviour said to the tree: "May no fruit grow on thee henceforward for ever" (Matt. 21:19), and: "May no man hereafter eat fruit of thee any more for ever" (Mark 11:14); and at the same instant the tree withered away to the very roots (Matt. 21:19; Mark 11:20). Usually a tree of this kind remains green for a time even after being cut down, for it does not need much nourishment and grows very easily, even in the dust of the high-roads. Now it had withered away in an instant, evidently by a miracle. And so the disciples considered it to be, as they saw next day that it was quite dead.

This miracle is the type of Israel's unfruitfulness till the end of the world, when the remnant of the people will be converted. Some, indeed many, of the Israelites received the faith, but the nation as such has never been converted or borne fruits of salvation. It had not kept the winter fruit of ancient times, nor yet begun to bear any in the spring; it had only leaves to show, which did not satisfy God's desires. It was felled at length by the axe of the Romans, as our Saviour had foretold on the preceding day (Luke 19:43), because it had borne no fruit as it could and should have done, but only feigned to do so.

3. MANIFESTATION OF THE MIRACLE, AND OUR LORD'S INSTRUCTION CONCERNING IT

On Tuesday morning our Saviour went along the same road with His disciples, and they saw the tree completely withered (Matt. 21:20). They had heard the curse on the preceding day (Mark 11:14), and now they recollected it. Peter, filled with astonishment, said: "Rabbi, behold the fig-tree which thou didst curse is withered away" (Mark 11:21; Matt. 21:20); and the Apostles asked in surprise: "How is it presently (i.e. at once) withered away?" (Matt. 21:20.) Thus the miracle was made manifest.

Our Saviour does not enter into a particular explanation of the miracle, but profits by the opportunity to give a practical lesson upon faith. He exhorts the Apostles to "have faith" (Mark 11:22), and gives them, first, motives for this; secondly, He specifies the condition upon which their faith will be efficacious. As a motive He adduces the power of faith, which is so great that it can work miracles like this and even apparently greater ones, such as moving mountains (perhaps our Lord here pointed to the Mount of Olives; cf. Matt. 21:21; Mark 11:23), and can moreover ensure the granting of our prayers (Matt. 21:22; Mark 11:24). But these prayers must be full of trust (Mark 11:23; Matt. 21:22), and made with a just and forgiving spirit towards our neighbor (Mark 11:25, 26; Matt. 6:14, 15).

This miracle is the eloquent expression of Jesus' longing for the salvation of the nation, and a silent but impressive warning of the judgment that awaits it, if it persists in its unbelief. It is, as it were, the continuation of the parable of the barren fig-tree, which He had lately brought forward with the same intention (Luke 13:6); He concludes it here by a striking phenomenon of nature, of a similar kind. Indeed, our Lord seems able to do nothing now but preach faith by threatening punishment, as His words reveal more and more clearly. A few months ago He had said in Peraea: "Your house shall be left to you desolate" (Luke 13:35); in the parable of the ten pounds the nobleman gives orders for his enemies to be killed before him (Luke 19:27); in His lament during the triumphal procession He depicts the ruin of the city to the people in vivid outlines (Luke 19:43 etc.); and now He holds out the prospect of the punishment of eternal barrenness, and plants a token of it before the gate of the city, just as the prophets had repeatedly made known God's decree to the people under material figures (Ez. 4:4; 12:5; Osee 1:2; Jer. 32).

The Purification of the Temple

Luke 19:45. And entering into the temple, he began to cast out them that sold therein and them that bought,—46. Saying to them: "It is written: My house is the house of prayer. But you have made it a den of thieves."—47. And he was teaching daily in the temple. And the chief priests and the scribes and the rulers of the people sought to destroy him:—48. And they found not what to do to him. For all the people was very attentive to hear him. . . .—20:1. And it came to pass that on one of the days, as he was teaching the people in the temple and preaching the gospel, the chief priests and the scribes with the ancients met together,—2. And spoke to him saying: "Tell us, by what authority dost thou these things? Or: Who is he that hath given thee this authority?"—3. And Jesus answering, said to them: "I will also ask you one thing. Answer me:—4. The baptism of John was it from heaven, or of men?"—5. But they thought within themselves, saying: "If we shall say, From heaven, he will say: Why then did you not believe him?—6. But if we say, Of men, the whole people will stone us; for they are persuaded that John was a prophet."—7. And they answered that they knew not whence it was.—8. And Jesus said to them: "Neither do I tell you by what authority I do these things."

MARK 11:15. And they come to Jerusalem. And when he was entered into the temple, he began to cast out them that sold and bought in the temple; and overthrew the tables of the money-changers, and the chairs of them that sold doves; —16. And he suffered not that any man should carry a vessel through the temple: —17. And he taught, saying to them: "Is it not written: My house shall be called the house of prayer to all nations? But you have made it a den of thieves."—18. Which when the chief priests and the scribes had heard, they sought how they might destroy him; for they feared him, because the whole multitude was in admiration at his doctrine.—19. And when evening was come, he went forth out of the city. . . .—27. And they come again to Jerusalem. And when he was walking in the temple, there come to him the chief priests and the scribes and the ancients; —28. And they say to him: "By what authority dost thou these things? And who hath given thee this authority that thou shouldst do these things?"—29. And Jesus answering said to them: "I will also ask you one word, and answer you me: and I will tell you by what authority I do these things.—30. The baptism of John was it from heaven, or from men? Answer me."—31. But they thought with themselves saying: "If we say, From heaven, he will say: Why then did you not believe him?—32. If we say, From men, we fear the people, for all men counted John that he was a prophet indeed."—33. And they answering say to Jesus: "We know not." And Jesus answering saith to them: "Neither do I tell you by what authority I do these things."

MATT. 21:12. And Jesus went into the temple of God, and cast out all them that sold and bought in the temple, and overthrew the tables of the money-changers, and the chairs of them that sold doves;—13. And he saith to them: "It is written: My house shall be called the house of prayer; but you have made it a den of thieves." . . .—23. And when he was come into the temple there came to him, as he was teaching, the chief priests and ancients of the people, saying: "By what authority dost thou these things? And who hath given thee this authority?"—24. Jesus answering said to them: "I also will ask you one word; which if you shall tell me, I will also tell you by what authority I do these things.—25. The baptism of John whence was it? From heaven, or from men?" But they thought within themselves, saying:—26. "If we shall say, From heaven, he will say to us: Why then did you not believe him? But if we shall say, From men, we are afraid of the multitude; for all held John as a prophet."—27. And answering Jesus they said: "We know not." He also said to them: "Neither do I tell you by what authority I do these things.—28. But what think you? A certain man had two sons, and coming to the first, he said: Son, go work today in my vineyard.—29. And he answering, said: I will not. But afterwards, being moved with repentance, he went.—30. And coming to the other, he said in like manner. And he answering, said: I go, Sir, and he went not;—31. Which of the two did the father's will?" They say to him: "The first." Jesus saith to them: "Amen I say to you, that the publicans and the harlots shall go into the kingdom of God before you.—32. For John came to you in the way of justice, and you did not believe him; but the publicans and the harlots believed him; but you seeing it, did not even afterwards repent, that you might believe him."

Early on Monday morning our Saviour came into the Temple, and immediately began to drive out the buyers and sellers.

1. OUR SAVIOUR PURIFIES THE TEMPLE

In the first place we must see how our Lord proceeds in the purification of His Temple. First, with prudence and moderation. Yesterday, after His entry, He had inspected the whole building (Mark 11:11). He saw with grief the same disorders and profanations from which He had purged it three years previously. The lowest class of market people had again established themselves in the sacred courts, in consequence of the apathy, indifference, and avarice of the High Priest and Temple officials. He had probably expressed His displeasure and threatened them with punishment on the preceding day. He now sees that this had been of no avail, and so He proceeds to forcible measures. Secondly, He sets about the purification with increased severity. He overturns everything and drives out the vendors with their stands (Matt. 21:12; Luke 19:45); indeed, He even forbids vessels to be carried across the Temple grounds, and effectually prevents this being done (Mark 11:15, 16). Probably the people took a short cut through the Temple from one part of the city to another, for convenience' sake; but this was against the Temple laws. Lastly, He performed the purification with impressive earnestness, majesty and intrepidity, exclaiming that according to Scripture His House was to be called "the house of prayer for all nations" (Isa. 56:7), but they had made it a den of thieves (Jer. 7:11). Probably the priests and rulers of the Temple let the outer court on hire, as a market-place for the animals destined for sacrifice. Our Saviour rightly showed more vehemence and threatened more severely than He had done at the first purification of the Temple (John 2:16).

The meaning of this purification was highly important, especially under these circumstances, and for three reasons. First, because it was a manifestation and exemplification of His mission. He simply asserts Himself here as Lord of the Temple and of all religion. He calls it His House. His task was to purify, fulfil and perfect the ancient religion (Matt. 5:17). He had begun His public ministry with the purification of the Temple, as a symbol of His vocation; and now He closes it with the same. Secondly, our Saviour gave His enemies by this act a new and potent reason for compassing His destruction. The chief priests and Temple officials regarded His step as an encroachment upon their office; He exposed their avarice and want of faith, at a time when so many pilgrims were there for the feast. They could not let this pass; either He or they must suffer for this, and therefore they sought to bring about His ruin (Mark 11:18; Luke 19:47). What He had said three years before—"Destroy this temple" (John 2:19)—is now about to be fulfilled. The third reason why the purification is so important is that it shows up the very climax of unbelief and hypocrisy on the part of the Israelites, in suffering the Temple to be thus profaned, opposing the Restorer of its honor, and branding His proceedings as presumption. On the other hand the purification of the Temple is a type and menace of the rejection of Israel. The Temple cries for vengeance, and they deserve to be cast out of it like the charlatans they suffer to trade there. It is not without purpose that our Saviour quotes the passage of Jeremias (Jer. 7:11) in which the prophet reproaches the Jews with their blasphemous boasting and reliance upon the Temple, whilst they profane it by all sorts of sinful abominations and make it a den for their theft and wickedness. Here the prophet also foretells the punishment of the Jews, reminding them of Silo and the tribe of Ephraim, who had been deprived of the honor of harboring the ark of the covenant and rejected, on account of similar abominations (Jer. 7:12).

2. OUR SAVIOUR IS CALLED TO ACCOUNT BY THE HIGH PRIESTS

As a matter of fact the chief priests did not let the deed pass unnoticed. For the moment they may have been surprised and at a loss what to do. But they recovered, and when our Saviour again appeared in the Temple on Tuesday morning and taught (Luke 21:7, 38), they called Him to account.

They evidently had in view some violent measure against Him, and therefore they called Him to account publicly, in the Temple and before the people, as He was walking about and giving instruction (Matt. 21:23; Mark 11:28; Luke 20:1). Moreover, they do it solemnly and officially, through a deputation taken from all the leading circles, chief priests, scribes, and ancients (Luke 20:1; Mark 11:28; Matt. 21:23), that is to say in the name of the

Sanhedrim, and probably they approached in a long procession, to make it very conspicuous; and lastly, they did it in a manner full of craft and arrogance. At the first purification of the Temple they had asked for a miracle to prove His authority (John 2:18); now they want to know by what authority He does these things (Luke 20:2; Mark 11:28; Matt. 21:3), whether He brings about His triumphal entry and purifies the Temple as prophet or Messias, in His own right or by God's commission. He might answer what He pleased; they thought they could entrap Him now, whether He said He did it of His own power, or as God's representative. Thus they were aiming at His destruction.

3. OUR SAVIOUR'S ANSWER

Our Saviour replied by a counter-question, as to whence John's baptism had been (Matt. 21:24, 25; Mark 11:29, 30; Luke 20:3, 4). The answer was evasive, because their question had been put insincerely. Our Lord's question was well framed because it obliged them to answer themselves and pronounce their own judgment; it was also clear because St. John had spoken plainly concerning the Person and authority of Jesus (Matt. 3:12; Luke 3:17). The "baptism of John" is here equivalent to "John's mission," and if the chief priests regarded it as proceeding from God, they had the answer to their question.

The priests would not recognize the divine origin of John's mission, for their own sakes, nor yet deny it publicly, on account of the people; and so they found a way out of the question by replying that they did not know (Matt. 21:25–27; Mark 11:31–33; Luke 20:5–7). The answer was cowardly and mean, a lie (cf. John 1:19) and a formal break with the past and with the prophets, of whom John was the last. To this very day Judaism still abides by this answer, "We know not."

It was only right that our Lord should refuse to give them information concerning the authority by which He purified the Temple (Matt. 21:27; Mark 11:33; Luke 20:8). He tells them that, since they had not troubled themselves about John's mission, they must give up questioning Him about His. He takes this opportunity first to hold up to the leaders of the people and to all Israel, as in a mirror, their spirit of unbelief and hypocritical ignorance; and secondly, to announce to them their rejection on this account. He depicts their spirit in the little parable of the two sons, one of whom says he will go to work in the vineyard as his father wishes, but does not do it; the other on the contrary declares that he will not go, and nevertheless does so (Matt. 21:28–31). So the leaders of Israel acted. They always proclaimed themselves obedient and despised sinners, whilst in reality they were always disobedient, and the sinners repented and became obedient. So it was in the time of John, who, fully conscious of the aim and end of the Old Covenant, showed and taught the "way of justice," by believing in Christ, proclaiming His advent, doing homage to Him, and preaching penance. John's mission was a ratification of our Lord's, and thus He showed them the way to acquire information concerning its nature. The priests had attacked John with the very same question (John 1:25) which they now put to our Saviour, and had not believed him (Matt. 11:18) any more than they now believed Christ (John 8:48). But the publicans and harlots had gone before them into the kingdom of heaven (Matt. 21:31) and had done penance (Matt. 21:32), just as they now also believe in Christ and do penance at His word. Here our Saviour only leaves the priests to guess at the punishment of their unbelief (which arises from immorality), but in the following parable He states it expressly.

In this mystery our Lord displays three glorious qualities. The first of these is extraordinary intrepidity. Under these circumstances the purification of the Temple was really fatal to Him, and was bound to raise the hatred of the whole priesthood to the highest pitch. The second is His zeal for the honor of God and His House. With the exception of the incident at His arrest, this is the only case in which our Saviour makes use of His exterior power and terrifying force. And He falls a victim to this zeal (Ps. 68:10). The third quality is His intellectual superiority and adroitness. Cunning as His enemies are, they find in Him a superiority of mind before which they must bow, and retire abashed. It is touching, too, to hear how He appeals at the last hour to John's testimony, evidently because their positions and the questions addressed to them both were so similar, and because the stubbornness and corruption of unbelief were reflected in these two events better than in anything else. With John our Lord begins His mission, and with John He concludes it.

The Parable of the Husbandmen

Luke 20:9. And he began to speak to the people this parable: "A certain man planted a vineyard and let it out to husbandmen; and he was abroad for a long time.—10. And at the season he sent a servant to the husbandmen, that they should give him of the fruit of the vineyard. Who beating him sent him away empty.—11. And again he sent another servant. But they beat him also, and treating him reproachfully, sent him away empty.—12. And again he sent the third; and they wounded him also, and cast him out.—13. Then the lord of the vineyard said: What shall I do? I will send my beloved son; it may be, when they see him, they will reverence him.—14. Whom when the husbandmen saw, they thought within themselves, saying: This is the heir, let us kill him, that the inheritance may be ours.—15. So casting him out of the vineyard, they killed him. What therefore will the lord of the vineyard do to them?—16. He will come, and will destroy these husbandmen, and will give the vineyard to others." Which they hearing, said to him: "God forbid."—17. But he looking on them, said: "What is this then that is written: The stone which the builders rejected, the same is become the head of the corner?—18. Whosoever shall fall upon that stone, shall be bruised; and upon whomsoever it shall fall, it will grind him to powder."—19. And the chief priests and the scribes sought to lay hands on him the same hour; but they feared the people: for they knew that he spoke this parable to them.

Mark 12:1. And he began to speak to them in parables: "A certain man planted a vineyard and made a hedge about it, and dug a place for the wine-vat and built a tower, and let it to husbandmen, and went into a far country.—2. And at the season he sent to the husbandmen a servant to receive of the husbandmen, of the fruit of the vineyard.—3. Who having laid hands on him, beat him, and sent him away empty.—4. And again he sent to them another servant; and him they wounded in the head, and used him reproachfully.—5. And again he sent another, and him they killed; and many others, of whom some they beat, and others they killed.—6. Therefore having yet one son, most dear to him; he also sent him unto them last of all, saying: They will reverence my son.—7. But the husbandmen said one to another: This is the heir; come, let us kill him, and the inheritance shall be ours.—8. And laying hold on him, they killed him; and cast him out of the vineyard.—9. What therefore will the lord of the vineyard do? He will come and destroy those husbandmen; and will give the vineyard to others.—10. And have you not read this Scripture: The stone which the builders rejected, the same is made the head of the corner;—11. By the Lord has this been done, and it is wonderful in our eyes?"—12. And they sought to lay hands on him; but they feared the people; for they knew that he spoke this parable to them. And leaving him they went their way.

Matt. 21:33. "Hear ye another parable: There was a man an householder who planted a vineyard, and made a hedge round about it, and dug in it a press, and built a tower, and let it out to husbandmen, and went into a strange country.—34. And when the time of the fruits drew nigh, he sent his servants to the husbandmen, that they might receive the fruits thereof.—35. And the husbandmen, laying hands on his servants, beat one, and killed another, and stoned another.—36. Again he sent other servants more than the former; and they did to them in like manner.—37. And last of all he sent to them his son, saying: They will reverence my son.—38. But the husbandmen seeing the son, said among themselves: This is the heir, come, let us kill him, and we shall have his inheritance.—39. And taking him they cast him forth out of the vineyard and killed him.—40. When therefore the lord of the vineyard shall come, what will he do to those husbandmen?"—41. They say to him: "He will bring those evil men to an evil end; and will let out his vineyard to other husbandmen, that shall render him the fruit in due season."—42. Jesus said to them: "Have you never read in the Scriptures: The stone which the builders rejected, the same is become the head of the corner; by the Lord this hath been done, and it is wonderful in our eyes?—43. Therefore I say to you, that the kingdom of God shall be taken from you, and shall be given to a nation yielding the fruits thereof.—44. And whosoever shall fall on this stone, shall be broken; but on whomsoever it shall fall, it shall grind him to powder."—45. And when the chief priests and Pharisees had heard his parables, they knew that he spoke of them.—46. And seeking to lay hands on him, they feared the multitudes; because they held him as a prophet.

The following parable seems to have followed immediately upon the preceding discourse.

1. AIM OF THE PARABLE

The parable of the vine-dressers continues the parable of the two sons under another and more familiar figure, supplements it and enlarges upon it, especially on two points. The first of these is the unbelieving spirit and obstinacy of the Jewish people. In this parable these sentiments find an outlet in mortal hatred and a plan of deicide.

The second point is the corresponding punishment. In the preceding parable it is only symbolized in the expulsion of the buyers and sellers, and in the parable of the two sons merely hinted at, in the statement that sinners will go before the leaders of Israel into the kingdom of heaven. But here the taking away of the kingdom from Israel and its transfer to others, together with the destruction of the stubborn nation, are quite plainly expressed.

2. DEVELOPMENT OF THE PARABLE

The parable deals with three points.

The first point describes God's loving solicitude for the Israelite nation, to whom He confides the means necessary for accomplishing the plan of Redemption. These means and Israel itself are represented under the well-known symbol of a vineyard, which occurs so often in Holy Scripture (Isa. 5:1 seq.; Jer. 2:21; Zach. 8:12), and with which all were acquainted. In the new Temple there hung at the entrance to the Holy of Holies an enormous golden vine, symbolizing the House of Israel. God had furnished this vineyard with everything desirable for its unity and independence (the hedge of the law), its protection and ornament (the tower—Temple and hierarchy), and its practical utility (the winepress; Matt. 21:33; Mark 12:1; Luke 20:9). This vineyard, the entire means of salvation, He gave over to husbandmen:

priests, lawyers, princes (Isa. 62:6), and people, that they might manage it and enjoy the profit of it, on condition of keeping it in order and delivering the fruits at the legally appointed time (Lev. 19:25). These fruits are honor, gratitude, obedience, and restitution if the lord of the vineyard returns and wishes to take over the management of it himself.

The second point describes the behavior of the husbandmen (the Israelites) towards the lord and the messengers sent by him to receive the produce. The husbandmen refused to deliver up anything; they ill-treated, chased away, and even killed the messengers, who were no others than the prophets. They banished Elias, killed Isaias, beat and imprisoned Jeremias, murdered John, and stained all Jerusalem with the blood of the prophets (Luke 13:34). It is the whole sad history of Israel's ingratitude for God's mercies (Luke 20:10–12; Mark 12:2–5; Matt. 21:34–36). At last He sends His only-begotten Son, expecting them to reverence Him. They know Him, know that He is the heir of the vineyard and of the House of David; and yet, full of envy and wickedness, they seize Him, cast Him out of the vineyard of the Israelite communion (by their proscription of Him), and kill Him (Hebr. 13:12). God's beloved Son has really "come unto His own" (John 1:11) in the Incarnation, and they ask Him for His authorization and are now about to put Him to death (Matt. 21:37–39; Mark 12:6–8; Luke 20:13–15).

The third point is the punishment. It is introduced by the question as to what the lord of the vineyard will do to these unfaithful husbandmen (Matt. 21:40; Mark 12:9; Luke 20:15), which our Saviour addresses to His hearers, the priests and people (Luke 20:9; Mark 12:1). They themselves, i.e. the hearers, give the answer, and by it pronounce their own sentence. He will destroy these wicked men in a terrible manner, and let the vineyard to others who will deliver the produce in due season (Matt. 21:41; Mark 12:9; Luke 20:16). So the punishment is a double one: destruction, loss of the salutary dispensation and its transfer to others. As some of the people now comprehend that He means them, and the hierarchy in particular, they exclaim: "God forbid" (Luke 20:16). Our Saviour cast a sharp and significant glance at them (Luke 20:17), and confirmed their sentence, repeating His words and adding the prophetic passage which says that "the stone which the builders rejected is become the head of the corner" (Ps. 117:22), and that it will be a "stone of stumbling and a rock of offence . . . a ruin to the inhabitants of Israel" (Isa. 8:14; 28:16; I Peter 2:7). In consequence of Israel's rejection of the corner-stone, the nation ceases to be God's people and the medium of salvation to the world. It collapses. Its vocation passes on to others. Israel itself will stumble and fall by its resistance to the corner-stone (Luke 2:34), and be "ground to powder" by the same in the judgment (Luke 20:17, 18; Mark 12:10, 11; Matt. 21:42–44; cf. also Luke 3:22). The punishment is therefore sure, terrible and just. They have passed their own sentence.

3. EFFECT OF THE PARABLE

The priests and Pharisees now saw that our Lord had been referring to them in the two parables. This enraged them, and they would have laid hands upon Him at once if they had not feared the people, who regarded Him as a prophet. This induced them to abandon their plan, and they went away (Matt. 21:45, 46; Mark 12:12; Luke 20:19).

Such was the result of the formal interview of the priests with our Saviour. Annihilated, but infuriated, the deputation retired before the overpowering truths which the parable cast in their teeth. The parable itself is a masterpiece in its truth, appropriateness, powerful development, and touching purport. Never had our Saviour shown the people and their leaders such a plain and uncompromising picture of their errors and the punishment to come.

The Parable of the Marriage-feast

MATT. 22:1. And Jesus answering, spoke again in parables to them, saying:—2. "The kingdom of heaven is likened to a king, who made a marriage for his son.—3. And he sent his servants to call them that were invited to the marriage; and they would not come.—4. Again he sent other servants, saying: Tell them that were invited: Behold, I have prepared my dinner, my beeves and fatlings are killed, and all things are ready; come ye to the marriage.—5. But they neglected; and went their ways, one to his farm, and another to his merchandise;—6. And the rest laid hands on his servants, and having treated them contumeliously put them to death.—7. But when the king had heard of it, he was angry; and sending his armies he destroyed those murderers, and burned their city.—8. Then he saith to his servants: The marriage indeed is ready, but they that were invited, were not worthy.—9. Go ye therefore into the highways, and as many as you shall find, call to the marriage.—10. And his servants going forth into the ways, gathered together all that they found, both bad and good; and the marriage was filled with guests.—11. And the king went in to see the guests; and he saw there a man who had not on a wedding-garment.—12. And he saith to him: Friend, how camest thou in hither not having on a wedding-garment? But he was silent.—13. Then the king said to the waiters: Bind his hands and feet, and cast him into the exterior darkness; there shall be weeping and gnashing of teeth.—14. For many are called, but few are chosen."

This parable is in appearance very similar to the one related by our Lord in the Pharisee's house in Peraea (Luke 14:16 seq.); but in reality it is quite distinct, and differs from the former parable in three respects.

1. AIM OF THE PARABLE

The aim of the parable in the Pharisee's house was to teach the hearers that a mere desire for the glorious Messianic kingdom, heaven, is not sufficient; in order to attain to it, we must accept our Lord's invitation, and enter the earthly Messianic kingdom, the Church. But this parable is chiefly concerned with the invitation itself, and our Saviour says that Israel will despise it, and will therefore not merely remain outside the Church, but will see it pass on to the Gentiles and suffer temporal destruction itself. This is the principal aim of the parable, and as far as that is concerned it is merely the repetition, continuation, development and confirmation of the one immediately preceding it.

But there is also a secondary aim, with reference to the Gentiles who enter the Church in place of the Jews. To them also our Saviour utters the warning that they can only remain in the Church and reach their heavenly goal if they fulfil the necessary conditions. Otherwise they too will lose the kingdom. This part of the parable is quite new, the other has received a new form by alteration of the circumstances.

2. DEVELOPMENT OF THE PARABLE

The first part presents, in conformity with its aim, the following new circumstances.

The host is here not merely a rich and influential man, but a king, with armies at his command. The acceptance of the invitation is probably to be regarded as an act of homage to the young king, his son, and therefore the refusal of it is so momentous. This royal host is evidently God the Father, and his son our Saviour (Matt. 22:2). The invitation itself is more pressing than in the former parable, and is also repeated; the king sends his servants twice. These servants are the Apostles (Matt. 22:3, 4). The invitation is first issued for the wedding itself, and later on for the actual marriage-feast, which is described (Matt. 22:4). In this the Church is plainly depicted. She is the bridal alliance of Christ with the human race, begun in the Incarnation and completed in heaven. The refusal on the part of the citizens and subjects here proceeds not merely from such unworthy motives as in the other parable—love of pleasure and desire of money-making—but from entirely hostile dispositions, with insult and injury to the king, inasmuch as they ill-treat and kill his servants (Matt. 22:5, 6). This refers to the mortal hostility of the Jews against our Saviour, His prophets and Apostles. Instead of following, they persecute them. The punishment is the complete destruction of the scorners and their city by armies (Matt. 22:7). This refers to the Roman legions, who execute this punishment upon Jerusalem and the people by fire and wholesale massacre (Luke 19:43). So far the parable is only the repetition and enlargement of the preceding one.

In the second part the invitation to the marriage-feast is issued to strangers and homeless wanderers on the high-roads and at the cross-ways; in a word, to everyone without distinction (Matt. 22:9). They accept the invitation, and the marriage is filled (Matt. 22:10). This alludes to the poor Gentiles, who were invited by the Apostles to enter the Church and accepted the invitation (Acts 12:46). Among those who entered was one who had sat down to table without putting on the wedding garment. As the king inspected his wedding company, he remarked the unworthy guest. Fully conscious of his own goodness and the respect due to him, he calls the man sharply to account, has him bound hand and foot and cast into outer darkness, where there is weeping and gnashing of teeth (Matt. 22:11, 12). The punishment is severe, but just, for the guest's behavior is most unworthy, ungrateful and insolent, an affront and an insult to the king. He does not even think it worth the trouble to don a wedding garment. So the culprit can find no excuse, and is dumb at the reproach and sentence (Matt. 22:12). This foretells that among the guests admitted some may and will be unworthy, and at the same time it is a threat of the punishment which will follow such unworthiness (Matt. 13:25, 47). Both Jews and Gentiles must fulfil these conditions; the Church and heaven are not given unconditionally. It is not enough to enter the Church by faith; we must combine faith with charity, i.e. put on the wedding garment of sanctifying grace. The people to whom the kingdom is transferred must yield its fruits (Matt. 21:43).

3. THE CONCLUDING SENTENCE

The concluding sentence: "Many are called, but few are chosen" (Matt. 22:14), which expresses the lesson and aim of the whole parable, refers to the Jews, and states that many, indeed all, of them are called to the Church, but only a few will enter it. It concerns the Gentiles only inasmuch as it teaches that even of those who do enter it—of the Gentiles, that is to say—all will not be saved. But our Lord never means to say that the greater part of those who belong to the Church will be damned. Only one among the Gentiles called (in the parable) was found unworthy. The same concluding sentence is found in the parable of the laborers in the vineyard (Matt. 20:16); but here it has another meaning, on account of its different aim. That parable is not immediately concerned with the attainment of salvation in general (for all the laborers receive the penny), but treats of the obtaining of special privileges with regard to it. Among the many who are called and who actually go to heaven, there will be a great difference of rank; some will occupy special posts of honor, and these posts will be distributed in quite a different order from that which we see here below.

In this parable the double punishment of Israel is again foretold in the most decided manner, and the grounds for it are also given. We see here how often our Saviour makes use of parables in order to propound unpleasant and ominous truths, and to bring them home to those whom they concern. It also exemplifies afresh how He makes figures, parables and similitudes that He has already employed, new and attractive by giving them some fresh turn, new aim or circumstances. It is remarkable how our Saviour now, since the parable of the pounds, reveals Himself more and more frequently in His character and attributes as King. These attributes are dignity, lively consciousness of His rank, justice, power, and goodness. They stand out in strong relief in His treatment of the Gentiles also. He receives them with indescribable goodness, as the wedding guests sent Him by His Father, but insists upon acknowledgment of His dignity and appreciation of His goodness. Where these are not forthcoming He administers punishment. The baseness and meanness of the abuse of His kindness on the part of the Gentiles is very well brought out. In this parable we see a confirmation of the truth that only faith combined with charity, or the possession of sanctifying grace, can ensure salvation.

The Coin of Tribute

Luke 20:20. And being upon the watch, they sent spies who should feign themselves just, that they might take hold of him in his words, that they might deliver him up to the authority and power of the governor.—21. And they asked him, saying: "Master, we know that thou speakest and teachest rightly; and thou dost not respect any person, but teachest the way of God in truth;—22. Is it lawful for us to give tribute to Caesar or no?"—23. But he considering their guile, said to them: "Why tempt you me?—24. Show me a penny. Whose image and inscription hath it?" They answering said to him: "Caesar's."—25. And he said to them: "Render therefore to Caesar the things that are Caesar's; and to God the things that are God's."—26. And they could not reprehend his word before the people; and wondering at his answer, they held their peace.

Mark 12:13. And they sent to him some of the Pharisees and of the Herodians, that they should catch him in his words.—14. Who coming, say to him: "Master, we know that thou art a true speaker, and carest not for any man; for thou regardest not the person of men, but teachest the way of God in truth; Is it lawful to give tribute to Caesar, or shall we not give it?"—15. Who knowing their wiliness, saith to them: "Why tempt you me? Bring me a penny that I may see it."—16. And they brought it him. And he saith to them: "Whose is this image and inscription?" They say to him: "Caesar's."—17. And Jesus answering said to them: "Render therefore to Caesar the things that are Caesar's; and to God the things that are God's." And they marveled at him.

Matt. 22:15. Then the Pharisees going, consulted among themselves how to ensnare him in his speech.—16. And they sent to him their disciples with the Herodians, saying: "Master, we know that thou art a true speaker, and teachest the way of God in truth, neither carest thou for any man; for thou dost not regard the person of men.—17. Tell us therefore what dost thou think, is it lawful to give tribute to Caesar, or not?"—18. But Jesus knowing their wickedness, said: "Why do you tempt me, ye hypocrites?—19. Show me the coin of the tribute." And they offered him a penny.—20. And Jesus saith to them: "Whose image and superscription is this?"—21. They say to him: "Caesar's." Then he saith to them: "Render therefore to Caesar the things that are Caesar's; and to God the things that are God's."—22. And hearing this they wondered, and leaving him went their ways.

1. CIRCUMSTANCES THAT OCCASIONED THE TEMPTATION

The chief priests and Pharisees did not dare to lay hands upon our Saviour, for fear of the people. They took counsel together and agreed to surround Him with spies and lay traps for Him, to try if they could not find in His words some pretext for delivering Him up to the authority and power of the Roman government (Luke 20:20; Matt. 22:15).

The tribute question afforded them an opportunity. The Jews practically recognized the supremacy of the Romans, and paid them tribute and taxes. The Emperor struck coins bearing his image, and these were in circulation. Nevertheless the various schools and parties disputed over the theoretical question, whether it was permissible to pay tribute to a foreign ruler and one that was a heathen besides, or whether according to a misconstruction placed upon the law (Deut. 17:15) it was not rather forbidden. The pious Ezechias had paid tribute (IV Kings 18:15); Jeremias warned the people not to rebel against Babylon (Jer. 27:12); Esdras and Nehemias saw no wrong in the Persian supremacy (I Esdr. 7:24; II Esdr. 5:4). The Pharisees and zealots denied the duty, asserting that taxes were due only to God, His Temple, and the priests. The Herodians, who, at any rate outwardly and from policy, held more to the Romans, nevertheless favored the supremacy of Herod, as a more national monarchy, rather than the despotic rule of Pilate. The question more or less concerned the family of Herod. So the Pharisees dragged in the Herodians, who were to be found everywhere, especially now at the time of the feast, in order that in union with them they might overthrow our Saviour. It was not the first time they had made common cause against Him. Their plan, then, was to entrap our Lord by getting Him to give some expression of opinion upon the tax question.

2. DANGER OF THE QUESTION

This was a very wily question in many respects.

First, the question itself was a critical one. It ran thus: "Is it lawful to give tribute to Caesar?" (Matt. 22:17; Luke 20:22.) They push the question of lawfulness into the foreground, a purely speculative one, because they did not wish to appear to contemplate actual refusal of the tax, since this would have got them into difficulties themselves. They only add: "Or shall we not give it?" (Mark 12:14) in quite a casual way, as if it were an after-thought. The question included in its range religion as well as politics, and was a very critical one to answer in every respect. If our Saviour declared that tribute was allowable, He would make enemies of the Pharisees and the popular party; if He denied it, even only theoretically, they would immediately draw from this the conclusion that He refused to pay tribute, and then He would get into trouble with the Romans, who looked very sharply after these tax-payments in the provinces, partly for the sake of the material profit, and partly on account of the recognition of their supremacy, which stood or fell with the right to exact tribute. Refusal of the State tax was a capital crime and most strictly inquired into.

The manner in which the question was put to our Lord made it more difficult. The priests and Pharisees did not come themselves, but sent their disciples, who were not so well known to our Saviour, accompanied by Herodians, in order that the question might not have the appearance of being the result of premeditation and agreement on the part of the Pharisees, but rather the outcome of accidental circumstances. They probably feared a summary dismissal.

The introduction to their question was equally likely to entrap Him. They come to our Lord with an air of great righteousness, fidelity to the law, and conscientiousness, as though they only put the question in order to have their doubts of conscience settled (Luke 20:20). They come to Him (so they say) because they consider Him to be a God-fearing man and a truth-loving teacher, who knows no fear nor human respect and teaches the way (i.e. the law) of God without any regard for persons, which other teachers, for fear of the Romans amongst others, did not do on these points (Matt. 22:16; Mark 12:14; Luke 20:21). They begin with praise, in order to gain His favor and His confidence. Nothing makes a man so affable and communicative as praise, and so they wished to arouse His vanity, in order at all events to get an answer out of Him, even if only in the shape of a personal or private opinion. For this reason they add, in quite a familiar and pressing manner: "Tell us, therefore, what dost thou think?" (Matt. 22:17.) He was to answer in public, before all the people; thus the Herodians, who were in high favor with the Romans, could bring the matter before Pilate and follow it up. It was probably for this reason that the Pharisees made use of them. Under these circumstances the question was not easy to answer.

3. OUR SAVIOUR'S ANSWER

There are three parts in our Saviour's answer. First, He unmasks the dishonorable intention of the tempters, and rebukes their insincerity. "Why do you tempt Me, ye hypocrites?" (Matt. 22:18; Mark 12:15; Luke 20:23.) He thus shows them that He sees through the whole plan and knows their intention. They had laid stress upon His love of truth; now He gives them a proof of it.

Secondly, He breaks through the snare they have set for Him

by an unexpected and practical stroke. He has a tribute-coin given to Him, one bearing Caesar's image, like those with which they are accustomed to pay the tax, and He asks whose image it bears. They answer: "Caesar's" (Matt. 22:19–21; Mark 12:16; Luke 20:24). So they themselves practically acknowledged the actual supremacy of Caesar, giving him the title Caesar, having his coins struck and circulated, and paying him tribute with them, all of which actions are a practical recognition of the royal prerogative. (Cf. I Mach. 15:6.) Our Saviour, therefore, rightly drew from their acknowledgment of Caesar's actual supremacy the conclusion that they should give to Caesar the things that were Caesar's, and, since God is likewise their Lord and Master, to God the things that were God's (Matt. 22:21; Mark 12:17; Luke 20:25). Thus all claims were satisfied, and all parties must be content. He drew the theory of the question from the practice, decided it from this point of view, and even obliged His opponents to give the decision themselves.

But our Saviour's answer does not stop there. It contains, thirdly, a great and important law for all ages. He does not say: "Caesar here and God there," but: "God and Caesar," thus founding the great law of the legitimacy of both great powers, the spiritual and the temporal, each in its own sphere, and also showing the possibility and the duty of satisfying both, as long as they do not exceed their powers. In one grand sentence our Saviour sums up the whole extent of the duties of man, intended as he is for the service of God, but having also to live in union with other men (Schanz). Thus the Church has always taught that the temporal authority must be obeyed, but not when at variance with God's commands (Rom. 13:1; I Peter 2:13, 14, 17; John 18:36; Acts 4:19). This is the principle of the union and the rational separation of the spiritual and temporal power, the law of genuine liberty of conscience, the great law that ensures the dignity of superiors and subjects, and suppresses arbitrary action and unbridled exercise of power on both sides.

The tempters were taken aback at this answer. They could find no cause of blame in our Lord, but remained dumb with astonishment and departed (Matt. 22:22; Mark 12:17; Luke 20:26).

How great and powerful is this mind, which so easily disperses the mists and lets the full sun of truth shine out! One does not know which to admire most, the loftiness and incorruptibility of this character, which is so proof against all human weaknesses; or the great wisdom that makes allowance for all circumstances; or the mildness which answers such provoking and malicious attacks so calmly, and even by conferring the benefit of a great revelation.

Repulse of the Sadducees

Luke 20:27. And there came to him some of the Sadducees, who deny that there is any resurrection, and they asked him,—28. Saying: "Master, Moses wrote unto us: If any man's brother die having a wife, and he leave no children, that his brother should take her to wife, and raise up seed unto his brother.—29. There were therefore seven brethren; and the first took a wife, and died without children.—30. And the next took her to wife, and he also died childless.—31. And the third took her. And in like manner all the seven, and they left no children, and died.—32. Last of all the woman died also.—33. In the resurrection, therefore, whose wife of them shall she be? For all the seven had her to wife."—34. And Jesus said to them: "The children of this world marry, and are given in marriage:—35. But they that shall be accounted worthy of that world and of the resurrection from the dead shall neither be married, nor take wives;—36. Neither can they die any more; for they are equal to the angels, and are the children of God, being the children of the resurrection.—37. Now that the dead rise again, Moses also showed, at the bush, when he calleth the Lord: The God of Abraham, and the God of Isaac, and the God of Jacob.—38. For he is not the God of the dead, but of the living; for all live to him."—39. And some of the scribes answering, said to him: "Master, thou hast said well."—40. And after that they durst not ask him any more questions.

Mark 12:18. And there came to him the Sadducees, who say there is no resurrection; and they asked him, saying:—19. "Master, Moses wrote unto us, that if any man's brother die, and leave his wife behind him, and leave no children, his brother should take his wife and raise up seed to his brother.—20. Now there were seven brethren; and the first took a wife, and died leaving no issue.—21. And the second took her, and died; and neither did he leave any issue. And the third in like manner.—22. And the seven all took her in like manner; and did not leave issue. Last of all the woman also died.—23. In the resurrection, therefore, when they shall rise again, whose wife shall she be of them? For the seven had her to wife."—24. And Jesus answering, saith to them: "Do ye not therefore err, because you know not the Scriptures, nor the power of God?—25. For when they shall rise again from the dead, they shall neither marry, nor be married, but are as the angels in heaven.—26. And as concerning the dead that they rise again, have you not read in the book of Moses, how in the bush God spoke to him, saying: I am the God of Abraham, and the God of Isaac, and the God of Jacob?—27. He is not the God of the dead, but of the living. You therefore do greatly err."

Matt. 22:23. That day there came to him the Sadducees, who say there is no resurrection, and asked him,—24. Saying: "Master, Moses said: If a man die having no son, his brother shall marry his wife, and raise up issue to his brother.—25. Now there were with us seven brethren; and the first having married a wife, died; and not having issue, left his wife to his brother.—26. In like manner the second, and the third, and so on to the seventh.—27. And last of all the woman died also.—28. At the resurrection therefore whose wife of the seven shall she be? For they all had her."—29. And Jesus answering, said to them: "You err, not knowing the Scriptures nor the power of God.—30. For in the resurrection they shall neither marry nor be married; but shall be as the angels of God in heaven.—

31. And concerning the resurrection of the dead, have you not read that which was spoken by God, saying to you:—32. I am the God of Abraham, and the God of Isaac, and the God of Jacob? He is not the God of the dead, but of the living."—33. And the multitudes hearing it were in admiration at his doctrine.

Another attack, consisting of another critical question, seems to have ensued immediately.

1. THE QUESTIONERS

The questioners who now advanced were Sadducees; these, we are told, denied the resurrection (Matt. 22:23; Mark 12:18; Luke 20:27), the world to come, the existence of the angels (Acts 23:8), the immortality of the soul, and consequently the resurrection of the body also. They accepted the five Books of Moses, but it was precisely on these that they based their denial of the resurrection. They were very hostile to the Pharisees; nevertheless they had to act with them in public life. They now came to put a question to our Saviour (cf. Introd., p. 11).

2. THE QUESTION

The answer to their question involved a decision on an imaginary case, which though conceivable was very futile and by no means edifying, based upon the law of leviration (Deut. 25:5). The question was, who in the resurrection was to have a woman who had been married to seven brothers one after another, all of them having died childless (Matt. 22:24–28; Mark 12:19–23; Luke 20:28–38).

The intention of the Sadducees is not clear. Perhaps they were actuated by curiosity. In all probability they had already puzzled the Pharisees with this case, and were desirous to see how our Saviour would answer it. Most likely they wished to do Him harm. If He decided for them, it was an injury to their enemies, the Pharisees, and also an injury to Himself, since the Pharisees and the people would be enraged with Him; and if He decided in favor of the Pharisees, He would be strengthening the influence of His declared enemies. In any case they thought they would gain something in favor of their dogma against the resurrection and the immortality of the soul, by making these latter appear ridiculous and impossible by means of this case. And what answer could be given, according to the grossly sensual theology of the Sadducees? Was no one to have the woman? And if anyone, who? The first husband, the last, or one of the intervening ones? That was incest. Or all of them? That was polyandry, and worst of all. That there could be a state of existence in which difference of sex could be found without sexual intercourse, did not occur to them, and they did not believe it. At all events there does not seem to have been so much malice in the question, nor can we perceive that the attack was made in collusion with the Pharisees. But the proposal and discussion of this question in public throws light not only upon the moral depravity of the sects, but also upon the degeneracy they had brought about in the moral condition of the people.

3. OUR SAVIOUR'S ANSWER

Our Saviour's answer may be divided into two parts.

In the first part He designates the supposition upon which the proposed case was founded as erroneous and false, and this in several respects (Mark 12:24), with regard to the nature of life after the resurrection and also with regard to the resurrection itself. These errors proceeded from their ignorance of the Scriptures, which bear testimony to the resurrection, and also from ignorance of the true conception of God, Whose omnipotence is able to institute a manner of life different from the present one (Matt. 22:29; Mark 12:24). According to the Jewish religious views "the resurrection" was synonymous with "immortality" (II Mach. 12:43–46).

In the second part of His answer our Lord refutes both errors, beginning by the one concerning the nature of life in the world to come. Those who are found worthy of the glorious resurrection will not rise again like the children of this world, who, being subject to death, can therefore marry. There will be difference of sex among them, certainly, but they will make no use of it, because they are immortal, "equal to the angels," "the children of God" (Luke 20:35, 36; Matt. 22:30; Mark 12:25). This glorious regeneration and transformation is designated by our Saviour a work of God's power (Matt. 22:29; Mark 12:24). He mentions the angels, probably because the Sadducees denied their existence. Thus the frivolous case in question is shown to be without foundation. As regards the immortality of the soul, our Saviour proves it from the very five Books of Moses which the Sadducees accepted as undoubtedly genuine, and by a text that was very familiar (Ex. 3:6). He says that, at the time when God had told Moses that He was the "God of Abraham, of Isaac, and of Jacob," these patriarchs had long been dead according to the flesh; but since God's word must be true, it follows that they still live and await the resurrection. Therefore there *is* a resurrection (Belser). Cf. Luke 20:27, 28; Mark 12:26, 27; Matt. 22:31, 32.

The effect produced upon the people who were listening to this discussion was astonishment and holy awe at the doctrine and wise words of our Lord (Matt. 22:33; Luke 20:39). It is indeed wonderful how He contrives to give such an edifying, elevating turn to this frivolous and disedifying interruption. How noble are the words and ideas in which He describes the wondrous state of the glorious resurrection, and how simple and telling are His proofs of immortality! We see here again the superiority of His glorious intellect, shedding light upon the most difficult questions with perfect calmness and majesty, however hard pressed by His enemies on all sides.

Last Repulse of the Pharisees

Mark 12:28. And there came one of the scribes that had heard them reasoning together, and seeing that he had answered them well, asked him which was the first commandment of all.—29. And Jesus answered him: "The first commandment of all is: Hear, O Israel, the Lord thy God is one God;—30. And thou shalt love the Lord thy God with thy whole heart, and with thy whole soul, and with thy whole mind, and with thy whole strength. This is the first commandment.—31. And the second is like to it: Thou shalt love thy neighbor as thyself. There is no other commandment greater than these."—32. And the scribe said to him: "Well, Master, thou hast said in truth, that there is one God, and there is no other besides him.—33. And that he should be loved with the whole heart, and with the whole understanding, and with the whole soul, and with the whole strength; and to love one's neighbor as one's self, is a greater thing than all holocausts and sacrifices."—34. And Jesus seeing that he had answered wisely, said to him: "Thou art not far from the kingdom of God." And no man after that dust ask him any question.—35. And Jesus answering said, teaching in the temple: "How do the scribes say, that Christ is the son of David?—36. For David himself saith by the Holy Ghost: The Lord said to my Lord, Sit on my right hand, until I make thy enemies thy footstool.—37. David therefore himself calleth him Lord, and whence is he then his son?" And a great multitude heard him gladly.

Matt. 22:34. But the Pharisees hearing that he had silenced the Sadducees, came together;—35. And one of them, a doctor of the law, asked him, tempting him:—36. "Master, which is the greatest commandment in the law?"—37. Jesus said to him: "Thou shalt love the Lord thy God with thy whole heart, and with thy whole soul, and with thy whole mind.—38. This is the greatest and the first commandment.—39. And the second is like to this: Thou shalt love thy neighbor as thyself.—40. On these two commandments dependeth the whole law and the prophets "—41. And the Pharisees being gathered together, Jesus asked them,—42. Saying: "What think you of Christ? Whose son is he?" They say to him: "David's"—43. He saith to them: "How then doth David in spirit call him Lord, saying:—44. The Lord said to my Lord: Sit on my right hand, until

I make thy enemies thy footstool?—45. If David then call him Lord, how is he his son?"—46. And no man was able to answer him a word; neither durst any man from that day forth ask him any more questions.

LUKE 20:39. And some of the scribes answering, said to him: "Master, thou hast said well."—40 And after that they durst not ask him any more questions.—41. But he said to them: "How say they that Christ is the son of David?—42. And David himself saith in the book of Psalms: The Lord said to my Lord, Sit thou on my right hand,—43. Till I make thy enemies thy footstool?—44. David then calleth him Lord; and how is he his son?"

After the Sadducees had departed, the Pharisees again appeared to dispute with our Lord.

1. THE PHARISEE'S QUESTION

The cause of the question seems to have been again an agreement among the Pharisees (Matt. 22:34). They had heard the discussion with the Sadducees, and rejoiced that our Lord had so thoroughly silenced these free-thinkers. Nevertheless they themselves would not yield, but resolved to make another attempt. A scribe offered himself for the purpose.

The questioner was a scribe, and it would appear a Pharisee also (Matt. 22:35; Mark 12:28; Luke 20:39). But he seems to have been a good and truth-loving man, for he appreciates and applauds our Lord's answer to the Sadducees (Mark 12:28; Luke 20:39), and later on the answer given by Jesus to his own question also (Mark 12:32). Still the question seems to have been a temptation, inasmuch as it was put by the scribe out of curiosity to see how our Lord would take it, and with the intention of depreciating His victory over the Sadducees if He did not answer correctly and in accordance with his (the scribe's) own opinion.

The question itself concerned the difference between great and small commandments of the law; what made a commandment great, and which one was the greatest and highest, as it were the epitome of all the commandments. This question was the subject of animated discussion in the rabbinical schools. Probably some Pharisees maintained that the outward observance of divine worship formed the chief commandment, as the scribe's answer appears to indicate (Mark 12:33). So the test lay in the question itself, and in this the discussion differs from a former and similar one (Luke 10:25). There the aim was a practical one; the lawyer inquired about ways and means of getting to heaven. Here it is merely speculative. The conclusion too was different in the former case. The scribe here asks whether there are great commandments in the law, and which they are (Matt. 22:36), or, more plainly and clearly expressing the questioner's meaning, which is the greatest of all commandments (Mark 12:28).

2. OUR SAVIOUR'S ANSWER

Our Saviour's answer is very beautiful, clear, ingenious and to the point. He first quotes the passage of the law which the Jews wore sewn upon the hem of their garments, in which God's unity and absolute supremacy are expressed: "Hear, O Israel, the Lord thy God is one God" (Deut. 6:4; Mark 12:29); and then He draws from this unity and absolute supremacy of God the inference of the unity of the commandments, or the chief commandment in which all others are contained. This is love of God above all things, the love which subjects man to God and directs to Him the whole man with all the powers of his body and soul and all the manifestations of his life, and which makes him love his neighbor also for God's sake (Mark 12:30, 31; Matt. 22:37–39). Our Saviour expressly adds that this is the chief commandment, which includes all the others and all the instructions of the prophets (Matt. 22:40).

The scribe followed our Saviour's conclusions thoughtfully and intelligently, grasped them completely, and expressed his assent to them, as opposed to the other doctrines of his party; saying that not the outward religious observance, but love alone was the adequate worship of God's unity, and the chief commandment (Mark 12:32, 33). Our Saviour answers him in an equally appreciative manner, praises him and encourages his good and truth-loving dispositions, saying that he is not far from the kingdom of God (Mark 12:34). Henceforth no one else dared to tempt our Lord again with questions (Mark 12:34; Luke 20:40).

3. THE COUNTERQUESTION PUT BY JESUS TO THE PHARISEES

Our Saviour was victor in all these debates. His opponents stood around Him, completely at a loss for words (Matt. 22:41). And now He began a contest, and put a counterquestion to them in presence of the people (Mark 12:35).

The subject of this question was not anything useless and unimportant, as had been the case with the inquiries of the Pharisees and Sadducees, but very important, in fact the gist and main point of their whole religious life; viz. who the Messias really was. It is plainly to be seen from Scripture that the Messias is also God, whilst the Jews, in their expectation of a political Messias, quite overlooked this attribute, and merely awaited him as the "son of David."

Our Saviour intends by this question not only to let His enemies feel their ignorance, but also to make it clear to them that the Messias is really God, and that He is therefore saying nothing contrary to the Scriptures in announcing Himself as the Messias and God; but that, on the contrary, their conception of the Messias is false and contradictory to Scripture itself. Perhaps He wished to warn His enemies against His murder, which they were planning for the very reason that He declared Himself to be God and the Messias.

The wording of the question is clear and comprehensive in the extreme. At first our Saviour asks them in an apparently harmless manner, quite as though it were of no particular consequence, what they think of Christ, and whose son He is (Matt. 22:42). That is to say, they were to state their opinion concerning the Messias, whether He were merely the son of David, or the Son of God also. It is assuredly not without a secondary intention that our Lord says: Whose son is the Messias? and not: Whose will He be? For He is there already. They answer, without suspecting anything, that He is the son of David, and no more. Our Saviour immediately confronts them with a difficulty by quoting the 109th Psalm, which was universally recognized as a Messianic and Davidical one, and asking how they can reconcile their statement that the Messias is merely the son of David and no more with what David says of the Messias in the Psalm in question, viz. that the latter is his Lord, and that God bids Him sit at His right hand (Ps. 109:1). He (the Messias) must therefore stand in a much higher relation to David than a mere son, viz. in that of his God. What is stated of the Messias in this Psalm—His share in God's throne, His generation in the bosom of God before the morning-star, His eternal priesthood, His office as Supreme Judge of peoples and kings—are all attributes that appertain to God. How, then, can He be merely the son of David? (Mark 12:35–37; Matt. 22:43–45; Luke 20:41–44.) So the Messias unites in Himself the royal, priestly, human, and divine rank and power.

No one was able to answer Him (Matt. 22:46), but the people listened to Him gladly (Mark 12:37). The reason is simply that His words were manifestations of His keen and lofty intelligence, His wisdom, sincerity, and humility, in short, of His whole glorious personality. How ingeniously He infers from the unity of God the unity of the law, in the commandment of love! How convincingly and irresistibly He overcomes the Pharisees with the question as to the "son of David," and how modestly He reveals His Divinity and character of Messias! How easy it was for a truth-loving heart to infer from this His Divinity! But the Pharisees do not do so, but persist in their design for His destruction. How earnestly the question about the greatest commandment and our Saviour's answer to it ring out at this moment: "Hear, O Israel; the Lord thy God is one God. And thou shalt love the Lord thy God with thy whole heart, and with thy whole soul, and with thy whole mind, and with thy whole strength!" (Mark 12:29, 30.) And this is the God they wish to kill!

The Censure of the Pharisees

Matt. 23:1. Then Jesus spoke to the multitudes and to his disciples,—2. Saying: "The scribes and the Pharisees have sitten on the chair of Moses.—3. All things therefore whatsoever they shall say to you, observe and do; but according to their works do ye not; for they say, and do not.—4. For they bind heavy and insupportable burdens, and lay them on men's shoulders; but with a finger of their own they will not move them.—5. And all their works they do for to be seen of men; for they make their phylacteries broad and enlarge their fringes.—6. And they love the first places at feasts, and the first chairs in the synagogues,—7. And salutations in the market-place, and to be called by men, Rabbi.—8. But be not you called Rabbi; for one is your Master, and all you are brethren.—9. And call none your father upon earth; for one is your Father, who is in heaven.—10. Neither be ye called masters; for one is your Master, Christ.—11. He that is the greatest among you shall be your servant.—12. And whosover shall exalt himself, shall be humbled; and he that shall humble himself, shall be exalted.—13. But woe to you scribes and Pharisees, hypocrites; because you shut the kingdom of heaven against men; for you yourselves do not enter in, and those that are going in, you suffer not to enter.—14. Woe to you scribes and Pharisees, hypocrites; because you devour the houses of widows, praying long prayers; for this you shall receive the greater judgment.—15. Woe to you scribes and Pharisees, hypocrites; because you go round about the sea and the land to make one proselyte, and when he is made, you make him the child of hell twofold more than yourselves.—16. Woe to you, blind guides, that say: Whosoever shall swear by the temple, it is nothing; but he that shall swear by the gold of the temple, is a debtor.—17. Ye foolish and blind; for whether is greater, the gold, or the temple that sanctifieth the gold?—18. And whosoever shall swear by the altar, it is nothing; but whosoever shall swear by the gift that is upon it, is a debtor.—19. Ye blind; for whether is greater, the gift, or the altar that sanctifieth the gift?—20. He therefore that sweareth by the altar, sweareth by it, and by all things that are upon it;—21. And whosoever shall swear by the temple, sweareth by it, and by him that dwelleth in it;—22. And he that sweareth by heaven, sweareth by the throne of God, and by him that sitteth thereon.—23. Woe to you scribes and Pharisees, hypocrites; because you tithe mint, and anise, and cummin, and have left the weightier things of the law, judgment, and mercy, and faith; these things you ought to have done, and not to leave those undone.—24. Blind guides, who strain out a gnat, and swallow a camel.—25. Woe to you scribes and Pharisees, hypocrites; because you make clean the outside of the cup and of the dish; but within you are full of rapine and uncleanness.—26. Thou blind Pharisee, first make clean the inside of the cup and of the dish, that the outside may become clean.—27. Woe to you scribes and Pharisees, hypocrites; because you are like to whited sepulchers, which outwardly appear to men beautiful, but within are full of dead men's bones, and of all filthiness;—28. So you also outwardly indeed appear to men just; but inwardly you are full of hypocrisy and iniquity.—29. Woe to you scribes and Pharisees, hypocrites, that build the sepulchers of the prophets, and adorn the monuments of the just.—30. And say: If we had been in the days of our fathers, we would not have been partakers with them in the blood of the prophets;—31. Wherefore you are witnesses against yourselves, that you are the sons of them that killed the prophets.—32. Fill ye up then the measure of your fathers.—33. You serpents, generation of vipers, how will you flee from the judgment of hell?—34. Therefore behold I send to you prophets, and wise men, and scribes; and some of them you will put to death, and crucify; and some you will scourge in your synagogues, and persecute from city to city;—35. That upon you may come all the just blood that hath been shed upon the earth, from the blood of Abel the just, even unto the blood of Zacharias the son of Barachias, whom you killed between the temple and the altar.—36. Amen I say to you, all these things shall come upon this generation.—37. Jerusalem, Jerusalem, thou that killest the prophets and stonest them that are sent unto thee, how often would I have gathered together thy children, as the hen doth gather her chickens under her wings, and thou wouldst not?—38. Behold, your house shall be left to you desolate.—39. For I say to you, you shall not see me henceforth till you say: Blessed is he that cometh in the name of the Lord."

MARK 12:38. And he said to them in his doctrine: "Beware of the scribes who love to walk in long robes, and to be saluted in the market-place,—39. And to sit in the first chairs in the synagogues, and to have the highest places at suppers;—40. Who devour the houses of widows under the pretence of long prayer; these shall receive greater judgment."

LUKE 20:45. And in the hearing of all the people he said to his disciples:—46. "Beware of the scribes, who desire to walk in long robes, and love salutations in the market-place, and the first chairs in the synagogues, and the chief rooms at feasts;—47. Who devour the houses of widows, feigning long prayer. These shall receive greater damnation."

Continuing His discourse to the disciples and people, our Lord now proceeded to pronounce a severe censure upon the Pharisees, publicly in the Temple. This discourse may be divided into three parts.

1. OUR SAVIOUR TESTIFIES THAT ISRAEL HAS FALLEN INTO SECTARIANISM

Our Saviour bears this testimony in the words: "The scribes and the Pharisees have sitten on the chair of Moses" (Matt. 23:2). By the chair of Moses He understands the authority to teach, to proclaim and interpret the law, faith and morals; especially the authority of the Sanhedrim. He does not speak expressly of the priesthood itself.

This authority to teach had now fallen into the hands of a religious party, a sect, viz. the Pharisees. In point of fact the Pharisees ruled at this period; they had the upper hand in the synagogues, in the schools, and even in the Sanhedrim, so that they almost decided the religious life of the people. The priesthood and the scribes were mostly of the Pharisaical persuasion (cf. Introd., pp. 11, 12).

Our Saviour also points out in what this sectarianism and Pharisaism consists, namely in every teacher wishing to be the leader and head of a special school of thought (Matt. 23:8, 16). Thus was founded the power of party opinion, or the "precepts of men" (Mark 7:7–9), and this power gradually overruled everything else.

2. OUR SAVIOUR GIVES THE PEOPLE RULES OF CONDUCT TOWARDS THE PHARISEES

The rules of conduct given by our Saviour contain two points.

First, He says that the Pharisees must be obeyed in their lawful position as interpreters and guardians of the Mosaic law. "Whatsoever they shall say to you, observe and do" (Matt. 23:3). The authority of the Sanhedrim to issue binding regulations in controversial cases concerning the meaning and the observance of the law was a rightful one, and as such it was not subordinate to the judgment of the people, but to God alone. He alone can dispense from obedience to the existing power, and transfer that power to others. Later on, at the Feast of Pentecost, He did so. Until then obedience was due to the Pharisees as teachers of the law, whenever they officially and as a teaching body declared and interpreted the law of Moses; but not to each one individually, when they followed party opinions and human precepts against which our Saviour had warned them and here repeats His warning (Matt. 23:16–22). Hence He says: "Beware of the scribes" (Mark 12:38; Luke 20:46). They might bring forward these falsifications of the law in their schools and in private intercourse, if they liked, but not when they were teaching officially.

The second point in these rules of conduct for the people was that they should not imitate the works and lives of the Pharisees (Matt. 23:3), because these were at variance with their official teaching. Our Saviour proves this by condemning their morals, that the people might not seek truth, salvation and holiness in their way of life. There are three blots upon the life and works of the Pharisees. The first is insincerity. They overburden the people with regulations as to the observance of the law, and do not keep these regulations themselves (Matt. 23:4). The second is vanity, pride and love of being honored. In order to make themselves conspicuous they walk about in long robes, such as are worn only by those in very high office (Mark 12:38); they wear broader fringes and hems to their garments (Num. 15:38), and showy phylacteries (Matt. 23:5; Deut. 6:8), that they may be considered models of exactitude in the Mosaic law; they seek the places of honor in the synagogues and at feasts (Matt. 23:6; Luke 20:46; Mark 12:38, 39), and openly claim the new titles of "Rabbi," "father," "master," under the pretext that each of them is the master of an accredited school and everyone must submit to them (Matt. 23:7, 8, 9, 10). This is the very essence of sectarianism. In opposition to it our Saviour depicts the nature of Christian teaching, saying that there is one Master and Father, viz. Christ, and from Him all doctrine and power proceed; all stand to Him in the relation of disciples, even the appointed teachers and pastors; indeed, the higher the position, the humbler and more self-sacrificing the holder of it must be (Matt. 23:9–12). The third blot upon the conduct of the Pharisees is that they harm and ruin the people. They close the kingdom of heaven to men, instead of opening it to them, by rejecting Christ, the Gate of heaven and the true Shepherd, and thus barring the door for themselves (Matt. 23:13); they consume the substance of pious widows under the pretext of long prayers (Matt. 23:14; Mark 12:40; Luke 20:47); their eagerness to make proselytes is only pride or avarice, and is the ruin of these converts, because they not only make them no better, but infect them with their own leaven and make them worse (Matt. 23:15); lastly, many of their casuistical decisions are wrong, false and absurd, as our Saviour demonstrates by the formulas of oaths (Matt. 23:16–22). He sums up the fundamental evil of Pharisaism by reproaching it with cant and hypocrisy, as manifested in their scrupulous observance of petty things and neglect of such important virtues as honesty, justice and mercy (Matt. 23:23, 24). They are like cups scoured and clean outside, but full of filth inside (Matt. 23:25, 26), or like the sepulchers, which looked trim outside when they were whitewashed at Easter, but remained full of putrefaction within (Matt. 23:27, 28). In vain do they restore the graves of the prophets in the vicinity of Jerusalem, and curse their fathers as the murderers of them. By this they merely testify themselves to be the sons of the murderers of prophets, and "fill up the measure of their fathers" by now wishing to murder the Lord of the prophets (Matt. 23:29–32).

3. OUR SAVIOUR FORETELLS JUDGMENT AND PUNISHMENT

After our Saviour has thus judged the Pharisaical party in Israel, He foretells their punishment and gives brief and concise reasons for it.

The punishment falls upon the Pharisees and the whole nation. The former first receive a severe rebuke in the epithets: "blind," "blind guides," "ye foolish" (Matt. 23:16, 17, 19, 24), "serpents," "generation of vipers," as John had called them (Matt. 23:33); the opprobrious word "hypocrite" is cast in their teeth at least eight times (Matt. 23:13–15, 23, 25, 27–29). Then He holds out to them the prospect of a terrible punishment, first expressed in general terms by the eightfold "woe" (Matt. 23:13–16, 23, 25, 27, 29), and then in particular: the punishment of humiliation (Matt. 23:12), a specially severe judgment (Matt. 23:14; Mark 12:40; Luke 20:47), and finally damnation (Matt. 23:33). Upon the whole nation, Jerusalem and the Temple, the punishment of desolation is pronounced (Matt. 23:36–38; cf. 7:27). God will forsake the city and Temple, and the Romans will demolish the empty shrine. This punishment of devastation and abandonment by God will last until the time when the remnant of Israel will be converted to the Messias (Matt. 23:39).

The grounds for the punishment are briefly and impressively given, in the constant contumacy and stubbornness with which the nation had met all tokens of God's favor, from the time of the prophets down to Christ. Under the touching figure of a hen that gathers her chickens under her wings with motherly care to protect them from the birds of prey, our Saviour holds up to the people this solicitude shown by God for Israel, and as opposed to it the wanton wickedness with which the nation kills His prophets and messengers and finally the Messias and His Apostles (Matt. 23:34, 35, 37). No one will now shield Israel from the approaching eagles of Rome. Its bloodguiltiness, which is as great as that of all former times (Matt. 23:35), can only be expiated by the blood of the whole nation. The mention of the murder of Abel (Gen. 4:10) and the High Priest Zacharias (II Par. 24:22) is very apt; Israel's crime is fratricide and the murder of the prophets.

Such is our Lord's censure of the Pharisees and of pharisaical Israel. He speaks as Judge. He comprises in one great picture all their moral depravity, justifies His words and proceedings with respect to them, and hurls the final sentence in their faces. But He does not do this without feelings of sorrow and regret. These were His last words in the Temple, the solemn farewell as it were to the Synagogue and the nation, represented by the countless pilgrims who had come to the feast from far and near and were now assembled round Him. It needed no little courage to speak such words and to judge and rebuke Judaism so unmercifully. The ruling party had really no more dangerous adversary than our Saviour, and therefore His removal was necessary. He sealed His doom irrevocably by this discourse, but that made no difference. He was come to bear testimony to the truth. His Heart was not inimical to anything but insincerity, pride and hardness of heart; but these were the very reasons why He could not be reconciled to this party (Isa. 50).

The Widow's Mite

Mark 12:41. And Jesus sitting over against the treasury beheld how the people cast money into the treasury, and many that were rich cast in much.—42. And there came a certain poor widow, and she cast in two mites, which make a farthing. —43. And calling his disciples together, he saith to them: "Amen I say to you, this poor widow hath cast in more than all they who have cast into the treasury.—44. For all they did cast in of their abundance; but she of her want cast in all she had, even her whole living."

Luke 21:1. And looking on, he saw the rich men cast their gifts into the treasury.—2. And he saw also a certain poor widow casting in two brass mites.—3. And he said: "Verily I say to you, that this poor widow hath cast in more than they all.—4. For all these have of their abundance cast into the offerings of God; but she of her want hath cast in all the living that she had."

1. Our Saviour Sits Down Opposite the Treasury

After His censure of the Pharisees our Saviour sat down in the women's fore-court, near the treasury, into the funnel-shaped openings of which the gifts of money for various ends were cast. It was Tuesday evening, probably, and our Lord might well seek a little rest after the exciting occurrences of this day. Perhaps it was after the evening sacrifice, and the native Jews and strangers who had offerings to make were acquitting themselves of their vows and promises of gifts by casting the amount into the sacred box. Our Saviour, surrounded by His disciples, sat there and watched the procession of donors, many of whom were wealthy and cast large sums into the box (Mark 12:41; Luke 21:1). He was waiting for a consoling incident.

2. THE WIDOW MAKES HER OFFERING

Amongst others there came at length a woman to the treasury and laid her offering in it. But whilst the money of the rich had rolled with a heavy clink through the openings into the box, one scarcely heard her gift. She only gave two mites, which made a farthing (Mark 12:42; Luke 21:2), almost nothing in comparison with the gifts of the rich.

But the woman gave in proportion incomparably more than all the others. They offered of their superfluity what they did not need, and without retrenching their expenses in the least on account of the gift; but she gave all that she had, her whole amount of ready money, so that she was now really in want and had nothing left (Mark 12:43, 44; Luke 21:3, 4). She was poor and a widow. Under these circumstances she was not bound to give anything, and would have done a great deal in offering only the half of what she possessed. But she had given it all.

This shows a noble mind which, filled with deep religious earnestness, is determined to fulfil all the duties of religion at any cost and under all circumstances, without regard for self.—It also shows deep trust in God. The poor widow has nothing more. God knows it and will now have to provide for her.—Lastly, it shows the spirit of generosity, which does not look at what one is *bound* to do, but at what one *can* do, and which does its utmost with a lofty mind and great reverence for God, and without esteeming its own act.

3. OUR SAVIOUR REWARDS THE WIDOW'S OFFERING

It was not without reason that our Saviour had sat there in the vicinity of the treasury. Perhaps no one would have paid attention to the poor widow among the rich donors, or perhaps her appearance and her offering itself attracted notice of a painful kind. Our Saviour sitting near saw it, and judged everything with nicety and exactness, noticing all the attendant circumstances; and according to these were determined His approbation and reward. He called His disciples together (Mark 12:43), pointed to the poor widow and made known to them her good deed, with all the circumstances that made it so precious in God's eyes. She "hath cast in more than they all" (the rich). "They did cast in of their abundance; but she of her want cast in all she had, even her whole living" (Luke 21:3, 4; Mark 12:43, 44). Even here below she already received the approval of all who heard, and from God she awaited an eternal reward.

Thus the dull and stormy day was brightened at its close by this beautiful, consoling gleam of sunlight. Touchingly beautiful is the deed of this poor, despised woman of the people, contrasted with the outward splendor of the Temple, the superficiality, frivolity, terrible selfishness, avarice and ambition, unbelief and godlessness of the upper and leading classes of Israel, a solitary flower amid ruins and wild undergrowth. The flower did not spring forth from the schools, but from the ever vigorous and fertile soil of the old economy of salvation and of simple observance of the same.

The Gentiles and the Vow of Sacrifice

John 12:20. Now there were certain Gentiles among them who came up to adore on the festival day.—21. These therefore came to Philip, who was of Bethsaida of Galilee, and desired him, saying: "Sir, we would see Jesus."—22. Philip cometh and telleth Andrew; again Andrew and Philip told Jesus.—23. But Jesus answered them saying: "The hour is come that the Son of Man should be glorified.—24. Amen, amen I say unto you, unless the grain of wheat falling into the ground, die;—25. Itself remaineth alone; but if it die, it bringeth forth much fruit. He that loveth his life shall lose it; and he that hateth his life in this world, keepth it unto life eternal.—26. If any man minister to me, let him follow me; and where I am, there also shall my minister be. If any man minister to me, him will my Father honor.—27. Now is my soul troubled. And what shall I say? Father, save me from this hour. But for this cause I came unto this hour.—28. Father, glorify thy name." A voice therefore came from heaven: "I have both glorified it, and will glorify it again."—29. The multitude therefore that stood and heard, said that it thundered. Others said: "An angel spoke to him."—30. Jesus answered and said: "This voice came not because of me, but for your sakes.—31. Now is the judgment of this world; now shall the prince of this world be cast out.—32. And I, if I be lifted up from the earth, will draw all things to myself."—33. (Now this he said, signifying what death he should die.)—34. The multitude answered him: "We have heard out of the law, that Christ abideth for ever; and how sayest thou: The Son of Man must be lifted up? Who is this Son of Man?"—35. Jesus therefore said to them: "Yet a little while the light is among you. Walk whilst you have the light, that the darkness overtake you not; and he that walketh in darkness knoweth not whither he goeth.—36. Whilst you have the light, believe in the light, that you may be the children of light." These things Jesus spoke; and he went away, and hid himself from them.

It was probably at the end of this memorable day that the important event recorded by St. John, viz. the meeting of Jesus with the Gentiles, occurred in the Temple.

1. THE APPROACH OF THE GENTILES TO JESUS

Whilst our Saviour was in the Temple some Gentiles were announced, who had applied to the disciples for an introduction to our Lord (John 12:20). Probably they were proselytes from Syria or Asia Minor, who had come to the feast. The report of the miracles of Jesus, and especially the events of the last few days may have excited in them the wish to make His personal acquaintance. They come very modestly, delicately and politely, according to the Greek etiquette, and seek an intermediary in Philip, whom they perhaps happened to meet first or had possibly become acquainted with in Galilee. They may have done this out of respect for Jesus, or because they as Gentiles were not allowed to go beyond the fore-court.

Philip does not dare to comply with the request immediately, whether from natural irresolution, from Jewish narrow-mindedness and prejudice against the Gentiles, or for fear of attracting the attention and rancor of the Jews, if our Lord were to converse with Gentiles in the Temple. He therefore asks Andrew, and both together communicate to our Saviour the request of the Gentiles (John 12:21). Thus we find the Apostles acting especially as intermediaries. And we see evidence of the attractive charm of our Saviour's character.

We are not told whether our Lord granted the request. His answer seems rather to point to the contrary.

2. SIGNIFICATION OF THIS APPROACH OF THE GENTILES

Instead of going out to the Gentiles, our Saviour explains to the disciples and the people the signification of this personal approach of the Gentiles to Him. Their arrival is a sure sign first of His Death, and secondly of His glorification (John 12:23).

This approach is first the sure sign of His Death. As surely as the grain of wheat must fall into the earth, disappear and decay before it brings forth fruit, so surely must He also die before the Gentile world, whose first pioneers are now announced, can bring forth the fruit of eternal life (John 12:24). Indeed, He even lays this down as a general law, for His disciples as well as for Himself, for He adds that one gains eternal life only by sacrificing the earthly one (John 12:25), and that whoever wishes to be His disciple must follow Him in earthly tribulation, and will then also participate in His heavenly glory (John 12:26). This thought of His Passion and approaching Death suddenly fills His soul with unspeakable fear and sorrow, the violence of which is revealed in the touching words that His "soul is troubled" even to its very depths. He is visibly struggling with the rising waves of natural repugnance and fear. What shall He do? Prompted by His nature and His lower will, He begs the Father to avert this hour of death: "Father, save Me from this hour." Then He gathers up all the strength of His higher will, and says: "But for this cause I came unto this hour," i.e. No, I will not ask that, for it was precisely to suffer and die that I came. "Father, glorify Thy Name," do what promotes the honor of Thy Name, glorify Thyself as Thou hast determined, by My Death (John 12:27, 28). The hour of agony on the Mount of Olives casts its shadow before, and as He is about to do there and did so often during His life, He ratifies the great sacrificial vow to glorify His Father by His Death (Ps. 39:8). And the Father on His side ratified the vow by saying in a mighty voice like thunder: "I have glorified it," i.e. My Name, hitherto by Thy miracles and Thy doctrine, "and will glorify it again," namely, by the sending of the Holy Ghost and the preaching of the Apostles (John 12:28). The bystanders thought the voice was a thunder-clap or the voice of an angel (John 12:29; cf. Gen. 21:17; 22:11). As at the beginning of our Lord's public life, so also now at its close, the voice of the Father bears witness to the Divinity of Jesus.

The Passion is but the passage to glory, and the arrival of the Gentiles is, in the second place, the pledge of this glory, which is threefold. The first glory is the conversion of the Gentile world. As His Heart had once exulted at the sight of the great harvest-field that was opened out before Him at Sichem (John 4:35), so it exults now. The countryman casts the grains of wheat into the furrows joyfully, without sorrow, in the certainty of the hundred-fold life and blessing that will spring from them. Perhaps our Saviour too may have thought here of the first sheaf of barley that was offered on the second Easter day, and was every year the glorious precursor of thousands of other sheaves (John 12:24, 25). The second glory is the dethronement of Satan, the prince and power of the world. The present vow of sacrifice and its early fulfilment are the judgment and condemnation of the spirit of the world, and the downfall of his power (John 12:31). By the expiation of sins, creation and humanity as a whole are withdrawn from the bondage of Satan, and though the individual may be tempted, he cannot be compelled by him to yield. The third glory that our Saviour's Death is to bring Him is His elevation and victorious power in heaven, for which His painful and shameful elevation on the Cross is the preliminary preparation. The purifying, gently attracting, all-conquering power of Christ takes the place of the tyrannical power of Satan and the world. By degrees, and with the grace of God, it will draw all to Him, as to the Source of all salvation; Jews and Gentiles, nations and individuals, in short the entire creation, uniting all in one kingdom of grace and truth, of which Christ is the Head. His Cross and Death will indeed cause countless numbers to turn to Him. At the Death of Jesus the Cross already begins to exercise this power of attraction, as we see in the good thief, the centurion, and the people who strike their breasts; and this it has continued to do ever since.

3. CONSEQUENCE AND EFFECT OF THE DISCOURSE UPON THE JEWS

The very fact of the Gentiles making their appearance to speak with our Saviour ought to have been for the Jews an exhortation to faith. But the greater part of the people had not really been made any better even by the events of the past week or those of that day itself. Incredulous, quarrelsome, and led astray by their carnal conception of the Messianic kingdom, they urge against the elevation of the Messias (by which they understood very well that He meant death on the Cross; John 3:14; 8:28), that the Messias was not to die, His kingdom would be eternal (Dan. 7:13, 14; Isa. 9:6, 7; Ps. 109:4). "Who is this Son of Man?" Not the Messias; He does not die (John 12:34).

In His answer our Saviour does not enter into discussion upon the point of contention, because He had already spoken plainly enough about it on the occasion of the Feast of Tabernacles (John 8:25, 58 seq.), and because the question was to be publicly decided within a few days. He contents Himself with an earnest exhortation to desist from this incredulity and believe at last. "This voice came not because of Me, but for your sakes" (John 12:30), i.e. not for My instruction, but to induce you to believe. He then clothes this thought in the similitude of walking in the sunlight (John 12:36). He is the Light, and has publicly called Himself the Light of the world (John 8:12). To "walk in His light" means to believe in Him and accept His doctrine. He adduces two motives for this: first, the shortness of the time that He would still be with them and that they would have until the destruction of their city (John 12:35); secondly, the danger of losing the light; one does not know where one is going in the darkness (John 12:35). It is much the same as He had already told the Jews on a former occasion, that they would not be able to follow Him, but would die in their sins (John 8:21). The fate of this unhappy nation has verified in a terrible way the words of our Saviour. Even now, in the midst of the light of Christianity, it is surrounded by darkness. The veil is not removed from its heart. These were the concluding words of the day, and indeed of our Lord's whole public teaching and revelation, an exhortation to faith.

Our Saviour now rises to quit the Temple and go out to Bethania (Matt. 24:1). It was the beginning of the prophesied desolation. He had taught in the Temple for the last time. He wished to pass the last two days among His own, and He never entered the Temple again. With His departure a momentous change set in. The Temple, throughout so many centuries God's dwelling, now ceased to be the seat of revelation and the spiritual center of humanity. Our Lord "went away and hid Himself from them" (John 12:36). With His departure went out the light of the Temple and the lamp of Israel, and the Temple had no longer any meaning.

The Discourse on Mount Olivet. First and Second Part Prediction of Persecutions, of the Chastisement to Overtake the City, and of the Tokens of the Last Judgment

Matt. 24:1. And Jesus being come out of the temple, went away. And his disciples came to show him the buildings of the temple.—2. And he answering said to them: "Do you see all these things? Amen I say to you, there shall not be left here a stone upon a stone that shall not be destroyed."—3. And when he was sitting on Mount Olivet the disciples came to him privately, saying: "Tell us, when shall these things be, and what shall be the sign of thy coming, and of the consummation of the world?"—4. And Jesus answering, said to them: "Take heed that no man seduce you;—5. For many will come in my name saying: I am Christ; and they will seduce many.—6. And you shall hear of wars, and rumors of wars. See that ye be not troubled; for these things must come to pass, but the end is not yet.—7. For nation shall rise against nation, and kingdom against kingdom; and there shall be pestilences, and famines, and earthquakes in places;—8. Now all these are the beginnings of sorrows.—9. Then shall they deliver you up to be afflicted, and shall put you to death; and you shall be hated by all nations for my name's sake.—10. And then shall many be scandalized, and shall betray one another, and shall hate one another.—11. And many false prophets shall rise, and shall seduce many.—12. And because iniquity hath abounded, the charity of many shall grow cold;—13. But he that shall persevere to the end, he shall be saved.—14. And this gospel of the kingdom shall be preached in the whole world, for a testimony to all nations; and then shall the consummation come.—15. When therefore you shall see the abomination of desolation, which was spoken of by Daniel the prophet, standing in the holy place (he that readeth, let him understand);—16. Then they that are in Judea, let them flee to the mountains;—17. And he that is on the house-top, let him not come down to take anything out of his house;—18. And he that is in the field, let him not go back to take his coat.—19. And woe to them that are with child, and that give suck in those days.—20. But pray that your flight be not in the winter, or on the Sabbath;—21. For there shall be then great tribulation, such as hath not been from the beginning of the world until now, neither shall be.—22. And unless those days had been shortened, no flesh should be saved; but for the sake of the elect those days shall be shortened.—23. Then if any man shall say to you: Lo, here is Christ, or there; do not believe him.—24. For there shall arise false Christs and false prophets, and shall show great signs and wonders, insomuch as to deceive (if possible) even the elect.—25. Behold, I have told it to you beforehand.—26. If therefore they shall say to you: Behold he is in the desert, go ye not out; Behold he is in the closets, believe it not.—27. For as lightning cometh out of the east, and appeareth even into the west; so shall also the coming of the Son of Man be.—28. Wheresoever the body shall be, there shall the eagles also be gathered together.—29. And immediately after the tribulation of those days the sun shall be darkened, and the moon shall not give her light, and the stars shall fall from heaven, and the powers of heaven shall be moved."

LUKE 21:5. And some saying of the temple, that it was adorned with goodly stones and gifts, he said:—6. "These things which you see, the days will come in which there shall not be left a stone upon a stone that shall not be thrown down."—7. And they asked him, saying: "Master, when shall these things be, and what shall be the sign when they shall come to pass?"—8. Who said: "Take heed you be not seduced; for many will come in my name, saying I am he; and, The time is at hand; go ye not therefore after them.—9. And when you shall hear of wars and seditions, be not terrified; these things must first come to pass, but the end is not yet presently."—10. Then he said to them: "Nation shall rise against nation, and kingdom against kingdom.—11. And there shall be great earthquakes in divers places, and pestilences and famines, and terrors from heaven, and there shall be great signs.—12. But before all these things they will lay their hands on you, and persecute you, delivering you up to the synagogues and into prisons, dragging you before kings and governors for my name's sake;—13. And it shall happen unto you for a testimony.—14. Lay it up therefore in your hearts, not to meditate before how you shall answer;—15. For I will give you a mouth and wisdom, which all your adversaries shall not be able to resist and gainsay.—16. And you shall be betrayed by your parents and brethren, and kinsmen and friends, and some of you they will put to death;—17. And you shall be hated by all men for my name's sake;—18. But a hair of your head shall not perish.—19. In your patience you shall possess your souls.—20. And when you shall see Jerusalem compassed about with an army, then know that the desolation thereof is at hand;—21. Then let those who are in Judaea flee to the mountains; and those who are in the midst thereof, depart out; and those who are in the countries, not enter into it.—22. For these are the days of vengeance, that all things may be fulfilled that are written.—23. But woe to them that are with child and give suck in those days; for there shall be great distress in the land, and wrath upon this people.—24. And they shall fall by the edge of the sword; and shall be led away captives into all nations; and Jerusalem shall be trodden down by the Gentiles; till the times of the nations be fulfilled.—25. And there shall be signs in the sun, and in the moon, and in the stars, and upon the earth distress of nations, by reason of the confusion of the roaring of the sea and of the waves;—26. Men withering away for fear and expectation of what shall come upon the whole world; for the powers of heaven shall be moved."

MARK 13:1. And as he was going out of the temple, one of his disciples saith to him: "Master, behold what manner of stones and what buildings are here."—2. And Jesus answering said to him: "Seest thou all these great buildings? There shall not be left a stone upon a stone, that shall not be thrown down."—3. And as he sat on the Mount of Olives over against the temple, Peter and James and John and Andrew asked him apart:—4. "Tell us, when shall these things be, and what shall be the sign when all these things shall begin to be fulfilled?"—5. And Jesus answering, began to say to them: "Take heed lest any man deceive you;—6. For many shall come in my name, saying I am he; and they shall deceive many.—7. And when you shall hear of wars and rumors of wars, fear ye not; for such things must needs be; but the end is not yet.—8. For nation shall rise against nation and kingdom against kingdom, and there shall be earthquakes in divers places, and famines. These things are the beginnings of sorrows.—9. But look to yourselves. For they shall deliver you up to councils, and in the synagogues you shall be beaten, and you shall stand before governors and kings for my sake, for a testimony unto them.—10. And unto all nations the gospel must first be preached.—11. And when they shall lead you and deliver you up, be not thoughtful beforehand what you shall speak; but whatsoever shall be given you in that hour, that speak ye; for it is not you that speak, but the Holy Ghost.—12. And the brother shall betray his brother unto death, and the father his son; and children shall rise up against the parents, and shall work their death.—13. And you shall be hated by all men for my name's sake. But he that shall endure unto the end, he shall be saved.—14. And when you shall see the abomination of desolation, standing where it ought not; he that readeth, let him understand; then let them that are in Judaea, flee unto the mountains;—15. And let him that is on the house-top not go down into the house, nor enter therein to take anything out of the house;—16. And let him that shall be in the field not turn back to take up his garment.—17. And woe to them that are with child, and that give suck in those days.—18. But pray ye that these things happen not in winter.—19. For in those days shall be such tribulations as were not from the beginning of the creation, which God created until now, neither shall be.—20. And unless the Lord had shortened the days, no flesh should be saved; but for the sake of the elect which he hath chosen, he hath shortened the days.—21. And then if any man shall say to you: Lo, here is Christ, lo, he is here, do not believe.—22. For there will rise up false Christs and false prophets, and they shall show signs and wonders, to seduce (if it were possible) even the elect.—23. Take you heed therefore; behold, I have foretold you all things.—24. But in those days, after that tribulation, the sun shall be darkened, and the moon shall not give her light;—25. And the stars of heaven shall be falling down, and the powers that are in heaven shall be moved."

1. OCCASION OF THE PREDICTIONS

The first cause of the predictions was the Apostles' cry of admiration at the sight of the extent and magnitude of the Temple buildings. As they were quitting the Temple, they cast a glance of astonishment at its magnificence, perhaps from the fore-court of the Gentiles, whence one could survey the whole majesty of the edifice. "Behold," the disciples said to our Lord, "what manner of stones and what buildings!" (Mark 12:1.) And they pointed to the buildings and the magnificent gifts with which they were adorned (Luke 21:5; Matt. 24:1). Indeed, the sanctuary with its golden Temple-house, with the beautiful porches and gates, the great courts and the majestic colonnades, and the costly votive offerings of princes (cf. Introd., p. 6), was one of the wonders of the world at that day, the very pride of Israel (Jer. 7:4), and a "stone of stumbling." The second circumstance which led to the prophecy was the question of the Apostles. Whilst ascending Mount Olivet the Apostles Peter, James, John, and Andrew sat down in sight of the Temple, and asked our Lord when the destruction which He had revealed would take place, since His words indicated that not a stone of all that magnificence would remain. The Apostles wished to know not only when this was to happen to the Temple, but also when our Lord's second advent would take place and when the end of the world would come, and by what signs this might be known (Luke 21:7; Mark 13:4; Matt. 24:3). The disciples had repeatedly heard from our Lord's lips the promise of His future glorious coming to judgment (Matt. 16:27; 19:28; 22:7; Luke 19:15, 27). They therefore connected in their thoughts and in their question the judgment upon Jerusalem and the Last Judgment, and our Lord responded accordingly. The prophets also connected both these facts, because they are closely related divine acts; namely the beginning and the completion of the world-sovereignty of Christ. The judgment upon Jerusalem is a token, prophecy and type of the universal Judgment; Israel is the type of the Messianic kingdom in its close as well as in other respects, and the universal Judgment is the conclusion of the earthly Messianic kingdom.

But since our Saviour prefaces His answer to the double question of the disciples by a general announcement of persecutions, His discourse upon Mount Olivet contains three parts. He first foretells a time of persecutions and afflictions for the world in general and for the Apostles (Matt. 24:4–14; Mark 12:5–13; Luke 21:8–19). Then He mentions the signs that will precede the destruction of Jerusalem (Matt. 24:15–21; Mark 13:14–19; Luke 21:20–24) and the Last Judgment (Matt. 24:22–39; 32–35; Mark 13:20–25; 28–31; Luke 21:25–26; 29–33). Thirdly, He describes the Last Judgment (Matt. 24:30, 31, 34–42; 25:31–46; Mark 12:26, 27, 32; Luke 21:27, 28, 34, 35).

2. PREDICTION OF PERSECUTIONS, OF THE JUDGMENT TO OVERTAKE THE CITY, AND OF THE TOKENS OF THE LAST JUDGMENT

Before our Lord answers the twofold question of His disciples, He unfolds before their eyes a great picture of the persecutions and afflictions that were to fall upon the Church, the Apostles and the faithful at various periods of the world's history. His intention in so doing was to encourage us all to exercise prudence, patience and perseverance, which is truly of far more importance than to become acquainted with the signs of the Last Judgment and the vengeance to come upon Jerusalem.

With regard to these periods of affliction He tells us, first, that many false prophets and Christs will arise and seduce many (Matt. 24:5, 11, 24; Mark 13:6; Luke 21:8); secondly, that great distress will be caused by wars, famines and earthquakes (Matt. 24:6, 7; Mark 13:7, 8; Luke 21:10, 11); thirdly, that the Apostles and the faithful will be hated, persecuted, delivered up and even killed, and by their own relatives too, so that these persecutions will be the occasion of much scandal, dissension and hatred, and also of the decline of religion and of love of God and one's neighbor (Matt. 24:9, 10, 12; Mark 13:9, 12, 13; Luke 21:12, 16, 17). Our Saviour here depicts the Church very much as He had done on a former occasion, showing how she must pass through conflict, suffering and persecution to her eternal goal.

Our Lord then proceeds to answer the questions of His Apostles. With regard to the destruction of the Temple and city He prophesies as follows. Generally speaking, their fate will be a terrible one, such as has never been seen or experienced (Matt. 24:21; Mark 13:19); these will be "days of vengeance" (Luke 21:22), such as the prophets have foretold (Num. 24:24; Deut. 28:49 seq.; Isa. 6:13, 65; Dan. 9:24; Osee 3:4). In particular our Saviour says that Jerusalem will be "compassed about with an army" (Luke 21:20); the people will fall by the sword and be carried away captive by the nations; Jerusalem will be devastated and trodden down, no stone of the magnificent Temple will remain upon another (Matt. 24:2; Mark 13:2; Luke 21:6); the sanctuary will remain profaned, until "the times of the nations be fulfilled" (Luke 21:20, 24; Matt. 24:15; Mark 13:14); it is therefore to be a permanent and complete ruin until the time of the Christian world, which consists of converted heathen nations, is fulfilled and the remnant of Israel saved. This is the judgment upon Jerusalem, the Temple and the people. Our Saviour mentions as tokens of this judgment the investment of the city by a besieging army (Luke 21:20), and the "abomination of desolation" (Dan. 9:27), by which may be understood in particular the abundance of shameful crimes and sacrileges with which the conflicting factions of the besieged within the city profaned the Temple and the Holy of Holies, as well as the entrance of the Gentiles into the sanctuary (Matt. 24:15; Mark 13:14).

Our Saviour also gives an answer concerning the Last Judgment, introducing it by the words that there will be "great tribulation" (Matt. 24:21, 22; Mark 13:19, 20). As tokens of the approaching end of the world He mentions, first, extraordinary doings and terrible display of power on the part of false prophets and Christs, so that even the elect might be deceived by their seeming miracles, if God permitted it (Matt. 24:24, 25; Mark 13:21, 22). This is probably an allusion to Antichrist (II Thess. 2:9–10). The second sign is that of terrifying phenomena in the heavens and on the earth (Matt. 24:29; Mark 13:24; Luke 21:25). There will be such fluctuations and disturbances in the equilibrium of the elements, in the course of the natural order of things in the firmament and on the earth, that it will seem as though day and night, spring and summer were intermingled; the stars will appear to fall from the sky, the sun and moon to vanish, the central forces around which the universe moves to be shaken, and the great machinery of creation to be unhinged. All this may perhaps be brought about by the influx of powerful meteoric masses into the atmosphere of our earth. The people on earth will nearly die of fear and terror.

Our Lord later on confirms all these predictions and signs, as well as the immediate preliminaries of the Last Judgment (namely, the rising of the dead and the appearance of Christ), in the most solemn words (Matt. 24:32–35; Mark 13:28–31; Luke 21:29–33).

3. RULES OF CONDUCT GIVEN BY OUR LORD TO HIS FOLLOWERS

Our Saviour does not content Himself with naming the signs of the Judgment; He also instructs His followers how to behave when these signs appear. There are four of these instructions.

First, our Saviour exhorts His disciples not to trust the false prophets and Christs, not to be deceived by them nor follow them (Matt. 24:4; Mark 13:5; Luke 21:8). In such turbulent times there is special danger of being led astray. Even the various rumors of temporal afflictions are not to lead them into the erroneous opinion that the final moment has now arrived. The end of the world is not to follow immediately after the judgment upon Jerusalem (Matt. 24:6, 8; Mark 13:7; Luke 21:9). With regard to the doings of the false prophets and Christs previous to the Last Judgment, our Lord especially warns us against following them, in whatever way they may make their appearance, secretly or openly. The advent of Christ will be like lightning, so clearly and palpably visible to all that it will not be necessary to go anywhere to find Him (Matt. 24:26, 27; Mark 13:21, 23). As the eagles sight their prey and flock round it, so the elect and all mankind will hasten to Christ to be judged (Matt. 24:28).

The second admonition is for the Christians, when they see the tokens of the judgment upon Jerusalem. They are not to take refuge in the towns, as is usually done in such cases, and especially not in Jerusalem, but to flee out of Judaea across the Jordan into the mountains of Peraea, and this with such haste that women in their pregnancy or with infants to carry are to be pitied on account of this hindrance; and all should pray that the flight may not fall in the winter season or on the Sabbath, i.e. at an inopportune time (Matt. 24:16–20; Mark 13:14–18; Luke 21:21). Although it was permissible in this case to flee a greater distance than a Sabbath-day's journey (about a mile), still many would perhaps have scrupled to do so, or the Jews might have hindered their flight, since it was founded upon Christ's warning.

Thirdly, our Saviour exhorts His followers to hope confidently for special help in persecution. The Holy Ghost will speak for the Christians before the judges, and not a hair shall fall from their heads (Matt. 10:30; Luke 21:14, 15, 18), i.e. they will be under God's especial protection on earth as well as in the life to come, and the Gospel will be propagated farther and farther until it has spread to all nations (Matt. 24:14; Mark 13:10).

The last instruction is to persevere in fortitude until the end (Matt. 24:13; Mark 13:13; Luke 21:19). As a motive for endurance our Lord gives the assurance that these days of tribulation will be shortened for the sake of the elect (Matt. 24:22; Mark 13:20). This evidently refers to the events preceding the Last Judgment.

This prediction of our Lord forms a most tragic scene. He has taken leave of the Temple (cf. Ez. 11:23), and is seated on the gentle slope of Mount Olivet, perhaps on the very spot where He had wept over Jerusalem, surrounded by His Apostles, and facing the city and Temple. There the city lies, with its unique Temple-buildings in renewed beauty and splendor, bathed in the last rays of the evening sun. But our Lord gazes sadly and earnestly at the proud, obstinate city. He beholds what the eyes of mere mortals do not see. Slowly, but with ominous threatenings, destruction is approaching her from all points of the compass. Our Saviour raises the mysterious veil. As Prophet, Judge, and King, He proclaims her downfall, the murderess of the prophets, the deicide. This prediction is important with reference to the prophetic character of Christ. No prophecy of the destruction and the events to precede it had ever been so clear. All has been fulfilled. Before the last investment of the city the Christians fled across the Jordan, especially to Pella; destruction and the abomination of desolation began, Titus penetrated into the Holy of Holies; not a stone remained upon another, and to this day Jerusalem, become the abode of infidels, is down-trodden. Everything is fulfilled. God has judged Jerusalem with the full severity of His judgment, because she willed to have it so; He has protected His own like a careful Shepherd and Father. How touchingly our Saviour's tender care for His followers in the time of distress is here displayed!

The Discourse on Mount Olivet. Third Part. The Last Judgment

Matt. 24:30. "And then shall appear the sign of the Son of Man in heaven; and then shall all tribes of the earth mourn; and they shall see the Son of Man coming in the clouds of heaven with much power and majesty.—31. And he shall send his angels with a trumpet and a great voice; and they shall gather together his elect from the four winds, from the farthest parts of the heavens to the utmost bounds of them.—32. And from the fig-tree learn a parable: when the branch thereof is now tender, and the leaves come forth, you know that summer is nigh.—33. So you also, when you shall see all these things, know ye that it is nigh even at the doors.—34. Amen I say to you, that this generation shall not pass, till all these things be done.—35. Heaven and earth shall pass, but my words shall not pass.—36. But of that day and hour no one knoweth; no, not the angels of heaven, but the Father alone.—37. And as in the days of Noe, so shall also the coming of the Son of Man be;—38. For as in the days before the flood they were eating and drinking, marrying and giving in marriage, even till that day in which Noe entered into the ark,—39. And they knew not till the flood came, and took them all away; so also shall the coming of the Son of Man be.—40. Then two shall be in the field; one shall be taken, and one shall be left.—41. Two women shall be grinding at the mill; one shall be taken, and one shall be left.—42. Watch ye therefore, because you know not what hour your Lord will come. . . .—25:31. And when the Son of Man shall come in his majesty and all the angels with him, then shall he sit upon the seat of his majesty;—32. And all nations shall be gathered together before him, and he shall separate them one from another, as the shepherd separateth the sheep from the goats;—33. And he shall set the sheep on his right hand, but the goats on his left.—34. Then shall the king say to them that shall be on his right hand: Come, ye blessed of my Father, possess you the kingdom prepared for you from the foundation of the world;—35. For I was hungry, and you gave me to eat; I was thirsty, and you gave me to drink; I was a stranger, and you took me in;—36. Naked, and you covered me; sick, and you visited me; I was in prison, and you came to me.—37. Then shall the just answer him, saying: Lord, when did we see thee hungry, and fed thee; thirsty, and gave thee drink?—38. And when did we see thee a stranger, and took thee in; or naked, and covered thee?—39. Or when did we see thee sick or in prison, and came to thee?—40. And the king answering, shall say to them: Amen I say to you, as long as you did it to one of these my least brethren, you did it to me.—41. Then shall he say to them also that shall be on his left hand: Depart from me, you cursed, into everlasting fire which was prepared for the devil and his angels;—42. For I was hungry, and you gave me not to eat; I was thirsty, and you gave me not to drink;—43. I was a stranger, and you took me not in; naked, and you covered me not; sick, and in prison, and you did not visit me.—44. Then they also shall answer him, saying: Lord, when did we see thee hungry or thirsty, or a stranger, or naked, or sick, or in prison, and did not minister to thee?—45. Then he shall answer them, saying: Amen I say to you, as long as you did it not to one of these least, neither did you do it to me.—46. And these shall go into everlasting punishment; but the just, into life everlasting."

Luke 21:27. "And then they shall see the Son of Man coming in a cloud, with great power and majesty.—28. But when these things begin to come to pass, look up and lift up your heads; because your redemption is at hand."—29. And he spoke to them a similitude: "See the fig-tree and all the trees;—30. When they now shoot forth their fruit, you know that summer is nigh.—31. So you also when you shall see these things come to pass, know that the kingdom of God is at hand.—32. Amen, I say to you, this generation shall not pass away, till all things be fulfilled.—33. Heaven and earth shall pass away; but my words shall not pass away.—34. And take heed to yourselves, lest perhaps your hearts be overcharged with surfeiting and drunkenness and the cares of this life, and that day come upon you suddenly;—35. For as a snare shall it come upon all that sit upon the face of the whole earth.—36. Watch ye therefore, praying at all times, that you may be accounted worthy to escape all these things that are to come, and to stand before the Son of Man."

MARK 13:26. "And then shall they see the Son of Man coming in the clouds, with great power and glory.—27. And then shall he send his angels, and shall gather together his elect from the four winds, from the uttermost part of the earth to the uttermost part of heaven.—28. Now of the fig-tree learn ye a parable. When the branch thereof is now tender, and the leaves are come forth, you know that summer is very near;—29. So you also when you shall see these things come to pass, know ye that it is very nigh, even at the doors.—30. Amen I say to you, that this generation shall not pass, until all these things be done.—31. Heaven and earth shall pass away, but my words shall not pass away.—32. But of that day or hour no man knoweth, neither the angels in heaven nor the Son, but the Father."

After our Saviour has prophesied and described the judgment upon Jerusalem, He passes on to the Last Judgment.

1. GENERAL FEATURES OF THE LAST JUDGMENT

There are three special characteristics of the Last Judgment.

First, it will be universal. "All tribes of the earth" will see the sign of the Son of Man appear (Matt. 24:30); He will come accompanied by all His angels, and "all nations shall be gathered together before Him" (Matt. 25:31, 32). Men will be judged individually in the particular judgment held at their departure from this life; but they will be judged again as members of society, of families, communities, nations, kingdoms, and of the whole human race. God is to be justified in His guidance of individual nations and of all humanity, and Christ also is to appear and be publicly and solemnly acknowledged as Head, King, and Judge of nations and men. Hence at this judgment the sentence will deal with man in relation to society (Matt. 25:40, 45). The Last Judgment is the grand finale of the whole history of the Church and of mankind.

The second feature is that the Judgment is certain in one respect, but uncertain in another. That it will come is certain. Apart from the predictions of the prophets (Isa. 2:12; 13:6; 34:8; Joel 1:15; 2:1; Dan. 7:9, 10; Amos 5:18; Abd. 1:15; Soph. 1:7, 14; Zach. 14:1), Christ Himself affirms it mostly solemnly (Matt. 24:35; Mark 13:31; Luke 21:33). To emphasize His words He pointed probably to some fig-trees close by, saying that as surely as one could conclude from the sprouting of the leaves and fruits on these trees that the warm season was approaching, so surely they might also conclude that the Redeemer was at hand, when these signs occurred (Matt. 24:32, 33; Mark 13:28, 29; Luke 21:29, 30, 31). And He adds that this generation will live to see it

(Matt. 24:34; Mark 13:30; Luke 21:32), which is true with regard to the judgment upon Jerusalem, for it occurred only about 36 years later, and correct also with regard to the Last Judgment if we understand by "this generation" the Jewish race, which will survive until the last. But with all this the day and hour of the Last Judgment is uncertain. No man, nor yet the angels, nor even the Son of Man, i.e. in His quality of God's messenger to men, knows the hour; only the Father, inasmuch as He is the eternal and deciding principle in the Most Holy Trinity, and this appertains to Him as such, and not to the Son (Matt. 24:36; Mark 13:32). This uncertainty is constantly emphasized and thrown into strong relief in the following parables, in which our Lord urges us to exercise watchfulness and zeal. And therefore though we are told that the tokens will commence "immediately after the tribulation" occasioned by the false prophets (Matt. 24:25), we must not forget that a thousand years are as one day with the Lord (II Peter 3:8).

The third feature is the unexpectedness and extraordinary suddenness with which the Judgment is to burst upon us. This suddenness is illustrated by our Saviour in several figures drawn from nature, life and history. It will come like the lightning, which flashes from one point of the horizon to the opposite one (Matt. 24:27); like a thief (Matt. 24:43) and a snare it will "come upon all that sit upon the face of the whole earth" (Luke 21:35); it will come as the flood came in the days of Noe and washed away all men in the midst of their sensual, worldly lives (Matt. 24:38, 39); so suddenly and with such vehemence will the Judgment fall upon the world, that of two who are working side by side in the field or at the mill, one will be saved, and the other will perish, just as they are found, without time for further preparation (Matt. 24:40, 41; cf. Luke 17:22–37).

2. COURSE OF THE LAST JUDGMENT

The Last Judgment may be divided into the preparation for it and the holding of the judgment itself.

This preparation is twofold. The first preparation is the resurrection of the dead. The Lord will send out His angels, and at their mighty trumpet-blast (probably a summons audible exteriorly) the earth will open and will give up her dead, wherever they lie (Matt. 24:31; Dan. 12:2). The resurrection of the bodies is the work of divine omnipotence; but the angels may cooperate in it in some way, either by issuing the exterior command or by collecting the scattered particles (I Thess. 4:15). The resurrection is universal, but diverse. For the blessed it is glorious. They will go forth from their graves in spirit-form, agile, beautiful, shining, like flowers and stars, and will be guided through the air to the place of judgment in a glorious procession, accompanied by angels. But the damned will creep out of their graves like toads and vermin, abashed and hideous, disfigured, and bearing to their exceeding shame the curse of their sins and vile crimes in their bodies; and they will be driven by evil spirits, like a herd of unclean animals, to the place of judgment. This place will be, according to many, the Valley of Josaphat (Joel 3:2), that is to say near the same place where our Lord made the prophecy of the Judgment, commenced His Passion and gloriously ascended to heaven (Acts 1:11, 12). The second preparation is the appearance of Christ to judge the world. It seems that the holy Cross, the sign of the Son of Man, is first to appear in the air, either in reality or as a beautiful luminous phenomenon. Then our Lord Himself will come, and His appearance will be glorious and majestic. Thus He Himself describes it in Holy Scripture. He will come with great power and glory, in the midst of wonderful phenomena in the clouds and atmosphere, and with all His angels as companions, witnesses and executors of the sentence; He will seat Himself as King upon the throne of His majesty (Matt. 24:30; 25:31, 34; Mark 13:26; Luke 21:27). This beseems His character as Head, Judge, King, High Priest, and God-Man, the more so that He has voluntarily lived in such great poverty, humility and lowliness here below. Now it is His will to reveal Himself with all His power and majesty; and if He wills it, He will also be able to do it. What an effect this appearance of Christ will produce! How joyfully the blessed will look up, exult and go in a glorious throng to meet Him and take their places at His side! Now has their redemption come (Luke 21:28). But the appearance of Christ will spread terror and dismay amongst the damned, like the autumn storm among leaves and chaff, or a flash of lightning in the darkness of night. This Jesus, whom they have denied, betrayed, despised, insulted, blasphemed, defied and persecuted, is now placed over them as their God and Judge. Will not the cry then be heard: "Ye mountains, fall upon us! Ye hills, cover us!" (Luke 23:30.)

The judgment itself consists, first, in the manifestation of consciences (Matt. 25:32). In an instant, by an effect of God's omnipotence, all consciences will suddenly be laid open and lit up as one enormous picture. It is the picture of the whole history of the Church, the world, and the human race, woven out of the ways and deeds of individuals, communities, states and nations; the picture woven out of the most secret thoughts, principles, intentions, plans, intrigues, crimes and shameful deeds of the damned, who will be confounded at the disgracefulness, meanness, baseness and uselessness of their counsels and works, and will cry out: "Therefore we have erred!" (Wisd. 5:6.) It is the picture woven out of the principles, intentions, virtues, and sufferings of the blessed, who were hidden, calumniated and persecuted here below, and who perished through the triumph of baseness and godlessness, but now stand justified by the eternal truth; it is the great picture of the city of God and that of the devil here below, made up of darkness and light, by the intermingling of heaven and earth, men, angels and devils, everywhere penetrated by the luminous ways of Divine Providence, transfigured in the light of the justice, wisdom, goodness and omnipotence of God. What a grand and wonderful spectacle! Man by man, nation by nation will stand there, judged already by the simple radiance of this picture.

The second act of the judgment is the sentence. Our Lord will then rise, and turning first to the blessed, will reward them with a kind and gentle mien; a very heaven of goodness, love and tenderness will beam upon them in His glance, as He says: "Come, ye blessed of My Father," ye children of election, who are predestined in and with Me by the Father's decree; come, draw near as My faithful servants and brethren. I recognize you as such; come now, and "possess the kingdom prepared for you from the foundation of the world." This will be a joy, an honor, a glory that the blessed cannot comprehend. They will ask how it comes that they are to receive so much in return for so little. But He will confirm the sentence, not in a manner exteriorly perceptible, but in the inward conviction of each, saying that their works, done out of faith and love to Him, deserve this; for what they have done to the least of men, they have done to Him (Matt. 25:34–40). But terrible as a thunder-storm, as lightning or blazing flame, He will turn to the damned with the words: "Depart from Me, you cursed!" Away from Me, your Lord, your Brother, your God and greatest good! A curse upon your intellect: you will never see God or know a consoling truth; a curse upon your will: never shall it be refreshed by love or bliss; a curse upon your body: it will burn in the eternal flames that were prepared for Satan and his angels. They (the wicked) have adhered to them, and now the devils' portion is their lot also. This sentence too finds its confirmation in the unbelief and want of mercy which they have shown not to men, but to Christ, in the person of the least of men (Matt. 25:41–45). The last act of the Judgment is the execution of the sentence passed. The abyss will open and swallow up the devils and their condemned adherents. It is sealed up, and the key deposited in the depths of God's justice and truth. No one will ever fetch it out, throughout all eternity. But under these terrible seals and gates, universal, terrible and eternal perdition will work upon the damned and render their misery complete. For the blessed, on the other hand, begins the eternal Alleluia, eternal bliss, eternal rejoicing, and eternal dominion with the Lamb. The new Jerusalem now descends (Apoc. 21:2), and the marriage-feast of the Lamb begins. Blessed are they who have part in it! The damned will "go into everlasting punishment, but the just into life everlasting" (Matt. 25:46; Apoc. 19:20, 21; cf. Dan. 12:3).

CONCLUSIONS

It was well that our Saviour extended and sealed His teaching by the prediction and revelation of the end of the world and what is to take place then, and we owe Him many thanks for so doing. This revelation contains important conclusions for us.

This unbelieving, proud and mighty Jerusalem, within sight of which the prophecy was made, is the expression and symbol of the godless world, her sin and her punishment. She will now triumph over God for a moment, but not for long. What remains of her glory, her lust and her defiance, when her walls stagger under the blows of the Roman besiegers, and the golden sanctuary is leveled to the ground in smoke and ruins? So will the world fare also. Its end will come. Not a stone of all its magnificence will remain upon another. The last cloud of smoke that rises from the universal conflagration and vanishes in the air is the soul and sum of the world's glory. The world is vain, transitory and wicked; it tempts us to sin, and sin makes us unhappy. That is the first conclusion to be drawn from the truth of the Last Judgment.

The Apostles, who draw closer to our Saviour's side in their fear and awe as they listen to His words, and through whose hearts such anxious presentiments of the immediate future are passing, are the precursors of the faithful, the followers of Christ. Here below they have a hard condition. Unbelief and vice triumph, and nothing is left for them but the desolation of Good Friday. But it will not always be thus. At the edge of the horizon of the world's duration the dark sky is illumined, as the setting sun may have cast a red glow across the sky while our Saviour was speaking. The evening of the world is ours. As long as we have our Lord's word for it, we, who are the disciples of disgrace and the offscouring of the world, will not despond. It will be a bright evening for us, and all tribulations and disfavor will melt away in honor and joy. Heaven and earth will pass away, but our Lord's words will not pass away (Matt. 24:35). Happy we! When all the world quails with fear, we have great confidence, we raise our heads, for our redemption is at hand (Luke 21:28). Confidence amid all afflictions is the second lesson to be drawn from the prediction of the Last Judgment.

The Person of our Saviour Himself, Who makes the prophecy, gives us the third. He will now be judged and crucified in this Jerusalem, and thus perish in shame and pain. What becomes of His kingdom? What of His royalty? They remain intact. This Death is only a temporary eclipse, but not the destruction of His kingdom; indeed, it is the beginning of His world-sovereignty. Henceforth Jerusalem will see Him as King and Judge. The judgment upon this city is the first, the Universal Judgment the last act of His judicial work, and the completion of His glorious kingship here below. At the end of time, when the battle has been fought out, He will stand on the battle-field, unfurl His victorious standard and gather all His faithful soldiers round Him. No one will be absent, and no one will lose His reward. It will be meted out in proportion to what each one has done for Christ's kingdom. Nothing is lost, even if all was lost. All temporal defeats of Christ's kingdom are only fluctuations of the victory. His kingdom, like Himself, is eternal. What an encouraging motive to adhere to Christ our Lord, to work, suffer and even die for His kingdom! He will awaken us all to life again, reward us, beatify us for ever!

PREPARATION FOR OUR LORD'S ADVENT
PARABLES OF THE PORTER, THE VIRGINS, AND THE TALENTS

MARK 13:33. "Take ye heed, watch and pray; for ye know not when the time is.—34. Even as a man who, going into a far country, left his house, and gave authority to his servants over every work, and commanded the porter to watch.—35. Watch ye therefore (for you know not when the lord of the house cometh; at even, or at midnight, or at the cock-crowing, or in the morning);—36. Lest coming on a sudden, he find you sleeping.—37. And what I say to you, I say to all: Watch."

LUKE 21:36. "Watch ye therefore, praying at all times, that you may be accounted worthy to escape all these things that are to come, and to stand before the Son of Man."

MATT. 24:42. "Watch ye therefore, because you know not what hour your Lord will come.—43. But this know ye, that if the good-man of the house knew at what hour the thief would come, he would certainly watch, and would not suffer his house to be broken open.—44. Wherefore be you also ready; because at what hour you know not, the Son of Man will come.—45. Who, thinkest thou, is a faithful and wise servant, whom his lord hath appointed over his family, to give them meat in season?—46. Blessed is that servant, whom when his lord shall come, he shall find so doing;—47. Amen I say to you, he shall place him over all his goods.—48. But if that evil servant shall say in this heart: My lord is long a-coming;—49. And shall begin to strike his fellow-servants, and shall eat, and drink with drunkards;—50. The lord of that servant shall come in a day that he hopeth not, and at an hour that he knoweth not;—51. And shall separate him, and appoint his portion with the hypocrites; there shall be weeping and gnashing of teeth.—25:1. Then shall the kingdom of heaven be like to ten virgins, who taking their lamps went out to meet the bridegroom and the bride.—2. And five of them were foolish, and five wise;—3. But the five foolish, having taken their lamps, did not take oil with them;—4. But the wise took oil in their vessels with the lamps.—5. And the bridegroom tarrying, they all slumbered and slept.—6. And at midnight there was a cry made: Behold the bridegroom cometh, go ye forth to meet him.—7. Then all those virgins arose and trimmed their lamps.—8. And the foolish said to the wise: Give us of your oil; for our lamps are gone out.—9. The wise answered, saying: Lest perhaps there be not enough for us and for you, go you rather to them that sell, and buy for yourselves.—10. Now whilst they went to buy, the bridegroom came; and they that were ready went in with him to the marriage, and the door was shut.—11. But at last come also the other virgins, saying: Lord, Lord, open to us.—12. But he answering said: Amen I say to you, I know you not.—13. Watch ye therefore, because you know not the day nor the hour.—14. For even as a man going into a far country called his servants, and delivered to them his goods;—15. And to one he gave five talents, and to another two, and to another one, to everyone according to his proper ability; and immediately he took his journey.—16. And he that had received the five talents, went his way, and traded with the same, and gained other five.—17. And in like manner he that had received the two, gained other two.—18. But he that had received the one, going his way digged into the earth, and hid his lord's money.—19. But after a long time the lord of those servants came, and reckoned with them.—20. And he that had received the five talents coming, brought other five talents, saying: Lord, thou didst deliver to me five talents, behold I have gained other five over and above.—21. His lord said to him: Well done, good and faithful servant, because thou hast been faithful over a few things, I will place thee over many things; enter thou into the joy of thy lord.—22. And he also that had received the two talents came and said: Lord, thou deliveredst two talents to me; behold I have gained other two.—23. His lord said to him: Well done, good and faithful servant; because thou hast been faithful over a few things, I will place thee over many things; enter thou into the joy of thy lord.—24. But he that had received the one talent, came and said: Lord, I know that thou art a hard man; thou reapest where thou hast not sown, and gatherest where thou hast not strewed;—25. And being afraid I went, and hid thy talent in the earth; behold, here thou hast that which is thine.—26. And his lord answering, said to him: Wicked and slothful servant, thou knewest that I reap where I sow not, and gather where I have not strewed;—27. Thou oughtest therefore to have committed my money to the bankers, and at my coming I should have received my own with usury.—28. Take ye away therefore the talent from him, and give it him that hath ten talents;—29. For to everyone that hath shall be given, and he shall abound; but from him that hath not, that also which he seemeth to have shall be taken away.—30. And the unprofitable servant cast ye out into the exterior darkness; there shall be weeping and gnashing of teeth."

As a conclusion to the prediction of His advent our Saviour adds the exhortation to watch, pray (Mark 13:33, 35, 37; Luke 21:36), be ready (Matt. 24:44; Luke 21:34), and make good use of our time, because the Lord's coming is certain but the hour is uncertain, and everyone will receive what his works deserve (Matt. 24:45–51). Our Saviour then develops these general thoughts very clearly, in three parables: vigilance in the parable of the porter; readiness in that of the virgins; and zealous labor in that of the talents. These various parables were probably propounded by Him in the course of the following days, in Bethania. The exhortation to watch, be ready, and work is intended not only for the Apostles, but for all; the hour of death for each individual is for him the coming of the Lord. What has been said of the Last Judgment holds good more or less for the hour of death also (Matt. 24:43, 44), and therefore our Saviour says: "What I say to you I say to all; watch!" (Mark 13:37.)

1. THE PARABLE OF THE PORTER (MARK 13:34–37)

In this parable our Lord lays stress upon three thoughts.

First, the lord of the house is far away, and leaves his house in charge of his servants, as trustworthy persons. They are empowered to manage everything in his name (Mark 13:34).

Secondly, he gives the command to watch. At least four times in succession he repeats the admonition (Mark 13:33, 34, 35, 37), this vigilance being specially recommended to the porter (Mark 13:34).

Thirdly, the lord will certainly come, but it is uncertain at what hour (Mark 13:35). And therefore the porter must be ready at every hour of the four night-watches, that he may not be unexpectedly surprised by his master (Mark 13:35, 36).

Our Saviour evidently intends by this parable to recommend vigilance as a preparation for His advent. And this watchfulness consists particularly in praying (Luke 21:36).

2. THE PARABLE OF THE VIRGINS (MATT. 25:1–13)

This parable lays particular stress upon preparation and being ready. Our Saviour clothes His thoughts in the figure of a marriage. At a Jewish wedding the bridegroom usually went in the evening to the bride's home, accompanied by his friends. The bridesmaids, friends of the bride, came to meet him and conducted him to her. Then the wedding procession went by torchlight with music and song to the house of the bridegroom, and the marriage-feast and dance followed. We may distinguish three parts in this parable.

The first part describes the preparation for the arrival of the bridegroom. The purpose of this preparation is participation in the wedding rejoicings. The wedding here signifies the coming of Christ (with the Church triumphant, His Bride), and His glorious mystical union with the human race and the Church after the Judgment, in the joys of heaven. From the earliest days a marriage had been to the Jews the sum-total of earthly joy, and at the same time the symbol of eternal bliss. The bridesmaids or "virgins" represent all who are called to heaven (Matt. 25:1; Ps. 44:15, 16). The preparation itself varies. The wise virgins do not content themselves with filling their "lamps" (sanctifying grace) with oil, but also take vessels of it with them in order to be prepared for all emergencies. The others, the foolish virgins, do not consider the possibility of a long delay on the bridegroom's part, and are satisfied with having filled their lamps with oil. The oil represents everything that helps to preserve sanctifying grace. Neither the bridegroom's delay nor even their falling asleep had any fatal consequences. Their calamity came from the failure of the oil, or rather from their neglect in not providing themselves with it. To be at times unmindful of the Lord's coming, which may be signified by this slumber, does at least no very great harm, if only one is in the state of grace (Matt. 25:2–4).

The second part of the parable is the arrival of the bridegroom. Three details are given with respect to it. First, the bridegroom keeps the virgins waiting (Matt. 25:5). Secondly, he comes suddenly and unexpectedly (Matt. 25:6), whether to the Last Judgment or to call us away by death. Thirdly, he passes by quickly and hurriedly, so that there is no more time to make preparations. Once he is past, he is past for ever (Matt. 25:7–10). The oil of justifying works cannot be borrowed from others. It is at most to be obtained from those who administer the Sacraments; but there is not always time for that.

The third part is the result of the different preparations made. The wise virgins are rewarded with happiness, joy and honor for ever (Matt. 25:10). Vexation, humiliation and unhappiness are the portion of the foolish ones. They are shut out (Matt. 25:10). All their contrition, their lamentations and longing entreaties are of no use. They are and remain rejected: "I know you not" (Matt. 25:12). They had not deserved these honors and joys, on account of their slight appreciation and esteem for them.

So our Saviour warns us here not merely to prepare for His coming, but also to keep ourselves in readiness. That is only the case when we remain in the state of sanctifying grace. Then we are sure of heaven, even if death should come unexpectedly.

3. THE PARABLE OF THE TALENTS (MATT. 25:14–30)

The object of this parable is to encourage us to prepare for the Lord's coming by making a zealous use of the goods entrusted to us. The principal points of this parable relate to the persons treated of, and show what use we are to make of these goods entrusted to us and what are respectively the consequences of a good or a bad use of them.

The lord goes "into a far country" and distributes his goods, natural and supernatural, among his servants. They are his own goods, and though he distributes, he does not make a present of them. He distributes them with circumspection and wisdom, giving to one more, to another less, according to the occupation and ability of each; and there is often a great difference. He distributes his goods in order that the servants may trade with and husband them. He will return after a while and demand an account (Matt. 25:14, 15, 19).

The faithful, clever and zealous servants at once begin to trade with the talents entrusted to them, and do so with skill and perseverance (Matt. 25:16, 17). On their master's arrival they immediately bring their accounts, show them joyfully to him and lay all their gains with fidelity and humility at his feet, one ten, another four talents, just twice as much as they had received (Matt. 25:19, 20, 22). Then they receive their reward; first in the recognition and praise of their good qualities, and then in the superabundant recompense and magnificent provision made for them by the share in their master's goods granted to them (Matt. 25:21, 23).

A third servant, who had received one talent, does not employ it according to his lord's wish. He does not steal or lose it, but buries it in the ground instead of turning it to account for the owner's profit (Matt. 25:18). When called to account he brings the talent back and excuses himself for the lack of interest by pleading his fear of his lord's severity, an excuse most insulting to his master (Matt. 25:24, 25). He is punished for this, first, by a reprimand for his worthlessness and sloth; his master rightly turns the excuse into an accusation, deprives him of the talent and gives it to the first servant (who has already been rewarded once), and finally delivers him up to his merited punishment (Matt. 25:26–30). He thus rightly receives a positive and a negative punishment. He has disregarded his lord's wish with regard to the employment of what was entrusted to him; he has injured his master's interests by his negligence and idleness. Idleness is in reality at the root of his fear.

In these three parables our Saviour gives us complete directions for preparing for death, which is for us the coming of our Lord. He teaches us how to prepare for death, and why; He gives us the manner of the preparation, and also the motives for it. In the first place we must watch, think of death, and not live on regardless of the future. The reason is that there is nothing surer and more important than death. This certainty and importance of death is emphasized in all the parables. Secondly, we must be ready, and not put off our preparation until the hour of death, because death may indeed come unexpectedly, and only comes once. This too is very clearly brought out in the parables. This preparation consists in the preservation of sanctifying grace. Thus our Saviour expressly warns us: "Take heed to yourselves, lest perhaps your hearts be overcharged with surfeiting and drunkenness and the cares of this life, and that day come upon you suddenly" (Luke 21:34). Lastly, we must carefully prepare for death by making a good use of the good things God gives us. The reckoning and recompense is sure, for the use as well as for the ill use and neglect of the goods entrusted. We cannot work too hard for such a great reward. And we do not work for God alone, but for ourselves also. We have as much bliss in heaven as we have earned here below. These are the last exhortations that our Saviour gives to His own in the two last days that He spends with them at Bethania. Words of farewell and departure are heard continually. Everything points to the stern truth of a great and ominous future, the end of all things, the Last Judgment, and the advent of the Lord; and the hour of death is this advent for each individual. To die well is the task and aim of our whole life.

G. Retrospect of the Public Life of Jesus

We shall here do well to follow St. John's example (John 12:37–50) and cast a glance back over the public life of our Saviour, in order to obtain a comprehensive view of it. This public ministry of our Saviour may be divided into three parts: His teaching, His miracles and His example of virtue.

The Teaching of Our Lord

Here there are again three points of importance.

1. AUTHORIZATION FOR OUR SAVIOUR'S OFFICE OF TEACHER

Teaching formed an important and integral part of our Saviour's task. Among the other details foretold of the Messias by the prophets, they always proclaim Him as a teacher (Isa. 30:20; Joel 2:23), "the light of the Gentiles" and "a witness to the people" (Isa. 49:6; 55:4; 61:1 seq.). He was expected by the people as a prophet and teacher (John 4:25); He announced Himself as such (Luke 4:18; John 13:13), and did so as a sign that He was the Messias (Matt. 11:5). He is the King of truth (John 18:37), Truth itself (Matt. 14:6). Teaching formed an essential part of the Redemption. No one can be saved except by faith and the supernatural knowledge of the end and the means of faith, and therefore it was necessary that Christ should teach us the way of salvation. By doing this He first becomes our Good Shepherd and Redeemer. And therefore His Church is before all things united in faith.

But the authority to teach can only come from God, because He alone knows and can teach the way to the supernatural goal. The office of teaching is a divine office, and it can and may only be undertaken and exercised in virtue of a commission from God. He alone can send prophets and apostles (Rom. 10:15; II Cor. 5:20). Our Saviour held His authority not from men, not from any school, but from His Father (Luke 9:35; John 7:16). Indeed, He had it in His own right, as a consequence of the union of His human nature with the Second Person of the Godhead. He Himself was God and the "Light which enlighteneth every man" (John 1:9). As God-Man He is High Priest, Lawgiver, Prophet, Head of angels and men, and can enlighten and teach all and lay upon them the obligation of accepting His doctrine and belief. Thus He has in the highest degree all the qualifications requisite for a teacher. He has knowledge and science, so that He needs not to be taught by anyone (John 3:31 seq.); He has holiness and truth (John 5:46); He possesses not merely the power, strength, and skill to impart instruction outwardly, but also by the power of His grace to enlighten the understanding, touch the heart, and even in an instant make ignorant men enlightened. What all others teach and effect by their teaching, they do only by His authority and His power.

2. EXERCISE OF THE OFFICE OF TEACHING

Here we must consider what our Saviour preached, and how.

The tenor of our Saviour's teaching could only have reference to the end of man and the means to this end. God is the origin and end of man (Matt. 23:9). All men are one family. Their Father is God in three Persons: Father, Son, and Holy Ghost (Matt. 28:19). This Father is almighty, all-wise and all-good; He knows everything, can do everything, guides and arranges everything (Matt. 6:8, 26), and wishes to make us all happy by making us heirs to heaven, a great, glorious and eternal kingdom (Luke 11:2). Our Saviour always holds out the prospect of this kingdom (Matt. 5:3 seq.; Mark 1:14) as the goal and reward of all good, even of the very smallest action, such as giving a cup of water (Mark 9:40). It is our aim and end.

The means of reaching it are summed up by our Saviour under two heads: the commandments and the means of grace. The commandments, upon which He always lays such stress (Matt. 19:17), refer to the virtues which must be practised in order to attain to the goal, and to these belong, before all, faith (Mark 16:16) and the great commandment of love of God and of our neighbor (Mark 12:30). Of moral virtues four especially are recommended by our Lord. These are first poverty in spirit and in fact—detachment of heart and that apostolic poverty which renounces and forsakes everything for the sake of the Gospel (Matt. 5:3; 19:29); secondly, purity of heart in thoughts, intentions, desires, and complete renunciation in celibacy (Matt. 5:8, 28; 6:22; 19:11, 12); thirdly, love of one's neighbor (Matt. 5:7) and of one's enemies (Matt. 5:44), and works of mercy; fourthly, patience and joy in suffering and persecution (Matt. 5:10). All this is the way and the narrow gate that lead to life, the law of mortification and self-denial. The means of grace specially recommended by our Saviour is prayer (Luke 11:2; 18), upon which He enlarges considerably, and which He urgently invites us to practise (Luke 11:9); next, the use of the Sacraments which He institutes and prescribes (Matt. 28:19, 20; Mark 16:16; John 6:54; Luke 22:19), and attendance at divine service. All this is not left to individual discretion, but regulated by definite institutions and appointed authorities in a definite social union; namely by the Church and in the Church (Matt. 18:17). Our Saviour speaks at length concerning this Church, her nature, task, constitution (Matt. 16:18; 18:18) and destiny (Matt. 13). His preaching may be summed up in the law of the Gospel, Christian faith and morals. How simple, how true, how grand, consoling and easy! Few commandments—nothing beyond the Ten Commandments of the Old Testament, except the command to believe and submit to the Church; but much grace.

As regards the manner in which our Saviour preached, we may distinguish exterior and interior characteristics. By the exterior we mean chiefly the form of address. He taught by all kinds of sermons. He preached moral sermons everywhere (Matt. 5; 6; 7); dogmatic sermons (John 5; 6:14–16) chiefly in Jerusalem, when He went to that city for the feasts, and on these occasions His discourse often took the form of controversy. Many instructive addresses are debates between our Saviour and the Jews (John 7:15; 8:12; 10:24). He very often makes use of the attacks of His enemies to give a positive enunciation of His doctrine (Luke 6:1; Matt. 15:10 seq.; 19:1 seq.).

Among the intrinsic characteristics of our Saviour's preaching His zeal is especially remarkable. How often we are told in Holy Scripture of His preaching and teaching everywhere (Matt. 9:35), in the country, on the mountains, in the towns and synagogues, on the sea-shore, in the desert (Matt. 16:14), on His journeys

(Luke 13:23)! Anything serves Him for a pulpit, from a well (John 4:6) to a boat (Luke 5:3). He never troubles about the number or class of those who listen to Him. He makes use of everything as a subject for His discourses: the lilies (Luke 12:27), the birds (Matt. 6:26), the trees (Luke 13:6, 19), life and customs (Luke 13:21), religious and political events (Luke 13:4). He never refuses a sermon; He feels simply constrained to preach. Secondly, our Saviour preaches in a dignified and majestic style. He does not quarrel or dispute with His opponents, does not hesitate concerning the law and the truth, nor base it on mere subtleties, as did the schools of the day. He decides with clearness and authority; He does not merely interpret, but lays down the law (Matt. 5:22), and His decision, supported by clear and convincing eloquence and a saintly life, admits of no contradiction. He spoke "as one having power" (Matt. 7:29); men felt that it was the Lawgiver Himself. Thirdly, our Saviour taught in a very natural and unaffected way. It is often recorded of Him that He sat teaching among His disciples and the people, like a father among his children. The words flowed easily and unconstrainedly from His lips. The whole domain of truth, natural and supernatural, lay before His great and glorious intellect like an open book. He saw clearly their reciprocal relations, how the one is foreshadowed, prepared for and typified in the other, and how ordinary everyday things are the type and copy, basis and interpretation of the lofty and sublime. Nothing therefore was needed but indications to discover the relations between them.

Our Saviour built His marvelous discourses of the natural and the supernatural, as a clever artificer combines with dexterous hand the most various threads in one gay texture of many colors. Thus were fabricated those magnificent parables, the depth and sublimity of which no mind can fathom, and the truth of which any child can comprehend. He did not speak like the prophets, whose power of expression often falters, and who under the unspeakable weight of the truths they contemplate seem at a loss for words. Our Saviour's mode of speech, although a true reflection of His own time, country and people, yet preserves, in contrast with the prophets, a character of universality in keeping with the beautiful expression of pure humanity that beseemed the Son of Man, and in keeping with the fact that His doctrine was intended for all times and nations. With the natural ease of a spring gushing forth, and the grace of a sower scattering his grains of seed, our Saviour cast abroad the golden seed of His doctrine. Even His outward form of address was only a refined conversation. Lastly, He preached with great unction. His words satisfied not merely the understanding of His hearers by their truth, clearness of expression, depth and loftiness of intellect; but also the will and the feelings, by the way in which He put His heart into His teaching. Our Saviour took men just as they were, with understanding and will, feeling and fancy, and appealed to all their faculties. He always presupposed unprejudiced, docile minds and good hearts in His hearers. He made no demands that He did not support by the noblest and most solid motives, and drew these motives from all sorts of things in the natural and the supernatural order. He raises men's minds, encourages them, shows them how right and profitable it is to follow His teaching. How often He says: Blessed is the man who does this or that! And He always holds out the prospect of the glorious kingdom of heaven as the end and reward of all sacrifices. If people will not listen to Him, one feels only too well how pained He is. He grieves over it, and bitterly laments the unhappiness they bring upon themselves. No one who heard Him could help feeling that His words were prompted by a kind heart.

3. THE EFFECT OF OUR LORD'S TEACHING

Such teaching did not fail to meet with success. Everyone felt that there was something extraordinary about it, and wondered (Luke 13:17). The people followed Him in crowds (Matt. 19:2), thronged and pressed round Him (Luke 5:1; 8:45; 12:1), so that houses (Luke 5:16), squares, and even the sea-shore did not afford room enough; they forgot food and home to listen to His words (Matt. 15:32). Even His enemies were forced to admit that no man had ever spoken as He did (John 7:46), and finally left the field to Him, since they met with nothing but defeat and confusion (Matt. 22:46). The tremendous power of His wisdom and eloquence, together with the fearlessness and force with which He exposed and stigmatized their incorrigible wickedness, was one of the very things that drove them to take extreme measures against Him. Even though the greater part of the unhappy people perished in their unbelief and obduracy, that did not prevent the success of His teaching. The Gospel He had preached passed over from the Jews to the Gentiles, and the

Christian civilization of the world and the salvation of the human race is and remains the result of Jesus' teaching.

And now, before we conclude this meditation, we must first thank our Divine Saviour for the great blessing of His teaching and for all the labor it cost Him. What do we need more than light and truth and faith? By His doctrine He has become our Teacher and Guide to salvation and wisdom before God (I Cor. 1:30). What unspeakable comfort His lessons afford us in every position in life! Secondly, it is right and of the highest importance for us that we should become acquainted with this doctrine, understand and apply it, enter into its spirit and become penetrated with it. To know Jesus' doctrine is to love it, and therefore the study of it should be our constant occupation. And whoever has the duty of preaching and teaching it should rejoice in this great honor and happiness. He should also have a high esteem for his office, for to preach is more than to baptize. Our Saviour and St. Paul preached, but did not baptize (John 4:2; I Cor. 1:17). One must overcome all weariness in preaching by the reflection that this very weariness is the cross that brings the blessing, and that an "exceeding great reward" is in store for all who preach Christ's doctrine. Our Saviour gives most beautiful motives for zeal in preaching (Matt. 4:21–25), and finally a special reward in heaven (Matt. 5:19). He also teaches us by His example what to preach, and how. We must preach His doctrine, preach what is necessary and useful, what enlarges the heart and gives courage; and therefore we must take counsel with our Saviour about the subject of our sermons, recommend the matter to Him, and seek to become penetrated ourselves with the lesson in theory and in practice. The Catholic preacher is not a Scripture-reader. He must be the very incorporation of his doctrine and sermons, in life and words; then he will do good work.

The Miracles of Our Lord

The second sphere of action in the public ministry of our Saviour was the performing of miracles.

1. Signification and Aim of the Miracles of Jesus

Our Saviour had a threefold end in view in working miracles, and this threefold end corresponds to a threefold signification in the miracles themselves.

The first end was the confirmation of His doctrine. The subject of His teaching was, in the first place, His testimony of His divine mission and of His Divinity itself, His rank as Messias and Son of God. He Himself declares repeatedly that He works miracles in order that they may bear testimony to Him and to the truth of His words (John 10:25, 36), and that these miracles must be believed (John 10:38; 14:12). When John sent a deputation to Him, He referred them to His miracles as a proof of His Messianic mission (Matt. 11:5). He proves His power to forgive sins by healing the man sick of the palsy (Mark 2:10). But His most solemn declaration with respect to the object of His miracles was made at the raising of Lazarus (John 11:42). Miracles were certainly the simplest, shortest and surest way to make people believe in Him, and were quite in keeping with His Divinity. All other proofs require time, observation and talent, and even then are not convincing. Supernatural truths which cannot be proved by reason are best confirmed by supernatural deeds and miracles. Thus God shows Himself to be the Author of the natural and the supernatural, of the visible and the invisible. Wherever a miracle is worked in proof of a truth, there is the finger of God; for He alone can work miracles, and what He bears witness to is infallible truth. Thus a miracle, a divine proof of power over visible nature, is an attestation or certificate, so to speak, which everyone understands, and which admits of no contradiction. The people understood this at once, and therefore they cried out: "What is this new doctrine? For with power He commandeth even the unclean spirits" (Mark 1:27). Our Saviour was bound to confirm His doctrine by miracles, because this had been foretold of the Messias by the prophets (Isa. 35:5 seq.), and because this was the only means of making so many people of such different dispositions believe in Him. This, then, was the first object of His miracles.

Our Saviour's miracles are also proofs of His goodness and mercy, and this is their second important feature. The imparting of blessings is quite a remarkable characteristic of Christ's miracles. Love and mercy, and the intention of saving and redeeming us had brought Him down from heaven, and His object and work of redemption are aided in several ways by His miracles. The redemption includes deliverance from unbelief, sin and the punishments of sin. Almost all His miracles, with the exception of the miracles in connection with the sea, are works of deliverance from the power of Satan as exemplified in possession by evil spirits, or of deliverance from sickness and death, and very often from sin at the same time (Matt. 9:2; John 5:14). It was especially by this that they served to propagate the faith. Faith is the accepting of revealed truths, not because one has any natural perception of them, but because God, the Wise and Infallible, reveals them. Faith, therefore, necessarily depends upon the wish to believe, and this good will was powerfully stimulated by the miracles of Jesus, inasmuch as they were proofs of His goodness and mercy and great blessings for the recipients of them. To this character of goodness and benevolence displayed in His miracles is to be ascribed the circumstance that, with few exceptions, they do not bear the imposing and terrifying outward stamp of those wrought by Moses and other prophets. Our Saviour did not come to judge, but to redeem; what He most wished was to benefit, not to frighten, to save, and not to punish. This quiet grandeur of His miracles is the result of the object of His coming, of His surroundings, and of His character. Nevertheless in spiritual greatness and importance they infinitely surpass the great miracles of the prophets, because they were Messianic miracles, miracles wrought in proof of His divine mission and His own Divinity; those of the prophets were only types of His.

Their third signification, lastly, consists in their being intended not merely as a confirmation of His doctrine, but as lessons themselves, and also as types and prophecies of future institutions in the Church. As in the parables, so also in His miracles and in the manner in which He worked them, our Saviour brought out many features and institutions of His future Church. They are, as it were, parables in action. That His miracles have a figurative meaning cannot be denied, and with regard to this characteristic they may be divided into two groups. Those of the first group are a figure of the Sacraments. The miraculous cures of the possessed, the deaf, the dumb, and the blind are types of the Sacrament of Baptism, and often display remarkable resemblance to it in their attendant ceremonies; the cures of the lame and the leprous, and the raising of the dead are types of the Sacrament of Penance; and the transformation of water into wine and the multiplication of loaves are types of the Holy Eucharist. The other group, the miracles connected with the sea, are worked for the benefit of the Apostles, and are meant to encourage them for their future apostolic ministry by showing them the privilege they have of being specially helped and protected in all difficulties, interior and exterior. They are real revelations and prophecies of the future experiences of the Church.

2. DESCRIPTION AND PURPOSE OF THE MIRACLES OF JESUS

As regards their variety as well as the manner in which they were worked, our Saviour's miracles had these various ends in view. They extended over four spheres of action. First, over irrational nature. Our Saviour changes water into wine, multiplies bread, stills the storm, walks upon the water, eclipses the sun, and splits the rocks; He is therefore Lord of the earth, the sea, the lower regions, and the firmament. The second sphere of action is the human body and sickness of all kinds. In this connection He worked innumerable miracles of all descriptions. The departed souls form the third sphere. They are subject to His command; He calls them back from eternity to earthly life. The evil spirits, whom He exorcises and expels, are the fourth. This is the climax of Christ's power, because He here confronts a positive, spiritual power. He subdues powers that hold sway over everything else, and that no one could master. Many of the miracles worked by Him are supernatural not merely as regards the way in which they were accomplished, but also in their intrinsic nature, such as the cure of the man born blind, the changes of the substance of things, the raising of the dead, and the expulsion of devils. There was no part of creation in which the power of Christ did not give evidence of His glorious supremacy. Amid His poverty and lowliness His miracles shine out like flashes of lightning over all forms of life.

What especially helped Him to attain His end was the manner in which He worked them. He did so openly, before friends and enemies; suddenly, without any preparation; in the most various ways, sometimes by ceremonies, sometimes by His mere word without any outward action (Mark 2:11; 10:52), and from a distance (John 4:50; Matt. 15:28). His miraculous power formed a part of Himself, as it were, so that it always stood at His command (Luke 6:19); and He accomplished these proofs of power not by the medium of His prayer, but by the immediate effecting of the miraculous result (Luke 9:16; Mark 5:30).

When we think connectedly over all this, we see that the miracles of Christ, together with the prophecies in which these Messianic marvels were foretold, sufficiently proved His divine mission and His own Divinity; that is to say, if one knew the prophecies and recognized the miracles as such. When His personal testimony with regard to these two truths (namely His divine mission and His Godhead) and the holiness which was clearly perceptible in His whole manner of life are taken into consideration, His miracles became so complete and overpowering a proof of His Divinity and mission as Messias, that with the aid of God's grace moral certainty was quite easily attainable.

3. EFFECT OF THE MIRACLES OF JESUS

The effect of these miracles was different upon different classes. The evil spirits must have learnt before the Death of our Lord that He was not merely the Messias but also the Son of God; for they knew the prophecies and the nature of His miracles (Mark 1:24; Luke 4:41). The people were, for the most part, led by His wonderful deeds to the conviction that He was a prophet (John 6:14) and sent by God (Luke 7:16), and to admit, though with hesitation and fluctuation of opinion, that He was the Messias (John 7:31, 41, 42; 10:24, 25); but they did not generally recognize Him as the Son of God. The Jews had as a rule too superficial and worldly a conception of the Messias. No more did well-educated Pharisees or the chief priests believe in the Divinity of our Saviour. They could indeed recognize Him as the Messias from the prophecies and His miracles, and their consciences must have urged them to believe in Him, but their passions stifled the voice of conscience. In any case their ignorance was culpable and their unbelief sinful (John 12:37, 40; 15:22; Luke 22:67). The Apostles, on the other hand, and many of the disciples and the faithful, such as Simeon, Anna, Elizabeth, Martha, the man born blind, and many others, recognized not only our Lord's divine mission as the Messias, but also His true Divinity.

As for ourselves, these miracles must first of all confirm our faith. Together with the prophecies they form the solid foundation of our faith in the true Divinity of Jesus. To this day we stand upon this foundation and enjoy the fruits of these miracles. How marvelously beautiful and surprising is the connection of the miracles of Jesus with His doctrine! How many of His statements did He immediately confirm by a corresponding miracle! He says: "I am the Light of the world," and He opens the eyes of the blind; He calls Himself the Bread of Life, and twice multiplies bread; He calls Himself the Resurrection and the Life, and restores innumerable sick people to health and raises the dead to life; He says He has power on earth to forgive sins, and immediately heals the palsied man. His word is also a divine and wonder-working act. Secondly, these miracles must fill us with confidence. The power of Christ penetrates the darkness of our sufferings, dispels our grief, averts punishment and frees us from the curse. Even on the threshold of eternity, when all human power is helpless, we may look trustfully up to our Saviour and say: "Thou canst help me." He has helped, has restored the shattered body and called back the departed spirit. Can we not throw ourselves with implicit confidence into the arms of such a power? Thirdly, these miracles also inspire us with love. In them the kind heart and lovable character of Jesus are revealed. He does not content Himself with working miracles only when He is asked to do so, but often works them spontaneously, as at the raising of the youth of Naim from the dead and the cure of the lame man at Bethesda. The two remarks: "And He gave him (the son) to his mother" (Luke 7:15), and "Jesus . . . cured the boy, and restored him to his father" (Luke 9:43), show us how tender and susceptible was His Heart. And is it not on the occasion of just such a miracle that His compassion moves Him to tears? All our evils and misfortunes drew from Him not only tears and words of consolation, but also the aid of His almighty power. He could do what He willed; and He willed, because He loved.

The Example of Virtue Set by Jesus

The third point in the public life is the example of virtue set by our Divine Saviour. This may be considered from three points of view: with relation to God, with relation to His fellow-men, and with relation to Himself.

Our Saviour's example of virtue in relation to God

The virtues relating to God may be considered under three heads, and in all these the Heavenly Father has the predominant place.

1. SUBMISSION TO THE WILL OF THE FATHER

This dependence upon His Father and submission and obedience to Him is a strongly marked characteristic of our Saviour's virtue and holiness as seen in His public life, in so far as we consider Him in His human nature.

Generally speaking, the fulfilment of the Will of His Heavenly Father was His special work (John 5:30; 6:38), the starting-point, rule, measure and aim of His plans, undertakings and actions, the element in which He moved (John 8:29), the food that formed His sustenance (John 4:34), His comfort and joy in everything (Matt. 11:26). It had been foretold that He would be the great servant and subject of God (Isa. 42:1; 49:3; 53:11; Zach. 3:8); He Himself calls the Father the "Lord of heaven and earth" (Matt. 11:25), and He showed Himself in all respects simple and childlike, submissive and obedient to His Heavenly Father.

This feature may be followed out in detail in all the stages of our Saviour's life. The first act of His will was an act of resignation to the Will of His Father (Ps. 39:9; Hebr. 10:5 seq.), and during His youth His obedience to His parents, the representatives of His Heavenly Father, is especially emphasized (Luke 2:51). Indeed, even at this early period He already testifies solemnly by word and deed that He is under the guidance of a superior, namely the Heavenly Father, and He follows His directions (Luke 2:49). In His public ministry He adheres strictly to the Will of His Father: first, with regard to the time of its commencement, at the age of thirty; secondly, with regard to the field of His labors, which He confines almost exclusively to Galilee and Judaea; thirdly, with regard to those whom He is to instruct, the Jewish nation, beyond which He does not work officially (Matt. 15:24); among the Jews He receives all whom His Father sends Him, even Judas (John 6:37), and says that all who do the Will of His Father belong to His family (Matt. 7:21); lastly, He is submissive and resigned with regard to the result of His teaching. All this—the time, place and result of His ministry—was really small and not in keeping with the dignity of His Divinity, but He submitted humbly and obediently to everything (John 4:37, 38). His obedience is equally shown in His Passion. It is the chalice that His Father gives Him. Must He not drink it, however bitter it is? (Mark 14:36; John 18:11.) He cannot die until He has fulfilled the last prophecy (John 19:28). His last word in the desolation of death is an acknowledgment of the Father and an act of resignation into His hands (Luke 23:46). Great and majestic events in connection with the Messias had been predicted by the prophets, such as His virgin Birth, His power as Prophet, Priest, and King, His Death and Resurrection; and also minor and less important ones, e.g. that He would be born in Bethlehem, make His entry into Jerusalem upon the foal of an ass, be sold for thirty pieces of silver, and suffer thirst in His dying agony. And all these were fulfilled to the letter. Naturally speaking, His public life seems strange in many respects. It was spent in constant wanderings from place to place. Sometimes He works His miracles publicly, as though on purpose to annoy His enemies, and sometimes He wishes them to be kept secret; He irritates the Jews by holding intercourse with those excommunicated and others of ill repute, and by offending against and neglecting their customs; and He scarcely makes any frank and plain declaration of His Divinity to the people. But there is no arbitrariness in all this; on the contrary, an infallible rule. He is guided and governed in everything by the Will of His Father. That is the golden thread that runs through His marvelous life and work, and the explanation of His plans and proceedings.

The first example of virtue that our Saviour gives us with relation to God is that of the submission which is due to Him. What does the creature owe more to its Creator than acknowledgment, submission and obedience? For our Saviour was a creature as regards His human nature, even though He was the true Son of God. Without this submission the greatest deeds are nothing but irregularity. Wisdom, holiness and success are only to be found in the fulfilment of God's Will. The priest and apostle is all the more obliged to obey God's Will, because he is His messenger and ambassador here below, and must follow His directions in every respect. Our Saviour gives us an example of trustworthiness and conscientiousness, in fulfilling the Will of God in everything, in never doing or undertaking anything contrary to it, and in submitting in every respect to what He in His wisdom, holiness and goodness permits. At every step we should ask ourselves: "Is this God's Will? Am I justified in doing this?" And we should always be able to say: "I do always the things that please Him" (John 8:29).

2. ZEAL FOR THE GLORY OF THE HEAVENLY FATHER

The second virtue with relation to God that our Saviour practised in His public life was His zeal for the glory of His Heavenly Father. He practised this virtue in three degrees of perfection.

First, He does not seek His own honor, but that of His Heavenly Father; and He declares this very often. "I seek not My own glory" (John 8:50). And yet He might have done so. He deserved glory, and would not have misused it. But He did not seek it; and His acts confirmed His words. He hides Himself, so to speak, under the shadow of His Father. How often He speaks of Himself as "sent" by God! (John 8:42; 12:49.) His doctrine is the doctrine of the Father (John 7:16); His miracles are the works of the Father (John 14:10); He is the way to the Father (John 14:6), and He Himself goes to the Father (John 14:12). In His parables the Father is the lord, the master of the house, the king; He is the Lord of all good things, and our Saviour obtains them from Him by His prayer for us (John 16:23); the aim and end of His life and work is simply His Father's honor (John 17:4); He desires His own glory only as a means of glorifying the Father (John 17:1).

Secondly, our Saviour seeks in all He does the greater glory of the Father, and therefore He does not do everything in the same way. He makes His choice, and selects what is more necessary, more useful, more comprehensive and lasting. He teaches first in Galilee, where it was more needed; He quits His native town, because there was nothing to be done there (Matt. 13:58); He seeks out sinners and lives on terms of intimacy with them, because they were lost (Luke 5:31); He prefers preaching to baptizing, apostolic work to the quiet repose of the contemplative life; He does not forget one town amid the wants of another (Luke 4:43). He restricts His intercourse chiefly to men (John 4:16, 27); He even leaves His holy Mother. He lets Himself be guided in everything solely by consideration for the greater glory of the Father.

Thirdly, our Lord seeks His Father's glory with self-sacrifice, at the cost of His own honor and even of His life. In order to save and restore the glory of His Heavenly Father, He incurs the enmity of the Jews, exposes their wickedness and corruption, and puts them publicly to shame. He even proceeds to active and forcible measures, twice purifying the Temple, His Father's House, protecting it from profanation, and expelling the buyers and sellers. Called to account for this, He answers in words full of meaning that they might destroy the temple of His Body, if they pleased; but nothing would prevent Him from promoting the glory of His Father (John 2:17, 19). And so it really came about.

He died on the Cross as an oblation to the glory of the Heavenly Father. If He had sought His own honor, He would have led a very different life. But He wished to receive glory from His Father alone (John 8:50; 17:1), and at the price of His own honor and His life. Hence, when Judas had gone out to betray Him, He exclaimed: "Now is the Son of Man glorified" (John 13:31). We may call this zeal for His Father's glory the very passion of our Saviour. It animated Him from the very first instant, when He said: "Behold, I come" (Ps. 39:8), to offer Myself as a sacrifice in place of the ancient sacrifices; and He sacrificed everything to it.

Our Saviour sets us in this a beautiful example, and we must follow it. Justice, first of all, demands it of us. God alone deserves all honor, because He is the Source of all our good, the greatest good, and all in all. To Him, therefore, above all others, honor is due; and not to render it to Him is a robbery. Let us seek, as is only right, the glory of God; then we shall be working for the same end as that for which all creation is consciously or unconsciously working, and for the same end as God Himself. Secondly, our own advantage requires it. If we do not seek God's honor, whose honor do we seek, but our own? And, if not from God, from whom do we seek it? Evidently from men. But such an endeavor can only degrade us. This striving after self-glorification is fatal. It was this very vice that kept the Jews from believing (John 5:44; 12:43). It is their spirit, and Satan's. Lastly, God Himself will glorify us if we glorify Him, as our Saviour Himself says and as happened in His case (John 8:50, 54; 12:28). This, then, will be true glory. Whoever has the spirit of our Saviour will seek in all things, even in his spiritual progress, nothing but the glorification of God in us; and will shun no work, no pains, and no sacrifice, in order that He may be acknowledged and loved by the hearts of men.

3. OUR SAVIOUR'S INTERCOURSE WITH HIS HEAVENLY FATHER IN PRAYER

The third example of virtue that our Saviour gives us in relation to God is His fervor in prayer.

What a perfect example He sets us! He not only spoke often of prayer, encouraged and taught people to pray, but He also practised it Himself. Interiorly He enjoyed the constant and uninterrupted vision of God; therefore He was constantly engaged in inward communion with the Father. But He also prayed outwardly; in private, at night (Luke 6:12), and also publicly and vocally (Matt. 6:9; John chap. 17), at ordinary times in the synagogue and elsewhere on various occasions (Matt. 11:26), and at unusual times before undertaking important projects (Luke 6:12; 9:18; John 6:11; 11:41). Thus He practised all kinds of prayer, and held the most constant intercourse with His Heavenly Father. For prayer is nothing else than intercourse, intimacy, converse with God; an exchange of thoughts and sentiments, in thanksgiving, adoration, praise, petition and atonement. Our Saviour prayed much and well; outwardly with great reverence, with raised eyes (John 11:41) and in a kneeling posture (Mark 14:35), and inwardly with deep recollection and devotion, and with infallible efficacy when His prayer was simple petition (John 11:42). His prayer was that of the Divine Mediator, the Son of God (Hebr. 5:7).

The reason of our Saviour's constancy in prayer was, first, that it was fitting and necessary that He should pray. According to His human nature He too was a creature, and as such He was bound to offer to the Father the tribute of prayer, adoration and thanksgiving. Prayer extends over the whole creation. Thus regarded it is the first end of the creature, whose duty it is to praise and thank God. The second reason was the sublimity of prayer, because it is intercourse with God. Even for our Saviour there was nothing higher, sweeter, or more important than communing with His Heavenly Father. The attainment of an end is the essence of perfection. In prayer we attain our last end, as far as it can be attained here below. The third reason was our Saviour's consideration for us; He prayed in order to set us an example, to make our prayer effective by His own, to gain graces for us, and to glorify God in us. He did not need to pray for graces for Himself, but for us. With regard to us He was subject to the same law as we are: the more prayer, the more grace; no prayer, no grace. God required of Him not only work and suffering, but also prayer as the price of our graces. Now it is easy to understand why He prayed so much. He had many to pray for, and much to ask for them. He regarded Himself, as He really was, as the Representative, Head, and High Priest of the whole human race and the Mediator for them with God in prayer, partly to glorify Him in the name of all, and partly to draw down graces upon them. Thus He had before His mind every individual human being, with his wants, concerns, duties, dangers and difficulties; He saw in spirit the whole Church, her history and development, her experiences, persecutions and successes, and the whole hierarchy, all the Popes, bishops, priests and faithful; He saw the entire human race, all ages, classes and nations to the end of time. All this passed before His eyes like a great panorama, and He prayed, wrestled and gave thanks for all. Everything was merited and settled by His prayers. Whatever grace, protection, strength and enlightenment we have comes to us from this source. Our Saviour stands there in prayer like a mighty tree. He spreads His roots throughout the world into every human life and heart, into the heart of the Church and of all families and nations, absorbs to Himself their duties to praise and acknowledge God, their wants and interests, offering them to God in union with His prayer, and drawing down and distributing everywhere the blessing and the grace bestowed by His intercession. The whole Church and the whole human race draw their life from His intercession, as well as from His grace and doctrine. Here we have a glimpse of the tenor of His prayer as God-Man, and of what occupied His mind in His long nocturnal prayers. They were truly the prayers of a God-Man. This may be seen from His words to St. Peter (Luke 22:32), as well as from His prayer for His disciples (John chap. 17) and the purport of the Our Father.

The conclusion to be drawn from this meditation is that we too must pray; and we are shown the way. The reasons that our Saviour had for praying, and for praying so much, apply to us also. We must pray, because there is really nothing higher and better than to converse with God, and nothing more necessary. Prayer is an indispensable means of obtaining graces for ourselves and others; it suffices for all our wants as well as for those of our neighbor, because its intrinsic efficacy is unlimited. What a grand and universal means of glorifying God is prayer! Our Saviour practised it so constantly, because He was working for His Father when He prayed. We are simply the children of His prayers. Would it not have been a great honor and happiness, if we had been able to pass an hour at our Saviour's side during one of those nights of prayer? We can do so; He is always inviting us when He inspires us to pray. Our prayer, made in His Name, is a continuation of His. But then it must be like His, too. We must pray as He did, that is, we must pray much, as much as the duties of our vocation demand and permit; that is how we learn to pray. We must also pray well. We do so when we pray as our Saviour did, with the desire that God may be glorified in us and others; and when we pray not only for ourselves and our little domestic wants and crosses, but for the whole Church and the entire human race. And thus we too can pray long, because we have to pray for many and ask for much. This is especially true of prayers of obligation, Holy Mass and the breviary. These are not private prayers, but ecclesiastical and universal ones. The priest reciting the Divine Office is the heart of the world. Every Mass, every canonical Hour, and every Our Father thus becomes a part of the history of the Church and the world.

In these three virtues the whole relation of our Saviour to His Heavenly Father is comprised. This relation may be fittingly called His devotion, and to this He also exhorts us in word and deed.

Our Saviour's example of virtue in relation to His neighbor

The second relation in which His example of virtue was seen in His public life was His intercourse with His neighbor, and this again in three respects.

1. FRANKNESS AND SINCERITY OF OUR SAVIOUR

The first thing that we owe to our neighbor is truth and sincerity. We see this in our Saviour. He was sincerity, truth and frankness itself to everyone. He wished everyone well, and was never anything but kindness itself in word and deed. He never made use of men for selfish ends, but spoke and acted openly, sincerely and uprightly, without circumlocution or ambiguity of speech. To all who wished to follow Him He told straightforwardly what they must be ready for, and what they had to expect (Luke 9:58); and in His predictions He spoke plainly of crosses and persecutions (Luke 12:51; Matt. 10:21; John 16:2). He required of everyone the same as He did and suffered Himself, and no more (Luke 9:23; 14:26; John 15:20; Matt. 10:24). When a reproof was needed, He gave it openly and fearlessly (Luke 11:50). For this reason He was the declared enemy of the Pharisees, because they were the exact opposite in all these respects (Matt. chap. 23).

This truthfulness and sincerity is a very important part of our duty to our neighbor, although very little known and esteemed. It is simple justice, the beginning of charity, and absolutely necessary for the exercise of the apostolic office, because this is the only way in which sincerity and confidence can be awakened, and without confidence no good can be done to anyone. If a man were a Saint in other respects, without this virtue he would not be a Saint according to the spirit of Jesus.

2. PATIENCE AND GENTLENESS

Another virtue of no less importance than sincerity in our intercourse with our neighbor is patience and gentleness. Gentleness, which we generally call patience, controls and restrains angry feelings and outbursts of anger.

Our Saviour sets us a magnificent example of this. What great demands were made upon His gentleness in His public life, from all sides, and how gloriously it stood the test! What a trial to His patience must His disciples have been, with their slowness of comprehension and inaptitude for their high vocation and intercourse with Him (Matt. 13:36; Mark 8:16, 17; Acts 1:6); the people, with their obtrusiveness, coarseness (Mark 3:10; 5:31; Luke 5:1; Matt. 14:13, 14), and selfishness (John 6:26); the upper classes, with their indifference, policy and contempt (John 7:48); His enemies, with their contradictions, molestations, and insinuations! Lastly, He was tried by His Heavenly Father, Who in His inscrutable decree restricted our Saviour's sphere of action, and only allowed Him to make slow progress. And yet with all this our Saviour does not complain, or only in very few instances (Mark 8:17–20; 9:18); does not get into a passion, does not bring about any change in His position and circumstances; but on the contrary allows everyone unrestricted liberty to make demands upon His time and patience. He might have altered much if He had chosen, but He did not choose. And yet how sensitive and susceptible He was! But all this had been predicted of Him (Isa. 42:1 seq.; Matt. 12:18).

Here we have a beautiful example to imitate. Patience is absolutely necessary to us. However much we try, we shall never be able to arrange matters so that there is nothing to provoke us to impatience. It is not possible. And patience is a powerful help in apostolic work. Patience procures us influence and good-will; it is the practice of charity and self-control, practical wisdom in daily life, strength of will, a good, humble and benevolent heart, and great virtue. Patience is virtue, practical virtue, mature virtue. The more spiritual progress a man makes, the more patient and gentle he becomes. Patience attracts people to us and makes them feel themselves at home with us. Impatience, on the contrary, drives them away. It does no good and much harm, especially in the case of a superior, a confessor, or those engaged in the education of children. And it is certainly not the spirit of Jesus. For the God-Man impatience was an impossibility. We are the pastors of the New Testament, and not of the Old, which was a law of fear; and as pastors we are not the offended parties, but reconcilers, not executioners, but physicians. The Good Shepherd does not strike the lost sheep when he finds it, but carries it with gentle force back to the fold. In order to be patient we must be recollected, consider all kinds of unpleasantness possible in this life, be prepared for anything, and let it be our principle that there is no good reason for getting impatient.

3. CHARITY

Charity is nothing but practical love of our neighbor, the endeavor to do good to him in soul and body; in short, mercy in the highest sense of the word.

We only need to look at the circles in which our Saviour moved, in order to gain an idea how charitable He was. The Apostles formed the first circle. The chief thing in their case was their training for the apostolic office. Our Saviour provided for the cultivation of their intellect by His discourses (Matt. 5:1) and special instructions (Matt. 13:10, 36; 15:15); for the training of their hearts by correcting their faults of ambition (Mark 9:32; Matt. 20:24), envy (Luke 9:50), and revengefulness (Luke 9:55), and by inculcating apostolic virtues, such as detachment from home and relatives (Luke 14:26), industry (Mark 6:51), abstinence (Matt. 12:1), patience under persecution (Matt. 10:16 seq.). With regard to externals, He provided for their temporal wants (Luke 22:35), protected them from the Pharisees (Mark 2:16), and exercised them in the duties of the apostolic office (Matt. 10:5; 15:35, 36). The second circle by which our Saviour was surrounded was composed of the faithful. What a good, kind friend Lazarus and his sisters have in Him! (John 11:5.) He does not overlook the temporal needs of His followers (Matt. 14:19; 15:36); He treats their faults with indulgence (John 2:3; Mark 5:36); does not overload them by requiring many things of them (Mark 2:18 seq.), but encourages them and praises their virtues (Mark 5:34; Matt. 8:10; 15:28). And how kind and friendly He is to children! (Mark 10:14.) The sick and distressed form the third circle. It is especially towards these unfortunates that His love and kindness is shown. He even seeks them out (John 5:2,6) and offers them His miraculous aid (Luke 7:13). Nearly all His miracles are cures of diseases, expulsions of devils, raising of the dead; He works them even to remove the most trivial difficulties (John 2:9). Everything about Him seems to acquire a healing and miraculous power on behalf of those in distress, His clothes (Matt. 9:21; 14:36; Mark 6:56; Luke 8:44), His saliva (John 9:6), and His hands (Matt. 8:3). He heals and comforts everyone. In some towns and villages there were no sick people left at His departure. He let no one go away dissatisfied or unconsoled in his suffering. The fourth circle consists of sinners, the most wretched of all the unfortunate; and it is towards these especially that His goodness and mercy are so wonderfully displayed. He does not despise them with a lofty and sanctimonious air, as did the Pharisees; He goes after them and tries to meet them (John 4:6); He encourages them by His sermons; for them He has the most touching parables (Luke 15:1 seq.); He receives them kindly (John 8:10), examines their consciences with the utmost delicacy (John 4:16), and gently admonishes them (Luke 7:50; John 5:14; 8:11). And when they are converted they become His friends, and He defends them warmly (Luke 7:40); they are admitted to the most familiar friendship with Him. Is He not truly a Good Shepherd and Mercy Incarnate?

How and why did our Saviour perform these acts of charity? Outwardly with great graciousness, friendliness and assiduity; inwardly with true supernatural virtue, kindness and good will. All His acts of benevolence were real virtue, the pure gold of love. And He was actuated by the holiest motives. He did us so much good for God's sake; He saw in us the creatures, the children and the image of His Heavenly Father. He did it also for His own sake, just because He was God, and our God; He would have had to do violence to His Heart to refrain from doing good. Lastly, He did it for our sakes, because we were really so miserable and so sorely in need of help, and because He wished to win us over to His teaching by His benefits.

Thus our Saviour passed through life in a manner worthy of God, bestowing blessings and benefits (Acts 10:38). What a beautiful example for us! The amount of misfortune and the number of the unfortunate in the world is so great, and we have so many means of alleviating misfortune; we have a heart, good thoughts, good words and works, and kind glances; and above all, we have supernatural powers, prayer and the priestly faculties. We ourselves need forgiveness of sins and comfort in prayer and at the hour of death. If we wish to do good and to win the world for our Saviour and the Church, let us have recourse to acts of charity and benevolence. We can do it all by these means, and win our Divine Saviour's Heart as well.

Our Saviour's example of virtue in relation to Himself

Our Saviour's example of virtue in relation to Himself in His public life likewise embraces three points.

1. POVERTY

Poverty is voluntary privation of external and material goods, for supernatural ends and for the sake of evangelical perfection.

Our Saviour's poverty was not absolute, but suited to His state of life and the apostolic ends He had in view; but it was nevertheless very great. He had no dwelling, at least no settled one of His own. He was at home everywhere and nowhere, always with strangers; by day in the streets and squares, by night under the open sky, or in caves or under trees, when no compassionate people gave Him shelter. He "had not where to lay His head" (Matt. 8:20). His supply of food was likewise very uncertain; today He eats with Larazus or a Pharisee, tomorrow He is in the desert with a crowd of people and they have only a few loaves, the next day on the high-road with His disciples in the noonday heat without a morsel of bread, so that the Apostles begin to rub the ears of wheat (Matt. 12:1). His clothing was respectable, as beseemed a teacher of the law, but simple and according to the custom of the country, without anything superfluous. At the Crucifixion we have all His garments enumerated (John 19:23). He carried no money on His person, not even enough to pay the Temple-tax (Matt. 17:26). He really lived upon alms, and allowed Himself to be supported by compassionate people (Luke 8:3; John 12:6). Indeed, His poverty was always on the increase. In Nazareth He had at least a home of His own, and His every need was provided for; but later on this was not the case, and at His Death His poverty was so great that He had not even a drink of water to quench His thirst, a piece of linen to cover Him, nor a grave in which to lie. Even His dead Body was confiscated and put under seal. What He said to the scribe came to pass: "The foxes have holes, and the birds of the air nests; but the Son of Man hath not where to lay His head." This is surely great poverty, and it is touching when we consider Who He is and what demands He might have made. He might have had all the pleasure-gardens, country-houses, and palaces by which He passed, in which people were leading a luxurious and pleasant life; and yet with how little He contented Himself! What prince ever asked for so little?

This is a very touching and solemn lesson, and it should make us reflect that we too must take example from Him, especially if the apostolic vocation is ours. He requires this poverty of the Apostles also (Matt. 10:9; 19:21), for their own perfection and security (Matt. 19:23), for the sake of good example, and in order to give them liberty and aptitude for their apostolic work (Luke 12:34); and lastly also for the sake of the temporal and eternal rewards which He promises to apostolic poverty (Matt. 19:28 seq.).

2. DETACHMENT FROM KINDRED, AND FROM HONOR AND FAVOR WITH MEN

We must be detached not only from external, material goods, but also from those which are more subtle and interior, such as love of relatives and honor.

In this respect also our Saviour sets us a most perfect example. He had no inordinate attachment to His home. He was only once or twice in Nazareth during the whole of His public life (Matt. 13:54; Luke 4:16). He never spoke of His home but to warn others (Mark 6:4), and with good reason. He did not flatter His fellow-citizens, nor they Him. And He showed just as little irregular attachment to His holy Mother. He left her as soon as God willed it (Matt. 3:13), and did not admit her to His presence at once, when she came during one of His discourses (Matt. 12:48). He always used this freedom towards His friends. He did not scruple to reprove Martha's irritation at her sister's behavior (Luke 10:41), nor to let both the sisters wait for Him three days when their brother Lazarus was sick (John 11:6). Neither did He hesitate to refuse the request made by the mother of two of His disciples, that her sons might occupy the first places in His kingdom (Matt. 20:22). He gave the Gentile woman from Phoenicia an apparently very harsh rebuff (Mark 7:27). He gave even His favorite disciples sharp reproofs (Matt. 16:23; Luke 9:55). Thus our Saviour was quite detached, and had no attachment to anything but God and His duty. Neither should we be attached to anything; first, for God's sake, because attachment to creatures takes our heart from God, and He cares for nothing but our love, for we must love Him with all our heart and with all our strength. Secondly, we must suffer no inordinate attachments to remain in our hearts, for our neighbor's sake, that we may be able to give others help and edification; without this detachment those among our fellow-men who most need help are often neglected. Lastly, we must try to be detached for our own sake, because in detachment alone is to be found purity, tranquillity, the necessary influence, strength through grace, and energy for work and sacrifice. The want of this detachment makes us effeminate, selfish and narrow-minded.

Our Saviour was equally detached from all inclination to human respect, which is in reality only lack of humility. He did not try to please the world. He did not appear at all as the carnal and worldly expectations of the people would have had Him. He came humble and poor, preached penance, exacted self-denial, and did not gratify the national vanity in any way. For this reason He says: "Blessed is he whosoever shall not be scandalized in Me" (Luke 7:23). Further, He openly opposed the ruling party of the Pharisees, exposed their secret and shameful doings, and censured them severely. Lastly, He incurred the displeasure of the Jews, by giving them plainly to understand that He, as the Messias and Son of God, was the Master in all ecclesiastical affairs; that He would found another religious and ecclesiastical system; that they would not belong to this new divine kingdom, and that through their own fault; that sinners and Gentiles would be called to take their places, and that they would bring upon themselves their ruin in this life and the next. This naturally displeased them, and thus He made enemies of all the Jews. He became an object of hatred and bloody persecution. But that did not make the least difference to Him. He sought before all things God and His justice, and was humble enough to take upon Himself the displeasure and disapproval of all. "Christ did not please Himself," as it is truly and beautifully put by Holy Scripture (Rom. 15:3). And without this thorough humility one can never be a faithful and reliable servant of God (Gal. 1:10).

3. FORTITUDE IN SUFFERING AND ADVERSITY

By "sufferings and adversities" we mean here only those endured by our Lord in His public life. Of these there were two kinds.

The first kind of sufferings were those which our Saviour inflicted on Himself by His active and fatiguing life. It was especially His great, uninterrupted and strenuous labor that caused Him suffering. He was always to be found going from one mission to another. Traveling, preaching, and healing the sick filled up His whole day and often part of the night (Matt. 8:16; 19:13); He often had no time to rest, and when He tried to do so He was disturbed, but never regretted it (Mark 6:34). He had no predilections or favorite pursuits, nothing but work, hard work and duty. It was tiring, and He often felt His weariness (Matt. 8:24; John 4:6). To this were often added the inclemency of the weather, bad roads and unpleasant districts. Lastly, He often increased these sufferings by great austerity of life, fasting (Matt. 4:2; Luke 6:12) and long nocturnal prayers. Who can tell what suffering all this caused Him? This cross, the cross of labor, is certainly the first and best for us to seek and choose. Our Saviour wants laborers, not idlers or those who play at work (Luke 10:2). An Apostle must be before all things a laborer. For this reason our Lord chose His Apostles mostly from the working class, and compared the apostolic office to the calling of a shepherd (John 10:11), a fisher (Mark 1:17), a vine-dresser and husbandman (Luke 9:62). Happy the feet and hands that grow weary in the service of the Church and of souls! How great will be their reward in heaven!

The second kind of sufferings that our Saviour had to bear were caused Him by His fellow-men. These fall to the lot of all who have the cure of souls. In the first place, there is want of success. One means well, labors and prays, and yet it seems to be of no use, and people get worse and worse. It is hard to bear; but our Saviour found it the same. No one ever labored more to do good. How many were His sermons, prayers and miracles! And yet almost all His efforts were frustrated by the stupidity, passion and malice of men. How it must have pained Him to see the poor people bringing such misery upon themselves! It brought tears to His eyes and forced deep sighs and bitter lamentations from His lips (Luke 19:41). Besides this want of success there were the constant annoyances, calumnies and other injuries that

He had to put up with from His enemies, who were bent upon thwarting and destroying the effect of His ministry upon the people. They picked to pieces everything that He did, and made the worst they could of it. If He preached, they said He had not studied (John 7:15); if He conferred a benefit upon the people, they said He only wished to lead them astray (John 7:12); if He accepted invitations from men of the upper classes, they called Him a wine-drinker (Matt. 11:19); if He worked miracles, they ascribed them to the power of the devil (Luke 11:15) and said that He Himself was possessed (Mark 3:22); if He proclaimed His Divinity, they accused Him of blasphemy (John 10:36). They dogged His steps everywhere (Matt. 12:2), and watched all that He did (Luke 14:1), trying to catch Him in His speech (Matt. 19:3; Luke 11:16) and even in His works of mercy (Luke 14:3); they openly cast in His teeth the most shameful affronts, before all the people (John 7:20; 8:48; 10:20). They drew everyone, the people and their rulers, away from Him, and brought things to such a pitch that no one knew what to think of Him (John 7:12), and many gave up all intercourse with Him and felt ashamed of having received His benefits. Animosity and dislike passed by degrees into mortal hatred and persecution. One only needs to read St. John's accounts of our Lord's visits to Jerusalem at the various feasts, to see how this hatred ever increased and even threatened His life. On the first Feast of the Pasch He drives the buyers and sellers out of the Temple, and the ill-feeling aroused is so great that Nicodemus dares visit Him only by night (John 2:18, 24; 3:2). On the second, He heals the lame man on the Sabbath, and the Jews begin to think of putting Him to death (John 5:16, 18). He does not go to the third Paschal Feast at all, in order to avoid the snares set for Him by the Jews (John 7:1). He does not dare to travel openly to the Feast of Tabernacles, and yet on this very feast they try to arrest Him (John 7:30, 32), and soon after to stone Him (John 8:59). On the Feast of the Dedication, when He speaks about His Divinity more clearly than on any other occasion, only by a miracle can He escape being arrested in the Temple and stoned (John 10:31, 39). Finally, when the fourth Feast of the Pasch occurs, He has fallen a sacrifice to their rage and is lying in the grave. At the very beginning of His public ministry, on His visit to Nazareth, He was already in danger of being cast headlong from the brow of the hill (Luke 4:29), and from this moment persecutions and attacks upon His freedom and His life never ceased. How often He had to go from place to place and from province to province to escape the snares set for Him by His enemies! (John 4:1; Matt. 12:15; 14:3, 13.) Thus His entire public life was a succession of moral and physical persecutions.

And how did He behave in the midst of it all? First, He bore it with patience. He did not call down fire from heaven like Elias (IV Kings 1:10), nor yet wish to give up His vocation like Moses (Num. 11:15), Jonas (John 1:3), and Jeremias (Jer. 20:14–18). Secondly, He bore persecution with fortitude. He exhorted and warned the people and His enemies unceasingly, by signs, miracles, instructions and reproofs, although He knew that all this was hastening His Death (Luke 13:32 seq.). Thirdly, He is full of gentle indulgence for His enemies. He never avoids them (Luke 7:36), always replies to their insincere questions, and even instructs them (Matt. 15:10); and it was certainly often on their account that He forbade persons whom He had healed to publish the miracle abroad, lest it might irritate them still more and increase their punishment. We must follow His example here below. Souls must be bought with sacrifices and blood, and not merely by work and prayer. We certainly cannot meet with any kind of suffering in the cure of souls that our Saviour has not experienced and that we do not find in the Gospels. He included all this in the program of His public life and work, that we might have an example before us, might sanctify ourselves and the souls under our care by suffering, and thus promote His kingdom.

Concluding Meditation upon the Active Life of Jesus. Results of His Teaching and Miracles

John 12:37. And whereas he had done so many miracles before them, they believed not in him;—38. That the saying of Isaias the prophet might be fulfilled, which he said: "Lord, who hath believed our hearing? And to whom hath the arm of the Lord been revealed?"—39. Therefore they could not believe; because Isaias said again:—40. "He hath blinded their eyes, and hardened their heart; that they should not see with their eyes, nor understand with their heart, and be converted, and I should heal them:"—41. These things said Isaias when he saw his glory, and spoke of him.—42. However, many of the chief men also believed in him; but because of the Pharisees they did not confess him, that they might not be cast out of the synagogue;—43. For they loved the glory of men, more than the glory of God.—44. But Jesus cried, and said: "He that believeth in me, doth not believe in me, but in him that sent me.—45. And he that seeth me, seeth him that sent me.—46. I am come a light into the world; that whosoever believeth in me, may not remain in darkness.—47. And if any man hear my words, and keep them not; I do not judge him; for I came not to judge the world, but to save the world.—48. He that despiseth me, and receiveth not my words, hath one that judgeth him; the word that I have spoken, the same shall judge him in the last day.—49. For I have not spoken of myself, but the Father who sent me, he gave me commandment what I should say, and what I should speak.—50. And I know that his commandment is life everlasting. The things therefore that I speak, even as the Father said unto me, so do I speak."

At the close of the active life of Jesus, viz. in Judaea, St. John makes a short meditation, giving a brief summary of the results of our Lord's ministry.

1. THE RESULT OF JESUS' TEACHING IS, GENERALLY SPEAKING, UNBELIEF

Our Lord's active life was passed, as we have seen, in imparting instruction, working miracles, and setting an example of virtue. St. John here (12:37) lays especial stress upon the miracles, because they confirmed our Saviour's doctrine and, together with His saintly life, furnished a convincing proof of His Divinity and mission as Messias. He says that Jesus had worked many and great miracles "before them" (i.e. the inhabitants of Judaea), such as the healing of the sick man at Bethesda, the cure of the man born blind, and the raising of Lazarus.

The result of this immense labor is summed up in a few words: "They believed not in Him." They believed neither in our Saviour's Divinity nor in His divine mission (John 12:37); on the contrary, they suppressed faith wherever it showed itself, even in prominent men like Joseph of Arimathaea and Nicodemus (John 12:42), and much more in the people, by means of such violent measures as exclusion from the synagogue (John 12:42; 9:22) or excommunication. This latter punishment consisted, in its milder form, in temporary exclusion from ecclesiastical and official intercourse; but in the severer and more solemn form it called down, by means of anathemas, the curse and punishment of God upon the person excommunicated (I Esdr. 10:8). Probably only the milder form is meant here.

2. CAUSES OF THIS UNBELIEF

St. John mentions two causes. First, ambition and human respect (John 12:43). Our Saviour was not what the Jews had fancied and expected, since He did not come as a secular ruler, but as a Redeemer from sin; He did not devote Himself to politics, but preached the truth, founded a religion not for the Jews alone but for the whole world, and did not pander to their passions in any way. On this account the more extreme Jews opposed Him, and the others out of human respect allowed themselves to be governed by the party in power. The words of the Evangelist: "They loved the glory of men more than the glory of God" (John 5:44; 12:43), apply to both classes. Human respect always proceeds from ambition, and ambition leads to apostasy.

The second cause is the obduracy of the Jews (John 12:38–41). The Messias, God Himself, comes, proves His identity by the greatest miracles, and yet finds scarcely anyone to believe in Him. Israel, which exists only in order to give the Messias to mankind, mistakes Him for an impostor, declares itself against Him, kills Him, and perishes itself. These facts are so extraordinary and inexplicable that the Evangelist seems to fear people would necessarily doubt the divinity of Jesus' mission and the success of God's work (cf. Rom. 9 seq.). He therefore illustrates and explains the fact by the prediction of the prophet Isaias (John 12:38–41). This prediction contains two important points. First, an exposure of the fundamental cause of unbelief, that is the obduracy and obstinacy (John 12:38–40) which had always been the hereditary evil of Israel (Ex. 32:9; Deut. 9:27; Isa. 46:12; Ez. 3:7; Acts 7:51; 28:25). They had not believed the words of the prophet, neither will they believe those of the Messias (John 12:38), solely because of their stubbornness, which proceeds from a bad will. Their hardness of heart and obstinacy, as the prophets had foretold, are directed against our Lord. Our Lord's words are not the cause of this ill-feeling, but are the means by which its existence is revealed. Secondly, the prophecy also contains a proof of the divinity of Jesus' mission and work. God's work does not suffer through unbelief. On the contrary, it is by that very unbelief that it is proved to be God's work, because that was just what had been predicted. The result of Jesus' mission speaks for its divinity, not against it. The reason not only explains the fact, but reconciles us to it and consoles us.

3. CONSEQUENCES OF UNBELIEF AND OF FAITH

In order to emphasize the consequences of unbelief the Evangelist repeats several passages from former testimony borne by Jesus Himself to His Divinity, viz. that He is one with the Father, not merely morally speaking by His sanctity and His office as God's ambassador, but essentially as His Son, and therefore He does not speak in His own name, but as commissioned by the Father

(John 12:49, 50); and whoever believes in Him and sees Him, sees and believes in the Father Who sent Him (John 12:44, 45; cf. John 5:31; 10:30, 38).

Thence is to be deduced, first, the punishment of unbelief. Whoever will not hear, accept and believe the Word, but despises it or does not keep what he has heard, is not judged at Christ's first coming, which is only to make known His goodness, mercy and redemption; but notwithstanding he has already a Judge, viz. the Father. He is already judged by Him in consequence of his sin of unbelief against His Word, and this will be the cause of his damnation on the Last Day (John 12:47, 48; cf. John 3:18; 8:50; 12:44). Secondly, the blessing of faith will preserve the believer from walking in the darkness of ignorance and sin in this world, and will lead him to eternal life in the next; for our Saviour is the Light that is come into the world, and all that He does and institutes in the Name and by the commission of the Father, His doctrine and Sacraments, are sources of eternal life (John 12:46, 50; cf. John 8:12).

This concluding meditation contains three significant truths. The first is the fatal power of ungoverned passion, which destroys all God's works, resists His most sublime and touching revelations, and can bring unspeakable misery upon individuals and even upon a whole nation. How sad is the fate of God's people, brought about as it was by blind, obdurate passion! The second truth is a consoling one, viz. that all apparent victories of evil, hell and the bad will of men do not upset or even injure God's plans. For this reason the obstinacy of the Jews, instead of being evidence against the divinity of the work and mission of Jesus, is rather a proof in favor of it. All had come to pass as had been foreseen and predicted. The third truth is the reiterated and glorious proof of the Divinity of Jesus. It is contained in the words of our Saviour quoted by St. John, and also in the vision of the prophet Isaias (6:1 seq.), in which, probably, the Most Holy Trinity was shown to him; hence the thrice-repeated "Holy" was heard. At all events the prophet also saw the "glory" of Jesus, i.e. His Divinity, and therefore he calls Him simply "the Lord." Many understand by "the arm of the Lord" not merely the power of God as displayed in the decree of the Redemption and its execution, but Christ Himself. In any case Isaias saw Him as God, and bore witness to Him. The Evangelist makes the testimony of the Old Covenant and our Lord's own testimony of His Divinity shine out with the majestic brilliancy of a sun, before this Divinity hides itself for a short time behind the dark, heavy clouds of the Passion.

III. THE LIFE OF THE PASSION, AND THE DEATH OF JESUS

Prediction of the Passion. Introduction to the Meditations upon the Passion

Matt. 26:1. And it came to pass, when Jesus had ended all these words, he said to his disciples:—2. "You know that after two days shall be the Pasch, and the Son of Man shall be delivered up to be crucified."

Mark 14:1. Now the feast of the Pasch and of the Azymes was after two days; and the chief priests and the scribes sought how they might by some wile lav hold on him and kill him.

Luke 22:1. Now the feast of unleavened bread, which is called the Pasch, was at hand.

"And it came to pass, when Jesus had ended all these words, He said to His disciples: You know that after two days shall be the Pasch, and the Son of Man shall be delivered up to be crucified" (Matt. 26:1, 2). These words, probably spoken on Tuesday, indicate that a new and important phase of our Saviour's life is beginning, viz. His Passion; and therefore He opens it Himself with a solemn announcement of His Passion and Death.

It will be quite in keeping with the significance of these words to insert here an introductory meditation on the Passion of Christ.

1. MOTIVES FOR MEDITATING UPON THE PASSION OF CHRIST

There are three principal motives for meditating upon our Lord's Passion.

The first is its sublimity. Everything about our Saviour, every word and deed of His is great and glorious beyond all measure; but this is especially the case with the mysteries of His Passion. These are the last steps in the life of the God-Man. Hitherto He had set an example first of virtue in ordinary life, and then of apostolic zeal by His teaching and miracles; now He completes the Redemption by His Passion and Death. Others also taught and worked miracles, but only our Saviour could redeem the world by His Death. The mysteries of His Passion and Death are the end and climax of His whole life, the summary and seal of His work on earth, and the supreme manifestation of the glorious prerogatives which He possessed. These prerogatives are three in number. Our Saviour is a King. He had come to blend heaven and earth into one great kingdom, in which all men should find peace and protection, and which should provide for their temporal and spiritual welfare. But this kingdom had to be conquered. Satan was the prince of this world, and he ruled it by sin, by the power of the passions, and through the instrumentality of the earthly rulers of the Jewish and heathen States. It is with Satan that our Saviour now has to cope in a wondrous duel (Isa. 63:3). He falls, and conquers in His fall. He frees man from the yoke of sin and passion, chooses His subjects and founds His kingdom, and wins His glorious Resurrection, His elevation to the right hand of God, and His divine office of Judge. Now the prince of the world is cast out; our Lord "lifted up" on the Cross, draws all things to Himself. His Passion is His accession to the throne. Our Saviour is also a Prophet and a Lawgiver. By His obedience to the Death of the Cross He fulfils the prophecies (Luke 24:44) and sets aside the ancient moral and ceremonial law; by His Passion He confirms the doctrine of the Cross, seals His love for the Heavenly Father and for us (John 14:31), and sets us a most sublime and glorious example of all virtues. Lastly, our Saviour is a High Priest, and by His Passion and Death He offers sacrifice, that sacrifice so great and glorious through the dignity of the Person Who offers it, the love with which He does it, and the intensity of pain and suffering which it involves, to which suffering the whole human race contributes by its representatives; He offers that sacrifice for which so great a preparation had been made by types and prophecies from the very beginning of the world; that sacrifice so unspeakably great in its results, for God by the honor and glory it procures for Him, and for us by the treasures of satisfaction, propitiation, merit and blessing that it places at our disposal. It is the Sacrifice of the eternal Covenant, which reconciles heaven and earth and sheds its life-giving light over time and eternity alike. By this sacrifice our Saviour becomes the "High Priest for ever." Thus He performs His life-work in the Passion, and nowhere does He reveal and exercise His glorious powers and offices with greater grandeur. That is why He spoke of it so often, longed for it and filled all ages with prophecies and types of it.

The second motive for meditating upon the Passion of Christ is fitness. It is most just that we should think of our Lord's Passion and meditate lovingly upon it; first because it cost Him more than anything else. It cost Him His most precious life, and amid what pain and anguish He gave it up! Surely it is not too much for us to think at least of what He suffered for us. Secondly, people pay so little heed to this Passion of our Lord. The thoroughfares of the world are crowded with people; but how few tread the Way of the Cross! How often our Saviour complains by the mouth of the prophets that He is left solitary, without comfort or sympathy! (Isa. 63:5.) And yet the remembrance of His sufferings, and the gratitude and love that we render Him on account of them, are all that He really gained for Himself by His Passion. He possessed everything else already in virtue of other rights. Who, then, can refuse Him this one recompense?

The third motive is our own interest. The Passion is holy, and makes holy. All the characteristics and blessings of a holy life spring from this source; above all, hatred and horror of sin. The merits and graces of the Passion of Christ are the means to atone for sin, and the remembrance of the Passion is the noblest and most powerful incentive to avoid sin. And if the sinner in his misery is tempted to despair, the Passion of Christ gives him new courage and shows him how much he is worth, and what love and sacrifice God and His Divine Son consider him worthy of. Holiness of life consists secondly in overcoming irregular passions. And what proves their terrible power more clearly than Christ's Death, of which they were the accursed instruments? If the Passion of Christ is the sublimest tragedy, the passions are the actors who stage and perform it. There is nothing that more powerfully incites us to fight against our passions than the example of our suffering Saviour. Strength and zeal to work and suffer for God and His holy kingdom form a third constituent of holiness of life. Under this heading we may place that precious heritage, the spirit of the Cross: love of the Cross, generosity and the desire to promote the kingdom of God's glory and the salvation of souls. And that is the very spirit with which the Passion of Christ so powerfully inspires and fills us. The Saints employed no means of becoming Saints oftener and more effectively than meditation upon the Passion of Christ. Thence they drew the spirit that made them what they became. These are some of the motives that may induce us to enter lovingly upon the meditation of Christ's Passion.

2. HOW TO MEDITATE UPON THE PASSION OF CHRIST

The Christian life offers us many ways of practising devotion to the Passion of Christ.

In the first place, there is devout and loving reflection upon the mysteries of the Passion. In order to practise this effectually it is well first to make ourselves acquainted with the dispositions of our Saviour with regard to His Passion, and to try to make them our own. He regarded it simply as His life's work (Matt. 20:28), always bore it in mind from the first moment of His life (Hebr. 10:5), and longed for it without ceasing (Luke 12:50). It often formed the subject of His conversations with His disciples. He regarded it as the chalice that His beloved Father had prepared for Him (John 18:11). When He wishes to give us an idea of His love for the Heavenly Father (John 14:31) and for us (John 15:13), He always points to His Passion; when He wishes to show us the greatness of the glory that is in store for Him and for us with the Father, He speaks of His Passion and Death as the price of it (Luke 24:26); and if ever His displeasure is excited, it is certainly when Peter wishes to deprive Him of His Cross (Matt. 16:23). These are the sentiments of His Heart with regard to the Passion, sentiments of reverence, love and desire. With these sentiments must we try to be filled, and in this spirit must we enter upon the meditation of the different mysteries of the Passion and go through them with great sympathy, love and gratitude, trying to picture them to ourselves and as it were live them through with our Lord; reflecting how His Godhead withdraws its protecting and beatifying effects and permits His Sacred Humanity to suffer in its faculties of soul and body, and remembering that He suffers all this voluntarily and for us, for each one of us in particular.

Other practices of devotion to the Passion of Christ are: the Sorrowful Mysteries of the Rosary, in which we take Our Lady's heart as a mirror, and consider the Passion as reflected there; the Way of the Cross, that beautiful and popular devotion in which we follow in particular the last steps of our Saviour, and as it were accompany Him; and lastly, the Holy Sacrifice of the Mass, which is the crown of all devotions to the Passion of Jesus, because its very essence is the renewal, representation, and actual continuation of the Sacrifice of the Cross.

A last and very important manner of honoring the Passion of

Christ is the practical imitation of the virtues and dispositions that are disclosed to us in the various mysteries. Thus we really suffer with our Saviour, and gain a far stronger and more vivid impression of all that He took upon Himself and went through for us. The virtues and good works that the meditation of the Passion thus produces in us are so many flowers and tokens of love that we strew on His path to Calvary, and with which we gladden His Heart. Will He not be grateful to us, if we walk thus at His side?

Judas Betrays Our Lord for Money

Luke 22:1. Now the feast of unleavened bread, which is called the Pasch, was at hand;—2. And the chief priests and the scribes sought how they might put Jesus to death; but they feared the people.—3. And Satan entered into Judas who was surnamed Iscariot, one of the twelve;—4. And he went and discoursed with the chief priests and magistrates, how he might betray him to them.—5. And they were glad, and covenanted to give him money.—6. And he promised. And he sought opportunity to betray him in the absence of the multitude.

Mark 14:1. Now the feast of the Pasch and of the Azymes was after two days; and the chief priests and the scribes sought how they might by some wile lay hold on him, and kill him.—2. But they said: "Not on the festival day, lest there should be a tumult among the people." . . .—10. And Judas Iscariot, one of the twelve, went to the chief priests, to betray him to them.—11. Who hearing it were glad; and they promised him they would give him money. And he sought how he might conveniently betray him.

Matt. 26:3. Then were gathered together the chief priests and ancients of the people into the court of the High Priest, who was called Caiphas;—4. And they consulted together, that by subtilty they might apprehend Jesus, and put him to death.—5. But they said: "Not on the festival day, lest perhaps there should be a tumult among the people." . . .—14. Then went one of the twelve, who was called Judas Iscariot, to the chief priests;—15. And said to them: "What will you give me, and I will deliver him unto you?" But they appointed him thirty pieces of silver.—16. And from thenceforth he sought opportunity to betray him.

1. The Great Council Decides upon the Arrest of Jesus

The circumstances under which this decision was taken were as follows.

As regards the time, it was probably on Tuesday that the council assembled, and most likely at the hour when our Lord positively assured His disciples that He would be crucified on the Feast of the Pasch (Matt. 26:1). The meeting-place of the council was not, it would appear, the assembly-room in the Temple, but the palace of Caiphas the High Priest (Matt. 26:3), because the decision was to be kept secret and all care taken to avoid attracting attention. Nevertheless the Sanhedrim seems to have been represented in every essential point, for the three classes of which it was composed are mentioned as being present (Matt. 26:3; Mark 14:1; Luke 22:2). It was therefore an official session.

The subject of the deliberations was no longer the putting to death of Jesus, for this had been decided upon long ago (John 11:53), but the manner in which it was to be accomplished, whether openly and by force, or secretly by a crafty surprise. The occurrences of the last few days, the complete defeats by which our Lord had put His enemies to shame, and His increasing influence all urged them to a sudden *coup de main.*

The decision seems to have been as follows. The arrest was to be made secretly, by craft. Our Lord was to be taken and executed when and how they best could; not on the feast-day, however, but after the Pasch was over (Matt. 26:4, 5; Mark 14:1, 2). The reason of this was their fear of the people (Luke 22:2). At the Paschal season there were great multitudes of people in Jerusalem, and the crowds were much inclined to disturbances and tumult; moreover our Lord had many adherents among them, especially among the excitable Galileans. So the Sanhedrim feared resistance and riot, as in that case the Romans would have been obliged to interfere. For this reason the arrest and execution were to take place secretly, and not until after the principal feast-day, when the people had dispersed. Such was the decision of the council, and such their dispositions for the great feast. They feared—not God, but the people.

Our Saviour, on the contrary, declares expressly and positively that He will die "after two days," on the Feast of the Pasch, and by a violent death. He knows the counsels of God and the hearts of men. Divine Wisdom had ordained that the typical and the actual sacrifice of the Covenant, the Paschal Lamb, should coincide, and our Saviour well knew how this was to be brought about.

2. JUDAS SELLS OUR LORD

Judas was the wretched instrument by which this prophecy was to be fulfilled. He seems to have been entertaining the thought of the betrayal for a long time. Now, probably late on Tuesday or early on Wednesday morning, after the Sanhedrim had charged the executive councilors to take steps in accordance with the decision of the previous day, he carried out his project. He went to the chief priests and offered to betray our Lord into their hands (Luke 22:4).

How did Judas come to take such a resolution? What were the causes of it? The fundamental cause was probably the shallowness, untrustworthiness and superficiality of his character. He seems to have been a man of no depth or moral stamina. The second cause was his worldliness, ambition and avarice. One can scarcely conceive of his ever having had any other idea of the Messianic kingdom than that which the majority of the Jews entertained. This unhappy bent of mind caused him to lose by degrees the faith that he had had at first, and so unbelief was the third cause of his resolve. Our Saviour had already said on the third Feast of the Pasch, in Capharnaum, that he was a devil and did not believe (John 6:65, 72). The fourth cause may have been the discomfort of the situation. He was tired of the constant journeying about and of the evidently disinterested aims of our Saviour; so he tried to make use of his position for temporal ends. Thus he acquired a regular habit of thieving from the purse that our Saviour had entrusted to him (John 12:6), and the charge of which he had perhaps pushed himself forward to obtain. Then followed the decisive measures taken by the Jews against our Saviour, and the latter Himself proclaimed His approaching Death (Matt. 26:1) and burial (John 12:7). And certainly the earnest mien of Jesus, and the private admonitions which He doubtless did not spare Judas, must have grown burdensome and intolerable to him; indeed, one can well imagine how the enthusiastic love and devotion of the Apostles and friends of our Lord must have annoyed him, and how exaggerated and extravagant they must have seemed to him, until at last he took a positive dislike to the Person of Jesus. This showed itself plainly at the anointing of our Saviour's Feet by Mary Magdalen, in Bethania. There is an amount of unbelief, irreverence and callousness in the words of Judas on this occasion that almost stuns us (Matt. 26:8; Mark 14:5). As a last cause (which, however, was already at work in all the other influences) is mentioned the influence and seduction of the devil (Luke 22:3; John 6:71; 13:2), which grew more and more powerful, the more Judas gave way to unbelief and passion. Thus it was that his resolution matured. Under these circumstances he wished to see the plans of Jesus thwarted and the whole Apostolic College dissolved, that he might be freed from his trammels; and he thought he might as well gain something by it too, if possible.

It is evident enough how disgraceful the deed of Judas was,

when we consider the circumstances. Judas the traitor was one of the Twelve. All the Evangelists who record his crime remark it (Matt. 26:14; Mark 14:10; Luke 23:3). That is to say, he was an Apostle and a friend of Jesus, a member of His family, so to speak. This must have meant no slight shame and no little pain for our Lord. And he took the step quite of his own accord. He hastens to the priests himself, and asks in the most shameless and unblushing manner what they will give him for his treachery (Matt. 26:15). He knew the men he had to deal with, and promised to deliver our Lord into their hands (Luke 22:6). And for what a wretched sum he sells his Benefactor, Master, and Lord—his God and greatest good! For thirty pieces of silver, about seventeen or eighteen dollars. It was no more than the price paid in compensation for killing a slave (Ex. 21:32). It is not without reason that God says to the prophet with indignant scorn, in predicting this crime: "Cast it to the statuary, a goodly price, that I was priced at by them" (Zach. 11:13). And it seems as though Judas would have done it for even less. One is almost bound to conclude that the Sanhedrim and even Judas himself did not regard the sum as the actual price of the deed, but rather as an acknowledgment, in return for something that ought to have been done in any case (John 11:56), or as compensation for the trouble and danger incurred. And to whom does Judas sell his Lord? To His worst enemies, who lie in wait to devour Him. The sequel shows what their projects with regard to Him were. And Judas delivered Him over to all these torments. How many misdeeds are included in this one act! Self-interest, avarice, ingratitude, cowardice, faithlessness, hard-heartedness and cruelty! The cruel and horrible deed of the brothers of the Egyptian Joseph cannot be compared to it. And what deep humiliation, what bitter pain it brought to our Saviour!

3. THE ENEMIES OF JESUS IMMEDIATELY DECIDE TO KILL HIM

Nothing could have been more opportune for the plans of the chief priests than Judas' proposal. They received him gladly, promised him the money he demanded, and gave it to him (Matt. 26:15; Mark 14:11; Luke 23:5). This unexpected occurrence gave the enemies of Jesus not merely hope of success, but also the means of carrying out their plan to arrest Him secretly. Probably no definite arrangement was made; everything depended upon finding a favorable opportunity. The circumstance that one of His own Apostles came to betray Him lowered the high opinion which the chief priests had held of the power and close cohesion of His followers. And perhaps Judas may have told them that our Lord quite expected His Death and had predicted it, and how full of fear and indecision the Apostles were. There was nothing to fear from the immediate surroundings of Jesus, and the priests hoped to manage the people without difficulty when once they had Him in their power and He could no longer appeal to the multitude for support.

Judas was now bound to help them. He did so, and tried to find an opportunity to make our Lord fall into His enemies' hands quietly and without attracting attention (Matt. 26:16; Mark 14:11; Luke 22:6). So he followed Him like a thief, dogging His footsteps, spying out all He did, and informing His enemies of everything, all the time simulating fidelity, sympathy, readiness to oblige and the most cordial friendship. Thus our Lord had in very truth the devil at His side (Luke 4:13). He knew it all, too, and endured it, in spite of His repugnance, without complaint. He only warns the traitor, and offers it all up for those in particular who will have to suffer ingratitude, faithlessness and treachery on the part of friends and relatives. The prophets have described to us the emotions of His Heart at this time (Ps. 54:13 seq.).

Thus all the threads of the cruel plot are drawn together, and the tragedy is about to begin. The prophecies of Jesus and the counsels of God are fulfilled, and our Lord's enemies are instruments to carry them out. They imagine they are gratifying their own hate, but in reality they are playing into God's hands. The type foreshown in the Paschal lamb must be fulfilled; and with what calm majesty our Saviour sees this terrible fulfilment approaching and becoming a reality! But who can understand Judas? Who does not look with horror at this tool by which the blackest and most shameful of deeds is accomplished! Must this accursed tool be an Apostle? The sight of this unhappy disciple as a traitor at the side of Jesus is surely calculated to fill us with the fear of God and distrust of ourselves; to strengthen us in the resolution to avoid danger and every proximate occasion of sin; to make us persevere in humble prayer; and lastly, to urge us to overcome our evil passions by acts of self-conquest. If we do not do this we are capable of anything, and no sin is beyond the range of possibility for us. It was truly a black and abominable crime that

Judas committed. But is not a similar crime committed in every mortal sin; every time that the grace of God, the gift of faith, and the interests of the Church and of souls are sacrificed for some temporal object? And how often that occurs in the world!

Preparation of the Paschal Lamb

LUKE 22:7. And the day of the unleavened bread came, on which it was necessary that the Pasch should be killed.—8. And he sent Peter and John, saying: "Go and prepare for us the Pasch, that we may eat."—9. But they said: "Where wilt thou that we prepare?"—10. And he said to them: "Behold, as you go into the city, there shall meet you a man carrying a pitcher of water; follow him into the house where he entereth in.—11. And you shall say to the good-man of the house: The master saith to thee: Where is the guest-chamber, where I may eat the Pasch with my disciples?—12. And he will show you a large dining-room furnished; and there prepare."—13. And they going, found as he had said to them, and made ready the Pasch.

MARK 14:12. Now on the first day of the unleavened bread when they sacrificed the Pasch, the disciples say to him: "Whither wilt thou that we go and prepare for thee to eat the Pasch?"—13. And he sendeth two of his disciples, and saith to them: "Go ye into the city; and there shall meet you a man carrying a pitcher of water, follow him;—14. And whithersoever he shall go in, say to the master of the house: The master saith: Where is my refectory, where I may eat the Pasch with my disciples?—15. And he will show you a large dining-room furnished; and there prepare ye for us."—16. And his disciples went their way, and came into the city; and they found as he had told them, and they prepared the Pasch.—17. And when evening was come, he cometh with the twelve.

MATT. 26:17. And on the first day of the Azymes the disciples came to Jesus saying: "Where wilt thou that we prepare for thee to eat the Pasch?"—18. But Jesus said: "Go ye into the city to a certain man, and say to him: The master saith: My time is near at hand; with thee I make the Pasch with my disciples."—19. And the disciples did as Jesus appointed to them, and they prepared the Pasch.

1. THE ORDER TO PREPARE THE PASCHAL LAMB

It was probably early on Thursday morning that our Lord commanded His disciples to prepare the Paschal lamb. In reply to their question as to where He wished to celebrate the Pasch, He mysteriously told them of a man who would meet them at the gate of the city; him they were to follow into his house, and there to prepare the meal. This was on the 14th of the month Nisan, the first day of unleavened bread. On this day all leaven and leavened bread had to be taken out of the houses (Luke 22:7–12; Mark 14:12–15; Matt. 26:17, 18). In this command of our Saviour's we have three beautiful virtues upon which to meditate.

The first is His loving and willing obedience. Wherever there is a law to be kept, the day and the hour find Him ready. He Himself gives the Apostles the order to go and prepare the Pasch.

The second virtue that He practises in making this arrangement is wise and prudent caution. He chooses Peter and John to go and make the preparations, not Judas, who seems to have performed such functions before (John 13:29). Neither does He name the man at whose house He intends to celebrate the Pasch, but only describes him mysteriously, saying that the two disciples would be met on entering the city by someone carrying a pitcher of water, whom they were to follow (Luke 22:10; Mark 14:13). Our Lord probably acted thus in order to avoid giving Judas an opportunity of betraying Him, because he might easily have informed the enemies of Jesus of the time and place of the meal, and then the arrest would have been made in the Coenaculum, and thus the Sacred Mysteries would have been disturbed and His host troubled. It may be, too, that our Lord wished by these mysterious words to give the Apostles another proof of His supernatural knowledge, and to show them that it was not the ordinary Pasch He intended to celebrate. Hence He gives them a message for the man full of friendly familiarity, as of a master to his disciple: "The Master saith: My time is near at hand; with thee I make the Pasch with My disciples" (Matt. 26:18). "Where is My refectory?" (Mark 14:14; Luke 22:11.) The inhabitants of the city were wont to arrange every available room at the time of the Pasch, to enable the stranger pilgrims to celebrate the feast in a becoming manner. Probably the man to whom the disciples were sent was a disciple of Jesus, possibly Nicodemus or Joseph of Arimathaea.

Thirdly, we may see here another instance of our Saviour's poverty. He is now about to institute the great mystery of the Blessed Sacrament of the Altar, and He has no house or room of His own in which to do it. He must appeal to the charity of men for every great thing that He does for the good of the world. How touchingly He asks the host to grant Him admittance for the last time, in order to institute the mystery that is to be such a blessing to the whole world! He had had no cradle, and was to have no grave of His own; and now He has no church in which to institute and deposit the chief Sacrament of the Church.

2. THE PREPARATION OF THE PASCHAL MEAL

The two Apostles went and found everything as our Lord had predicted. The man met them and showed them a large furnished room, and there they made all preparations (Luke 22:12, 13; Mark

14:15, 16; Matt. 26:19). Tradition says that the Coenaculum in which our Lord celebrated the Pasch was in a house near the present Mosque of David, on Mount Sion, in the highest part of the upper city. It is a large room, about 20 yards long and 11 broad, divided into two parts by a couple of pillars. This is the spot sanctified by the first and holiest Christian memories: by the Last Supper, by several visits of Christ after His Resurrection, and by the Descent of the Holy Ghost. Our Blessed Lady is said to have lived and died in a house hard by.

The room itself had to be prepared and furnished by the Apostles with tables, utensils, couches for reclining, and carpets. The host would probably help them in this, and perhaps also some of our Lord's adherents of both sexes. Then there was the Paschal lamb to be bought, shown in the Temple in the afternoon, killed, flayed and disemboweled. In the evening it had to be spitted upon two pieces of pomegranate wood in the form of a cross, and roasted. There were also cakes of unleavened bread, bitter herbs (wild lettuce, parsley, cress and horse-radish), a thick, brick-colored pottage made of dates, almonds, figs and cinnamon, and lastly wine and water to be provided.

The Apostles made all these preparations gladly and lovingly. St. Peter and St. John are the representatives of faith and love respectively. And thus everything was well done. Our Lord's command and also, we may be sure, the exact fulfilment of His prediction with regard to this preparation, combined with His words about this being His last Paschal meal, sufficed to inspire them with zeal. What would they not have done if they had had a clear idea of the great mysteries that were to be celebrated in this room, and during this meal! For it was the first church that they were arranging and decorating. And they were preparing for the instituting of a Sacrament that would henceforth be the heart and soul of spiritual life in the Church.

3. OUR SAVIOUR'S WALK TO JERUSALEM

In the evening our Saviour went with the disciples from Bethania to the dining-room in the upper town (Matt. 26:20; Mark 14:17; Luke 22:14).

Before they set out He must have bidden farewell to Bethania and the dear friends who had shown Him so much love and reverence, and whose hospitality He had so often enjoyed. It was His last visit to the house of Lazarus and his sisters in the beautiful little hamlet under the shade of the fig, olive, and almond-trees. He was never to return thither in this life. The Saints who have meditated upon this mystery draw us a touching picture of this farewell of Jesus to His holy Mother, to Lazarus and many of His other friends. Such a parting is painful to every grateful and feeling heart, and so it must surely have been to our Saviour. We do not know whether the leave-taking took place in public or in presence of only a few; but there can be no doubt that it was loving, touching and sorrowful on both sides. And we may be sure our Saviour expressed His warm gratitude for the faithful love of His friends, and they on their side their grief that He was never to return, but to go to His Death. How affectionately our Lord would embrace Lazarus, and with what deep sorrow He must have taken leave of His holy Mother! And how inconsolable were Martha and Mary! Often He had left them before, but now it is a final farewell. His presence had been their joy and comfort; now His departure brings them the more grief.

The walk itself over the Mount of Olives and down the vale of Cedron, through Ophel up to the dining-room in the upper city, was very silent and sorrowful. There in the gloaming lay the city with its towers and walls, dark and threatening, like a mighty prison-house or place of execution, ready to receive Him and put Him to a cruel death. But our Lord walks on towards His goal with firmness and decision, and neither the clear consciousness that His hour has come nor the shrinking fear that fills His Heart can delay His steps for a moment.

This farewell to Bethania and walk to Jerusalem are a very profitable as well as touching subject for our meditation. Our Lord was a man like ourselves, and susceptible to all natural feelings, as far as His will was concerned. It must have cost Him much to leave such faithful and loving friends and cause sorrow to them as well as to Himself. He would remember how gently they desired His welfare, how heartily they loved Him, and how happily He might have lived with them. He would think too of where He was now going, into whose hands. He was about to deliver Himself to His enemies, and what a fate was in store for Him! How hard it must have seemed to Him at that moment to fulfil His vocation! But He overcame all His pain and repugnance, in order to set us an example and gain for us the graces we need when we are called upon to part from dear friends, favorite occupations and beloved spots. At such times we must call to mind how our Saviour too went through all this for our sakes, and that His sacrifice calls for ours in return.

The Legal Paschal Meal. First Part of the Last Supper

Luke 22:14. And when the hour was come he sat down, and the twelve apostles with him;—15. And he said to them: "With desire I have desired to eat this Pasch with you before I suffer.—16. For I say to you, that from this time I will not eat it, till it be fulfilled in the kingdom of God."—17. And having taken the chalice he gave thanks, and said: "Take, and divide it among you;—18. For I say to you, that I will not drink of the fruit of the vine, till the kingdom of God come. . . .—21. But yet behold, the hand of him that betrayeth me is with me on the table.—22. And the Son of Man indeed goeth, according to that which is determined; but yet woe to that man by whom he shall be betrayed."—23. And they began to inquire among themselves, which of them it was that should do this thing.—24. And there was also a strife amongst them, which of them should seem to be greater.

Mark 14:18. And when they were at table and eating, Jesus saith: "Amen I say to you, one of you that eateth with me shall betray me."—19. But they began to be sorrowful, and to say to him one by one: "Is it I?"—20. Who saith to them: "One of the twelve, who dippeth with me his hand in the dish.—21. And the Son of Man indeed goeth, as it is written of him; but woe to that man by whom the Son of Man shall be betrayed; it were better for him, if that man had not been born."

Matt. 26:21. And whilst they were eating he said: "Amen I say to you, that one of you is about to betray me."—22. And they being very much troubled, began everyone to say: "Is it I, Lord?"—23. But he answering said: "He that dippeth his hand with me in the dish, he shall betray me.—24. The Son of Man indeed goeth, as it is written of him; but woe to that man, by whom the Son of Man shall be betrayed; it were better for him, if that man had not been born."—25. And Judas that betrayed him, answering said: "Is it I, Rabbi?" He saith to him: "Thou hast said it."

John 13:21. When Jesus had said these things, he was troubled in spirit: and testified, and said: "Amen, amen, I say to you, one of you shall betray me."—22. The disciples therefore looked one upon another, doubting of whom he spoke.—23. Now there was leaning on Jesus' bosom one of his disciples, whom Jesus loved.—24. Simon Peter therefore beckoned to him, and said to him: "Who is it of whom he speaketh?"—25. He therefore leaning on the breast of Jesus saith to him: "Lord, who is it?"—26. Jesus answered: "He it is to whom I shall reach bread dipped." And when he had dipped the bread, he gave it to Judas Iscariot, the son of Simon.—27. And after the morsel, Satan entered into him. And Jesus said to him: "That which thou dost, do quickly."—28. Now no man at the table knew to what purpose he said this unto him.—29. For some thought, because Judas had the purse, that Jesus had said to him: "Buy those things which we have need of for the festival day:" or that he should give something to the poor.—30. He therefore having received the morsel, went out immediately. And it was night.—31. When he therefore was gone out, Jesus said: "Now is the Son of Man glorified, and God is glorified in him.—32. If God be glorified in him, God also will glorify him in himself: and immediately will he glorify him."

The legal Phase or Paschal meal, which forms the first part of the Last Supper, now began.

1. CEREMONIES OF THE LEGAL PASCHAL MEAL

The company at table (Ex. 12:3, 4), who were not to be less than ten nor more than twenty in number, took their places round the table, arrayed as for a journey, girded and with staves in their hands. The head of the family said the prayer and performed the ceremony of washing the hands. The first chalice was blessed and passed round; with it were taken bitter herbs dipped into the mess of fruit. The second chalice was handed round during a short explanation of the Paschal meal. The cakes of unleavened bread were now broken and distributed, together with bitter herbs, and not until then did the company proceed to eat the Paschal lamb and the meat of the peace-offering. In later times it had become customary to recline upon couches during this part of the meal. Then followed the washing of hands, whereupon the third chalice, the chalice of blessing, was poured out, whilst Psalms (the 112th and 113th) were sung and longing prayers for the coming of the Messias recited. Lastly, the Little Hallel (Ps. 114–117) was sung and a fourth chalice handed round. After the last morsel of the Paschal lamb had been consumed and the fourth chalice drunk, no more food was touched and no more wine passed round; only on condition of singing the Great Hallel (Ps. 119–136) was it permissible to drink a fifth chalice, but this was a matter of choice. Such were the customary ceremonies at the legal Paschal meal. Thus it is easy to picture to oneself the course of the Last Supper down to the washing of the feet, and to fit in the different parts of the conversation recorded by the Evangelists.

2. THE CONVERSATION BETWEEN OUR SAVIOUR AND THE APOSTLES

The conversation between our Saviour and the Apostles during the legal Paschal meal turned upon three topics.

The first was its significance for them under the present circumstances. Our Lord very probably pointed out this peculiar significance conjointly with the ordinary one, while the second chalice was being passed round, saying among other things: "With desire I have desired to eat this Pasch with you before I suffer. For I say to you, that from this time I will not eat it, till it be fulfilled in the kingdom of God. . . . I will not drink of the fruit of the vine, till the kingdom of God come" (Luke 22:15–18).

This Supper, combining the ceremonies of the Old Testament with the reality of the New, is the last meal of Jesus before His farewell to His loved disciples and to the world; it is the fulfilment of the great types of the Old Covenant, and is itself the type and introduction to the eternal banquet in heaven (Matt. 26:29; Apoc. 19:7). It is the climax of the love of the God-Man, shown in the accomplishment of the astounding mysteries that this Supper was to witness: the washing of the feet, the institution of the Blessed Sacrament of the Altar, and His parting discourse, so that we may truly say of it: "Having loved His own who were in the world, He loved them unto the end," i.e. to the very utmost, giving them on this occasion an extraordinary proof of His love (John 13:1). All these mysteries were included in the significance of this Supper for Jesus, His disciples, and the Church; all this unrolled itself before our Saviour's mental vision at the very beginning of the meal, and so He greeted it in the words above cited, with the most ardent longing and heartfelt joy.

The second subject upon which the conversation turned was the impending Passion of our Lord. He already touches upon it in the above words, when He says that this is His last meal before He suffers (Luke 22:15); but He speaks of it more fully in the prediction of His betrayal by Judas. The manner in which He predicts it is very solemn and distinct; He employs the formula of asseveration: "Amen I say to you" (Mark 14:18; Matt. 26:21), indicates the traitor in plain though considerate terms, saying that he is one of the disciples, who is sitting at table and dipping his hand in the dish with Him and therefore necessarily sitting quite near Him (Matt. 26:21, 22; Mark 14:18, 20; Luke 22:21; Ps. 40:10). Lastly, He expressed His horror of the abominable deed, by comparing His own fate with that of the traitor (Mark 14:21; Matt. 26:24; Luke 22:22) and proclaiming the punishment of the crime. The lot of Judas is apparently preferable; he sells his Master, makes profit, lives, and makes friends amongst the ruling party, whilst our Saviour, forsaken and sold into their hands, goes to His Death. But in truth the fate of Judas is incomparably worse. Our Saviour by love and obedience passes through death to glory; Judas is on his way to suicide, to the rope and unutterable punishment, so that it would have been better for him if he had never been born (Isa. 53:10; Ps. 108:8 seq.). Our Lord's reasons for predicting His betrayal were these: He wished to prove that He knew everything and suffered voluntarily; to warn the unhappy Apostle and deter him from committing his sin; to show how this treachery pained Him; and lastly, to prepare the other Apostles for what was to come, and to strengthen their faith. Hence He added a little later: "I know whom I have chosen; but that the Scripture may be fulfilled . . . At present I tell you, before it come to pass; that when it shall come to pass, you may believe that I am He" (John 13:18, 19). At these words, we are told, our Lord was "troubled in spirit" (John 13:21), and even His outward appearance betokened the deep emotion of His Heart—His sorrow, compassion for the traitor, and horror of the deed and its punishment—in order to make the prediction and warning more impressive and deter the betrayer.

This prediction brought great consternation and sorrow upon the Apostles, as we may well imagine; and though every one of them except Judas was convinced that such a thought had never entered his head, still they grew bewildered, and fearing their own weakness anxiously asked our Saviour: "Is it I, Lord?" (Mark 14:19; Matt. 26:22.) And they also began to ask each other who it could possibly be (Luke 22:23). Peter, always accustomed to act on the spur of the moment, made a sign to St. John, who was sitting where he could lean his head on our Saviour's breast (John 13:23), and told him to ask who it was (John 13:24). So John inclined his head towards our Lord and said: "Lord, who is it?" (John 13:25.) Then our Saviour revealed the traitor. He did not make the revelation openly, however, but only to St. John, by means of a sign, saying: "He it is to whom I shall reach bread dipped" (John 13:26). Our Lord acted thus in order to spare the traitor, to protect his honor and perhaps his life, for the disciples might very likely have laid violent hands on him; and lastly, in order not to hinder His own Passion and Death. He now gave the morsel to Judas (John 13:26), an action which was regarded as a mark of special love and tenderness. Judas had the shamelessness to ask in his turn if he were the traitor. Our Lord replied in the affirmative (Matt. 26:22), but in an undertone, and added that, if he was determined to betray Him, he should do it at once (John 13:27). This was not a command to commit the sin, but rather a confirmation of His prediction and at the same time another form of dissuasion and reproach for Judas. Perhaps, too, the latter may have intended to wait until our Saviour left the Coenaculum. But our Lord wished to be alone with His faithful disciples now, so He gave Judas an opportunity to get away, since the disciples did not understand what He meant, and only thought He was giving him a commission to procure something for the feast or perform some act of charity to the poor, as He seems to have been accustomed to do (John 13:28, 29).

Judas, on the other hand, maintained all his callousness and hardness of heart. Perhaps he thought himself exposed now, or at all events did not feel safe among the Apostles any longer, after our Lord's disclosures. It was now near the end of the legal Paschal meal, so he rose and hurried away, at the same instant falling deeper and deeper into the power of Satan, who urged him on to the black deed (John 13:27). As the Evangelist remarks, it was already dark outside, the right time for such a hideous crime. It was dark, too, in the heart of the wretched Apostle; never-ending night and the power of darkness reigned there.

Scarcely had Judas departed when our Lord exclaimed: "Now is the Son of Man glorified; and God is glorified in Him. If God be glorified in Him, God also will glorify Him in Himself; and immediately will He glorify Him" (John 13:31, 32). The betrayal was the first step leading to the Passion; and God is glorified by the Passion, because it is the victory over the world and the devil, and the revelation of His own justice and mercy. And God in His turn will immediately glorify our Saviour by various miracles during His Passion and by His Resurrection.

The third topic of conversation among the disciples was a dispute about precedence. A question may have arisen with regard to the places at table, upon the order of which the Jews set a very high value (Luke 14:7); or it may have been about the order in which the chalice and the various dishes were to be passed round. Our Lord may perhaps have made some special, exceptional arrangement as to their places at table for this evening; at all events He must have made Judas sit quite near Him, since He handed him the morsel and spoke to him in an undertone (John 13:26–29). Or the prediction concerning the traitor may have led to the dispute, the disciples asking each other who it might be, and each one claiming to be more attached to our Saviour than the others. Lastly, the mention of His departure (Luke 22:15) may have reawakened the old jealousy about the first places in the kingdom which, according to their idea, was to be made manifest after our Lord's return. In short, however it may have been, a dispute arose among these bewildered, anxious and troubled hearts.

3. VIRTUES PRACTISED BY OUR LORD AT THE LEGAL PASCHAL MEAL

Our Lord practises the most beautiful virtues even in the first part of the Last Supper.

In the first place, He shows great exactitude in the performance of the legal ceremonies. Even the day was exactly in accordance with the legal regulation. According to this, the 14th of Nisan was the first day of unleavened bread, the day on which the Paschal lambs were slaughtered; and the 15th was the day of the Pasch itself (Ex. 12:6, 18; Lev. 23:5; Num. 28:16–18). The first three Evangelists refer to this regulation (Matt. 26:17; Mark 14:12; Luke 22:7). Indeed, had we only these three accounts, we should undoubtedly conclude that our Lord died on the 15th of Nisan, the actual day of the Pasch. But the fourth Evangelist tells us clearly and plainly that He did not die on the feast-day, but on the Parasceve of the Pasch (John 19:14, 31; cf. Luke 23:54). The Paschal feast must therefore have been transferred to Saturday, the 16th of Nisan. Perhaps there was some special reason for transferring it that year; or possibly it was the custom always to do so when the 15th of Nisan fell on a Friday. Moreover, on account of the great number of the Paschal lambs, it was permissible to slaughter some of them a day earlier. Thus it is generally assumed that our Lord celebrated the Pasch on the 14th of Nisan and died on Friday, the 15th. At all events it is certain that He held the Pasch in accordance with the law.

Secondly, we may notice the piety and deep recollection, the calmness and dignity with which He performed the ceremony. He recognized as no other could do the meaning and significance of the prescribed ceremonies, and accompanied them with acts of heartfelt gratitude to God for the great benefit of which they were destined to perpetuate the memory. He rejoiced that He was now able to fulfil their typical meaning by the reality. The reason why our Saviour combined the institution of the Holy Eucharist with the celebration of the legal Pasch, in almost immediate connection with His Passion, was without doubt that, on the one hand, no type symbolized the Eucharist as sacrifice and sacrament so minutely as the Paschal lamb, which was at once a sacrifice and communion; and that, on the other hand, the Eucharist itself is a type and memorial of His Passion and Death.

Thirdly, our Saviour displays wonderful serenity and unselfishness at this Paschal meal. His Passion was near, and everything reminded Him vividly of it: His surroundings, the disciple Judas, the Paschal lamb which lay there pierced by a spit in the form of a cross, the terrible instrument of His Death; and even the Holy Eucharist. Thus His mind and heart were besieged by these terrifying figures of death, and yet He is calmness and serenity, friendliness, love and tenderness itself. He rejoices over this Last Supper, and has longed for it, because He can do us such infinite good by the mysteries that He now institutes.

Lastly, our Saviour sets us an example of the most magnanimous love of enemies. Judas, the traitor, sits at His table, even at His side. Our Lord knows his thoughts and his devilish plan, and yet how He loves him! He is not angry with him, does not expose him, but respects his honor and good name even in the prediction of the betrayal, and seeks to save the soul of His unhappy disciple and Apostle at any cost. Is not this a love of surpassing generosity?

What an insight into the Sacred Heart this mystery once more affords us! With what touching fidelity the Good Shepherd pursues the lost sheep, and tries by every possible means to recover it! How carefully and conscientiously He protects the good name and ensures the safety of the reprobate Apostle! He discloses no more of the mystery of wickedness than higher considerations require Him to do. And we can see from His grief and "trouble of spirit" what pain the treason, the wretchedness, impenitence, and the very presence of Judas were to Him. He exults with joy and relief when the traitor had gone. It is a divine and wondrous joy, the cause of which, naturally speaking, could only pain, depress and terrify a human heart. He sends away the traitor, and thus draws the meshes of the net more closely round Him; He will not escape from it again. Freely and joyfully He enters the terrible precincts of His Passion, because this is the glorification of the Father and the beginning of His own glorification. How marvelous are the sentiments and dispositions of His Sacred Heart!

Christ Washes His Disciples' Feet. Second Part of the Last Supper

John 13:1. Before the festival day of the Pasch, Jesus knowing that his hour was come that he should pass out of this world to the Father; having loved his own who were in the world, he loved them unto the end.—2. And when supper was done, the devil having now put into the heart of Judas Iscariot, the son of

Simon, to betray him;—3. Knowing that the Father had given him all things into his hands, and that he came from God, and goeth to God;—4. He riseth from supper, and layeth aside his garments; and having taken a towel, girded himself.—5. After that he putteth water into a basin, and began to wash the feet of the disciples, and to wipe them with the towel wherewith he was girded.—6. He cometh therefore to Simon Peter. And Peter saith to him: "Lord, dost thou wash my feet?"—7. Jesus answered and said to him: "What I do, thou knowest not now, but thou shalt know hereafter."—8. Peter saith to him: "Thou shalt never wash my feet." Jesus answered him: "If I wash thee not, thou shalt have no part with me."—9. Simon Peter saith to him: "Lord, not only my feet, but also my hands and my head."—10. Jesus saith to him: "He that is washed, needeth not but to wash his feet, but is clean wholly. And you are clean, but not all."—11. For he knew who he was that would betray him; therefore he said: "You are not all clean."—12. Then after he had washed their feet, and taken his garments, being set down again, he said to them: "Know you what I have done to you?—13. You call me Master and Lord; and you say well, for so I am.—14. If then I, being your Lord and Master, have washed your feet; you also ought to wash one another's feet.—15. For I have given you an example, that as I have done to you, so you do also.—16. Amen, amen, I say to you: the servant is not greater than his Lord; neither is the apostle greater than he that sent him.—17. If you know these things, you shall be blessed if you do them.—18. I speak not of you all; I know whom I have chosen; but that the Scripture may be fulfilled: He that eateth bread with me, shall lift up his heel against me.—19. At present I tell you, before it come to pass; that when it shall come to pass, you may believe that I am he.—20. Amen, amen, I say to you: He that receiveth whomsoever I send, receiveth me; and he that receiveth me, receiveth him that sent me."

LUKE 22:24. And there was also a strife amongst them, which of them should seem to be greater.—25. And he said to them: "The kings of the Gentiles lord it over them; and they that have power over them, are called beneficent.—26. But you not so; but he that is the greater among you, let him become as the younger; and he that is the leader, as he that serveth.—27. For which is greater, he that sitteth at table, or he that serveth? Is not he that sitteth at table? But I am in the midst of you, as he that serveth.—28. And you are they who have continued with me in my temptations;—29. And I dispose to you, as my Father hath disposed to me, a kingdom,—30. That you may eat and drink at my table in my kingdom; and may sit upon thrones judging the twelve tribes of Israel."

1. OUR LORD'S OBJECT IN WASHING HIS DISCIPLES' FEET

Our Saviour had a twofold aim in view in performing this unusual action at the Last Supper.

First, He intended to give the Apostles a significant answer to their dispute about the order of their rank. He wishes to teach them humility and charity, and therefore He once more instructs them as to the true meaning of superiority in the Church. The aim of ecclesiastical rule is not an autocratic and tyrannical power, nor the gratification of selfishness and love of authority, but the welfare of the people. The exercise of ecclesiastical office, therefore, is a "service," rendered not as a mark of condescension and kindness, as is the case for example with a "beneficent" emperor, but as a matter of duty; a service of loving humility and humble charity (Luke 22:25–27). This is the lesson our Lord wished to inculcate upon all His Apostles.

The second aim was undoubtedly a mystical one, viz. to impart to the Apostles purity and conformity with Christ, that they might perform their apostolic office worthily and perseveringly; possibly too the ceremony was to be their immediate preparation, by an increase of purity and faith, for the reception of the Blessed Sacrament, as our Saviour Himself mysteriously hints (John 13:7, 8, 10). This perfect purity, freedom not merely from mortal sin, but even from lesser transgressions (John 13:10), is symbolized by the washing of the feet. But since this virtue is so necessary for communion with Christ and for the apostolic office (John 13:8), our Lord does not rest content with merely typifying it, but actually confers it, by the working of His grace and the overwhelming force of His example. This example must surely have awakened in the hearts of the Apostles acts of love and humility, thus purifying them and preparing them in the best possible manner for the reception of the Holy Eucharist.

2. HOW OUR SAVIOUR SEEKS TO ATTAIN THIS END

Our Saviour seems to have been most anxious to impress this lesson deeply upon the minds of His Apostles. This is shown by the way in which He gives it.

In the first place, He does so more strikingly than on any previous occasion. He had taught the Apostles this lesson twice before (Matt. 18:2 seq.; 20:25 seq.), but never in such an earnest and impressive manner.

Secondly, He does this just before His Death (John 13:1, 2), so that the lesson forms, so to speak, a part of His last will.

Thirdly, He uses every means to impress it upon His Apostles by word and deed, first washing their feet and then explaining in the above sense what He has done.

3. MOTIVES CONTAINED IN THE MYSTERY FOR PUTTING THIS LESSON IN PRACTICE

How necessary this lesson is, is shown by the fact that the Apostles had fallen into a dispute about rank even under such circumstances. There is in everyone of us a touch of the egotism which loves to rule. But our Saviour gives us powerful motives to overcome it and acquire the virtues of humble charity and loving humility.

The first motive is His own example, which we learn to comprehend in some measure when we reflect Who He is. Great stress is laid upon this in the words of St. John, that our Saviour did this "knowing that the Father had given Him all things into His hands, and that He came from God, and goeth to God" (John 13:3), that is to say, in the full possession and consciousness of His dignity as God-Man. He calls Himself a little later on "Master and Lord," and draws the special attention of His disciples to the position in which He stands to them (John 13:13, 14), adding that "the servant is not greater than his Lord, neither is the Apostle greater than he that sent him" (John 13:15, 16; Luke 22:26, 27). Who can compare himself to our Lord? And yet He performs in person this office of love and humility. And upon whom? Upon His Apostles and servants. And in what does this service consist? In washing their feet (John 13:4, 5), that is to say, performing the lowest and most servile office, that was usually done by slaves. What, then, ought *we* not to be ready to do for our fellow-men? What may we consider beneath our dignity? St. Peter puts the significance of this motive in the true light when he says that he will never permit our Lord to wash his feet (John 13:6, 8).

The second motive is our Saviour's express wish. He says He has given us this example in order that we may imitate it (John 13:15).

The third motive is the reward that our Lord promises for this humility and charity. He promises that we "shall be blessed" (John 13:17). And how happy men would be, princes and subjects, if this spirit prevailed amongst them! But on the other hand our Lord says that whoever will not accept the lesson, whether in regard to purity of heart, charity or humility (John 13:8), will have no part with Him, no part in His spirit, His character or His life. He also points to the future reward in heaven. There service and sacrifice cease, and are replaced by rest, abundance and dominion, even by special power and glory (Luke 13:29–30); and they earn honor and respect even here on earth, for whoever receives the representatives or messengers of Jesus, receives Jesus Himself, and whoever receives Jesus, receives the Father Who has sent Him (John 13:20).

This is the great and important lesson that our Saviour gives us all by washing His disciples' feet: charity and humility, loving humility and humble charity. We must have both. Humility without charity is like the bright but cold light of the moon; charity without humility is but a transient flame that soon expires, and often but veiled selfishness. It is the union of these two virtues which characterizes the Church and Christianity. The Church, the Saints, and the pastors according to the Heart of Jesus have always borne this character. That is why our holy Mother the Church has the ceremony of washing the feet repeated by her prelates on the Thursday in Holy Week, and calls it the Mandatum, or Maundy. But the Mandatum is not to be confined to Maundy Thursday. Every exercise of the ecclesiastical functions is a "mandatum," and ought to be performed with the dispositions with which Jesus washed His disciples' feet, dispositions of humility and charity. What progress have we made in these virtues? We should consider him happy who possessed some relic of the first Maundy, such as the basin, or a piece of the towel with which our Lord girded Himself and wiped the feet of the Apostles. Yet every opportunity that presents itself of performing like acts towards our neighbor is a memorial of this mystery.

The Institution of the Holy Eucharist
Third Part of the Last Supper

Matt. 26:26. And whilst they were at supper Jesus took bread, and blessed, and broke, and gave to his disciples, and said: "Take ye, and eat; this is my body." —27. And taking the chalice he gave thanks; and gave to them, saying: "Drink ye all of this.—28. For this is my blood of the new testament, which shall be shed for many unto remission of sins.—29. And I say to you: I will not drink from henceforth of this fruit of the vine, until that day when I shall drink it with you new in the kingdom of my Father."

Mark 14:22. And whilst they were eating, Jesus took bread: and blessing broke, and gave to them, and said: "Take ye; this is my body."—23. And having taken the chalice, giving thanks he gave it to them; and they all drank of it.—24. And he said to them: "This is my blood of the new testament, which shall be shed for many.—25. Amen I say to you, that I will drink no more of this fruit of the vine, until that day when I shall drink it new in the kingdom of God."

Luke 22:19. And taking bread, he gave thanks, and brake, and gave to them, saying: "This is my body which is given for you; do this for a commemoration of me."—20. In like manner the chalice also, after he had supped, saying: "This is the chalice, the new testament in my blood, which shall be shed for you."

After our Lord had washed the feet of the Apostles, He proceeded to institute the Holy Eucharist. This is the center and soul of all that takes place at the Last Supper, and the fulfilment of the great promise made by Him at Paschal-tide the year before, in the synagogue of Capharnaum; it is a mystery of the highest importance and widest range for the whole Church and the Christian religion.

1. WHAT OUR SAVIOUR DOES IN THE INSTITUTION OF THE HOLY EUCHARIST

By instituting the Holy Eucharist our Saviour does four very important things.

First, He founds quite a new phase of His existence and personal presence in this world. This new existence of His has four qualities. In the first place it is a real, true and substantial presence of Jesus, of His Body and Blood, Humanity and Divinity, although He is invisible, concealed under the appearances of bread and wine. This follows from the simple words by which it is instituted: "This is My Body, this is My Blood," which in accordance with the promise (John 6:56) are to be taken literally; it follows also from the purpose of the institution, inasmuch as our Lord wishes, in accordance with His wisdom, power and love, to make His last will and leave us nothing less than Himself; and lastly it follows from the teaching and belief of the Church, which in this particularly, as in all other respects, has never varied. Secondly, this presence of His is most marvelous; indeed, it is entirely produced and maintained by miracles. Without ceasing to be a true body, the Body of our Lord here assumes an entirely spiritual property, in some respects even more glorious than in heaven, where It does not exist in many places at the same time and without extension; but here It is present, as we say, after the manner of a substance without extension and in innumerable places at the same time; and yet the appearances of bread remain, but inasmuch as they have lost their natural support in the substance of bread, they are sustained by the power of an abiding miracle. Thirdly, His presence is continual, never-ending, and multiplied a countless number of times, so that He is now in all parts of the world, which He has promised never to forsake. Formerly He was to be found only in the Promised Land, and only in one place at a time; and His visible presence was entirely lost to us at His Ascension. Formerly, too, He had to be sought by those who wished to be with Him; now He seems to follow us, and makes Himself everywhere our fellow-citizen. Lastly, His presence is very efficacious, because it elevates the Church and makes her the true Bride and mystical Body of Christ, comforts her in the exile of this life, and lastly reanimates her and adorns her with a precious crown of the most touching devotions, which arise in the first instance from this true and perpetual presence of Jesus in the Blessed Sacrament. Such are, for instance, the Exposition in the Monstrance, the service of Benediction, the solemn processions of the Blessed Sacrament: all favorite devotions, dear to the hearts of the Catholic people.

Secondly, our Saviour institutes in the Holy Eucharist the Sacrifice of the New Testament. Our Church, which is that of the New Covenant, was to have a visible sacrifice: a sacrifice, because this is the soul and highest act of religion; and a visible one, because it had been prophesied that our religion would have a true and visible sacrifice, never-ceasing and offered "from the rising of the sun even to the going down" (Mal. 1:11; Ps. 109:4). Without such a sacrifice, the public worship of the Christian religion would have been far more imperfect than that of the Old Covenant. But now our religion possesses a true, a worthy and glorious sacrifice, that of the Holy Mass. Christ has instituted the Holy Eucharist by a sacrifice, or made a sacrifice by instituting it, and has ordained that this sacrifice should be continued throughout all ages. The very words with which He instituted it denote a sacrifice, and not merely a sacrament. He says: "This is My Body, which is given for you" (Luke 22:19), "My Blood which shall be shed for you" (Luke 22:20); or as the Greek text of St. Paul's words has it: "My Body which shall be broken for you" (I Cor. 11:24). To shed blood for the remission of sins is, in other words, to sacrifice. At the same time the words and the two separate species express the essential relation of the Eucharistic Sacrifice to the Sacrifice of the Cross, as well as its relation to the typical Paschal lamb. The consecration, by which the Eucharistic Sacrifice is accomplished, has also all the characteristics of a true sacrificial act. It withdraws the sacrificial gift from any human use, and effects a great change in it, inasmuch as the substance of bread is converted into the substance of the Body of Christ, which thus becomes present; on the one hand in a state of mystical death and annihilation, but on the other hand in such a wondrous form of life that God is glorified in every way. Whether the essence of sacrifice be regarded as consisting in the real or mystical destruction and change of the gift or in the offering and consecration of it for sacrificial purposes, all this is found in the Consecration at Mass, in which the sacrificial action is, in fact, actually accomplished. Lastly, we have in the Holy Mass, which is precisely the Sacrifice of the Last Supper, a sacrifice of the greatest value and of infinite glory; and this on account of the celebrating High Priest, who is none other than Christ Himself, truly present there as High Priest and officiating as such, especially by the transubstantiation of the bread and wine into His Body and Blood, a change which can be effected only by divine power; also on account of the sacrificial gift, which again is Christ under the appearances of bread and wine, under the symbols of His youthful, suffering, and glorious life; lastly, on account of its glorious effects for God and the whole Church—militant, suffering and triumphant.

Thirdly, our Saviour hereby institutes the Blessed Sacrament of the Altar. He appoints and defines, first, the essence of this Sacrament. It consists in the substance of the Body and Blood of Christ under the appearances of bread and wine. Further, He indicates the effects of the Sacrament in the words by which He institutes and regulates it. It is the most intimate union with Christ under the form of food. Thus the Eucharist is the Sacrament of life, inasmuch as it preserves and increases the life of sanctifying grace and marvelously develops it, especially through the actual graces it bestows for the extirpation of sinful concupiscence and the increase of love, joy, zeal and courage, which may rise even to the highest works of supererogation, to virginity and martyrdom. Lastly, our Saviour also commands us to receive this Sacrament, in the words: "Take ye, and eat . . . drink ye all of this" (Matt. 26:26, 27; Mark 14:22). The Eucharist is the greatest and most glorious Sacrament, the end, crown, perfection and seal of all Sacraments, by virtue of what it contains, Christ Himself, and of its glorious effects.

Fourthly, our Saviour also founds in the institution of the Holy Eucharist the Catholic priesthood, which is to perpetuate the Sacrament in this world. It is certain that, in the words: "Do this for a commemoration of Me," He made the Apostles priests of the New Covenant (Trid. Sess. 22, cap. 1, can. 2). All the power of the priesthood has its source in the Eucharist. Its highest manifestation is its power over the true Body of Christ. Its other power, over the mystical Body of Christ, the faithful, is only an amplification of the first, which is its end and aim. It is likewise from the Eucharist that the priesthood derives all its influence and honor among the Catholic people, and lastly the powerful spirit that animates it: its purity, holiness, strength and invincible might. Everything comes to the priesthood from this most holy of Sacraments, even its temporal sustenance, in part (Hebr. 13:10). And our Saviour accomplishes all these great and magnificent works, in the first instance, by the institution of the Holy Eucharist.

2. HOW OUR SAVIOUR INSTITUTES THE HOLY EUCHARIST

Our Saviour institutes the Holy Eucharist, first, with infinite love for God and for us. It is the Sacrament of love, the supreme act of His love. Love is self-sacrifice, and the Eucharist is a sacrifice, a constant and never-ending sacrifice. Love is the communication of oneself; and our Saviour could not give more than He gives us in the Eucharist, nor could He do it in a more gracious and loving way. How completely He lays aside all His glory here, and how lowly and familiar He makes Himself! We can scarcely imagine our Saviour having instituted this great mystery of love otherwise than in an ecstasy of love. The very words with which He began the Last Supper: "With desire I have desired to eat this Pasch with you," point to this. They referred especially to this mystery.

Secondly, our Saviour instituted the Eucharist with great joy, on account of the glorious results that were to proceed from it. It is itself a great and glorious world of grace and holiness. He saw when He instituted it all the Holy Masses, all the Communions, all the altars that He would make His thrones, all the moments that He would pass in this world, all those who would approach to the Holy Eucharist; He saw all the streams of grace, sanctification, comfort and zeal that they would draw from this source; all the honor and glory that God would derive from its nature and use. What a grand and wonderful creation it is! With the Eucharist our Saviour founds the entire holiness, power and beauty of His Church. Its institution was the amplification of His Incarnation, advent, work and Passion. Here He communicates Himself to every human heart, and becomes in very truth the vine that bears God's plants, sending the sap of His Divine Life into all its branches and shoots, and causing them to blossom and bear the fruit of eternal life. The Blessed Sacrament is the force by which He draws all men to Himself and makes them one with Him. Our Saviour saw all this, and His Sacred Heart rejoiced unspeakably over it.

Lastly, it was also with feelings of pain and sorrow that Christ instituted the Eucharist. He saw this Eucharistic life surrounded and clouded by dark and terrible shadows of ingratitude, unbelief and outrage. The precursor of the men who would make Him this unworthy return—a living example of this unbelief, callousness and ingratitude—had been sitting by His side during the celebration of the legal Pasch, and was now gone to seek His enemies and take the preparatory steps for His betrayal and Death. In him our Lord saw the whole terrible future of His Eucharistic Passion; for the unworthy reception of Holy Communion is rightly compared to the treason of Judas. It was a bitter chalice in return for the chalice of sweetness and salvation that He was offering to humanity. Surely His Heart must have shuddered at it. But these tempestuous waves of sorrow did not terrify Him; His love unhesitatingly pursued its way to our hearts.

3. HOW THE APOSTLES RECEIVED THE HOLY EUCHARIST

The Apostles made their First Communion, in the first place, with childlike, simple faith. The Holy Eucharist is above all things a mystery of faith. Our Saviour would probably begin the institution of it with a full instruction, and continuing the lesson He had commenced in the synagogue of Capharnaum, would explain everything to them, telling them that He was now about to put into actual execution what He had then promised. And the Apostles receive our Saviour's words with childlike faith now, as they had done then, because He, their dear Master, Teacher, and God, speaks them (John 6:69, 70).

The Apostles received the Body of our Lord, secondly, with great purity of heart. Our Saviour Himself affirmed this, saying that they were all pure except Judas and only needed to be cleansed from slight stains (John 13:10). This cleansing was accomplished by means of the washing of their feet, in consequence of the heartfelt acts of humility and love that our Saviour's example evoked from them.

Thirdly, they received the Holy Communion with a great desire to participate in the marvelous treasures and graces that our Lord promised them. How the hearts of Peter and John must have burned at the reception of the wondrous food!

Lastly, the Apostles received the Body of our Lord with heartfelt gratitude and ardent love. Love is the best thanksgiving and the most beautiful effect of Holy Communion. And they remained faithful to this love in the main, even in the most terrible hours of the Passion that were just coming upon them. Surely it was the virtue of this Sacrament that strengthened them and preserved their faith and love for Him.

Such was the celebration of the first Holy Communion and the first Mass. What great things our Saviour does in this one mystery! He becomes an integral part of creation, so to speak, by this new form of existence; institutes the Most Holy Sacrifice of the New Testament, and founds the Catholic priesthood. Is not this the same thing as founding the whole Church? Now death may come and rob us of the visible presence of our Saviour; He remains nevertheless truly and essentially with us and in His Church. She is now in very deed the Church of Christ, Who is present in her, His true Bride and mystical Body. Without the Eucharist, we should have suddenly lost our Saviour from this earth nineteen centuries ago. But now we have our God truly with us; and even this earth, our place of exile, becomes home-like through His presence. What we shall possess and actually behold in heaven, we now possess in faith, no less truly and essentially than there. Now we have a new and glorious Sacrifice of the Covenant; and how precious our earth becomes by this Sacrifice, precious even to God Himself! It has become His land of gold and frankincense by the honor and joy that this Sacrifice affords Him. Not less are the advantages that we derive from the Holy Eucharist through Holy Communion. What could this earth offer us, without the Blessed Sacrament? Our souls would pine away and die, in spite of all abundance of temporal things. For all other nourishment that we find on earth is perishable, except this Bread. And what a happiness, what an honor it is for so many thousands of the children of men, that they can now participate in the true and glorious priesthood of Christ! The institution of the Holy Eucharist was indeed the dawn of a new life and happiness both for heaven and earth. How shall we ever be able to thank our Saviour enough for it? How we should rejoice that we have a special feast in order to celebrate worthily all the benefits we received in that holy hour of the first Maundy Thursday! This most holy of all Sacraments ought in truth to be the center and magnet of our thoughts and hearts, indeed of our whole lives.

The Farewell Discourse. Fourth Part of the Last Supper. Introduction to the Farewell Discourse

John 13:33. "Little children, yet a little while I am with you. You shall seek me; and as I said to the Jews: Whither I go, you cannot come; so I say to you now.—34. A new commandment I give unto you: That you love one another, as I have loved you, that you also love one another.—35. By this shall all men know that you are my disciples, if you have love one for another."—36. Simon Peter saith to him: "Lord, whither goest thou?" Jesus answered: "Whither I go, thou canst not follow me now; but thou shalt follow hereafter."—37. Peter saith to him: "Why cannot I follow thee now? I will lay down my life for thee."—38. Jesus answered him: "Wilt thou lay down thy life for me? Amen, amen I say to thee: the cock shall not crow, till thou deny me thrice."

Luke 22:31. And the Lord said: "Simon, Simon, behold Satan hath desired to have you that he may sift you as wheat;—32. But I have prayed for thee that thy faith fail not; and thou being once converted, confirm thy brethren."—33. Who said to him: "Lord, I am ready to go with thee both into prison and to death."—34. And he said: "I say to thee, Peter, the cock shall not crow this day, till thou thrice deniest that thou knowest me." And he said to them:—35. "When I sent you without purse and scrip and shoes, did you want anything?"—36. But they said: "Nothing." Then said he unto them: "But now he that hath a purse, let him take it, and likewise a scrip; and he that hath not, let him sell his coat, and buy a sword.—37. For I say to you, that this that was written, must yet be fulfilled in me: And with the wicked was he reckoned. For the things concerning me have an end."—38. But they said: "Lord, behold here are two swords." And he said to them: "It is enough."

We have reached the fourth and last part of the Last Supper, the ever-memorable farewell discourse of our Lord. It consists of three parts: the introduction, the discourse properly so-called, and our Saviour's prayer for His disciples.

The introduction itself strikes the key-note of the whole discourse, determining its attendant circumstances, its subject and tenor, and lastly its tone and character.

1. THE ATTENDANT CIRCUMSTANCES

The first circumstance to be noted is that the traitor had departed; he was away doing his evil work. So the atmosphere was pure and the surroundings safe. Our Lord was no longer among cold, indifferent, malevolent and unbelieving men, as hitherto. He was surrounded only by simple but pure, childlike, loving hearts, sincerely devoted to Him. So He could lay aside all reserve and open His Heart to them, giving confidence for confidence and love for love. This circumstance made it possible for Him now to communicate unreservedly the last and deepest secrets of His Heart, and thus to reach the climax of the revelation He wished to make.

The second circumstance was that His departure and the hour of His Death were rapidly approaching. This thought already occupied and oppressed our Saviour as well as the Apostles, making itself felt in emotions of anxiety and inconsolable sorrow; the more so that our Lord did not and could not conceal from them the terrible certainty of it all. These two circumstances exercise an unmistakable influence upon all the remainder of the farewell discourse.

2. THE TENOR OF THE DISCOURSE

The circumstances naturally made it necessary for our Lord to speak upon three topics. First, He had to reveal to the Apostles His departure and the sufferings that would ensue upon it. Secondly, He had to console them. Thirdly, He had to give them His last directions and charges. These three notes are already struck in the introduction.

Our Lord predicts to the Apostles His departure and the train of sufferings and trials that will follow upon His Death. "Little children, yet a little while I am with you. You shall seek Me; and as I said to the Jews: Whither I go, you cannot come: so I say to you now" (John 13:33; Luke 17:22; cf. John 7:34). "For the things concerning Me have an end. . . . This that was written, must yet be fulfilled in Me: And with the wicked was he reckoned" (Luke 22:37). So a speedy and shameful Death is awaiting Him. Still more, this Death will have the saddest consequences for all the Apostles, especially for Peter. Our Saviour's prediction of His departure leads St. Peter to ask whither He is going. And as Jesus replies that Peter cannot follow Him thither now (because he is still too weak, and because he has first to govern the Church), but adds that he shall do so later, the impetuous Apostle seizes the opportunity to express his fidelity and resolution, saying that he will give his life for our Lord and is ready to go to prison and to death (John 13:36, 37; Luke 22:33). But our Lord warns him of the temptation of Satan, which will be violent and terrible, like the sifting of wheat (Luke 22:31); and finally foretells his denial (John 13:38; Luke 22:34). Our Saviour's Death will mean for the Apostles a complete and painful change; the very conditions of their life will not be as hitherto. Until now He had provided for everything, protection as well as maintenance; they had only needed to trust Him. He asks them if anything had been lacking to them, when He sent them out without purse, scrip, or shoes. They answer that they had wanted for nothing (Luke 22:35). But now it will be otherwise; now they must make provision for their own sustenance and defence. Our Saviour here employs the similitude of a journey into a far country, where one has to provide for everything oneself, for food (scrip), money (purse), and weapons. Indeed, weapons will be more necessary to them now than even the most indispensable articles, so that they should even sell their coats in order to be able to buy a sword (Luke 22:36); for the shameful end of their Master (Luke 22:37) will have evil consequences for them also, will deprive them of all protection and hospitality and expose them to contempt and persecution. The disciples understood our Lord's words about the "sword" in the literal sense, and showed Him two swords that they had procured on account of the danger they foresaw: "Behold, here are two swords" (Luke 22:38). These were terrible disclosures, and one can well imagine the bewilderment, grief and anxiety with which they filled the disciples.

But our Lord comforted them. He promises all of them, in the person of Peter, a happy issue out of the temptation; he (Peter) will not perish, but on the contrary will rise again from his fall, confirm his brethren, and later on follow our Lord to death (Luke 22:32; John 13:36). Far in the future beyond the darkness of this night our Lord shows Peter the glory of his martyr's confession, and of the infallibility in the teaching office by which he is to enlighten and strengthen all ages.

Lastly, our Lord gives them even thus early the commandment of love (John 13:34, 35), as His last great charge before leaving them. A little later, when He has fairly entered upon His farewell discourse, He will explain this commandment more fully; here He only mentions it, and does so for very obvious reasons. His statement that one of the Apostles would betray Him had greatly disquieted them, and as He did not openly name the real traitor, they might suspect that he was still in their midst, even after Judas had departed. This thought would naturally make them suspicious and distrustful. It is in order to restore their familiarity and guileless, cordial feelings towards one another that He lays such stress upon the commandment of love, calling it "a new commandment," new, that is to say, with regard to its proclamation, motive, and model. This model can be no other than His own love for us. Indeed, He even makes love the token by which His disciples are to be known, and the condition of being one of their number. This is the love of Christianity, so different in its character from that of the Old Covenant.

3. TONE AND CHARACTER OF THE DISCOURSE

The circumstances also determine the tone and character of the farewell discourse. The key-note is struck here and continued throughout the whole discourse. It has three characteristics.

The first is its tender and familiar love. The very first words of the introduction, the form of address, "Little children" (John 13:33), bear this stamp. All the words and deeds of Jesus are inspired and accomplished by love, which is the secret source of their power. But here love breaks through the mysterious veil, and shows and expresses itself. These words of our Saviour's are revelations of love demanding reciprocation. It is as if the love of the God-Man, which had been working in His Heart throughout His whole life, here forces an outlet for itself at last, and now wells forth in a mighty flood, carrying away with it the whole human race to a union with the Father and the Holy Ghost (John 17:23). This discourse is truly the canticle of love.

The second characteristic is the tone of gentle melancholy occasioned by the thought of the impending separation and the bitter Passion and Death of our Lord, and also by the prospect of its fatal reflex action in the shape of the endless suffering and persecution that was to befall His beloved disciples and all who would believe in Him through their word. The loving union of that last meal and the peace of the last hour spent together are repeatedly interrupted and disturbed, as it were, by the world's cries of hate and rage and the sighs of the faithful throughout all ages. Our Lord knows and sees all this, and that is why He is so deeply affected. His voice falters, and it is only with difficulty that He can master His emotion; His whole discourse is interspersed with revelations of future sufferings.

But His courage conquers at last, and He raises their spirits and His own by revealing to them consoling truths. Thus consolation forms the third characteristic of His discourse. This farewell address has been rightly called the charter of consolation, the fund of comfort for all Christendom (Keppler). And such indeed it is. Such real and abundant comfort may be derived from it, that not merely is sorrow alleviated, but the heart is filled with joy at the clearness and truth of the grounds for consolation that Christ gives us.

Thus everything is introduced in these few preliminary words. The circumstances under which the farewell discourse is made are sketched, the principal headings of its purport are given, and the note that will sound to the very end is struck.

The farewell discourse itself may be divided into two principal parts: our Saviour gives His last directions, and comforts His followers.

The Farewell Discourse. First Part: The Last Charge

John 14:1. "Let not your heart be troubled. You believe in God, believe also in me." . . .—6. Jesus saith to him: "I am the way, and the truth, and the life; no man cometh to the Father, but by me.—7. If you had known me, you would without doubt have known my Father also; and from henceforth you shall know him, and you have seen him,"—8. Philip saith to him: "Lord, show us the Father, and it is enough for us."—9. Jesus said to him: "So long a time have I been with you; and have you not known me? Philip, he that seeth me, seeth the Father also. How sayest thou: Show us the Father?—10. Do you not believe that I am in the Father, and the Father in me? The words that I speak unto you, I speak not of myself. But the Father who abideth in me, he doth the works.—11. Believe you not that I am in the Father, and the Father in me?—12. Otherwise believe for the very works' sake. Amen, amen I say to you, he that believeth in me, the works that I do, he also shall do, and greater than these shall he do; because I go to the Father.—13. And whatsoever you shall ask the Father in my name, that will I do; that the Father may be glorified in the Son.—14. If you shall ask me anything in my name, that will I do.—15. If you love me, keep my commandments. . . . —21. He hath my commandments, and keepeth them; he it is that loveth me. And he that loveth me, shall be loved of my Father; and I will love him, and will manifest myself to him."—22. Judas saith to him, not the Iscariot: "Lord, how is it that thou wilt manifest thyself to us, and not to the world?"—23. Jesus answered, and said to him: "If anyone love me, he will keep my word, and my Father will love him, and we will come to him, and will make our abode with him.—24. He that loveth me not, keepeth not my words. And the word which you have heard is not mine, but the Father's who sent me. . . .—15:1. I am the true vine; and my Father is the husbandman.—2. Every branch in me that beareth not fruit, he will take away; and everyone that beareth fruit, he will purge it, that it may bring forth more fruit.—3. Now you are clean by reason of the word which I have spoken to you.—4. Abide in me; and I in you. As the branch cannot bear fruit of itself, unless it abide in the vine; so neither can you, unless you abide in me.—5. I am the vine, you the branches; he that abideth in me, and I in him, the same beareth much fruit; for without me you can do nothing.—6. If anyone abide not in me; he shall be cast forth as a branch, and shall wither, and they shall gather him up, and cast him into the fire, and he burneth.—7. If you abide in me, and my words abide in you; you shall ask whatever you will, and it shall be done unto you.—8. In this is my Father glorified, that you bring forth very much fruit, and become my disciples.—9. As the Father hath loved me, I also have loved you. Abide in my love.—10. If you keep my commandments, you shall abide in my love, as I also have kept my Father's commandments, and do abide in his love.—11. These things I have spoken to you, that my joy may be in you, and your joy may be filled.—12. This is my commandment, that you love one another, as I have loved you.—13. Greater love than this no man hath, that a man lay down his life for his friends.—14. You are my friends, if you do the things that I command you.

—15. I will not now call you servants; for the servant knoweth not what his Lord doth. But I have called you friends; because all things whatsoever I have heard of my Father, I have made known to you.—16. You have not chosen me; but I have chosen you, and have appointed you, that you should go, and should bring forth fruit; and your fruit should remain; that whatsoever you shall ask of the Father in my name, he may give it you.—17. These things I command you, that you love one another. . . .—16:23. And in that day you shall not ask me anything. Amen, amen I say to you: if you ask the Father anything in my name, he will give it you. —24. Hitherto you have not asked anything in my name; ask and you shall receive, that your joy may be full.—25. These things I have spoken to you in proverbs. The hour cometh when I will no more speak to you in proverbs, but will show you plainly of the Father.—26. In that day you shall ask in my name; and I say not to you, that I will ask the Father for you;—27. For the Father himself loveth you, because you have loved me, and have believed that I came out from God."

Our Saviour is evidently telling His disciples here His last and most important wishes, before He leaves them. They are all contained in one charge; or rather, they are in reality but one charge and one commandment.

1. WHAT THIS LAST CHARGE IS

The last wish and most urgent request of all who love one another tenderly and are regretfully compelled to part is, naturally, to remain united in spirit at least. And so it must have been with our Saviour as He was about to deprive the Apostles of His bodily presence; the more so that this spiritual union was of such supreme importance for them. His first and last charge to them, therefore, is to remain united with Him in spirit. He says to them: "Abide in Me, and I (abide) in you" (John 15:4; 14:20). And this union is to be a very close and vital one, to denote which He employs the beautiful similitude of the vine and the branches. As the branch is organically united to the vine and has a common life with it, so was their union with Him to be (John 15:1). And in truth Christ is the spiritual Vine which supports and gives vitality to the whole Church and the entire human race.

Our Saviour adduces beautiful motives for the maintenance of this union. First, the special love and care of the Father, Who, as the Lord of the vine, has an equal love for the stem and the branches, and shows this love by pruning them, cutting off the dead branches, and freeing the sound ones from all that may injure or impede their growth, that they may bear more fruit (John 15:2; cf. Matt. 25:29; Mark 4:25; Luke 8:18). The second motive is the bearing of fruit, which is entirely conditional upon the vital union of the branch with the vine. As long as this union exists, there is abundance of fruit; without it the branch can only wither away in a natural and still more in a supernatural respect, and be cut off and burnt (John 15:4–6). The third motive is the honor and glory of the Father, and His joy at finding abundance of fruit, like the joy of the vine-dresser when the vine flourishes; thus we become the disciples of Jesus in the fullest sense (John 15:8, 16). The fourth motive sums up everything in those words of our Lord which are so full of meaning: "I am the way, and the truth, and the life: no man cometh to the Father, but by Me" (John 14:6). In answer to the disciples' question as to the way our Saviour was to pursue and the goal of His journey, He replies that His Father is the goal, and He Himself the way, precisely because He is the truth and the life. Whoever wishes, therefore, to attain to the possession of God, of eternal bliss, must be united to Christ, because He is the only way to heaven, by the truth that He teaches and is, and by the life that He gives and is. We are all bound to seek Christ and remain united to Him as the sole means of our salvation. Without Christ there is no salvation, no bliss.

2. HOW THIS CHARGE IS FULFILLED AND REALIZED

This vital union with Christ consists in three distinct things.

The first is faith. This is the first thing that our Saviour emphasizes in this last discourse: "You believe in God, believe also in Me" (John 14:1). He gives the following motives for this union with Him by faith. First, His consubstantiality with the Father. As the disciples desire to know and see the Father, the goal of eternal bliss, our Saviour replies that if they know Him, they know the Father also, and now see Him . . . for whoever sees Him, sees the Father. He is in the Father, and the Father in Him (John 14:7–11). It follows from this that His doctrine is divine truth, and that He teaches it not of Himself alone, but in union and consubstantiality with the Father; and also that He Himself is the truth, and that by believing in and accepting Him as such we attain eternal bliss (John 14:6). The second motive for faith in our Lord is to be found in the works and miracles that the Father Who is in Him does, which are a still clearer proof of His Divinity (John 14:10–12). As a third motive our Saviour gives the promise that those who believe in Him will do still greater works than He Himself (John 14:12). By this He means the work in the service of His kingdom, the foundation and extension of which was accomplished apparently by the Apostles, because Christ had withdrawn His visible presence and wrought everything by means of the faith of the Apostles and the other faithful. Lastly, He promises special efficacy to prayer that is offered to the Father in His Name, in this vital union with Him.

The second constituent of this union with Christ is love, love of God and of one's neighbor. He expressly says that the bond of union consists chiefly in love of Him: "Abide in My love" (John 15:9). He then goes on to teach us wherein love essentially consists, viz. in keeping the commandments (John 14:15, 21, 23, 24; 15:10, 14); not in words nor in feelings, but in the pure, supernatural faculty of love, and in the deeds of love. Both are contained in the observance of the commandments, by which we are to keep ourselves in the state of sanctifying grace and virtue, and manifest the same. Our Saviour points to His own example in this respect (John 14:31; 15:10). His life has been passed in loving obedience. The transgression of the commandments, on the contrary, is the death of love (John 14:24). As a motive for this love our Saviour points, first, to the love we shall receive from the Father in return, and to His own reciprocal love. He loves His disciples with the same love with which the Father loves Him (John 15:9), and is now manifesting this love to them, since He is on the point of laying down His life for them all, friends and enemies, which is the greatest possible proof of love (John 15:13). He has shown them this love, further, by admitting them to His friendship, and not treating them as mere servants, but telling them all that He has heard from the Father (John 15:15), that is to say, not merely informing them of the will and commands of the Father, but also giving them an insight into His counsels and intentions, and making familiar friends of them; and lastly, by choosing them out for salvation and the apostolic ministry, to build up His kingdom on earth (John 15:16). As a second motive for love of Him our Saviour promises a future and far higher manifestation of love on His side and His Father's. Whoever has His commandments and keeps them, that is, whoever loves Him, will be loved by the Father, and the Son also will love him and manifest Himself to him (John 14:21), not outwardly, as the Apostle Judas Thaddaeus thought (John 14:22), but inwardly; and both, the Father and the Son, will come and make their abode with him (John 14:23). In these words the deepest, sublimest and sweetest mystery of grace is expressed. By imparting sanctifying grace the Divine Persons give not merely their gifts, but in a certain sense themselves. In sanctifying grace lies the foundation of a special relation to the Divine Persons (the Holy Ghost included; John 14:17), Who manifest their personal attributes to the favored soul by the gift and preservation of this sanctifying grace and by exceptional attachment and special protection, bringing it into a special relation to themselves, taking possession of it, as it were, and imbuing it with their own interior life. This gracious relation, manifestation and immanence is the source of the purest and most perfect joy here below (John 15:11), and may be gradually increased and made more glorious, until we attain to the Beatific Vision in heaven.

But our Saviour will not have love of God separated from love of our neighbor (John 15:12). The reason for this is that love of one's neighbor is most intimately connected with man's relations to God in life and love, and cannot be eliminated from them. For love of God consists, as our Lord Himself said, in the observance of the commandments; and one of His commandments, indeed the chief of them (John 13:34; 15:12), is that we should love one another. It is His new commandment (John 13:34), new on account of the example of Jesus, Who loved us more than Himself (i.e. His life), spontaneously, without being first loved by us, and for God's sake; new, because it is given afresh, and more emphatically than it had ever been enjoined in the Old Testament. Indeed, it is one and the same with the commandment of love for God, because this commandment has two objects, God and our neighbor, and one and the same motive, viz. God (John 15:12, 17). If love of our Saviour makes us all branches of the same vine, there must also be loving union among these branches by their participation in the same life. As a measure of this love our Lord gives us nothing less than His own love for us. We are to love one another as He has loved us (John 15:12); that is, from the same motive and with the same kind of generosity, which went so far with Him that He gave Himself and His life for us, His creatures, brethren and enemies (John 15:13; I John 3:16).

The third constituent of union with Christ is prayer, by which also this union is manifested and preserved. Our Saviour first teaches us what the characteristics of this prayer must be. It is to be made in His Name (John 14:13, 14; 15:7, 16; 16:23, 26), i.e. in intimate union of life with Him by faith and love; with His intentions, for the advancement and weal of the kingdom of God;

on the ground of His merits; under the invocation of His Name; and, since it is made in His spirit, at His desire. He then gives us the most beautiful motives for this prayer; we only need to see how He regards it. Now He speaks of it as a manifestation of faith and the glorification of God (John 14:13, 14); now as a token of union with Him (John 15:7); again as a very important part of apostolic work (John 15:16); at another time as a means of intercourse with Him after His departure (John 16:24). In short, it is under all circumstances a manifestation and means of union with Him in faith, love and work. Prayer is, as it were, the absorption and reception of the vivifying sap of the vine (John 15:7), the inhalation of faith and love (John 14:13), the mightiest means of promoting Christ's kingdom, because it is always at our command and its effects can extend over all places and times (John 15:16). In a word, it is the substitute for the bodily presence of Jesus. What our Saviour did for the Apostles as long as He was visibly with them, He will now do by means of prayer; it is to teach them (John 16:23), protect and comfort them, and provide them with all they need. Our Saviour says the reason why they have not hitherto prayed in His Name is, that He was with them (John 16:24). What a beautiful motive for prayer this is, that it is a compensation for the loss of His visible presence, and a substitute for it! The other motive that our Saviour adduces for prayer, viz. its effects, corresponds to this. These effects are great, incalculable, divine, like His own presence; by faith in Him and love for Him, by compliance with His intentions, and by union with His merits, the prayer of the Apostles becomes as it were His own prayer, and is therefore all-efficient (John 14:14; 15:7, 16; 16:23, 26). There are no limits to be set to its efficacy. This is so true, that a prayer made in the Name of Jesus does not even need a special recommendation or help from Him (John 16:26), for "the Father Himself loveth you, because you have loved Me, and have believed that I came out from God" (John 16:27). What motives more beautiful and more sublime than these could be urged in recommendation of prayer?

3. WHAT FOLLOWS FROM THIS LAST CHARGE

This, then, is our Saviour's first and chief recommendation to His Apostles and to us also before His departure: union with Him by faith, love, and intercourse in prayer. By these three acts man with all his faculties is completely united to our Saviour, and forms a part of Him, so to speak. By faith he obtains the spirit and principles of the God-Man, and shares in the rich treasures of His truth and wisdom. By love, which consists in keeping the commandments and precepts of Jesus, he acquires His virtues and manner of acting, and walks in His footsteps. In prayer he keeps up a continual intercourse and exchange of thoughts, sentiments and feelings with our Saviour, and draws down His graces upon himself. Thus he really remains in our Lord, takes root in Him, and loses himself in Him. Thus he really "puts on" Christ; it is no longer he who lives, but Christ in him.

The first thing that must induce us to strive after this is the desire, will and prayer of Jesus. It is His Heart's desire, His last wish. Ought we not to hold it dear and sacred? The second motive is our own progress. He is our way, our truth, and our life. In Him we must grow, until we attain our full growth in heaven. He is the way that leads to the Father, and there is no other. The last motive is the glory of God and the salvation of men. What glorious strength and power this union with Christ gives us, to glorify God and save the world: Christ's truth, Christ's strength, Christ's merits, and Christ's prayer!

The Farewell Discourse. Second Part: The Last Words of Comfort

John 14:2. "In my Father's house there are many mansions; if not, I would have told you; that I go to prepare a place for you.—3. And if I shall go, and prepare a place for you; I will come again, and will take you to myself, that where I am, you also may be.—4. And whither I go you know, and the way you know. . . .—16. And I will ask the Father, and he shall give you another Paraclete, that he may abide with you for ever,—17. The Spirit of truth, whom the world cannot receive, because it seeth him not nor knoweth him; but you shall know him; because he shall abide with you, and shall be in you.—18. I will not leave you orphans; I will come to you.—19. Yet a little while, and the world seeth me no more. But you see me; because I live, and you shall live.—20. In that day you shall know that I am in my Father, and you in me, and I in you. . . .—25. These things have I spoken to you, abiding with you.—26. But the Paraclete, the Holy Ghost, whom the Father will send in my name, he will teach you all things, and bring all things to your mind, whatsoever I shall have said to you.—27. Peace I leave with you, my peace I give unto you; not as the world giveth, do I give unto you. Let not your heart be troubled, nor let it be afraid.—28. You have heard that I said to you: I go away and I come unto you. If you loved me, you would indeed be glad, because I go to the Father; for the Father is greater than I.—29. And now I have told you before it come to pass; that when it shall come to pass, you may believe.—30. I will not now speak many things with you; for the prince of this world cometh, and in me he hath not anything. . . .—15:18. If the world hate you, know ye that it hath hated me before you.—19. If you had been of the world, the world would love its own; but because you are not of the world, but I have chosen you out of the world, therefore the world hatheth you.—20. Remember my word that I said to you: The servant is not greater than his master. If they have persecuted me, they will also persecute you; if they have kept my word, they will keep yours also.—21. But all these things they will do to you for my name's sake; because they know not him that sent me.—22. If I had not come and spoken to them, they would not have sin; but now they have no excuse for their sin.—23. He that hateth me, hateth my Father also.—24. If I had not done among them the works that no other man hath done, they would not have sin; but now they have both seen and hated both me and my Father.—25. But that the word may be fulfilled, which is written in their law: They hated me without cause.—26. But when the Paraclete cometh whom I will send you from the Father, the Spirit of truth, who proceedeth from the Father, he shall give testimony of me;—27. And you shall give testimony, because you are with me from the beginning.—16:1. These things have I spoken to you, that you may not be scandalized.—2. They will put you out of the synagogues; yea, the hour cometh, that whosoever killeth you will think that he doth a service to God;—3. And these things will they do to you, because they have not known the Father, nor me.—4. But these things I have told you; that when the hour shall come, you may remember that I told you of them.—5. But I told you not these things from the beginning, because I was with you; and now I go to him that sent me; and none of you asketh me, Whither goest thou?—6. But because I have spoken these things to you, sorrow hath filled your heart.—7. But I tell you the truth; it is expedient to you that I go; for if I go not, the Paraclete will not come to you; but if I go, I will send him to you.—8. And when he is come, he will convince the world of sin, and of justice, and of judgment;—9. Of sin: because they believe not in me;—10. And of justice: because I go to the Father, and you shall see me no longer;—11. And of judgment: because the prince of this world is already judged.—12. I have yet many things to say to you; but you cannot bear them now.—13. But when he, the Spirit of truth, is come, he will teach you all truth; for he shall not speak of himself; but what things soever he shall hear, he shall speak; and the things that are to come he shall show you.—14. He shall glorify me; because he shall receive of mine, and shall show it to you.—15. All things whatsoever the Father hath, are mine. Therefore I said: That he shall receive of mine, and show it to you.—16. A little while, and now you shall not see me; and again a little while, and you shall see me; because I go to the Father."—17. Then some of his disciples said one to another: "What is this that he saith to us: A little while, and you shall not see me; and again a little while, and you shall see me; and, Because I go to the Father?"—18. They said therefore: "What is this that he saith, A little while? We know not what he speaketh."—19. And Jesus knew that they had a mind to ask him, and he said to them: "Of this do you inquire among yourselves, because I said: A little while, and you shall not see me; and again a little while, and you shall see me.—20. Amen, amen I say to you, that you shall lament and weep, but the world shall rejoice; and you shall be made sorrowful, but your sorrow shall be turned into joy.—21. A woman, when she is in labor, hath sorrow, because her hour is come; but when she hath brought forth the child, she remembereth no more the anguish, for joy that a man is born into the world.—22. So also you now indeed have sorrow, but I will see you again, and your heart shall rejoice; and your joy no man shall take from you. . . .—28. I came forth from the Father, and am come into the world; again I leave the world, and I go to the Father."—29. His disciples say to him: "Behold now thou speakest plainly, and speakest no proverb;—30. Now we know that thou knowest all things, and thou needest not that any man should ask thee. By this we believe that thou camest forth from God."—31. Jesus answered them: "Do you now believe?—32. Behold, the hour cometh, and it is now come, that you shall be scattered every man to his own. and shall leave me alone; and yet I am not alone, because the

Father is with me.—33. These things I have spoken to you, that in me you may have peace. In the world you shall have distress; but have confidence, I have overcome the world."

We see even from the introduction to this discourse that the Apostles were very sad and dispirited on account of the situation in which they found themselves. There were two grounds for their fear and sorrow: first, our Saviour's departure, which He had clearly and repeatedly declared to be impending (John 14:4, 19, 28; 16:5, 16, 18); and secondly, the sufferings and persecutions that awaited them. So our Saviour immediately begins to comfort and console them: "Let not your heart be troubled" (John 14:1). But He does not content Himself with general words of encouragement. He gives the Apostles reasons for consolation in all kinds of sorrow and apprehension, consolation for His departure and for their future sufferings.

1. COMFORT WITH REGARD TO OUR LORD'S DEPARTURE

Our Lord first comforts the Apostles with regard to His departure by telling them that it will not alter the Father's decision to give them the kingdom (Luke 22:29, 30). On the contrary, He was only going to prepare a place for them in the palace of the great King, where there were many mansions; since no one could enter there without Him, and they themselves must also first be prepared for this dwelling. And He confirms this statement by adding that, if it were not so, He would have told them, for He was going to prepare a place for them (John 14:2). So He is only going on their account, and as soon as He has prepared this place for them in heaven (and indeed within themselves, by the sending of the Holy Ghost), He will come again and fetch them, either at their death or at the Last Judgment, that they may be there with Him in an eternal union (John 14:3). The comfort He gives them, in other words, is this: You will not become homeless through my departure. We have a Father's house, a home in heaven, which is large, beautiful, and secure from all evil. We shall see each other again. I am only going for your sakes, and will come again to fetch you home. This is a beautiful and thoroughly Christian thought to console us in that feeling of being alone and forsaken, homeless and homesick, which comes over us when we have to suffer (Keppler). Our Saviour also takes especial care to set aside the fear the Apostles might have entertained on account of His saying that they could not follow Him where He was going (John 13:36). They will all have a place in His kingdom, and in order that nothing may be wanting to complete this consolation, our Saviour adds that they now know whither He is going, and by what way (John 14:4). And as St. Thomas replies that they know neither the one nor the other (John 14:5), our Saviour responds that God the Father is the goal, and He, the God-Man, the way; they need only follow Him (John 14:6).

He now gives the Apostles a second ground of consolation for His departure, in the words: "You have heard that I said to you: I go away and I come unto you. If you loved Me, you would indeed be glad, because I go to the Father; for the Father is greater than I" (John 14:28). Our Lord's departure is certainly a cause for sorrow, regarded from the disciples' point of view, but it is a subject of real joy if we look at it from His own, in unselfish love. He now calls the Apostles' attention to this joy. His going to the Father is the beginning of greater and more perfect blessings, the beginning of His glory. He is inferior to the Father as regards His human nature, and especially in the state of His earthly life, which is a state of abasement. This abasement now ceases, and is replaced by the glory which He possessed from the beginning with the Father. If they really loved Him, they should rejoice at this glory, and in this joy forget or at any rate abate their sorrow. They did love Him, and it was on His account that they sorrowed. Now the cause of their sorrow is to become a joy to them, and His departure a token by which they may believe that He has entered into the glory of the Father (John 14:29).

Yet a third and beautiful ground of consolation for His departure is given to the Apostles by our Saviour, viz. that the separation will not last long; He will return (John 14:18, 19, 20, 28), and very soon too, to their exceeding joy. "A little while, and now you shall not see Me; and again a little while, and you shall see Me" (John 16:16). This can only refer to their meeting with Him after the Resurrection, and, if we take into account the following verses (John 16:20–22), probably to the time after the Descent of the Holy Ghost also, since all the circumstances of this meeting agree only with this period. The "little while" during which they are not to see our Lord is the time of His Passion and Death, which He does not expressly name, lest it should grieve them too much at this moment. He speaks of it merely as a time when they will weep, whilst the world will rejoice (John 16:20);

but their pain, though it will be intense, will be transient (John 16:21), quickly changing into great and unalterable joy (John 16:22). When this time of joy has arrived, they will no longer need to ask Him about His departure and return, because they will see everything fulfilled, and He will teach them no longer in figures, but directly and openly about His return to the Father, the aim and end of all revelation. They will then ask in His Name, but their prayer will have such strength and efficacy as to need no special assistance from Him (John 16:23, 26, 27). All this agrees with the happy time after the Resurrection and the Descent of the Holy Ghost. It is the dawn of a new age, of new and perfect spiritual life under the guidance of the Holy Ghost.

And this is the fourth ground for consolation, viz. the promise of the Holy Ghost. This promise is a glorious revelation with regard to the Person and Nature as well as the operation of the Holy Ghost.

The Holy Ghost is God, and a true Divine Person. He is the Spirit of truth (John 14:17; 15:26), the Spirit Who *is* truth absolute and essential, and Who teaches all truth (John 14:26; 16:13), knows and predicts the future, and imparts the gift of prophecy (John 16:13); and Who, as regards His origin, proceeds from the Father and the Son (John 15:26; 16:7, 13–15). The Father and the Son send Him (John 16:7; 20:22); for the Father sends Him in the name of the Son (John 14:26), i.e. at the request (John 14:16) of the Son and in consideration of His merits, in union and common action with Him. This temporal sending is the eternal procession, revealed and imitated by a supernatural operation upon the creature; and so the Holy Ghost can receive nothing from the Son but His origin. His personal name is "the Holy Ghost" (John 14:26), because, in consequence of His procession from the Father and the Son, and by their reciprocal love, He is the common Spirit of both, the Divine Spirit, personified holiness and love of God. So it is a Person of equal rank with Himself whom our Saviour sets in His own place.

Our Lord gives a general idea of the operation of the Holy Ghost by saying that He will be His substitute, the "Paraclete" or Comforter, Advocate and Counsellor (John 14:16, 26; 15:26). What our Saviour was to the Apostles with respect to their apostolic vocation, that the Holy Ghost is to be to them, and this in three ways: in the first place, with regard to their own personal preparation and training, secondly with regard to the world, and thirdly with regard to our Saviour. The Apostles personally are above all things the holders and teachers of the faith, and therefore they themselves must be led into the full possession of the treasure of faith. The Holy Ghost will do this. He will remind them of all that our Saviour has taught them (John 14:26); further, He will teach them all truth, i.e. will lead them to an intelligent and connected comprehension of the truths of faith, give them clear insight, deep knowledge, and lofty wisdom (John 14:26), and even widen the circle of truth and teach them what our Saviour had not yet propounded (John 16:12, 13). He will therefore complete the revelation made to the Apostles, and close it with them. It is quite certain that the Holy Ghost taught the Apostles many new truths, e.g. that their letters were inspired (II Peter 3:15); and that He made known to them many future events (Rom. 11:25; I Cor. 15; II Peter 3; I Thess. 4:15; I Cor. 2:12; II Thess. 2:3; Acts 10; cf. Trid. Sess. 4, decr. de can. Script.). With these words the Church and the Chair of Peter arc assured of infallibility in the proclamation, preservation, and continual development and perfection of the truths of faith imparted to them; in a word, of that interior progress in the knowledge of the faith which has been so brilliantly verified down to the present day. All the light that shines forth from the Councils and from the teachings and writings of the doctors of thc Church is an outcome of this promise. With regard to the world, the operation of the Holy Ghost consists in convincing it of sin, justice, and judgment, with a view to its conversion and penance (John 16:8). He convinces it of sin, by showing that it is unbelieving, and that unbelief is sin and the source of all sin (John 16:9); without faith in Jesus it is impossible to get rid of sin (John 8:24; 9:41). He convinces it of justice, because Christ, having ascended into heaven, sanctifies all the faithful by the Holy Ghost (thereby proving His own innocence and holiness, as opposed to the unjust judgment of the Great Council), and because He has thus become the Source of all holiness (John 16:10). Lastly, the Holy Ghost convinces the world of the judgment to come upon it, by the fact that judgment has already been pronounced upon the prince of the world (John 16:11); that is to say, the ruin of His kingdom has begun with the Death of Jesus, is continued by the Church in virtue of her invincibility, and completed at the Last Judgment.

The operation of the Holy Ghost regarding Christ is comprised in the brief words: "He shall give testimony of Me" (John 15:26) and "glorify Me" (John 16:14). The testimony that the Holy Ghost gives is the infallibility of the Church's teaching, the administration of the means of holiness, the manifestation of the gifts of grace, miracles and prophecy, and the wonderful success of the Apostles among the Gentile races, the kingdom of the prince of this world; and also occasional cases of remarkable judgments, such as the chastisement of Jerusalem, which herald the Last Judgment like flashes of sheet-lightning before a storm. In short, the whole work and history of the Church is nothing but the testimony of the Holy Ghost (Keppler). He is the Spirit of truth, the Spirit of prophecy, miracles and holiness. What the Apostles and the Church do is done by the Holy Ghost, and that is why our Saviour says: "The Spirit of truth . . . shall give testimony of Me, and you shall give testimony" (John 15:27). The aim of this great display of power on the part of the Holy Ghost, which is to be seen in the Church in all ages, is the glorification of Jesus. By the power of preaching, by the means of sanctification appointed by Christ, by the miracles and gifts of grace in His Church, and by their marvelous results, unbelief is constantly being convinced of the Divinity of Christ, His holiness, and His judicial power to punish; which power no one can escape. This is the testimony that the Holy Ghost gives to the world through the Apostles. In the Apostles themselves His operation manifests itself in other ways. Our Saviour promises that He will not leave them orphans, but will soon return; the world will not see Him then, but they will see Him, because He will live and they also (i.e. He is life, has life in Himself, and will also give them life, now and hereafter); and in that day they will know that He is in the Father, and they in Him, and He in them (John 14:19, 20). This was fulfilled in the happy days after His Resurrection and the Descent of the Holy Ghost, when they caught a glimpse of the Godhead of the Son shining in the brilliancy of His glorious life; saw Him, as it were, in the glory of the Father, and at the same time received an interior share in this divine life by the possession of the Holy Ghost. Christ is in the Apostles, and in us, by the Holy Ghost. And this testimony was confirmed by the fulness of the peace that our Lord gave them and left with them (John 14:27; 16:33), not a false peace such as the world gives, but peace in its very essence (John 16:27); and also by the superabundance of their inalienable and imperishable joy (John 15:11; 15:22).

This could only be the operation of the Holy Ghost, for He is love; and peace and joy are the effects of love and fruits of the Holy Ghost. This is His work with regard to our Saviour. He glorifies Him, and the aim of His action in the Church and the world is this glorification of Jesus. And rightly; for the Holy Ghost proceeds from the Son as well as from the Father, and receives from Him His origin and the communication of all the glories of the Divine Nature; as God, Christ sends Him, and as God-Man He has effected His sending by the merit of the Redemption and His own prayer (John 14:16). Having entered the kingdom of the creation, the Holy Ghost now fills the world and leads it back to the Son, and through the Son to the Father. And this Holy Ghost, this Helper, Guide and Comforter, this Giver of all gifts, is what our Saviour promises His Apostles in His own stead. The Holy Ghost is to be in them, not merely outwardly to teach and guide them; He will abide in them, and not be taken from them like the bodily presence of Jesus. And they will recognize Him by all His glorious operations in themselves and in their ministry, and by an infallible inward testimony (John 14:16, 17). Could the Apostles imagine or wish for more glorious consolation than the Comforter Himself? And so our Saviour is right when He says: "I tell you the truth; it is expedient to you that I go, for if I go not, the Paraclete will not come to you; but if I go, I will send Him to you" (John 16:7). Thus it was decreed by Divine Providence that all the Persons of the Most Holy Trinity should cooperate in the salvation of mankind: the Father by sending the Son and drawing all to Him; the Son by instructing and redeeming the world; and the Holy Ghost by perfecting and sanctifying the redeemed and filling them with His gifts.

2. COMFORT WITH REGARD TO PERSECUTIONS

In the introduction to His discourse our Saviour had characterized His departure in brief but portentous words as the cause of hard trials and afflictions for the Apostles (Luke 22:35–37); and so it was well to speak cheering words of encouragement with respect to these also (John 14:1, 27; 16:33). Therefore our Saviour gives them definite and solid grounds of consolation.

The first consists in the plain predictions which our Lord makes to the Apostles concerning many of these persecutions, with the intention of encouraging them; for adversities that are predicted and expected are not so hard to bear, since they prove by their very occurrence that they are dispositions of Divine Providence. So our Saviour tells the Apostles that the godless and unbelieving world, both heathen and Jewish, hates them (John 15:18, 19). In particular He foretells that they will be expelled from the synagogues and be killed by the Jews, out of religious fanaticism, so that these countrymen of theirs will think they are doing a religious act, well-pleasing to God, in killing them (Ex. 32:29; Deut. 13:9; 17:7; 18:20). This was really the case with the Jews (Acts 6:11; 8:3; 9:1; 26:9; Rom. 10:2; Gal. 1:13), to whom our Saviour here refers, and later on with the Gentiles also. Our Lord had not told them before (John 16:5) of this circumstance, that they would be persecuted and killed by their own people for the sake of religion (John 16:2, 3); but He does so now, that they may not be scandalized when it happens (John 16:1), but think of His prediction (John 16:4).

The second motive for comfort in persecution is the example of our Saviour (John 15:18), Who was also persecuted in this manner by the Jews, even to death, for the sake of religion (Matt. 26:65; John 9:24; 18:30). The Apostles are not to forget what He told them before, that the servant is not more than his lord (John 13:16; Matt. 10:24); the Jews would behave with regard to their words as they had done towards His, i.e. only very few of them would accept them (John 15:20). This might have been a cause of disquietude and scandal even for the Apostles (cf. John 12:37 seq.).

The third motive is drawn from the reason of the hatred and persecution. It has no other foundation than their adherence to our Saviour. They are separated from the world and devoted to Him, His Person and His cause (John 15:19); they are persecuted in His Name and for the confession of His Name as that of the Ambassador and Son of God the Father, Whom the world does not know (John 15:21). Its hatred is a sin, an inexcusable sin (John 15:22), simply hatred of God (John 15:23); because our Lord has sufficiently proved Himself to be the Ambassador and Son of God by His miracles, which are so great and significant precisely because they are Messianic miracles and confirmations of His divine mission. So it is the Father Whom the world has seen and hated in our Lord (John 15:24). There is beautiful and solid consolation in these words. The world's hatred is a natural thing, proceeding from the rule of opposites, and it was foreseen and predicted in the law: "They have hated Me with an unjust hatred" (Ps. 24:19), just as the prophets too were hated. It is a sweet and honorable thing to be hated and persecuted for the sake of the Name of Jesus. As a matter of fact, this was the Apostles' sweetest consolation later on (Acts 5:41; 21:13; 26:9). But as, in spite of our Saviour's words, the disciples still remained sad and depressed on account of the persecutions they were to endure without Him (for He again lays stress upon His departure; John 16:5, 6), He goes still farther, and promises that the Holy Ghost will help them to gain the victory in the struggle with this unbelieving world that so hates them (John 16:7–15). Their sorrow will be changed into joy, their distress into victory.

3. CONCLUSION OF THE FAREWELL DISCOURSE

So our Saviour had comforted His beloved Apostles and helped them to put aside all their grief; indeed, this clear and glorious disclosure of the reasons and object of His departure (John 16:28) had so completely solved their doubts and made such an impression upon them, that they broke into a joyful and enthusiastic confession of His Divinity (John 16:29, 30). The Apostles are consoled; but nevertheless a hard time is impending for them and for our Lord, the time of His Passion. It is touching to see with what pain He reverts to it. It will be a personal and decisive combat between Him and Satan, the prince of the world (John 14:30), and no one will give Him any aid therein (John 16:32). But He immediately encourages Himself to engage in this combat. The enemy will have no power over Him (John 14:30), because He is innocent; the Father is with Him (John 16:32); His Death is not the effect of external violence, but the most glorious offering of voluntary obedience and love for His Father (John 14:31), and at the same time the entrance to His glory. "I came forth from the Father, and am come into the world; again I leave the world, and I go to the Father" (John 16:28). That is the great and glorious significance of His departure and Death, and it leaves neither Him nor the Apostles any room for hesitation, doubt, or grief. So He exclaims with enthusiasm: "Arise, let us go hence" (John 14:31). "In the world you shall have distress; but have confidence, I have overcome the world" (John 16:33).

This is the comfort our Saviour gives His Apostles; and with this He has comforted us all. It suffices for all ages and every earthly sorrow (II Cor. 1:3–7; 6:4–10; 7:4). It has never failed and never been exhausted. The foundation of this comfort is heaven: God Himself, the Holy Ghost, with His imperishable, undisturbed peace and superabundant joy; and even earthly suffering is itself a comfort, when we reflect how short it is, and that we bear it for Christ and His kingdom and in order to gain our glorious goal, eternal happiness in heaven. This is the very essence of Christian consolation, which sweetens all sorrow and changes it into heavenly joy. How many have been made happy by these comforting words of our Saviour! How many tears they have dried! It was in these very same thoughts that our Saviour found His own encouragement during this terrible night. We can thus follow His train of thought and the emotions of His Heart, and raise our own spirits by this means. There is divine strength and inexhaustible abundance of grace in these ever-memorable words.

Christ's Prayer for His Disciples

John 17:1. These things Jesus spoke; and lifting up His eyes to heaven, he said: "Father, the hour is come, glorify thy Son, that thy Son may glorify thee;—2. As thou hast given him power over all flesh, that he may give eternal life to all whom thou hast given him.—3. Now this is eternal life; that they may know thee, the only true God, and Jesus Christ, whom thou hast sent.—4. I have glorified thee on the earth; I have finished the work which thou gavest me to do;—5. And now glorify thou me, O Father, with thyself, with the glory which I had, before the world was, with thee.—6. I have manifested thy name to the men whom thou hast given me out of the world; thine they were, and to me thou gavest them; and they have kept thy word.—7. Now they have known that all things which thou hast given me are from thee;—8. Because the words which thou gavest me, I have given to them; and they have received them, and have known in very deed that I came out from thee, and they have believed that thou didst send me.—9. I pray for them; I pray not for the world, but for them whom thou hast give me; because they are thine;—10. And all my things are thine, and thine are mine, and I am glorified in them;—11. And now I am not in the world, and these are in the world, and I come to thee. Holy Father, keep them in thy name, whom thou hast given me; that they may be one, as we also are.—12. While I was with them, I kept them in thy name. Those whom thou gavest me have I kept; and none of them is lost but the son of perdition, that the Scripture may be fulfilled.—13. And now I come to thee; and these things I speak in the world, that they may have my joy filled in themselves.—14. I have given them thy word, and the world hath hated them, because they are not of the world, as I also am not of the world. —15. I pray not that thou shouldest take them out of the world, but that thou shouldest keep them from evil.—16. They are not of the world, as I also am not of the world.—17. Sanctify them in truth. Thy word is truth.—18. As thou hast sent me into the world, I also have sent them into the world.—19. And for them do I sanctify myself; that they also may be sanctified in truth.—20. And not for them only do I pray, but for them also who through their word shall believe in me. —21. That they all may be one, as thou, Father, in me, and I in thee, that they also may be one in us; that the world may believe that thou hast sent me.—22.

And the glory which thou hast given me, I have given to them; that they may be one, as we also are one.—23. I in them, and thou in me; that they may be made perfect in one; and the world may know that thou hast sent me, and hast loved them, as thou hast also loved me.—24. Father, I will that where I am, they also whom thou hast given me may be with me; that they may see my glory which thou hast given me, because thou hast loved me before the creation of the world.—25. Just Father, the world hath not know thee; but I have known thee; and these have known that thou hast sent me.—26. And I have made known thy name to them and will make it known; that the love, wherewith thou hast loved me, may be in them, and I in them."

Our Saviour closes His farewell discourse with a sublime prayer. It is sometimes called His priestly prayer, because He is truly a High Priest, whether He is actually engaged in the sacrificial action or not; further, because the objects and aims of this prayer are really priestly, being concerned with the great subjects of His mediation between God and men. It is so called also because it sums up the whole result of His previous priestly activity and turns it to account; and lastly, because it is almost immediately connected with the approaching Sacrifice of the Cross and that of the Last Supper which had just been completed. It thus forms the thanksgiving for the one and the solemn introduction and consecration of the other. Thus it is truly an official prayer. With regard to its nature, it is a true and real prayer, a prayer of praise and thanksgiving, but more especially of impetration. Its object could be no other than that of every prayer, viz. the acknowledgment of God's sovereignty by praise, thanksgiving, and petition; and secondly, our profit and that of the Apostles. This profit consists in the obtaining of the blessings asked, and in the incidental effects of the prayer: tranquillity, comfort and encouragement, in consequence of the sublime and consoling truths that are expressed in it (John 17:13). In this respect it is not merely the continuation, but it is also the crown and seal of the farewell discourse, in the form of a prayer; and that is why our Lord pronounces it audibly and openly, standing in the midst of His disciples. This prayer may be divided into three parts, corresponding to the subjects of His petitions.

1. WHAT OUR LORD ASKS FOR HIMSELF (JOHN 17:1–5)

In this case also our Lord observes the suitable and traditional form of every good prayer; He begins with an invocation and then offers His petitions.

The form of invocation is simply: "Father" (John 17:1); it is that which He had formerly taught (Matt. 6:9) and constantly used. This word often recurs in the course of the prayer, and gives to the whole a tone of childlike deference, love and familiarity.

The subject of the petition is, first, His own glorification, the time for which has now arrived, with "His hour" of suffering (John 13:1). A little later He explains wherein this glorification consists: "Glorify Thou Me, O Father, with Thyself, with the glory which I had, before the world was, with Thee" (John 17:5); that is, the heavenly glory for His Humanity, which was appointed Him as the Son of God, and to which He had a right from the very first moment of His existence, but of which He had hitherto deprived Himself. Now He asks for it, and wishes to enter upon and possess it also in virtue of His prayer and of the merits He has gained upon earth. This glory began with the marvelous events at His Death and His Descent into Limbo, was increased at His Resurrection, and completed at His Ascension. Still He does not desire this glory on His own account alone, but for the sake of the Father's glory: "that Thy Son may glorify Thee" (John 17:1). The Father is the origin and the last end of everything, and therefore our Saviour seeks in all things the honor and glory of the Father, as His life's aim. The honor of the Son is the honor of the Father. The exaltation of the Son is also a revelation to men of the glory of the Father. This, then, is the subject of His petition; His own glory in the first instance, and then, as its end and aim, the Father's glory.

Our Saviour then adds motives as touching and beautiful as the petition itself. The first is drawn from the object of His lifework, and is indicated in the words: "As Thou hast given Him power over all flesh, that He may give eternal life to all whom Thou hast given Him" (John 17:2). The Father has given to the Son a royal, judicial and sacerdotal power over the whole human race; but He has given Him the elect in a special manner, and to these the Son is to give eternal life. And eternal life consists in this: "that they may know Thee, the only true God, and Jesus Christ, whom Thou hast sent" (John 17:3). This knowledge is the saving faith that finds its perfection and completion in the vision of God in heaven. But this faith can only be given to the elect by the exaltation of Jesus. Our Saviour here calls Himself for the first time by His full and most sacred Name, and confesses His Divinity by including Himself in the object of the Beatific Vision. The second motive is His faithful fulfilment of

His mission as God-Man. "I have glorified Thee on the earth: I have finished the work which Thou gavest Me to do" (John 17:4). It is the motive of justice and equity, founded upon perfect, unselfish sanctity and fidelity to vocation. The third and last motive is His absolute claim to this glory, which He had from all eternity as the Son of God (John 17:5). This motive throws a glorious light upon the sacrifice of self-abasement made by Him in His earthly life, and brings our Saviour very close to us, since He, like ourselves, will enter upon His heavenly glory as the reward and in virtue of the merits He has gained. The whole petition is touchingly human, and yet sublime.

2. WHAT OUR LORD ASKS FOR HIS APOSTLES (JOHN 17:6–19)

Our Saviour now passes on to the petitions for His Apostles. Of these there are two.

The first petition is that the Father may vouchsafe to guard them in two respects. Our Lord asks that He may prevent them from being infected with the sinfulness of the world, and that He may keep them in knowledge, faith, and communion with the Father, "that they may be one, as We also are" (John 17:11, 12), i.e. one among themselves by the unity of the life of grace, as We are one by the unity of Our nature. The Father had given this unity to the Son, that He might communicate it to others by faith and grace. The mention of the unhappy Judas and the sinful world, which, as such, has no part in this communion, confirms this interpretation of the petition. Our Saviour adduces the following motives for it. In the first place, He says, they are Thine, the children of Thy eternal election and fatherly love, and therefore they are also Mine, for Thou hast given them to Me (John 17:6); all that is Thine is Mine also, and they are My heritage and the instruments of My glorification by their faith, love and future work (John 17:10). Secondly, the Apostles have believed. They have accepted the revelation of Thy Nature and Thy Name, and the preaching of Thy truth, and have recognized that I came out from Thee; they have believed that Thou hast sent Me, and have kept Thy word (John 17:6–8). So they (not the world, for our Lord expressly says that He is not now praying for the world) deserve protection and help on account of their faith and fidelity, which are of such value in the eyes of our Saviour and His Father. Thirdly, the Apostles are in the world. Hitherto, our Lord says, I have kept them all except one, but now I am no longer in the world; I come to Thee, and therefore Thou must protect them (John 17:11, 12). Our Saviour makes this petition audibly, in presence of the Apostles, before He leaves them, in order that they may derive courage, confidence and joy from seeing themselves so beloved and recommended to the Father's care by Him (John 17:13). And He also prays that the Father will protect them against the hostility and persecution of the world and its prince. By the faith they have accepted, the Apostles are separated from the world, placed in opposition to it, like our Saviour Himself. The world hates them, persecutes them (John 17:14, 16), and therefore our Lord asks for protection and deliverance from evil: from the devil, the prince of the world, and his attacks, and all the more because they are not to be placed beyond range of these, but on the contrary to remain entangled in them.

The second petition on behalf of the Apostles is a positive one: "Sanctify them in truth" (John 17:17). The sanctification here spoken of is not a merely personal one, consisting in preservation from sin and union with God by the state of grace; it also includes the necessary endowments for aiding in the sanctification of others. The Apostles are to become instruments of the sanctification of others, like the priests (Ps. 105:16), the prophets (Luke 1:70), and Christ Himself (Mark 1:24; John 10:36). So our Saviour means here: Sanctify them for ever in the exercise of their vocation, by the requisite graces and gifts. He then urges reasons for this. First, it is their vocation to preach Thy word. But Thy word is truth, and nothing but truth, and therefore they too must be entirely true and holy (John 17:17). Secondly, the Apostles are appointed to the same vocation as He Himself has been appointed to by His Father (John 17:18); and as He has been sanctified by the Father, so must they be also; ordination is necessary for orders. Thirdly, our Saviour sanctifies (i.e. sacrifices) Himself for the Apostles, that they may be sanctified (John 17:19). The sacrificial Death of Jesus effected the sending of the Holy Ghost, by Whom the Apostles were "sanctified in truth" for their vocation. The Holy Ghost is holiness personified and the Spirit of truth. By Him they were kept and consecrated for their office. The sending of the Holy Ghost is the Apostles' baptism. In asking this for them, our Saviour has asked everything.

3. WHAT OUR LORD ASKS FOR THOSE WHO WILL BELIEVE IN HIM (JOHN 17:20–26)

The Apostles do not stand alone, nor does our Lord intend that they shall. They are the seeds of the whole Church and all the faithful. In them our Lord sees the men of all ages who will receive and accept the faith through their instrumentality (John 17:20); and He lovingly includes these also in His prayer. He makes two petitions for the faithful, as He had done for the Apostles.

The first petition is, that they may be one (John 17:21), "made perfect in one" (John 17:22, 23); all of them, the faithful and the Apostles (John 17:11), the former through the latter. The unity of the Father with the Son is held up as the ideal of this perfect unity: "Thou, Father, in Me, and I in them, that they also may be one in Us" (John 17:21); that is to say, there is to be in the Church, in spite of diversity, the greatest possible unity, in faith, in love, and in the life of grace in the Holy Ghost (I John 1:3; 4:13; Eph. 4:4). In this manner our Lord is really in the faithful, and since the Father is in Him, they are also one with the Father (John 17:23); and therefore their unity is like that of the Father and the Son, because they are one with the Father and the Son. Our Saviour also gives reasons for the granting of this union. First, He asks it in order that the world may believe that the Father has sent Him. Amid the dissensions and divisions which prevail in this sinful world such a power of unity is a real miracle, and bears witness to the Divinity of Christ, Who brought it about (John 17:21); indeed, the world is to recognize by this not merely that the Founder of the Church is the Son of God, but also that the faithful are the adopted children of God, beloved by the Father with a love similar to that which He bears to His own Son (John 17:23). The second motive is that Christ has done everything to bring about this unity (John 17:22). He has given the faithful His "glory," i.e. grace and truth (John 1:14), faith and sanctifying grace (Col. 1:11; Eph. 1:5, 6; 3:16; II Peter 1:3, 4). Their unity is based upon the communication of this grace (John 1:12; I John 3:1).

Our Saviour's second petition for the faithful, in which He again especially includes the Apostles (John 17:24, 25, 26; cf. 6, 9, 11, 12), is that they may be where He is, and may see His glory (John 17:24). This glory is nothing else than the glory of the

Divine Sonship, including the created, acquired glory of the God-Man. He asks that the Apostles and the faithful may contemplate this glory and enjoy it with Him (Rom. 8:17; Col. 3:4; II Tim. 2:12). Our Lord makes this petition with great emphasis and earnestness. He repeats the name of "Father," and says: "I will." It is, so to speak, His last will, by which He disposes of what the Father has given Him, as well as of the glory that He had bestowed upon Him when He loved and begot Him, before the creation of the world; and He lays all the more stress upon this volition of His, because it coincides with the Will of His Father.

This marvelous prayer concludes with an invocation of the justice of the Father, in order to commend to Him these petitions for the Apostles whom He had given to Jesus in a special manner (John 17:6) and who had been the first to acknowledge His Divinity (John 17:25), and also the petitions for the faithful. In corroboration of His prayer He points, on the one hand, to the world, which does not and will not recognize the Father in the Son, and on the other hand to the disciples and the faithful, who receive the knowledge of Him from the Father and joyfully take part in the work of the revelation of His glory (John 17:26). This work of revelation has no other object than that "the love, wherewith Thou hast loved Me, may be in them, and I in them." This love of the Father in the Apostles and in us is a fatherly love, not merely as regards the affection, but also in reality and in truth, since He has received us as His children by the gift of adoption and the communication of the Holy Ghost, Who is the personal love of the Father and the Son (Rom. 5:5; I John 4:13). In this manner the love of the Father and the Son is in us.

Thus this priestly prayer for His disciples is really the evening prayer and last blessing of our Saviour. Full of gratitude to His Father, He glances back over His ministry, lays a magnificent account of it at His feet, and asks for the glory He has earned, His Father's blessing, before He lays down His head in death. And He Himself blesses and prays for His own. He presents them all, the Apostles especially, to His Heavenly Father; He has a prayer and a blessing for all, save the world. It is sad and terrifying to hear what He says of the latter. He and the Apostles are not of the world (John 17:14, 16); it does not know Him, nor the Father (John 17:25), nor the Holy Ghost (John 14:17); He does not pray for the world here (John 17:9); He leaves its fate to the justice of the Father (John 17:25). But still He does not lose sight of it, nor of those of its children who are capable of amendment. His Church and her prayers (Matt. 5:44; Luke 22:34), the riches of her means of redemption (I John 2:2), and the glorious spectacle of her firmness and unity are to be their salvation and a token to them (John 17:21, 23). And with the blessing of this glorious unity His prayer ends. He has nothing more to say, nothing more to give. In this unity everything is included and consummated, all blessings for time and eternity, all interior glory and exterior power and efficacy.

On casting a glance over this grand farewell discourse, we are immediately struck by its double significance with regard to our Saviour. It is the climax of the revelation of His doctrine, and also of the magnificence of His character. It is not without reason that He calls attention to the fact that He says all this now, and not before (John 14:29; 15:11; 16:1, 4, 5, 33; 17:13). The discourse is a sketch and summary of the greatest mysteries of the faith. It sends rays of light in all directions, and reveals the whole cycle of Christian truth. The entire mystery of the Most Holy Trinity is revealed: the glory of the Father as the Last End of all things, the Principle of predestination, and the Origin of the procession of the Divine Persons (John 14:16, 28; 15:1, 26; 17:6, 7); the Divinity of Christ (John 14:6, 14, 20; 15:26; 16:15; 17:3, 5, 8, 24); and especially the Divinity of the Holy Ghost, and His work in the Church (John 14:17, 26; 15:26; 16:7 seq., 13). Here is also revealed the mystery of the Church, in her mission (John 17:18), in the infallibility of her teaching (John 14:16, 17, 26; 16:13), in her wonderful gifts (John 14:12; 16:13), her victorious battle with the world (John 16:18 seq., 33), her unity (John 17:11, 21, 23, 26), the nature of her state of grace (John 14:23; 15:4, 5), the power of her prayer (John 14:13; 15:7, 16; 16:23). All this shines forth in the light of this discourse and this prayer.

But not less sublime and full of charm is the revelation it affords us with respect to the Person, character and spirit of our Saviour. In the first place, it shows us His holiness, in His reverential and childlike submission to His Father. He ascribes everything to Him (John 17:7); goes to his Death out of obedience and love for Him (John 14:31); the end and object of His work and even of His glorification is the glory of the Father (John 17:1, 4 seq.). "I have glorified Thee on the earth; I have finished the work which Thou gavest Me to do" (John 17:4). Who but He Who is holiness itself can speak thus of His life? And in what grand outlines He reveals to us His majesty and full consciousness of His consubstantiality with the Father, as the Son of God, when He demands His glory as His portion from all eternity (John 17:5); when He disposes of heaven as His heritage (John 17:24), and seals His prayer with an invocation of the Father's justice (John 17:25)! Lastly, we feel the promptings of His Sacred Heart in all His words, His truly human, tender compassionate Heart, so open to all human emotions of joy, fear, compassion, melancholy and sadness, so full of true humanity, friendship and love. It is Love indeed that speaks here (Keppler), Love revealing Himself and seeking a return of love; Love showing Himself in sweet words of comfort and promise, and lifting His hands to offer this marvelous prayer and give a last blessing. Who does not feel, in the broken words of petition for the disciples and the faithful, in the even more urgent and impressive prayer for union with us that goes to our very hearts, the whole resistless power and abundance of the love that welled up in this Heart and sought an outlet in order to communicate itself to us? The kiss imprinted by a father or mother upon the lips of a child at parting conveys their longing wish to retain their place in this beloved heart for ever. The parting words of Jesus signify no less. They are the most profound revelation, the last will and testament of the love of Jesus. "Having loved His own who were in the world, He loved them unto the end" (John 13:1).

The Walk to the Mount of Olives

MATT. 26:30. And a hymn being said, they went out unto Mount Olivet.—31. Then Jesus saith to them: "All you shall be scandalized in me this night. For it is written: I will strike the shepherd, and the sheep of the flock shall be dispersed.—32. But after I shall be risen again, I will go before you into Galilee."—33. And Peter answering, said to him: "Although all shall be scandalized in thee, I will never be scandalized."—34. Jesus said to him: "Amen I say to thee, that in this night before the cock crow, thou wilt deny me thrice."—35. Peter saith to him: "Yea, though I should die with thee, I will not deny thee." And in like manner said all the disciples.

MARK 14:26. And when they had said a hymn, they went forth to the Mount of Olives.—27. And Jesus saith to them: "You will all be scandalized in my regard this night; for it is written: I will strike the shepherd, and the sheep shall be dispersed.—28. But after I shall be risen again, I will go before you into Galilee." —29. But Peter saith to him: "Although all shall be scandalized in thee, yet not I." —30. And Jesus saith to him: "Amen I say to thee, today even in this night, before the cock crow twice, thou shalt deny me thrice."—31. But he spoke the more vehemently: "Although I should die together with thee, I will not deny thee." And in like manner also said they all.

LUKE 22:39. And going out he went according to his custom to the Mount of Olives. And his disciples also followed him.

JOHN 18:1. When Jesus had said these things, he went forth with his disciples over the brook Cedron, where there was a garden, into which he entered with his disciples.

1. OUR LORD LEAVES THE COENACULUM

After the sublime and glorious mysteries of the Last Supper had been accomplished, our Lord rose and quitted the house in which He had celebrated the feast. We may here consider why He did not wish to be arrested there. There were probably three reasons.

First, He wished to go to His Passion and Death of His own free will, and to avoid even the semblance of an involuntary surprise. In this respect no cloud was to be cast upon the majesty of His Passion. This was one of the points upon which His nobility of character made Him keenly sensitive.

Secondly, our Lord did not wish His kind host to incur the annoyance, disturbance, or damage to property, which would have been inevitable in the case of a sudden armed attack.

Thirdly, He would not have the last hour of leave-taking, the quiet solemnity of the Paschal meal, the first celebration of the Sacred Mysteries, and His last familiar disclosures, warnings, and words of comfort disturbed and broken off by the violence of His enemies. The last hours of His freedom were to be passed in His wonted tranquillity and majesty. That is why our Saviour did not rise until He had completed all that He intended to do, and then quitted with His disciples the Coenaculum on the heights of the upper city, Sion.

2. OUR LORD GOES TO THE MOUNT OF OLIVES

We must now consider our Saviour's emotions and the conversation He holds with His disciples during this walk.

First, He is full of gratitude to God; for we are expressly told that He caused a hymn to be sung (Matt. 26:30; Mark 14:26). If the Eucharist was instituted at the drinking of the fifth chalice, this hymn of praise must have been the Great Hallel (Ps. 119–136). We may be sure that His Heart was full of joy and overflowing with gratitude to God for the many and great mysteries that He had instituted, and which were to have so many glorious results for God and for us. And He certainly did not omit to thank His host also, on taking leave of him. The second emotion our Lord experienced was sadness. Everything was calculated to make Him sorrowful. His Passion was approaching with giant strides.

It was His last walk. Probably His path led through the suburb of Ophel, on the south side of the Temple hill, into the valley of Josaphat. There is scarcely a gloomier or more somber place in the world than this valley. In the midst of it lies the dry bed of the winter-brook Cedron; on either side are ravines, rugged rocks, barren hills, and stunted trees, and the whole is overshadowed by the city walls that stretch along its margin. Perhaps its aspect may have been otherwise formerly, when the heights were wooded and the many aqueducts of the Temple kept the brook running. But in any case it was a dreary walk in the dark. David had once trodden the same path with covered head and bare feet, as he crossed the bed of the Cedron on his flight from Absalom, his rebellious son, in order to retreat into the desert with some of his loyal subjects (II Kings 15:16). Our Saviour may well have been reminded of this as He passed over one of the bridges of the Cedron and, walking up the valley along the left side of the brook (John 18:1), gazed upon the somber city, where another rebellious son, an apostate Apostle, was collecting officials and soldiers for the perpetration of his mysterious crime. The nearer our Lord came to Gethsemani, the more His sorrow and anxiety increased, and probably what was passing in His Heart became visible by outward signs as well. The disciples too were very downcast as they walked at His side, and listened anxiously to His words. But however sad our Lord felt, His will never wavered in its fortitude and determination, nor did He for a moment delay His steps as He drew near to the fatal scene of His Agony and arrest.

The conversation during this walk turned upon His impending Passion and Death and the flight of His disciples. He tells them beforehand that they will all be scandalized in Him this night (Matt. 26:31; Mark 14:27), and quotes the prophetic words of Zacharias: "Awake, O sword, against My shepherd, and against the man that cleaveth to me, saith the Lord of hosts: strike the shepherd, and the sheep shall be scattered" (Zach. 13:7; John 16:32). Our Lord expresses in plainer language the last words of the prophet: "And I will turn My hand to the little ones," by saying: "But after I shall be risen again, I will go before you into Galilee" (Matt. 26:32; Mark 14:28). The disciples, on the other hand, protest against the prediction and assure Him that they will rather die with Him than ever forsake Him (Matt. 26:35; Mark 14:31).

Peter in particular again asserts that, although all the others should forsake our Saviour, he will never be scandalized in Him. Our Lord, however, assures him that this very night, before the cock has crowed twice, he will thrice deny Him. But Peter insists that he will rather die than do this (Matt. 26:33–35; Mark 14:29–31). These words of St. Peter's certainly imply incredulity, undue estimation of himself, and perhaps a little self-exaltation over the other Apostles; but they also show heartfelt love and sincere resolution, and probably the endeavor to inspire our Saviour and the other Apostles with courage. Who is not here reminded of Ethai and the faithful servants who, weeping, followed David over the Mount of Olives, whilst Absalom was the sad prototype of Judas? (II Kings 15.) And although this assurance of fidelity was not to be brilliantly verified, still our Saviour does not receive it ungraciously; on the contrary, although so sorely in need of comfort Himself, He comforts the Apostles by referring to the Scriptures, and promising that the trial will be but transient and that He will not abandon His plans for them. How truly does He show Himself the Good Shepherd! Who will not appreciate His words of comfort, spoken under such circumstances?

3. OUR LORD ENTERS THE GARDEN OF GETHSEMANI

Gethsemani was a farm (Matt. 26:36; Mark 14:32), with a garden (John 18:1) of olive-trees, situated on the western slope of the Mount of Olives (Luke 22:39). It had also probably a country-house and an olive-oil press. A part of this farm is still intact, and encloses within its precincts eight very ancient olive-trees, which tradition says were in existence in the time of our Lord and were witnesses of the Agony of the God-Man. They stand in a quiet, ever flowering garden of rosemary and those well-known red immortelles sometimes called Messias-blood. It is a bright and cheering little spot in the midst of the dreary, sepulchral valley of Josaphat. It was this garden that our Saviour now entered with His disciples, in order to pray there as He was wont (John 18:2; Luke 21:37), and to begin His Passion.

And why did He wish to begin His Passion in this garden, and with prayer? The fall of our first parents had taken place in a garden, under the trees of Eden; and therefore the reparation of this fall was also to be made in a garden. That question of Almighty God: "Adam, where art thou?" that had once resounded through the garden, demanding satisfaction from the first Adam, had hitherto remained unanswered. No one appeared to offer the required expiation. But now our Saviour, the second Adam, comes, and offers Himself to make full satisfaction, saying: "Behold, I come" (Ps. 39:8). In the second place, it was from Mount Olivet that our Saviour was to make His Ascension to the throne of His glory; how fitting, then, that His Passion too should begin there! Lastly, no more majestic introduction to the Passion could be imagined than prayer. There was not a single important undertaking in the public life of our Saviour that He did not begin with prayer; how much more, then, His blessed and saving Passion! The prayer on Mount Olivet is thus the majestic gate and vestibule of the sanctuary of His Passion, and the first station of the Passion itself. He well knew that this very prayer was to cost Him unspeakable anguish and the sacrifice of His freedom. But He does not forbear to make it. He had foreseen it and had again and again foretold it.

Thus our Saviour entered the terrible precincts of His Passion.

The Agony on Mount Olivet

MATT. 26:36. Then Jesus came with them into a country place which is called Gethsemani, and he said to his disciples: "Sit you here, till I go yonder and pray." —37. And taking with him Peter and the two sons of Zebedee, he began to grow sorrowful and to be sad.—38. Then he saith to them: "My soul is sorrowful even unto death; stay you here and watch with me."—39. And going a little further, he fell upon his face, praying, and saying: "My Father, if it be possible, let this chalice pass from me; nevertheless not as I will, but as thou wilt."—40. And he cometh to his disciples, and findeth them asleep, and he saith to Peter: "What! could you not watch one hour with me?—41. Watch ye, and pray that ye enter not into temptation. The spirit indeed is willing, but the flesh weak."—42. Again the second time he went, and prayed, saying: "My Father, if this chalice may not pass away, but I must drink it, thy will be done."—43. And he cometh again, and findeth them sleeping; for their eyes were heavy.—44. And leaving them, he went again, and he prayed the third time, saying the self-same word.—45. Then he cometh to his disciples, and saith to them: "Sleep ye now and take your rest; behold the hour is at hand, and the Son of Man shall be betrayed into the hands of sinners."

MARK 14:32. And they come to a farm called Gethsemani. And he saith to his disciples: "Sit you here, while I pray."—33. And he taketh Peter and James and John with him; and he began to fear and to be heavy.—34. And he saith to them: "My soul is sorrowful even unto death; stay you here and watch."—35. And when he was gone forward a little, he fell flat on the ground; and he prayed that if it might be, the hour might pass from him.—36. And he saith: "Abba, Father, all things are possible to thee, remove this chalice from me; but not what I will, but what thou wilt."—37. And he cometh, and findeth them sleeping. And he saith to Peter: "Simon, sleepest thou? Couldst thou not watch one hour?—38. Watch ye, and pray that you enter not into temptation. The spirit indeed is willing, but the flesh is weak."—39. And going away again, he prayed, saying the same words. —40. And when he returned, he found them again asleep (for their eyes were heavy); and they knew not what to answer him.—41. And he cometh the third time, and saith to them: "Sleep ye now, and take your rest. It is enough; the hour is come; behold, the Son of Man shall be betrayed into the hands of sinners."

LUKE 22:40. And when he was come to the place, he said to them: "Pray, lest ye enter into temptation."—41. And he was withdrawn away from them a stone's cast; and kneeling down he prayed,—42. Saying: "Father, if thou wilt, remove this chalice from me; but yet not my will, but thine be done."—43. And there appeared to him an Angel from heaven, strengthening him. And being in an agony, he prayed the longer.—44. And his sweat became as drops of blood trickling down upon the ground.—45. And when he rose up from prayer, and was come to his disciples, he found them sleeping for sorrow.—46. And he said to them: "Why sleep you? Arise, pray, lest you enter into temptation."

On entering the garden our Lord left eight of the Apostles behind, exhorting them to pray, lest they should enter into temptation (Luke 22:40; Mark 14:32; Matt. 26:36); and took only Peter, James, and John a little way further with Him. In their presence His Passion already began, so, repeating His exhortation to pray, that they might not fall into temptation, He quitted them also and went further into the garden (Matt. 26:37–39; Mark 15:32–35; Luke 22:41).

1. THE NATURE OF HIS SUFFERINGS

As regards the nature of our Lord's sufferings on Mount Olivet, they were not external, but purely internal, that is to say mental sufferings, sufferings of the soul. But suffering of soul can be much worse than bodily pain, for the very reason that it is interior and mental, and it often communicates itself to the body.

With regard to their number these sufferings were manifold and various. Three in particular are enumerated: first, fear and apprehension (Mark 14:33); secondly, repugnance and horror and aversion (Mark 14:33); and thirdly, sadness and depression (Matt. 26:37, 38). Even one mental suffering can make us unhappy enough. Here it was not a question of one only, but of many; the waves of affliction came surging in upon the Sacred Heart of our Saviour from all sides. There is no conceivable phase or form of mental suffering that He did not go through in His Agony.

And what shall we say of the depth and violence of these sufferings? We can form some idea of their terrible intensity from the variability of our Lord's outward behavior. Now He shuns the companionship of His Apostles, now He goes to seek them; now He prays, now complains of His abandonment; in short, His whole nature is in a tumult of agitation, and He betrays great inward perturbation. The intensity of these interior sufferings finds vent, secondly, in His words. He says: "My soul is sorrowful even unto death" (Matt. 26:38; Mark 14:34). Our Saviour was not wont to exaggerate. When He says, then, that He is "sorrowful unto death," this sorrow really is such depression, sadness and abandonment as are experienced only in death; a sadness that would be capable of causing His death, did not His Divinity support and strengthen His human nature. Still more; He asks (not unconditionally, but "if it be possible") that this bitter chalice of sadness and anguish of soul may be taken from Him. "Father, if it be possible, let this chalice pass from Me" (Matt. 26:39, 42; Mark 14:36; Luke 22:42). And He repeats this prayer more than once. It must indeed have been terrible anguish, if He, Who had hitherto longed and prayed for this chalice, He, the Strength of God, finds it so unspeakably bitter and insupportable that He would fain have it taken from Him, and turns from it with repugnance and horror. And the last peculiar sign and striking proof of the vehemence of these mental sufferings is the actual sweat of blood that they force from His veins. "Being in an agony . . . His sweat became as drops of blood trickling down upon the ground" (Luke 22:44). There is no doubting the fact; this sweat of blood was so copious that it trickled down on the ground. This shows us on the one hand how delicately constituted was our Lord's Sacred Body, and on the other the force of His mental anguish and struggle. It must have been an exceedingly vehement resistance of the higher will to the attacks of the lower volition, for the force of this resistance to press the blood from His Heart through the delicate tissues of His Body. Thus it was a real agony, a true death-struggle, and even His outward aspect must have been a pitiable spectacle. His face was pale, His limbs trembled; His breast heaved convulsively, and His respiration grew short and spasmodic; His terrified glance wandered from heaven to earth, and then to the Apostles, as a dying man turns his anxious gaze first upon one, then upon another of those around him (cf. Ps. 17:5, 6; 68:2, 3; 114:3).

2. CAUSES OF THESE SUFFERINGS

Our Lord's three principal sufferings in His Agony may be traced to three corresponding causes.

His fear and apprehension were caused by the certainty and proximity of His Death and the sufferings that were to bring it about. Life is sweet, and it is a hard and bitter sacrifice, indeed the greatest of all sacrifices, to give it up. Our Saviour recognized more fully than anyone the value of His life, its merit, holiness, and priceless worth for heaven and earth, and especially for His holy Mother and His friends. And this life He was to sacrifice while yet so young, and by a death so unjust, so unworthy of Him, and of such unheard-of cruelty. He pictured these sufferings to Himself, and His vivid fancy conjured up all the scenes of the coming Passion: all the ignominy, ill-treatment and pain that the fury and cruel malice of His foes, the faithlessness and inconstancy of His friends, and the base cowardice of those in authority were to cause Him. He saw all the instruments that were to torture His Body, and His limbs seemed to feel their sharpness and strength already. He recognized the signification of all His torments, and let the consciousness of the sins He had undertaken to expiate cast its shadows over His whole nature, like the thousand spreading branches of a mighty tree. How terribly a human heart can be affected by fear of a misfortune, or by terror and mortal agony! And what must our Lord have felt, with His vivid fancy and sensitive temperament, presuming that He surrendered Himself up to these impressions! And very probably Divine Justice, in order that He might expiate the contempt with which it meets from men, so worked upon His mind by terrible representations and revelations as to make Him tremble and quiver like an aspen-leaf. For what is even a God-Man against the terrific justice of God, Who crushes like a lion (Isa. 38:13), and Whose voice "breaketh the cedars of Libanus" and "shaketh the desert" (Ps. 28:5, 8)? Our Lord writhed under its force, and found no escape from its terrors. He trembled and shook at the magnitude of the atoning suffering that Divine Justice required of Him.

The repugnance, disgust and aversion experienced by our Lord arose from the knowledge of the sins for which He was to suffer so much and so terribly. He saw and recognized them in all their dreadful multiplicity, the sins of all men and races and ages; He saw all their vileness, baseness, wantonness and malice; saw them in their shocking contradiction to God's supreme authority, justice, beauty and goodness; saw their fearful ravages among the human race, and their fatal effects upon men for time and eternity. What abominable pictures of sins, in all their lust, vileness and insolence, crowded upon Him! He saw as it were a mingled torrent of the sinful filth of all ages and races pouring down upon

Him. He saw it before Him in one loathsome, unfathomable sea of crime, and every single hateful drop of it must have filled His sensitive Sacred Heart with unutterable repugnance and horror. And all these sins called for bitter expiation. The human race itself was a second cause of His repugnance. What must He have seen there! What are men to Him, these men, to atone for whose sins He was now to suffer and die? The greater part of mankind, in all ages, sunk in the depths of heathenism and unbelief: what are they to Him? And all who hold aloof from Him in heresy, mortal sin, indifference, worldliness and lukewarmness: what are they to Him? Are there not Christians who stand up in crowds against Him, as His personal enemies, full of ferocity and hate? Do they not persecute Him in the souls of men, in His Church, His doctrine, His Sacraments, His representative the Pope, and His own Person? How well He deserved our love and reverence, as our Lord and our God! How good was His will towards us all! And yet, what does He see? Throughout all the centuries, whole troops of Christ-haters drawn up in battle array, and raging against Him with all the weapons at their command. How small the handful of His faithful followers looks against this army of foes! And how does it stand even with these trusty soldiers? Which of us can say that he does all his duty, and serves so good a Master with zeal, constancy, unselfishness and generosity? Oh, how soon we all tire! How we grudge and weigh our service, how soon it is "too much" and "too hard"! We chaffer and haggle over every sacrifice, and how often our Saviour gets the worst of the bargain! He saw all this. He saw too His own Divine Person and all its claims to service, loyalty, love and generosity, as opposed to our slothfulness, indifference and unbounded selfishness. Is it any wonder that He felt unspeakable repugnance, disgust and aversion for these men, who would do nothing for Him?

His sadness, lastly, was caused by His knowledge of the small result He would gain by all His sacrifices. In the Incarnation He had espoused Himself to the human race as His bride, in order to lead it to the Heavenly Father. To this end He had founded the Church and instituted her doctrine, Sacraments and priesthood; and now He was going to die for men. But what was to be the fruit of all this? What is the use of it all? Do they take advantage of it? No. They neglect it all, or misuse it to their own ruin. Our Lord saw the tree of sound doctrine imbued by proud heretics with such deadly poison that millions would die of the fatal fruits; saw the living fountain of the Sacraments neglected and desecrated and profaned by administrators as well as recipients, or stopped up altogether in wanton and criminal stupidity; the priesthood despised, mocked, persecuted; His "seamless coat," His Church, torn, tattered and soiled. He saw the altar of His most holy Sacrifice and Sacrament become a stone of stumbling and separation, and disappear from whole countries; saw countless souls saved but by a hair's breadth, and many other precious souls—nay, whole nations—torn from His mystical Body for ever, to wander astray and go to their eternal ruin. He gave His infinitely precious Life and Blood for all, and the magnitude of this price He paid for them gave Him a right to expect that all would be saved. And now He saw so many perish! The loss of every soul gave Him infinite pain. At that time they were still members of His mystical Body, and He felt the loss of each one as acutely as though a limb had been torn from His material Body. Oh, the grief it caused Him! How many were to perish even on account of His bitter Passion, because they reviled and despised it! All these terrible pictures rose before Him in endless array, and cut Him to the very heart. He mourned, lamented, sighed and prayed in His agony and distress, bathed in perspiration and blood. It seemed as though all the horrors of earth and hell were besieging the grotto and crowding round Him. This is what made Him come to the Apostles so often, to flee from these oppressors, so to speak, and seek comfort. But He always found them overcome with weariness and drowsiness, and they afforded Him no relief. Thus Gethsemani was truly a wine-press, in which His precious Blood was forced from the veins of His Sacred Body, as the juice and oil are pressed from the crushed grape and pounded olive.

3. MANNER IN WHICH OUR SAVIOUR SUFFERED

The circumstances of the Passion lead us to consider the manner in which our Saviour suffered on Mount Olivet.

In the first place, He suffered voluntarily. He was absolute master of His emotions. If He suffered, then, and suffered much and terribly, it was of His own free will and choice. He Himself opened, so to speak, the flood-gates of the bitter waters of affliction that surged over His Heart; He immersed Himself of His own accord in their terrible depths. He was like one who, though suffering intensely, will not make use of a remedy that is certain to ease the pain, because He wishes to suffer. More than this; theologians find a deep mystery in this mental suffering of our Saviour on Mount Olivet. How was it possible that, in spite of the clear vision of God that shed a beatific light upon His Passion, He could yet be sorrowful, not merely in His Body and sensual appetitive faculty, but also in His higher, purely spiritual will? It was as though the same object at once gave light and joy, and yet frightened Him by its darkness. Of course it may be said that our Saviour had different faculties with which to regard His Passion, and could therefore rejoice at it in one respect and sorrow over it in another; but nevertheless it remains a deep and inscrutable mystery and a miracle worked by our Lord, that He should be able to suffer thus. Indeed, it cannot be denied that this clear vision of God itself increased the pain, horror and aversion to sin in His higher will. Does not this free volition make the sacrifice doubly dear and deserving of our love and reverence? How glad we feel when the load of some oppressive sadness is at last removed from us, and how great should we consider the sacrifice if we were asked to bear this state of suffering still longer, and even inflict it upon ourselves! But this is what our Saviour did. He shed His first Blood Himself, and how copiously! Truly He has trodden the wine-press Himself, and alone (Isa. 63:3). How noble, how lovable, precious and venerable this free and voluntary endurance renders His Passion!

Secondly, our Saviour suffers with beautiful humility. This suffering on Mount Olivet was, in the eyes of men, a state of great weakness. Nevertheless He allows His disciples to witness it; not all of them, indeed, because they could not all have borne it, but the three chief of the Apostles, who had also witnessed His Transfiguration. And He shows the same touching humility in His prayer; for in His distress He takes refuge in prayer. He prays most fervently and with the most touching words, crying again and again: "Father, Abba, My Father" (Matt. 26:39, 42; Mark 14:36; Luke 22:42); He prays repeatedly (Matt. 26:44; Mark 14:39) and with perfect resignation to His Heavenly Father's Will. However hard it is for His nature to acquiesce in His Passion and Death, still He protests again and again that the Will of His Heavenly Father shall be done. He also shows His humility by not aspiring to the greatest and loftiest flight of generosity in His petitions and asking for suffering, but contenting Himself with lowly submission to the Will of God. Lastly, He shows loving and humble solicitude for the Apostles, repeatedly going to watch over them, warning them, encouraging them to pray, and excusing their slowness to respond. "Simon, sleepest thou? Couldst thou not watch one hour with me? Watch ye, and pray that ye enter not into temptation. The spirit indeed is willing, but the flesh is weak" (Matt. 26:40, 41; Mark 14:37, 38).

Lastly, our Saviour suffers with constancy and perseverance, and triumphs gloriously. The battle was indeed a hard one; the fear, repugnance and sadness of His inmost nature were unutterable, and so His higher will had a long and hard siege to sustain and a terrible charge to repulse. But He stood firm and won the victory. He kept fast to God's Will, that He should redeem us by His Passion and Death; and so He was comforted. "There appeared to Him an angel from heaven, strengthening Him" (Luke 22:43). Such a degree of self-forgetfulness and humiliation as He showed in His Agony on Mount Olivet deserved an outward sign from heaven. This was often the case in our Saviour's life; e.g. at His Nativity, after His fast in the desert, and again here. He did not absolutely need this comfort, it is true; but still it was consoling to His Sacred Humanity to see a messenger from His Heavenly Father approach Him in visible form, and in His touching humility and gracious condescension He deigned to accept an external consolation of this kind. But how did the angel strengthen our Saviour? Certainly he could not really offer Him anything, exteriorly or interiorly, that He did not know and possess already, or might not have procured for Himself. Probably the heavenly messenger strengthened our Lord in the same way as we comfort a friend, by praising his constancy and drawing his attention to the glorious results of suffering well borne. Thus the angel may possibly have shown our Saviour in vision all the grand and glorious consequences, so salutary for men and so conducive to the glory of God, that were to result from His Passion. Perhaps He may have seen all the Saints of the Old and the New Testament, vested in the glory merited for them by His Passion, passing before Him in one long, glorious procession, formed from out all ages of the Church, all a wondrous and manifold reflection of His most sacred Life and Passion, and a glorious crown of victory destined for His brow. Certainly the sight of this must have comforted and encouraged our Saviour, so that, freed from the inward struggle and the anxiety of His lower nature, He could enter upon the work of the Redemption.

4. AIM AND INTENT OF THE AGONY ON MOUNT OLIVET

Our Lord's chief intention in suffering this Agony was certainly to give us a conclusive proof of His true and complete human nature. We have here indeed a confirmation of the fact that there were two wills in Christ, one will divine and one human; for He says: "Not My will, but Thine be done" (Luke 22:42; Matt. 26:39). Further, we have a palpable proof that He had, like ourselves, an inferior will with all its natural impulses and emotions; the only difference being that in His case even the very beginning of an emotion was dependent upon His higher will. Lastly, He wished to teach us that these emotions are not faults or even imperfections, as long as they remain subject to reason. The emotion of fear experienced by our Saviour in this case was not an imperfection; for no one can be said to fear, who only fears when he wills to do so.

Secondly, our Saviour intended in this mystery to experience in His own Person all interior sufferings, and this in a very high degree; just as He was also about to take upon Himself all exterior sufferings. That is why He fills the chalice of mental suffering to the very brim, and drains it to the last drop.

Thirdly, He intended to satisfy for the sins and imperfections that we are often guilty of in these interior trials: impatience, rebellion against the Will of God, want of generosity, neglect of prayer, unfaithfulness to resolutions, inordinate seeking for comfort from creatures and complaining to them. Our behavior is often very different from that of our Saviour on Mount Olivet. He wished to do penance for this.

Fourthly, our Saviour wished to comfort us by His example, when we cannot find comfort anywhere else. How pained He felt at finding no one to console Him and having to bear the whole weight of His suffering alone! Here we have an example to comfort us, when we can find no other solace. And is it not a sweet consolation, to think that our Saviour had to suffer the same, and that He too found no comfort?

Lastly, our Lord intended to merit special grace and strength for us when we have interior trials and sufferings to bear. We are sorely in need of it then. Our Saviour has won it for us; let us go to Him and ask for it. We too shall have our hours on Mount Olivet. But there will be one hour in particular that will be very like that of our Saviour's Agony, the hour of our death, our mortal agony, when similar anguish of soul, fear, lassitude and sadness will unman us, and we shall be quite alone. What a consolation it is for us then, that our Saviour has gone through this hour, and that we find in Him a Heart that can understand our distress and help us! Let us often ask for a share in the blessings, graces and victorious strength of the Agony of Jesus. How sweet it will be then to think that we have often paid it loving veneration! But, generally speaking, perhaps the resolution most in accordance with the intention and signification of this mystery will be never to desist from our good resolves nor abate our generosity in the service of our Lord on account of interior difficulties, such as distaste, fear or sadness. Let us never forget what a combat He had to sustain in His Heart, and how hard it was for Him to undertake the Passion for us, but yet how that loving Heart never wavered in its love and fidelity to us. What a happiness, what an honor for us, if the Angel of Comfort included us also in his consoling representations, and pointed to us as being among those who, out of gratitude and reverence for His Passion, would stand the test of interior affliction victoriously!

The Arrest of Jesus

John 18:2. And Judas also, who betrayed him, knew the place; because Jesus had often resorted thither together with his disciples.—3. Judas therefore having received a band of soldiers and servants from the chief priests and the Pharisees, cometh thither with lanterns and torches and weapons.—4. Jesus therefore knowing all things that should come upon him, went forth, and said to them: "Whom seek ye?"—5. They answered him: "Jesus of Nazareth." Jesus saith to them: "I am he." And Judas also, who betrayed him, stood with them.—6. As soon therefore as he had said to them: "I am he"; they went backward, and fell to the ground. —7. Again therefore he asked them: "Whom seek ye?" And they said: "Jesus of Nazareth."—8. Jesus answered: "I have told you that I am he; if therefore you seek me, let these go their way."—9. That the word might be fulfilled which he said: "Of them whom thou hast given me, I have not lost anyone."—10. Then Simon Peter having a sword, drew it, and struck the servant of the high priest, and cut off his right ear. And the name of the servant was Malchus.—11. Jesus therefore said to Peter: "Put up thy sword into the scabbard. The chalice which my Father hath given me, shall I not drink it?"—12. Then the band, and the tribune, and the servants of the Jews took Jesus, and bound him.

Matt. 26:45. Then he cometh to his disciples, and saith to them: "Sleep ye now and take your rest; behold the hour is at hand, and the Son of Man shall be betrayed into the hands of sinners.—46. Rise, let us go; behold, he is at hand that will betray me."—47. As he yet spoke, behold Judas one of the twelve came, and with him a great multitude with swords and clubs, sent from the chief priests and the ancients of the people.—48. And he that betrayed him gave them a sign, saying: "Whomsoever I shall kiss, that is he, hold him fast."—49. And forthwith coming to Jesus, he said: "Hail, Rabbi." And he kissed him.—50. And Jesus said to him:

"Friend, whereto art thou come?" Then they came up, and laid hands on Jesus, and held him.—51. And behold one of them that were with Jesus, stretching forth his hand, drew out his sword, and striking the servant of the high priest, cut off his ear.—52. Then Jesus saith to him: "Put up again thy sword into its place; for all that take the sword shall perish with the sword.—53. Thinkest thou that I cannot ask my Father, and he will give me presently more than twelve legions of Angels? —54. How then shall the Scriptures be fulfilled, that so it must be done?"—55. In that same hour Jesus said to the multitudes: "You are come out as it were to a robber with swords and clubs to apprehend me; I sat daily with you teaching in the temple, and you laid not hands on me."—56. Now all this was done, that the Scriptures of the prophets might be fulfilled. Then the disciples all leaving him, fled.

MARK 14:41. And he cometh the third time, and saith to them: "Sleep ye now, and take your rest. It is enough; the hour is come; behold, the Son of Man shall be betrayed into the hands of sinners.—42. Rise up, let us go; behold, he that will betray me is at hand."—43. And while he was yet speaking, cometh Judas Iscariot one of the twelve, and with him a great multitude with swords and staves, from the chief priests and the scribes, and the ancients.—44. And he that betrayed him had given them a sign, saying: "Whomsoever I shall kiss, that is he, lay hold on him, and lead him away carefully."—45. And when he was come, immediately going up to him, he saith: "Hail, Rabbi"; and he kissed him.—46. But they laid hands on him, and held him.—47. And one of them that stood by, drawing a sword, struck a servant of the chief priests, and cut off his ear.—48. And Jesus answering, said to them: "Are you come out as to a robber with swords and staves to apprehend me? —49. I was daily with you in the temple teaching, and you did not lay hands on me. But, that the Scriptures may be fulfilled."—50. Then his disciples leaving him, all fled away.—51. And a certain young man followed him, having a linen cloth cast about his naked body; and they laid hold on him.—52. But he, casting off the linen cloth, fled from them naked.

LUKE 22:47. As he was yet speaking, behold a multitude, and he that was called Judas, one of the twelve, went before them; and drew near to Jesus, for to kiss him. —48. And Jesus said to him: "Judas, dost thou betray the Son of Man with a kiss?" —49. And they that were about him, seeing what would follow, said to him: "Lord, shall we strike with the sword?"—50. And one of them struck the servant of the high priest, and cut off his right ear.—51. But Jesus answering, said: "Suffer ye thus far." And when he had touched his ear, he healed him.—52. And Jesus said to the chief priests, and magistrates of the temple, and the ancients that were come unto him: "Are you come out, at is were against a thief, with swords and clubs?—53. When I was daily with you in the temple, you did not stretch forth your hands against me; but this is your hour, and the power of darkness."—54. And apprehending him, they led him to the high priest's house; but Peter followed afar off.

1. OUR SAVIOUR GOES TO MEET HIS ENEMIES

Fortified by the angel and having regained His strength and composure, our Saviour came to the Apostles for the third time. He found them sleeping again, and said to them: "Why sleep you?" And then, in gentle and loving reproof: "But sleep ye now, and take your rest; it is enough," i.e. enough of struggling against drowsiness and sorrow.[1] "Rise up, let us go; behold, he that

[1] According to others, our Lord here kindly invites the disciples to rest a little; and later on, when the enemies appear, He says: "It is enough."

will betray me is at hand. The hour (of the Passion) is come, and the Son of Man shall be betrayed into the hands of sinners," i.e. Gentiles, heathens (Matt. 26:45, 46; Mark 14:41, 42; Luke 22:45, 46).

Perhaps our Lord pointed, as He spoke these words, to the valley-path, along which the band of men who were to arrest Him was coming. For this purpose Judas had received a Roman cohort with its captain, part of the Temple guard (which consisted of Levites), and some of the servants of the chief priests and influential Pharisees (John 18:3). There were also a few priests of higher rank, magistrates of the Temple, and ancients of the people among the company (Luke 22:52). They had been deputed by the Great Council to make the arrest, and were therefore armed with swords and clubs, and carried lanterns (Matt. 26:47; Mark 14:43; John 18:3). Judas, as their leader (Acts 1:16), walked in front of them all, perhaps at a little distance, in order that our Saviour might not think he had anything to do with the rabble. A kiss to be given by Judas on meeting Him had been agreed upon as the sign by which the soldiers were to know our Saviour, and he had recommended them to be very cautious (Matt. 26:48; Mark 14:44).

So this was the rabble our Lord went to meet, probably along the path that runs parallel with the Garden of Gethsemani as far as the grotto known in our days as the Grotto of the Agony. The eight other Apostles had probably joined Him again by this time. It is an impressive sight to gaze upon, our Saviour going to meet His foes. In this also He maintains the majestic character of freedom and spontaneity that marks His Passion throughout. He will not be surprised by His enemies. What a contrast He presents to His foes, as He stands face to face with them! On His side heavenly calmness, peace, purity and courage; on theirs, uncertainty, haste, agitation and violence! He is the only quiet and steady point in the surging billows around Him. We have here a striking picture of the Church in this world, as opposed to her enemies and persecutors.

2. OUR SAVIOUR MEETS HIS ENEMIES

There are two circumstances about this meeting that call for consideration.

First, the manner in which our Saviour is recognized. This was to take place, in the first instance, by means of Judas' treachery.

He stepped up to our Lord, greeted Him with "Hail, Rabbi!" and gave Him the customary kiss (Luke 22:47; Matt. 26:49; Mark 14:45). Many, probably most, of the soldiers did not know our Saviour. Besides, it was dark, and therefore easy to make a mistake. But what is the portent of this kiss? What hypocrisy and baseness, so to abuse the sign of friendship and discipleship for the purpose of betrayal! What malice and callousness, thus to give the signal for the terrible process of torture to commence! (II Kings 20:9, 10.) And how does our Saviour take this abominable deed? He does not refuse the kiss; no, He permits it, receives and returns it, precisely because it is the signal for His Death, and He wishes to suffer and die. Further, He accompanies the kiss He gives with words of most incomprehensible gentleness: "Friend, whereto art thou come? Dost thou betray the Son of Man with a kiss?" (Matt. 26:50; Luke 22:48.) He says this to show Judas that He knows everything and reads thoughts, and to touch his heart (if possible) by this exposure of his intention, and by His own unfathomable love and gentleness. What a marvelous grace! How many Saints and servants of Jesus would gladly have accounted a kiss from Him as the very highest reward for their fidelity and labor, and did not receive it! But He bestowed this favor upon Judas. What a length His love for sinners, His desire to save them, and His longing for suffering carries Him! But probably the treacherous sign was not sufficiently remarked in the darkness and confusion, and so our Lord was recognized, secondly, by His own words: "I am He." He repeated them twice (John 18:5, 8), after having received (in response to His question whom they sought) the answer that they sought Jesus of Nazareth (John 18:5, 7). These words of His sufficiently revealed His identity; but in order that no doubt might be left, He accompanied them with a miracle, causing those of the rabble who stood next to Him and answered His question to fall to the ground, simply by speaking these words: "I am He" (John 18:6). He did this partly to prove His freedom, and partly to frighten His enemies and so deter them from committing the crime; but chiefly in order to divert their attention from the Apostles to Himself, as He shows in the words: "If you seek Me, let these go their way" (John 18:8, 9). "The Good Shepherd giveth His life for His sheep" (John 10:11). The Apostles were indeed in danger of being arrested along with their Divine Master.

The second circumstance to be remarked about this meeting was our Saviour's hindrance of the Apostles' resistance. As the soldiers were about to lay hands upon Him, Peter cried out, asking Him if they should strike with the sword; and then, without waiting for our Lord's answer, he drew his sword and with one blow struck off the ear of Malchus, a servant of the High Priest (Matt. 26:51; Mark 14:47; Luke 22:49, 50; John 18:10). But our Saviour reproved him for his action, and bade him put his sword into the scabbard. He gave two reasons for this: the first being that everyone who takes up the sword must expect to be met with the sword, to his own disadvantage (these words of Jesus seem to have been a proverb); and the second, that it is not the Father's Will nor His own to offer resistance. He could have help from the angels, if He chose, but He wishes to drink the chalice that His Father gives Him, and the Scriptures must be fulfilled (Matt. 26:52–54; Luke 22:51; John 18:11). Resistance would therefore have been superfluous and foolish, unworthy of our Lord and contrary to the Divine Will. Thus the opposition was checked, and our Saviour mercifully healed the wound that Peter had inflicted upon Malchus (Luke 22:51). But He also rebuked the priests and magistrates of the Temple for their unworthy, despicable act of violence, saying that they had come out against Him as though He were a robber, and yet He had been with them in the Temple every day, and they could easily have apprehended Him. But this was their hour and the power of darkness; and it must happen thus, that the Scriptures might be fulfilled (Matt. 26:55, 56; Mark 14:48, 49; Luke 22:52, 53). With these words our Saviour proves to them His innocence and voluntary submission to the Will of God, reminds them of His benefits, and frightens them by His reference to their deed, which cannot be good, since it seeks the cover of darkness and is prompted by Satan.

3. OUR SAVIOUR IS APPREHENDED BY HIS ENEMIES

At these words the soldiers laid hands upon our Saviour (Matt. 26:57; Luke 22:54; Mark 14:46; John 18:12), bound Him and led Him away, probably with rough ill-treatment and insulting jests. But our Lord patiently submitted to it all. Thus His Hands, that might have proved themselves stronger than Samson's, were bound, and He quietly suffered Himself to be led away. It was at His arrest that our Saviour made the actual sacrifice of His freedom, His honor, and His life. Henceforth He is only the Victim of His enemies' cruelty, and of our sins. And He made this sacrifice with infinite patience, love and humility.

In the meantime the Apostles dispersed and fled in all directions (Matt. 26:56; Mark 14:50). Only one young man, whose identity is unknown, clad merely in an undergarment, followed the procession that led our Saviour away towards the city. He was seized by the soldiers, but escaped, leaving his linen garment in their hands (Mark 14:51, 52). Thus our Saviour's words and the Scriptures were fulfilled. All had fled, and our Saviour, alone and forsaken, was in the power of His rough and insolent enemies. This flight of the disciples is one of the bitter dregs of His cup of suffering, and the prophets had foretold it long before (Ps. 21:12; 87:9, 19).

The arrest of Jesus is the majestic inauguration of the Passion. How great, how glorious, and how lovable He appears in it! In the first place, it reveals His omniscience. He knew that Judas had fixed upon this spot and hour (John 18:2); in spirit He saw the rabble approaching, and knew all that was to happen (John 18:4). And how gloriously His power and divine freedom are displayed! He needs no defender, and will have none. If He had cared to be defended, and the Heavenly Father had not decided otherwise, the slightest sign from Him would have sufficed to summon all the heavenly hosts that stood at His command. But He does not need the angels; He transfixes the whole mob with a word. Lastly, He shows His touching kindness of heart towards Malchus as well as towards His Apostles, taking care that no harm should befall them (John 18:8, 9), and even extending His loving solicitude to Judas. The Church is always the Bride of Christ and the faithful reflection of His spirit. She always behaves in this manner to the world, which persecutes, reviles and despoils her, and curtails her freedom. She has always met its cunning and violence with the same temper and principles. She does not resort to sword and club; her power lies in the Will of God, in suffering and endurance. When she is fettered, she continues to bless, and does good to those who injure her. The bonds she wears for Christ are her most beautiful and precious adornment, and the supreme pledge of her victory. Her cry is ever: "We suffer violence; thanks be to God!"

The First Judicial Sitting in Caiphas' House

Matt. 26:57. But they holding Jesus led him to Caiphas the high priest, where the scribes and the ancients were assembled. . . .—59. And the chief priests and the whole council sought false witness against Jesus, that they might put him to death;—60. And they found not, whereas many false witnesses had come in. And last of all there came two false witnesses,—61. And they said: "This man said, I am able to destroy the temple of God, and after three days to rebuild it."—62. And the high priest rising up, said to him: "Answerest thou nothing to the things which these witness against thee?"—63. But Jesus held his peace. And the high priest said to him: "I adjure thee by the living God, that thou tell us if thou be the Christ, the Son of God."—64. Jesus saith to him: "Thou hast said it; nevertheless I say to you, hereafter you shall see the Son of Man sitting on the right hand of the power of God, and coming in the clouds of heaven."—65. Then the high priest rent his garments, saying: "He hath blasphemed, what further need have we of witnesses? Behold, now you have heard the blasphemy;—66. What think you?" But they answering said: "He is guilty of death."

Mark 14:53. And they brought Jesus to the high priest; and all the priests and the scribes and the ancients assembled together. . . .—55. And the chief priests and all the council sought for evidence against Jesus, that they might put him to death, and found none.—56. For many bore false witness against him; and their evidences were not agreeing.—57. And some rising up, bore false witness against him, saying:—58. "We heard him say: I will destroy this temple made with hands, and within three days I will build another not made with hands."—59. And their witness did not agree.—60. And the high priest rising up in the midst, asked Jesus, saying: "Answerest thou nothing to the things that are laid to thy charge by these men?"—61. But he held his peace, and answered nothing. Again the high priest asked him, and said to him: "Art thou the Christ, the Son of the blessed God?"—62. And Jesus said to him: "I am; and you shall see the Son of Man sitting on the right hand of the power of God, and coming with the clouds of heaven."—63. Then the high priest rending his garments, saith: "What need we any further witnesses?—64. You have heard the blasphemy; what think you?" Who all condemned him to be guilty of death.

John 18:12. Then the band, and the tribune, and the servants of the Jews took Jesus, and bound him;—13. And they led him away to Annas first, for he was father-in-law to Caiphas, who was the high priest of that year.—14. Now Caiphas was he who had given the counsel to the Jews: that it was expedient that one man should die for the people. . . .—19. The high priest therefore asked Jesus of his disciples, and of his doctrine.—20. Jesus answered him: "I have spoken openly to the world; I have always taught in the synagogue, and in the temple, whither all the Jews resort; and in secret I have spoken nothing.—21. Why askest thou me? Ask them who have heard what I have spoken unto them; behold, they know what things I have said."—22. And when he had said these things, one of the servants standing by gave Jesus a blow, saying: "Answerest thou the high priest so?"—23. Jesus answered him: "If I have spoken evil, give testimony of the evil; but if well, why strikest thou me?"—24. And Annas sent him bound to Caiphas the high priest.

Luke 22:54. And apprehending him, they led him to the high priest's house.

Our Saviour was now led away into the city, probably by the same path that He had taken on His way to the Mount of Olives, and was first brought before Annas (John 18:13), because he was the father-in-law of Caiphas and an influential man (Acts

4:6). Perhaps, too, his house may have been on the way to the palace of Caiphas, and whilst our Lord was detained before Annas the Great Council had time to assemble at the High Priest's residence. But the delay at Annas' house seems to have been merely casual, and did not last long. The goal of the procession was really the house of Caiphas, which, like that of Annas, stood on the heights of the upper city; and the actual judicial sitting probably took place there (Luke 22:54; Matt. 26:57; Mark 14:53; John 18:24). All the various grades of the Great Council were represented: chief priests, scribes, and ancients (Matt. 26:57; Mark 14:53). But it is uncertain whether all its members were present. We are told that all condemned our Saviour at this sitting (Mark 14:64), so it would seem that His friends, Joseph and Nicodemus, were not present, perhaps not invited at all. At these judicial proceedings of the Sanhedrim the court was arranged in the following manner. The members sat in a semi-circle, so that they could see one another. Two clerks took their places in front of them, one on the right side, the other on the left, to note down the speeches for and against the accused. Before them sat the scribes in three rows. The accused appeared clad in mourning. Each member stood up to give his vote, beginning at the youngest. The whole proceedings may be divided into three principal parts.

1. THE PERSONAL CROSS-EXAMINATION OF JESUS

The proceedings began from the very outset with a contravention of the ordinary judicial usage. Instead of giving our Saviour a counsel for the defence, hearing the evidence in His favor, formulating the accusation definitely and confirming it by witnesses, the High Priest began immediately (probably through embarrassment) with a cross-examination of our Lord concerning His doctrine and disciples. He was to declare Himself with regard to these two points (John 18:19). In the first place, this cross-examination was quite superfluous, for the condemnation of Jesus was a foregone conclusion. Secondly, it was very unjust, for no defendant is bound to accuse himself; and lastly, it was very crafty, because they only hoped to find something in His answers that could be turned against Him.

Our Saviour says nothing about His disciples, because He always screens them, and with regard to His doctrine He merely replies that He has always taught in public, and not in secret; the High Priest should therefore ask those who have heard Him (John

18:20, 21). This answer was very humble, for it recognized the jurisdiction of the High Priest; very just, because no court obliges the defendant to accuse himself; and lastly, very wise and moderate, because no one can expect an accused man to make a statement that would incriminate himself, and because this was a most modest way of demanding a trial.

At this reply of our Saviour one of the soldiers (probably because he wished to curry favor and was encouraged by the displeasure and irritation shown by the High Priest at Jesus' words) gave Him a blow in the face, saying: "Answerest thou the High Priest so?" (John 18:22.) The enormity of this ill-treatment becomes clear in some measure, when we consider, first, in what it consisted. It was a gross public affront, at once insulting and painful. Secondly, to Whom was this affront offered, and by whom? To the Son of God, by a common servant. Where, and before whom? At a public assembly, before the whole Council. And why? Because our Lord had given a most just and gentle answer. How painful and sad it must have been to see the fettered figure of our Saviour stagger under the heavy blow, and how most likely the blood poured from His mouth, and the whole Council applauded the vile stroke with mocking laughter!

But our Saviour turned to the man quite composedly, and said: "If I have spoken evil, give testimony of the evil; but if well, why strikest thou Me?" (John 18:23.) He repudiates this ill-treatment as unjust, in order not to let the imputation of disrespect to the High Priest rest upon Him; secondly, in order to teach us by His own example that self-defence is allowable, as long as it remains within proper bounds; and lastly, in order to indicate with all modesty that He insisted upon a trial. So the Great Council was compelled to examine the witnesses.

2. THE HEARING OF THE WITNESSES

The High Priest and the Council were now obliged to proceed to the examination of the witnesses; for the law required that at least two witnesses should agree exactly (Num. 35:30; Deut. 17:6; 19:15). They had already been on the look-out for witnesses, and false ones too (Matt. 26:59; Mark 14:55); for the Death of Jesus was already decided upon. Therefore many hired witnesses appeared for the prosecution. We are not told all that they said against our Saviour. But whatever it may have been, it was false, malicious, invented, or at best misrepresented; and as the witnesses were heard separately, according to the ordinary judicial usage, the result was deplorable. Their statements did not agree even in the main points, and no use could be made of them (Matt. 26:60; Mark 14:56, 59). At last two witnesses appeared, who stated that our Lord had spoken contemptuously of the Temple and said that He would destroy it and build another, not made with hands, within three days (Matt. 26:61; Mark 14:57, 58). This was supposed to be the answer given by our Saviour on the first Paschal Feast of His public ministry, when the priests asked Him by whose authority He had dared to cleanse the Temple (John 2:19). This evidence was also false, as regards both the words and the sense. Our Lord's answer on that occasion had been: "Destroy this temple," not "I will destroy it," and He had been referring to the temple of His Body.

And how did our Saviour behave in the face of this evidence? He held His peace and answered nothing. Even when the High Priest, in order to get some avowal from Him, asked what He had to say to the statements of the witnesses, He was silent, and spoke no word of reply (Matt. 26:62, 63; Mark 14:60, 61). And why did He give no answer? It was wise and most prudent of Him to act thus, for any answer or defence would be unnecessary in the face of the contradiction and invalidity of the depositions (Ps. 26:12), and quite useless in the present disposition of the Council; and lastly, His silence showed fortitude, independence and humility. Our Divine Saviour wished hereby to set us an example not to be too eager in our own defence, and also to satisfy for the faults which this eagerness to justify ourselves causes us to commit.

3. CAIPHAS' SOLEMN ADJURATION OF JESUS

The reason of this adjuration was, in the first place, the position of extreme embarrassment and difficulty in which the Great Council was placed by the depositions of the witnesses. Secondly, there was nothing left to be done, according to the legal regulations, but to resort to the administration of an oath. So the High Priest, making use of the ordinary formula for putting the judicial oath, adjured Him "by God" to declare if He was the Son of God, the Messias (Matt. 26:63; Mark 14:61). Perhaps the last accusation may have prompted this question, because the Messias alone could introduce innovations and alterations in matters of religious worship; or perhaps this accusation had played an important part in the depositions. Our Saviour Himself had repeatedly declared, in plain enough terms, that He was the Messias and Son of God, and many of those who came to Him to be healed had called Him so. And besides, this was the quickest way of bringing matters to a close, for the very claim to be the Messias or a prophet counted as blasphemy with them (Deut. 18:20; Lev. 24:16). That is why Caiphas asked this question, thus going straight to the point of the whole affair. The question was put in official form, as solemnly as possible. He adjured our Saviour by the Living God, in the name of God, as High Priest and representative of God and the whole nation. Our Saviour was bound to give an answer to this; silence would have been tantamount to denial. Caiphas' intention in making this solemn adjuration was the very worst possible, viz. to deliver our Saviour up to certain death, and that of the most painful and shameful kind, on the charge of blasphemy.

And so our Saviour, thus solemnly adjured, gave a clear, solemn and majestic answer. He replies to Caiphas' question in the affirmative. "Thou hast said it," or "Amen," was the customary affirmative answer to the judicial oath (Deut. 27:15). He had never before spoken so frankly and plainly in presence of the people. But now He does so; His answer, which leaves nothing to be desired in the way of clearness, is addressed to the High Priest and the Great Council, and (since these are the representatives of the people) to the entire nation and the whole human race. And He goes still farther. He confirms His testimony by predicting the glory in which He will reveal Himself as the Messias and Son of God, and threatens them with the Judgment at which He will appear as their Supreme Judge. "Nevertheless" (or in spite of the state of abasement in which I now stand here as accused, and in spite of your unbelief) "I say to you, hereafter you shall see the Son of Man sitting on the right hand of the power of God, and coming in the clouds of heaven" (Matt. 26:64; Mark 14:62). Our Lord here unmistakably alludes to the prophecy of Daniel (Dan. 7:13, 14; Ps. 109).

Scarcely had our Lord given this answer when the High Priest rose and declared it blasphemy: "He hath blasphemed!" And in order to express his indignation and fill those present with the same holy anger, he rent his upper garment from the neckband to the girdle, as was often done on occasions of great mourning and horror (IV Kings 18:37; I Mach. 11:71; Acts 14:13). Then he turned to the Council, and cried: "You have heard the blasphemy; what need we any further witnesses? What think you? But they answering said: "He is guilty of death." And they "all condemned Him to be guilty of death" (Matt. 26:65, 66; Mark 14:63, 64). With this the trial was at an end, the facts established, our Lord found guilty of blasphemy on His own evidence, and the motion for punishment of the crime formulated (Lev. 24:16). The Council could be satisfied with the result of this night's work. All was now in readiness for the final sentence of the Great Council, which had to be passed in the day-time.

The whole proceeding was a mockery, a mere travesty of right and justice, a court over which the most unblushing malice and hypocrisy reigned supreme. It was an assembly at which passion, confusion, precipitation, hatred, vindictiveness, unbelief, and all the demons of hell presided. It shows us how far envy, insincerity and infatuation can go. How these Pharisees and sinners, whom our Saviour had crushed and branded, wreaked their long-suppressed rancor and fury upon Him, now that they had Him in their power! Fettered, bowed, in pitiable plight, He stands among them, a helpless lamb, at the mercy of their teeth and claws. And yet He stood as far above them as God above man, and the dark and stormy background of this scene in the court only serves to throw up the glorious outlines of His figure: His dignity and calmness, His wisdom and moderation, the humility and meekness with which He meets such insupportable outrages, and the fortitude and love of truth and of us that He displays in the glorious testimony to His Divinity. This testimony possesses a high importance and significance. In the first place, for the Jews. It was necessary that they should have it, for otherwise their unbelief would always have taken refuge behind the less plain statements of Jesus with regard to His Divinity. Now they had an answer, clear, plain and unequivocal, an answer so solemn and official that it left nothing to be desired. With this reply our Saviour explains and confirms all the main points of the prophecies concerning the Messias: His state of abasement, His exaltation, and particularly His judicial office, which He describes in almost the very words of Daniel the prophet (Dan. 7:13, 14). And this testimony was of the greatest importance for our Saviour also. It is the sum-total of His doctrine, the explanation of His miracles, and the seal of His holiness, His truthfulness, His obedience and love for His Father, His constancy and fortitude; for it was no slight matter to confess His Divinity in His present state of abasement and weakness. Lastly, the testimony was of immense importance for the whole creation. Heaven exulted with joy; hell trembled and quaked, and felt its judgment in these words; and the farthest ages and ends of the world began to revive and sun themselves in the beautiful light of this saving truth. Such is the grand testimony of our Saviour. Eternal thanks be to Him for it!

Peter's Denial of Jesus

John 18:15. And Simon Peter followed Jesus, and so did another disciple. And that disciple was known to the high priest, and went in with Jesus into the court of the high priest.—16. But Peter stood at the door without. The other disciple therefore who was known to the high priest, went out and spoke to the portress, and brought in Peter.—17. The maid therefore that was portress, saith to Peter: "Art not thou also one of this man's disciples?" He saith: "I am not."—18. Now the servants and ministers stood at a fire of coals, because it was cold, and warmed themselves; and with them was Peter also standing, and warming himself. . . . —25. They said therefore to him: "Art not thou also one of his disciples?" He denied it and said: "I am not."—26. One of the servants of the high priest (a kinsman to him whose ear Peter cut off) saith to him: "Did not I see thee in the garden with him?"—27. Again therefore Peter denied; and immediately the cock crew.

Luke 22:54. And apprehending him, they led him to the high priest's house; but Peter followed afar off.—55. And when they had kindled a fire in the midst of the hall, and were sitting about it, Peter was in the midst of them.—56. Whom when a certain servant-maid had seen sitting at the light, and had earnestly beheld him, she said: "This man also was with him."—57. But he denied him, saying: "Woman, I know him not."—58. And after a little while another seeing him, said: "Thou also art one of them." But Peter said: "O man, I am not."—59. And after the space as it were of one hour, another certain man affirmed, saying: "Of a truth this man was also with him: for he is also a Galilean."—60. And Peter said: "Man, I know not what thou sayest." And immediately as he was yet speaking, the cock crew.—61. And the Lord turning, looked on Peter. And Peter remembered the word of the Lord, as he had said: "Before the cock crow, thou shalt deny me thrice";—62. And Peter going out wept bitterly.

Matt. 26:58. And Peter followed him afar off, even to the court of the high priest. And going in, he sat with the servants, that he might see the end. . . .—69. But Peter sat without in the court; and there came to him a servant-maid saying: "Thou also wast with Jesus the Galilean."—70. But he denied before them all, saying: "I know not what thou sayest."—71. And as he went out of the gate, another maid saw him, and she saith to them that were there: "This man also was with Jesus of Nazareth."—72. And again he denied with an oath: "That I know not the man."—73. And after a little while they came that stood by, and said to Peter: "Surely thou also art one of them; for even thy speech doth discover thee." —74. Then he began to curse and to swear that he knew not the man. And immediately the cock crew.—75. And Peter remembered the word of Jesus which he had said: "Before the cock crow, thou wilt deny me thrice." And going forth, he wept bitterly.

Mark 14:54. And Peter followed him afar off even into the court of the high priest; and he sat with the servants at the fire, and warmed himself. . . .—66.

Now when Peter was in the court below, there cometh one of the maid-servants of the high priest;—67. And when she had seen Peter warming himself, looking on him she saith: "Thou also wast with Jesus of Nazareth."—68. But he denied, saying: "I neither know nor understand what thou sayest." And he went forth before the court; and the cock crew.—69. And again a maid-servant seeing him, began to say to the standers-by: "This is one of them."—70. But he denied again. And after a while they that stood by, said again to Peter: "Surely thou art one of them; for thou art also a Galilean."—71. But he began to curse and to swear, saying: "I know not this man of whom you speak."—72. And immediately the cock crew again. And Peter remembered the word that Jesus had said unto him: "Before the cock crow twice, thou shalt thrice deny me." And he began to weep.

1. THE HISTORY OF PETER'S FALL

The history of Peter's denial is as follows. Peter and John had followed our Lord at a little distance into Caiphas' house (Matt. 26:58; Mark 14:54; Luke 22:54; John 18:15). John, who was acquainted with the High Priest, succeeded in gaining admittance to the inner court-yard of the house for himself and Peter (John 18:15, 16). There a fire was burning on account of the chilliness of the night. Peter joined the servants of the High Priest, who were sitting and standing about it, and warmed himself (John 18:18; Matt. 26:58; Mark 14:54; Luke 22:55). Presently the portress who had admitted Peter came, and looking attentively at him as he sat by the fire, said: "Art not thou also one of this man's disciples?" whilst perhaps another maid may have added, in confirmation of her words: "Thou also wast with Jesus of Nazareth" (John 18:17; Luke 22:56; Mark 14:67; Matt. 26:69). Peter answered: "I am not. I know him not. I neither know nor understand what thou sayest" (John 18:17; Luke 22:57; Mark 14:68; Matt. 26:70). This was the first denial, and the cock crew for the first time (Mark 14:68). Peter now rose, and as he was going out of the gate, another maid said to the bystanders: "This man also was with Jesus of Nazareth." And someone else present may have interposed: "Thou also art one of them." Thereupon Peter denied it for the second time, and with an oath, saying: "I am not, I know not the man" (Matt. 26:71, 72; Mark 14:69, 70; Luke 22:58). This was the second denial. Peter now went into the outer court, but soon returned to the inner one, and (as it appears) again sat down among the servants at the fire. After about an hour had elapsed, another man returned to the charge, saying: "Surely thou art one of them," whilst a second and a third added: "Thou art a Galilean," and "Thy speech doth discover thee." Indeed, one of those who had been present at our Lord's arrest, a kinsman of Malchus, insisted: "Did not I see thee in the garden with him?" Then Peter denied it for the third time, with an oath and an imprecation upon himself (I Kings 3:17; 14:44; II Kings 3:35), asseverating: "I am not, I know not this man of whom thou speakest"; and immediately the cock crew again (Matt. 26:73, 74; Mark 14:70–72; Luke 22:59, 60; John 18:26, 27). The thrice-repeated denial graduates to a climax. The first time it was rather an evasive answer; the second time Peter denies all acquaintance with "this man," and the third time he formally forswears Him.

Such is the history of Peter's denial. The gravity and ignominy of the fall becomes evident when we consider how many unworthy features this action included. There lay in it a want of character, miserable human respect, a lie, then a false asseveration, an oath and an imprecation upon himself, and lastly a denial of our Lord. Peter avers and swears that he is not a disciple of His, that he does not even know "the man." Who is it that swears thus? And with Whom does he aver that he has no acquaintance? Once it was his glory and his greatest happiness to be one of the Apostles, indeed their head. Only a few hours ago he was ready to die for our Lord, and had drawn the sword in His defence. Now he does not know the Man whom he had so often called Master and Father, and whose Divinity he had repeatedly and solemnly confessed. And before whom is it that he does not dare to confess Him? Before maids, serving-men, and common menials. How little even the best and noblest men are to be depended upon! Further, the greatness of his fall becomes evident when we consider what pain and humiliation it caused our Saviour. How ingratitude, faithlessness and contempt hurt a master, benefactor or father! One Apostle betrays and sells Him, all forsake Him, and the first of His disciples denies Him and swears that he never knew Him. To what a depth our Lord's humiliation has reached! Is He not, humanly speaking, quite abandoned? Great and lamentable indeed was this fall of Peter.

2. CAUSES OF PETER'S FALL

One cause of Peter's fall was certainly his neglect of prayer, in spite of the earnest and repeated admonition addressed to him and the other Apostles with regard to this by our Saviour, Who foresaw what would happen. A second cause was a certain self-confidence. He thought that, with his love for our Saviour, he could do anything, and that disloyalty or a fall on his part was not to be thought of (Matt. 26:33). Such was his impetuous character. Lastly, it was certainly imprudent of him to venture needlessly and uselessly into this evident danger and remain in it so long.

Nevertheless, we must not disregard the circumstances that diminish the gravity of his fall and excuse him to a certain extent. It was certainly the most heartfelt sympathy, ardent love and lively compassion, combined with an irresistible desire to know what was being done with our Saviour, that urged Peter and John to follow Him so closely into the very house of Caiphas (Matt. 26:58). Besides, the circumstances show that Peter was in a very excited and bewildered state, in consequence of the sad and unexpected events that had followed in such quick succession that night, and that he was completely under the sway of his impressions and feelings. Add to this the fear and anxiety, the menacing and intimidating scenes that met him everywhere, and the attacks that were made from all sides one after another, upon his fortitude and presence of mind. He escaped from one danger only to fall into another. So we may well assume that in the case of St. Peter great allowance must be made for unfavorable circumstances: the pressure put upon him, his fear, distress and bewilderment, his mental and bodily weariness and exhaustion, and the precipitation of his character. Which of us would have been made steadfast under such circumstances?

3. EXPIATION OF THE FALL. PETER'S REPENTANCE

We must above all consider Who it was that prompted Peter's repentance. It was no other than our Saviour Himself. The first exhortation came from Him. Probably our Lord was just passing by at the moment of the last denial, led by soldiers, and either quitting the assembly-room after the provisory condemnation or being brought from the courtyard into a dungeon. Peter was near, and our Lord, Who had hitherto turned a deaf and unresponsive ear to His surroundings, and had not even moved or flinched under the hands of His tormentors, turned to the side on which Peter was standing, and looked at him sadly and significantly (Luke 22:61). And why did He looked at him? Was it a glance of reproach or indignation? Did it indicate punishment or death? No, it was a life-giving glance. Who can comprehend all that it conveyed? An earnest warning, surely, and acute pain; but also infinite mercy and encouragement to have confidence.

It was a great and powerful grace, a glance full of the infinite mercy of God, Who makes in a single moment saints of sinners, and Apostles of deniers and persecutors. Peter now saw the awful chasm into which he had fallen; but he also saw the Hand outstretched to help him, so he seized it as he had once done on the Sea of Galilee, and it drew him out. He thought of the words our Lord had spoken to him: "Before the cock crow, thou shalt deny me thrice" (Luke 22:61), and: "I have prayed for thee that thy faith fail not; and thou being once converted, confirm thy brethren" (Luke 22:32).

This was the part our Saviour took in Peter's repentance. The rest was for him to do; and he did it, perfectly and completely. The sight of our Saviour, maltreated and condemned to death in spite of His innocence, struck him to the heart and awakened in him the full consciousness of his guilt. He had sinned against One who had warned him so faithfully and so earnestly, One who was his Father, his Friend, his God and his all. He began to weep bitterly, and quitted the court (Luke 22:62). He surely feared no longer lest he should be spoken to; he would have told anyone who he was and what a great sin he had committed. Probably he went quite outside the city, in order to give free vent to his tears and contrition.

So our Saviour had to bear this grief and humiliation too. The fact that He foresaw Peter's fall did not lessen its bitterness; foreseeing an evil is a very different thing from experiencing it. But our Lord permitted this fall of Peter's in order to comfort us when we are forsaken and denied by friends. Secondly, He wished to warn us against rashness and over-estimation of ourselves. Let us not trust the love that is not humble and discreet. It only makes us unhappy. Thirdly, our Saviour wished to teach us to trust Him and hold fast to Him in all circumstances. These are the lessons we may learn from that glance of His, related in this mystery. Peter understood it completely and never forgot it as long as he lived, nor his transgression either. By day he thought of his office, of saving souls and propagating the kingdom of Christ; by night he rose to weep over his fall, so that (as the legend says) the copious tears he shed gradually made furrows in his cheeks. This is the foundation of his apostolic work. His love had grown humble now, and the tortures in store for him will find him faithful.

The Rest of the Night of the Passion, in Caiphas' House

Luke 22:63. And the men that held him, mocked him and struck him.—64. And they blindfolded him, and smote his face; and they asked him, saying: "Prophesy, who is it that struck thee?"—65. And blaspheming, many other things they said against him.

Mark 14:65. And some began to spit on him, and to cover his face, and to buffet him and to say unto him: "Prophesy"; and the servants struck him with the palms of their hands.

Matt. 26:67. Then did they spit in his face, and buffeted him, and others struck his face with the palms of their hands,—68. Saying: "Prophesy unto us, O Christ, who is he that struck thee?"

The rest of the night after the provisory condemnation was passed by our Saviour in the house of Caiphas amid manifold sufferings.

1. SUFFERINGS OCCASIONED BY CIRCUMSTANCES

After all the sorrowful and agitating events of the night—the Agony on Mount Olivet, the ill-treatment He had suffered at His arrest and on the way into the city—our Saviour must naturally have been overcome with weariness and exhaustion, and tormented by hunger and thirst. But His captors left Him no rest, and would not even let Him sit down in a quiet corner. They brought Him out of the judgment-hall into the court-yard, and there He had to suffer new and prolonged injuries, standing on His wearied Feet. It is very unlikely that they even gave Him a drink of fresh water. To this was added the biting cold of a night in the early spring. Whilst His tormentors from time to time warmed themselves at the open hearth (Luke 22:56; Mark 14:54), our Saviour, scantily clad as He was, had to stand on the cold stones of the court, shivering and trembling with frost and cold. He was Lord of the elements, and might have caused the night of His Passion to be mild and temperate as the loveliest spring; but He wished to include this suffering also in the plan of His Passion, that nothing might be wanting.

2. SUFFERINGS OCCASIONED BY MEN

Instead of leaving our suffering Lord a little rest after the stormy scene of the court, they subjected Him to the coarsest and most revolting ill-treatment.

The authors and instruments of this ill-usage seem to have

been not merely the soldiers to whose keeping He was entrusted (Luke 22:64) and some of the servants, but even some of the members of the Great Council (Matt. 26:67; Mark 14:65). They too, it seems, did not consider it beneath their dignity to take part in the unworthy sport.

Three kinds of ill-treatment are mentioned. They first mocked Him, jeered at Him, and ridiculed His high offices and attributes. They blindfolded Him, struck Him in the face, and then asked Him who had done it (Matt. 26:68; Mark 14:65; Luke 22:64); and uttered many other blasphemies against Him (Luke 22:65). Secondly, they spat upon Him (Mark 14:65; Matt. 26:67), an outrage considered by the Israelites as the greatest possible insult (Deut. 25:9; Num. 12:14; Job 30:10). Lastly, they proceeded to acts of positive violence, struck Him in the face and buffeted Him (Luke 22:64; Mark 14:65; Matt. 26:67). This was the fulfilment of the words of the prophet: "I have given my body to the strikers, and my cheeks to them that plucked them; I have not turned away my face from them that rebuked me and spit upon me" (Isa. 50:6).

The enormity of this ill-treatment appears, first, from the circumstances in which our Saviour found Himself. It was not merely an act of barbarity thus to ill-use a poor defenceless man who was already in such a pitiable condition; it was also a crying injustice. An accused man has a right to public protection, and it is the duty of those in authority to protect him from any arbitrary ill-usage. Here it was the magistrates themselves who looked on at the revolting scene. The enormity of it all becomes evident, secondly, when we consider Who this ill-used Man was. The threshold of the Temple might not be defiled by spittle; we ourselves would not dare to spit upon the floor in presence of anyone who had a claim to our respect, and now the Face of the Living God is made the object of this abominable outrage. The most abject wretch can vent his coarse and wanton vulgarity upon our Lord. And He Who is now covered with filth and spittle is the same Who received the homage of the prophets on Mount Thabor. But He suffers it all, accepts it all with unspeakable patience, humility and devotedness.

3. THE SUFFERINGS IN PRISON

Who knows all that our Saviour had to suffer, and how long the hellish spectacle lasted? Tradition says that He was finally brought into a prison-cell, there to be kept until the Great Council assembled in the early morning. In the Catholic districts of South Germany one often comes across a very touching picture, high up on the mountains or far in the solitary depths of the forest. Our Lord is represented sitting in a narrow cell, with His Hands bound and an iron ring round His neck, by which He is fastened to the wall; the noble, suffering Head is bowed, as though seeking a resting-place and finding none; He is quite alone, and His gaze is grave and sad. The picture is called "God in distress." This is a fair description of our Saviour's position in the prison. Rest was not to be thought of. He suffered, and with a keen feeling of abandonment. We may fitly apply to Him the words: "Weeping he hath wept in the night, and his tears are on his cheeks; there is none to comfort him among all them that were dear to him; all his friends have despised him, and are become his enemies. . . . Therefore do I weep, and my eyes run down with water; because the comforter, the relief of my soul, is far from me; my children are desolate, because the enemy hath prevailed" (Lament. 1:2, 16).

Day-break probably found Him sitting thus, and the first rays of light that fell through the prison-grating greeted the Face of our Saviour. And He, too, greeted the dawn, raised His eyes towards the light, and began His morning prayer, His last. What may it have been? It was always the same. From the first moment of His Conception He had been awaiting this day with longing anticipation; it was constantly in His thoughts, as it slowly but surely approached. And now it was come. Hesitatingly as an executioner it came, to announce to our Lord His Death. And He received it readily, joyfully. We may reverently imagine that He raised His eyes to His Heavenly Father, and thanked Him for the dawn of this great day; that He offered Him all His sufferings, His Life and Death, for the glory of His Name and for us sinners. Thus began the ever-memorable day of our Redemption, and it was probably with these and similar sentiments that our Saviour greeted its first rays (Ps. 53).

Final Sentence of the Great Council

Luke 22:66. And as soon as it was day, the ancients of the people and the chief priests and scribes came together, and they brought him into their council, saying: "If thou be the Christ, tell us."—67. And he said to them: "If I shall tell you, you will not believe me;—68. And if I shall also ask you, you will not answer me, nor let me go.—69. But hereafter the Son of Man shall be sitting on the right hand of the power of God."—70. Then said they all: "Art thou then the Son of God?" Who said: "You say that I am."—71. And they said: "What need we any further testimony? For we ourselves have heard it from his own mouth."—23:1. And the whole multitude of them rising up, led him to Pilate.

MATT. 27:1. And when morning was come, all the chief priests and ancients of the people took counsel against Jesus, that they might put him to death.—2. And they brought him bound, and delivered him to Pontius Pilate the governor.

MARK 15:1. And straightway in the morning the chief priests holding a consultation with the ancients and the scribes and the whole council, binding Jesus led him away, and delivered him to Pilate.

JOHN 18:28. Then they led Jesus from Caiphas to the governer's hall. And it was morning.

1. CONVOCATION OF THE GREAT COUNCIL

The Great Council was convoked, and representatives of all its three estates—chief priests, scribes, and ancients—were summoned to attend. Indeed, it would appear that all its members (excepting possibly the friends of Jesus) were present (Mark 16:1).

The time of the assembly was day-break, "in the morning" (Mark 15:1; Matt. 27:1; John 18:28), "as soon as it was day" (Luke 22:66). They made this despatch in order to get the affair finished before the Paschal Feast began, on the evening of the 15th of Nisan. "The feet of the sinners run to evil, and make haste to shed innocent blood" (Isa. 59:7; Ps. 13:3; Prov. 1:16).

The chief priests' object in convoking the Great Council was to kill our Lord (Matt. 27:1), i.e. to do everything in their power to bring about His Death, to pronounce final sentence upon Him and deliver Him up to the Roman governor with a view to His execution; and probably also to consult upon the steps to be taken in order to attain this end. The proceedings of the previous night could pass only for a preliminary examination; for the ordinary course of the law required that sentence should not be passed until the second day of the trial, and it might not be given at night.

2. THE TRIAL

In order to formulate the verdict and obtain it as speedily as possible, they merely fixed upon the chief point of the proceedings of the previous day, concerning which our Saviour Himself had already given His evidence and made His avowal. They asked Him if He were Christ (Luke 22:66). Their question, therefore, concerned the Messianic rank of Jesus. Our Saviour replied that any answer or discussion would be of no avail. "If I shall tell you, you will not believe Me, and if I shall also ask you (what right you have to treat Me thus), you will not answer Me." So there is nothing left for you but the judgment, which I shall pronounce upon you. You will not have Me as your Messias and Redeemer; you shall have Me, therefore, as your Judge, in the power and by the authority of the Father (Luke 22:67–69). He gave them to understand this in much the same words as He had used in the nocturnal assembly (Matt. 26:64). Thereupon they all asked: "Art thou then the Son of God?" Our Saviour replied firmly: "You say that I am" (Luke 22:70).

This short discussion sufficiently shows, on the one hand, the insincerity, obduracy and utter want of principle of the Jews. They understood the drift of the question perfectly, and were only trying to elicit from our Saviour a clear avowal of His Messianic rank and His Divinity, in order to condemn Him to death as a blasphemer on the ground of this declaration. But on the other hand, it also shows us the fortitude and goodness of Jesus. He gives them a full and clear explanation in His plain testimony, thus depriving their unbelief of its last pretext, and directs their attention (in His first answer) to their own malice and bad dispositions, which are more unseemly in a judge than in others; He warns them against the terrible consequences of their conduct by His reference to the Judgment, showing that He, Who now stands before their judgment-seat, will one day pronounce judgment upon them. It needed no little courage to bear this testimony at this moment, for He knew that it was all they were waiting for, and that it would infallibly cost Him His life. But nevertheless He made the avowal with steadfast firmness.

3. VERDICT AND SENTENCE

With the words: "What need we any further testimony? For we ourselves have heard it from His own mouth" (Luke 22:71), they rise to give their verdict, and condemn our Lord to death on the ground of His declaration that He is the Messias and Son of God. We can well imagine with what hypocritical expressions of indignation, with what fury and threatening cries they accompanied this sentence. So the Just One is condemned to death by the representatives and administrators of the law; the Messias, by His own people; God, by His own creatures. We know not whether to feel more horror or grief at such a spectacle, or whether rather to smile at the immense incongruity. There is reason for all three. Such a terrible crime, and committed with such obduracy, malice, and wantonness! They themselves acknowledge that they have a full and valid testimony from His own lips, and they pass sentence of death upon Him, as a blasphemer and false Messias, for giving them what they ought to have thanked Him for on bended knee. Now our Saviour's fate was settled. The ecclesiastical trial was ended and the die cast.

And how did our Lord hear and accept this sentence of His people? We may feel sure, with humility, resignation, constancy, and great love to God and to us. He rejoiced to be able to bear this testimony once more with all solemnity, and to die for it. It is for the glory of God, for His own glory, and for our salvation. Does it not give Him a right to our most devoted faith and heartfelt gratitude, and even to the sacrifice of our life for this faith? His own nation hates Him, curses Him, delivers Him up to death for His testimony; all the more, then, are we bound to give Him satisfaction, adoration, and unconditional devotion. How many have counted themselves happy to lay down their life in confession of the Divinity of Christ! It was but the fit response to our Saviour's confession. Shall we not here kneel down in spirit on the spot where our Saviour was condemned to death for this testimony, and cry in adoring gratitude and reparation: *Deus sanctus, Deus fortis, Deus immortalis, miserere nobis!*

Steps were immediately taken to put the sentence into effect. The whole assembly broke up and conducted our Saviour, with hands bound in order to mark Him conspicuously as a condemned malefactor, to the residence of Pilate, the Roman governor, in order to deliver Him over to him for execution (Matt. 27:2; Mark 15:1; Luke 23:1; John 18:28). This had to take place, because our Saviour had predicted that He would be delivered up to the Gentiles and be crucified by them (Matt. 20:19; John 18:32); and also because the Jews wished Him to suffer the most ignominious death, namely that of crucifixion, and to this He could be sentenced only by the Roman governor. Another secondary reason for this step on the part of the Jews may have been a wish to support and confirm their sentence by that of the governor, and thus secure themselves against any eventual popular demonstration in favor of our Saviour.

So this strange procession, consisting of the chief priests, the Great Council (Luke 23:1), and some armed men, went with our Saviour through nearly the whole city, from the heights of the upper town (Sion) westwards, past the Temple, and through the outskirts to the northern part of the city, to the palace of Pilate, the governor. This palace (also called Praetorium) was situated either in the citadel Antonia, at the north-west corner of the Temple square, or in the immediate vicinity. Our Saviour must have suffered much discomfort, humiliation and grief during this procession, since it intentionally passed in a most conspicuous manner through the principal parts of the city, and the streets were teeming with pilgrims come to the feast. But on the other hand, it was also an honorable testimony to His rank and importance, since everyone took part in it. It was the memorable procession in which Israel went to deliver its Messias to the Gentiles to be put to death.

The End of Judas

Matt. 27:3. Then Judas, who betrayed him, seeing that he was condemned, repenting himself brought back the thirty pieces of silver to the chief priests and ancients,—4. Saying: "I have sinned, in betraying innocent blood." But they said: "What is that to us? Look thou to it."—5. And casting down the pieces of silver in the temple, he departed; and went and hanged himself with an halter.—6. But the chief priests having taken the pieces of silver, said: "It is not lawful to put them into the corbona; because it is the price of blood."—7. And after they had consulted together, they bought with them the potter's field, to be a burying-place for strangers.—8. For this cause that field was called Haceldama, that is, the field of blood, even to this day.—9. Then was fulfilled that which was spoken by Jeremias the prophet, saying: "And they took the thirty pieces of silver, the price of him that was prized, whom they prized of the children of Israel;—10. And they gave them unto the potter's field, as the Lord appointed to me."

1. How Judas Repents of His Deed

It was the condemnation of Jesus by the Great Council and His being led away to Pilate (Matt. 27:3) which brought Judas to repentance. He now saw with his own eyes the terrible consequences of his treachery, and began to repent of his deed.

As regards the nature of his contrition and penance, it seems to have been perfect in many respects, at all events exteriorly. He recognizes the infamy and horror of his crime, and repents of it. He openly confesses it before the chief priests and ancients, who had perhaps remained behind in the house of Caiphas to transact other business, or had gone into the Temple (Matt. 27:3). He testifies in their presence to the innocence of Jesus, as opposed to the verdict of "guilty" which they had pronounced upon Him, and acknowledges his own guilt, saying that he has betrayed innocent blood and thereby sinned (Matt. 27:4). Lastly, he tears himself away from his idol, the money that had seduced him to sin, and casts it down in the Temple (Matt. 27:5). What, then, was wanting to his contrition and penance? It was the important —nay, essential—virtues of hope, confidence, and love. He saw only the magnitude and dreadfulness of his offence, and not the possibility of pardon, and so he despaired, as Cain had once done (Gen. 4:13). His sorrow was therefore not a sorrow unto life, but unto death (II Cor. 7:9 seq.).

And how was this? Some are of opinion that Judas had thought our Saviour would certainly not be killed, but would contrive to escape from the hands of His enemies, as He had so often done before; but this expectation had not been fulfilled, and so he was the first to be guilty of the blood of our Lord. And therefore he despaired. But even apart from this, the whole course of what passed in his soul is very natural. At first, blinded by passion and tempted by the devil, he had only seen in the deed the enticing prospect of gain, and now it was accomplished he saw only the horror of it. A complete reaction set in, and so now he could not even endure to keep the money that had had such an attraction for him before. Such is the natural interior course of every sin, and in this case his own fickle, unstable character together with the influence of the devil contributed to bring it about.

2. HOW JUDAS WAS RECEIVED BY THE PRIESTS

The way in which the priests received Judas is odious for two reasons.

The first of these is their callousness and heartlessness. They meet Judas' repentance and confession of guilt with the answer: "What is that to us? look thou to it" (Matt. 27:4). They do not comfort him by saying that our Saviour is a blasphemer and false Messias. They throw all the responsibility on him, and leave him to despair. Thus do evil communications bring about their own punishment.

The second odious feature in the conduct of the priests is their hypocrisy. They do not accept the money, in order not to appear to repent of their deed and thus contradict themselves. As a matter of fact, they had not bought Jesus, but had only paid for the act of treachery. On the other hand they will not put the money into the Temple treasury, because it is blood-money and the price of sin (Deut. 23:18). They reckon this as sin, and take care not to commit it; but they do not hesitate to take upon themselves the actual blood-guiltiness and retain it (Matt. 27:6, 25), although Judas' repentance was an impressive warning to them not to commit the crime. For he did not repent of his deed after the Resurrection, but at the time of the deepest humiliation of Jesus. So at length they hit upon the expedient of purchasing with the money a piece of land known as the "potter's field," whether because it belonged to a potter, or because potter's clay was to be found there. This field was to serve in future as a burying-place for strangers (Matt. 27:7, 8). It was called the "field of blood" (Haceldama), and retains the name to the present day (Matt. 27:8; Acts 1:19). The place is still distinguishable by the many vaults there. Thus the Jews set up a perpetual memorial of their crime, and fulfilled the prediction of the prophets Jeremias and Zacharias. The latter foretold the price for which the Messias would be sold (Zach. 11:12), and the former indicated the field that was to be purchased with the money (Jer. 18:1–3; 19:1–2; 32:8–14). St. Matthew combines both prophecies, because they now found their complete fulfilment (Matt. 27:9, 10).[1]

3. THE END OF JUDAS

After Judas had cast the pieces of silver into the Temple he fled, driven by despair and the Evil One, out of the city to the vale of Hinnom. What a terrified glance would he now cast at the Mount of Olives, at the foot of which the Garden of Gethsemani lies! Would he not think of those words of our Saviour's: "Friend, whereto art thou come?" and: "It were better for him, if that man had not been born!" Did he not think too of Absalom, who expired hanging on a tree? Did not the Evil One shout into his ears the terrible execrations and curses that the prophet (as it appears, with reference to him) had foretold: "They repaid Me evil for good, and hatred for My love. . . . May the devil stand at his right hand. When he is judged, may he go out condemned; and may his prayer be turned to sin. . . . May there be none to help him. . . . He loved cursing, and it shall come unto him. . . . It went in like water into his entrails, and like oil in his bones. . . . May it be unto him like a garment which covereth

[1] The words: "Then was fulfilled that which was spoken by Jeremias the prophet" etc. appear to refer merely to the purchase of the field, of which Jeremias alone speaks.

him, and like a girdle with which he is girded continually" (Ps. 108:4 seq.). Overpowered by remorse of conscience and despair, the unhappy wretch hanged himself. The body burst asunder in the midst (Acts 1:18).

What an example, and what a terrible lesson! An Apostle ends his days as a suicide, the impeacher and avenger of his own crime. What more is needed to teach us how fatal it is not to resist our evil passions? Is not every passion a very Satan, that can make us miserable for time and eternity? But still even passion and its bitter fruit, sin, could not have compassed his ruin if only he had not lost confidence and despaired. Peter had fallen, too. But he seized the saving Hand of Jesus by his love and trust. How very differently Judas would have been received by Peter, John, and Mary, if he had fled to them in his contrition and cast himself into their arms, instead of going to the chief priests! How great is the evil of losing confidence and falling into despair!

First Hearing before Pilate

John 18:28. Then they led Jesus from Caiphas to the governor's hall. And it was morning; and they went not into the hall, that they might not be defiled, but that they might eat the Pasch.—29. Pilate therefore went out to them, and said: "What accusation bring you against this man?"—30. They answered and said to him: "If he were not a malefactor, we would not have delivered him up to thee." —31. Pilate therefore said to them: "Take him you, and judge him according to your law." The Jews therefore said to him: "It is not lawful for us to put any man to death."—32 That the word of Jesus might be fulfilled which he said, signifying what death he should die.—33. Pilate therefore went into the hall again, and called Jesus, and said to him: "Art thou the king of the Jews?"—34. Jesus answered: "Sayest thou this thing of thyself, or have others told it thee of me?"—35. Pilate answered: "Am I a Jew? Thy own nation and the chief priests have delivered thee up to me; what hast thou done?"—36. Jesus answered: "My kingdom is not of this world; if my kingdom were of this world, my servants would certainly strive that I should not be delivered to the Jews; but now my kingdom is not from hence."—37. Pilate therefore said to him: "Art thou a king then?" Jesus answered: "Thou sayest that I am a king. For this was I born, and for this came I into the world, that I should give testimony to the truth; everyone that is of the truth, heareth my voice."—38. Pilate saith to him: "What is truth?" And when he said this, he went out again to the Jews, and saith to them: "I find no cause in him."

Luke 23:2. And they began to accuse him, saying: "We have found this man perverting our nation, and forbidding to give tribute to Caesar, and saying that he is Christ the king."—3. And Pilate asked him, saying: "Art thou the king of the Jews?" But he answering, said: "Thou sayest it."—4. And Pilate said to the chief priests and to the multitudes: "I find no cause in this man."—5. But they were more earnest, saying: "He stirreth up the people, teaching throughout all Judaea, beginning from Galilee to this place."—6. But Pilate hearing Galilee, asked if the man were of Galilee.

Mark 15:2. And Pilate asked him: "Art thou the king of the Jews?" but he answering, saith to him: "Thou sayest it."—3. And the chief priests accused him in many things.—4. And Pilate again asked him, saying: "Answerest thou nothing? Behold in how many things they accuse thee."—5. But Jesus still answered nothing, so that Pilate wondered.

MATT. 27:11. And Jesus stood before the governor, and the governor asked him, saying: "Art thou the king of the Jews?" Jesus saith to him: "Thou sayest it."—12. And when he was accused by the chief priests and ancients, he answered nothing. —13. Then Pilate saith to him: "Dost not thou hear how great testimonies they alleage against thee?"—14. And he answered him to never a word, so that the governor wondered exceedingly.

1. HISTORICAL COURSE OF THE PROCEEDINGS

The trial was held, it would appear, in the market-place or forum, which enclosed a guard-house for soldiers, the tribunal where Pilate gave judgment, and the pillar of flagellation. Pilate's palace seems to have adjoined this market-place, and communicated with it by broad flights of steps and a terrace from which conversation could be held with the people in the forum. Pilate's judgment-hall was probably behind this terrace. The chief priests and Jews kept at a certain distance in the market-place, and did not enter Pilate's palace or judgment-hall, because intercourse with a Gentile would have rendered them legally unclean until the evening, and thus excluded them from the sacrifices in the Temple (John 18:28; Acts 10:28). Probably they had already given Pilate notice of their business and requested him to transact it with them from the terrace.

So Pilate went out to them there and made inquiries about the accusation. This seems to have annoyed the Jews from the outset; for they had probably sent word to him that the criminal was already condemned and the sentence only needed to be ratified and put into effect. And now Pilate seemed to be beginning the whole affair over again, which would occupy a considerable time. So they answered in an irritated tone that if the accused had not been a malefactor, they would not have delivered Him up to him (John 18:30). But Pilate had no mind to be made use of by the Jews as a public executioner, and answered (probably under the impression that it was only a matter of some point of religion) that they had better punish the condemned man as far as their jurisdiction allowed (John 18:31). The Jews thereupon replied that it was a question here of a political offence against the Roman executive power (Luke 23:2)—a most critical case, that is to say—and they had no longer the power to put anyone to death (John 18:31). On hearing this Pilate ordered our Lord to be brought into the judgment-hall, where he questioned Him about

His alleged kingship (John 18:33; Luke 23:3; Mark 15:2; Matt. 27:11). Our Saviour explained to him that He laid claim only to a spiritual kingdom (John 18:36, 37). Pilate was satisfied, and, convinced that there was no question here of an offence against the State, he went back to the Jews and gave his opinion in favor of the innocence of Jesus (John 18:38; Luke 23:4). They hereupon began to lend weight to their assertion by many serious accusations, especially by charging our Lord with having incited the people to revolt, from Galilee down to Judaea (Luke 23:5; Mark 15:3). The persistent silence maintained by our Lord, even when Pilate called upon Him to defend Himself, confirmed the governor still more in his opinion of our Saviour's innocence. But since the Jews seemed so unruly, he sought to get rid of the affair under the pretext that our Lord was Herod's subject and the matter must therefore be referred to him. So he sent the Jews to Herod with our Saviour (Luke 23:6, 7).

2. THE ACTORS IN THIS SCENE; THEIR BEHAVIOR

In the first place there are the accusers, the Jews. In them we have an illustration of the power of passion. All the chief priests and the Great Council, appear before Pilate, probably in order to influence him; and they demean themselves to the common rôle of prosecutor (Luke 23:2; Mark 15:5; Matt. 27:12). They do this before the hated Roman governor, who treats them in a most off-hand manner, and yet in spite of this they make the ignominious admission that they have no power over life and death (John 18:31). All these sacrifices they make in their hatred of Jesus. The accusation itself is most slanderous and malicious, and is thoroughly calculated to entangle the governor in the matter. At the meeting of the Great Council they had condemned our Saviour on the charge of blasphemy (Matt. 26:65, 66; Luke 22:70, 71). But here they drop this accusation, and impeach Him of a political crime amounting to high treason, viz. of seducing the people and inciting them to revolt, refusing to pay tribute, and giving Himself out for the Messias, of course in their and the governor's sense of that dignity, namely as a political sovereign (Luke 23:2, 3). They convert the ecclesiastical case into a political one. In the second onset they let fall the name of "Galilee," perhaps with the intention of placing our Lord in an unfavorable light from the very first, because the Galileans were very restless and often took part in risings against the Romans. Thus the accusation was a mixture of ambiguity and downright falsehood. Our Saviour had never forbidden anyone to pay the tribute (Matt. 22:21). But their aim was to force the Roman governor into the matter, since his first duty was to look sharply after the payment of the tribute and uphold the prestige of the Roman name with all the means at his command.

Pilate himself comes next. He is a fair sample of a Roman official of the day. We see in him above all the haughty pride of the Roman patrician and his contempt for all the conquered races, especially the Jews. He treats them in a most disdainful manner, and sends them away with their object unattained. "Am I a Jew," that I should trouble myself about the so-called Messias? he himself replies to our Saviour in an irritated tone, when the latter asks him if he inquires about His high rank of his own accord, or on account of the statement of the Jews (John 18:35). On the other hand, we also remark in him a certain smooth compliance, which makes him show consideration for the religious feelings and customs of the Jews and go out on the terrace to speak to them, and even propose to them to punish our Lord themselves (John 18:31). At the same time, one cannot overlook in him a certain sense of justice and sound judgment. He sees through the Jews' tissue of lies at once, and does not let himself be influenced by mere words of accusation, but disregards the first two charges on account of their evident falsehood, and only inquires for facts to prove that our Saviour has aspired to the secular sovereignty and actually arrogated to Himself its rights, as they allege (John 18:35). Not finding any, he publicly proclaims the innocence of Jesus (Luke 23:4), and admires the calmness and nobility of character He shows in not replying a word to all the accusations of the Jews (Mark 15:4, 5; Matt. 27:13, 14). But lastly, Pilate shows from the first his indecision, shallowness, insincerity, and time-serving policy. He sees that our Saviour is innocent, and yet he does not take Him under his protection, but turns the matter over to Herod, either because he hoped the latter would keep our Lord with him, or because he wished to gain time and show Herod a mark of attention (Luke 23:12). Pilate is insincere even to himself, since he scorns to be taught the way of truth by our Saviour (John 18:38). A thoroughly worldly statesman, lax, unscrupulous, and sceptical, he regarded the search for truth as mere romantic enthusiasm. Our Saviour is in his eyes nothing but a harmless, fanatical dreamer.

Our Saviour is the third to be considered. They are weighty words with which St. Matthew begins his account of our Lord's appearance before Pilate: "And Jesus stood before the governor" (Matt. 27:11). It was the first official meeting of our Saviour with the holder of the Roman executive power; the future Heir to the world stands before the representative of the actual world-empire, innocence and holiness before the sullied Gentile, God before His creature. Yes, God, though poor, humble, stripped of all exterior power, rejected and accused by His own people, and delivered up to the Gentile to be tried and judged by him. And how does our Saviour behave? His conduct is, first, very humble and submissive. He acknowledges Pilate's jurisdiction and submits to it. He replies with great calmness, lucidity and modesty to the question concerning His kingly rank, and shows His great ascendancy of mind by immediately asking Pilate if he put it in consequence of his own conviction or merely on account of the Jews' accusation (John 18:34). Taking the words in this sense, our Lord is certainly inquiring about the charge brought against Him, but assuredly with the intention of cross-examining Pilate also, so to speak, awakening his conscience and warning him not to pander to the lying accusations of the Jews if he did not consider Him guilty himself. The question betokens great clearness, composure and majesty. And what does He say of His kingdom, its origin and nature? That it is upon the earth, certainly, but not *of* the earth; it is a spiritual, supernatural kingdom, the kingdom of truth. It docs not fight with weapons of steel, but with the power of conviction, and conquers by this means the hearts that by right belong to it; He Himself, our Saviour, is witness to this truth, and is Himself the Truth (John 18:36, 37). What clear and majestic words, and yet how modest! What might He not have said of his kingdom, and how little He does say! Finally, He gives Pilate another earnest warning in the words: "Everyone that is of the truth, heareth My voice" (John 18:37). When our Saviour speaks, He does so humbly, wisely, and in a manner that commands reverence. But He knows how to be silent, too, and His silence is like His speech, full of wisdom, humility, power and majesty. He opposes silence to the persistent accusations of the Jews, and preserves it even in the face of Pilate's repeated exhortation to speak (Mark 15:4; Matt. 27:13, 14). He could easily have defended Himself and turned all the charges against the accusers themselves, if He had chosen. But He did not choose, in spite of the fact that His life and honor were at stake. And why not? Because it was unnecessary after the information He had already given Pilate; the Jews themselves well knew what their accusations were worth. Besides, He would have nothing more to do with them; His cause had passed to another juridical authority. Further, our Saviour wished to warn us against the inordinate desire of always defending ourselves, to satisfy for the sins it leads us to commit, and to comfort those who cannot defend themselves. So this silence of His was not, as ours might be, due to impotence and stupidity, obstinacy or pride; it was prompted by majestic patience, wisdom, humility, intrepidity, nobility of sentiment, and love of God and of us.

3. CONCLUSION

Our Lord's delivery into Pilate's hands marks a new development in the tragedy of His Passion, and this scene in court is, as it were, the first act, in which the actors and moving forces present themselves and give an idea of the issue of the play and their own parts in it. Here we have all the agents who appear in the future course of the history of the Passion. First of all, the Jews, representatives of the great force and inventive power of the passions, with their fierce, implacable hate, their unbelief, malice and utter want of principle, who shrink from no means that can lead them to their end. Opposed to them is Pilate, in possession of all the means of the executive power, with evident appreciation of truth and justice, but as unprincipled and unreliable as a statesman can be who regards the expediency of the moment, and not truth and justice, as his highest law. It is not difficult to guess who will be victor here. Between them stands our Saviour, a Lamb between the fox and the wolves. He has nothing at His command but the majesty of truth and holiness, humility and voluntary suffering, and yet it is equally certain that in the end He will vanquish both His adversaries with these means. Truth and justice are eternal. Even here in His state of powerlessness and humiliation our Saviour is the object of Pilate's respect, admiration and reverence. It is certainly most significant that He is here accused by the Jews before the Roman governor, the representative of the world-monarchy of that age, on account of His kingly rank; that He gives him an account of its signification; and that the governor himself finds nothing criminal about Him, but declares His guiltlessness and harmless character. If only the Roman government had abided by this judgment! Unhappily it afterwards went over to the Jews, and sided with them against the Innocent One. And so the Lamb will fight with the great beast (Apoc. 17:14; Dan. 7:7, 13, 14), vanquish it, and change its temporal sovereignty into a spiritual one. St. Peter and his successors in Rome are the living witnesses to this spiritual kingdom in the world. The claim made by our Saviour to this kingdom in the presence of the Roman governor, and His explanation with regard to its nature, certainly belong to the prime significance of this mystery. This testimony borne by our Saviour before Pilate is the "good confession" of our faith (I Tim. 6:13).

Jesus before Herod

Luke 23:7. And when he understood that he was of Herod's jurisdiction, he sent him away to Herod, who was also himself at Jerusalem in those days.—8. And Herod seeing Jesus, was very glad; for he was desirous of a long time to see him, because he had heard many things of him, and he hoped to see some sign wrought by him.—9. And he questioned him in many words. But he answered him nothing.—10. And the chief priests and the scribes stood by earnestly accusing him.—11. And Herod with his army set him at naught; and mocked him, putting on him a white garment, and sent him back to Pilate.—12. And Herod and Pilate were made friends that same day; for before they were enemies one to another.

1. The Journey to Herod's Palace

Herod's palace was probably situated on the hill Bezetha, to the north of the official dwelling of the Roman governor, and not far distant from it. In spite of the short distance this journey was a very bitter and painful one for our Saviour, for two reasons.

First, it was very humiliating for Him to be treated thus by Pilate. It was only from policy and cowardice that the latter shifted the affair on to Herod's shoulders. He could pass it on to him, according to the law, but was not bound to do so. But he saw plainly enough that he could not in justice condemn our Lord, and on the other hand he did not wish to irritate the already exasperated Jews. So the rightful authority would not hold itself responsible for our Lord, and washed its hands of Him. Besides, the present case afforded Pilate a good opportunity of paying Herod a mark of attention and effecting a reconciliation with him (for they had quarreled about several matters; amongst others, possibly, on account of the Galileans whom Pilate had had massacred in the Temple; Luke 13:1). Also Herod happened to be in Jerusalem at the time (Luke 23:7, 8). It was humiliating for our Saviour to have to appear before this prince. He had always shunned him, had spoken of him in no flattering terms, and had also been persecuted by him (Luke 13:31, 32; Mark 8:15). And now He had to go to him, and His fate lay in his hands.

Secondly, the journey was rendered very bitter to Him by the ill-usage He had to submit to on the way. This reference of the matter to Herod was very annoying for the Jews, first on account of the delay and loss of time it entailed; secondly of the danger of a demonstration in favor of Jesus on the part of His followers and the people; and lastly of the humiliation of having to go round the town begging for a final condemnation, especially at the hands of Herod, whom they so detested. We can hardly doubt that they made our Saviour pay dearly for their vexation, by all sorts of outrages and ill-treatment.

2. THE MEETING WITH HEROD

In order to gain a correct idea of this encounter we must first consider the attendant circumstances. In the first place, Herod was an effeminate and notorious voluptuary, sufficiently judged and branded by public opinion (Luke 3:19; Matt. 11:8). Further, he was a frivolous, shallow man, with a desire to witness marvels and wonders (Luke 23:8); and lastly, he was vain and, as a "fallen star," very eager to regain the prestige of his person and house. This reference of the affair to him was a capital opportunity of gratifying all his passions. He received a mark of distinction from the Roman governor, was publicly acknowledged by him and chosen as judge in a celebrated case. The Great Council and the priesthood appeared before him with their petitions and accusations against our Saviour (Luke 23:10); the latter Himself, Whom he had long wished to see, and of Whom he had heard so much, was now in his power; thus he received public recognition and honor from all sides. And if only our Saviour too would acknowledge and honor him in His own way, this day would be the most glorious of Herod's life. This was what made him so glad to see and receive our Lord (Luke 23:8). He would, we may be sure, have mustered all his military retinue for the occasion.

And how did this meeting pass in reality? How did our Saviour behave? His exterior was by no means attractive to an effeminate man like Herod, nor was it calculated to inspire him with respect; on the contrary, He presented a disfigured and pitiable appearance. Herod's curiosity and love of the marvelous found just as little gratification. For others our Saviour was wont to have words of instruction, friendly advances, and even miracles; for Herod and his innumerable questions He has no answer, not a word (Luke 23:9). Neither was his vanity to receive the least satisfaction; our Lord does not vouchsafe him the slightest acknowledgment, not a word of petition, not even a glance. Herod was as nothing to Him. By this persistent silence and striking reserve He censures and exposes him, and condemns him before all the people and his own courtiers.

The effect of this behavior was, first, to convince Herod that there was no truth in all the charges brought by the priesthood against our Saviour of aspiring to the monarchy; but it served also to excite him to exasperation and anger at the slight put upon him by our Lord. So he derided and mocked Him with all his court, ridiculed His alleged royal and Messianic pretensions by having a white garment put upon Him, such as was worn by princes, generals and priests, and finally sent Him back to Pilate (Luke 23:11). Thus Herod too gained his end: he flattered Pilate and returned his compliment by sending our Saviour back to him; he satisfied the Jews to some extent at least by the disgrace and humiliation he inflicted upon Jesus; and did himself the greatest service of all by getting rid of the disagreeable business. Well indeed did he deserve the name of "fox." In this way Pilate and Herod became friends (Luke 23:12).

3. SIGNIFICATION OF THE MYSTERY

By this mystery is signified the mocking of the kingship of Jesus by earthly royalty, in the person of Herod. This also was to take place. His universal monarchy had to be bought at the price of being mocked at on all sides. But Herod himself showed by this how unworthy he was of his kingly office.

Our Saviour on the contrary displays the full majesty of true royalty in every sense of the word, by the nobility of His truly royal spirit. In the first place, He will not throw Himself away, nor degrade His wisdom and power to the level of conjuring tricks. Herod had become His lawful judge by Pilate's act, it is true, but then he did not subject Him to any proper judicial cross-examination. He simply played with Him and treated Him as a charlatan; and our Saviour had not come into the world to provide amusement and entertainment at Court. Besides, it was our Lord's will to die by the hands of the Gentiles and thus redeem us.

If He had condescended to do anything to please Herod, the latter might have kept Him in his retinue. But we were dearer to our Saviour than was the friendship of kings. Lastly, He wished to instruct us and set us an example of how we should behave in our intercourse with the great ones of the world. If we will not and cannot treat them as for good reasons He did here, at least we must not sacrifice human, Christian and priestly dignity and simplicity. This lesson is very necessary for us, because our vanity and natural inclination very easily lead us into flattery, untruthfulness, and parade of our wisdom and greatness, in order to curry favor with the world and appear to be on a par with it, to some extent at least. And yet, what is the world? May we respect and love it, this world that our Saviour rejects and does not vouchsafe to look at? May we be the adherents of that world which ill-uses our Saviour, and treats Him as a fool? And shall we have part and lot with Jesus, if we do? This meeting of Jesus and the world shows what the latter is. It smiles upon and flatters us as long as we flatter and smile at it, and in order that we may do so. But if we do not, we have nothing but the most savage and venomous fury to look for from it. For it seeks itself alone in all things (Gal. 1:1; James 4:4). We do well to be on our guard against its seductions and its deceptive promises.

Second Appearance before Pilate. Barabbas. Pilate Washes His Hands

Matt. 27:15. Now upon the solemn day the governor was accustomed to release to the people one prisoner, whom they would;—16. And he had then a notorious prisoner, that was called Barabbas.—17. They therefore being gathered together, Pilate said: "Whom will you that I release to you: Barabbas, or Jesus that is called Christ?"—18. For he knew that for envy they had delivered him.—19. And as he was sitting in the place of judgment, his wife sent to him, saying: "Have thou nothing to do with that just man; for I have suffered many things this day in a dream because of him."—20. But the chief priests and ancients persuaded the people that they should ask Barabbas, and make Jesus away.—21. And the governor answering, said to them: "Whether will you of the two to be released unto you?" But they said: "Barabbas."—22. Pilate saith to them: "What shall I do then with Jesus that is called Christ?"—23. They say all: "Let him be crucified." The governor said to them: "Why, what evil hath he done?" But they cried out the more, saying: "Let him be crucified."—24. And Pilate seeing that he prevailed nothing, but that rather a tumult was made; taking water washed his hands before the people, saying: "I am innocent of the blood of this just man; look you to it."—25. And the whole people answering, said: "His blood be upon us, and upon our children."

Mark 15:6. Now on the festival day he was wont to release unto them one of the prisoners, whomsoever they demanded.—7. And there was one called Barabbas, who was put in prison with some seditious men, who in the sedition had committed murder.—8. And when the multitude was come up, they began to desire that he would do as he had ever done unto them.—9. And Pilate answered them, and said: "Will you that I release to you the king of the Jews?"—10. For he knew that the chief priests had delivered him up out of envy.—11. But the chief priests moved the people, that he should rather release Barabbas to them.—12. And Pilate again answering saith to them: "What will you then that I do to the king of the Jews?" —13. But they again cried out: "Crucify him."—14. And Pilate saith to them: "Why, what evil hath he done?" But they cried out the more: "Crucify him."

LUKE 23:13. And Pilate calling together the chief priests, and the magistrates, and the people,—14. Said to them: "You have presented unto me this man, as one that preverteth the people, and behold I having examined him before you, find no cause in this man in those things wherein you accuse him.—15. No, nor Herod neither; for I sent you to him, and behold, nothing worthy of death is done to him.—16. I will chastise him therefore and release him."—17. Now of necessity he was to release unto them one upon the feast day.—18. But the whole multitude together cried out, saying: "Away with this man, and release unto us Barabbas,"— 19. Who for a certain sedition made in the city, and for a murder, was cast into prison.—20. And Pilate again spoke to them, desiring to release Jesus.—21. But they cried again, saying: "Crucify him, crucify him."—22. And he said to them the third time: "Why, what evil hath this man done? I find no cause of death in him; I will chastise him therefore, and let him go."—23. But they were instant with loud voices requiring that he might be crucified; and their voices prevailed.

JOHN 18:39. "But you have a custom that I should release one unto you at the Pasch; will you therefore that I release unto you the king of the Jews?"—40. Then cried they all again, saying: "Not this man, but Barabbas." Now Barabbas was a robber.

Thus our Saviour came back from Herod to Pilate, and the latter was compelled to take up the matter again. The sequel consisted of efforts on his part to save Jesus, and counter-efforts of the Jews to compass His Death.

1. PILATE'S EFFORTS TO SAVE OUR LORD

Pilate made several attempts to thwart the Jews' purpose of having our Saviour sentenced to death. He first called all the people together, with the intention of proclaiming the Paschal amnesty (Luke 23:13, 18; Matt. 27:17, 25). On this he formed his plan, since he knew it was only the chief priests, and not the people, who were hostile to our Lord (Matt. 27:18). He hoped that the latter would out-vote the chief priests and their party. Secondly, he immediately declared again in the most solemn manner, in presence of all the people, that our Saviour was innocent of all the charges brought against Him, and that even Herod had found "nothing worthy of death" in Him (Luke 23:14, 15). Nevertheless, in order to meet their wishes to some extent, he was ready to make the concession of having Him scourged before he set Him free (Luke 23:16). In order to gain his end, Pilate thirdly made use of the customary Paschal ceremony of extending pardon to a condemned criminal. The Jews had been wont to grant some criminal his life at the Feast of the Pasch, in memory of the nation's deliverance out of Egypt, and the Romans had allowed them to retain the custom. So Pilate, with the intention of freeing our Saviour, purposely selected a criminal of the very worst repute, Barabbas, a revolutionary, robber and murderer (John 18:40; Mark 15:7; Luke 23:19), and probably had him brought out and set beside Jesus, offering the people their choice between the two. At the same time, in order to work upon the feelings of the crowd, he laid stress upon the excellence and dignity of our Saviour as compared with Barabbas: "Whom will you. . . . Barabbas, or the king of the Jews (Mark 15:9; John 18:39), that is called Christ?" (Matt. 27:17.) Fourthly, as the people, contrary to his expectation, still demand the release of Barabbas, Pilate makes another attempt (Luke 23:20), and tries to put them into a dilemma by asking what in that case he should do with Jesus (Matt. 27:22; Mark 15:12). Upon their answering shout that he should have Him crucified, he declared the innocence of Jesus for the third time, and repeated his offer to have Him scourged (Luke 23:22; Mark 15:14; Matt. 27:23). Fifthly and lastly, as they repeated their mad shouts of "Crucify Him" (Matt. 27:23; Mark 15:14), Pilate endeavored to make a greater impression upon them by even going through the ceremony of washing his hands, and saying: "I am innocent of the blood of this just man; look you to it" (Matt. 27:24).

And what induced Pilate to make all these efforts? In the first place, his conviction of the innocence of Jesus. He saw plainly enough that it was nothing but envy and hatred that had prompted the chief priests to deliver Him up (Matt. 27:18; Mark 15:10). A second motive may have been a secret fear and dread of the supernatural and of the air of mystery that seemed to hover about our Saviour and mark Him as belonging to a higher sphere; for the Gentiles were commonly very superstitious. Lastly, he may have been influenced by the message sent to him by his wife during the trial, to beware and have nothing to do with that just man, for she had had to suffer a great deal on his account during the night (Mark 27:19). Since the time of Augustus the law forbidding governors to take their wives into the provinces with them had fallen into abeyance. Many of the Roman ladies showed a great predilection for Judaism, and this may have been the case with Pilate's wife. Probably she had heard of Jesus before; and it is quite possible that the dream was a divine inspiration, sent as a warning to Pilate.

2. FRUSTRATION OF THESE ATTEMPTS TO SAVE JESUS

There were two reasons for the miserable failure of all these efforts on Pilate's part.

The Jews were the first cause; above all, the stubbornness with which they kept to their plan. They rejected Pilate's conciliatory offer to scourge our Saviour, although he twice repeated it (Luke 23:16, 22), and demanded that Barabbas should be set free (Luke 23:18; Matt. 27:21) and our Saviour put to death (Matt. 27:23; Mark 15:13; Luke 23:21). Further, there was the chief priests' activity and skill in exciting the passions of the mob. It was they who instigated the people to demand the release of Barabbas and the crucifixion of Jesus (Matt. 27:20; Mark 15:11). Lastly, there was the exasperation and uproar of the multitude and the threatening attitude assumed by the chief priests and the excited rabble, which made the place a perfect Babel. Time after time the shouts rang out: "Away with Him!" (Luke 23:18.) "Crucify Him!" (Luke 23:21; Mark 15:14; Matt. 27:23.) By degrees a veritable tumult ensued (Matt. 27:24), and all the people cried like madmen, with ever rising fury, that Pilate should have our Lord crucified (Luke 23:23).

But as far as Pilate was concerned, the frustration of his effort to release Jesus was due to his uncertain mode of action. He had no fixed plan, and so he falls back upon one expedient after another, just as they chance to present themselves. It was secondly due to his inconsistency; he declares the innocence of Jesus and orders Him to be scourged in the same breath (Luke 23:22); and thirdly, to his weakness. He had nothing but words, declarations of innocence, negotiations; but no deeds, or at least only weak, half-hearted ones, such as the ceremony of washing his hands. This ceremony sometimes signifies innocence and immunity from an alleged crime, sometimes cleansing from a real crime (Deut. 21:6); but it can never have the sense of shaking off the responsibility of an act that one regards as unjust and yet voluntarily commits, as Pilate did here, and as his words sufficiently express (Matt. 27:24). But the Jews did not trouble themselves about that at this exciting moment. The last cause was the wretched policy which sacrifices the life of an innocent man, though fully perceiving his innocence, from considerations of State and fear of an insurrection, and tries to exculpate itself by protesting its freedom from guilt. If Pilate had at once shown sternness and threatened the rabble with the sword, as he had often done before and as the Romans were accustomed to do, he would have come off victor. As it is, he retreats step by step before the systematic and pertinacious attack of the Jews, and already gives a virtual consent to the crucifixion (Luke 23:16, 22), although he does not yet pronounce the sentence in due judicial form, but orders the scourging first, in the hope of satisfying the Jews and finally saving our Saviour's life.

3. SUFFERINGS THAT THESE EFFORTS OF PILATE AND THE JEWS CAUSED OUR SAVIOUR

These sufferings consist in slights, humiliations and wrongs, which are showered upon our Lord from all sides.

From Pilate He has to suffer this humiliating injustice, that the legal authority, the representative of justice, instead of espousing His cause and protecting Him, gradually deserts Him for reasons of policy, and out of weakness. However, a most outrageous injustice and humiliation is offered to our Lord by Pilate when he places Him before the people, side by side with Barabbas and on a par with him, and leaves them to choose whom they will, with the words: "Whom will you that I release to you, Barabbas or Jesus?" (Matt. 27:16, 17.) To realize how deep a degradation this was for our Lord we must consider Who He was and who Barabbas; by whom He is thus insulted and exposed, viz. by Pilate himself, with the intention of saving His life at the cost of His honor; before whom this indignity is put upon Him, in presence of all the people; and lastly, what the result of this degrading attempt to save Him is, that He is rejected and Barabbas preferred to Him. What a degradation of His innocence, His merits, His Person and dignity! How humiliated our Saviour must have seemed as He stood there beside Barabbas, before the whole crowd! He loses His cause against a robber and murderer.

From the people our Saviour has to suffer all that can wound and grieve the heart. They not only prefer Barabbas to Him, but demand that He shall be put to death, and in the most painful and shameful way, by crucifixion; and as Pilate declares Him innocent and solemnly repudiates all responsibility for His execution, they cry with one accord: "His blood be upon us, and upon our children" (Matt. 27:25). How much is contained in this act, and in these words! In the first place, the most revolting ingratitude. He had done no one any harm. How many of those who joined in this shout had He healed, instructed, and comforted! With how much reason and truth might He have cried to them: "O My people! What have I done to thee, that thou coverest Me thus with opprobrium and demandest My death?" Secondly, it was the most crying injustice. Most of the people certainly did not know the truth of the matter. They simply let the chief priests dictate the sentence to them. Thirdly, these shouts expressed a terrible hate, that could rest satisfied with nothing short of the disgrace—nay, even the blood—of the hated man. Lastly, they showed an indescribable contempt for our Saviour. Pilate, heathen as he is, calls their attention to the responsibility they will incur by the shedding of innocent blood, the crime they are committing upon a human life. But they cry: "His blood be upon us!" The words, "Thy blood be upon thee," are those with which the judge casts the responsibility for the execution upon the condemned criminal's own head; and this is the cry of the Jews. They are quite ready to answer for the blood of the Nazarene; they take all the consequences upon themselves and their children, and are sure they will not find them too heavy to bear. In their eyes our Lord is no more than the vermin that one treads under foot without compunction. Yes, He is a criminal, and they are sanctifying themselves by shedding His blood, and meriting God's blessing instead of punishment. How terrible is the position of our Saviour now! All His friends are absent and powerless to help Him, the authorities do not protect Him, and His enemies have everything their own way; He is hated, despised and rejected by the whole nation.

From this mystery we may learn what sin is. What Pilate proposed to the people has a counterpart in every sin that is committed. It is a choice between God and a creature. Secondly, we may learn the value of policy and half-measures; their result is to deliver Christ over to be scourged and crucified. Thirdly, this mystery clearly shows what popularity and favor with men are worth. Today the cry is "Hosanna"; tomorrow, "Crucify Him." Nothing is more fickle and uncertain. Lastly, we learn what slights and humiliation really are. Whatever may befall us in this way, it can never be compared with what our Saviour experienced.

The Scourging

John 19:1. Then therefore Pilate took Jesus, and scourged him.

Mark 15:15. And so Pilate being willing to satisfy the people, released to them Barabbas, and delivered up Jesus, when he had scourged him, to be crucified.

Matt. 27:26. Then he released to them Barabbas; and having scourged Jesus delivered him unto them to be crucified.

1. THE PUNISHMENT OF SCOURGING

Generally speaking, the punishment of scourging is an exceedingly severe and terrible one. It is one of the chief mysteries in the Passion of Christ, and therefore our Saviour usually mentions it when predicting His sufferings (Matt. 20:19; Mark 10:34; Luke 18:33).

This punishment was severe and terrible, first, on account of the degradation and ignominy of it. Thoroughly low, bad men—robbers, murderers, slaves—and brute beasts are scourged. With the former the whip has to make up for the deficiencies of conscience, with the latter for the lack of reason. Whoever had once been touched by the lash was for ever branded, degraded and ruined. That was why St. Paul did not suffer himself to be scourged by the Romans (Acts 22:25). The punishment was also degrading on account of the denudation, although the delinquent was usually stripped only to the waist. Secondly, the scourging was terrible on account of the pain and torture it inflicted. Elm sticks or rods were used for the purpose (Acts 16:22; II Cor. 11:25), or else scourges plaited of strips of leather, to which little hooks, claws, stars, and pieces of bone or wood were often attached. These last were the worst. The classical expressions for the effects of these various kinds of scourging answer to the English terms: striking, lashing (literally "cutting"), lacerating, bruising, and crushing. As regards its object, scourging was employed either as a simple corrective and an independent form of punishment (Luke 23:16, 22); as an integral part of the penalty of crucifixion (forming, as it were, the introduction and terrible preface to it); or sometimes as a torture, for the purpose of extorting a confession. The scourging of our Saviour may be taken either in the first or in the second sense. When scourging was employed as a torture, no particular duration was prescribed; the roughest ill-usage was not excluded, but was regarded as a means to an end. Except in this case, however, the number of stripes given might not exceed forty (Deut. 25:3). With the Romans sixty-six were allowed. From the effects of even this limited number of stripes many died or remained broken in health for the rest of their lives. The scourging might be either private or public. In this case it seems to have been inflicted in the forum (Matt. 27:27; Mark 15:16). The pillar to which the culprit was bound was either half the height of an ordinary man, so that he had to receive his stripes with bent back (Deut. 25:2), or else so high that the hands of the delinquent could be drawn up and fastened to it in such a manner as only to allow his toes to touch the ground. The scourging was generally performed by four soldiers. All this shows that it was an excruciatingly painful punishment.

In our Saviour's case, too, there were other circumstances that tended to increase the torment. First, the crying injustice of the punishment made it all the more bitter. Secondly, Pilate's object in having our Lord scourged was to inspire the Jews with pity for Him; that was why he separated the scourging from the crucifixion, and had it inflicted in the forum, before his palace. And with this same motive he may perhaps have had it executed with unusual severity and even cruelty, so that it assumed the barbarity and duration of a torture. Lastly, there was the extraordinary tenderness and delicate constitution of our Saviour's body. The intensity of pain certainly depends greatly on the physique of the sufferer, and whether his life, habits and occupation have braced and hardened his body against the sensation of pain or not.

2. THE SCOURGING ITSELF

One can well imagine with what emotions of natural fear and dread our Saviour took His stand at the terrible pillar, and what a torture even the partial stripping was for His sense of modesty. His wrists were bound with cords and His body was drawn up and made fast, so that His face was turned to the pillar. And now the strokes of the rods or scourges hiss through the air and fall with terrible force upon His back and shoulders. The flesh swells up and becomes inflamed; red and brown weals appear. The skin breaks, at first in little cracks, then little furrows open out, ever deeper and longer; the flesh parts asunder and the blows fall upon the very bones. The blood wells forth, trickles down in little streams, and then flows in torrents, until the whole body is bathed in it and it is sprinkled upon the dirty market-place and forms pools around the pillar. And the pain! At first dull and aching, then sharp and stinging as fire and salt, it penetrates our Lord's whole body, rages in the limbs, pierces its way to the very soul, and forces tears from His eyes and gentle moans and sighs from His lips. Oh, how His Heart must have cried to heaven, how pleadingly His eyes must have gazed up to His Father there! But it goes on: blows, wounds, blood, and burning pain, until the poor Victim threatens to perish under the torture.

At last they loose Him from the pillar, and probably He sank prostrate to the ground beside it. See how He lies there in His blood, like a crushed and trodden worm! How pitiable is His condition, with the hard ground for His bed, without help, relief or loving care! He must painfully gather up His own clothing, and wrap it round His lacerated shoulders. No one moves a hand to help Him. Where, one may well ask, were all those who had seen Him, honored, loved and followed Him in better days, all upon whom He had bestowed health, comfort and life? Where are Lazarus, Peter, Magdalen, John? Is there then no balm, no oil nor linen for His wounds, in the land that flows with oil and balsam? No hand to help Him, no eye to compassionate Him? How many saw Him and knew Him well, but were ashamed to own it; and how many even mocked at Him in His pain! How completely the prophecies have been fulfilled! Truly, "the wicked have wrought upon my back: they have lengthened their inquiry" (Ps. 128:3).[1] "There is no beauty in Him, nor comeliness. . . ." He is "despised, and the most abject of men, a Man of sorrows . . . and His look was as it were hidden and despised. . . . Surely He hath borne our infirmities and carried our sorrows; and we have thought Him as it were a leper, and as one struck by God and afflicted" (Isa. 53:1–4).

3. OUR SAVIOUR'S DISPOSITIONS AND INTENTIONS IN SUFFERING THIS SCOURGING

Our Saviour endured this terrible suffering with the holiest dispositions. He was not so much occupied with His exterior pain that He did not accompany it with the loftiest acts of virtue. He bore the scourging with heavenly patience, constantly raising His

[1] Or, as the Hebrew text of the Psalm has it: "The plowmen have plowed upon my back and made long furrows." (Translator's Note.)

Heart to God; He suffered with admirable love for all men, even for His torturers, for Pilate and the Jews.

It is not difficult to see what His intentions were in enduring this frightful suffering. Scourging is chiefly a physical pain, a suffering of the sense of touch. Who does not perceive that His principal intention here was to take upon Himself the punishment due to the sins of the flesh and to satisfy for them? It was for such sins that the law prescribed the punishment of stripes (Lev. 19:20). Let whoever has indulged in this sin look at our scourged and lacerated Saviour and His bleeding wounds, and earnestly ask himself why our Lord underwent this intolerable physical agony, and how much pain the scourges inflicted upon Him. But let no one lose courage and fall into despair at the sight of this terrible suffering. There is superabundance of satisfaction and grace for amendment here, and He offers it to us with touching love.

Further, our Saviour wished by this suffering to set us an example of how we should treat our body and use it in God's service. Should this service of His supreme majesty cost us our physical beauty, health and strength, then let us see how our Saviour sacrifices His Body and all its faculties. To what rough and violent ill-usage He submits it! What terrible instruments lacerate it! And yet how pure, noble and beautiful this Body was, and of what high birth; with what miraculous powers was it gifted! Our bodies cannot be compared to it in any of these respects. So let us make of them a pleasing and holy sacrifice to God, by laboring and suffering till death.

Our Lord Is Mocked and Crowned with Thorns

Matt. 27:27. Then the soldiers of the governor taking Jesus into the hall, gathered together unto him the whole band;—28. And stripping him, they put a scarlet cloak about him,—29. And platting a crown of thorns, they put it upon his head, and a reed in his right hand. And bowing the knee before him, they mocked him, saying: "Hail, king of the Jews."—30. And spitting upon him, they took the reed, and struck his head.

Mark 15:16. And the soldiers led him away into the court of the palace, and they call together the whole band;—17. And they clothe him with purple, and platting a crown of thorns, they put it upon him.—18. And they began to salute him: "Hail, king of the Jews."—19. And they struck his head with a reed; and they did spit on him, and bowing their knees, they adored him.

John 19:2. And the soldiers platting a crown of thorns, put it upon his head; and they put on him a purple garment.—3. And they came to him, and said: "Hail, king of the Jews"; and they gave him blows.

1. OCCASION AND CIRCUMSTANCES OF THE CROWNING WITH THORNS

After the scourging the soldiers brought our Saviour into the court of the Praetorium, either the yard outside the guard-house, or the inner court-yard of the governor's palace (Mark 15:16; Matt. 27:27), there to be kept in custody until final sentence could be pronounced. They whiled away this interval (either from pure wantonness or at Pilate's instigation and with his permission) by making our Saviour the butt of a brutal pastime. This exactly fell in with Pilate's object of satisfying the Jews to a certain extent and thus saving His life. The soldiers had evidently caught up the idea of this cruel jest from Herod and the Jews, who had already derided our Saviour's kingship. So now they are going to do the same by making a mock king of Him.

The first thing that made this rude pastime so inexpressibly painful was its injustice and the utter want of authorization for such an outrage. It was contrary to all the rules of law. The person of an accused man must be treated as sacred and protected against illegal ill-usage. "*Res sacra reus*" were the words of the judicial regulation, and now the myrmidons of the law permit themselves such an arbitrary act of wantonness against our Saviour before the very eyes of the governor, and perhaps even at his instigation. Secondly, one can form an idea of the brutality of the scene, when one considers who are its instruments and agents: rough soldiers, accustomed to bloody work, willing tools of despotism, and full of contempt for foreign nations, especially for the Jews. Our Lord is completely at their mercy, and they can wreak their wanton will upon Him. They call together the whole band of armed men on duty (Matt. 27:27; Mark 15:16), and what was lacking to the cruel ingenuity of one was supplied by another. The jests of such a class of men are never wont to be of the most delicate and refined order. Lastly, the object of their buffoonery is no other than our Saviour, Who is so gentle, pure and modest, of high birth and peaceful occupation, so different in every way from these rough soldiers. But this circumstance only irritated them and increased their wantonness. This man, people said, had pretended to be a king, and wanted to drive away the Romans. So they intended to teach him a lesson. And our Saviour had just been scourged, and was still quivering in every limb with the pain. How intolerably must all this have increased His suffering!

2. HOW THE MOCKING WAS CARRIED OUT

The idea of the coarse jest, then, was a ridiculous mimicry of the ceremony of paying homage to a king.

The first thing necessary for such a solemn act of fealty was the purple, the distinguishing mark of earthly royalty. Herod had had our Saviour vested in a white robe, because he wished to mock at His spiritual, Messianic pretensions. But the soldiers are only thinking of a secular and military potentate, and therefore a purple mantle such as emperors and generals wore must be procured. But they do not go to Tyre or Sidon for it. A ragged soldier's cloak was good enough for their purpose. So they tore the clothes from His bleeding shoulders, and covered Him with the mantle (Matt. 27:28; Mark 15:17; John 19:2). The broken base of a pillar, the "*columna improperiorum*" that is still shown in the Church of the Holy Sepulcher, probably served for a throne, and they made our Lord sit down upon it. Then they put a reed in His bound hands to represent a scepter (Matt. 27:29; Mark 15:19). The crown was not the diadem of Melchom that His forefather David had worn; it was not made of gold and precious stones, not even of iron, nor yet woven of olive-twigs and flowers; no, a perfectly devilish impulse prompted them to twine it of tendrils set with long, sharp thorns (Matt. 27:29; Mark 15:17; John 19:2). And this terrible crown they placed upon our Saviour's head. The royal insignia being thus provided, the homage began. They bowed the knee before Him (Matt. 27:29; Mark 15:19) and did reverence to Him, hailed Him as king (Matt. 27:29; Mark 15:18), all in mockery and with ridiculous gestures (Matt. 27:31; Mark 15:20; John 19:3). Then they sprang to their feet, struck Him, spat upon Him, and struck His head with the mock-scepter so that the thorns wounded Him and pierced His head (Matt. 27:30; Mark 15:29; John 19:3); pushed Him perhaps from His throne, amid shouts of mocking laughter; derided Him in every imaginable way, and vented all their wanton cruelty upon Him.

What a scene, what a sight! There our Saviour sits, bowed with pain, the picture of utter wretchedness, His beautiful forehead half-concealed and pressed upon by the crown of thorns, His hair tangled and caught in its twists, His Sacred Face almost hidden by it. The blood trickles from all sides of His head, runs in little rivulets over His temples and neck, suffuses His eyes, reddens His shoulders, and makes His hair hang together in matted locks. How many sharp thorns are buried in His temples, those most sensitive parts of the body! And every jerk, every push, every movement drives them deeper, and sends a burning throb of smarting pain through body and soul. What agony, what ignominy! And Who sits there among these inhuman barbarians, and upon Whom are such pain and contumely showered? Truly it is a greater than Solomon, the favored of God, in all his wisdom and glory; greater than the unapproachable majesty of Assuerus; greater than David clad in his battle array; it is the Living God, Who at this very moment wields His scepter over myriads of radiant angel-hosts. They lie at His feet waiting for a sign, and He sits here in shame and pain, in the power of a miserable rabble, by whom He is "filled with reproaches" (Lam. 3:30). He is the Messias, the long-expected of this nation; and behold, thus His people treat Him on the day when He stretches out His hand to receive a pledge of love and homage from them. An unnatural mother, in truth, has the synagogue, His Bride, become to Him. She crowns Him with the diadem of shame and suffering, and the Promised Land of His fathers has but thorns and thistles for Him.

3. SIGNIFICATION OF THIS MOCKING AND CROWNING WITH THORNS

This mystery is the mocking of Christ's royalty by the Gentiles, by the nation that then ruled the world. It was enacted in the Roman praetorium, by Roman soldiers, before the eyes (and perhaps at the instigation) of the Roman governor. By this mocking our Saviour gains the sovereignty of the world. This crown of thorns shall become a crown of glory; this miserable reed, the iron staff with which in due time He will shatter thrones and kingdoms. The jeering soldiers will make way for the kings and nations of the earth who will come to adore Him. Through this mocking the Roman world-empire has fallen to His heritage.

And the thorn-crowned Saviour is also the atoning Victim for the sins of pride and for the lust of power that comes over all Adam's children at times, to their torment; the Victim for the unjust strife for honor and authority; for all injury done to the honor and influence of others; for all impatience under scorn and derision; for all insult and resistance to rightful authority, and especially against the majesty of the Church. How bitterly our Saviour had to suffer for all this!

And He also wished to teach us how deeply unjust derision wounds. Sneers and irony are thorns with which we torture our neighbor. But our Lord's example in this mystery also teaches us how we must bear such wrongs.

Last Stage of the Proceedings under Pilate

John 19:4. Pilate therefore went forth again, and saith to them: "Behold, I bring him forth unto you, that you may know that I find no cause in him."—5. (Jesus therefore came forth bearing the crown of thorns and the purple garment.) And he saith to them: "Behold the Man!"—6. When the chief priests therefore and the servants had seen him, they cried out, saying: "Crucify him, crucify him." Pilate saith to them: "Take him you, and crucify him; for I find no cause in him." —7. The Jews answered him: "We have a law, and according to the law he ought to die, because he made himself the Son of God."—8. When Pilate therefore had heard this saying, he feared the more.—9. And he entered into the hall again; and he said to Jesus: "Whence art thou?" But Jesus gave him no answer.—10. Pilate therefore saith to him: "Speakest thou not to me? Knowest thou not that I have power to crucify thee, and I have power to release thee?"—11. Jesus answered: "Thou shouldst not have any power against me, unless it were given thee from above. Therefore he that hath delivered me to thee, hath the greater sin."— 12. And from thenceforth Pilate sought to release him. But the Jews cried out, saying: "If thou release this man, thou art not Caesar's friend; for whosoever maketh himself a king, speaketh against Caesar."

The last proceedings, by which our Lord's condemnation was finally brought about, fall naturally into three separate scenes, each showing a renewed attempt on Pilate's part to save Him and a counter-effort of the Jews to frustrate it.

1. ECCE HOMO!

The first scene opens with Pilate's leading our Saviour, scourged, crowned with thorns and clad in the purple garment, to some place where He could be seen by the people. Pilate begins with a new declaration of the innocence of Jesus, and ratifies his former judgment (John 19:4). At the same time he seeks to excite the compassion of the people by pointing to our Saviour, Who stands there in such a pitiable plight, ruined in health and honor, with the touching words: "Behold the Man!" (John 19:5), i.e. Behold, what a man! or: Look at the poor man! Even he, Pilate himself, who, as a Roman, was used to similar sights in the amphitheater, seems touched, and appeals to the human instinct of the Jews, if they have a spark of it left in them. And indeed, the people too seem to have been touched and remained silent; for we are only told that the chief priests and the servants shouted: "Crucify Him, crucify Him!" (John 19:6.)

But Pilate at once rejected this demand, with the declaration that Jesus was innocent and he could not crucify Him; but he was willing to permit them to do so themselves, on their own responsibility. But our Lord's foes would not have this on any account, perhaps for fear of the people. Pilate must condemn Him and have Him crucified. So, in their embarrassment, they dropped the original charge, that Jesus set up to be the Christ and a king (Luke 23:2), and cried out that they had a law and according to this law He must die, because He made Himself out to be the Son of God (John 19:7).

This was taking the question into a province unfamiliar to Pilate. They appealed to the judgment of the Great Council and to the law that decreed death for blasphemous presumption (Lev. 24:16; Deut. 18:20). Pilate was in a great dilemma on hearing this, and began to fear this mysterious Being (John 19:8). Superstition and unbelief are often found together. The Romans, from motives of policy, made a practice of leaving the conquered races their own customs and laws; but since Pilate had once taken the matter in hand, and the Jews made a new accusation based upon their own law, he was bound to follow them thither also and consent to a new examination.

2. SECOND EXAMINATION

The second scene is the examination which the new turn in the impeachment of our Saviour compelled Pilate to make. He did this in the judgment-hall, and questioned Him concerning His origin, who He really was (John 19:9).

Our Saviour gives him no answer (John 19:9). He remains silent, and rightly. Obviously He could not deny His Divinity. But He could not admit it either, because Pilate would not have understood it nor, probably, have acted up to the recognized truth if he had done so; and perhaps our Saviour's silence may also have been intended as a punishment, because he would not hear truth in the former examination (John 18:38). Besides, Pilate already knew enough from the previous proceedings; he was convinced of our Lord's innocence.

Irritated by the silence of Jesus and perhaps also by the embarrassment in which he found himself, Pilate said to our Lord: "Speakest Thou not to me? Knowest Thou not that I have power to crucify Thee, and I have power to release Thee?" (John 19:10.)

He tries to extort an answer by threatening Him with his arbitrary power and holding out the prospect of his good will.

Our Saviour does not answer the question concerning His origin; He simply replies to Pilate's assertion of his power. In this reply He does two things. He recognizes Pilate's power, but warns him against abusing it, by referring to a higher Authority from Whom he derives it and to Whom he will one day have to answer for the use he has made of it. This abuse of his power would be a sin; a greater one in the case of the Jews, certainly, because they voluntarily and maliciously delivered Jesus up to be punished as a criminal, and thus caused His Death; whilst Pilate did so only under duress. Nevertheless, it would still be a sin if he condemned Him (John 19:11). The correctness of the answer, the composure, gentleness and plain-speaking of Jesus, and the majesty of the innocence and justice that shone forth in His reply, filled Pilate with fear and dread, and he tried now to set our Lord free at any cost (John 19:12).

3. LAST DECISIVE WORDS

The third scene probably opened with a new declaration of our Saviour's innocence on the part of Pilate, whom the Jews in response at once attack on a weak point. They too threaten him with a higher judge, and hint that they will accuse him to the Emperor of favoring and promoting high treason, if he does not condemn Jesus, since the latter sets up to be a king and is an enemy of Caesar. "If thou release this man, thou art not Caesar's friend (loyal subject); for whosoever maketh himself a king, speaketh against Caesar" (John 19:12). As a matter of fact no more fatal accusation could be brought against a man under Tiberius than that of high treason. Judaea was a remote province, very wavering in its allegiance, and Pilate had repeatedly been accused to the Emperor of having given cause for discontent and disturbance. And if the Jews themselves were now to impeach him of high treason, Tiberius would certainly think it must be true. This had its effect upon Pilate. He gave up all attempt to set Jesus free, and proceeded to pronounce His condemnation.

Thus the Jews had carried their point, but by dint of such craftiness, stubbornness and dishonesty, and with such fierce hatred, that no human and right-feeling heart can fail to be struck with horror and astonishment that such a thing could be possible.

It was truly a terrible moment and a heart-rending spectacle, when the Son of God, overcome with weakness, the reed-scepter in His fettered hands, clad in the old red mantle that barely sufficed to cover His torn and bleeding body, His head crowned with a wreath of thorns and streaming with blood, appeared on the terrace, racked with pain, and looked at His people from under the dreadful crown of thorns with boundless grief, gentleness and forgiving love, as though to beg for His poor life at the price of such suffering and degradation. And it was not granted Him. After a moment of dead silence, during which perhaps the pricks of conscience may have awakened a gentler feeling in many a heart, the chief priests and their most intimate adherents vociferated still more fiercely, as though startled at the terrible picture of their guilt as reflected in our Lord's appearance: "Away with Him, crucify Him!" And in an instant they had carried the entire crowd with them, so that the whole market-place resounded with the furious shout: "Crucify Him!" Such is the power of party sway. It is the worst thing that can befall a nation, to get into the hands of unprincipled and infatuated leaders. This party spirit, together with the indomitable pride of the Jewish nation and its fearful abuse of the great graces lavished upon it by Almighty God, was the most efficacious instrument in its crime of deicide, and finally brought about the downfall of the whole Jewish State. Our Saviour had told them this beforehand (John 5:43; 8:21; 10:8, 10).

Pilate, the other party in this disgraceful trial, had no moral strength to oppose to the resolute and ingenious passion of the Jews, and so he was vanquished. He has not even, like them, the sorrowful distinction of owing his ruin to a great passion. He feared his conscience, but he feared Rome more, and his own interests were more to him than anything else. So he succumbed to cowardice, human respect and self-seeking. This last vice was the pest of the Roman officials of the time. It made Pilate a coward, a criminal, an unjust judge, and a murderer of the Son of God. Such is the terrible part played in the Death of our Saviour by the passions and sins of the great and powerful.

But who can fathom the pain and grief felt by our Lord during these occurrences at the ingratitude and mortal hatred of His people and the unhappy fate awaiting them, at Pilate's unscrupulous violation of his duty, and the grievous guilt incurred by all concerned in His condemnation? He had done no one any harm; He had good will towards all. He had bestowed the greatest benefits upon countless numbers of these people; He was the Lord and Messias of them all, and not one of all these thousands raises his voice in His favor. They are silent, or they demand His death with brutal fury, and only a heathen Gentile feels human pity for Him and seeks to obtain His deliverance. How painful and humiliating this was for our Lord! With how much truth might He have made to these people the reproaches that the Church puts into His mouth on the day on which we celebrate the memory of His Passion: "My people, what have I done to thee, or wherein have I grieved thee? I led thee out of Egypt and cast Pharao into the Red Sea, and thou hast delivered Me up to the chief priests; I went before thee in a pillar of cloud, and thou hast led Me to Pilate's praetorium; I fed thee with manna, and thou hast scourged Me; I struck down the kings of the Canaanites, and thou hast struck My head with a reed; I gave thee a kingly scepter, and thou hast crowned Me with thorns; I exalted thee with great power, and thou wilt raise Me upon the Cross! What more could I have done to thee, that I have not done?" No, He could not have done more. There was nothing left for Him to do, but to let the people have their bitter will and consummate the terrible fate the nation was about to incur by its own fault.

Condemnation of Jesus

John 19:13. Now when Pilate had heard these words, he brought Jesus forth; and sat down in the judgment-seat, in the place that is called Lithostrotos, and in Hebrew Gabbatha.—14. And it was the parasceve of the Pasch, about the sixth hour, and he saith to the Jews: "Behold your king."—15. But they cried out: "Away with him, away with him, crucify him." Pilate saith to them: "Shall I crucify your king?" The chief priests answered: "We have no king but Caesar."—16. Then therefore he delivered him to them for to be crucified. And they took Jesus, and led him forth."

Luke 23:24. And Pilate gave sentence that it should be as they required.—25. And he released unto them him who for murder and sedition had been cast into prison, whom they had desired, but Jesus he delivered up to their will.

Mark 15:15. And so Pilate being willing to satisfy the people, released to them Barabbas, and delivered up Jesus, when he had scourged him, to be crucified.

Matt. 27:26. Then he released to them Barabbas; and having scourged Jesus delivered him unto them to be crucified.

1. Preliminary Circumstances of the Condemnation

The circumstances of the condemnation are given in considerable detail.

As regards the time, it was towards noon (John 19:14) on the day of preparation for the Feast of the Pasch (known as the Parasceve). St. Mark, therefore, in saying that the Crucifixion took place at the third hour, either means during the third part of the day (viz. from 9 to 12 o'clock according to our reckoning), or he is speaking of the Crucifixion in a general sense, including all that belonged to it (our Lord's scourging, carrying of the Cross, and being nailed to it), or else he merely means to give an approximate idea of the time. The place where the sentence was pronounced was a raised seat of stone in the forum. There was always a flooring of mosaic beneath the judgment-seat. This spot was called in the Hebrew tongue Gabbatha, in the Greek Lithostrotos. The Roman governors passed sentence in the open air, sitting on the judgment-seat, and with great solemnity.

So Pilate, wearing the insignia of his office and accompanied by soldiers, went thither and mounted the judgment-seat, and our Saviour was placed before him as a criminal. Then another unusual scene ensued. Pilate, either wishing to annoy the Jews and reproach them with sharp irony for the injustice of their infamous deed, or else to compel them to make a public acknowledgment that he had done his duty towards the Emperor, pointed to our Saviour and cried to the Jews from his seat: "Behold your king!" (John 19:14.) "Away with Him, away with Him," was their immediate answer; "crucify Him." "Shall I crucify your king?" responded Pilate.—"We have no king but Caesar," replied the Jews. These were their last words in the matter (John 19:15).

2. THE CONDEMNATION

After this incident Pilate proceeded to pronounce the sentence, and condemned Jesus to the death of the cross. "*Ibis ad crucem! Lictor, expedi crucem!*" were usually the concluding words of such a sentence, and were probably addressed to our Saviour. So this was Pilate's final judgment. And what a judgment! First, it was the most unjust one ever passed; he had four or five times solemnly averred that our Saviour was innocent, and yet in the end he condemns Him to death. Secondly, it was an exceedingly cruel sentence, because the punishment to which it condemned our Lord was torture and protracted. The other capital punishments in vogue with the Jews were speedy and not particularly cruel; but our Saviour was to suffer long and acutely. Lastly, the sentence was most ignominious and degrading. Among the Romans only slaves and vile criminals suffered death on the cross. The Jews were only accustomed to hang the corpses of very great criminals on the gallows, after their execution, as a deterrent and a warning to others. That was why the law said: "He is accursed of God that hangeth on a tree" (Deut. 21:23; Num. 25:4). But our Saviour is to suffer all the pain and horror of death on the cross. Yet even here we may see the finger of Divine Providence. In the first place, God had ordained this manner of death for our Lord. He Himself had predicted it to Nicodemus (John 3:14; Num. 21:9), later on to the Jews (John 12:32), and repeatedly to the Apostles. By His Death on the Cross He freed Israel from the obligation of observing the law and from its curse (Gal. 3:13). And the Cross had been typified by the wood of the Ark, the rod of Moses, and the brazen serpent. Cruel and disgraceful as death on the cross was, it was nevertheless more suitable for our Saviour than any of the Jewish capital punishments: beheading, strangling, stoning, or burning. On the Cross He could make His last arrangements, impart comfort, reveal His holiness in all its greatness and glory, and die in a majestic manner, visibly of His own free will. The Cross became the altar of His sacrifice, the pulpit of His last and loftiest sermon, and the standard of His kingdom. Nor could any other kind of capital punishment have been more suited to the object of Jesus' Death. He wished thereby to give the sinful world a complete representation of the justice of God, as opposed to sin (Rom. 3:25). The dreadfulness of this death is quite in keeping with the hatefulness of sin, and the spectacle it sets forth works upon the heart, imagination and conscience of the beholder, and fills him with fear and contrition.

3. CONSEQUENCES AND EFFECTS OF THE CONDEMNATION

There were several groups of people who heard this sentence, and they did so with very different sentiments.

In the first place, there were our Saviour's enemies, the chief priests and Pharisees, who hated Him so bitterly. How they exulted! They had gained all they wanted, and their victory was complete. Their worst adversary and foe was to die on the Cross. What a splendid revenge for all the humiliations and defeats they had suffered at His hands! And the deluded crowd rejoiced with them. The enemies of Jesus had procured a public and solemn condemnation of the Messias, and made a declaration of loyalty to the Emperor in His place. How dearly the nation was to pay for this! Theocracy was now at an end. They renounced the Messias, the

Angel of the Testament, their God-King, and give themselves up to the Emperor. The Emperor will come and crush them, and there will be no Messias at hand to save them. These foolish trees would not have the olive of peace, the fig of sweetness, and the vine of joy for their king, but chose instead the bramble to rule over them, and lo! fire came out from the brambles and devoured them, their houses, and their children (Judges 9:15). The still waters of Siloe did not please them; they preferred the rushing torrent, and it came upon them and carried them away, and scattered them among the nations (Isa. 8:6). They themselves have but just now testified that our Saviour gave Himself out to be the Son of God, and therefore they put Him to death (John 19:7); and thus they become deicides and incur the punishment of their terrible crime.

And the judge: could he be satisfied with his sentence? This appearance of Jesus before the highest judgment-seat of the world was of the greatest significance, not merely for Pilate, but also for the power of which, in his office as judge, he was the representative. It was a true test of that power as to its love of justice. The Supreme Judge, Eternal Justice Itself, submits Himself unknown before the highest representative of this world-empire, to be judged by him. Long did the judge resist injustice; but finally he succumbed to it, and not our Saviour, but he, His judge, and in his person the whole Empire which he represented, went away judged and condemned. Our Saviour says to Pilate: The Jews have "the greater sin"; but the judge has sinned too, because he has acted contrary to justice and right in the exercise of his office. Such an act could not fail to be fatal to him and to the power whose deputy he was.

But there were also friends and disciples of Jesus present; His Mother, with John and Magdalen and the other holy women. Perhaps they were standing aside in the portico or vestibule that surrounded the forum, and saw and heard everything. Who can describe the grief and pain this sentence caused them? All was over now, all hope of His deliverance gone, His cause entirely lost. He was condemned to the most shameful and cruel of deaths. With unutterable pain they gazed at Him and heard the words of the sentence of death, and their hearts were ready to break with grief and sorrow.

And our Saviour? Surely He felt to the full the injustice, cruelty and ignominy of this sentence, for He was more conscious than anyone of His holiness and divine dignity. But He stood there full of humility, His head gently bent, and accepted it willingly and lovingly. He did not contradict, did not protest, did not appeal. He regarded Himself as a surety for the punishment due to the sins of the whole world, and submitted to the sentence as a well-merited one, without any bitterness against its authors, Pilate and the Jews; on the contrary, with great love for them, for God, and for us all. He saw therein the sentence of His Heavenly Father, and kissed with submission, reverence and gratitude the Hand that condemned Him. If He appealed, it was only to the justice and mercy of the Father in favor of all poor sinners, on the ground of the injustice of this sentence passed upon Him by men.

Should we not in spirit fall down and adore our Lord on the spot where for our sakes He received so unjust and ignominious a sentence, by which His life was declared forfeited? We must thank Him from the bottom of our hearts for having submitted to it. It ought to have been passed upon us. And here, too, we poor sinners may learn to suffer, if need be, an unjust judgment patiently, and to bear contemptuous treatment in silence. What else have we deserved, if we have ever committed a mortal sin, but hell? And our Saviour, the incarnate purity, innocence, justice and holiness of God, silently allows Himself to be condemned to death. Ought not this truth to incline us to modesty in our assertion and pursuit of our rights? Finally, we may here ask of our Saviour Himself the grace of a mild sentence, when we one day come to stand before His judgment-seat. By suffering this unjust sentence He has merited the power to be Judge of all. Let us offer Him the compassion we have now had for His unjust condemnation, that He may show mercy to us.

The Carrying of the Cross

Matt. 27:31. And after they had mocked him, they took off the cloak from him, and put on him his own garments, and led him away to crucify him.

Mark 15:20. And after they had mocked him, they took off the purple from him, and put his own garments on him; and they led him out to crucify him. . . . —22. And they bring him into the place called Golgotha; which being interpreted is the place of Calvary.

John 19:16. Then therefore he delivered him to them to be crucified. And they took Jesus, and led him forth.—17. And bearing his own cross he went forth to that place which is called Calvary, but in Hebrew Golgotha.

1. OUR LORD IS LADEN WITH THE CROSS

According to Oriental custom the sentence was immediately put into effect. Our Saviour was divested of the mock-purple, and His own clothes were restored to Him. The soldiers and the officials assemble, the two malefactors are led up, and the crosses brought. Criminals were executed, with few exceptions, by day and in public, and had to drag their crosses to the place of execution themselves, in order to increase their pain and disgrace. No exception was made in our Saviour's case; He was treated as a common criminal. The Cross was from 8 to 10 feet long, and about 20 to 40 pounds in weight. The cross-piece was bound upon the main stem.

And how did our Saviour receive the Cross? Hardly without natural fear and shrinking. It was the very embodiment of all suffering and shame. But He also received it with resignation and reverence—nay, with love and desire. Perhaps He kissed and embraced it, perhaps even knelt to receive it. For He looked beyond the shame and pain, and saw in the Cross the adorable Will of His Father, the instrument of our salvation and of all blessing, and the scepter of the honor and power that was hereafter to be His. We read of St. Andrew that he greeted his cross from afar with words of heartfelt love and longing; and some holy martyrs are said to have approached theirs on their knees. Whence should they have derived those marvelous dispositions, if not from our Saviour Himself, Who during His life-time greeted His Cross with the words: "How am I straitened until My baptism be accomplished!" (Luke 12:50; Hebr. 12:2.)

2. THE CARRYING OF THE CROSS

And now our Saviour started on His last and bitterest journey, from the citadel Antonia to the place of execution outside the city. The road led in a south-westerly direction through the city, and, passing through the second city-wall, out through the so-called execution-gate to the place of execution. This road is about a thousand paces long, and is called the "*via dolorosa.*" Along this road the sad cortège passed. A Roman centurion rode in front; then followed the condemned men, each accompanied by four soldiers; after these came the executioners and their assistants with the instruments of death and the penal titles on poles; and in the rear and on either side of the procession walked countless throngs of people, high and low, especially Pharisees, both strangers and those of the city. And in the midst of the crowd there walked a Figure, bowed and tottering, scarcely visible under the heavy Cross and the overshadowing crown of thorns. It is our Lord, our Saviour bearing His Cross.

And how does He carry His Cross? In the first place, He suffers great shame and ignominy. It is a criminal procession, and He is the principal culprit, condemned everywhere and by everyone as a false prophet and blasphemer. Countless numbers of people are awaiting Him; they stare at Him and jeer at Him from doors, windows, and roofs (Ps. 68:13). He traverses the same streets along which He had formerly passed respected, sought after, and feared. Secondly, He bears His Cross painfully. The way was long enough, uneven and steep too at parts. The other two condemned men were not scourged until they had reached Mount Calvary, immediately before their crucifixion, and so they could accomplish the journey with their crosses without great difficulty. But our Saviour had been scourged already, and was worn out with the ill-usage of that day and the previous night. All His limbs were bleeding and sore, His shoulders lacerated, and the exhaustion caused by loss of blood unspeakable. One can well imagine how hard this journey must have been for Him under the weight of the Cross. Tradition says that He fell from three to seven times. Lastly, He carried the Cross without finding compassion or relief. We feel sorry even for a poor beast when it falls, and try to help it up again. But our Saviour met with no pity. Most likely they even ill-treated Him for falling. And if at last they relieved Him of His Cross, it was only because He seemed about to succumb under it. Cruelty was their only motive; they simply wanted Him to die on the Cross. And He Himself puts forth His utmost remaining strength; He too wishes to die on the Cross.

The goal of the procession was the place of execution. The path from the execution-gate led, curving round from north-east to south-west, through a rather broad ravine between rocky elevations of the soil. Westwards, on the right hand, the ravine or hollow was bounded by a rocky hill, where Joseph of Arimathaea had made his sepulcher in a garden; eastwards, on the left, was the detached rocky summit known as Golgotha or Calvary, perhaps because it resembled a flattened skull. That was the place of execution. With the Jews this was usually outside the city, at some public place (Lev. 24:14; III Kings 21:13; Acts 7:57). The procession ascended the rocky height on the north-east side, and arrived at the place of crucifixion.

3. SIGNIFICATION OF THE CARRYING OF THE CROSS

Our Lord's carrying of His Cross has a double meaning.

First, it is the fulfilment of ancient types and prophecies. The types fulfilled by it were Cain's leading Abel out to murder him (Gen. 4:8), and Isaac's carrying the wood up the mountain upon which he himself was to be slaughtered as a sacrifice (Gen. 22:6). The beasts for sacrifice whose blood was brought by the High Priests into the sanctuary on the Feast of Atonement were burnt outside the city (Hebr. 13:11, 12). And the words of the prophet, that the Lord had "laid on Him (Christ) the iniquity for us all," were likewise here fulfilled (Isa. 53:6).

The second meaning of the carrying of the Cross bears reference to us. What our Saviour did and suffered here, we shall all have to do and suffer. Christ's Way of the Cross is the path which all must take. And herein lie two lessons. In the first place, we must carry the cross. Our cross consists in penance; in bearing the yoke of God's commandments; in overcoming our irregular passions; in enduring the exterior evils that befall us. No one can escape from this multiform cross. As men, as Christians, as priests and religious we must carry the cross, if we wish to live according to the dictates of reason, to belong to Christ, save our souls, attain to perfection, and win heaven. As our Saviour Himself says: "If any man will come after Me, let him . . . take up his cross, and follow Me" (Matt. 10:38; 16:24; Mark 8:34; Luke 9:23; 14:27). That is the first lesson. And the second is that we must also carry our cross well. We carry it well when we carry it for Jesus, in spiritual union with Him, whether this union merely consists in the possession of sanctifying grace or in believing and loving thought of Him. We carry it well when we carry it with the same dispositions and in the same manner, inwardly and outwardly, as our Saviour did. He did not carry His Cross with proud gait, but yet He bore it with noble dignity. Neither did He try to lighten it or disembarrass Himself of it. He bore it humbly, lovingly and courageously to the end, and died upon it.

The Escort of Our Cross-bearing Saviour

Luke 23:26. And as they led him away, they laid hold of one Simon of Cyrene coming from the country; and they laid the cross on him to carry after Jesus.—27. And there followed him a great multitude of people, and of women who bewailed and lamented him.—28. But Jesus turning to them, said: "Daughters of Jerusalem, weep not over me, but weep for yourselves, and for your children.—29. For behold the days shall come, when they will say: Blessed are the barren, and the wombs that have not borne, and the paps that have not given suck.—30. Then shall they begin to say to the mountains: Fall upon us; and to the hills: Cover us.—31. For if in the green wood they do these things, what shall be done in the dry?"—32. And there were also two other malefactors led with him, to be put to death.

Mark 15:21. And they forced one Simon a Cyrenian who passed by, coming out of the country, the father of Alexander and of Rufus, to take up his cross.—22. And they bring him into the place called Golgotha; which being interpreted is the place of Calvary.

Matt. 27:32. And going out they found a man of Cyrene, named Simon; him they forced to take up his cross.

Our Saviour did not carry His Cross alone; He was accompanied by many. Indeed, all who walked with the procession to the place of execution took part in the carrying of the Cross, each in his own way. We may distinguish three different groups among them.

1. THOSE WHO LOAD OUR SAVIOUR WITH THE CROSS

Those who lay the Cross upon our Saviour's shoulders are the authors of His Passion, viz. the Jews, the priests, the Pharisees, the soldiers, and the executioners and their assistants. They are all guilty of His Passion, and increase it by their cruelty and mockery. They themselves carry a cross, too, the cross of their vile passions and sins. They are the tools of Satan, and it is his yoke that they drag along. This is an inglorious cross, a fatal cross, which leads not to redemption, but to eternal death. Whoever does not carry the Cross of Jesus must bear that of Satan.

And in a wider sense we and all men belong to those who load our Saviour with the Cross. They are our sins that He is now so painfully carrying; our sins, that are pressing upon Him with such cruel weight. Which of us has not contributed his quota to them? How just and fitting it is, then, that we should accompany our Lord, and now at least recompense Him for the hardships of this journey by the little joy our compassion and gratitude can afford Him!

2. THOSE WHO LITERALLY CARRY THE CROSS WITH OUR SAVIOUR

The two malefactors are the first in this group. They go with Jesus and carry their crosses to the place of execution (Luke 23:32). But they do not carry them for Jesus, for faith and virtue, but on account of their crimes and misdeeds. Nor do they carry them as Jesus did His, but only under compulsion, raging and gnashing their teeth, and—one of them at all events, the thief on the left side—with evil consequences. For him it probably became the instrument of eternal damnation. But in the heart of the good thief the first emotions of the contrition and penance that he so touchingly completed on the cross may very likely have just now been beginning to stir, during the carrying of the cross.

Another of those who literally carry the Cross with Jesus is Simon of Cyrene, who actually carried it part of the way in His stead. How did this happen? He was returning from the country, and, as it appears, just entering by the city-gate; for we are told that the soldiers found him as they were going out (Matt. 27:32), laid hold of him, and forced him to take up our Saviour's Cross. And why? Because the weakness and exhaustion of Jesus were so great that they feared He would succumb on the way under its weight. And how did Simon carry the Cross? It was really laid upon him, and our Saviour walked before him freed from the burden (Matt. 27:32; Mark 15:21; Luke 23:26). He probably carried it very unwillingly at first. It must have seemed to him a great piece of ill-luck and also a degradation to have to carry a criminal's cross for him. But by degrees he became more willing, and at last he carried it with faith and love, and we may feel sure that as long as he lived he reckoned it as a great grace and his greatest happiness to have done so. And it was a great grace to render our dear Saviour this service, and thus to cooperate in the redemption of the world, to become a model for all the elect and obtain his own salvation. How celebrated has he become by this act! All Christian races and ages have been edified by his example. His sons seem to have been much looked up to in the Church of Rome, since their names are mentioned by St. Mark (Mark 15:21). And how, then, was this change of heart brought about? Probably by the sight of our Saviour's heavenly patience and gentleness. He felt pity for Him, and this pity drew down great graces upon him, which led him to faith and love. An involuntary cross is often the beginning of great blessings, and Simon is a model for all who are obliged against their will to bear outward misfortunes and sanctify themselves thereby.

3. THOSE WHO PARTICIPATE IN SPIRIT IN OUR SAVIOUR'S CARRYING OF THE CROSS

In this group we find first of all the women of Jerusalem and other good people who compassionated our Saviour's fate. For a great multitude of people followed Him (Luke 23:27), and many among them were His disciples, or at any rate well-disposed towards Him. They commiserated Him and gave vent to their pity and grief in loud lamentations. This expression of their grief was right and required great courage, since it was made in the presence and hearing of our Lord's triumphant foes. What was imperfect about it was that they regarded our Lord's Passion as a pure misfortune, and bewailed it as such. Our Saviour rewards them for their compassion. He vouchsafes to address them, and in His turn offers His pity for them and their children (Luke 23:28). He tells them that unhappily they and their children are far more to be pitied than He, on account of the terrible punishment that will overtake them. As a rule sterility was regarded by the Jews as a great misfortune and a reproach (Gen. 30:23; I Kings 1:6; Osee 9:14; Luke 1:25). But now those who have no children should esteem themselves happy, for days of such terrible distress will come that people will wish not to have been born (Job 3:11), or at least will be glad to have no children, that they may not have the sufferings of these to bewail as well as their own. Their affliction will be so terrible that they will wish for a speedy and sudden death (Luke 23:29, 30; Osee 10:8). Our Lord illustrates and confirms the prophecy of these afflictions by representing them as a punishment for the sins of the people, contrasting His own innocence with the guilt of Israel, and comparing their respective sufferings. In the Scriptures a just and innocent man is often compared to a green and flourishing tree (Ps. 1:3; Jer. 17:8), and the sinner to dry wood (Isa. 30:33; Ez. 20:47). If then such lamentable things are done to the just, what will be done to the sinner? (Luke 23:31.) As a matter of fact, the Romans came and felled Israel, the dry tree, with their axes, and burnt it. These women and other compassionate people are a type of the souls who feel pity for the sufferings of our Saviour, but do not follow up their pity by deeds. But He accepts even this token of love graciously, and returns it in His own way.

According to tradition our Lord was met on His way to Calvary by a woman named Veronica or Berenice. She was probably a disciple of His, and wished to give Him a proof of her attachment and compassion at this moment of distress and abandonment. Her pity is practical, noble and courageous. She pushes her way through the crowd to Him and hands Him her veil that He may wipe His Face. It was a slight service, but a courageous confession of her discipleship; it was all she could do at this moment, and she did it with a generous and loving heart. And how magnificently our Saviour rewards her for this act of charity! Tradition says that He took the veil, wiped the blood and perspiration from His Face, and gave it back to her; and when she reached home and unfolded it, she beheld His Face miraculously imprinted on its folds. This is how our Saviour rewards even the smallest act of charity, and encourages us to give Him heartfelt tokens of our love, even though we can do but little.

Lastly, we find in this group our Lord's own Mother, who (as tradition says) also awaited Him on this painful journey, and pushed her way up to Him to exchange but one glance, one word, one gesture of reverence and sympathy, grief, comfort and love. Who can fathom the anguish of these two hearts at this moment? This is the noblest and most sublime participation in our Saviour's Cross, because nothing could equal the courage and love of His Mother and her desire to suffer with her Son. Mary is here already the highest model of all who bear the cross.

Thus everyone—high and low, friend and foe, the just and sinners—all take part in our Saviour's Cross, either actually or in spirit, in hate or in love. All have a cross to carry; the cross of sin and passion, the cross of misfortune permitted by God, or the cross of penance and love. Thus the Way of the Cross is a true and living type of the Church and the whole human race. Whoever we are, voluntarily or involuntarily we must form part of the escort of the cross-bearing Saviour. All that is left to our choice is, to which division of the company we will belong. And surely the choice is not difficult.

The Crucifixion

Luke 23:33. And when they were come to the place which is called Calvary, they crucified him there; and the robbers, one on the right hand, and the other on the left.—34. And Jesus said: "Father, forgive them, for they know not what they do." But they dividing his garments, cast lots.

Mark 15:23. And they gave him to drink wine mingled with myrrh; but he took it not.—24. And crucifying him, they divided his garments, casting lots upon them, what every man should take.

Matt. 27:34. And they gave him wine to drink mingled with gall. And when he had tasted, he would not drink.

John 19:18. They crucified him, and with him two others, one on each side, and Jesus in the midst.

1. PREPARATIONS FOR THE CRUCIFIXION

At length our Saviour reached the hill of Calvary, pale, blood-stained, and completely exhausted. Whilst the preparations for the crucifixion were being made—the two thieves scourged, the crosses pieced together, and the holes in which to set them dug—our Lord is said to have been confined in a sort of rocky cleft or grotto at the foot of the hill, on the north side. The site is still shown in the Church of the Holy Sepulcher. Without doubt He spent the time here in prayer, and thus recited the Introit to His sacrifice on the Cross.

As soon as the preparations were finished, the soldiers brought our Lord to the place of crucifixion. Again they tore off His clothing, even the under-garments, thus scourging Him as it were a second time, since all His wounds, to which the clothes had been made to adhere by the blood that had clotted and dried during the carrying of the Cross, were torn open afresh. Probably they left Him the loin-cloth. This was customary even with the Romans, still more with the Jews. But otherwise our Saviour was completely stripped, and we may well imagine what a bitter pain this was to His pure Heart. Then the myrrh- or palm-wine was given to Him. It was the custom for compassionate women of gentle birth to prepare for poor criminals about to suffer crucifixion a strong drink, consisting of wine mixed with myrrh, aloes, and calamus, in order to stupefy the unfortunate men and render them less sensible to the pain (Prov. 31:6). Since this wine contained bitter ingredients, it is not incorrect when we are told that they gave our Lord gall to drink (Matt. 27:34). The mixture was probably prepared for Him by some of the women who had been His disciples. And what did He do with it? He did not refuse it altogether, in order to give these good women the consolation of His having tasted it. So He took a sip, but did not drink, because He would not lessen His pain, but wished to make the great sacrifice with full consciousness, as beseemed Him (Mark 15:23; Matt. 27:34).

2. THE CRUCIFIXION ITSELF

The soldiers now formed a circle round the place of crucifixion, and the executioners entered the ring. Must not our Saviour's heart have quailed and His whole being have trembled at this moment, before the terrible execution that was now about to begin? Ought we not to adore every pulsation of His beating Heart? It is not certain how the crucifixion really took place. According to ancient tradition, the cross was first erected, and the criminals were hoisted up and bound to it with ropes; then the executioners, sitting astride on a block of wood, nailed their hands and feet fast. But the culprits might also be nailed to the cross on the ground, and then raised together with it. This is how our Lord's crucifixion is usually represented.

Our Saviour, then, was seized by the executioners and thrown down on the Cross, like a helpless Victim, if indeed He had not already stretched Himself upon it voluntarily. How touchingly beautiful He is as He lies there in His disfigurement, how venerable in His shame, the Eternal God upon the Cross, with His eyes upraised to heaven! The executioners bound the upper part of His Body to the stem of the Cross; one may have knelt on His breast, another on His right arm, whilst a third seized the right hand, placed the rough, three-sided nail, filed to a sharp point, in the palm, and drove it with powerful blows through the tendons in the hollow of the hand into the hole already made for it in the Cross. A tremor of infinite pain passes through our Saviour's limbs; the blood spurts up and round about, and the fingers contract convulsively round the nail. Now the left hand is to be affixed. The arms are barbarously dislocated, the breast heaves and the muscles strain, and the same torture is repeated with this hand. And now the feet, which He has drawn up in His pain. They are violently pulled down, and with a splitting, cracking sound the nail is driven through the instep into the hole in the place for the feet. And now He lies there, nailed to the Cross. His whole Body is terribly distended; every nerve is twitching and quivering with exquisite anguish; His Face is deathly pale and bespattered with blood; tears, sighs and gentle moans mingle with the terrible blows of the hammer, while the blood pours from the gaping wounds. Can we not imagine the horror and anguish of our Lord's Blessed Mother, St. John and the holy women, who were standing close by and heard the strokes of the hammer and the groans of the innocent Victim?

And what does our Saviour think? What does He feel? His own words tell us best. "Father," He says, "forgive them, for they know not what they do" (Luke 23:34). He asks forgiveness for them all—for His torturers, the chief priests, and the Jews—all who have a hand in His suffering and Death. And He asks it so pleadingly, supporting His petition by the most touching motives. He makes use of the tenderest form of address, the name of Father. He pleads in His quality of Son, and conjures the Father by His obedience unto death, by all His wounds and sufferings, and by the love that the Father bears Him. His second motive is taken from His tormentors themselves. He excuses their crime by their ignorance. It was certainly a culpable ignorance, at all events as far as the Jews were concerned, as our Saviour Himself had testified (John 15:22). But nevertheless the plea is correct enough if we take into consideration the force of human passion and the superficiality of human nature (I Cor. 2:8; Acts 3:17). Lastly, He pleads with success. Those of the Israelites who were converted on the Feast of Pentecost and subsequently, and those who will be converted at the end of the world, are the fruit of this touching and urgent entreaty. As the sweet olive, grape and balsam yield their oil, wine and sweet perfume when they are pounded and crushed, so excess of pain and the fearful malice of His foes could extort nothing from His Sacred Heart but this precious prayer. Our Lord hereby wished to teach us by His example how we should treat our enemies and persecutors. All who have His spirit act as He did, and so it has always been (Acts 7:59).

3. THE ERECTION OF THE CROSS

And now the Cross with its burden was pushed to the place where it was to stand, raised by means of ropes and ladders with many a reel and stagger, and lowered into the cavity prepared. Undoubtedly every jerk and movement must have caused our Lord the most intolerable pain, especially the dreadful shock with which the Cross fell into the hole. His Body was dragged down by its own weight, tearing the wounds still farther and making the blood flow more copiously than before.

It was an ever-memorable moment, at once touching and terrible, when the Cross rose totteringly on high and at last stood there overlooking the whole surrounding country. Hell raised its cry of rage and victory, in the persons of the executioners and numerous Pharisees and other enemies of Jesus who surrounded the place of execution and looked on at the scene from various points of vantage on the surrounding heights. It was their moment of victory, and they celebrated and proclaimed it with godless jubilation. But there were also others hearts, other eyes, other voices, and other hands there, and they were raised too as the Cross was erected, and greeted it with their lamentations, love and adoration. They were those of Mary and John, and of the holy women, all friends and relatives of Jesus. How terrible was the sight for them!

So the Cross was erected, and overshadowed the earth for the first time, as an inscrutable token of the justice and mercy of God. Look at it in spirit, and reflect upon the sight. There our Saviour hung, between heaven and earth, outside the city, cast out by His people as an execrable criminal, suspended between two malefactors as the principal of the three, a very picture of the most terrible misery, abandonment and pain. His head had sunk on His breast beneath the weight of the thickly-woven crown, and the blood trickled into His eyes and mouth. His breast was stretched and strained, the shoulders hollow and strained, the form had almost disappeared under the tension of the body, and rivulets of blood flowed from the wounds of the feet and hands over the arms and feet and down the stem of the Cross. Such is His terrible condition. Who would have thought that this life would end under such fearful circumstances? The prophets saw Him in spirit, and cried out: "Who hath believed our report? and to whom is the arm of the Lord revealed? . . . We have thought him as it were a leper, and as one struck by God and afflicted. But he was wounded for our iniquities . . . and the Lord hath laid on him the iniquity of us all. He was offered because it was his own will, and he opened not his mouth; he shall be led as a sheep to the slaughter, and shall be dumb as a lamb before his shearer, and he shall not open his mouth. . . . He is cut off out of the land of the living" (Isa. 53:1–8). The Cross is the most terrible revelation of justice. But it is also the sign of mercy and the instrument of grace. The true tree of life is planted now. The ripe and rosy fruit that gives life to all nations hangs upon it, and streams of grace flow down upon the earth to atone for the curse of its sins and transform it into a paradise. No grace and no salvation is given, except in this sign. Lastly, the Cross stood erect as the great standard and ensign of God, to which the nations hasten and around which they muster (Isa. 11:10). On the steep western summit of the rock of Calvary our Saviour hangs on the Cross, His back turned towards ancient Jerusalem and His face towards the Occident. Thence, like a mighty general, He begins the great campaign in which He is to subdue the nations, not by the sword, but by that very Cross—not to their ruin, but to their salvation. "If he shall lay down his life for sin, he shall see a long-lived seed, and the will of the Lord shall be prosperous in his hand. Because his soul hath labored, he shall see and be filled. . . . Therefore will I distribute to him very many, and he shall divide the spoils of the strong, because he hath delivered his soul unto death, and was respected with the wicked; and he hath borne the sins of many, and hath prayed for the transgressors" (Isa. 53:10–12). All these glorious mysteries are contained in the erection of the Cross, on that first Feast of the Exaltation of the Cross. How just it is that we should adore the holy Cross with the dispositions with which Mary and all the followers of Jesus looked at it for the first time! The more so, since the posterity of His enemies of that day has not disappeared even yet, but blasphemes it and loads it with mockery, scorn and execration.

The Title over the Cross

John 19:19. And Pilate wrote a title also; and he put it upon the cross. And the writing was: Jesus of Nazareth the King of the Jews.—20. This title therefore many of the Jews did read; because the place where Jesus was crucified, was nigh to the city; and it was written in Hebrew, in Greek, and in Latin.—21. Then the chief priests of the Jews said to Pilate: "Write not, The King of the Jews; but that he said: I am the King of the Jews."—22. Pilate answered: "What I have written, I have written."

Luke 23:38. And there was also a superscription written over him in letters of Greek, and Latin, and Hebrew: This is the King of the Jews.

Mark 15:26. And the inscription of his cause was written over: The King of the Jews.

Matt. 27:37. And they put over his head his cause written: This is Jesus the King of the Jews.

It was customary to inscribe the grounds for the condemnation of a criminal upon a tablet, which was carried before him and fastened upon his cross. Sometimes he had to carry it himself to the place of execution, and in this case it was suspended round his neck.

1. THE TITLE

Pilate wrote the inscription in three languages: the official tongue, the one in vogue in ordinary intercourse, and the language of the country (John 19:19). In Latin the title was probably worded: "The King of the Jews" (Mark 15:26); in Greek: "This is the King of the Jews" (Matt. 27:37; Luke 23:38); and in Hebrew: "Jesus of Nazareth, the King of the Jews" (John 19:19).

And why did Pilate select this incription? In the first place, probably, because it was a fair summary of the accusation (Luke 23:2) and specified the main point of the trial (Luke 23:3; John 19:15); secondly, in order to clear himself of the charge of being implicated in high treason; and thirdly, to annoy the Jews, because they had forced him to condemn Jesus against his will and against his better judgment. And fourthly, this inscription was in reality the work of the finger of God.

2. THE JEWS PROTEST AGAINST THE TITLE

The Jews appear not to have seen the title until it was placed over the Cross, or at any rate about to be placed there. Perhaps Pilate had not had it carried before our Saviour at all; or our Lord may have carried it Himself round His neck, so that it could not well be read; or the Jews had overlooked it. But when they did catch sight of it they were exasperated at Pilate's having put such an affront upon them, and hurried to him with the request that he would write instead: "He said: I am the king of the Jews" (John 19:21). We have here a further proof of the hatred the Jews bore to Jesus, as well as a sign of their evil conscience and the incompleteness of their victory. The success of the wicked is after all but partial.

3. FRUITLESSNESS OF THE PROTEST

But they found Pilate less compliant than they expected; he seems to have been weary of the whole matter. He was determined to be firm at last and to take his revenge on the Jews. But in reality he was only a tool in God's hands. He carries out His design that the royalty of Jesus should be officially expressed in all the principal languages of the world, and that He should be proclaimed to all nations as King. And it is precisely the Roman governor, the representative of the sovereign power that ruled the world at that day, who has to do this, and thus to prophesy himself that our Saviour would be the heir and future ruler of the Roman Empire. Thus does God turn the mockery and the evil intentions of men to His own honor. How wonderful are His ways! At the very moment when our Saviour dies, He has Himself proclaimed King. The title on the Cross is the proclamation of His royalty and the condemnation of the Jews. He is their King, although they will not have Him as such, but deny and reject Him and lead Him away to death. They thus pronounce their own judgment. They read it in the inscription, and that is why they rise up against it. This is the beginning of Christ's kingdom and glory on earth.

But how did Mary and the holy friends of Jesus regard the title? What must His Blessed Mother have felt as her glance rested on the sweet names "Jesus" and "Nazareth," and what wellsprings of pain these dear memories must have opened in her heart! Jesus in Nazareth, and Jesus here! What a contrast! And besides, the words expressed the blood-guiltiness of her poor countrymen and the condemnation of her nation. But nevertheless she and the other friends of our Lord were the first to acknowledge and greet the title. He had long been King over their hearts, and they had but one wish, that He might become King over all others.

The Division of Our Saviour's Garments

John 19:23. The soldiers therefore when they had crucified him, took his garments (and they made four parts: to every soldier a part) and also his coat. Now the coat was without seam, woven from the top throughout.—24. They said then one to another: "Let us not cut it, but let us cast lots for it, whose it shall be." That the Scripture might be fulfilled saying: "They have parted my garments among them; and upon my vesture they have cast lot." And the soldiers indeed did these things.

Matt. 27:35. And after they had crucified him, they divided his garments, casting lots; that it might be fulfilled which was spoken by the prophet, saying: "They divided my garments among them, and upon my vesture they cast lots."

Mark 15:24. And crucifying him, they divided his garments, casting lots upon them, what every man should take.

Luke 23:34. But they dividing his garments, cast lots.

1. How the soldiers divided our Saviour's garments

According to ordinary custom the soldiers had a right to the garments of those who had been executed. Our Saviour's clothing consisted of sandals, a girdle, mantle, upper coat, and under-garment. The soldiers took them and divided them into four portions, for which they cast lots (Mark 15:24; Matt. 27:35; Luke 23:34), perhaps because these portions were not of equal worth. But our Lord's under-garment was a seamless tunic, "woven from the top throughout." So they did not tear it, because that would have rendered it useless to them all; but cast lots a second time as to who should have it (John 19:23, 24). They did this in rough soldier-fashion, close to the Cross, with coarse and cold-blooded indifference. Then they sat down to guard the place of execution, that no one might ill-treat our Saviour and the other two crucified men, nor yet try to take them down (Matt. 27:36).

2. HOW OUR SAVIOUR AND HIS HOLY MOTHER REGARDED THE DIVISION OF HIS GARMENTS

The division of our Saviour's garments was certainly a sad spectacle for Him. His last possessions were being disposed of. Now He had nothing more, not even a shroud. He was quite poor and despoiled of everything (Ps. 21:19). But He also saw in these torn garments the symbols of His merits, graces and sacraments; and as the former now fell to the lot of sinners, so He saw the whole heritage of His graces apportioned to all humanity, to worthy and unworthy recipients. All was to be for the profit of the world, of mankind. The entire human race was to be blessed in the garments of Jesus, like Jacob formerly in the garments of Esau (Faber). Our Saviour saw also in His seamless tunic the emblem of the unity of His Church, and His Heart was ready to break at the thought of the dissensions and heresies that were to tear and mutilate that beloved Church.

And how did Mary and the other holy women look on at this division of our Lord's garments? Surely they too grieved sorely at it. How precious these holy relics were to them! Perhaps they had made them for our Lord themselves, lovingly and reverently, and given them to Him. They had been consecrated by contact with His Sacred Body and sanctified by His Precious Blood; and of how many graces and miraculous cures had they not been the medium! How the holy women must have envied the fortunate soldiers and burned with the ardent desire to acquire the precious garments at any price and preserve them to the Church!

3. WHAT THIS DIVISION OF OUR LORD'S GARMENTS TEACHES US

The division of our Lord's clothing teaches us, first, love of poverty. We see how few garments He had. No more than it was customary to possess and wear, simply what was common and necessary. These necessaries were not costly, but neither were they unbecoming. They could still be of service to the winners of them, whilst our Lord Himself lost everything. So this division of His garments teaches us to be satisfied with little, to use that little in the spirit of poverty, and lastly to do without even this, if needs be. Death will finally deprive us of everything in any case.

And it also teaches us to make good use of the graces of Jesus and turn to account every opportunity of doing good and gaining merits for heaven. Every day, every minute, every inspiration is a relic of our Saviour, which can sanctify us and work wonders with us.

Finally, the division of our Lord's clothing teaches us to love, esteem and respect very highly the unity of the Church. He would not have His tunic sundered, for therein lay the symbol of the unity and concord of the Church, and this unity was His last wish (John 17:21). And of what use would the Church be to us without unity? Just as little as a torn coat.

Jesus Is Mocked on the Cross

MATT. 27:39. And they that passed by blasphemed him, wagging their heads, —40. And saying: "Vah, thou that destroyest the temple of God and in three days dost rebuild it, save thy own self; if thou be the Son of God, come down from the cross."—411. In like manner also the chief priests with the scribes and ancients mocking, said:—42. "He saved others, himself he cannot save; if he be the king of Israel, let him now come down from the cross, and we will believe him.—43. He trusted in God; let him now deliver him, if he will have him; for he said: I am the Son of God."—44. And the self-same thing the thieves also, that were crucified with him, reproached him with.

MARK 15:29. And they that passed by blasphemed him, wagging their heads, and saying: "Vah, thou that destroyest the temple of God, and in three days buildest it up again;—30. Save thyself, coming down from the cross."—31. In like manner also the chief priests mocking said with the scribes one to another: "He saved others, himself he cannot save.—32. Let Christ the king of Israel come down now from the cross, that we may see and believe." And they that were crucified with him, reviled him.

LUKE 23:35. And the people stood beholding, and the rulers with them derided him, saying: "He saved others, let him save himself, if he be Christ, the elect of God."—36. And the soldiers also mocked him, coming to him, and offering him vinegar,—37. And saying: "If thou be the king of the Jews, save thyself." . . .—

39. And one of those robbers who were hanged, blasphemed him, saying: "If thou be Christ, save thyself and us."

In addition to all His physical pain our Lord had also to endure the mental suffering of mockery and derision.

1. BY WHOM OUR SAVIOUR IS MOCKED

There seems to have been scarcely anyone among the bystanders who did not deride our Lord; at all events there were no groups or divisions of the spectators where there were not mockers to be found. A great many people looked on at the sad scene (Luke 23:35). Mount Calvary lay on the open high-road to Joppe and Caesarea, so there were many passers-by. On seeing the Cross they remembered the words in which He had promised to manifest His power (John 2:19), and shook their heads (Matt. 27:39; Mark 15:29) in sign of contempt (IV Kings 19:21; Ps. 108:25; Lam. 2:15). And the priests, too, even the chief priests, showered derision and opprobrium upon Him (Matt. 27:41; Mark 15:31), as did also the scribes and ancients (Matt. 27:41; Luke 23:35). Lastly, the soldiers (Luke 23:36) and even one of the thieves who were crucified with our Lord (Matt. 27:44; Mark 15:32; Luke 23:39) took part in the mockery. Thus scorn was poured upon Him from all sides, as the prophet had predicted (Ps. 21:8).

2. IN WHAT RESPECTS OUR SAVIOUR WAS MOCKED

Our Saviour was not only mocked at from all sides, but also in all His relationships, offices, and dignities. He was mocked as a prophet who had said that he would destroy the Temple and build it up again (Matt. 27:40; Mark 15:29); mocked in His quality of Son of God (Matt. 27:40, 43); mocked as a miracle-worker who healed others and could not help Himself (Matt. 27:42; Luke 23:35; Mark 15:31); mocked for His sanctity and confidence in God (Matt. 27:43); mocked as Messias and King of Israel (Matt. 27:42; Mark 15:32; Luke 23:35, 37, 39). If He freed Himself now from the Cross, they cried, they would believe in Him (Matt. 27:42; Mark 15:32); and the soldiers held a sponge soaked in vinegar to His lips, but (as it appears) only to torment Him without allowing Him to drink (Luke 23:36). Thus there was nothing that they did not misuse in order to deride Him.

3. HOW THIS MOCKERY MUST HAVE HURT OUR SAVIOUR

Mockery and scorn always wound, and especially such mockery as this. In the first place, it was indescribably coarse and inhuman under such circumstances. They would not even grant Him a moment of peace or a quiet spot in which to die. It is wrong to hurt anyone's feelings; much more in time of trouble and misfortune, and most of all in the hour of death, and death under such terrible circumstances (Eccli. 7:12; 8:8). Secondly, this mockery was black ingratitude. They mock and deride Him for that for which they ought to have been eternally grateful, viz. the revelation of His Divinity and all the tokens of His love and power. All the use they make of these is to torture His Heart with them. Even His trust in God is derided. Lastly, mockery is in this case nothing less than blasphemy, and thus our Redeemer's gentle Heart is oppressed not only by the injury done to Himself but also by the gravity of the offence against God. This again shows us exactly the spirit of this hard, obdurate and cruel people. Even the priests, in their fury, do not consider it beneath their dignity to make common cause with the rabble in deriding and abusing our Lord. In truth, "his inheritance is become to him as a lion in the wood; it hath cried out against him" (Jer. 12:8), and "the daughter of his people is cruel, like the ostrich in the desert" (Lam. 4:3). In the hour of His utmost distress they satisfied their hatred and fury by shooting arrows of scorn at their poor Victim, since they could no longer reach Him with their hands. But He said nothing. He locked within His Heart the pain their mockery caused Him, like "a deaf man . . . that heareth not and that hath no reproofs in his mouth" (Ps. 37:14, 15).

The Good Thief

Luke 23:40. But the other answering, rebuked him, saying: "Neither dost thou fear God, seeing thou art under the same condemnation.—41. And we indeed justly, for we receive the due reward of our deeds; but this man hath done no evil."—42. And he said to Jesus: "Lord, remember me when thou shalt come into thy kingdom."—43. And Jesus said to him: "Amen I say to thee, this day thou shalt be with me in Paradise."

1. HOW THE GOOD THIEF DOES PENANCE AND HONORS OUR SAVIOUR

Whilst all around were deriding and mocking our dying Saviour, the thief on His right hand began to reflect and repent. The excellence of his penance is shown in the following acts.

First, he loudly reproves the wicked thief, and with him the Jews also, for their godless behavior to our Saviour, by pointing to the punishment that they are both already suffering and to the avenging justice of God, which chastises them now and will do so still more severely if they do not repent. "Neither dost thou fear God" (dost not thou fear God either, any more than the other Jews), "seeing thou art under the same condemnation" (i.e. and yet thou art on the point of appearing before God with us? Luke 23:40). So he had begun to fear God, and that is the beginning of true penance.

Secondly, he openly confesses his guilt and expresses his willingness to bear his punishment (Luke 23:41).

Thirdly, he acknowledges the innocence of our Saviour, thus condemning the Jews (Luke 23:41). He had recognized this, by the grace of God, from the heavenly patience of Jesus and His prayer for His tormentors, and particularly from His giving God the appellation of "Father."

Lastly, he even confesses the Divinity of Jesus, by entreating Him to remember him in His kingdom (Luke 23:42). So he belived that our Saviour would live and reign in the world to come, and that He had power over souls and eternal bliss. The crucified, forsaken Jesus, reviled and despised by all others, is in his eyes all-powerful, the Lord of heaven and eternity. He had understood the title on the Cross well. His petition is full of deep humility and trust. Our Saviour has just prayed so touchingly for His executioners; now the thief begs Him to remember His poor companion in suffering as well. But he only asks for a remembrance; he leaves everything else to our Saviour and His mercy. This, then, was perfect penance, a penance full of honor and glory for our Saviour.

2. HOW OUR SAVIOUR RECEIVES THE THIEF'S PENANCE

Our Saviour receives his penance with loving attention, although He was Himself immersed in a very sea of pain; receives it with readiness and magnanimity. He gives the thief infinitely more than he had asked. He forgives him his sins and gives him a share in His kingdom and eternal bliss; and he is to enter upon it this very day, immediately after his death. What generosity! He gives the poor sinner the heaven that costs Him so much more than words can tell. He gives this to one who has committed horrible crimes, and gives it immediately, without delay. He grants it in return for a contrite sigh and a courageous confession (Luke 23:43).

3. WHAT THIS PARDON GRANTED TO THE THIEF TEACHES US

In the first place, this pardon reveals to us all the loving kindness and majesty of our Saviour. How pitiful, how good, and how powerful He is! He notices everything, nothing escapes Him. He hears the softest sigh. Here on the place of execution, Himself judged and condemned by human justice, He judges souls, forgives and retains sins, bestows heaven, and condemns to hell. Is not this spectacle on Mount Calvary a type and anticipation of the Last Judgment? How marvelously our Lord raises up confessors of His innocence and Divinity, even in the midst of the deepest shades of a criminal's death!

And this pardon also shows us the power of grace and its entire spontaneity as far as God is concerned, as also the independence and terrible freedom of the human will. Wonderful graces of conversion knocked at the hearts of both the thieves, desiring admission. One of them listens, and goes from the Cross to Paradise. The other remains obdurately impenitent, and goes to hell. To be damned, at the side of the dying Saviour and His Blessed Mother! The miscreant can hear the sighs of the Redeemer, and the Precious Blood is poured out around his cross as though it would besiege the heart of the sinner and ward off God's justice from its victim; and yet the miserable wretch remains unshaken in his wickedness. There is deep earnestness in this truth, and it teaches us better than anything else to be neither presumptuously confident nor yet pusillanimously despairing (Faber).

The Mother of Jesus and His Friends and Relatives beneath the Cross

JOHN 19:25. Now there stood by the cross of Jesus his mother, and his mother's sister, Mary of Cleophas, and Mary Magdalen.—26. When Jesus therefore had seen his mother and the disciple standing, whom he loved, he saith to his mother: "Woman, behold thy son."—27. After that, he saith to the disciple: "Behold thy mother." And from that hour the disciple took her to his own.

LUKE 23:49. And all his acquaintance, and the women that had followed him from Galilee, stood afar off beholding these things.

MARK 15:40. And there were also women looking on afar off; among whom was Mary Magdalen, and Mary the mother of James the Less and of Joseph, and Salome;—41. Who also when he was in Galilee, followed him and ministered to him, and many other women that came up with him to Jerusalem.

MATT. 27:55. And there were many women afar off who had followed Jesus from

Galilee, ministering unto him;—56. Among whom was Mary Magdalen, and Mary the mother of James and Joseph, and the mother of the sons of Zebedee.

1. HOW MARY AND THE RELATIVES OF JESUS STAND BENEATH THE CROSS

Among the spectators on Mount Calvary there were also relatives and acquaintances of our Saviour (Luke 23:49), the holy women who had followed Him from Galilee and many others (Mark 15:40, 41; Matt. 27:55, 56). The Mother of our Lord, St. John (John 19:26), Mary of Cleophas, Mary Magdalen and Salome are mentioned by name. They seem to have stood in different groups, some nearer, some farther away from the Cross, probably because they were often repulsed and driven back by the Jews; only a few of them—the Mother of Jesus, St. John, Magdalen and Mary of Cleophas—appear to have been permitted to come gradually nearer and nearer, until they stood quite close to the Cross (John 19:25).

It was of course their intention to be present at the Passion and Death of Jesus. They had followed Him in Galilee in happier days and ministered to Him with their alms and the work of their hands; and now they will follow Him to the Cross and offer Him their tears, their compassion, their very lives if it might be. They had come up with Him to the joyous Paschal Feast. O God, what a feast it had become for them! All were there, and with unspeakable pain they beheld it all, the crucifixion, the erection of the Cross, and our Lord's suffering as He hung upon it (Luke 23:49; Mark 15:41).

But greater and more indescribable than any other was the compassion of the Mother of Jesus. Who can fathom her sorrow? What does not a mother endure at the death-bed of her child, and where was there ever such a death-bed as this, so terrible in its torture and shame? And what a Child was suffering there! Never was one more glorious or more beloved; never did child honor its mother more or render her happier than Jesus did His Mother. And never yet was there a mother whose heart was capable of a greater, deeper or more comprehensive love—and therefore also of greater pain—than the heart of the Mother of Jesus. The whole awful scene was enacted before her eyes; she saw it all: the nails and the wounds; she heard it all: the strokes of the hammer, the imprecations against her Son, His own words and sighs; she stepped close up to the Cross, and could look into His dying Face.

Who can form an idea of her pain? And she suffered all this voluntarily. No one, nothing but her own love could impose upon her the sacrifice of being present in person at the Death of Jesus; but she made it courageously and undauntedly, in spite of the threats and invectives of His foes. She held up until the day with all its horrors was over, and accompanied it all with the most magnificent acts of adoration, love, compassion and all other virtues. And why did the Mother of Jesus act thus? Precisely because she was His Mother, and wished to participate in the suffering and shame of her Son. She recognized to the full the great significance of His Death; it was the great Sacrifice of the Redemption, and she must cooperate in it, as Eve had once taken an active part in the Fall. What drew Our Lady to the Cross and held her there was her faith, which revealed to her all the glory of the Cross; the love that is stronger than death; and the unfathomable humility that made her ashamed to be treated better than her Divine Son.

2. HOW MARY AND JOHN ARE REWARDED

Such faithful, motherly and heroic love as Mary showed was bound to be rewarded by our Saviour. He too saw everything: her actions, her thoughts, and her suffering; He comforted and cared for her. She was not to die with Him, but to survive Him a long time, and therefore it was fitting that He should make provision for her. So, glancing at John, He said to her: "Woman (i.e. second Eve), behold thy son" (John 19:26). Thy Son Jesus is dying, and can no longer care for thee; John is now to take My place, he shall tend thee henceforth. I give him to thee. And to St. John He said: "Behold thy Mother" (John 19:27). Take My place with her now, honor and love her and take care of her as I have hitherto done.

These words smote on Mary's heart with a new thrill of unutterable pain. They were His actual leave-taking, a formal renunciation of her. Everything seemed to vanish from her heart and before her eyes; her whole life, the soul and center of which this Son of hers had been, seemed now as nothing. His place was now taken by John: the beloved disciple, it is true, but still only the disciple instead of the Master, the son of Zebedee for the Son of God. It was a cruel exchange. But she consented to the loss of our Saviour with the same humility with which she had once consented to His Conception. "Behold the handmaid of the Lord, be it done to me according to thy word" (Luke 1:38). And John also obeyed our Lord's will with great humility and confusion, readiness and love. He immediately took possession openly of His sweet legacy (John 19:27) by taking her to his own house; and inwardly he did so by adopting the dispositions of reverence, love and solicitude that our Saviour had cherished for His Mother throughout His whole life. St. John had merited this great privilege to a certain extent by his virginity, his courage and fidelity at the Death of Jesus, and his childlike love for Our Lady.

3. WHAT CONCLUSIONS MAY BE DRAWN FROM THE MYSTERY

In the first place, this mystery teaches us how our Saviour respects and fulfils the Fourth Commandment. He will not die without having provided for His holy Mother. He thinks of everything, even under such circumstances as these.

Secondly, it is clearly to be seen from this mystery that St. Joseph was dead already, and that Mary was quite forsaken and alone in the world; otherwise our Saviour could not have commended her to St. John's care. This also proves that she had no other son.

Thirdly, the mystery shows us how we must love and honor Mary as our Mother. Since the twelfth century a beautiful view of this mystery has gained ground in the Church. It shows St. John as the representative of all Christendom; so that our Saviour, in giving him Mary for his Mother, gave her to us all, and likewise inspired her with motherly love for us and prepared for us the grace of childlike dispositions towards her. Thus He made His will here, as it were, and left His nearest and dearest possession on earth as a legacy to the Apostles, the Church and all the faithful, with the wish that we should all enter into these filial dispositions towards His holy Mother.

Lastly, it is also evident from this mystery what an advantage it is to stand by the Cross and persevere there to the end. How magnificently St. John was rewarded for his love and loyalty to our suffering Saviour! From being a disciple and an Apostle he became a brother of Jesus and son of the Mother of God.

The Eclipse of the Sun

LUKE 23:44. And it was almost the sixth hour, and there was darkness over all the earth until the ninth hour.—45. And the sun was darkened; and the veil of the temple was rent in the midst.

MARK 15:33. And when the sixth hour was come, there was darkness over the whole earth until the ninth hour.

MATT. 27:45. Now from the sixth hour there was darkness over the whole earth until the ninth hour.

1. THE ECLIPSE OF THE SUN

Towards mid-day, and probably very shortly after the crucifixion, the sky began to grow dark and lowering, and by degrees a complete eclipse of the sun set in, which lasted until about 3 o'clock in the afternoon, when our Saviour's Death took place (Luke 23:44, 45; Mark 15:33; Matt. 27:45). This could not have been an ordinary, natural eclipse, for the moon was at the full, and it lasted nearly three hours. Therefore it must have been produced by quite exceptional causes. Either the moon suddenly came between the earth and the sun; or God obscured the latter and thus hindered its rays from falling on the earth; or some other unusual event occurred. Whether the eclipse extended over the whole earth or not is uncertain. Probably it was confined to Palestine.

2. SIGNIFICATION OF THE ECLIPSE OF THE SUN

This sign was evidently given as a testimony to the innocence and Divinity of Jesus. He is the Head of the whole human race, and so it was fitting that His Death should be indicated to the entire creation, particularly at this moment, when He was condescending to undergo such deep humiliation for its salvation. As the appearance of a miraculous star had proclaimed the Birth of Jesus, so now the eclipse of the sun proclaimed His Death. He was the spiritual Light of the earth, and thus it was right that the sun, the source of its material light, should mourn at His departure.

The eclipse of the sun had a special purpose with regard to the Jews. They had repeatedly desired a sign from heaven (Matt. 12:38; Luke 11:16). Now they had a sign, and a very great one. And this sign was given to them to show them what a terrible crime they had committed, and to lead them to amendment and penance by announcing the punishment to come. Darkness and obscurity betoken in the Scriptures approaching judgment and the anger of God (Amos 8:9; Isa. 5:30; Joel 2:31; Ex. 10:22).

3. EFFECT OF THE ECLIPSE OF THE SUN

There is always something very weird about an eclipse of the sun, and this was especially the case here, since it began so suddenly, lasted so long, and was so terrible to behold. The birds in the gardens grew dumb, the beasts wandered timidly about or sought for hiding-places. Men were terror-stricken and all cast awed and anxious glances at the heavens. Those who had just been jeering and boasting of their victory over the Nazarene became frightened and dejected, and we may hope that grace began to work in many souls; whilst many another may have denied the fear he inwardly felt, sought to explain everything by natural causes, and grown still more hardened in his impenitence.

The Desolation of Jesus on the Cross

Matt. 27:46. And about the ninth hour Jesus cried with a loud voice, saying: "Eli, Eli, lamma sabacthani?" that is: "My God, my God, why hast thou forsaken me?"—47. And some that stood there and heard, said: "This man calleth Elias."—48. And immediately one of them running, took a sponge, and filled it with vinegar, and put it on a reed, and gave him to drink.—49. And the others said: "Let be, let us see whether Elias will come to deliver him."

Mark 15:34. And at the ninth hour Jesus cried out with a loud voice, saying: "Eloi, Eloi, lamma sabacthani?" Which is being interpreted: "My God, my God, why hast thou forsaken me?"—35. And some of the standers-by hearing, said: "Behold, he calleth Elias."

In the midst of the silence and obscurity that surrounded Mount Calvary, and towards the end of the three hours of agony, when the darkness and terror had reached their climax, our Lord suddenly made the air ring with the loud cry: "My God, My God, why hast Thou forsaken Me?" (Matt. 27:46; Mark 15:34.)

1. WHAT THIS CRY OF OUR SAVIOUR SIGNIFIES

These words express the whole depth and immensity of our Lord's suffering on the Cross; they lay bare His complete desolation, the suffering Humanity of Jesus forsaken by God, and deprived of all protection and every consoling fruition of the Divinity. In point of fact the Second Person of the Godhead never actually withdrew from the Sacred Humanity, nor, consequently, the Divinity either; nor was the union with the other two Divine Persons ever interrupted. But the Humanity had, with the exception of the immediate vision of God, no sensible perception of this union, no more refreshing effects of enlightenment, protection, comfort or joy. It was engulfed in an abyss of unspeakable suffering of every description. Our Lord experienced the utmost degree of abandonment, exterior as well as interior.

There our Saviour hangs in mid-air, rejected by earth and not received by heaven. The last tie that bound Him to earth is severed. His garments are divided, the very Mother who bore Him is given away; everyone has forsaken Him, His disciples are absent, His adherents have fallen off or dispersed; the whole nation has rejected Him. As far as His eye can reach He is surrounded by a crowd of foes and tormentors, men who hate Him and gloat over His misery, abuse and revile Him. From the Cross on which He hangs He can see only faces full of malignant exultation and fury, threatening hands and fierce gestures. All that He hears is bitter insults, inspired and animated by the spirit of hatred and revenge (Matt. 27:47–49; Mark 15:35). The little circle of faithful souls is kept at a distance; they can do nothing but increase His pain by their sorrow, helplessness and inconsolable grief. How their pain went to His Heart! Thus He receives nothing from earth but suffering.

And from His Body too all divine protection is withdrawn. He hangs stretched out upon hard, rough wood, on the terrible bed of the Cross. His shoulders and back are raw and bleeding; He is but one wound from head to foot. His hands and feet, pierced by the cruel nails, burn like fire; the thorns in His head and temples torture Him like pointed flames. The unnatural position, the cruel strain and distension of the limbs gradually causes numbness and checks all regular vital functions; the lungs, overfilled with blood, dilate painfully and uneasily in the oppressed breast; the heart beats slowly and heavily, and a terrible oppression weighs Him down with mortal fear. The blood cannot force its way back from the heart on account of the tension of the veins, and produces a dull, paralyzing, yet throbbing pain in the temples and neck. The brain is on fire with intolerable fever, and the countless wounds, exposed to the air, gradually begin to mortify, causing excruciating pain. Thus our Saviour felt really but one pain throughout His whole being, and there was no refuge or relief on earth. Nothing was left Him but heaven and His Father.

But heaven also, His Father, the refuge and comfort of all the forsaken, in Whom is all the mercy, fidelity and fatherhood of heaven and earth, has forsaken Him. This is the most awful suffering of all. When men forsake us, God still remains, and it is easy to do without all human comfort when one has the divine. But when He too departs, Who is the Supreme Good and the inmost life of the soul, then nothing more is wanting to render our misery complete; then the last star is extinguished, it is darkest night, and life is nothing but a kind of hell. But there was never a soul that loved God more or held more intimate intercourse with Him than the Soul of our Lord, in consequence of the union of His human nature with the Second Person of the Godhead, and also on account of His direct vision of God and the love, joy and bliss that proceeded from it. And now this communication of peace, enjoyment and consolation was completely broken off, and never was there a greater anguish of soul than this desolation of our Lord on the Cross. This was perhaps the most terrible and torturing pain He endured in the course of His whole Passion. It is an inscrutable mystery, like His sadness in the Garden on Mount Olivet; but here His suffering was much greater and more acute, because the exterior circumstances also oppressed His Heart with new grief and pain. From the very fact that He utters a cry to express His abandonment, it is clear how great this suffering was.

He calls, not upon His Father, but upon God. It is the cry of the soul for the Supreme, Eternal Good. Touching and thrilling are the words spoken by the prophets of this suffering and its attendant circumstances. "O God, my God . . . why hast Thou forsaken me? . . . I shall cry by day, and Thou wilt not hear. . . . In Thee have our fathers hoped; they have hoped, and Thou hast delivered them. They cried to Thee, and they were saved. . . . But I am a worm, and no man; the reproach of men, and the outcast of the people. All they that saw me have laughed me to scorn; they have spoken with the lips, and wagged the head. He hoped in the Lord, let Him deliver him. . . . For Thou art He that hast drawn me out of the womb: my hope from the breasts of my mother. . . . From my mother's womb Thou art my God. Depart not from me, for tribulation is very near; for there is none to help me. Many calves have surrounded me; fat bulls have besieged me. They have opened their mouths against me, as a lion ravening and roaring. I am poured out like water; and all my bones are scattered. . . . My strength is dried up like a potsherd, and my tongue hath cleaved to my jaws; and Thou hast brought me down into the dust of death. For many dogs have encompassed me; the council of the malignant hath besieged me. They have dug my hands and feet; they have numbered all my bones. And they have looked and stared upon me. They parted my garments amongst them, and upon my vesture they cast lots. But Thou, O Lord, remove not Thy help to a distance from me; look towards my defence" (Ps. 21). In the following passages also the Church finds a description of the desolation of Jesus on the Cross: "He hath led me, and brought me into darkness, and not into light. Only against me he hath turned and turned again his hand all the day. My skin and my flesh he hath made old, he hath broken my bones. He hath built round about me, and he hath compassed me with gall and labor. He hath set me in dark places, as those that are dead for ever. . . . Yea, and when I cry and entreat, he hath shut out my prayer. . . . I am made a derision to all my people, their song all the day long. He hath filled me with bitterness, he hath inebriated me with wormwood. . . . And my soul is removed far off from peace, I have forgotten good things. . . . My end and my hope is perished from the Lord. Remember my poverty and transgression, the wormwood and the gall. I will be mindful and remember, and my soul shall languish within me" (Lam. 3). Terrible Calvary! Never was there a more God-forsaken place, nor a more desolate and comfortless hour. Our Saviour is so hated that everyone wrongs and hurts Him; so despised, that no one will show Him any kindness: and so forsaken, that God Himself withdraws from Him, and this at the very moment when He gives Him the greatest proof of His love and dies for His honor.

2. WHY OUR SAVIOUR UTTERS THIS CRY

Our Saviour does not utter this cry through reluctance to suffer and weariness of the magnitude of His pain; but, first, in order to reveal to us that He took this suffering of interior desolation upon Himself, and that He suffered without any interior consolation. Further, He wished to show that all the prophecies with regard to the manner of His Death were now fulfilled; that is why He chose for this cry the first words of the very Psalm in which the principal prophecy is contained. Lastly, our Saviour intended this cry to be a comfort to us when we too have to suffer without human or divine consolation. By His complete abandonment He has left a precious treasure for the benefit of all the desolate, to the end of time. Here He merited and prepared for us the strength not to despond when we stand in the midst of the desert, in darkness and solitude, and not to despair even at our last hour. We are not alone there; our Saviour has been there before us and erected His Cross to be a comfort to us. This cry is like the voice of a friendly guide and powerful helper, proclaiming His presence in the pathless waste and offering His aid.

3. HOW HIS CRY OF AGONY WAS RECEIVED

This touching cry evoked only fresh mockery and scorn from our Saviour's foes. "Behold, he calleth Elias. . . . Let us see if Elias come to take him down" (Matt. 27:47; Mark 15:35). It is not certain if it was Jews or Romans who said this. Probably Jews; or perhaps the Jews said it first, and the Romans took up the cry. They seem not to have quite caught our Lord's words, and thought He had called Elias, who was regarded as the forerunner of the Messias, the helper in great distress and persecution, and the defender of God's people. At all events their words were a fresh expression of derision.

But how did Mary and John hear this cry of Jesus' crucified soul? The deep, mysterious abysses of His dereliction and mortal agony lay open before them; they themselves were plunged therein, and accompanied our Saviour in all His pain, all His conformity of will and love to His Heavenly Father, and all His noble love for us sinners, when we too shall be surrounded by this desert and engulfed in this abyss.

The Thirst of Jesus on the Cross

John 19:28. Afterwards Jesus knowing that all things were now accomplished, that the Scripture might be fulfilled, said: "I thirst."—29. Now there was a vessel set there full of vinegar. And they putting a sponge full of vinegar about hyssop, put it to his mouth.

Matt. 27:48. And immediately one of them running, took a sponge, and filled it with vinegar, and put it on a reed, and gave him to drink.

Mark 15:36. And one running and filling a sponge with vinegar, and putting it upon a reed, gave him to drink, saying: "Stay, let us see if Elias come to take him down."

1. HOW GREAT THIS SUFFERING WAS

It is plain that the suffering our Saviour's thirst caused Him was excessively great, from the mere fact of His complaining of it. He says nothing about His other torments—the thorns, the scourges, the nails—great as they were; but here He complains, and asks for alleviation. The circumstances were such that He was bound to experience torturing thirst. Great pain always provokes thirst, and it is always one of the most acute sufferings that accompanies death by crucifixion. No refreshment had passed our Lord's lips since the drinking of the blessed chalice at the Last Supper. His blood had been shed in torrents during the scourging, the crowning with thorns, and the crucifixion. The life-spring was exhausted, and His very bones had grown dry with the fever-heat He suffered; and the open wounds, exposed as they were to the air, must have caused this heat to alternate with feverish chills that made His whole Body tremble as if with ague. His lips were parched, His tongue black, His throat and palate dry and burning. What shipwrecked sufferer was ever consumed by such thirst as our Saviour's? This torment alone is so great that it can deprive men of their reason, and there is scarcely any death more terrible than to die of thirst.

2. HOW OUR SAVIOUR COMPLAINS OF HIS THIRST

Our Saviour complains of His terrible thirst very modestly. He asks for nothing, and only mentions His suffering late, very late. Indeed, He really did it chiefly in order to make known that He had this also to suffer, and spared Himself nothing of the bitter chalice of crucifixion; as also in order to fulfil the prophecies (John 19:28; Ps. 21:16), and to reveal that He was tormented by quite another thirst, of which this bodily one is but a feeble image, the thirst for the salvation and redemption of men, the Jews not excepted. Our Saviour's longing was not so much for what the Jews and His tormentors could offer Him to allay His bodily thirst, as for their own souls. He saw all men with His mind's eye, and burned with desire to save them; and this thirst was infinitely greater and more torturing. For what else did He suffer and die, but for the redemption of the human race, His creatures whom He so loved?

3. HOW THIS THIRST OF OUR SAVIOUR'S WAS RELIEVED

Our Saviour's implied request was fulfilled, but with a niggardly heartlessness. They gave Him no drink of refreshing water or strengthening wine, but only vinegar, and very little of that; and even this scanty refreshment was to be embittered by mockery and scorn. A soldier was pitiful enough to soak a sponge in vinegar, a vessel of which stood near at hand, and was about to hold it to our Saviour's lips on the end of a stalk of hyssop (Matt. 27:48; Mark 15:36; John 19:29). But others, Jews, perhaps, wished to prevent his act of charity, and told him to let it be, they would see whether Elias would come and deliver Him (Matt. 27:49). However, the soldier seems to have done it in spite of their protest (John 19:30). He refreshed our Saviour, in order to see if Elias would come (Mark 15:36). That was all the refreshment He received in His mortal agony: He, Who gives men everything in abundance, all the springs, all delicious wines and other beverages. His creatures do not even give Him a drink; water is refused to Him as it is to the rich glutton in hell. And just as scantily, nay rather more scantily, is His thirst for souls relieved; even the two thieves do not satisfy it. One of them refuses to give Him his soul, and prefers to give it to Satan. And so it was to continue. All men pass by His Cross; and how many of them refuse Him their souls, and carry them to hell!

This was a great grief to His Mother and the holy women also. They had no less courage and zeal than David's warriors (I Par. 11:18), and were just as ready as these to fetch a drink of water at the risk of their lives. But what could they do? They looked into His pale, dying Face, they saw His dry, parched lips, and they had nothing to give Him but their good will, their grief, their love and their souls.

The Death of Jesus on the Cross

Luke 23:45. And the sun was darkened; and the veil of the temple was rent in the midst.—46. And Jesus crying with a loud voice, said: "Father, into thy hands I commend my spirit." And saying this, he gave up the ghost.—47. Now the centurion seeing what was done, glorified God, saying: "Indeed this was a just man."—48. And all the multitude of them that were come together to that sight, and saw the things that were done, returned striking their breasts.—49. And all his acquaintance, and the women that had followed him from Galilee, stood afar off beholding these things.

Mark 15:37. And Jesus having cried out with a loud voice, gave up the ghost.—38. And the veil of the temple was rent in two, from the top to the bottom.—39. And the centurion, who stood over against him, seeing that crying in this manner he had given up the ghost, said: "Indeed this man was the Son of God."—40. And there were also women looking on afar off; among whom was Mary Magdalen, and Mary the mother of James the Less and of Joseph, and Salome.

Matt. 27:50. And Jesus again crying with a loud voice, yielded up the ghost.—51. And behold the veil of the temple was rent in two from the top even to the bottom; and the earth quaked, and the rocks were rent,—52. And the graves were opened; and many bodies of the saints, that had slept, arose,—53. And coming out of the tombs after his resurrection, came into the holy city and appeared to many.—54. Now the centurion and they that were with him watching Jesus, having seen the earthquake and the things that were done, were sore afraid, saying: "Indeed this was the Son of God."—55. And there were many women afar off who had followed Jesus from Galilee, ministering unto him;—56. Among whom was Mary Magdalen, and Mary the mother of James and Joseph, and the mother of the sons of Zebedee.

JOHN 19:30. Jesus therefore when he had taken the vinegar, said: "It is consummated." And bowing his head, he gave up the ghost.

1. EVENTS IMMEDIATELY PRECEDING OUR LORD'S DEATH

Our Saviour had already hung on the Cross for three torturing hours. And now the end was at hand. His Body began to droop down heavily from the Cross, as though the nails would no longer support it. He became more and more pallid, and the little channels of trickling blood showed up darker and plainer. His face grew longer, His features thinner, sharper and narrower; the cheeks fell in, the blue lips were slightly opened, and the bloodshot eyes gazed fixedly into space. . . . He was silent, and awaited the approach of death in mysterious suffering and communing with His Father.

All at once He painfully raised His thorn-crowned head, and cried: "It is consummated" (John 19:30). He meant by this: Pain and ill-treatment have exhausted Me, and Death claims its rights; My life-work is ended, God's Will and the prophecies are fulfilled and the duties of My office and vocation accomplished; sin is atoned for, justice is satisfied; grace and glory are prepared and My work and merits completed; it only remains for Me to die. And then He cried with a mighty voice, and with an upward glance of infinitely touching resignation and childlike confidence: "Father, into Thy hands I commend My spirit" (Luke 23:46). He wished hereby to teach us how to die, viz. in prayer, and with dispositions of love, resignation and unbounded confidence. Above all our Saviour acknowledges the Father as the origin of all things, His own life and being not excepted. He gives back His soul, His life, into His Father's hand, whence He received it (Ps. 30:6). And more than this. It might seem hard that the Father should have forsaken Him in His mortal agony on the Cross and deprived Him of all protection and joy. But this inexorable justice had not been able to diminish His childlike love one iota. "Thou art He that hast drawn me out of the womb; my hope from the breasts of my mother. I was cast upon Thee from the womb; from my mother's womb Thou art my God" (Ps. 21:10, 11). "Although He should kill me, I will trust in Him" (Job 13:15). He calls Him Father, and now that He is about to yield up His soul, His dearest possession, He knows no one to whom He can entrust it more gladly or more confidently than to His Heavenly Father. He surrenders it into His hands as one entrusts one's most precious possessions to the care of a friend, when setting out on a journey.

2. THE DEATH OF JESUS

And so death drew nigh: death, the last extremity, so hard and bitter to our nature; death, the deepest humiliation, when soul and body are torn asunder like associates in crime; death, the obstinate struggle, when life, besieged and forced back on all sides, makes its last desperate resistance; death, the sharpest pain, the acuteness of which is so often displayed in a tear and an unspeakably bitter, drawn expression about the mouth; death, that harsh and bitter child of sin, who touches all Adam's descendants with his destroying scepter, and turns them to dust; death, even death was now to come. And was he to stretch out his hand over the All-Holy one, the Giver and Author of all life, and to subject Him also to his bitter dominion? Yes, so it was to be, because He Himself willed it.

And when our Lord had cried with a loud voice, the death-struggle began. A cold perspiration breaks from His limbs; the pale hue of death overspreads the whole body, and a tremor of pain passes through it; the arms extend; the whole body sinks downwards, and the knees fall in and turn side-ways; the head sinks on the breast; He heaves a deep sigh and breathes out His spirit (John 19:30; Luke 23:46; Mark 15:37; Matt. 27:50). The disembodied soul, glorified in the same moment, descended like a bright flash of lightning to the lower world, and the body hung on the Cross broken and nerveless, an inanimate corpse.

Our Saviour died at 3 o'clock in the afternoon, after He had hung on the Cross for about three hours, and in consequence of the crucifixion and the sufferings and loss of blood attendant upon it, which together made up the great and painful Sacrifice of the Cross. Thus He really and truly died the death of the Cross. But He died of His own free will, because He wished to do so (Isa. 53:7; John 10:18). The sufferings He had endured since entering the Garden of Gethsemani were naturally mortal and sufficient to cause death; but nevertheless they could not deprive Him of life without an actual consent on His part. He gave this consent at the moment when He bowed His head. Scripture seems to indicate this, too, by saying that He bowed His head and then expired

(John 19:30). Under ordinary circumstances death sets in first, and then the head sinks. Further, three Evangelists remark that our Lord uttered a loud cry at the moment of His Death (Luke 23:46; Matt. 27:50; Mark 15:37), so that the centurion on guard saw therein an extraordinary sign and an evidence of the true Divinity of Jesus, and confessed Him to be the Son of God (Mark 16:39). Thus His Death bears not only the mark of the weakness of His true human nature, but also the majestic imprint of His self-mastery as God and God-Man. Lastly, He died with all the marks of the most perfect holiness, in the practice of the most glorious virtues: acknowledgment of the Father's supremacy, obedience, resignation, trust, and the most touching love of God and of us men. His Death is not only precious in the sight of the Lord, like that of every Saint (Ps. 115:15); it is also the model, crown, perfection and source of all holy deaths; yes, and of all life. We live simply by His life-giving Death. He has merited all this for us by that bitter Death. There His Body hangs now on the Cross—ill-treated, shattered, disfigured, and slain, as an adorable and holy Victim of His Heart's infinite love of God and of us men. The sacrifice is now complete. At the same time, probably, the slaughtering of the sacrificial lamb had just begun in the Temple, and from its fore-courts the longdrawn, wailing trumpet-blasts resounded, proclaiming to heaven and earth and to those under the earth that the true Sacrificial Lamb was slain.

3. EFFECTS OF THE DEATH OF JESUS

But the effects of the Death of Jesus became visible in other signs, particularly in the inanimate creation. At the moment of His decease the earth began to rumble and quake, as though in great agitation. A terrible and wonderful rent cleft the rocks of Calvary, graves fell in and opened, and after our Lord's Resurrection many Saints of the Old Testament appeared to bear witness to Him. And in the Temple also there was great destruction and confusion. The large and costly curtain between the sanctuary and the Holy of Holies (Ex. 26:33; II Par. 3:14) was rent in two from top to bottom, so that the Holy of Holies lay open to view (Matt. 27:51–53; Mark 15:38; Luke 23:45). Either the magnificent curtain (several times the thickness of a hand) rent asunder of itself, or the two upper posts gave way in consequence of the earthquake and tore it by their fall. This rending of the curtain signifies the cessation of the Old Testament, the rejection of the

Temple, the fulfilment of all types and mysteries, and the direct access of the people to Jehovah (Hebr. 9:8).

Among men the first to be affected by this cry were the centurion and the soldiers under his command. On hearing the powerful cry and perceiving how the earth immediately began to quake and the rocks under their feet were cleft, they feared exceedingly, and the centurion, enlightened by grace, glorified God and confessed the innocence and Divinity of Jesus: "Indeed this was a just man and the Son of God" (Luke 23:47; Mark 15:39; Matt. 27:54). The soldiers may have become Christians later on. And as for the people who stood near the Cross and on the surrounding heights, watching the spectacle, they were panic-stricken at these terrible signs. They gave ear to the voice of conscience, struck their breasts, lamented aloud, and fled in consternation to the city (Luke 23:48). There too, in all probability, a panic of fear had seized all.

But what was the effect of the Death of Jesus upon His friends, upon the holy women, John, and Mary? Grief and reverence probably cast them all upon their knees at this moment. John, although his heart was rent with unspeakable grief at the Death of his well-beloved Lord and Master, seems nevertheless not to have forgotten his vocation for an instant, but observed closely all that took place, in order to record it in his Gospel as the appointed witness. And our Lord's Mother? Lost in contemplation of her Son and motionless with grief, she at length perceived with unutterable horror the signs of the death-struggle. She knew all; her crucified soul, instead of dying, rose, assisted by powerful grace, to the supreme and most terrible of sacrifices. She made it. "Behold the handmaid of the Lord. Be it done to me according to Thy word," was surely her prayer now as heretofore. The Eternal Son offered the Father the sacrifice of His life on the arms, so to speak, of His Mother, whose soul was crucified with Him. Perhaps His last dying glance fell upon her, as His childish eye had greeted her before any other visible being. His holy Soul passed by her on its way to Limbo, and she stood there, a childless Mother (Faber).

These were the spectators and witnesses of the Agony and Death of Jesus. They indicate the effects that it should produce in us, and show us the dispositions and sentiments with which we should be animated in order to commemorate it worthily. They believed, above all, in His Divinity, confessed and adored it; they repented, Mary excepted, of their sins and loudly bewailed them; their hearts were crucified with the dying Saviour in love, pity and grief, and inanimate nature accompanied their homage with the terrible testimony of her mourning and horror. But it is especially Mary's heart that should teach us how to commemorate the Death of Jesus in our hearts. It was the living altar on which the Lamb offered Himself for the sins of the world, and no one accompanied the terrible act of sacrifice with such appropriate and marvelous sentiments and feelings as did Mary. As she had represented the entire human race by her love and adoration at the Conception and Nativity of our Lord, so she represented it now at His Death. The first adoration of the Cross, which the Church so touchingly celebrates every year on Good Friday, took place here. "Behold the wood of the Cross, upon which the salvation of the world hung! Come, let us adore. Holy God, Strong God, Immortal God, have mercy upon us!" (Liturgy of Good Friday.)

4. SIGNIFICANCE OF THE DEATH OF JESUS

Such was the Death of Jesus. How great is its significance for our holy religion! Above all it is the confirmation and illustration of the great truths of faith. First, of the Incarnation and true human nature of Jesus. If Christ really died, He must have died as man (I John 5:8). But His Death also bears witness to His Divinity. What a holy man dies for must be true; and our Saviour died for the testimony He had borne of His Divinity, and this testimony was confirmed by the miracles that took place in inanimate nature. His Death is the seal of all prophecies and types both of the shame and of the glorification of the Messias, which reciprocally depend upon, explain, and shed light upon each other. It is the touching witness of the infinite love of the Father for us, shown in His giving His Son for us; and lastly, it is the witness to the value of our immortal souls, which have their origin in God and are reckoned worthy to be purchased at such a price. Not less important is the Death of Jesus in the moral sphere, above all in the clear testimony it bears to the glory of our supernatural end and the majesty of the divine law which leads to it; to the gravity and atrocity of sin, which is a transgression of this eternal law; and to effacement and atonement of sin by Christ. To blot out sin, atone to God for the violation of the law, and deliver us from eternal damnation, a God must die. And He does it voluntarily and with the most touching dispositions of obedience and love, thus fulfilling to excess the requirements of the law in every virtue. We are redeemed now from the curse of sin and the law; Satan's power is broken, and the Death of Jesus is the pledge of the certainty of our redemption. Then further, how great is the significance of the Death of Jesus as regards the economy of grace! The treasure of Christ's merits, from which flow all the graces of the Sacraments as well as all actual graces required for our justification and for all the needs of the Christian life, is now deposited and completed. The essentials of our holy Sacrifice are founded. The Death of Christ gives us the very model of the new life in which, dead to sin, we are to live for God in the blessed hope of the resurrection of our bodies (Rom. 6:10). His Death is the source of all our blessings: the forgiveness of sins, grace, glory, and the resurrection of our flesh. As the uplifted serpent of Moses healed all who looked at it believing, so Jesus heals those who contemplate Him on the Cross with faith (John 3:14; Num. 21:9).

Thus the Death of Jesus is a confirmation and abridgment of our whole religion. His Death teaches us how to live and die, and how to live and die for Him. In His exceeding love and goodness He has suffered death for us, and by this Death has won us life. What more just than that we should use this life for Him? "Christ died for all; that they also who live may not now live to themselves, but unto Him Who died for them and rose again" (II Cor. 5:15). Our Saviour's voluntary sacrificial Death has become for Him the basis and title of His glory and world-sovereignty. "I will declare Thy name to my brethren; in the midst of the Church will I praise Thee. . . . When I cried to Him He heard me. . . . All the ends of the earth shall remember, and shall be converted to the Lord; and all the kindreds of the Gentiles shall adore in His sight. For the kingdom is the Lord's; and He shall have dominion over the nations. . . . And to Him my soul shall live; and my seed shall serve Him. There shall be declared to the Lord a generation to come; and the heavens shall show forth His justice to a people that shall be born, which the Lord hath made" (Ps. 21:23–32; Isa. 53:10–12; Hebr. 2:9–18). So His gravestone has become the foundation of His throne and kingdom, and His Cross the scepter of His power. "Whether we live or whether we die, we are the Lord's" (Rom. 14:8).

Our Saviour's Death gives Him a claim upon our death also, and sanctifies it. Since He died, death has no terror for the Christian. Christian death, death in grace, faith, love, and union with the dispositions of the dying Saviour, is a copy and reproduction of Jesus' Death, it is an infinitely precious sacrifice, the crown of the Christian life. Since the Death of Jesus, death has become so beautiful that without it there would be something wanting to our perfection, viz. the complete resemblance to Him. If the choice were left to us, we should even choose to die, because He too chose and suffered death for us. We have nothing to fear; our Saviour has won for us by His Death powerful graces to enable us to die well, like Christians. His last dying sigh: "Father, into Thy hands I commend My spirit," is a protection against the powers of darkness in the hour of death; that is why it has become the favorite prayer of the dying. With these words Jesus placed us also, as a dear legacy, in His Father's hands. We only need to draw upon these graces for ourselves and for all the dying. So let us not fear the dark portal! Jesus is there. And where Jesus is, Mary is also, because she was present at the Death of Jesus, her first-born Son. Does not Catholic feeling express this, by concluding the favorite prayer of all Catholics to Mary with the petition that she may "pray for us at the hour of our death"? And shall this petition, so often and so fervently made, fail to be granted?

The Opening of Jesus' Side

John 19:31. Then the Jews (because it was the parasceve), that the bodies might not remain upon the cross on the sabbath-day (for that was a great sabbath-day) besought Pilate that their legs might be broken, and that they might be taken away.—32. The soldiers therefore came; and they broke the legs of the first, and of the other that was crucified with him.—33. But after they were come to Jesus, when they saw that he was already dead, they did not break his legs,—34. But one of the soldiers with a spear opened his side, and immediately there came out blood and water.—35. And he that saw it hath given testimony; and his testimony is true. And he knoweth that he saith true; that you also may believe.—36. For these things were done that the Scripture might be fulfilled: "You shall not break a bone of him."—37. And again another Scripture saith: "They shall look on him whom they pierced."

After the Death of Jesus the darkness thereupon came to an end, and the sun, welcome after the gloom, shone again upon the hills and heights. Its light fell also upon the place of execution on Mount Calvary and the three crosses with the condemned men, at whose feet a Roman guard was still stationed and the friends of Jesus were standing and sitting in deepest grief. And now there came from the city soldiers with ladders and clubs, to break the arms and legs of the crucified men and to kill them. They immediately began their cruel and murderous work, to the terror and horror of the Mother of Jesus and her companions. But they did not maltreat the Body of Jesus in this manner; but one of them opened His side with a lance.

1. CAUSE OF THE OPENING OF JESUS' SIDE

Crucifixion does not of itself cause death speedily, but the sufferers expire slowly by the gradual loss of strength. For this reason the Romans were accustomed either to burn crucified criminals on the cross, to kill them with a lance, cast them to wild beasts, or sometimes leave them to die of hunger. According to the Jewish law the executed criminal whose body had been hung on the gibbet to increase his disgrace had to be taken down and buried before evening (Deut. 21:23). The Jews now took their stand upon this law, and asked Pilate to send soldiers to go and break the bones of the crucified men with clubs (to compensate for shortening their pain on the cross), to kill them and take them down from the gibbets to be buried. They urged as a reason for this that the following day was the Sabbath, and the "great Sabbath" too, because it was the one upon which the Paschal Feast fell this year. The Parasceve or day of preparation was already nearing its close, and it was high time to act (John 19:31). Other reasons were probably their evil consciences, the terror with which the dreadful natural phenomena and other occurrences had inspired them, and their fear of the people. They wanted to end the matter and consign it to oblivion. So Pilate sent soldiers to do as the Jews wished.

2. THE OPENING OF JESUS' SIDE

But in the meantime our Saviour had already expired, and so the soldiers, perhaps at the entreaty of His Mother and the holy women, forbore to profane His Body (John 19:33). But one of them, probably from the soldier's instinct of obedience and in order to make sure of our Saviour's Death, thrust his spear into His side (John 19:34). It was the right side, according to tradition, and the powerful thrust pierced to the heart. The wound must have been deep and wide, since St. Thomas could put his hand into it (John 20:27).

This thrust drew forth a stream of blood and water (John 19:34). That blood should flow was natural, because it does not coagulate until about four hours after death. But the water (and we are expressly told that it was water) really seems to have been a miraculous fact. The holy Fathers explain it thus, and the strong emphasis laid by St. John upon the incident seems to indicate it as such: "He that saw it hath given testimony; and his testimony is true. And he knoweth that he saith true; that you also may believe" (John 19:35). So the thrust must have pierced the pericardium and probably part of the heart itself.

3. SIGNIFICATION OF THE OPENING OF JESUS' SIDE

St. John's words, that "these things were done that the Scripture might be fulfilled" (John 19:36), point to great mysteries and divine intentions. In the first place, our Saviour doubtless intended the opening of His side to be a new and irrefutable proof of His real and true Death. Death must at least be the consequence of this spear-thrust, even if it had not occurred before; and St. John is here chiefly bearing witness to the truth of the Death of our Saviour. So this is the sacrifice of His last drop of blood.

Secondly, this mystery was the fulfilment of several prophecies and prophetic types. This spear-thrust had been foretold by the prophet Zacharias. "And I will pour out upon the house of David, and upon the inhabitants of Jerusalem, the spirit of grace and of prayers; and they shall look upon me, whom they have pierced; and they shall mourn for him as one mourneth for an only son, and they shall grieve over him, as the manner is to grieve for the death of the first-born" (Zach. 12:10). Jehovah will be killed by the Jews, and they will turn to him in faith and penitence. This was already taking place with many of the people (Luke 23:48), and also with the friends of Jesus, particularly the women, who are specially mentioned in this prophetic passage (Zach. 12:13, 14; 13:1). On the Feast of Pentecost this prophecy will be realized to a greater extent (Acts 2:37), and will finally be completely fulfilled at the end of time.

With regard to types, we find in this mystery the fulfilment of the peculiar circumstance in the sacrifice of the Paschal Lamb, that its bones were not broken, but that it was placed whole upon the family table, and had to be wholly consumed by the family and the family alone (Ex. 12:43–58; Num. 9:12). This signifies not merely the relationship and union between the partakers, but also their communion with the whole, undivided sacrificial lamb. We become partakers of the whole Body of Christ, which dies no more and cannot be divided (I Cor. 10:16 seq.). And the holy Fathers and the Church see here the fulfilment of yet another type. As Eve was taken from the side of the sleeping Adam (Gen. 2:21–24), so the new Eve, the Church (with her two principal Sacraments, Baptism and the Blessed Sacrament of the Altar, symbolized by the water and the blood), proceeded from the side of Jesus, the second Adam, in the sleep of death.

A third mystical signification lies in the relation of this mystery to two great devotions that arose in the Church later on: the devotions to the Precious Blood and to the Sacred Heart of Jesus. Both of them, especially the latter, have their origin in this mystery. The opening of Jesus' side is the last mystery in the Passion, and by it His Heart was laid bare, so to speak, and revealed as the seat of love, the hidden mainspring of life and of all mysteries, the source of all virtues and merits, the last sacrifice for us, and, by means of the devotion to this Sacred Heart, an important instrument of the graces in the meriting of which it had played such an exceptionally prominent part.

Such is the signification of the opening of Jesus' side; a mystery full of deep meaning and practical efficacy. We have now considered its brighter side. But there were dark shadows enough, and they surrounded the poor Mother and the little handful of faithful souls at the foot of the Cross. What pain and terror must have seized them as the soldiers were about to strike the Body of our Saviour! Perhaps they pushed Him irreverently, to see if there was any life in Him. And when the soldier unexpectedly thrust his spear into Jesus' side, must not a general cry of pain have been raised, and every hand have been stretched out as though to ward off the thrust? And what of His Mother? Was there a more sacred object on earth for her faith and love than the Body of our Saviour? Can a mother bring herself to be present at the opening of her child's corpse? And now she is forced to look on at this desecration by such a rough hand! Surely the spear could scarcely have pierced our Saviour more painfully, even had He been living, than it transfixed the heart of His Mother. With what holy care and bitter tears she sought to save the blood and water that poured out upon the rock! Could she contemplate the cruel wound otherwise than on bended knee? This was, as it were, the first homage of love and reparation to the Sacred Heart, the first public devotion paid to It. And thus the devotion to the Sacred Heart of Jesus is revealed, founded and established, with its object, the material heart as the seat and token of love, and its touching motives and practice, which are no other than love and reparation.

The Descent from the Cross

JOHN 19:38. And after these things Joseph of Arimathaea (because he was a disciple of Jesus, but secretly for fear of the Jews) besought Pilate that he might take away the body of Jesus. And Pilate gave leave. He came therefore and took away the body of Jesus.—39. And Nicodemus also came, he who at the first came to Jesus by night, bringing a mixture of myrrh and aloes, about an hundred pound weight.—40. They took therefore the body of Jesus, and bound it in linen cloths with the spices, as the manner of the Jews is to bury.

LUKE 23:50. And behold there was a man named Joseph, who was a counselor, a good and a just man,—51. (The same had not consented to their counsel and doings), of Arimathaea, a city of Judaea, who also himself looked for the kingdom of God.—52. This man went to Pilate and begged the body of Jesus;—53. And taking him down, he wrapped him in fine linen.

MARK 15:42. And when evening was now come (because it was the Parasceve, that is the day before the Sabbath),—43. Joseph of Arimathaea, a noble counselor, who was also himself looking for the kingdom of God, came and went in boldly to Pilate, and begged the body of Jesus.—44. But Pilate wondered that he should be already dead. And sending for the centurion, he asked him if he were already dead.—45. And when he had understood it by the centurion, he gave the body to Joseph.—46. And Joseph buying fine linen and taking him down, wrapped him up in the fine linen.

MATT. 27:57. And when it was evening, there came a certain rich man of Arimathaea, named Joseph, who also himself was a disciple of Jesus;—58. He went to Pilate, and asked the body of Jesus. Then Pilate commanded that the body should be delivered.—59. And Joseph taking the body, wrapped it up in a clean linen cloth.

1. HEART-BREAKING SITUATION OF THE MOTHER OF JESUS

In the meantime it had been growing quieter and quieter around the Cross, and the evening was drawing in (Mark 15:42; Matt. 27:57). The soldiers were occupied in dragging the bodies of the dead thieves down the hill to the common burial-place. And during this time our Lord's white Body, streaked with the dark blood that had flowed over it, hung on the Cross, at once touching and awe-inspiring.

With unutterable pain Mary contemplated this holy Body that the Holy Ghost had formed in her womb, now robbed of all form and beauty, even of its Soul, torn and shattered, borne down by its own dead weight on the Cross. What should she do with her dead Son? She could not even take Him down, and had no grave for Him. Indeed, He did not belong to her any more; He was the property of Pilate and the Jews. Any request from her might result in grosser desecration. She feared every instant that the soldiers would come back and drag away her dear Son's Body to the burial-place of criminals. It was considered a disgrace among the Jews not to be buried in one's own family sepulcher (III Kings 13:22; Jer. 26:23). The Mother of Jesus had always been poor, poor in Bethlehem also, but never had she felt her poverty so bitterly as here in sight of her Son's corpse.

2. THE DESCENT FROM THE CROSS

These were indeed moments of anguish. But God comforted her. He had already inspired good men to come and pay the last honors of burial to our Saviour. They came, accompanied by servants and provided with all necessaries.

These men were Joseph of Arimathaea and Nicodemus. Joseph was from Arimathaea or Ramatha (Rentis), a rich (Matt. 27:57) and respected member of the Great Council (Mark 15:43), otherwise Pilate would certainly not have given him the Body; he was also pious and just (Luke 23:50). That he practised the works of mercy is seen in his burying Jesus (Tob. 1:21). He expected the kingdom of God and the Messias (Luke 23:51; Mark 15:43), and was a disciple of Jesus, although hitherto only in secret, for fear of the Jews (John 19:38; Matt. 27:57). But he had not consented to the general verdict against Jesus at the sitting of the Council (Luke 23:51), and by this dissent had publicly broken with the party of His enemies. This first step, together with the unheard-of injustice and cruelty practised upon our Lord, prepared him for a second, far more important act. He determined to give our Saviour an honorable burial, though according to Jewish custom those who had been executed received only a shameful one. He possessed a new sepulcher hewn in the rocks near Mount Calvary, and in this he would lay our Lord (Matt. 27:60). So he went boldly to Pilate (Mark 15:43) and asked in the name of the friends and relatives for Jesus' Body, and for permission to take Him down from the Cross (John 19:38). This was allowable according to Roman law. Pilate wondered that Jesus should be dead already, for the Jews had just been there to obtain the order for Him to be killed on the Cross (John 19:31). In order to make sure he sent to inquire of the centurion in command of the guard at the Crucifixion. On hearing that our Saviour was really dead (Mark 15:44) he gave Joseph the Body (Mark 15:45), permitted him to take it down from the Cross (John 19:38), and gave orders that it should be delivered to him (Matt. 27:58). Pilate did this partly because it was the usual custom, partly out of respect for Jesus, and partly from dislike of the Jews. Joseph now bought fine Indian linen, such as the priests (Lev. 16:4) and rich men (Luke 16:19) wore (Mark 15:46), and began his task at once with his servants. The other man was Nicodemus, likewise a disciple of Jesus (John 19:39) and an influential lawyer and ruler (John 3:1, 10). We have already made his acquaintance on the first Feast of the Pasch, when he came to have an interview with Jesus. He too wished to share in His burial, and bought a hundred pounds of ointment, aloes, myrrh, and spices (John 19:39).

We can well imagine how Mary welcomed the arrival of these good men, and with what respect and compassion they greeted the Mother of Jesus. With what feelings they contemplated the dead, outraged Body, and what reverence and adoration they paid it! Then they placed ladders against the Cross, mounted them, and began their sad service of love. The crown of thorns and the nails were handed down one after another, and surely passed from hand to hand till they reached the Mother of Jesus. At last the Body, wrapped in cloths, was slowly and carefully lowered. St. John took it in his arms and laid it in those of the Mother, who received her Son on her knees at the Foot of the Cross (John 19:40; Matt. 27:59; Luke 23:53; Mark 15:46). These men of high degree did all this with great reverence, loving care and indescribable compassion. Their thoughts and hearts were filled with grief, adoration and love. No priest can treat the Blessed Sacrament with more care and reverence than these holy men did the Body of Jesus. How dear they must be to us for their love of our Saviour and His holy Mother, and for the generosity with which they gave not only their property—Nicodemus his wealth and Joseph his sepulcher (Gen. 23:6)—but also themselves, the personal service of their hands; and lastly, for their courage! It is not without significance that we are told Joseph went "boldly" to Pilate (Mark 15:43). It really needed courage to do this, seeing the fanatical hatred borne by the chief priests to Jesus and the victory they had gained over Him. This sympathy for the fate of the Crucified, their intervention for Him and the public burial they gave Him, might well be regarded as a demonstration of opposition, and might have the worst consequences for themselves. But they care nothing for all this. These are noble-minded men, and their act is the first victory of the Death of Jesus and a fruit of our Lord's gentleness and patience. He did not take it amiss that they kept the fact of their discipleship secret for a time. He waited patiently, and now His patience has borne fruit. And this is all the more wonderful, seeing that they were the only ones of all the disciples and Apostles (St. John excepted) who openly declared themselves for Jesus and espoused His cause.

3. OUR SAVIOUR ON HIS MOTHER'S LAP

Thus (as tradition tells us) Our Lady took the dead Body of Jesus on her lap. And what does she do? After a moment of speechless adoration she surveys the cruel havoc: the terrible ill-usage, the wounds, deep and large and small. With infinite woe she lives through the whole Passion again, following it out by the dreadful traces it has left. Now she can see it all close at hand. She arranges the tangled hair, touches, kisses, and closes the wounds. And of what does she think? Surely of happier times, of the glorious hour of the Last Supper, the majesty and nobility of His manly prime, and the sweet days in Bethlehem and Nazareth, when as a winsome Child He had lain in her arms, and she had rendered Him similar services. And what does she feel? The terrible sword foretold by Simeon, piercing her heart a thousandfold at the sight of every wound (Luke 2:35); unutterable pain and love, love of Jesus and love of us. She was not angry with us. She had given Him to us as the most beautiful and lovable of all the children of men, the vessel of all beauty, truth and love, for our joy and profit. And how does she receive Him back? In a plight worse than that of the prodigal son; poor, torn, a shattered and empty vessel, a mutilated and lacerated corpse, from us, whom He had come to restore to health and life. See! the Babe of Bethlehem has come back to His Mother's lap. But how differently His arms are stretched out now! They are so cruelly dislocated, so stiffened in His death-struggle, that she can scarcely bend them. He lies in the form of a cross on the knees and in the arms of His Mother (Faber). But of what do all these wounds speak to her, if not of His love for us? We were the price of this blood, these wounds, and this life. How could she help loving us? How could she forget us? We are graven on her heart in a thousand wounds.

And we must not forget her either. As long as the Death of Jesus is preached, as long as a cross is left standing in the world, the devotion to His Mother cannot die. Everyone who passes by the Cross sees the Mother there with her dead Son on her lap, and blesses God for having confounded our enemies through her means, saying: "Blessed art thou . . . above all women upon the earth. Blessed be the Lord who . . . hath so magnified thy name this day that thy praise shall not depart out of the mouth of men who shall be mindful of the power of the Lord for ever; for that thou hast not spared thy life . . . but hast prevented our ruin in the presence of our God" (Judith 13:23 seq.). The repose of the Virgin beneath the Cross has become the refuge of all the sorrowful. How many tears have been dried, how much grief has been comforted there! An inexhaustible spring of blessing and comfort for the world has welled forth from the place where Mary suffered so unspeakably.

The Burial of Jesus

John 19:41. Now there was in the place where he was crucified a garden; and in the garden a new sepulcher, wherein no man yet had been laid.—42. There therefore, because of the parasceve of the Jews, they laid Jesus, because the sepulcher was nigh at hand.

Luke 23:53. And taking him down, he wrapped him in fine linen, and laid him in a sepulcher that was hewed in stone, wherein never yet any man had been laid.—54. And it was the day of the parasceve, and the sabbath drew on.—55. And the women that were come with him from Galilee, following after, saw the sepulcher, and how his body was laid.

Mark 15:46. And Joseph buying fine linen and taking him down, wrapped him up in the fine linen and laid him in a sepulcher which was hewed out of a rock; and he rolled a stone to the door of the sepulcher.—47. And Mary Magdalen and Mary the mother of Joseph beheld where he was laid.

Matt. 27:59. And Joseph taking the body, wrapped it up in a clean linen cloth,—60. And laid it in his own new monument, which he had hewed out in a rock. And he rolled a great stone to the door of the monument, and went his way.—61. And there was there Mary Magdalen and the other Mary sitting over against the sepulcher.

The evening shadows grew longer, and the Parasceve was rapidly nearing its close. So the men made haste to bury Jesus.

1. PREPARATIONS FOR THE BURIAL

Joseph of Arimathaea and Nicodemus lifted the Body of Jesus from His Mother's lap and carried it to the stone of anointing, which is still shown and venerated in the Church of the Holy Sepulcher. There they prepared it for burial according to the Jewish custom (John 19:40). It was only in very rare cases that corpses were burnt (II Kings 21:12; II Par. 16:14; 21:19; Jer. 34:5; Lev. 20:14; 21:9); as a rule they were washed (Acts 9:37) and wrapped up in linen with spices. This the men did now. They wrapped the Body of Jesus in fine linen cloths and bands (Mark 15:46; Luke 23:53), and placed spices and bunches of sweet-smelling herbs between It and the linen; sprinkled the linen itself with sweet perfumes (John 19:40), and covered the Head with a napkin (John 20:7). Perhaps Mary herself performed this last duty, and with what woe she gazed for the last time upon the dead Face of her beloved Son! The sun of her life had really set with the covering of Jesus' Head. The preparation of the Body for burial was such as rich and respected men received. This became the dignity of Jesus and also the position and rank of the two noble-hearted men. The quantity of spices employed was intended to ward off corruption as long as possible.

2. THE INTERMENT

The preparations being completed, they proceeded to inter the Body. It was already late (Matt. 27:57; Mark 15:42), probably about 5 o'clock in the evening. The site where our Saviour was to be interred was situated about 50 paces north-west of the place where the Cross stood. It lay in a garden (John 19:41), which was probably planted with palms, olives, balsam-shrubs, bushes, and flowers, for it was customary among the Jews to surround their family sepulchers with foliage. It was fortunate that the distance was so short, on account of the nearness of the Sabbath. The sepulcher that was to receive our Saviour was hewn in the rocks (Matt. 27:60; Mark 15:46) and thus protected by nature against violation and profanation. It consisted of an antechamber and an inner room, the sepulcher properly so-called, containing a long, trough-shaped tomb, on the right-hand side of the low door-way between the ante-room and the grave-chamber. The sepulcher was quite new (Matt. 27:60; Luke 23:53; John 19:41) and unused, as befitted our Saviour, in Whose vicinity everything must be pure and inviolate as had been the womb of His holy Mother, to which the Holy Sepulcher is often compared (Num. 19:2; Deut. 21:3; I Kings 6:7; Luke 19:30). Joseph had had this sepulcher prepared for himself, and now it served for his Lord and Master. So it was a friend's grave, and this fact alone bears witness to the poverty of our Lord and the love of His followers for Him. He had neither a crib nor a sepulcher of His own. And as a Joseph had once helped His Mother to lay the Babe in the manger, so it was a Joseph too who helped her now to lay Him in the grave (Faber).

So the little procession of mourners went down the hill, through the ravine, straight across to the garden; the three or four men bearing the Body of Jesus carefully enveloped in the linen, His Mother, the holy women, and a few servants. These few faithful souls carried the Creator to the grave hard by the city, which, wrapped in darkness and silent in remorse of conscience, did not disturb our Saviour's last journey. But what a sad and heart-rending journey it was for Mary! It led to the grave, to separation. In the sepulcher they were probably obliged to use torches on account of the darkness. Gently they lowered the Sacred Body into the stone coffin. The instruments of the Passion were probably also placed in the tomb. One last glance of deep sorrow, one act of adoration, and the pall covered the beloved Dead; the door was closed, and a large stone rolled before it (Matt. 27:60; Mark 15:46; John 19:42). Many graves have closed and left broken hearts to weep over them, but none like this. The prophet describes this mourning in the words: "They shall mourn for Him (Jehovah) as one mourneth for an only son, and they shall grieve over Him as the manner is to grieve for the death of the first-born. In that day there shall be a great lamentation in Jerusalem, like the lamentation of Adadremnon. . . . And the land shall mourn; families and families apart . . . and their women apart" (Zach. 12:10, 11 seq.). It seems that the holy women, probably on account of the narrowness of the grave-chamber, could not enter the sepulcher itself, but watched the interment from outside (Luke 23:55; Mark 15:47; Matt. 27:61). Our Saviour had found His resting-place now; but not so His Mother. She set out on her way home, the way of exile and bereavement. She had no real home any longer. Like a ship that has lost its sails and helm, she arrived on Mount Sion, accompanied by the holy women.

3. SIGNIFICANCE OF OUR LORD'S BURIAL

The significance of our Lord's burial consists chiefly in its being a new proof of His true Death. His friends would never have buried Him if they had not been convinced that He was dead; and the eye and heart of a mother are not to be deceived in this respect. Secondly, the burial and three days' repose in the grave are the fulfilment of the prophecies; first, of the sign of Jonas, who passed three days in the belly of the fish and was then miraculously restored to the light of day. Our Saviour Himself had referred the Jews to this sign (John 2:19; Matt. 12:40). And His burial is also the fulfilment of the prophecy that His grave would be appointed Him with the ungodly, but His tomb would be given Him with a rich man (Isa. 53:9).[1] Thirdly, there is also a mystical signification of our Saviour's burial. He wished to pass through this last phase of human life, to bless and sanctify it by His presence and fill it with merit and consolation, by planting in the habitation of death the germ of life and making the tree of immortality sprout forth from the grave. St. Paul also sees in our Lord's burial a type of complete death to sin, in order to prepare ourselves for the glorious resurrection (Rom. 6:4; Col. 2:12).

The Great Sabbath

Matt. 27:62. And the next day, which followed the day of preparation, the chief priests and the Pharisees came together to Pilate,—63. Saying: "Sir, we have remembered that that seducer said, while he was yet alive: After three days I will rise again.—64. Command therefore the sepulcher to be guarded until the third day; lest perhaps his disciples come, and steal him away, and say to the people: He is risen from the dead; and the last error shall be worse than the first." —65. Pilate said to them: "You have a guard; go, guard it as you know."—66. And they departing, made the sepulcher sure, sealing the stone, and setting guards.

Luke 23:56. And returning they prepared spices and ointments; and on the sabbath-day they rested according to the commandment.

Mark 16:1. And when the Sabbath was past, Mary Magdalen and Mary the mother of James and Salome bought sweet spices, that coming they might anoint Jesus.

The Sabbath now began, a day of quiet mourning and hope. Its character is a mixed one; the dusk of Good Friday and the dawn of Easter Sunday seem to blend together on this day. A glance at Our Lady's house in the city, at the Sepulcher of our Lord, and into Limbo, will give us an idea of its events.

1. THE HOUSE ON MOUNT SION

The house on the heights of the upper city (Sion), in the neighborhood of which the Blessed Virgin probably dwelt, encloses all that is left of the Apostolic College, the whole Church. The occupants of the house are quiet, very quiet (Luke 23:56). They have much to reflect upon, much to mourn over, much to repent of. One sees only eyes reddened with weeping and tears still flowing; one hears only quiet sighs. Little is spoken. The preceding day with all its terrible incidents oppresses every heart with bitter pain. Our Saviour had suffered, was dead, lay buried outside the city. Our whole life ought really to be like this. We ought

[1] See the Hebrew text. The literal translation of the passage is: "They give him his grave with the ungoldly, but he is with a rich man after his death."

never to forget that our dear Lord has suffered and died, even though it happened long ago. A noble heart is never indifferent to this thought.

How still are the occupants of this house! And yet what deep consolation they find in the thought that they have remained true to our Lord to the end: John, Magdalen, and the holy women! The Apostles and disciples probably came one after another, returning from the hiding-places to which they had fled on their dispersion. They come humble and shamefaced, and softly ask for admittance. The others make friendly advances, encourage and comfort them. Peter too, probably, came and confessed his fault with many tears. But all the Apostles were very sad and inconsolable (Mark 16:10). They dared not think of the past, nor yet of the future. And who was now their comfort and support? Our Blessed Lady. In the midst of all the pain and woe that rent her heart, she was still quiet, firm, unshaken in her trust, and a comfort to them all; now already the Mother, the life, sweetness, and hope of the Church. In remembrance of this consolatory office exercised by Mary on this day, the Church (among other ordinances) has set apart the Saturday in each week for the special veneration of the Mother of God.

In the evening of the Great Sabbath, as the first day of the week commenced, the holy women already began to think again of their service to our Lord (Mark 16:1). They bought and prepared spices, in order to supply what had been unavoidably omitted in the preparation of our Lord's Body for burial on Friday evening, on account of the near approach of the Sabbath (Luke 23:54). Thus one good work incites and inclines to another.

2. THE SEPULCHER OF OUR LORD

Our Lord's resting-place, the Holy Sepulcher, was truly glorious.

In the first place, it was glorious in itself. It lay in a quiet and beautiful spot, in a blossoming garden, the flowers of which shed a perfume as of spring around the well-hewn vault. There our Lord's Body lies, motionless as a marble statue; it is full of wounds, but the blood has ceased to flow from them. The spices, bunches of herbs, and perfumes give forth a sweet odor. The Divinity, which never quitted the Body, sheds a quiet radiance round about; probably angels were there continually adoring. This repose of our Lord in the grave is a beautiful emblem of the Blessed

Sacrament of the Altar, a marvelous union of concealment and glory, life and death.

And our Lord's Sepulcher was also glorious on account of the love and reverence paid to it by the Apostles, the holy women, Our Blessed Lady, and in short by all His followers. As the bees and butterflies played round the flowers and blossoms of the surrounding garden, so the sad thoughts and feelings of all His disciples hovered round the grave. These are but the harbingers of the wonderful train of pilgrims from all Christian nations to the Holy Sepulcher of our Lord, the attraction that has found such widespread and imposing expression and manifestation in the course of the centuries. Like a magnet the Holy Sepulcher draws to itself all Christendom, and indeed the whole world.

Lastly, our Lord's Sepulcher is glorious in the fear with which it inspires His enemies. On the Sabbath itself (Matt. 27:62), probably in the evening, the chief priests and Pharisees went to Pilate and said they had remembered some declarations made by "that seducer," to the effect that He would rise again from the dead after three days. Possibly some of the disciples had let fall intimations of the kind, and the signs at our Lord's Death must have alarmed the Pharisees. So they now begged Pilate to have the Sepulcher guarded for three days, that the disciples might not come and take away the Body and say that He had risen from the dead; for this (political) fraud would naturally be worse than the first (Matt. 27:62–64). The first fraud had been the commotion excited amongst the people by Jesus in consequence of His assumed title of Messias. The second would be the tumult raised by the disciples' pretence that He was risen again. The Jews imputed a political significance to both, in order to frighten Pilate. So they themselves are afraid, and do not trust to their victory; indeed, they admit that the Resurrection or anything like it would be the worst danger of all. Pilate replied that they had the Temple guard, which he usually put at their disposal; or they might muster another force and do what they could with it; he would have nothing to do with the matter (Matt. 27:65). He is always the same, now compliant, now disdainful towards the Jews. So the chief priests went away and posted sentinels of their guard, a detachment of sixteen men, before the Sepulcher, and sealed the stone with bands crossed and recrossed (Matt. 27:66). That was a double precautionary measure, against the soldiers as well as the disciples. Thus they themselves provided with the utmost acuteness for the incontrovertibility of the miracle of the Resurrection, and placed at the Sepulcher a guard of honor and unimpeachable witnesses to what they were making such efforts to hinder. Thus our Lord's Sepulcher is truly glorious, and, as ever, He finds His glory in abasement.

3. LIMBO

At the moment of Christ's decease His Soul descended to Limbo (I Peter 3:19), already glorious, impassible and victorious, accompanied by a glorious escort of holy angels. By "the spirits in prison" we are doubtless to understand the Saints in their place of sojourn. It is uncertain whether our Saviour's personal presence penetrated into the abode of the damned also. At all events His power and the effect of His presence were felt there.

With what intent did the Soul of Christ descend into Limbo? First, in order to reveal His power and Divinity, as He had done on earth. Secondly, in order to confound and humiliate the evil spirits. What fear, shame, and terror must have seized them! They would not acknowledge Him at their time of trial, long ago; in their malice they had seduced the Jews into murdering Him, and now they saw that this very work of theirs had helped to complete the redemption of mankind. They had wounded themselves with the edge of their own sword. Terribly indeed did Christ let them feel His power now; in His Name every knee was compelled to bow, even in the nether world, Gehenna, or hell properly so-called (Phil. 2:10; Isa. 45:24). Thirdly, Christ's glorious Soul descended into Limbo in order to free the Saints of the Old Testament from the punishment of their sojourn there, under which they still sighed. He had conquered Satan, and now He freed his prisoners. His coming was to these holy souls as light and dew and fresh morning breezes. All of them, from our first parents downwards—the patriarchs, the prophets, kings, and High Priests, the blood-relations of our Lord, down to John, Elizabeth, and St. Joseph—adored Him in blissful ecstasy and exulted with holy joy and praise of God, after thousands of years of waiting and longing. They adored His Soul, and thanked Him for the redemption of the world and the fulfilment of all the prophecies and types; for the happiness that had fallen to their lot, of having resembled Him in their life, virtues and portion and contributed in some degree to the foundation of His kingdom. How loving it was of Him to come Himself to the holy souls, reveal Himself to them and set them free; rejoice them with the sight of Himself, and impart to them the immediate vision of God! He loved them, like us, as members of His mystical Body, and embraced them as parts of His world-redeeming life. Probably our Lord remained with the patriarchs until His Resurrection.

III

THE GLORIOUS LIFE OF JESUS

We now come to the glorious life of Jesus, the brilliant reverse of His earthly life, which, in spite of the miracles and prophecies by which God's glory was manifested in it, nevertheless bore throughout the stamp of poverty, labor, suffering and humiliation, in short, the "form of a servant."

Christ entered upon this glorious life by three gradations. Immediately after His Death His Soul was glorified, i.e. its lower faculties also entered into the state of beatitude. In the Resurrection His Body too was glorified, by being reunited to the beatified Soul. And at the Ascension His glory reached its climax and consummation.

Thus we have two periods of the glorious life to consider: the Resurrection and the glorious life on earth until the Ascension; then the Ascension and the glorious life in heaven.

1. THE GLORIOUS LIFE OF JESUS ON EARTH

The Resurrection of Christ

Mark 16:9. But he rising early the first day of the week appeared first to Mary Magdalen, out of whom he had cast seven devils.

The first mystery of Christ's complete glorification is the Resurrection. In the Resurrection His entire Humanity, Body and Soul, entered into essential glory, and hence Easter is the most glorious feast of the God-Man and of all Christendom, as the Martyrology so beautifully and rightly expresses it: "The feast of feasts, the Resurrection of our Lord and Redeemer Jesus Christ."

1. TRUTH AND REALITY OF THE RESURRECTION

Christ truly rose from the dead. All assure us of this: the Holy Scriptures (Mark 16:9), the holy angels (Matt. 28:6; Luke 24:6), the holy women (Mark 16:10; Luke 24:9, 22; John 20:18), and the Apostles (Luke 24:34), who doubted at first, but were afterwards convinced of the fact and preached their testimony of the Resurrection throughout the world. Indeed, the whole system of Christianity bears witness to the Resurrection; its very essence and stability stand and fall with this truth (I Cor. 15:14).

And Christ was bound to rise from the dead (Luke 24:46). This had been prophesied of Him (Ps. 15:10; Acts 2:31) and proclaimed in His types, Isaac (Hebr. 11:19) and especially Jonas. Christ Himself had often and solemnly predicted it to His Apostles (Matt. 15:22; 20:19; Mark 9:30; 10:34; Luke 18:33) and even to the Jews; at first mysteriously (John 2:19) and then quite plainly. He repeatedly refers them to the miracle of Jonas as a sign in confirmation of His mission, His Messianic office, and His Divinity (Matt. 15:4; Luke 11:29). So the Jews themselves awaited the third day after His Death in eager suspense (Matt. 27:63). All eyes were directed to this Sepulcher. If He did not rise again, all was over with Him, with His Person, His plans, and His work. This last failure would truly be worse for Him than anything. Thus it behoved Christ to rise from the dead, and He has risen in truth. "*Surrexit Dominus vere, alleluia. . . . Scimus Christum surrexisse a mortuis vere*" (Missal).

2. NATURE AND ATTENDANT CIRCUMSTANCES OF THE RESURRECTION

The essence of the resurrection consists in the reunion of the body and the soul to a glorious life. The transfigured soul reanimates the body; but the result of this reanimation is no longer an earthly life, but an entirely new and marvelous one. The body is now not merely a perfectly pliable instrument, which opposes no further resistance nor obstruction to the action of the soul; it is also a glorious instrument on a par with the soul, which it supports and to which it offers undreamed-of sources of knowledge, joy and power. For without ceasing to be a body it assumes spiritual qualities, the attributes of glorified bodies. They are these: first, immortality, which is complete impassibility and a complete independence with regard to life, youth and strength of exterior conditions and influences, such as food and sleep; secondly, clarity, which consists in radiant beauty and glory; thirdly, freedom, which excludes and overcomes everything difficult or base; lastly, agility, subtlety, and fulness of power, which knows no restrictions of matter, time, or distance. In consequence of these attributes a glorified body is a most wonderful thing, a masterpiece of God's wisdom and power (I Cor. 15:26, 38 seq.).

So Christ rose again. After He had laid aside all the consequences of this earthly life, which is burdened with the curse of sin (Rom. 6:10), He walked in this newness of life (Rom. 6:4), as a Body of glory (Phil. 3:21) which displayed the whole plenitude and magnificence of this glorious life. For He is the "first-fruit" (I Cor. 15:20), the "first-born from the dead," the Author and Model of all the glorified (Col. 1:18), and the true Son of God, Who merited for Himself the crown of glory and honor by His suffering and Death (Hebr. 2:9). The servile form has disappeared, and the Divinity now shines forth through the glorified Body, so that the Father can say as at the eternal generation: "Thou art My Son, this day have I begotten Thee. Ask of Me, and I will give Thee the Gentiles for Thy inheritance, and the utmost parts of the earth for Thy possession" (Ps. 2:7 seq.). Who can comprehend the floods of joy and rapture that now pour into the Soul of the God-Man through the transfigured senses of this glorious Body, and flow together into His Sacred Heart? His glorified Humanity receives a vast kingdom of honor, power and joy, and diffuses it again on all sides in streams of light, beatitude and strength. He now reigns in truth. In the agility, power and freedom of His glorified existence no point of His kingdom is remote from Him, and His scepter reaches to the utmost boundaries of His vast dominion. The holy women who come to Him are the harbingers of millions of adorers; for in place of the one nation which has rejected Him all the nations of the earth will be His portion. From His grave the angels proclaim His Resurrection and send the soldiers as heralds of it into the city, which, in the midst of her victory, trembles before the Risen Lord. And what sets the seal of perfection upon all His happiness and glory is its immutability, permanence and eternity. "Christ rising again from the dead dieth now no more, death shall no more have dominion over Him" (Rom. 6:9). The bright and beautiful day of a blissful eternity has risen for the God-Man, and it will never wane nor set.

Such is the essence of the Resurrection. Its attendant circumstances were as follows: first, it took place three days after Christ's Death. Three days sufficed for a valid proof of His real Death; there was no reason for a longer period.

Secondly, the Resurrection took place unseen. No mortal eye looked on; it was beheld with exultant joy only by eternity and the choirs of angels and patriarchs. Of the latter some shared in this glorious Resurrection, either temporarily or permanently. As the God-Man had once gone forth at midnight from the virginal womb of His Mother without violating its integrity, so His glorious Humanity now made its exit from the shade of the Sepulcher without breaking its seals, and unnoticed by men. The result of the Resurrection was a life that no longer belonged to his world.

Thirdly, the Resurrection was accomplished by Christ's own divine power. The raising of the dead is exclusively the work of divine omnipotence. This omnipotence originates in the Father, and therefore we are told that the Father raised up Jesus from the dead (Rom. 8:11), and that He lives by the power and glory of the Father (I Cor. 6:14; Rom. 6:4). But in virtue of the eternal generation the Son likewise possesses this omnipotence, and so the Resurrection is also the work of His own divine power. And since the latter operates independently of time and means, it (the Resurrection) was accomplished in a moment, as will be the case with us also (I Cor. 15:52). This self-resuscitation is a peculiar glory of the Resurrection of Christ. The God-Man resumes His life, as He had laid it down, of His own free volition (John 2:19; 10:18).

3. SIGNIFICANCE OF THE RESURRECTION

The great significance of the Resurrection consists in its being the crown of the life and work of Christ and the completion of the Redemption, and this in three respects.

The first aim of Christ's ministry was to prove His true Divinity, in order that we might be justified by faith. His teaching and miracles had this for their immediate object. But there was still a link wanting in the chain of this great proof, the most important link of all, viz. His Resurrection. Our Saviour Himself had held out the prospect of it to the Jews as His principal miracle and the most irrefutable proof of His Divinity. Now He works this miracle, and it is in very deed far greater than any other that His foes could have demanded of heaven (Mark 8:11), because it is wrought upon His own Body and life. So the Resurrection is the last and supreme proof of His Divinity. All other miracles rest upon this and receive from it their confirmation. Thus the glory of the Resurrection is reflected back upon the whole life and work of Jesus, surrounding it with a halo of radiant brightness.

The second object of Christ's ministry was our deliverance from the tyranny of Satan. With three mighty forces—the power of the passions, sin and death— the prince of darkness had subjugated the human race to his sway, and robbed men of all God's gifts: peace, grace and the immortality of the body. Our Saviour had already overcome the first two of these, the power of the passions and sin, by the example of virtue He set us throughout His life, by His Passion and Death, and by the grace that He thereby merited for us. It only remained for Him to vanquish the last enemy, Death. This He does now by His Resurrection, conquering this foe in his own securest stronghold, the grave (I Cor. 15:26, 55 seq.). As Samson lifted and carried away the gates of the city where he was imprisoned, so our Lord unhinged the terrible bolts and gates of death and bore them off in triumph, thus opening the prison of eternal death, that we might all escape (Judg. 16:3). By His Resurrection He has vanquished death for us, and our resurrection is now as certain as His (I Cor. 15). The fearsome grave, the death of all earthly hope, has become the place of life, and the garden around it is the new Paradise in which the Risen Saviour offers to mankind the gift of immortality. Thus the Resurrection is a new victory of the Redemption, a great and glorious victory, complete and universal, because it has been won for us all.

Thirdly, the Resurrection is the crown and perfection of the life and work of the God-Man, because it is His essential glorification, the entrance into His kingdom and the beginning of the glorious life that was due to Him from the first as the Son of God, and which was also the prize and reward of His suffering life. This divine life was in reality the destined end of the God-Man; the Passion was only a transition period and a preparation for the life of glory. And now He has entered upon this glory; for in His Resurrection He did not return to His former passible life, but began quite a new and most glorious one, truly immortal and divine. This glorious life is the type, pledge and cause of the glorious life that is in store for us. With it the Redemption is consummated. Thus the Resurrection of Christ is the completion of the Redemption and of His entire work as God-Man. Everything is now accomplished. All foes are defeated, all possessions and blessings are recovered; all God's plans for the human race are re-established, nay, infinitely furthered. Now all is peace, a blessed and eternal peace. Now there is nothing more to be done but to enjoy and use what He has won.

4. CONCLUSION TO BE DRAWN FROM THE MYSTERY OF THE RESURRECTION

The first fruit of the mystery is joy. Alleluia is the watchword, the cry of supreme and everlasting peace (Tob. 13:22; Apoc. 19:1). All rejoice; Heaven rejoices; the angels appear clad in the white garments of joy, and bid men rejoice; our Saviour, the Apostles and the whole Church rejoice. "*In resurrectione tua, Christe, coeli et terra laetentur!*" (Roman Breviary.) And who would not rejoice, both for our Saviour's sake and our own? Let us rejoice, then, and congratulate Him with all our hearts on His day of triumph. How well He has earned it! The eye that saw such evil days; the ear that heard so much contradiction and mockery, and so many blasphemies; the heart that broke with fear, grief, and the terrible anguish of death—how meet it is that they should all rejoice! Oh, how different everything has become! "*Tu Rex gloriae, Christe, tu Patris sempiternus es Filius*" (*Te Deum*). "*Jesu, Rex admirabilis et triumphator nobilis, tibi laus, honor nominis et regnum beatitudinis!*" (Hymn "*Jesu dulcis memoria.*") Let us unite ourselves in spirit with all the thanksgivings, praises and expressions of joy of heaven and earth; for this is truly "the day which the Lord hath made. Let us be glad and rejoice therein" (Ps. 117:24).

The second lesson of this mystery is love for our Divine Saviour. Every reason urges it. In the first place, we see here how great a Master we have in Him, glorious, immortal, powerful and gracious beyond all measure. It is this very mystery which shows us what a sacrifice He made for us in renouncing His glory for so long. Moreover His glory is our glory, His Resurrection our resurrection. He cannot forget us; He obtains everything for us, and shares everything with us.

The third lesson is hope, courage and confidence. What have we to fear, now that we no longer need to fear death? "*Surrexit Christus, spes mea!*" (Missal.) "I am the Resurrection and the Life; he that believeth in Me . . . shall not die for ever" (John

11:26). Christ is immortal; everything about Him and everything that is united to Him is immortal: His doctrine, His Church, His elect and their thoughts, words, works, sufferings and death. We Christians cannot be conquered by death. The Holy Sepulcher is the proof of it. Where is the stone? Where are the guards, the seals? Where is death? Let those who do not believe in Christ fear and despair! We hope and exult: "Thanks be to God, who hath given us the victory through our Lord Jesus Christ" (I Cor. 15:57). How sorely to be pitied are His enemies and adversaries! Let us pray for them, that they too may become participators in His joy and peace. "*Tu nobis, victor Rex, miserere. Amen.*" (Missal.) *Alleluia! Agnus Dei, qui tollis peccata mundi, dona nobis pacem.*" Love, joy and courage: these are set before us today with the "newness of life" to which Christ's Resurrection calls us (Rom. 6:4).

For reading and meditation: "*Victimae Paschali*" (Missal); "*Te Deum*"; (Ps. 2; 117; 138).

The Glorious Life from the Resurrection to the Ascension. Aim and Signification of This Life

The object of this intermediate sojourn on earth was twofold. First, the revelation of the truth and nature of the Resurrection; to prove that our Saviour was truly risen, and to a glorious life. And in all likelihood He also intended to show us what awaits our body after this life. Secondly, the completion of the organization of the Church, in which many very important points were still wanting. All our Saviour's appearances after His Resurrection are made in pursuit of these ends; sometimes of the former, sometimes of the latter, sometimes of both together.

The necessity of this revelation of the Resurrection lies in the extraordinary importance of this fact for the life-work of Jesus, for the whole Church, and indeed for the whole world. It is the foundation of all religion. That is why it is written that Christ "was delivered up for our sins and rose again for our justification" (Rom. 4:25), i.e. for the confirmation of the faith, hope and charity by which we are justified. So the Resurrection must of necessity in some way be proclaimed and made manifest.

As for the manner of this proclamation, it was not to take place through Christ Himself, by His rising again in presence of all the people. The life of the Resurrection is quite a new and extraordinary life, and does not belong to this world, but to the kingdom of glory. It was therefore advisable that the revelation should be made by means of intermediary agents and in ways appointed by God alone.

And by whom, then, was it made? First by angels, who are at times the connecting links between this world and the world beyond, and whom God employs to reveal His eternal decrees, as was the case with the mystery of the Incarnation, at the Annunciation and Nativity of Christ. This service by angels also gave proof of Christ's supremacy and power. Probably the Saints whose bodies were now resuscitated, and who appeared to many people in the city, were also charged to make known the fact of His Resurrection (Matt. 27:52, 53).

And to whom was the revelation to be made? Not to all the people, but to the "witnesses preordained by God" (Acts 10:41; 13:30 seq.; I Cor. 15:5), the Apostles. After His Resurrection Christ no longer held personal intercourse with the people. They are now referred to the Apostles. It is better so for their faith and for their submission to the Church in its established form.

The Revelation of the Resurrection to Christ's Enemies

Matt. 28:2. And behold there was a great earthquake. For an angel of the Lord descended from heaven; and coming, rolled back the stone, and sat upon it;—3. And his countenance was as lightning, and his raiment as snow.—4. And for fear of him the guards were struck with terror, and became as dead men. . . . —11. Some of the guards came into the city, and told the chief priests all things that had been done.—12. And they being assembled together with the ancients, taking counsel, gave a great sum of money to the soldiers,—13. Saying: "Say you, His disciples came by night, and stole him away when we were asleep.—14. And if the governor shall hear of this, we will persuade him, and secure you."—15. So they taking the money, did as they were taught; and this word was spread abroad among the Jews even unto this day.

1. Why Christ Reveals His Resurrection to His Enemies

Christ reveals His Resurrection to His enemies, in the first place, that He may be true to His word. He had held out the sure prospect of it to them, as well as to His Apostles, and so they too were to receive certain tidings of it.

Secondly, He did this out of goodness and mercy. The great miracle of the Resurrection was to remove the last pretext for their obdurate unbelief.

Lastly, He did it in pursuit of a plan of His wisdom, according to which the measures they had already taken to frustrate the Resurrection, as well as those they were about to take in order to deprive it of credence, should become the most brilliant testimony in its favor and also bear witness to the holiness of Jesus and their own wickedness.

2. HOW CHRIST REVEALS HIS RESURRECTION TO HIS ENEMIES

Our Lord first reveals His Resurrection to the soldiers on guard, through an angel, and with every token of terrific power. The angel descends like a flash of lightning, the earth trembles and quakes; he rolls away the stone and seats himself quietly and majestically upon it, in the midst of the soldiers who are set to guard the Sepulcher, so that they could convince themselves that it was empty, if they liked (Matt. 28:2, 3). The angels meet those who oppose violence to Christ with terrific and overwhelming power.

As for His enemies in the city, the chief priests, our Saviour reveals His Resurrection to them through the guards. Half-dead with terror, the soldiers fled. Some of them ran at once into the city and told the chief priests, under whose orders Pilate had placed them, what had happened (Matt. 28:4, 11). These witnesses are quite unimpeachable, partly on account of their calling and office and because they were in no way implicated in the matter, and partly because they must have been more inclined to speak in accordance with Pilate's and the chief priests' wishes than otherwise. And nevertheless they acknowledge the true facts of the occurrence. Thus the chief priests receive official information of the Resurrection against their will, and through the very guards they had posted to prevent any fraud.

3. WITH WHAT RESULT CHRIST REVEALS HIS RESURRECTION TO HIS ENEMIES

The chief priests take counsel with the ancients (Matt. 28:12); and their decision is therefore an official one. Instead of yielding, as they had promised to do (Matt. 27:42), or explaining away the whole occurrence by ascribing it to sorcery, against which even armed force was powerless, they evidently acknowledge it to be a fact; but in order to get out of the dilemma they induce the soldiers to tell a lie, bribe them with a large sum of money (Matt. 28:13, 14), and promise to secure them against punishment even from Pilate. They were to say that the disciples had taken away the Body whilst they slept. Under these circumstances Pilate might well feel little inclination to make an ado about the matter, in his own interest as well as in that of the soldiers and Jews. He had enough on his conscience. This measure of the chief priests was not simple unbelief, but the basest dishonesty. Every word is a crime and a fatal snare for themselves, as St. Augustine demonstrates (*"In Ps. 63. Mentita est iniquitas sibi, Ps. 26:12"*). By their lies they bring themselves into a dilemma, and win shame and hell as their portion. And yet, although their tissue of lies came to light, the tradition that the disciples took away the Body remained prevalent among the Jews, as St. Matthew tells us (28:15). We may here notice in passing the rôle that money plays in our Saviour's destiny; it is always that of iniquity and injustice (Luke 16:9, 11).

With this act of dishonesty the Great Council disappears from the Gospels. It has throughout perseveringly played the part of the impious State, in league with the temporal power of the day: first in pursuit of its object, viz. to stand its ground against God and the truth; secondly in its employment of means to this end, viz. bribery, lying, official manipulation of seals, confiscation, and suppression by brute force; and thirdly in the result of all this, which is nothing else than defeat and destruction in shame and terror. And this was actually the fate of the Jewish State a few years later. "The truth of the Lord remaineth for ever" (Ps. 116:2).

On the other hand, how glorious is our Saviour in His all-merciful goodness! He thinks of His unhappy persecutors, and sends them angels to instruct and embarrassments to warn them. And then in His supremacy and power. He does not show Himself to His foes again, nor ask them to bear witness to His Resurrection. He lives, above them and among them. He shows Himself everywhere, and everywhere witnesses are loudly preaching His Resurrection. What a terrible thought for His foes! Oh that the mighty ones of this world might at last "learn where is wisdom, where is strength, where is understanding," and "know also where is length of days and life, where is the light of the eyes, and peace!" (Bar. 3:14.) Where else than with God? How significant, in the light of this mystery, is the Office of Easter-week, in which we find depicted on the one hand the indestructible beauty of the Just One, Christ's divine power and royal triumph, and on the other the vain and futile efforts of His foes, and their miserable defeat and destruction.

Christ Appears to His Blessed Mother

1. WHETHER OUR LORD REALLY APPEARED TO HIS MOTHER OR NOT

This is not an article of faith. No mention is made of it in the Holy Scriptures. But Saints and spiritual authors of great repute are of this opinion (Bened. XIV., *De festis* . . . 8:45; Rupertus, *De div. offic.* 7:25; Eadmer, *De excell. B. M.* 6; Maldon.; Tolet.; Suarez; S. Bonav. [?] in the "Life of Christ" 96; S. Ign. in his "Exercises"). And it is quite natural; indeed, it seems almost a matter of course. Everything in the life of Christ was in accordance with what is fitting, and bore the mark of delicate consideration. So we can read a great deal between the lines of Holy Scripture that is not actually expressed.

2. HOW HE APPEARED TO HER

The first thing to be considered here is the way in which Our Blessed Lady prepared for her Son's appearance. In the first place, by a firm and lively faith. There is no wavering nor perplexity with her, as was the case with the holy women and the Apostles. To her Christ's words were perfectly clear, and she expected the Resurrection on the third day. So she did not accompany the other women to the Sepulcher, either because He had already appeared to her, or because she regarded the service they proposed as useless. Further, she awaited the Resurrection with great longing and ardent desire. One only needs to know the heart of a mother, and such a Mother, to understand this. The longing of Tobias' mother and Jacob's desire for his son Joseph were but feeble images of her longing (Tob. 10; 11:5, 6; Gen. 45:28). And she represented this faith and longing of hers to God in long and fervent prayer, as she had formerly done before the Incarnation (Cantic. 5:1; 4:16).

How, then, did our Saviour appear to her, and how did He comfort her? In the only way which can comfort a mother; namely by making it evident to her that her child lives, is happy, and loves her (Gen. 46:30). Surely our Lord revealed to no one the splendor of His glorious state so fully and so tenderly as He did to her. We may well assume that He raised her to a sublime and incomprehensible height of contemplation and participation in His glory, in His love for her and the compassion He felt at seeing her still in the garment of this mortal life. What new and glorious depths of knowledge respecting our Saviour and the glory of heaven must have been imparted to her then! Probably He also revealed to her His reasons for remaining on earth for some time yet, and all that He meant to do for His Church before He ascended to heaven, and appointed her her share in this glorious work.

It is evident enough why our Lord was so gracious to His holy Mother. She was His nearest and dearest in the order of nature and of grace. He had received from her the life that was now so glorious; she had had the most intimate share in the accomplishment of the mysteries of which this glory was the exceeding great reward, viz. the mysteries of His Passion, in which she had suffered so unspeakably and so generously. How fitting, then, that she should now have a special share in His glory!

The appearance of Jesus filled her with consolation and joy, a joy that was first so great and heartfelt as only a divinely-gifted being like herself could taste and bear. She could not see enough of His glory, happiness and honor, could not rejoice enough over it. Secondly, it was a pure and spiritual joy. Its object was her Divine Son and His glory (Gen. 45:28). Thirdly, it was a quiet, interior, modest joy. She does not seem even to have mentioned His appearance at all. The Mother of Jesus is ever the same in her modesty, following her Son so faithfully, keeping and pondering everything in her heart (Luke 2:19, 51), and never pushing herself forward, except where she will incur shame and suffering. Lastly, it was a noble and perfect joy, that extended to the Apostles and ourselves as well. She rejoiced at all the great and glorious benefits that the Resurrection brought us, and took the heartiest interest in every token of our Saviour's goodness and graciousness to His friends, when the news of it was brought to her. And doubtless she interceded warmly for the Apostles, and especially for those who most needed consolation and were worthy of it. That is how Mary keeps holy Easter and Eastertide.

3. WHAT RESULTS FOR US FROM OUR SAVIOUR'S APPEARANCE TO HIS MOTHER

In the first place, let us rejoice in Our Lady's joy and congratulate her with all our hearts; for she has well deserved it of us.

Secondly, we see how we too can attain to true Easter joy, viz. by always following our Lord faithfully and generously wherever He goes. Thirdly, let us learn wherein true Easter joy consists and how we must manifest it. In this Mary is our model. The object of our joy must be our Saviour and spiritual things; the manner of it must be quiet and interior, in prayer and recollection; and lastly, it must be noble and unselfish, not excluding others. All this finds a beautiful expression in the Easter anthem, which we may here briefly consider, in order to recite it well. *Regina coeli, laetare, Alleluia!* She is now no longer the Mother of Sorrows, but the Queen of heaven, i.e. of honor, power and joy. To be the Mother of God is now a joy. *Quia, quem meruisti portare, Alleluia!* All the joy of the Easter Feast is peculiarly her own. She is the Mother of the Risen Saviour. She gave Him birth and bore all His sorrows and sufferings with Him till His Death. *Resurrexit, sicut dixit, Alleluia!* O joy! By His Resurrection thy Son has confirmed everything: His doctrine, His word, and His Divinity. All is gloriously consummated. *Ora pro nobis Deum, Alleluia!* Pray for us, as thou then didst for the Apostles and the whole Church. Obtain for Christ's kingdom by thy glorious intercession an increase of faith, hope and love, and for the whole world participation in the true Easter joy in Christ, here below and in a blissful eternity.

The Holy Women at the Sepulcher

Mark 16:1. And when the Sabbath was past Mary Magdalen and Mary the mother of James and Salome bought sweet spices, that coming they might anoint Jesus.—2. And very early in the morning, the first day of the week, they come to the sepulcher, the sun being now risen.—3. And they said one to another: "Who shall roll us back the stone from the door of the sepulcher?"—4. And looking, they saw the stone rolled back. For it was very great.—5. And entering into the sepulcher, they saw a young man sitting on the right side, clothed with a white robe; and they were astonished.—6. Who saith to them: "Be not affrighted; you seek Jesus of Nazareth, who was crucified; he is risen, he is not here; behold the place where they laid him.—7. But go, tell his disciples and Peter that he goeth before you into Galilee; there you shall see him, as he told you."—8. But they going out, fled from the sepulcher; for a trembling and fear had seized them; and they said nothing to any man; for they were afraid.

Luke 24:1. And on the first day of the week very early in the morning the women came to the sepulcher, bringing the spices which they had prepared;—2. And they found the stone rolled back from the sepulcher.—3. And going in, they found not the body of the Lord Jesus.—4. And it came to pass, as they were astonished in their mind at this, behold two men stood by them in shining apparel.—5. And as they were afraid and bowed down their countenance towards the ground, they said unto them: "Why seek you the living with the dead?—

6. He is not here, but is risen; remember how he spoke unto you, when he was yet in Galilee,—7. Saying: The Son of Man must be delivered into the hands of sinful men, and be crucified, and the third day rise again."—8. And they remembered his words.—9. And going back from the sepulcher, they told all these things to the eleven, and to all the rest.—10. And it was Mary Magdalen, and Joanna, and Mary of James, and the other women that were with them, who told these things to the Apostles.—11. And these words seemed to them as idle tales; and they did not believe them.

MATT. 28:1. And in the end of the Sabbath, when it began to dawn towards the first day of the week, came Mary Magdalen and the other Mary to see the sepulcher. . . .—5. And the angel answering said to the women: "Fear not you; for I know that you seek Jesus who was crucified.—6. He is not here; for he is risen, as he said; come and see the place where the Lord was laid.—7. And going quickly tell ye his disciples that he is risen; and behold he will go before you into Galilee; there you shall see him. Lo, I have foretold it to you."—8. And they went out quickly from the sepulcher with fear and great joy, running to tell his disciples.—9. And behold Jesus met them, saying: "All hail." But they came up and took hold of his feet, and adored him.—10. Then Jesus said to them: "Fear not; go, tell my brethren that they go into Galilee, there they shall see me."

JOHN 20:1. And on the first day of the week Mary Magdalen cometh early, when it was yet dark, unto the sepulcher: and she saw the stone taken away from the sepulcher.

1. DISPOSITIONS AND LOVING ZEAL OF THE HOLY WOMEN

Who were these holy women? The Evangelists mention Mary Magdalen, Mary of James (or of Cleophas, the "other Mary," as she is called by St. Matthew, 28:1), Salome, Joanna, and "other women" (Matt. 28:1; Mark 16:1; Luke 24:1, 10).[1]

These holy women started off to the grave with ointments and spices on Sunday morning, or, as St. Matthew says (Matt. 28:1), at the end of the Sabbath and towards the dawn of the first day after it, at a very early hour (Luke 24:1; Mark 16:2). It was still dark when they quitted the house (John 20:1); but when they reached the Sepulcher the sun had just risen (Mark 16:2),[2] so that they were able to distinguish everything clearly.

And what did they intend to do? They wished to do honor to our Saviour's Body and show their love for Him, by bringing the ointments and perfumes they had bought on Saturday evening, which were perhaps still more costly than those provided by Joseph of Arimathaea, to make up for all that it had not been

[1] Some commentators distinguish two parties of the holy women who undertook this labor of love towards our Divine Saviour. The first party prepared spices before the Sabbath (Luke 23:56), the second did not buy them until after its close (Mark 16:1); the first came to the Sepulcher before dawn (John 20:1), the second after the sun had risen (Mark 16:2); the first saw two angels (Luke 24:4), the other saw one (Mark 16:5; Matt. 28:5).

[2] If we assume that the women visited the Sepulcher in different parties, there is no contradiction in the statements.

vouchsafed to them to do on Friday evening; for then they had only been able to look on. On the way they began to ask each other how they should get the grave-stone rolled away, for it was very large and quite beyond their strength; but even this difficulty did not deter them from their purpose (Mark 16:34). They seem not to have known that the Sepulcher had been sealed and guarded by soldiers, and probably hoped to persuade the gardener to help them roll away the stone. At all events they intended to go and look at the Sepulcher, and see what could be done (Matt. 28:1).

Here we see the true spirit of the women who followed Jesus: zeal, undaunted courage and intrepidity, generosity and self-sacrifice. They count as nothing all they have done for our Saviour in life; they think they cannot show Him love and service enough in death. They sacrifice money, rest and security, everything; nothing can keep them back, neither darkness, nor risk, nor any difficulty whatever. They are determined at least to see for themselves, on the spot, if anything can be done. They had learnt well in the school of Jesus. Theirs is true good will.

2. THEIR REWARD

The reward of these holy women is twofold: that which they received at the time of their visit and that which they enjoy now.

The reward they received at that time consisted first in the apparition of the angels. As they enter the antechamber of the Sepulcher, they see the stone rolled away, and on advancing into the inner room (Mark 16:5) they find the tomb empty (Luke 24:3). Whilst they stand there bewildered, two angels (SS. Matthew and Mark only mention one) appear on the right side of the tomb. The women, terrified, cast down their eyes. But the angels show them great honor and friendliness; first in their exterior appearance, by the sight of their white and glittering garments of joy and their youthful beauty, which like eternity never grows old (Mark 16:5); secondly and more particularly, by the words in which they address them. They first reassure the women: "Fear not you," "Be not affrighted"; and they show them that they know their good intentions and thoughts: "You seek Jesus of Nazareth, who was crucified." In these words high commendation is given to the women for having come at such cost to themselves to serve the Crucified. Then the angels announce the Resurrection to them in words fraught with deep meaning: "Why seek you the living with the dead?" (Luke 24:5.) "He is risen." In proof of their statement they point to the empty tomb: "Behold the place where they laid Him" (Mark 16:6), and they remind them of Jesus' own prediction (Luke 24:7). Lastly, they commission the women to go and inform the disciples and Peter especially (Mark 16:7) of the Resurrection, and indicate a spot in Galilee as the place of their meeting with our Lord. The holy women now remember the words of Jesus (Luke 24:8), and hasten away from the Sepulcher full of joy, which, however, is not unmixed with fear (Mark 16:8). Some of them, probably the first party, did not venture to deliver the message to the Apostles (Mark 16:8), until the evidence of the others, the second party, encouraged them to go together and communicate to them what they had seen and heard (Luke 24:9). But the Apostles regarded their statements as idle tales, and did not believe them (Luke 24:11; Mark 16:11). In these angelic apparitions it is worthy of note with what friendliness and respect the angels treat the holy women, whilst inspiring the guards with such terror. Further, our Saviour Himself rewarded the women by appearing to them, probably whilst they were on their way to the Apostles (Matt. 28:8), in the vicinity of the garden where the Sepulcher was, and addressing them with the most gracious friendliness. This was, however, after He had appeared to Magdalen (Mark 16:9). He greeted them lovingly: "All hail"; reassured them: "Fear not"; permitted them to kiss His feet (Matt. 28:9; cf. IV Kings 4:27); and confirmed the statement of the angels, repeating the message to the Apostles, His "brethren" (Matt. 28:10), as He graciously calls them.

And the reward the holy women now enjoy consists first in the gladness of the eternal Easter of heaven, where vision, adoration, joy and exultation do not pass away; and also in a mark of honor which they receive from the Church Militant year by year. Every Easter Sunday all Catholic Christians, Pope and Emperor not excepted, must stand bare-headed to hear the Gospel of the day read at Holy Mass. And what is read there? What is related? How the holy women rose early in the morning, what they said to one another, and what they did and intended to do for Christ's honor. This is a distinction that no great man of the world, however fêted he may be, ever meets with. To this day they are constantly receiving new honor and joy (Mark 14:9).

3. CONCLUSIONS

We see in this mystery, with which the Gospels take leave of the holy women, how faithfully they follow their vocation of serving our Lord and the Gospel. So we first met them (Luke 8:3), and so we find them today. In them we see delineated the vocation of women in the Church. First, in its aim, viz. to make themselves useful and promote Christ's kingdom indirectly, by corporal works of mercy. They are also commissioned by Christ to deliver a message; but not a public message, only a private one, to the household of the faith. Some must serve as messengers in Christ's kingdom also, and women are well fitted for that. Secondly, woman's vocation is depicted in the beautiful virtues it requires; indefatigable energy, generosity, zeal and love. Thirdly, in the reward it receives, which is so great and signal a favor; the holy women are the first to whom the two angels and Christ Himself graciously appear. He makes them the first heralds of His Resurrection, and our faith rests upon their testimony also. A woman was the cause of the curse; women are to cooperate in the Redemption, in the way we have indicated. They can prevent an immense amount of evil in Christ's kingdom, and do an infinite amount of good. The mystery also teaches us how good our Saviour is and how He rewards everyone without exception, in proportion to the zeal and love displayed in His service. "In the state of glory neither sex is at a disadvantage," says St. Thomas, because all depends upon love and zeal. The holy women saw our Saviour first, because they sought Him first. This is worthy of remembrance.

Peter and John at the Sepulcher. Our Lord Appears to Peter

John 20:1. And on the first day of the week Mary Magdalen cometh early, when it was yet dark, unto the sepulcher; and she saw the stone taken away from the sepulcher.—2. She ran therefore and cometh to Simon Peter and to the other disciple whom Jesus loved, and said to them: "They have taken away the Lord out of the sepulcher, and we know not where they have laid him."—3. Peter therefore went out and that other disciple, and they came to the sepulcher.—4. And they both ran together, and that other disciple did outrun Peter, and came first to the sepulcher.—5. And when he stooped down he saw the linen cloths lying, but yet he went not in.—6. Then cometh Simon Peter, following him, and went into the sepulcher and saw the linen cloths lying,—7. And the napkin, that had been about his head, not lying with the linen cloths, but apart, wrapt up into one place.—8. Then that other disciple also went in, who came first to the sepulcher; and he saw, and believed.—9. For as yet they knew not the Scripture, that he must rise again from the dead.—10. The disciples therefore departed again to their home.

Luke 24:12. But Peter rising up ran to the sepulcher; and stooping down he saw the linen cloths laid by themselves, and went away wondering in himself at that which was come to pass. . . .—34. (The disciples said:) "The Lord is risen indeed, and hath appeared to Simon."

1. PETER AND JOHN GO TO THE SEPULCHER

This visit was in consequence of the tidings of Magdalen, who ran back (perhaps even before the angels appeared), as soon as she saw that the Sepulcher was open, to bring the Apostles the news that the stone was rolled away and the Body removed (John 20:1, 2).

Peter and John immediately hasten to the Sepulcher. In this eager visit of the two Apostles we see, in the first place, their intellectual ascendancy over the rest; they do not reject Magdalen's tidings off-hand as mere fancy, as the other Apostles did a little later on hearing the statements of the women. They wish to look into the matter first, and in the meantime suspend their judgment. But a deeper cause was their warm interest in everything that concerned our Lord, and the heartfelt love they bore their Master. Every tiding of Him is of priceless value to them, and they consider it worthy of respect, let it come whence it may. In John this loving, youthful ardor is especially displayed, in the haste with which he outran Peter (John 20:4). Lastly, we see in Peter, in addition to his love, unselfishness and childlike confidence. He does not shun meeting our Lord, in spite of the fault he has committed. Probably he does not even think of himself at all, in his desire to obtain some news of his Master.

Thus should we also act, especially at times of spiritual dryness, and even after committing faults. Love and zeal for the interests of Jesus and His kingdom must not suffer from our excessive self-consciousness, self-interest, or dejection. These dispositions of St. Peter are most excellent and the best preparation for comfort.

2. THE DISCIPLES VIEW THE SEPULCHER AND BELIEVE

Arrived at the Sepulcher, John bends down and looks through the door-way. He sees the linen cloths lying there, but does not enter. He waits for St. Peter to come up, either through modesty and respect for him, or from youthful timidity (John 20:5). But Peter resolutely enters the Sepulcher, sees the linen cloths and the napkin that had been about our Lord's head, the latter folded up and lying apart from the rest in the tomb itself (John 20:6, 7). John also entered now, and probably they discussed together the manner in which the Body had been prepared and buried, and arrived at the conviction that there could be no question of its having sunk during the earthquake or having been stolen.

The effect of their examination was that John now firmly believed in the Resurrection (John 20:8). As for Peter, we are told that he went home full of wonder at what had happened (Luke 24:12). The reason why John needed the evidence of his eyes in order to believe, and Peter went away wondering, was that they had hitherto either not known or not practically comprehended the predictions of the Resurrection contained in the Scriptures and in our Lord's own words (John 20:9). At all events they quitted the Sepulcher in quite a different frame of mind from that in which they had come. What a difference there is between mere belief and a living faith, between hearing a thing and perceiving it! And how very differently the truth dawns upon us when God enlightens our minds!

The cause of this consolation received by the Apostles was first Christ's prayer for Peter (Luke 22:32); secondly, the way in which they had prepared for it, and the love for our Divine Saviour that had led them to the Sepulcher; and lastly, the use they made of reason and faith, by examining into the facts and reflecting upon them. To reflect thoroughly upon the truths of faith and take them to heart, this is our comfort and true Easter joy.

3. OUR LORD APPEARS TO ST. PETER AND THUS CONFIRMS HIS FAITH

We do not read that our Lord appeared to St. John. Perhaps He really did not do so, because his faith was already sufficiently firm; or perhaps the Apostle did not wish to mention the fact. With the exception of James, then, St. Peter is the only one of the Apostles to whom a special apparition was vouchsafed.

And why did our Lord appear to Peter especially? Because he, it would seem, needed to be specially strengthened in his faith, and also specially comforted on account of his fall; further, he was the head of the Apostolic College, and a personal appearance of our Saviour to him was calculated to confirm his influence and authority. Besides, his testimony would certainly be a powerful inducement to the other Apostles to believe in the Resurrection.

What took place at this meeting? It was a beautiful and touching circumstance that our Lord should come to St. Peter at all, and then how gracious and full of condescension He must have been to him! He wished to be Himself the one to bring to the Apostle the assurance of His forgiveness. He comforted and encouraged him, and bade him confirm his brethren in the faith. And surely He said to Peter also: "Peace be to thee . . . fear not, it is I . . . thy sin is forgiven thee. . . . I make all things new . . . confirm thy brethren."—And Peter? How humbly he asked forgiveness, and how this new favor increased his love and trust! How disinterestedly he would leave everything to our Saviour! "I am not worthy to be Thy Apostle . . . give me only Thy grace and love, and I shall be rich enough."

St. Peter immediately communicated this vision to the other Apostles, thus powerfully promoting their faith, as we see from St. Luke (24:24, 34). Thus he too has a joyous Easter, and immediately begins his apostolic work.

St. Mary Magdalen

John 20:11. But Mary stood at the sepulcher without, weeping. Now as she was weeping, she stooped down and looked into the sepulcher;—12. And she saw two angels in white, sitting one at the head and one at the feet, where the body of Jesus had been laid.—13. They say to her: "Woman, why weepest thou?" She saith to them: "Because they have taken away my Lord; and I know not where they have laid him."—14. When she had thus said, she turned herself back, and saw Jesus standing; and she knew not that it was Jesus.—15. Jesus saith to her: "Woman, why weepest thou? Whom seekest thou?" She thinking that it was the gardener, saith to him: "Sir, if thou hast taken him hence, tell me where thou hast laid him, and I will take him away."—16. Jesus saith to her: "Mary." She turning saith to him: "Rabboni" (which is to say, Master).—17. Jesus saith to her: "Do not touch me, for I am not yet ascended to my Father; but go to my brethren, and say to them; I ascend to my Father and to your Father, to my God and your God."—18. Mary Magdalen cometh and telleth the disciples: "I have seen the Lord, and these things he said to me."

Mark 16:9. But he rising early the first day of the week, appeared first to Mary Magdalen, out of whom he had cast seven devils.—10. She went and told them that had been with him, who were mourning and weeping.—11. And they hearing that he was alive and had been seen by her, did not believe.

1. MAGDALEN VISITS THE SEPULCHER

St. Mary Magdalen had followed the Apostles back to the Sepulcher, and after they had returned home she still lingered, unless it be assumed that she hurried on in front of them and saw our Lord there before they arrived. However that may have been, she stood or knelt at the Sepulcher and wept (John 20:11). The grave was all that was left her of our Saviour, and that made it dear to her. She wept, probably for His Death in the first instance; but also on account of the supposed new profanation and disturbance of His repose in the grave, and because she did not know what had become of His Body. Everything had been taken from her now. She stoops down and looks through the doorway into the Sepulcher, and there she sees two white-robed angels, one at the head, the other at the foot of the tomb (John 20:12). They ask her why she weeps. She feels neither fear nor pleasure, but simply replies: "Because they have taken away my Lord" (He was still her Lord, He was not dead to her), "and I know not where they have laid Him" (John 20:12). That was her only thought, her only grief. In her uneasiness she looks round. Our Lord is standing behind her. She takes Him for the gardener, perhaps because He had changed His outward appearance, or because in her grief and sorrow she did not look at Him closely, and thought no one but the gardener could be there at such an early hour (John 20:14). He too asks why she weeps, and whom she seeks. "Sir," she answers, probably in the hope of inducing the gardener to help her, "if thou has taken Him hence, tell me where thou hast laid Him" (John 20:15). She only cares about the gardener because he may possibly give her some news of our Saviour; she does not name our Lord, because she thinks everyone must know Him and be only occupied with Him. "And I will take Him away," wherever He may be, and at whatever cost. I will procure Him a grave such as He deserves.

All this shows us the depth and genuineness of this holy disciple's love. She thinks only of our Saviour, seeks only Him; He is all in all to her, and she cares for nothing else except in so far as it may lead her to Him. Her thoughts, words, works and feelings—the whole power of her will and all her faculties—her entire being is possessed with this noble love, the love of appreciation and affection. What a joy the sight of such a loyal, loving heart must have been to our Saviour, and how well she deserved some signal comfort!

2. OUR SAVIOUR REVEALS HIMSELF TO MAGDALEN

And in truth our Saviour did not long withstand such faithful love; He manifested Himself to her. And how? By a single word, and also, probably, by presenting Himself to her under His own well-known form, though transfigured and glorious beyond all measure (John 20:16). It is but one word He speaks; but what does it not contain! It is a word of revelation: Mary, it is I; dost thou not know Me? It is a word of comfort and reassurance: Mary, set thy heart at rest; be comforted, weep no more for Me. Lastly, it is a word of familiarity and approval: It is well, Mary, thou art true to thyself; thou hast given me sufficient proof of thy love. This one word was as sweetest music to her ear; it did more to comfort and gladden her than a hundred exhortations and books could have done.

The effect it had upon Magdalen was to make her recognize our Lord at once, and to fill her with rapturous joy. She too finds but one word for all that is passing in her heart: "Rabboni," My Master! (John 20:16.) But this word also contains all that she knows, feel and loves; it is the sum and abridgment of her whole life and being. In this one word is depicted the noblest, most touchingly beautiful relation of a child towards its teacher; loving respect, devotion and gratitude, in short, her whole relation to our Saviour. But who shall describe the greatness of her happiness? Oh, how happy she is to have renounced the whole world and chosen our Saviour for the Lord of her heart and life! It seems as though she could not cease kissing our Saviour's feet; all the more since she thought it was but a transitory visit from heaven, and that He would return thither and take her with Him (John 14:3). So He said to her: "Do not touch Me (any longer now), for I am not yet ascended to My Father" (John 20:17). He does not reject her act of homage, He permitted the other women to pay Him the same; He only retains her because she seems unable to cease, and evidently thinks she is now to enjoy His society for ever. That, at least, is how many great commentators explain these words.

3. OUR SAVIOUR SENDS MAGDALEN TO THE APOSTLES

Thereupon our Lord commissioned Magdalen to go to the Apostles and say to them in His name: "I ascend to My Father and to your Father, to My God and your God" (John 20:17). Why does this vision also end with a message to the Apostles? Because they are the final object our Lord has in view in all His apparitions, even the private ones; either on account of their dignity as heads of His kingdom, or of their weakness and need of comfort.

And what was contained in the message? He sends word to them not merely that He is risen, but also that He will ascend into heaven. Thus it contains a wider view of the aim and end of the glorious life on earth. In the first visions He had indicated Galilee as their place of meeting, that there His will on important matters might be made known; now He mentions heaven, as the conclusion of His life as God-Man and the last end of all men. The message taught them likewise that His sojourn here below would not last for ever, but would soon close with the Ascension. So it is not the same life as He had previously led on earth, but in this respect also quite a different, exceptional and transient life. This signification also lies in those other words of His to Magdalen: "Do not touch Me, for I am not yet ascended to My Father." These words are a preparation for the leave-taking, the separation which will ensue when He begins a glorious life to which the present is but an introduction.

And in what form does He send this message to the Apostles? In most loving words. He again calls them His "brethren," and in the words "to My Father and to your Father, to My God and your God," He adds not merely the basis of this fraternal relation (inasmuch as by the completion of the Redemption the bond of our adoption as God's children is made fast, and we thus have a common Father with Him), but also the perfection of this adoption, in our common possession of God and heaven. Our Saviour will take possession of heaven not only for Himself, but also for us. So this is a glorious expansion of the significance and scope of the Resurrection, and Magdalen hastened joyfully to the Apostles, and communicated it to them (John 20:18).[1]

There is scarcely any other vision in which everything so powerfully attracts our thoughts to heaven and to the supernatural as in this. It is as though our Saviour wished here to lay special stress upon this attraction and bring the force of it home to our hearts (Col. 3:1, 2). In this mystery we see also how He makes everything, even the most private matters, tend to the good of the loyal

[1] For the sake of gaining a clearer view of the apparitions, we may arrange them as follows: The holy women go to the Sepulcher early in the morning (Mark 16:1; Luke 24:10). As soon as Mary Magdalen sees that it is open, she hastens away before the angels have appeared, to bring the tidings to the Apostles (John 20:1, 2). Whilst the angelic vision is being vouchsafed to the other women (Mark 16:5 seq.), Mary delivers her information, but immediately hurries back to the Sepulcher, even before St. Peter and St. John have arrived there. After the two Apostles have inspected the grave and departed, Mary remains there, sees our Lord, and hurries back to the city to deliver His message (John 20:11–18; Mark 16:9). In the meantime our Lord appeared to the other holy women, who had probably lingered in the vicinity of the garden (Matt. 28:9, 10).

subjects of His kingdom. The Church and the Apostles are the final object of all His thoughts, and to them He directs the thoughts of His friends and followers. Should we not do the same, especially if we are consecrated in any special way to the service of the Church? The Apostles are the first in Christ's love. Should not Christ and the Church have the first place in their hearts also? Should they love Him less than Magdalen does? "Dost thou see this woman?" (Luke 7:44.) She how zealous and loving, how generous, how unshaken in her fidelity she is. And shall we be less so? May our Lord grant us the grace of such love and loyalty, through the intercession of this handmaid of His, whose faithful love so gladdened His Heart.

The Disciples on the Way to Emmaus

Luke 24:13. And behold, two of them went the same day to a town which was sixty furlongs from Jerusalem, named Emmaus;—14. And they talked together of all these things which had happened.—15. And it came to pass, that while they talked and reasoned with themselves, Jesus himself also drawing near went with them;—16. But their eyes were held that they should not know him.—17. And he said to them: "What are these discourses that you hold one with another as you walk, and are sad?"—18. And the one of them, whose name was Cleophas, answering, said to him: "Art thou only a stranger in Jerusalem, and hast not known the things that have been done there in these days?"—19. To whom he said: "What things?" And they said: "Concerning Jesus of Nazareth, who was a prophet, mighty in work and word before God and all the people;—20. And how our chief priests and princes delivered him to be condemned to death, and crucified him;—21. But we hoped that it was he that should have redeemed Israel; and now besides all this, today is the third day since these things were done.—22. Yea, and certain women also of our company affrighted us, who before it was light were at the sepulcher,—23. And not finding his body, came, saying that they had also seen a vision of angels, who say that he is alive.—24. And some of our people went to the sepulcher: and found it so as the women had said, but him they found not."—25. Then he said to them: "O foolish, and slow of heart to believe in all things which the prophets have spoken!—26. Ought not Christ to have suffered these things, and so to enter into his glory?"—27. And beginning at Moses and all the prophets, he expounded to them in all the scriptures the things that were concerning him.—28. And they drew nigh to the town whither they were going; and he made as though he would go farther.—29. But they constrained him, saying: "Stay with us, because it is towards evening, and the day is now far spent." And he went in with them.—30. And it came to pass, whilst he was at table with them, he took bread, and blessed and brake, and gave to them.—31. And their eyes were opened, and they knew him; and he vanished out of their sight.—32. And they said one to the other: "Was not our heart burning within us, whilst he spoke in the way, and opened to us the Scriptures?"—33. And rising up the same hour they went back to Jerusalem; and they found the eleven gathered together, and those that were with them,—34. Saying: "The Lord is risen indeed, and hath appeared to Simon."—35. And they told what things were done in the way; and how they knew him in the breaking of bread.

MARK 16:12. And after that he appeared in another shape to two of them, walking, as they were going into the country;—13. And they going told it to the rest; neither did they believe them.

1. HOW SORELY THE DISCIPLES NEEDED COMFORT

In the afternoon of Easter Sunday two disciples, one of whom was named Cleophas, went out of the city into the country (Mark 16:16), to the village of Emmaus, about sixty furlongs north-west or west of Jerusalem. They were sad (Luke 24:17), and the causes of their depression may easily be deduced from the conversation they held with each other and with our Saviour (Luke 24:14, 18, 19).

The first cause was His deplorable end. They took it sorely to heart that such a great man, a prophet and (as they had hoped) the true Redeemer of Israel (Luke 24:19, 20, 21), should perish so miserably and through the "chief priests and princes" of the people. They wondered that the stranger could ask them of what they were speaking and why they were sad.

The second cause of their sorrow was the complete failure, as they supposed, of the ministry of Jesus and of His Messianic vocation (Luke 24:21). They were led into this erroneous idea, in the first place, by His Death; but still more by the circumstance that, although three days had elapsed since then, He had not yet fulfilled the promise of His Resurrection by appearing in triumphant glory, to accomplish at once the deliverance of Israel. That was what they had been expecting, and instead of this the only certain information they had received was that His Sepulcher had been found empty by some women who fancied they had seen a vision of angels; but this evidence appeared too uncertain to convince them of His Resurrection. All this bewildered the disciples, and they did not know what to think. In this uncertainty they could not reconcile His Death on the Cross with their idea of the Messias, and the former seemed to them an irretrievable frustration of all the hopes that they and so many others had entertained. Thus it was the mystery of the Cross that disquieted them, and from which their intellect and heart recoiled. This is why our Saviour calls them "foolish and slow of heart to believe" (Luke 24:25).

Lastly, their present circumstances were also calculated to depress them. They had identified themselves with our Saviour's cause before all the people. Now they felt themselves deceived. They could scarcely appear in public without disgrace and danger, and perhaps it was on this account that they were leaving the perilous precincts of the city and retiring into the country. In short, they were very sad and greatly in need of comfort.

2. HOW OUR SAVIOUR COMFORTS THEM

It is under these circumstances that our Saviour joins them unrecognized, perhaps under the appearance of a pilgrim returning home from the feast, and with loving skill draws all the bitterness out of their hearts by the instruction and solace of His conversation. He first removes the scandal they had taken at the Cross, by showing them that His Passion and Death were not unexpected and unforeseen, nor yet a misfortune and a failure; but that on the contrary these events had been for centuries foretold by the prophets and foreshadowed in the history of the nation, and that the very fact of His having suffered all this proved Him to be the Messias. He probably drew this out in detail, unfolding before them the great picture of the Messias in the various features of His Passion and glory, and disclosing the whole divine plan of the Redemption from the beginning, the main idea of which lies in the thesis: "Christ ought to have suffered these things, and so to enter into His glory" (Luke 24:26). Secondly, He convinces the disciples that He is really and gloriously risen. He gives them every proof of it; He walks with them, talks with them, instructs them, eats with them, transforms Himself at will (Mark 16:12), and suddenly vanishes from their sight (Luke 24:16, 31). All this would also reassure them concerning their own future.

Here we must also consider the manner in which our Saviour does this, viz. with extraordinary graciousness, friendliness and kindness. He joins the disciples unasked, sympathetically inquires into the cause of their dejection, holds a long Scriptural discourse, and this merely for the benefit of two men who were not even Apostles, but simple disciples. His words are so cheering and so sublime that their hearts burn within them (Luke 24:32); He accepts their invitation to enter the house and sits down to table with them. Lastly, He reveals Himself to them by the manner in which He breaks the bread (which it was perhaps the privilege of an honored guest to do), performing this action under the form of His glory. Some of the holy Fathers assume that Christ here administered to the disciples His Sacred Body in the Holy Eucharist. This would certainly have been the very excess of goodness, that the inn-table should thus be transformed into an altar, and the supposed pilgrim to whom they had shown hospitality unveil Himself as the glorious High Priest of the New Testament.

And what was the effect of this gracious apparition upon the disciples? In the first place, they were now convinced of the Resurrection; their prejudices against the Passion, the want of understanding and the repugnance they had felt for it vanished from their hearts, which now burned with ardent love for their kind Master; and this love and joy gave them so much courage and strength that they immediately hastened back to the city, without even stopping to rest, in order to bring the Apostles the tidings of His appearance to them (Luke 24:33, 35). There they are met with the news that our Lord had appeared to Simon (Luke 24:34). Thus faith, hope and joy gradually gain ground in the Apostolic College, but still slowly; they (the Apostles) do not quite discard all doubt even on hearing the news brought by the two disciples (Mark 16:13).

3. WHY THE DISCIPLES RECEIVED THIS COMFORT

In the first place, they received it through the goodness of our Lord, to whom the sorrow of the Cross, borne in His service, is always an inducement to render help and comfort. Secondly, the disciples had merited this consolation by the high esteem of our Lord and faithful attachment to Him which their own words testify. Thirdly, they had deserved it by their pious conversation about our Saviour. When such discourse is held, our Lord is always close at hand (Matt. 18:20). Lastly, by their friendly and grateful invitation. Had they not given it, He would have gone on His way; but as it was, they were abundantly rewarded. Hence the proverb handed down to us from the good old times: *"Hospes venit, Christus venit."*

In this mystery we have another excellent example of our Lord's excessive love and goodness towards His own. How well He knows them all, how He goes after all, how prompt He is with comfort and advice, and how He exhausts Himself in tokens of His goodness! Secondly, we receive instructions of the highest importance with regard to the significance of the Cross in the Life of Jesus, the life of the Church, and the life of each and all of the elect. The Cross is an essential element in the Christian life. Christ had to die, and thus to enter into His glory; and this applies to us also. Therefore let us be prepared for it, the Cross, many crosses, inexplicable, repugnant crosses. Our Saviour was evidently endeavoring here to remove from the hearts of His disciples the scandal at the Cross to which our nature is prone. A great grace, this. O that He would teach us also to see how many blessings suffering and humiliation can bring us!

Christ's Manifestation of Himself to the Apostles in the Coenaculum

John 20:19. Now when it was late that same day, the first of the week, and the doors were shut, where the disciples were gathered together for fear of the Jews, Jesus came and stood in the midst, and said to them: "Peace be to you."—20. And when he had said this, he showed them his hands and his side. The disciples therefore were glad, when they saw the Lord.—21. He said therefore to them again: "Peace be to you. As the Father hath sent me, I also send you."—22. When he had said this, he breathed on them: and he said to them: "Receive ye the Holy Ghost;—23. Whose sins you shall forgive, they are forgiven them; and whose sins you shall retain, they are retained."

Luke 24:36. Now whilst they were speaking these things, Jesus stood in the midst of them, and saith to them: "Peace be to you; it is I, fear not."—37. But they being troubled and frighted, supposed that they saw a spirit.—38. And he said to them: "Why are you troubled, and why do thoughts arise in your hearts?—39. See my hands and feet, that it is I myself; handle, and see; for a spirit hath not flesh and bones, as you see me to have."—40. And when he had said this, he showed them his hands and feet.—41. But while they yet believed not and wondered for joy, he said: "Have you here anything to eat?"—42. And they offered him a piece of a broiled fish, and a honeycomb.—43. And when he had eaten before them, taking the remains he gave to them.—44. And he said to them: "These are the words which I spoke to you while I was yet with you, that all things must needs be fulfilled, which are written in the law of Moses and in the Prophets and in the Psalms concerning me."—45. Then he opened their understanding, that they might understand the Scriptures.

1. The Feeling That Prevailed in the Apostolic College

After the arrival of the disciples from Emmaus all the Apostles, Thomas excepted, were assembled in the Coenaculum. In spite of the various revelations and assurances of the Resurrection that had been vouchsafed to several among them, the general feeling in the Apostolic College still remained that of uncertainty, wavering, doubt, disquietude and fear.

The holy women had hesitated at first to tell the Apostles of the Resurrection (Mark 16:8), and when they at length brought themselves to do so (Luke 24:9; Matt. 28:8), they met with no credence (Luke 24:11). Nor did Magdalen fare better with her message (Mark 16:11). Even the testimony of St. Peter and the disciples from Emmaus did not completely satisfy the Apostles (Mark 16:13). So the attitude that prevailed among them on the evening of Easter Sunday was still that of uncertainty and fear with regard to three things.

First, they feared the Jews, as St. John expressly states (20:19), and had therefore shut all the doors. Secondly, they felt uncertain about the Resurrection; and lastly, they were probably doubtful about their position as Apostles. Our Saviour had called them His brethren in the greeting He had twice sent them, it is true; but still they doubted whether He would abide by the choice He had formerly made, and continue His work through their instrumentality. So they stood there like a forlorn, forsaken flock looking in helpless bewilderment for its shepherd.

2. CONSOLATION BESTOWED BY OUR LORD

The Apostles were still conversing about the vision vouchsafed to the two disciples (Luke 24:36), when suddenly our Lord stood in their midst and comforted them.

He addressed them with the words: "Peace be to you; it is I, fear not" (Luke 25:36). He thus encourages them to lay aside all uneasiness and fear; He is with them again, He Himself and no other, and just as He had been before, their Master, Lord, Defender and Protector. His words are an assurance of peace, an exhortation to courage and confidence, an application, so to speak, of all the blessings of the Redemption He had accomplished and of His future glorious life. The miraculous manner of His appearance, too, and His transfigured form, as well as the friendly and loving way in which He addressed them and the interior and efficacious grace by which His words were accompanied, must have filled the Apostles with courage and confidence, even with regard to the Jews. As a matter of fact they met with no molestation from this quarter until after the Descent of the Holy Ghost. Thus does our Saviour understand and show consideration for all weaknesses, and such is the wisdom, prudence and indulgence with which He deals with them.

Secondly, He comforts the Apostles with regard to His Resurrection. They shrink from Him in terror and consternation, thinking Him to be a spirit (Luke 24:37). But our Saviour now gives them sure and sufficient proofs that it is He Himself, and that He is therefore risen again and in a glorious state. He reveals to them His knowledge of their doubts and thoughts (Luke 24:38), shows them His Hands and Feet and Side (John 20:20) with the marks of the wounds, and probably lets them feel and handle Him. And as they still do not believe for very joy and wonder, He has a piece of fish and a honeycomb brought, and eats before them and with them in the old familiar way. One can imagine how joyfully the Apostles watched Him and shared His meal. And that He was risen in a glorious state was proved by His sudden appearance and disappearance in spite of the closed doors, and perhaps also by the ethereal aspect of His Body.

Lastly, our Saviour effectively reassured the Apostles with regard to their office, inasmuch as He extended their apostolic power by adding to it two important constituents. First, He imparted to them the comprehension of Holy Scripture (Luke 24:44, 45), so that they recognized the meaning of it and could make use of its words as exigency required. This was shortly after verified at the election of St. Matthias as Apostle, and also on the Feast of Pentecost (Acts 1:16, 29; 2:16). Secondly, He gave them the power to forgive sins, which is a component part of the sacerdotal power (John 20:23). He imparted this power in a solemn and official manner with the words: "Peace be to you. As the Father hath sent Me, I also send you. Receive ye the Holy Ghost," i.e. the power to absolve (John 20:21–23). The Holy Ghost is the holder and bestower of all ecclesiastical authority, and in order to express this in a still more concrete and forcible manner our Saviour breathed upon the Apostles. Breath is a symbol of the Holy Ghost, and signifies His being and nature, as well as His origin from the Father and the Son in their mutual love.

3. SIGNIFICANCE OF THE APPARITION

The significance of this apparition consists, to begin with, in its being the first that was vouchsafed to the entire Apostolic College. Hitherto our Lord had only appeared to individual disciples, and had announced His Resurrection to the Apostles as a body by means of these intermediaries. Probably He had delayed His appearance in person in order to prepare the Apostles for His coming and increase their desire of it; perhaps, too, they were not all assembled until the evening. Our Saviour here fulfils the promise He had given to the Apostles, that He would return and make their joy full (John 14:18; 16:16, 22).

The second thing that makes this apparition so significant is that our Lord here reveals and fulfils all the aims of His temporary sojourn on earth after His Resurrection, viz. to comfort His followers by giving them proofs of this Resurrection and tokens of His exceeding graciousness, and to continue and complete the organization of the Church. We have already seen how many gracious proofs of His Resurrection He gives the Apostles. And He continues to work at the organization of the Church by imparting to her a most important gift of grace, viz. the understanding of Holy Scripture, and by instituting the Holy Sacrament of Penance (Council of Trent, Sess. XIV. c. 1, can. 3). What important stones are these in the edifice of the Church! What great benignity towards the Apostles and what benefits for the whole world are comprised especially in the latter gift, the institution of the holy Sacrament of Penance! The power thus conferred is truly divine; divine in its origin from God through our Saviour, as He says here: "As the Father hath sent Me, I also send you"; divine in its truth and reality: the Apostles really remit sins, they do not merely declare them to be remitted by God; divine in its extent, for it reaches as far as man's weakness and malice can go on the one hand and God's mercy on the other; divine, lastly, in its beneficent operation, inasmuch as it remits so many sins, saves so many souls, allays despair, and imparts so much comfort, peace and joy. There is scarcely another Sacrament that has been instituted under such sweet auspices; on Easter evening, at our Saviour's first visit to the Apostles, whilst He shows them His Sacred Wounds, greets them with the salutation of peace, breathes upon them the breath of immortality, and gives them the Holy Ghost, Who is the goodness and love and sweetness of God. The gentle peace and comfort that reigned at the institution of this Sacrament still hover around it, diffusing their sweet perfume. It is the true Easter greeting of our Saviour to the whole world. He brings the whole merit of His Redemption with Him out of eternity, and makes of it in this Sacrament an inexhaustible and ever-flowing fountain for the forgiveness of sins. Here we see so truly the goodness and loving kindness of our Divine Saviour. How we should thank Him for the inestimable benefit of the institution of this holy Sacrament! What would have become of us all without it? With what confidence, what joy and zeal we should make use of it, since in receiving it we receive the price of His Precious Blood and His Five Sacred Wounds!

Our Lord Appears to St. Thomas

John 20:24. Now Thomas, one of the twelve, who is called Didymus, was not with them when Jesus came.—25. The other disciples therefore said to him: "We have seen the Lord." But he said to them: "Except I shall see in his hands the print of the nails, and put my finger into the place of the nails, and put my hand into his side, I will not believe."—26. And after eight days again his disciples were within, and Thomas with them. Jesus cometh, the doors being shut, and stood in the midst, and said: "Peace be to you."—27. Then he saith to Thomas: "Put in thy finger hither, and see my hands, and bring hither thy hand, and put it into my side; and be not faithless, but believing."—28. Thomas answered, and said to him: "My Lord and my God."—29. Jesus saith to him: "Because thou hast seen me, Thomas, thou hast believed; blessed are they that have not seen, and have believed."

1. CAUSES OF THE APPARITION

The first cause was the absence of St. Thomas at our Saviour's first appearance among the Apostles (John 20:24). The second cause is the disposition of mind of the Apostle. He will give no credence to the assurance of all the other Apostles (John 20:25) that they have seen our Lord, and declares that he will not believe in the Resurrection until he has put his finger into the print of the nails in our Lord's Hands and his hand into the wound of His Side; and by this determination he abides.

These words reveal no little obstinacy and tenacity of opinion as well as want of respect for all the other Apostles, whose testimony certainly deserved acceptance; further, they imply a certain amount of irreverence even towards our Saviour; and lastly, they denote unbelief, because Thomas himself fixes the conditions upon which he will believe. Such an attitude would make faith impossible. What if the Gentiles to whom the Apostle afterwards preached our Lord's Resurrection had received his words with the same reservations?

But at the same time St. Thomas was whole-hearted in his devotion to our Lord and also loyal and self-sacrificing (John 11:16); the fear and grief of the last few days seem to have depressed him and led him to shun the companionship of others. Here we see the kindness of our Lord. He makes allowance for men in whom there are failings as well as good points. And if they are only sincere and well-meaning, He knows how to overlook many faults and correct them in His own way.

2. THE APPARITION ITSELF

St. Thomas had certainly deserved a reproof. What should we have done, and what does our Lord do? Eight days later He again appears to all the Apostles, when St. Thomas is with them (John 20:26). And how does He treat him? He falls in with Thomas' almost presumptuous idea, complies with all his conditions, and takes him at his word. And what is the reproof that He gives him? He repeats word for word what Thomas had said, to show him that He knows everything, and then says to him: "Be not faithless, but believing" (John 20:27). Lastly, He accepts the Apostle's confession of faith, but on the other hand extols the simplicity and faith of those who believe without having seen (John 20:29). And what was the punishment? According to many commentators, it consisted in our Lord's insisting that Thomas should now do as he had said, and touch His Five Sacred Wounds. Others deny this. As ever, our Lord's behavior is the very excess of indulgent kindness. Such is His way, to bring good out of faults and overcome evil by good (Rom. 12:21). Here we may learn to "think of the Lord in goodness" (Wisd. 1:1). It seems as though His kindness and mild indulgence had increased with His Passion and glorification (Hebr. 4:15).

3. EFFECT OF THE APPARITION

The effect produced upon St. Thomas was surely an overwhelming sense of confusion, humility, and contrition for his fault; but the apparition also filled him with faith and love. All this is contained in that beautiful utterance: "My Lord and my God!" (John 20:28.) It is a clear, complete, touching and sublime confession of lively faith in the Divinity of Christ and entire devotion and submission. How his love must have increased at this kindness of our Lord! What must he have felt as he put his fingers into the print of the nails in his Master's Hands and his own hand into His Side, almost touching the Heart that is the central fire of all love and goodness! Can we doubt that he was completely cured of his fault and made a great stride forward in all virtues?

The apparition must have had a similar effect upon the other Apostles. The reason why our Lord did not appear to Thomas alone, but in presence of all the rest, was probably His wish to strengthen their faith also by the new proofs of the Resurrection elicited by Thomas's unbelief, and to increase their love by the kind and gracious way in which He cured him of his fault.

And the mystery should produce the same effect upon us. Our unbelief finds its cure in that of St. Thomas. It can no longer be assumed that the Apostles were precipitate in their belief. And how encouraging it is for our faith that our Lord pronounces a special blessing upon those who believe without having seen! The loving way in which He brings St. Thomas to believe should strengthen in us as in the Apostles the spirit of love and confidence. We see how longsuffering He can be in bearing with faults and bringing good out of them. Has He not shown similar kindness and patience towards us?

Another motive for faith and love lies in the fact that it was our Saviour's will to retain the marks of His Five Sacred Wounds in His glorified Body. There can be no doubt of this. It was already hinted at in the previous mystery, by His showing the Apostles His Hands, Feet, and Side (John 20:20); but here it is stated as an indubitable fact. And why did He retain the Sacred Stigmata? First, as an eternal memorial of His victory and triumph over death and hell, by His Death and Resurrection. Secondly, as a glorious adornment of His Body, because these Wounds shine by love to the eyes of the soul, and by a bright and luminous radiance to those of the body. Thirdly, as an irrefutable proof of His love for us, inasmuch as He has graven us in His Hands and Heart (Isa. 49:16). Fourthly, to lend weight to His petitions for us with the Father and obtain graces for us. Lastly, for the confusion and condemnation of His foes on the Day of Judgment. These are Christ's weapons. We may honor these Sacred Wounds by devoutly kissing the Crucifix, by reciting prayers to the Five Wounds, and by petitioning through their merits for protection in temptations and the bestowal of merits and graces. Each of these modes of veneration glorifies the Five Sacred Wounds and rejoices our Risen Saviour.

The Apparition at the Lake of Genesareth

John 21:1. After this Jesus showed himself again to the disciples at the sea of Tiberias. And he showed himself after this manner:—2. There were together Simon Peter, and Thomas who is called Didymus, and Nathanael who was of Cana in Galilee, and the sons of Zebedee, and two others of his disciples.—3. Simon Peter saith to them: "I go a-fishing." They say to him: "We also come with thee." And they went forth and entered into the ship; and that night they caught nothing.—4. But when the morning was come, Jesus stood on the shore; yet the disciples knew not that it was Jesus.—5. Jesus therefore said to them: "Children, have you any meat?" They answered him: "No."—6. He saith to them: "Cast the net on the right side of the ship, and you shall find." They cast therefore; and now they were not able to draw it for the multitude of fishes.—7. That disciple therefore whom Jesus loved, said to Peter: "It is the Lord." Simon Peter, when he heard that it was the Lord, girt his coat about him (for he was naked) and cast himself into the sea.—8. But the other disciples came in the ship (for they were not far from the land, but as it were two hundred cubits), dragging the net with fishes.—9. As soon then as they came to land, they saw hot coals lying, and a fish laid thereon, and bread.—10. Jesus saith to them: "Bring hither of the fishes which you have now caught."—11. Simon Peter went up, and drew the net to land, full of great fishes, one hundred and fifty-three. And although there were so many, the net was not broken.—12. Jesus saith to them: "Come and dine." And none of them who were at meat, durst ask him: "Who art thou?" knowing that it was the Lord.—13. And Jesus cometh and taketh bread and giveth them, and fish in like manner.—14. This is now the third time that Jesus was manifested to his disciples, after he was risen from the dead.—15. When therefore they had dined, Jesus saith to Simon Peter: "Simon, son of John, lovest thou me more than these?" He saith to him: "Yea, Lord, thou knowest that I love thee." He saith to him: "Feed my lambs."—16. He said to him again: "Simon, son of John, lovest thou me?" He saith to him: "Yea, Lord, thou knowest that I love thee." He saith to him: "Feed my lambs."—17. He said to him the third time: "Simon, son of John, lovest thou me?" Peter was grieved, because he had said to him the third time: "Lovest thou me?" And he said to him: "Lord, thou knowest all things; thou knowest that I love thee." He said to him: "Feed my sheep.—18. Amen, amen I say to thee: When thou wast younger, thou didst gird thyself, and didst walk where thou wouldst; but when thou shalt be old, thou shalt stretch forth thy hands, and another shall gird thee, and lead thee whither thou wouldst not."—19. And this he said, signifying by what death he should glorify God. And when he had said this, he saith to him: "Follow me."—20. Peter turning about, saw that disciple whom Jesus loved following, who also leaned on his breast at supper, and said: "Lord, who is he that shall betray thee?"—21. Him therefore when Peter had seen, he saith to Jesus: "Lord, and what shall this man do?"—22. Jesus saith to him: "So I will have him to remain till I come, what is it to thee? Follow thou me."—23. This saying therefore went abroad among the brethren, that that disciple should not die. And Jesus did not say to him: He should not die; but: "So I will have him to remain till I come, what is it to thee?"

This is our Lord's first appearance in Galilee, where He had bidden His Apostles await His coming, and the third in presence of several Apostles (John 20:14). It is principally concerned with St. Peter. His equipment for the apostolic vocation, that part of it at least which was peculiar to him, is here completed.

1. OUR SAVIOUR SPECIALLY ENCOURAGES ST. PETER TO EXERCISE THE APOSTOLIC OFFICE

This exhortation certainly applied also to the other Apostles who were present (John 21:12), but it was especially intended for St. Peter, because he had proposed that they should go and fish (a symbol of the apostolic ministry; Luke 5:10; John 21:3) and thus furnished the occasion for the apparition, and also because he was the leader (John 21:11).

Our Saviour encouraged them in the first place by appearing to them (John 21:4); by expressing His desire for something to eat with the bread He had prepared, viz. fish (John 21:5); and by urging them to make a new trial after an unsuccessful night (John 21:6). Our Lord longs for the souls that are gained through apostolic work, partly on His own account, because He loves men and is glorified by their salvation; partly on the Apostles' account, because they merit a great reward in heaven by their labors; and partly on account of the men who are thereby made happy for time and eternity.

The encouragement our Saviour gave the Apostles consisted secondly in His miraculous help, which was almost the same as at the first miracle of the draught of fishes. There are new circumstances here, however; first, that the quantity of fish caught appears to have been still greater than on the previous occasion, and yet the net did not break (John 21:6, 11), for the Church is never overwhelmed by the greatest conquests of souls that can be made; and secondly that Peter, instead of recoiling in reverential fear, precipitates himself into the water in his love and eagerness to reach our Lord (John 21:7), as soon as St. John tells him that it is He who is standing on the shore. Our Saviour wins St. Peter for the apostolic vocation and confirms him in it for ever, by a miracle similar to the one of former days.

The third encouragement was to be found in the eternal reward of apostolic work, which is symbolized by the pleasant morning meal on the seashore. Here as in eternity the nightly labor and fatigue is over; the shore is safely reached; and here as there our Lord is Author, sharer, and component part of the enjoyment (John 21:12, 13). The means is miraculous, and all are full of joy and wonder at His goodness; all see and know Him, and no one asks His Name (John 21:12). And the souls who have been won form a part of the joy (John 21:10). In truth, our Lord gives here a beautiful, touching and sublime encouragement.

2. OUR LORD CONFERS THE PRIMACY UPON ST. PETER

Hitherto St. Peter had only received the promise of the Primacy (Matt. 16:18). But after this morning meal our Lord finally confers it upon him. In the first place, He declares him in plain and unequivocal terms to be now actually in possession of this office (John 21:15, 16, 17); and this He does most solemnly, in the presence of several other Apostles (John 21:2). Further, He confers it upon him in all its plenitude and majesty. It is truly divine power; divine, first, in its origin and nature, for it represents our Saviour Himself: "Feed My lambs" (John 21:15). It is divine, secondly, in its compass; it extends over the whole Church, the hearing (the lambs) as well as the teaching body (the sheep), and includes the entire and supreme power, indicated in the Scriptural mode of expression by "feeding" (II Kings 5:2; Ps. 22:1; 77:71; Matt. 2:6). Thirdly, it is divine in its operation and significance for the whole Church, whose being, attributes, stability, life, growth and work stand and fall with the Primacy. Life, progress and efficacious work is only found under the sway of Peter.

But our Saviour also appoints the conditions upon which He will confer this dignity upon St. Peter, viz. a love which is both great and humble (John 21:15). This is the meaning of the thrice-repeated question whether Peter loves Him and loves Him more than the other Apostles do, evidently a reference to his premature protestation of his fidelity before the Passion (Mark 14:29) and to the threefold denial. St. Peter's modest answer proves that his love was now really humble, and so our Lord could entrust him with the highest dignity. Only in love and humility can any office be exercised in a Christian and useful way; otherwise office and power merely tend to bring about our ruin (Luke 22:24–27). St. Peter had now reached this point, through our Lord's wise training, and therefore the Church had in him a head according to God's own heart.

3. OUR LORD PROMISES ST. PETER THE GLORIOUS DEATH OF A MARTYR

After conferring upon him the highest dignity in the Church, our Lord predicts to St. Peter that he will die the death of a martyr (John 21:18); or, to be more explicit, that he will be taken prisoner in his old age, bound ("girded"), and led to the martyrdom of the cross, since his hands were to be "stretched forth" upon it (John 21:19; II Peter 1:14; cf. John 13:36).

At the same time our Saviour assures St. Peter that his profession of love is sincere, and that he will seal this love for Him and for his flock like a good shepherd, with the victorious constancy of martyrdom. He praises the courage of his old age, contrasting it with the weakness he has shown in the prime of life. Otherwise, as a rule, people are courageous and independent in their youth, but timid and dependent upon others in their old age. With Peter the opposite will be the case. This, then, is the perfect "following" after our Lord to which He calls St. Peter and no other Apostle (John 21:19): to follow Him in His office and follow Him in the death of the Cross. Now St. Peter is perfectly comforted.

And when Peter, following our Lord, sympathetically (though, as was often the case, over-eagerly) inquires about the destiny of

St. John, who, uninvited, was also following Jesus (John 21:20), our Saviour replies in the negative, though somewhat indefinitely: "So (if) I will have him to remain till I come, what is it to thee?" (John 21:22, 23.) John is to be preserved from violent death and to remain until our Lord comes again to fetch him home by a natural death (John 14:3). St. John remarks that these words of Jesus are not to be taken to mean that he will not die at all, but only that he will not die a violent death (John 21:23). Besides, our Lord further observes to Peter, he is not to trouble himself about the special vocation of St. John or anyone else, but simply to strive to follow Him in his own (John 21:22). Special graces and peculiar vocations concern our Lord alone. Everyone loves and is loved in a special manner. To St. John, perhaps, more tender love, greater familiarity, and more personal privileges were vouchsafed; Peter was distinguished by greater proofs of esteem and higher official prerogatives. To John our Lord granted the grace of virginity, and perhaps also deeper knowledge, higher contemplation, and a special work in the Church in this respect; Peter excelled in courage, energy and maturity of judgment. To John our Lord entrusted His dear Mother; to Peter, the Church (S. Thom. 1, q. 20, a. 4 ad 3).

This is another very important mystery. On the one hand we see the inexhaustible love and kindness of our Saviour towards His Apostles, and especially to Peter. When He has once given His love to anyone, He does not recall it (Rom. 11:29). How gentle and loving is His allusion to the thrice-repeated denial! On the other hand, we again see His untiring care and activity on behalf of His Church. He institutes the Primacy, and hereby gives the Church a firm basis and a head. How many blessings come to us from God through the Pope, Christ's vicar and the ruler of the kingdom of God on earth! Eternal thanks be to our Saviour for this inestimable benefit!

The Apparition on the Mountain

Matt. 28:16. And the eleven disciples went into Galilee, unto the mountain where Jesus had appointed them.—17. And seeing him they adored; but some doubted.—18. And Jesus coming spoke to them, saying: "All power is given to me in heaven and on earth;—19. Going therefore teach ye all nations; baptizing them in the name of the Father, and of the Son, and of the Holy Ghost;—20. Teaching them to observe all things whatsoever I have commanded you; and behold I am with you all days, even to the consummation of the world."

Mark 16:15. And he said to them: "Go ye into the whole world, and preach the Gospel to every creature.—16. He that believeth and is baptized, shall be saved; but he that believeth not, shall be condemned.—17. And these signs shall follow them that believe: In my name they shall cast out devils; they shall speak with new tongues;—18. They shall take up serpents; and if they shall drink any deadly thing, it shall not hurt them; they shall lay their hands upon the sick, and they shall recover."

I Cor. 15:6. Then Jesus was seen by more than five hundred brethren at once.

1. CIRCUMSTANCES OF THE APPARITION

This is probably our Lord's last appearance in Galilee, after He had instituted the Primacy and completed the organization of the Church. According to the prophecy (Isa. 9:1; Matt. 4:15) Galilee was the principal scene of His teaching and miracles and the home of most of the Apostles. There He had begun the structure of the Church, and there He now completes it by the institution of the Primacy; there too were the Apostles to receive their final mandate to go forth into the world and found the Church. The mountain upon which our Lord appeared was perhaps Thabor or the Mount of the Beatitudes.

If this apparition is identical with the one mentioned by St. Paul (I Cor. 15:6), the Apostles, disciples, and a great number of the faithful, about five hundred, were assembled together. So it was one of the most glorious and solemn of all, quite in keeping with its high importance, and in all likelihood one of those that had been promised to the Apostles (Matt. 28:7; Mark 16:7). As regards the disposition of those assembled, some of them, probably the Apostles, to whom our Lord had already appeared, adored Him (Matt. 28:17); "but some doubted," most likely those who had not yet seen Him in His glorious state.

2. IMPORTANCE OF THE APPARITION

Its importance lies in the fact that our Lord, after having appointed the various orders and states in the Church, once more confers upon the Apostles plenary ecclesiastical power, and commissions them to exercise it throughout the world.

He first confirms the legitimacy of this power and the commission to exercise it, by pointing to its origin and nature: "All power is given to Me in heaven and in earth" (Matt. 28:18). Our Lord possesses the plenitude of all power, the teaching, priestly, kingly and judicial authority in the whole sphere of God's dominion; and not merely does He possess it for Himself, but He can also impart it to others. He possesses this power in His own right as

Son of God and Creator of the world (John 1:10); He has inherited it as God-Man (Col. 1:15), earned (Hebr. 2:10) and purchased it (I Peter 1:19) by His Death. And all these titles are included in the authority granted to the Apostles.

Secondly, our Saviour defines the extent of the apostolic power. It is simply His "power," and He thus explains it (Matt. 28:19): Teach (make the people your pupils), baptize (incorporate them into My kingdom), and teach them to "observe all things whatsoever I have commanded you"; that is to say, it is the teaching, priestly and pastoral power; it confers all authority to establish, maintain, govern and propagate Christ's kingdom, each according to his own proper degree of power under the guidance of St. Peter. And this power extends over the whole world (Mark 16:15), all nations, the whole human race (Matt. 28:19) and all time, as long as the present order of grace shall last, "to the consummation of the world" (Matt. 28:20). It even reacts upon eternity (Matt. 28:18), and is completely independent of temporal power. The boundaries of the great kingdom are marked out; the barriers between the nations and even between heaven and earth are broken down. Heaven and earth are now merely two provinces of the same kingdom. In conferring this power upon the Apostles our Lord also imposes upon them the duty of exercising it, and upon all men that of submitting to it. No one is excepted or declared exempt from the authority of His representatives.

Thirdly, our Saviour adds to the charge a promise of reward and punishment; for mankind in general, who will be saved or damned according as they believe or do not believe (Mark 16:17), and also for the holders of the power, to whom for the easier and surer exercise of it He promises miraculous gifts, such as authority over evil spirits, power to heal the sick, the gift of tongues (Mark 14:17), and a special divine aid that will never cease (Matt. 28:20), until the Church Militant passes over into the Church Triumphant.

3. CONCLUSIONS

The first fruit that all may derive from this significant and important apparition should be that of heartfelt thanksgiving for the final and solemn institution of Holy Baptism as the entrance-door of the Church and means of adoption into Christ's kingdom; secondly, respect and submission to the ecclesiastical hierarchy, which stands before us invested with such glorious and truly divine power; and lastly, faith and gratitude with regard to the clear and solemn manifestation of the mystery of the Most Holy Trinity, which forms the keystone and crown of the whole revelation.

And those who have the happiness and honor to share in the apostolic power in any way should be led by this mystery to strive to acquire and manifest the apostolic spirit. This apostolic spirit consists first in a certain expansion of heart, for the Apostle is for the whole world and the whole world is for him; he must not cling too much to his native land, nor indeed to any country in particular. Secondly, the apostolic spirit consists in invincible courage amid all difficulties and dangers. Christ is with us and lends us His divine aid; who then should lack courage? A third peculiarity of this spirit is a certain dignity and full consciousness of one's position, such as the Apostles felt, expressed and maintained against all temporal potentates. Lastly, the apostolic spirit consists in love of the Cross and humility, for the apostolic power owes its origin to the Cross, and our Saviour would only possess His in right of His bitter Passion and Death. Everything in this mystery is sublime, grand, and of vast extent. The words that are spoken here are like the words of blessing formerly pronounced over the completed creation (Gen. 1:28). The echo of them never dies away in the Church; they still continue their work in her. All the power of extension and propagation, all the efficacy of life and blessing, all the resisting force and victorious strength of the Church in her members and orders comes from this commission and blessing. How we ought to pray that the divine virtue of these words may be truly efficacious in us all! How glorious would then be the state of Christ's kingdom!

Retrospect of the Glorious Life on Earth

Acts 1:1. The former treatise I made, O Theophilus, of all things which Jesus began to do and to teach—2. Until the day on which, giving commandments by the Holy Ghost to the Apostles whom he had chosen, he was taken up;—3. To whom also he showed himself alive after his passion by many proofs, for forty days appearing to them and speaking of the kingdom of God.

This life has three characteristics, corresponding to the various ends of this intermediate sojourn on earth from the Resurrection to the Ascension.

1. IT IS A GLORIOUS LIFE

This life is glorious, first, because it is impassible, in consequence of our Lord's immortality. And it is impassible because He is exempt not merely from suffering and death, but even from the ordinary necessities of this earthly life, from dependence upon rest and nourishment. He has the well-spring of life within Himself, independently of any exterior source, and when He takes food it is for higher purposes than the preservation of life, viz. in order to demonstrate the truth and reality of His material Body.

It is glorious, further, because it is a divine life. In consequence of its clarity, agility and subtlety, even His Body now displays the divine attributes in a special manner. He is now here, now there, and manifests even in the body what one might almost call a kind of omnipresence. His omnipotence is seen in the wonderful power that He exercises over nature (John 21:6, 9) and over His own Body, to which He can give any appearance He pleases (John 20:15, 19, 26; Luke 24:16). Lastly, the glory of His Godhead shines out in the marvelous beauty and clarity of His risen Body.

2. IT IS AN ACTIVE LIFE

We are told that our Lord spoke to His disciples during these forty days of the kingdom of God, i.e. of the Church (Acts 1:3). Indeed, He worked actively in all sorts of ways at the development and firm establishment of the Church.

The first essential element of the Church is faith. And faith, especially in the Resurrection, was now marvelously strengthened. This was one of the principal intentions our Saviour had in view in various apparitions. In fact He gives every possible proof of the Resurrection: indirect proofs, such as quotation of the Scriptures and the testimony of angels, and direct, positive proofs in His own Person that He is really risen in a true, tangible human body (Luke 24:39), the same that He formerly had (John 20:20, 27). And this Body is animated by a human soul, and therefore He leads a truly human life even in His glory; a vegetative life, when He chooses to exemplify it as such (Luke 24:43); a sensitive life, because He hears, answers, greets His followers (Matt. 28:9); lastly, an intelligent life, since He expounds the Scriptures (Luke 24:27). And yet it is withal a glorious life, because it is superior to the conditions of ordinary earthly life, as is seen by His sudden appearance and disappearance (Luke 24:31, 36; John 20:19, 26).

By this glorious life He also confirms our faith in our own future resurrection and immortality, indeed in all His miracles and doctrine.

The second constituent of the Church is the possession of the Sacraments and the gifts of grace. During the forty days of His glorious life on earth our Saviour instituted no less than two Sacraments, Penance (John 20:23) and Baptism, at all events inasmuch as He then proclaimed the general command and obligation to receive them (Matt. 28:19). And as regards the gifts of grace, He conferred upon the Church the understanding of Holy Scripture (Luke 24:45) and the gift of miracles (Mark 16:17 seq.).

The third foundation upon which the Church rests is the hierarchy. Our Saviour completes its organization by the institution of the Primacy (John 21:15 seq.), and invests the Apostles with the most complete authority (Matt. 28:19), commissioning them to exercise the same and solemnly assuring them of His divine aid (John 21:6; Matt. 28:20; Mark 16:15; Luke 24:47).

3. IT IS A LOVING AND LOVABLE LIFE

This life is worthy of our love on account of the abundant proofs it gives us of the inexhaustible goodness, grace, love and kindness of our Lord towards everyone without exception. His Apostles and disciples as well as the holy women, friends and foes, just and sinners. He bestows His benefits and His blessings upon the whole world and in the most lovable and winning way. We may briefly call to mind the holy women, Magdalen, the disciples of Emmaus, Peter, and Thomas.

We can represent to ourselves our Lord's tenderness and goodness during this period in three pictures which His various appearances conjure up before our minds. Magdalen took Him for a gardener (John 20:15). This represents our Saviour in His risen life. A violent storm had devastated His garden and made havoc of everything. Now, after His Resurrection, He re-enters the garden, carefully raises every drooping shrub and plant, tends what has suffered injury, plants, waters everything with His gentle comfort, and refreshes it with the sunlight of His joy. In a short time the havoc has disappeared and order is restored. The disciples on the way to Emmaus see our Lord as a wanderer. Truly, His love for us makes Him remain as a pilgrim on earth for forty days longer, although He is already in His glorified state (Luke 24:15). What a faithful, cheering companion He is on the way! How winningly

He shortens and cheers the sad and weary journey by His sweet converse and comfort, and how He strengthens and encourages the disciples by the breaking of bread! This is a beautiful picture of our Lord's whole life. By the Incarnation He really made Himself our companion in the pilgrimage of life, and now He continues to live and journey with us in the Holy Eucharist. "*Se nascens dedit socium, convescens in edulium*" (Roman Breviary). And at the Lake of Genesareth we find Him as the Supreme Pastor. What a Good Shepherd He is in His risen life! He does not forsake His sheep; He comes at once to call them and goes after them all. How the Heart of the Good Shepherd rejoices when He has found and assembled them all again! And He does not go away until He has found and trained a shepherd after His own Heart; nor does He entrust the flock to him until He has exacted from him a solemn promise to lead it in the spirit of love which animates that Heart (John 20:15). Is He not indeed the good and faithful Shepherd of our souls?

2. THE GLORIOUS LIFE OF JESUS IN HEAVEN

The Ascension

Luke 24:46. And Jesus said to the disciples: "Thus it is written, and thus it behoved Christ to suffer, and to rise again from the dead the third day;—47. And that penance and remission of sins should be preached in his name unto all nations, beginning at Jerusalem.—48. And you are witnesses of these things.—49. And I send the promise of my Father upon you; but stay you in the city, till you be endued with power from on high."—50. And he led them out as far as Bethania; and lifting up his hands he blessed them.—51. And it came to pass, whilst he blessed them, he departed from them, and was carried up to heaven.—52. And they adoring went back into Jerusalem with great joy.

Mark 16:19. And the Lord Jesus, after he had spoken to them, was taken up into heaven, and sitteth on the right hand of God.

Acts 1:4. And eating together with them, he commanded them that they should not depart from Jerusalem, but should wait for the promise of the Father, "which you have heard" (saith he) "by my mouth;—5. For John indeed baptized with water, but you shall be baptized with the Holy Ghost not many days hence."—6. They therefore who were come together asked him, saying: "Lord, wilt thou at this time restore again the kingdom to Israel?"—7. But he said to them: "It is not for you to know the times or moments, which the Father hath put in his own power;—8. But you shall receive the power of the Holy Ghost coming upon you, and you shall be witnesses unto me in Jerusalem, and in all Judaea, and Samaria, and even to the uttermost part of the earth."—9. And when he had said these things, while they looked on, he was raised up; and a cloud received him out of their sight.—10. And while they were beholding him going up to heaven, behold two men stood by them in white garments,—11. Who also said: "Ye men of Galilee, why stand you looking up to heaven? This Jesus who is taken up from you into heaven, shall so come as you have seen him going into heaven."—12. Then they returned to Jerusalem from the mount that is called Olivet, which is nigh Jerusalem within a sabbath-day's journey.

With the Ascension the earthly life of our Divine Saviour comes to a close. It is the last mystery of His pilgrimage here below and the first of His glorious life in heaven. With it His glorification reaches its climax.

1. REASONS FOR THE ASCENSION

It was necessary that our Saviour should complete His glory by taking possession of heaven; in the first place, on His own account. He had spoken of it beforehand (John 1:51; 16:28; 20:17). This earth is not a permanent abode for man, it is merely a place of preparation and not the goal; least of all could it be so for the God-Man. As God-Man He had a right to heaven and was bound to take possession of it, in order to complete His glory. To all intents and purposes it had become His at the Resurrection; there was wanting only the accidental joy and glory that heaven itself could afford Him as the place of His abode, and these He now acquired by the Ascension. Thus the fulness of His glory was complete (Eph. 4:10).

And on our side also there were reasons for our Lord's Ascension. He had finished His work and completed the structure of the Church. His return to the Father would be of very great use to us, but His presence here was no longer needed. By His Ascension He promoted the life of faith (John 16:10; 20:29); strengthened our hope most powerfully, inasmuch as He already took possession of heaven for us (John 14:2, 3); and increased our love in like measure by the glorious gifts that He sends us from heaven (Ps. 67:19), especially by the Holy Ghost, Who is love itself and infuses love into our hearts. Had our Lord not ascended into heaven, the Holy Spirit would not have come (John 16:7), neither would heaven itself have been opened to us (Eph. 4:8). Thus the Ascension does not merely confer an honor on our nature, inasmuch as it raised humanity, in Christ, above all the orders of heaven to the joint possession of all divine honors with the Godhead (John 1:21); but it is also a source of blessing, inasmuch as it strengthens and elevates our life of virtue, and enables our Saviour to take possession of heaven for us and be there our Advocate with the Father (Hebr. 7:25). Thus by His Ascension He procures us new means of grace, and completes His doctrine by setting before us the sure and elevating hope of heaven, the glorious goal of all the efforts of God and men. The God-Man certainly could not have concluded His life more gloriously than with the Ascension.

2. HOW THE ASCENSION TOOK PLACE

The preparation for the Ascension consisted first in our Lord's command to the disciples to remain in Jerusalem. Thence, from the city of the throne of David, He wished to ascend to heaven and enter into His kingdom (Ps. 109:3; Mich. 4:7; Luke 1:32). There too He partook of a familiar repast with His disciples, as He had been wont to do during His earthly life, and gave them His last instructions (Luke 24:46–49; Acts 1:4, 5). He bade them remain in the city and await the Holy Ghost, and then go forth thence to exercise their office and preach to the whole world. Nevertheless the Ascension was not to take place in Jerusalem itself nor in presence of the people, because this mystery does not belong to His earthly life.

Accordingly our Saviour led the disciples out towards Bethania, to the Mount of Olives (Luke 24:50). There, where He had begun His Passion and whither He will one day come again in Judgment (Acts 1:11), it was His will to ascend to heaven. On the way thither, as it seems, the disciples inquired whether the Messianic kingdom was to be made manifest now, or if not, when it would be revealed (Acts 1:6). Our Saviour does not deny its manifestation, but will have the "when" and "how" left to the Heavenly Father. But in His next words He indicates plainly enough that, as it is written in the books of the prophets (Isa. 44:3; Jer. 31:33), the kingdom of God, though not yet complete will nevertheless begin with the Descent of the Holy Ghost, through their glorious testimony. He opens out to them a magnificent vista of the future history of the Church. Having ascended the Mount of Olives, He bestows a farewell blessing upon all His disciples (Luke 24:50) in His quality of High Priest, and with more powerful effect than the blessing of Jacob produced upon his sons (Gen. 49). We were all included in this blessing.

The Ascension itself was accomplished by the power of the God-Man Himself, and, as far as human eyes could see, gradually (Acts 1:9) and with manifestations of great power and glory. How great this glory was is seen from the fact that a "cloud," i.e. a magnificent atmospheric phenomenon, appeared. (Acts 1:9); secondly, from the fitness of things, for it was meet that the

God-Man should ascend to heaven with all the display of power becoming His dignity; thirdly, from the effect that the Ascension had upon the Apostles, who, instead of mourning over our Saviour's departure, rejoiced and adored Him (Luke 24:52), a sign that He must have caused a divine glory to surround His Person at this moment especially; and lastly from the words of the angels: "Jesus . . . shall so come as you have seen Him going up into heaven," i.e. to the Judgment, when, as we know, He will appear with great exterior splendor.

But who shall describe the glory that the Apostles' eyes did *not* see? What must have been our Saviour's thoughts as He glanced down to this earth that was gradually vanishing from His sight? Oh how short is this life, how small this world! How quickly all His sufferings and sacrifices had passed, and yet they had done so much good! And what did He feel as He glanced up to the heaven that was opening to Him, a vast kingdom of honor, joy and power, in which He is now to reign as King and Son of God for all eternity! How glorious must have been His entry there, with the throngs of redeemed Saints of the Old Covenant; how glorious the homage of the heavenly hosts, the reception He met with from the Father and the Holy Ghost, and His instalment in His place at God's right hand! (John 17:5, 24; Apoc. 5:12; Eph. 4:8; Ps. 46:6, 7; 67:19.)

3. EFFECTS OF THE ASCENSION

The effect produced by the Ascension upon the Apostles was wonder and admiration (Acts 1:10, 11), adoration and joy (Luke 24:52). This was but natural; for they had had as it were a glimpse of heaven, and heaven is full of joy and courage. There they stood, as though they could never see enough of the grand and magnificent spectacle. Filled with this joy they quitted the mountain, and the glad memory of this sight remained with them for the rest of their lives.

And the Ascension must fill us also with joy, joy in our Divine Saviour and for His sake. He has now reached His goal and is in possession of His full glory; nothing lies before Him now but joy and honor unending. "Of His kingdom there shall be no end" (Luke 1:33). And we must rejoice on our own account also. Heaven is ours; our Saviour has taken possession of it for us as our common heritage. "I ascend to My Father and to your Father, to My God and your God" (John 20:17). Our good Saviour, our

Brother, will not withhold from us our share. So let us rejoice. No one can take this joy from us. Secondly, the Ascension must fill us with courage and confidence. The vanguard of our army already stands victorious upon the battlements of the Eternal City, and our Lord is reigning in the heavenly Jerusalem. What can discourage us? Sooner or later we shall be there too. And the last effect that the Ascension must produce upon us is love and longing. In heaven is our Saviour, God, everything that is good and beautiful; heaven is our home, whence we came and whither we go. Where else, then, should our hearts be? So let us think of heaven very often, and also long for it. We can think of nothing more beautiful, nothing more useful to us. The thought of heaven detaches our hearts from earth and gives us joy and courage for work and sacrifice. Whoever believes in heaven never has a really sad moment here below.—For reading: "Imitation of Christ," Book III, chaps. 21, 47, 48, 49.

Christ's Sitting at the Right Hand of God

Mark 16:19. And the Lord Jesus, after he had spoken to them, was taken up into heaven and sitteth on the right hand of God.

Ps. 109:1. The Lord said to my Lord: "Sit thou at my right hand, until I make thy enemies thy footstool."

We will now consider the life of the God-Man in His glory. This is briefly indicated in the words of St. Mark: "Jesus . . . sitteth on the right hand of God."

1. CHARACTERISTICS OF THIS LIFE

This sitting at the right hand of God is first a life of the most sublime, supreme and divine power, majesty and glory. It signifies nothing less than the full possession and equal share of the power and glory of the Father and all divine honors. This place on the Father's throne belongs to our Saviour by right as God-Man, inasmuch as the Person of the God-Man is the Second Person in the Godhead. But as regards His human nature the "sitting at the right hand of the Father" signifies merely a place of honor near the Godhead and precedence over all other creatures, because this human nature surpasses every other created being in holiness and abundance of gifts and dignities. The seat at the right hand is always a special honor and distinction. So, take it as we will, this expression denotes a peculiar privilege of Christ's, which He shares with no one else. Whilst all the other creatures of God who have attained to bliss, even the highest among the angels, stand round the Father's throne and serve Him (Dan. 7:10), the God-Man has His place on the throne itself (Hebr. 1:13; 12:2), and receives conjointly with the Father the highest divine honor, the homage, praise and adoration of the blessed spirits who surround the Divine Majesty in a million circles, casting their crowns at His feet and adoring Him with incessant thanksgiving and divine praise, as the Apocalypse testifies (Apoc. 4:3 seq.; 5:8 seq.; 11:15 seq.). This heavenly service never ceases day or night.

Secondly, Christ's sitting at the right hand of the Father is a life of the sweetest rest and securest peace. That is why it is called "sitting," for this term expresses the immutability and indestructibility of this kingdom of honor, power and joy. Christ now rests from His journeys, labors and fatigues, in blissful repose. He only works exteriorly by His word of command and through His servants. No foe can reach the sublime elevation of His throne; unbounded peace hovers over His kingdom, and as far as the horizon of eternity extends the heavens are unclouded and blissfully serene. What a beautiful picture of peace is presented to us in the heavenly stronghold whose gates stand open day and night (Apoc. 21:25; Isa. 60:11), and where death and mourning and sorrow shall be no more (Apoc. 21:4), but everywhere the beauty and contentment of peace! What can be compared to this heavenly repose and imperishable peace?

Thirdly, this peace does not hinder His life from being one of great activity. The occupation of the God-Man is the government of His kingdom on earth and in heaven. As Head of the whole creation and universal Mediator, as King and High Priest, He is the noble instrument of all God's exterior communications, the intermediary of all graces and rewards, and the executor of all judgments and punishments. He is constantly shedding beams of joy and rapture upon the Church Triumphant, comfort and alleviation upon the Church Suffering, light, strength and purity upon the Church Militant, and pouring down the sweet sunshine of the light of faith upon the heathen world. He is always praying for us and offering the immeasurable price of His Wounds, together with our prayers and works, to the Father; at every moment He is judging souls and deciding their eternal fate. As Moses stood upon the shore of the Red Sea and directed the passage of his people through the depths of the water, Christ stands upon the heights of heaven and guides His Church through the stormy sea of time. But time is no longer the boundary of His empire; everything, temporal as well as eternal, is subject to His command. His hand gathers up the threads of the government of the world; He guides the destinies of individuals and of nations; He exalts and degrades, calls, effaces, rewards and punishes; He takes away the lives of princes—He, "the terrible with the kings of the earth" (Ps. 75:13), and no mortal can escape His power. Such is the activity of the God-Man in heaven.

Fourthly, Christ's sitting at God's right hand is a life of the most wonderful success and victorious triumph. He reigns as God. His power is over all, and is not felt; it works everywhere, and is not perceived; He forces no one, and yet all serve Him; He leaves His creatures the most untrammeled freedom, and weaves their criminal abuse of it into the texture of His plans; He draws back from them as though He were obstructed and vanquished, and yet entices them whither He wishes to lead them. The government of the God-Man is like His life, without mistake or repentance. Calmly and with divine joy He watches from His throne the rush and hurry of mundane affairs, and their impetuous course "maketh the city of God joyful" (Ps. 45:5); however wild and unruly they seem, they are only His servants, and accomplish His will to the glory of His Father and the weal of the elect throughout all ages of the world, until the last wave rolls up and breaks on the shore of eternity. Then He will rise to judge the world, separate the just from the wicked, and put all things under His Father's feet (I Cor. 15:26, 28). The Apocalypse gives us a vivid description of this life and reign of the God-Man at God's right hand. There we see the Lamb upon the throne of His glory (Apoc. 5:6; 7:17; 14:14); the seals of the destiny of the world and of each individual are in His hand (Apoc. 5:5); He executes this destiny (Apoc. 14:14; 19:11); He is the source of the bliss of the elect (Apoc. 2:26; 3:21; 7:17; 14:1; 21:22; 22:1) and the object of royal and divine honor (Apoc. 5:12; 7:10).

2. CONCLUSIONS

And what conclusions are we to draw from our meditation upon this glorious life?

Its first fruit should be admiration, adoration, praise and devoted service of our Divine Saviour. He sits upon the throne of the

Father in unity with Him and the Holy Ghost, as one God; so let us honor and serve Him as our God. Our homage and adoration here below is but an echo of the eternal song in heaven, as is so beautifully expressed in the liturgical hymn of praise *Gloria in excelsis Deo*. Let us rejoice at our Saviour's glorious and joyful reign and congratulate Him upon it (Ps. 144).

Secondly, we shall one day share with our Saviour the glory of this active and powerful life and reign with Him (Apoc. 2:7; 14:13; Ps. 149:5 seq.; Eph. 2:6). So let us reflect upon it with interest and love in order to encourage ourselves to work here below for Christ's kingdom. Heaven, with its honors and joys and eternity, is the glorious part of this kingdom, whilst to the Church on earth is allotted the stress of the fighting and labor. Christ wishes our prayers, our work, our conflicts and our sufferings. They are the material for heaven, so let us not grow weary. We cannot devote our lives to a more glorious cause; success is sure, glorious and eternal.

Thirdly, let us not despond when the scales of the fight tremble and the issue seems to waver in the balance. God permits this to try our confidence. If we feel our strength failing, let us cast an upward glance at the peace and bliss of the eternal kingdom, past whose rocky base the history of the world sweeps and melts into space without disturbing its peace, and on whose pinnacles the reflection of the final victory is already shining, that victory that will end the battle in the evening of the world's existence and establish for ever the supremacy of Christ. Oh that this kingdom of His might be the object of our work, the constant subject of our prayer, the motive of our sufferings and labors, and the beginning and completion of our joy! (Ps. 136:5 seq.)

The Days Preceding the Descent of the Holy Ghost

Acts 1:13. And when the disciples were come in, they went up into an upper room, where abode Peter and John, James and Andrew, Philip and Thomas, Bartholomew and Matthew, James of Alpheus and Simon Zelotes, and Judas the brother of James;—14. All these were persevering with one mind in prayer with the women and Mary the mother of Jesus, and with his brethren.—15. In those days Peter rising up in the midst of the brethren, said (now the number of persons together was about an hundred and twenty):—16. "Men, brethren, the Scripture must needs be fulfilled which the Holy Ghost spoke before by the mouth of David concerning Judas, who was the leader of them that apprehended Jesus;—17. Who was numbered with us, and had obtained part of this ministry.—18. And he indeed hath possessed a field of the reward of inquity, and being hanged burst asunder in the midst; and all his bowels gushed out.—19. And it became known to all the inhabitants of Jerusalem, so that the same field was called in their tongue Haceldama, that is to say, the field of blood.—20. For it is written in the book of Psalms: Let their habitation become desolate, and let there be none to dwell therein; and his bishopric let another take.—21. Wherefore of these men who have companied with us all the time that the Lord Jesus came in and went out among us,—22. Beginning from the baptism of John, until the day wherein he was taken up from us, one of these must be made a witness with us of his resurrection."—23. And they appointed two, Joseph, called Barsabas, who was surnamed Justus, and Matthias.—24. And praying, they said: "Thou, Lord, who knowest the hearts of all men, show whether of these two thou hast chosen—25. To take the place of this ministry and apostleship, from which Judas hath by transgression fallen, that he might go to his own place."—26. And they gave them lots; and the lot fell upon Matthias, and he was numbered with the eleven apostles.

LUKE 24:53. And the disciples were always in the temple, praising and blessing God.

1. THE DAYS BETWEEN THE ASCENSION AND PENTECOST WERE A PREPARATION FOR THE COMING OF THE HOLY GHOST

All that Holy Scripture tells us about the Apostles during these days points to a preparation for the Descent of the Holy Ghost. Our Saviour's directions to the Apostles have the same meaning. They are to remain in the city and wait for the Holy Ghost (Luke 24:29; Acts 1:4). This, then, is the meaning of these days; they are a time of rest for the Apostles, the solemn vigil of the holy Feast of Pentecost.

2. MANNER OF THE PREPARATION

The Apostles prepare for the reception of the Holy Ghost in three ways.

The first preparation consisted in solitude and quiet recollection. According to our Saviour's instructions they were not to return to Galilee, to their families and occupations, but to stay quietly in the city and "wait for the promise" (Luke 24:49; Acts 1:4). These days were to be days of rest for the Apostles. And we are also told that they went up into the Coenaculum, "into an upper room," and there abode (Acts 1:13). This room, the first Christian church, sanctified by so many sacred memories of the past few weeks, helped them to be recollected and to reflect. And they seem only to have quitted it during these days in order to go into the Temple (Luke 24:53). Retreat—solitude and recollection—is the beginning of everything good. Recollection always costs something to our distracted minds and our sensuality. But it is here that a man gains strength and prepares the way for God to come and speak to his heart (Osee 2:14). This is the first preparation for Pentecost. One must rest, i.e. abstain from all unnecessary occupations and distractions, and retire to the "upper room" of the soul.

The Apostles' second preparation was prayer. This is expressly mentioned (Acts 1:14). It was a continual and persevering prayer, common and unanimous, made in union with the Mother of Jesus, the holy women, and the rest of the faithful; and it was also a fervent and eager prayer, because they had been told to expect the Holy Ghost (Acts 1:4). They prayed now in the Coenaculum, now in the Temple (Luke 24:53), and were constantly occupied in praise and petition. As the fervent cry for the coming of the Redeemer had been handed down from father to son in the Old Covenant, so the supplication for the Holy Ghost now passed from mouth to mouth and was continued from hour to hour. The little Christian community on Mount Sion was the representative of the world, which had to prepare for the Holy Ghost. All graces must be striven for in prayer. And their prayer united in itself all the conditions necessary to ensure a favorable answer, because it was persevering and general, made "in the Name of Jesus" (John 16:23; Matt. 18:20) and in union with the Mother of Jesus. The Old Covenant had never mustered such powerful forces for prayer.

A third and peculiar form of preparation for the coming of the Holy Ghost was the choice of St. Matthias as Apostle to fill the void left in the Apostolic College by the defection of Judas. It was necessary that the number of the Apostles (twelve according to God's appointment and according to the number of the tribes of Israel) should be complete before the Holy Ghost descended upon the Church. The election took place by St. Peter's order (Acts 1:15 seq.). The condition laid down for eligibility was that the candidate should have personally witnessed the teaching and deeds of Jesus from beginning to end, because the very essence of the Apostolate consists in bearing testimony to facts witnessed. The manner of the election was as follows: they selected two disciples, Barsabas and Matthias, and then (after fervent prayer) drew lots, thus leaving the final choice between the two to be decided by God Himself (Acts 1:23 seq.). The lot fell upon Matthias, and he was forthwith numbered among the Apostles. There were precedents for "God's arbitrament," as the choice by lot is sometimes called, in the Old Covenant (Luke 1:9; Num. 17:2; I Kings 10:20); and the resort to this method, though unusual, was justified here by the circumstance that it was a question of election to the apostolic office, which of its very nature is quite an extraordinary one, and also by the fact that the other Apostles (even St. Paul, later on; Gal. 1:1) were all chosen directly by Christ Himself. Here we already see the whole Church in her various orders and ranks, with St. Peter acting as her head, ordering, directing and manifesting the gift of understanding of the Holy Scriptures (Acts 1:16 seq.) that our Lord had conferred upon him and the other Apostles (Luke 24:45). Thus did the primitive Church prepare for the Descent of the Holy Ghost.

3. MOTIVES FOR THIS PREPARATION

The first motive was evidently the wish and direction of our Divine Saviour (Luke 24:49; Acts 1:4). Everything that He said to His Apostles before His Ascension tends to show that He wished them to prepare for the Holy Ghost in a special manner, and by this preparation, to a certain extent, to merit His coming for themselves and the whole world. Here as everywhere God's work must be supported by the cooperation of man. The Old Covenant had also to undergo a long preparation for the Redeemer, and our Lord Himself always began His important undertakings with special prayer. The more zealous and careful the preparation, the greater the fulness of blessing.

The second motive was the dignity of the Guest for whom they were preparing. He was no less than a Divine Person. Our Saviour had sufficiently instructed the Apostles concerning the nature and dignity of the Holy Ghost, especially during the latter part of His sojourn among them (John 14:16–18, 26; 15:26; 16:7–15).

Another motive, lastly, lay in the magnificent effects which the Holy Ghost would produce in them, the prospect of which our Lord had held out to the Apostles. He had termed the Descent of the Holy Ghost a new "baptism" (Acts 1:5), the Messianic baptism in the highest sense of the word. They were to become quite different beings. They were to be baptized with the baptism of the apostolate. Hence our Saviour explains it as a being "endued with power from on high" (Luke 24:49; Acts 1:8), and as an endowment fitting them to "be witnesses unto Him . . . even to the uttermost part of the earth." Great indeed was the transformation they underwent on the Feast of Pentecost. And the transformation of the Apostles led to the transformation and renovation of the whole human race. To sum up all in a word, our Saviour called the Descent of the Holy Ghost the fulfilment of "the promise of the Father" (Luke 24:49). So the Holy Ghost is the seal of all God's graces and favors and the crown and perfection of all His communications. Our Saviour had mysteriously linked even the beginning of His kingdom, which the Apostles were so impatiently awaiting, with the coming of the Holy Ghost (Acts 1:7, 8). And the Holy Ghost Himself in all probability instructed the Apostles by interior graces of enlightenment concerning the importance of His advent, and prepared their hearts for their great task. The infant Church in the Coenaculum is for all ages the model of preparation for the Feast of Pentecost.

Let us make our preparation also. The first Feast of Pentecost is not yet over. The annual feast is not merely a commemoration of this former Descent of the Holy Ghost, but a renewal and continuation of it. Pentecost returns every year, in order to apply the graces of the first feast to all ages and generations. We have the same motives for preparing for the Holy Ghost as the Apostles had, and in so doing we are surely fulfilling the wish of our Divine Saviour. The dignity of the Guest we expect is infinite; He is our God, and well deserves that we should devote a part of the year to His honor. The power of His operation is not lessened, and its effects are very precious and necessary for us and everyone. So let us set to work. Let us unite with the whole Church in this. She goes in spirit to the Coenaculum every year, in order to receive the Holy Ghost, and Our Lady and the holy Apostles will willingly lend us their aid in this preparation, if we remind them what blessings the first Feast of Pentecost brought them and ask their glorious intercession.

The Descent of the Holy Ghost

Acts 2:1. And when the days of the Pentecost were accomplished, they were all together in one place;—2. And suddenly there came a sound from heaven, as of a mighty wind coming, and it filled the whole house where they were sitting.—3. And there appeared to them parted tongues as it were of fire, and it sat upon every one of them;—4. And they were all filled with the Holy Ghost, and they began to speak with divers tongues according as the Holy Ghost gave them to speak.—5. Now there were dwelling at Jerusalem Jews, devout men out of every nation under heaven.—6. And when this was noised abroad, the multitude came together, and were confounded in mind, because that every man heard them speak in his own tongue.—7. And they were all amazed and wondered, saying: "Behold, are not all these that speak Galileans,—8. And how have we heard every man our own tongue wherein we were born?—9. Parthians, and Medes, and Elamites, and inhabitants of Mesopotamia, Judaea, and Cappadocia, Pontus and Asia,—10. Phrygia, and Pamphilia, Egypt and the parts of Lybia about Cyrene, and strangers of Rome,—11. Jews also, and proselytes, Cretes, and Arabians;

we have heard them speak in our own tongues the wonderful works of God."—12. And they were all astonished and wondered, saying one to another: "What meaneth this?"—13. But others mocking said: "These men are full of new wine."—14. But Peter standing up with the eleven, lifted up his voice, and spoke to them: "Ye men of Judaea, and all you that dwell in Jerusalem, be this known to you, and with your ears receive my words.—15. For these are not drunk, as you suppose, seeing it is but the third hour of the day;—16. But this is that which was spoken of by the prophet Joel:—17. And it shall come to pass in the last days (saith the Lord), I will pour out of my Spirit upon all flesh; and your sons and daughters shall prophesy, and your young men shall see visions, and your old men shall dream dreams.—18. And upon my servants, indeed, and upon my handmaids will I pour out in those days of my Spirit, and they shall prophesy;—19. And I will show wonders in the heaven above, and signs on the earth beneath, blood and fire, and vapor of smoke;—20. The sun shall be turned into darkness, and the moon into blood, before the great and manifest day of the Lord come.—21. And it shall come to pass: that whosoever shall call upon the name of the Lord, shall be saved.—22. Ye men of Israel, hear these words: Jesus of Nazareth, a man approved of God among you by miracles and wonders and signs, which God did by him in the midst of you, as you also know;—23. This same being delivered up, by the determinate counsel and foreknowledge of God, you by the hands of wicked men have crucified and slain;—24. Whom God hath raised up, having loosed the sorrows of hell, as it was impossible that he should be holden by it.—25. For David saith concerning him: I foresaw the Lord before my face always; because he is at my right hand, that I may not be moved;—26. For this my heart hath been glad, and my tongue hath rejoiced; moreover my flesh also shall rest in hope;—27. Because thou wilt not leave my soul in hell, nor suffer thy Holy One to see corruption.—28. Thou hast made known to me the ways of life; and thou shalt make me full of joy with thy countenance.—29. Ye men, brethren, let me freely speak to you of the patriarch David, that he died, and was buried; and his sepulcher is with us to this present day.—30. Whereas therefore he was a prophet, and knew that God had sworn to him with an oath that of the fruit of his loins one should sit upon his throne;—31. Foreseeing this, he spoke of the resurrection of Christ, for neither was he left in hell, neither did his flesh see corruption.—32. This Jesus hath God raised again, whereof all we are witnesses.—33. Being exalted therefore by the right hand of God, and having received of the Father the promise of the Holy Ghost, he hath poured forth this which you see and hear.—34. For David ascended not into heaven; but he himself said: The Lord said to my Lord: Sit thou on my right hand,—35. Until I make thy enemies thy footstool.—36. Therefore let all the house of Israel know most certainly, that God hath made both Lord and Christ, this same Jesus, whom you have crucified."—37. Now when they had heard these things, they had compunction in their heart, and said to Peter and to the rest of the Apostles: "What shall we do, men and brethren?"—38. But Peter saith to them: "Do peance, and be baptized everyone of you in the name of Jesus Christ, for the remission of your sins; and you shall receive the gift of the Holy Ghost.—39. For the promise is to you, and to your children, and to all that are far off, whomsoever the Lord our God shall call."—40. And with very many other words did he testify and exhort them, saying: "Save yourselves from this perverse generation."—41. They therefore that received his word were baptized; and there were added in that day about three thousand souls.—42. And they were persevering in the doctrine of the Apostles, and in the communication of the breaking of bread, and in prayers.—43. And fear came also upon every soul; many wonders also and signs were done by the Apostles in Jerusalem, and there was great fear in all.—44. And all they that believed were together, and had all things common.—

45. Their possessions and goods they sold, and divided them to all, according as everyone had need.—46. And continuing daily with one accord in the temple, and breaking bread from house to house, they took their meat with gladness and simplicity of heart,—47. Praising God and having favor with all the people. And the Lord increased daily together such as should be saved.

At length our Lord's promise was fulfilled, and the Holy Ghost descended upon the Apostles. It was the tenth day after His Ascension, the Feast of Pentecost, which was celebrated under the Old Covenant in thanksgiving for the wheat-harvest (Ex. 34:22; Lev. 23:15; Deut. 16:9) and the giving of the law on Mount Sinai (Ex. 19:1 seq.).

1. WHY THE HOLY GHOST DESCENDED

We can form no adequate idea of the significance and importance of the Descent of the Holy Ghost. It will help us to understand it in some measure, if we consider why He came.

In the first place, the Holy Ghost comes to fulfil and perfect the Old and the New Covenant. He had been promised as the crown and completion of both, the Old (Isa. 44:3; Jer. 31:31 seq.; Ez. 11:19; 36:25–27; Joel 2:28) as well as the New. John the Baptist had spoken of His coming, telling the people that the Messias would "baptize them with the Holy Ghost and with fire" (Matt. 3:11; Luke 3:16); and our Saviour also had repeatedly promised it (John 14:16–18, 26; 15:29; 21:7–15). St. Peter alludes to this significance of the Descent of the Holy Ghost in the first part of his sermon to the Jews (Acts 2:14–21). All is now fulfilled. The Holy Ghost is therefore rightly called "the promise of the Father" (Acts 1:4). His coming is the glorious conclusion and completion of all the personal revelations and communications made by God to the world in general, and the crown and seal of all His ordinances of grace.

Secondly, the Holy Ghost comes to reveal and communicate Himself to the whole world, and to take possession of it by a new presence. Hitherto the prophets and our Saviour had revealed Him to the people, and if He appeared Himself (as at Christ's baptism and on Mt. Thabor) it was only in a transient vision for some particular end. But now the Author both of the Old Law and prophetic dispensation and of all sanctification under the New Law appears in Person with a mission to the whole human race.

Thirdly, the Holy Ghost comes to glorify Christ. This object had already been specified by our Saviour Himself (John 16:8, 14). As a matter of fact the Holy Ghost convinced and still continues to convince the world of the Divinity of Christ's Person and work. He was to continue and complete Christ's work, and thereby prove it to be the work of a God. This testimony to the Divinity of Christ began with the preaching and miracles of St. Peter (Acts 2:22–36) and the other Apostles, and is perpetually continued in the Church. The Church can only be propagated by faith in Christ's Divinity, and by her propagation she bears witness to her divine origin from Christ, in the Holy Ghost. All her gifts and faculties, her whole life and being, have Christ for their immediate object. So the Holy Ghost, by preserving, guiding and animating the Church and her activity, glorifies Christ, and thus the whole life of the Church and the operation of the Holy Ghost is one great glorification of Jesus.

Fourthly, the Holy Ghost comes to reveal and inaugurate the long-promised Messianic kingdom, the kingdom of God and Christ, as our Saviour had signified to His Apostles immediately before His Ascension. For this purpose it was necessary to terminate Judaism by the proclamation of another economy of grace; and war and judgment had to be declared against heathendom, as the world-empire of Satan. Both these tasks were performed by Peter. He proclaimed baptism in the Name of Jesus as the appointed means of salvation (Acts 2:38); and to the prince of the world he announced the coming of the Holy Ghost as the beginning of the future universal Judgment (Acts 2:19, 20). And since Jerusalem, the royal city of the Messias, was the chosen place of the revelation (Isa. 60:1) and the seat of the law and of justice (Isa. 2:3), it was fitting that the Holy Ghost should descend there and that the envoys of the new kingdom should set forth thence (Acts 1:8; Ps. 109:2).

But this kingdom is the Church, and it was in order to give her life and activity that the Holy Ghost descended. Today for the first time she makes her appearance in public, under the guidance of the Holy Ghost, as she had been organized and constituted by Christ. Today the glorious faculties, the teaching, priestly and pastoral power, that had hitherto lain dormant in the Apostles, began to work. Today the brilliant gifts of grace and miracles were revealed (Acts 2:4, 17 seq., 43). Today for the first time the victorious power and efficacy of apostolic preaching was manifested, in the conversion of three thousand people and the foundation of the first Christian community, which displayed the new Christian spirit in all its glory: poverty, zeal for prayer, obedience, and charity (Acts 2:42, 44 seq.). All these glorious forces were set in motion by the Descent of the Holy Ghost, and began to work in a marvelous manner, speeding as though winged throughout the world and renewing the face of the earth. Christ founded and organized the Church; the Holy Ghost gave her life and activity. In this sense the Feast of Pentecost is the birthday of the Church. From this hour the Holy Ghost undertook the preservation, guidance and government of the Church, as our Saviour had prophesied (John 14:26; 16:13). The Holy Ghost constantly preserves in the Church the right doctrine, the life-giving Sacraments, and the valid power of the keys. Armed, guided and impelled by Him, the Apostles went out and preached everywhere, whilst our Lord aided their work and confirmed their words by accompanying signs (Mark 16:20). The whole glory of the Church's history is summed up in the blessing brought by the Descent of the Holy Ghost.

2. HOW THE HOLY GHOST COMES

He came in a manner becoming His majesty and the dignity of God, under circumstances and with signs that reveal His Divine Nature, His Person and attributes, and His task and mission as Author and Herald of the New Covenant.

In the first place, His coming was glorious, that is, perceptible, visible, public and solemn. It took place before the eyes of the whole city and of countless throngs of strangers who had assembled from all quarters of the globe for the Feast of Pentecost (Acts 2:5 seq.); and it was accompanied by most significant and glorious symbols. The rushing and roaring "as of a mighty wind coming" signifies the proceeding of the Holy Ghost from the Father and the Son by love, and also His Name and the moving, cooling, purifying and all-conquering power of His Nature. This rushing is as it were an after-breeze of the creative breath with which He imparted life to the lifeless creation in the beginning, an echo of the thunder heard at the giving of the law on Sinai, and a true symbol of the heavenly origin and vivifying, all-conquering power of the New Law, which blows away what is dead and decayed and opens new germs. And not less glorious are the flaming tongues of fire. According to Biblical signification they are symbols of spirituality (Isa. 4:4), of holiness (Ez. 1:4), of the purifying (Mal. 3:2), clarifying (IV Kings 2:11), judging and consuming power of God (Isa. 66:15). All lofty, divine emblems. It was from the burning bush that the word of Jehovah once went forth for the deliverance of Israel from Egyptian bondage (Ex. 3:4); and out of the descending flames the Holy Ghost proceeded for the renewal of the world.

Secondly, the Holy Ghost came laden with rich graces. We are told that the Apostles were "filled" with the Holy Ghost (Acts 2:4). It was truly a fulness of grace that accompanied His Descent; the fulness of sanctifying grace (Acts 2:41), the fulness of *grâces d'état* (Acts 2:38), the fulness of gifts of grace (2:4, 16 seq., 43), so that the Apostles were not only filled with the Holy Ghost themselves but also became the instruments of His communication to others (John 7:38), that is to say, the fulness of grace for the hearing as well as the teaching Church; a fulness that included not merely the gifts of grace, but the Giver of graces Himself; such a fulness that the Feast of Pentecost is the unrivaled type and inexhaustible source of grace for all ages.

Thirdly and last, the Holy Ghost came graciously. He is the God of love, benevolence, mercy and peace. So His coming is not a judgment for the destruction of Jerusalem or the world, although they had deserved it (Acts 2:23); on the contrary, He came to save and redeem not only the Jews but the whole world (Acts 2:21, 36, 39). He comes to honor, sanctify, comfort and gladden the world by a new presence; He comes, never to forsake it again (John 14:17). This presence of His is not any longer dependent on the faith of an individual or one nation, but is bound up with the stability of the Church. As long as she exists in the world, the Holy Ghost is in the world also, with the blessing of truth and grace. He will never be taken from the Church (John 14:16).

3. CONCLUSIONS THAT RESULT FROM HIS COMING

These are the mysteries of the Descent of the Holy Ghost. And what obligations does His so gracious advent impose upon us? In the first place, we must welcome Him upon earth with all our hearts, just as though we had been present in Jerusalem at the first Feast of Pentecost. We must pay Him our homage and adore Him, for adoration is the homage that is due to Him. He comes not merely as God's envoy, but as our Lord and God Himself, as the Creator and Owner of heaven and earth. How sublime is the beginning of the Office of the Feast: "*Alleluia! Spiritus Domini replevit orbem terrarum, venite adoremus! Alleluia!*"

Secondly, we must rejoice at the Descent of the Holy Ghost and thank Him with all our hearts for all that His advent has brought us. Innumerable are the treasures and graces that the Feast of Pentecost has showered upon us. It brought us the Holy Ghost Himself; it brought us the Church and all the blessings and graces she bestows; it brought us Christian life and the Christian world, Christian laws, Christian morals, and Christian virtues. All this is beautifully and touchingly exemplified in the first Christian community at Jerusalem. And the whole world would be like it, if only it would accept the blessings of the Holy Ghost.

Thirdly, we must also worship the Holy Ghost and practise a constant and loving devotion to Him. He is our God, and as such He is our Lord and Creator, our greatest good and our last end, just as much as the Father and the Son. We receive nothing from them that we do not owe to the Holy Ghost also. And in His own Person He is worthy of all our love. He proceeds from the Father and the Son by love, and so He is the Spirit of the Father (Matt. 10:20), the Spirit of the Son (Gal. 4:6), the Personification of love, goodness, benevolence, peace and joy, one might almost say the Heart of the Godhead. Further, the Holy Ghost bestows on us infinite benefits. He receives us into the Church, makes us children of God in Baptism, forgives us our sins in the Sacrament of Penance, strengthens us in Confirmation, protects, directs, guides and trains us, and leads us to the beautiful heavenly country. Lastly, the Holy Ghost is so near us. Indeed, He is in our very hearts; He Himself is given to us (Rom. 5:5), and we are His living temples (I Cor. 6:19). We are and we live in His Church; and the Church is His kingdom, her guidance and government His work, her history His Gospel. He is the Ruler of the Church, and His coming marks the beginning of our era; by being in the Church we stand under His especial care and guidance. How many motives we have, then, to love and honor the Holy Ghost!

And fourthly, if the Holy Ghost has brought us so many and such great blessings, then we must gratefully remember from Whom He came to us. It was our Lord and Saviour Who promised Him to us, merited Him for us and sent Him to us. The Holy Ghost is the beautiful fruit of the Life and Passion of Jesus, the highest gift of His love, and His Divine Substitute and Representative with us. All that our Saviour is to us and does for us, He is and does by the Holy Ghost. Through Him He wishes to be glorified in us. So let us love the Holy Ghost in our Saviour; He is our Saviour's Spirit and His Heart's sweet love.

IV

MYSTICAL LIFE OF JESUS IN THE CHURCH

The life and work of the God-Man here below does not cease with the Ascension, the enthronement on the right hand of the Father, or the Descent of the Holy Ghost. As He had a former life previous to His Advent on earth, so He has also an after-life; and this after-life in and through the Church is much grander and more glorious than His actual earthly or previous life, with regard to time, place, and manifestation.

This after-life is a twofold one: a personal life in the Holy Eucharist, and a moral life of power and activity in the various members and orders of the Church.

THE LIFE OF JESUS IN THE HOLY EUCHARIST

The Holy Eucharist, which our Saviour instituted in the Church immediately before His Passion and Death and for all ages, preserves and continues His life in a threefold manner.

1. THE HOLY EUCHARIST IS THE CONTINUATION OF THE TRUE AND PERSONAL PRESENCE OF JESUS

What lends an unrivaled dignity to this most holy of Sacraments and gives it pre-eminence over all others is the fact that our Saviour is really present in it. According to the teaching of the Holy Scriptures and the Church we believe that He is present in the Holy Eucharist, not merely in sign and symbol, but in truth; not merely according to the faith of the recipient, but really and actually; not merely as an effective grace, but substantially, with His Divinity and Humanity, as He once lived here on earth and now is in heaven; not merely transiently and at the moment of the Holy Sacrifice and sacramental Communion, but permanently and continuously, as long as the Eucharistic appearances remain, and as a sacrifice and a sacrament.

This pre-eminence of the Eucharist is something wonderful and divine, but it completely tallies with the words of its promise and institution, with the constant belief and interpretation of the Church, and with many other reasons that arise from the intimate relations of the God-Man to the Church and to us. In the first place, our Saviour perfectly fulfils His promise that He would not leave us orphans (John 14:18), if He leaves us as a substitute for His visible presence not only the Holy Ghost and the promise of His own speedy return, but nothing less than His true, though veiled, sacramental presence. Moreover the Church, in virtue of her immediate origin from Christ, her lofty task of making us children of God and preparing us for the direct vision of Him, and her nature as the Bride and mystical Body of Christ, is so sublime that nothing but Christ Himself can suffice to be her sacrifice and sacrament. The child of God has a right to divine and celestial food, and the Bride has a right to the Body of the Bridegroom. As God Christ creates all things and preserves and governs them by His own power; as God-Man He does the same for His Church. He is not merely her Founder and Builder, but infinitely more, something organic, that cannot be separated from her, her Head and the prime cause of her life and being. Thus a merely transient appearance of Christ, or compensation for His absence in the shape of any substitute whatever, cannot suffice, but only His true, continual presence. Only thus can the Church Militant be a worthy link between the Church of Types and the Church in heaven. She is on a par with the latter and superior to the former. We have no cause to long for the pillar of fire, the holy Tabernacle, the manna, or the miraculous water. We have the truth, not merely the shadow. We have indeed "come to Mount Sion and to the city of the Living God, the heavenly Jerusalem, and to the company of many thousands of angels, and to the Church of the first-born . . . and to Jesus the Mediator of the New Testament, and to the sprinkling of blood which speaketh better than that of Abel" (Hebr. 12:22–24). Thus our Saviour provides for the deepest need of the human heart. It wishes to pay God divine honor, to know where its God is, to possess and enjoy Him. Everything about man, everything within him asks: "Where is thy God?" (Ps. 41:4, 11.) So the deep longing of his heart for the "Strong Living God" (Ps. 41:3) is completely satisfied and the name of the Christian religion justified, because Christ is its all in all.

2. THE HOLY EUCHARIST IS THE CONTINUATION OF THE MYSTERIES OF THE LIFE OF JESUS

Not only is our Saviour really present in the Church by the Eucharist; He also continues His life therein, and constantly renews the mysteries of His life in His own way.

First, He renews in the Holy Eucharist the mysteries of His youth: the Incarnation, the Nativity, the Epiphany, the Presentation, and His Hidden Life. Every day our Lord is born again in the Blessed Eucharist in a state that bears a great resemblance to that of the Incarnation, because here also the Eucharistic species exist without their own substance, as the human nature existed there without a natural personality of its own; He is produced here as He was there by the word of a virgin, and is laid in virginal hands. In the Eucharist also He appears wrapped in the pure white swaddling clothes of the accidents, and is adored and offered to God. He renews His Hidden Life in the deep stillness and concealment by which He veils even His human nature; in His great poverty and the unselfishness with which He abandons Himself entirely to us; in His matchless obedience to the priests and dispensers of the Sacraments; and lastly, in His quiet and invisible work in souls. It is not without reason that the two mysteries of the Incarnation and Transubstantiation are constantly interchanging in the liturgical hours and the Eucharistic hymns. The preface of the Mass of the Blessed Sacrament is that of the Incarnation and Nativity, and apparitions of Christ in the Eucharist have often taken place under the figure of His holy and lovable Childhood.

And no less striking is the way in which our Saviour mystically renews His Public Life in the Holy Eucharist. Who does not see in the multiplication of His Presence in all countries and at all places, in His noiseless walking through our streets and fields, the indefatigable Teacher and Shepherd of our souls Who in His Public Life never wearied of journeying through the country from one end to the other, teaching, blessing, comforting and healing? How many of His parables—for example the parables of the Great Supper and the marriage feast, or that of the merry-making at the return of the Prodigal Son—find their deepest and most sublime interpretation and fulfilment in the Eucharist! Is He not constantly renewing the great miracles of the changing of water into wine and the multiplication of the loaves? And how many spiritually dumb, blind, deaf, lame, and possessed by evil passions He heals here! In consequence of its intrinsic nature the Blessed Sacrament is a continual exhibition of the very greatest miracles, greatest because they are miracles wrought upon our Lord's own Body. With what supreme magnanimity and liberality He here practises the lovable social virtues of His public ministry: patience, kindness, mercy and beneficence! In the Promised Land of yore He was in only one place at a time, but now He is everywhere; He follows us everywhere, we can find Him everywhere, He waits for us everywhere, day and night, always ready to receive us, to listen to us, to comfort and protect us. With what a heavenly atmosphere of grace the beneficent Presence of our Saviour in the Blessed Sacrament surrounds us! With how many touching devotions it beautifies and enriches the Church's life: visits to the Blessed Sacrament, Benediction services, the Perpetual Adoration, and the inspiring processions that are an imitation of the triumphal entry of Jesus into Jerusalem!

It is scarcely necessary to point out how the mysteries of the Passion are contained in the Holy Eucharist. It is throughout the memorial of the Death of Jesus. The Sacrifice of Holy Mass is at once the perfect renewal of the Sacrifice at the Last Supper and the Sacrifice on the Cross. With the former it coincides even in the sacrificial action; with the latter it is essentially connected, because it is not merely a memorial, but also a pictorial representation, a continuation and renewal of this Sacrifice on the Cross in every particular except the bloody rite, and a completion (because an application) of its graces. And alas! often the Holy Eucharist is also the renewal of sufferings that our Saviour did not desire and did not seek, and that do no honor to men. The Coenaculum is never free from secret Judases in disguise, who come to meet our Lord and give Him the kiss of peace with soiled and traitorous lips and hearts. And oh! how often the "upper room" of the banquet of faithful love is changed into the dark court-yard of Caiphas, and scenes are enacted that mock description! The Eucharistic life is an abyss almost equally as regards its miracles, its love, and the ingratitude shown towards it. And lastly, the repose of Jesus in the Tabernacle has also many features in common with His rest in the Holy Sepulcher.

And the glory of the Risen Life also is renewed in the Holy Eucharist. Our Saviour is here in the Body, in a transfigured state, in some respects still more glorious and wonderful than He was at His Resurrection. The state of the Eucharistic Body of Jesus is the utmost extent of transfiguration and glory of which a body is capable, the highest and most brilliant victory of grace and glory over material substance. And our Lord imparts this glory to our bodies by the Eucharist; it is for this He is there, and for this reason we receive Him. Who does not see in the loving and blissful intercourse of Jesus with men in the Blessed Sacrament a charming picture of His appearances to His Apostles and His intercourse with them after His Resurrection? He makes Himself the friendly companion of our pilgrimage, as He did to the wanderers on the way to Emmaus; He watches us from the quiet Tabernacle, comforts us by His friendly encouragement in the difficulties of our journey, and blesses the unfruitfulness and uselessness of our work with wonderful success, as He blessed Peter's fishing.

Thus our Saviour renews all the mysteries of His life in the Holy Eucharist; but not the Ascension, for He does not leave us. No. His presence in the Tabernacle compensates us for being separated by time and place from the blissful days of His earthly life. We need not wish ourselves in the Promised Land, nor back in those happy days when all flesh saw the salvation of the Lord; for here we have Nazareth, Bethlehem, Thabor, Jerusalem, Calvary, and the Holy Sepulcher. Without faith it would be of no use to have been a contemporary and witness of our Lord's life; and faith is easier for us now than it was then, because we have incomparably more motives for it.

3. THE HOLY EUCHARIST IS THE CONTINUATION OF THE EFFECTS OF THE LIFE OF JESUS

Where our Saviour is with His whole life, there must be a superabundant blessing of fruitfulness and efficacy. This fruit and these effects are of three kinds.

The first effect relates to God. It is that of honor and glory. If the angels rejoiced and broke into exultant song at the glory resulting for God from the first Advent of Christ, how much more must they rejoice at the work of His glorification achieved in the

Eucharist! Assuredly quite new and abundant sources of His glory are opened here: first, on account of the marvelous constitution of the Eucharist and the wondrous state of Christ's Body therein; secondly, on account of Its sacrificial character, since nothing glorifies God so much as sacrifice, especially in such a state of annihilation and mystical death as that in which Christ sacrifices Himself here; thirdly, on account of the wonderful multiplication of His presence and sacrifice as regards time and place. The manger stood in one place only; the Cross was erected on Calvary alone. But now God's Eye beholds His Son engaged in sacrifice and adoration everywhere, at every moment, on countless altars and in Tabernacles without number. The glory of the Incarnation now encompasses the whole earth, which is wrapped in the sweet fragrance exhaled from innumerable altars. And as the moon in her transit attracts the waters of the sea and causes the tide to run high, so this Eucharistic presence and Eucharistic sacrifice of our Lord attracts from all sides the waves of piety, prayer and worship, and swells them into mighty billows whose foaming crests rise heavenwards and form a grand and imposing spectacle for the City of God. These are the days that the prophet saw in vision, in which "the fruit of the earth shall be high . . . and the Lord will create upon every place of Mount Sion . . . a cloud by day, and a smoke and the brightness of a flaming fire in the night" (Isa. 4:2, 5). "And the sacrifice of Juda and Jerusalem shall please the Lord as in the days of old" (Mal. 3:4). And "from the rising of the sun even to the going down His Name is great among the Gentiles, and in every place there is sacrifice, and there is offered to His Name a clean oblation" (Mal. 1:11).

The second effect reflects back upon our Saviour Himself. One of His intentions in the institution of the Eucharist was that we should not forget Him, but always bear Him in remembrance (Luke 22:19; I Cor. 11:25). That is why He wished to remain really close to us, to come to our country and penetrate even into our hearts, and dwell among us. How could we forget Him, since He is even willing to be our food, our very life? In truth, our Saviour has won a great deal, won our whole hearts, by the nearness and use of the Holy Eucharist. We cannot possibly forget Him. By the many-sided use of the Eucharist He makes too deep an impression upon our faith, our religious life and our hearts, for that to be the case. It is in the Eucharist that faith, love, necessity and gratitude urge us to seek Him, to pay Him the homage of our belief, adoration and love, and crown Him with a never-fading wreath woven of a thousand many-hued flowers of worship and reparation for all the shame and suffering of His Life and Death. It is extraordinary what imposing monuments the Holy Eucharist has erected for itself in the world. It has pressed everything into its service: all the treasures of the earth, all the magnificence of art, and all the inventive power of love. The Eucharistic cult is the center and acme of our religious service. This mystical rose of Eucharistic devotion has blossomed forth with fresh splendor since the 13th century, when the mystery of Christ's perpetual dwelling with us, even outside the time of the Eucharistic Sacrifice and the reception of the Sacrament, was practically realized. Thus the glorious life of Jesus in the Eucharist is only a just compensation and necessary redintegration for the dark side of His former actual life on earth.

The third effect of the Eucharist is a precious fruit that falls to the lot of the Church and of us all. By this constant dwelling of our God and Saviour among us, the Church and even the world become dear and homelike to us. We have our God with us at all times; we can find Him whenever we have a petition to present. The silent glimmer of the sanctuary lamp in our churches is like a guiding star, showing us where He is. And when the quiet visit expands into a public audience, a service ending with Benediction of the Blessed Sacrament, and this again into the pomp and splendor of the Forty Hours Prayer or the heart-stirring demonstration of the Corpus Christi procession, then the melancholy strains of our exile pass into the triumphant songs of the celestial country, and we seem to be already joining in the perpetual adoration of the Lamb in heaven. No one is lonely, no one forsaken or helpless, not even the dying; for our Lord is with us. From His quiet watch-tower, the Tabernacle, He watches us and lends us His aid. Thus the Eucharist, considered as the perpetual dwelling of our Saviour with us, makes our lives homelike, joyous, and full of consolation. And as a Sacrifice it makes us so rich that we can thereby satisfy all God's demands, cover all our debts, and offer to the Divine Majesty a superabundance of praise, honor and joy. Not only does it bestow a hundred blessings upon our fields, houses and towns; it even penetrates the dusk of Purgatory with its gentle rays of comfort and soothing relief. How poor we should all be without this Sacrifice! As a Sacrament the Holy Eucharist combats with divine power the tyranny of sin and passion; it refreshes, strengthens and elevates the soul, and transforms us little by little through love, courage and joy, until we have "put on Christ." The all-assimilating power of this Sacrament, although it works so quietly, transforms everything by degrees, gives a Christlike and Eucharistic coloring to the whole Church (John 6:58), and endows her with the beauties of virginity, martyrdom and the Apostolate.

Such is the life of Jesus in the Eucharist. It is His whole life, only invisible under the appearances of the Sacrament and in souls. But if He were visibly present and working in the Church He could not do more. All her riches, all her light, all her strength and power, all her grace and beauty come to her from Jesus in the Blessed Sacrament. He is the basis of her unity, her activity and her very existence. Take the Blessed Sacrament away from the Church, and she will be no more. We see in the various communions of our separated brethren what becomes of her without Jesus in the Blessed Sacrament. They are religions of an absent Christ, and that is saying everything. Nothing can then fend off the devastation of unity, of the life of sanctity, of the Sacraments, and even of the Christian faith. A Christian religion without the Eucharist is like a firmament without a sun, a land without water, a body without a soul. Earth has no real, substantial link to unite her to heaven then, for she lacks God's highest communication to her and her highest gift to God. But the Church possesses all this in the Blessed Sacrament, and that is why it is the nearest, first and sublimest object of her worship and love.

Christ in the Church

In the Eucharist Christ continues His real presence and life. But only in the Eucharist. In all other respects Christ is and lives in the Church only morally or spiritually, by His influence and operation. The first thing we must now consider is the Church as a whole and in general. And here Christ's relation to her is threefold.

1. The Church is Christ, who continues to live in her

Christ continues to live in the Church morally, but yet not merely accidentally; for He is her very essence, and is seen in her principal attributes.

The Church is intrinsically a social union, a corporate body which strives after the same goal, with the same means and under a common guidance. The principal thing about a social organism is its head, its government. The head is the principle upon which society and the State are formed; upon the head unity, strength and stability depend. In the Church this Head is Christ. By His assumption of human nature the Second Person of the Godhead is the born Head of the whole creation, of the entire human race and especially of the Church, which He not only rules in things belonging to the natural order, but also influences supernaturally and leads to a supernatural end. Thus in the Incarnation Christ assumed as it were a double body, His real, physical Body and also a spiritual or mystical one; and this latter is the Church. So the Church is not merely His work, His foundation, His kingdom and His family, but His Body. This view of the Church is very frequent in the Scriptures. "He . . . hath made Him Head over all the Church, which is His body" (Eph. 1:22, 23; Col. 1:18). "Now you are the body of Christ and members of member" (I Cor. 6:15; 12:27). That is the reason why the Church is called the Bride of Christ (II Cor. 11:2; Eph. 5:23, 25). And as the head holds the first place in the body by its very position, by the dignity and excellence of its organism and by its guiding, preserving and deciding influence, so Christ also takes the supreme and decisive rank in the Church by His position, His dignity, and His all-pervading, all-influencing operation (Eph. 4:16). He is in the real, true sense of the word the Head of the Church. Life, light, strength and activity all proceed from Him. He is the real basis of her existence and nature.

And the Church's chief attributes proceed in like manner from this intimate relation of Christ to her. They are sketched and modeled from the attributes of the real Body of Christ. The Body of Christ is one, and one also is the Church; for Christ is not divided (I Cor. 1:13) and has not two bodies (Eph. 4:4). The Body of Christ is substantially visible and perceptible to the senses; so also the Church. This is so true that Christ has even given her a visible head, who represents Him and forms an integral part of her constitution. Christ is the invisible and supreme Head of the Church, the Pope the representative and visible head. And as the true Body of Christ is indestructible and imperishable, so the Church also is indestructible and unchangeable, so that she can neither suffer interior dissolution nor yet be removed by an extraneous power (Rom. 6:9) nor separated from Christ. Lastly, as the Body of Christ was holy in itself and was moreover sanctified by the grace of its personal union with the Divinity and by the possession of all supernatural blessings and the Holy Ghost, so the Church also is holy in her continual union with Christ by the communication of supernatural treasures: sanctifying grace, virtues and gifts, and the Holy Ghost Himself. The Body of Christ has never been without the Holy Ghost, and the Church also constantly enjoys His presence. In this she differs from the rest of the human race, which is also the Body of Christ in a wider sense; inasmuch as she participates through Christ in His supernatural life, the supernatural communication of His Sonship and all corresponding blessings (Eph. 5:27).

Thus Christ really fills the whole being of the Church. She is His Body, and He animates her supernaturally, as our soul animates our body naturally. Sanctifying grace, the primary element of the supernatural life, is only a communication of the Sonship of Christ (Rom. 8:15; 9:26; Gal. 4:6; Eph. 1:5; 5:1); the virtues are infusions of the Son of God (II Cor. 4:6; Gal. 2:20; 5:5, 6), the sweet odor of Christ (II Cor. 2:15); the gifts of the Holy Ghost are traits of similarity to Christ (Luke 4:18; Isa. 61:1); the influences of actual grace for the exercise of these gifts in good works are Christ's operation in us (John 15:1, 5 seq.). The beginning, progress and completion of the Christian life are nothing else than the birth, growth and attainment to "the measure of the age of the fulness" of Christ (Gal. 4:19; Eph. 4:13, 15). So the Church is in reality nothing but a creature in Christ (Gal. 6:15; Eph. 2:10; II Cor. 5:17), the Christ in us (Gal. 4:19; II Cor. 13:5). How true, then, are the words in which our Saviour Himself describes His relation to the Church: "I am the vine, you the branches"! (John 15:5.) Whatever we have of supernatural life comes to us through Him. He is our life (Gal. 2:20; Phil. 1:21), and thus the Church is really the living Christ.

2. THE CHURCH IS CHRIST, WHO CONTINUES TO WORK IN HER

The Church has life only in order to work; and Christ is in her in order to work. But this work includes an object, the requisite forces, and a definite way of exercising these forces. In all three respects we see again the intimate alliance of Christ with the Church.

Christ's object in life was to promote God's glory by the salvation and eternal beatification of men. He came "to save that which was lost" (Luke 19:10), "not to judge the world, but to save the world" (John 12:47). To obtain for men eternal life and heaven—heaven, that sum-total of all God's works and creations, that city where He is seen face to face, and where He is all in all; to obtain for men this infinite degree of happiness, honor, and glory—that was the glorious object of our Saviour's life (John 6:47; 12:50; Rom. 15:22). That was why He founded the Church, placed us in this kingdom of His love (Col. 1:13), and made us His children and joint-heirs with Himself (Rom. 8:17). The Church has entered into this aim of the God-Man and made it her own object also; and all her endeavors are directed towards the attainment of this end.

For this purpose she employs all the forces at her command. To these forces and powers belongs, first, the preaching office, the competence to preach the faith everywhere with authority and infallible certainty. That is the first and most necessary condition of salvation, because without faith no one can arrive at a supernatural knowledge of God or please Him. Secondly, the power to administer the Sacraments and thereby impart spiritual life to man, preserve and perfect it in him, and give a supernatural character to his whole earthly life. Thirdly, the pastoral power, i.e. the power to rule the Church by laws, regulate the administration of them, and uphold the appointed order in every respect. And the fourth constituent of the Church's equipment is formed by the gifts of grace, special miraculous faculties which enable her to give additional emphasis to the preaching of the faith by proofs of a higher power. These gifts are enumerated by the Apostle Paul (I Cor. 12; II Cor. 12:12; Rom. 12:6 seq.).

This magnificent endowment of the Church is nothing but an emanation of Christ, a communication made by Him to His Church, which gives her a certain similarity to Him. Everything has Christ for its source; all comes from Him. Her preaching is only a participation in the prophetic office of our Saviour, Who alone is truth (John 14:6), Who alone is commissioned by God to preach His commandment (Ps. 2:6), Who alone can make the Church the pillar and ground of the truth (I Tim. 3:15), as Whose ambassadress she speaks (II Cor. 5:20), and Who gives to her words the power of enlightenment (II Cor. 4:6), marvelous fertility (Rom. 1:18; 15:19), and power to overcome (I John 5:4). And the priestly power of the Church is likewise a participation in the priestly office of Christ, Who instituted the Sacraments, offered the Sacrifice, and left this power to the Church (I Cor. 3:5, 9; 4:1). The pastoral power is an emanation of Christ's kingship, whether the Church in the exercise of it makes laws (I Cor. 7:10), inflicts punishments (II Cor. 13:3), or excommunicates (I Cor. 5:4). Lastly, the gifts of grace are really an endowment proper to the prophetic and Messianic office of Christ (Isa. 35:5). He exemplified them Himself and left them to the Church (Matt. 10:8; Mark 16:17) as the brilliant seal of His unique and eternal alliance with her.

And the Church exercises and manifests these glorious powers in the same way as our Saviour Himself once did. First, she does so under the guidance of the Holy Ghost. As our Lord always allowed Himself to be guided by the Holy Ghost in His public ministry (Luke 3:22; Acts 10:38), so the Church was not to enter upon her work until after the Descent of the Holy Ghost, but to exercise all the functions of her office under His influence (John 14:16, 26; 15:26; 16:13, 14; I Cor. 12:11; Hebr. 2:4). Secondly, the Church exercises her powers with the same mildness, love and patience (I Thess. 2:7–9), the same unwearying zeal (II Tim. 4:2) and the same devotion (II Cor. 12:11–15) that our Saviour manifested in His public ministry. It is the love of Christ that presses her (II Cor. 5:14). Lastly, her exercise of these powers is marked by the same divine success that Christ had; and therefore she is catholic, working everywhere to the very ends of the earth and incorporating the nations into herself. This is the virtue of the divine commission and blessing with which Christ sent out His Church into the whole world (Matt. 28:18–20). In her all nations of the earth are blessed (Gen. 12:3; Rom. 15:9–15).

Thus the Church is in this respect also the true Body and Bride of Christ. As God gave Eve to Adam as his helpmate for the propagation and training of the human race, and made her similar to him in all things (Gen. 2:20–24), so that he could say: "This is bone of my bone, and flesh of my flesh"; so the Second Person of the Godhead, wishing to redeem and restore the human race, not only assumed for the accomplishment of this great work a human nature, but also took the Church to be His mystical Body, made her like Himself, and filled her with His spirit and His strength. And it is through her and with her that He continues to accomplish the redemption of the world.

3. THE CHURCH IS CHRIST, WHO CONTINUES TO FIGHT AND TRIUMPH IN HER

The Church cannot carry on this work of redemption without conflict and opposition. Our Saviour already experienced this in His own Person, and predicted it to His Church (Matt. 10:16–23; John 16:2), not omitting to point out the reason of this opposition. The reason is no other than Himself. It is on His account that the Church is persecuted and calumniated (Matt. 5:11), precisely because she belongs to Him, and not to the world (John 15:19). As a matter of fact it is only the teaching office of Christ and the proclamation of His doctrine and law, that make the world excited and angry. The Church aims at bringing every intellect into captivity unto the faith (II Cor. 10:5); she knows and preaches only Christ crucified, a foolishness to the Gentiles and a stumbling-block to the Jews (I Cor. 1:23). It is Christ's priestly office that the world rejects, because it upbraids her with her sins and reminds her of the mediation of Jesus for her salvation (John 16:10). When the Church speaks of chastity and judgment, the world shudders (Act 24:25). And if we go to the root of the matter, it is only Christ's pastoral office and kingship that the world will not submit to. It was for this title of King and Messias that our Saviour had to die (John 19:7, 15; Luke 19:14). These are the real and lasting causes of the battle. Christ will not abdicate, nor the Church either. So the struggle is really directed against Christ. The Church is His captive also (Eph. 3:1). She could free herself from her fetters, if only she would consent to give up preaching in the Name of Jesus (Acts 4:18). But she will not do that, and so it is in reality He Who continues to fight in the Church.

And it is Christ, too, Who continues to conquer in the Church. This victory is threefold. First, the Church always escapes from the spite of her enemies. Like our Saviour Himself, Who so often escaped from the hands of His enemies and evaded their weapons and stones (Luke 4:30; John 7:44; 8:59; 10:39), she also evades the snares of her persecutors. She does not let herself be captured. Her word cannot be fettered (II Tim. 2:9). Even prisons cannot confine her (Acts 5:19; 12:11; 16:26). What save a body can be laid hold of and bound? One can no more fetter the spirit, faith, grace, or authority than one can seize and bind the light. If the Church disappears in one place, she reappears in another. Secondly, all opposition only serves to make the Church show her strength and manifest herself all the more plainly in the world (Phil. 1:12, 13). As the storm-wind scatters the seeds of trees, so persecutions propagate the Church. Thirdly, the Church can in no case perish or be extirpated. Even death and the grave could not fetter our Saviour, and for the Church there is no grave other than the whole earth. She really lives by her defeats, and cannot die, because our Saviour died for her and made her immortal. Heaven and earth will pass away sooner than the Church. Like her Lord she is crucified and yet liveth (II Cor. 13:4).

The Church is truly a great mystery in Christ. She is His Body and fulness (Eph. 1:23). As the members of the body are the complement of the soul, because its organs serve as the instruments of the latter's manifold activity, so the Church with her construction, her manifold organization and her life is the instrument and organ of Christ. Her whole activity is only "the edifying of the body of Christ" (Eph. 4:12), and her success is the attainment of the "measure of the age of the fulness of Christ" (Eph. 4:13). She is truly the living, working, fighting and conquering Christ. Thence we may see what reverence we ought to have for the Church, in which everything leads us to Christ and where He meets us at every turn. And we may also learn here how we must value union with the Church and stability in her communion, and regard it as the highest grace and the pledge of all blessings. What Christ is to us, He is in the Church and through the Church. We too may say here: "Lord, to whom shall we go? Thou hast the words of eternal life" (John 6:69). And the last conclusion we must draw is to thank God and rejoice that we belong to His Church.

Christ Continues to Live in the Christian People

By far the greater part of the Church consists of the people. They form the hearing or lay Church. And in them also Christ continues to lead a mystical life in three ways, corresponding to the circles in which the life of the Christian people moves and is spent and to the elements of which it is formed. These forms of life are matrimony, the family and the State.

1. MATRIMONY

The first and deepest foundation of the life of the people is matrimony. And Christ belongs essentially to Christian matrimony. He is its founder, its restorer, and the necessary condition of its being.

As God, Christ instituted matrimony in Paradise (Gen. 2:20–24). The ideal He had before Him in so doing was, as St. Paul writes (Eph. 5:22, 23), the alliance upon which He was hereafter to enter with the Church; and He gave to matrimony even then the attributes corresponding to this mystery, viz. holiness, unity, indissolubility and fertility. Later on these qualities became defaced and disfigured. Christ restored matrimony to its original form, raising it out of the shameful and degraded state into which it had fallen among the heathens, and removing the clouds that had obscured its luster among the Jews. He re-established its primitive constitution and added to this the blessing, the sanctification and the sublime character of the Sacrament (Matt. 19:3–10).

Christian matrimony is really a Sacrament, and, like the union of Christ with the Church, it is one, holy and indissoluble (I Cor. 7:10, 11). Even the mutual duties of married people—submission, love, and mutual sanctification (Eph. 5:22, 23; I Cor. 11:3)—are deduced by the Apostle from the relation of Christ to the Church. The fulfilment of these duties is made possible and also facilitated by an abundance of actual graces and a thousandfold blessing, such as beseems the sacramental character of Christian matrimony.

So matrimony is an image, spiritually similar though imperfect, of the union of Christ with the Church, and a part of His mystical life in the human race. Christ is essentially built into the base and groundwork of the life of a Christian people, and thus it is true here also that there is no foundation but Christ (I Cor. 3:11).

2. THE FAMILY

From matrimony the family springs, and the family is the second foundation and groundwork upon which a healthy and vigorous life among the people is built up and thrives. But to this end it is necessary that the people should exercise themselves in submission, work and prayer, in accordance with their duties. These are the necessary manifestations of family life. Submission puts the family into the right place with regard to Church and

State by religious and civic obedience, and regulates it interiorly as well in unity, peace and happiness, inasmuch as all the members of the family, children as well as servants, obey the common head. Labor procures for the family a permanent abode, maintenance, prosperity, education and influence. And prayer, lastly, unites it to God, its eternal end, and procures it the blessings of the temporal and eternal promises. In this manner the family is regulated and ordered internally and externally, and possesses all the conditions of natural and supernatural welfare.

Our Saviour is no stranger to family life. He Himself proceeded as Man from a family, and passed long years, indeed the longest and pleasantest part of His life, in the bosom of a family. It was at the foundation of a family and for the comfort of a family that He worked His first great miracle. How many families did He restore to happiness by means of miracles, cures of the sick and raising of the dead!

He is not only the benefactor of the family, but also the model of the virtues that make up its happiness and its task in life. These virtues consist precisely in the three manifestations of our Saviour's youthful life that are mentioned in the Scriptures. The first thing remarked and emphasized is His obedience. "He was subject to them" (Luke 2:51), not only to His parents but also to the civic and religious authorities. He gives us quite a superabundance of examples of submission in this respect. He remained in this domestic dependence for the greater part of His life, longer than most children do; and His submission was in no respect less than that of servants, because in poor families the children are servants. This is a great and impressive example for our ungoverned nature, which is full of proud rebellion and unruly love of freedom, and wishes to shake off the trammels of dependence and submission as soon as possible. Our Saviour was moreover a working-man, and His work in the family was not of a superior and intellectual kind, but ordinary, hard, laborious and humble manual work. It is written of Him that He was the "carpenter's son" (Matt. 13:55; Mark 6:3), and probably He Himself also practised this craft, not merely for occupation's sake, but in order to earn His daily bread. If work, even manual work, is now held in honor, it is certainly due chiefly to the example of Christ's labor. He made work tolerable, ennobled it, and blessed it not merely with temporal but also with eternal rewards. Not only the earth but heaven also must be earned by labor. Lastly, our

Saviour prayed and took part in public worship in the synagogue (Luke 4:16), and also assisted at the great national feasts (Luke 3:42); and He would certainly not have omitted to join in private family worship.

In all these domestic virtues our Saviour set a most beautiful example, which was followed by His Blessed Mother and His holy foster-father, and thus the life of the Holy Family at Nazareth presents the most charming and elevating model of well-regulated family life. To imitate it as far as possible would make any family holy, rich and happy here below.

3. THE STATE

The union of families and communities gives rise to the State. The State is the last and highest development of the natural life of the people. They cannot throw off this form of society, but exercise a decisive influence upon it, salutary or pernicious, according to the condition in which matrimony and the family, the foundations of all social life, happen to be. The family depends upon matrimony, and the family is the type and source of all social federation, and is of the greatest importance even for the Church. The life of the community, of the State, the Church, heaven and earth is derived from the family. It is the natural root of all blessing, strength and prosperity. "If the root be holy, so are the branches" (Rom. 11:16); but only in Christ.

The Christian family diffuses innumerable blessings, spiritual as well as material, over the life of the people and thence over the whole State, imprinting characteristic features and qualities upon it. The first blessing consists in the health and strength of the growing generation; this proceds from the holiness of matrimony. The second is a good measure of true and noble education and culture; it owes its being to the work and prayer of the family. A third blessing consists in dignity, noble self-respect, and the spirit of true Christian freedom, which so favorably distinguish the Christian from the heathen State. This spirit of freedom is a noble fruit of the religion of Christ, and the result of the humility and submission of Jesus, Who, although He possessed a Divine Nature, "emptied Himself, taking the form of a servant, being made in the likeness of men, and in habit found as a man" (Phil. 2:6, 7). Our Saviour hereby brought about the greatest and most blessed revolution in the world, the abolition of slavery (Gal. 3:26–28; I Cor. 7:20–23; 12:13; Col. 3:11, 12), and made the servant a member of the family (Phil. 16, 17). This spirit of self-respect and freedom manifests itself among the Christian people in three special ways.

In the first place, a Christian people will have freedom for its conscience. According to the instructions of Christ (Matt. 22:21) and the Church (Rom. 13:1 seq.), the Christian respects every rightful authority, regarding this as a duty which he is in conscience bound to fulfil, and rejecting every proposal of unlawful rebellion. But he will just as little allow himself to be seduced to rebellion against God, his Supreme Lord and Master. He knows very well that the State is not the goal and end of man, but a means to the attainment of his end. He has entered the union of the State not in order to lose his eternal salvation, but in order to have in the State a help towards the attainment of this end. And so he holds fast to all the means that law and justice afford him of keeping the freedom that Christ has given him; a truly Christian people is always a liberty-loving people.

Further, a Christian people will have freedom for the family. It upholds the rights that God and nature have given it for the preservation, maintenance, training and independence of the family, and defends them against violence in any shape or form, whether it come from high or low. And it does this not only from the natural instinct of self-preservation and love of its rights, but also because it wishes well to the State and desires the general good. The family is the unit of life in the State; to oppress or injure it is to injure the common weal. The State must not be the suppressor but the protector and shield of individual rights. To act contrary to them is to rule not over free and healthy men full of life and vigor, but over slaves, cripples and dead men.

Lastly, a Christian people will have freedom for its Church, for her servants, her institutions, and everything that belongs to her life and development; freedom for its religious wants, not only in the seclusion of the home but also in public life. The populace itself is a great and important constituent of the life of the State, and it regards every restriction of its Church's freedom as an attack upon its own liberty, honor and independence. Nothing brings its own reward so surely as respect on the part of the State for the Church and the religious feeling of the people. It is certain that the piety of the Christian people, its zeal for prayer, its pilgrimages, processions, and other public professions of faith are not only a powerful witness in favor of the Catholic religion, but also the instrument of great things and much blessing in the life of the nations. When the Church musters the forces of the Christian people for prayer, neither heaven nor hell can resist the assult (Acts 12:5). Prayer preserves the balance between temporal aims and the needs and interests of the soul, between the number and weight of offences and the influx of grace and mercy, and stamps all public life with the sacred mark of religious feeling and the fear of God.

Such are the relations of our Saviour to the Christian people. They are the most intimate imaginable. Christ loved the people, and went forth from their ranks Himself; He lived among them and shared their daily bread, their labor, poverty, joys and sorrows. How often His eyes filled with tears at the sight of their desolate state! (Matt. 9:36.) And it was a not unimportant point in the charge upon which He was condemned to death, that He was a "seducer of the people" (John 7:12; Luke 23:5). Christ belongs to the people and is built up into their very being, life and history. In short, He founded the Christian State, and He preserves it on the one hand by the spirit of Christian government—love, humility, and self-devotion for the good of the people (Matt. 20:25–28; Luke 22:25–29; John 10:11–17; 13:12–17)—and on the other hand by the spirit of humility and submission, the labor and prayer of the people themselves. Christ accomplished the greatest things, indeed everything, through the Christian people. Through them He rules the world. If they keep true to Him and His Church, peace will never be disturbed on earth. If only the Christian populace knew and constantly bore in mind that nothing, nothing in the world can resist its piety, activity and enterprising effort, its endurance and perseverance is asserting and vindicating its rights, as long as it only employs right and legitimate means! But it must not forsake Christ and listen to other prophets (Matt. 24:5, 23). The people need Christ, and Christ's cause needs the people, especially in our days, when no government will espouse the cause of His Church.

Church and the Religious State

Another form in which Christ continues His life in the Church is the religious state. This life of His may be considered under three aspects: the religious state in its essence, its use and application, and its rewards.

1. ESSENCE OF THE RELIGIOUS STATE

The essence of the religious state comprises its end as well as the means to that end.

The end and aim of the religious state is the attainment of Christian perfection. Perfection itself consists in union with God by love and special service. To strive after perfection is the first and fundamental duty of the religious state; and this striving is not merely occasional and accidental, attendant upon other duties of this vocation, but is itself an intrinsic and essential duty, so that religious make this their exclusive task in life and enter upon it and pursue it as their calling. The religious state is simply the state, i.e. the unalterable way of life, in which one binds oneself to strive after perfection. And the essential means of the religious state consist in the observance of the three evangelical counsels: poverty, chastity, and obedience. These three counsels are not perfection itself but only means to it; indeed, the peculiar characteristic of the counsels is that they are only special means to perfection, which are not obligatory but left to everyone's free option. And they are special means to perfection precisely because they are optional and presuppose a higher degree of zeal, generosity and love; and also because they remove the chief hindrance to love of God, viz. self-love, which sometimes takes the form of attachment to exterior goods, sometimes that of predilection for sensual enjoyments, and sometimes that of love of freedom and self-guidance. And therefore the observance of the three counsels has always been regarded as an indispensable condition and essential foundation of the religious state.

This constitution was given to the religious state by our Saviour Himself. It is an institution that He has founded in the Church. When as a twelve-year-old child He remains behind in the Temple, separates Himself from His parents, leads a life of poverty and detachment from flesh and blood, appears and teaches in the Temple, and, on being found by His parents and asked for an explanation of these proceedings, solemnly answers that He must be about His Father's business (Luke 2:49), all this is only a prelude to His future public ministry, and this again is the type and model of the end, means, and utilization of the religious state. Later on this institution of His was more and more plainly revealed, and it became a reality and a fact with the calling of the Apostles (John 1:43; Luke 5:27; Mark 1:20; Matt. 19:27) and others (Luke 9:57–62), especially the rich youth (Matt. 19:16–21). Here we see an evident distinction made between two states of life in the Church: that of ordinary Christian life, or necessary love of God, which contents itself with the observance of the commandments as its essential duty; and another life that takes for its aim perfection, a higher degree of love and service of God (Matt. 19:21), and to this end decides to observe the counsels also, which thus become the essential obligations of this state. So we have here an institution and a law of Christ, and these we see realized in the religious state. This state really owes its origin to Christ, and is a continuation of His spirit and life; it is the practical expression of Christian perfection, because in it the perfection of Christ's moral law, which consists in the evangelical counsels, has been realized and made the essential constituent of a state of life. Lastly, it is the perfect imitation of the life of Jesus, because it has chosen for its sole object in life the exclusive service of His Heavenly Father, and for its means, as a necessary consequence, the perfect renunciation of personal property, detachment from flesh and blood, and a poor and celibate life. This object, namely the exclusive service of God, and these means, complete detachment, certainly form one of the grandest and most beautiful traits of the spirit and life of our Saviour, and the religious state has chosen this for its peculiar characteristic and possession. And our Saviour instituted the religious life because it is only meet and right that there should be a state in the Church and world exclusively devoted to God's service. There is no mode of life to which men do not dedicate themselves, and it is chiefly by adopting a profession that men make their efforts durable, persevering and successful. Besides, there will always be hearts in the world which are repelled by the uselessness and danger of earthly aspirations, and seek higher, better and more lasting things; hearts which will be free to serve God and belong to Him alone, which wish to be generous towards their Maker and Redeemer. For such He has created the religious state, and thereby satisfied the most noble and justifiable craving of the human heart. All that our Saviour realized and established in Himself and His Apostles during His earthly life, as Teacher and Lawgiver, has found the grandest and most lasting expression in the Church through the religious Orders.

2. THE FUNCTION OF THE RELIGIOUS STATE

The religious state has a double function in the Church, according as the immediate aim and object of an Order is contemplative or active. The Orders diverge in these two directions. In their last end, the striving after perfection, and in the common means, the observance of the evangelical counsels, they are one; but they differ in the particular means that they employ for the manifestation of charity or perfection. Some Orders, the contemplative ones, are occupied directly and solely with the practices that promote their own personal sanctification, and only indirectly with the world. Others exercise a direct influence upon the world and sanctify themselves by works of spiritual or corporal mercy; these are the active Orders. The contemplatives sanctify the world by their expiatory prayer, their life of sacrifice and their example; the active Orders by mission-work, teaching, participation in the Church's cure of souls, and works of corporal mercy. It can scarcely be conceived how much the Orders as a body have done for the propagation and defence of the Church, the cultivation and promotion of science and art, and even the promotion of the material well-being of the world.

And in this they are simply imitating our Saviour. He gave to the world and the Church in Martha the model of the active, and in Mary the ideal of the contemplative life. But both Martha and Mary are merely types of vocations and fractions of the complete life of Jesus, which unites in itself both the active and the contemplative vocations (Luke 10:38–42). The contemplative Orders find their model in the Saviour Who, full of the joy of the Holy Ghost, went from the Jordan into the wilderness, in order to give us an example of how we may sanctify ourselves by prayer, penance and conflict with the Evil One (Matt. 4:1–11). And the active Orders take their example from the Saviour Who went forth in the strength of the Holy Ghost from the desert into Galilee and preached in the synagogues (Luke 4:14, 15), returning, when His work was done, into the desert to pray (Luke 5:16). He Himself repeatedly indicated the observance of the evangelical counsels as the means of practising apostolic zeal, and apostolic work as the aim and end of the evangelical counsels (Luke 9:60; Mark 10:29). By their observance the apostolic laborer acquires freedom, strength and energy of action, the blessing of good example, and the strength of sacrifice. Thus all apostolic men have labored, and our Saviour continues His ministry in the activity of the religious Orders.

3. THE REWARDS OF THE RELIGIOUS STATE

Our Saviour has promised two rewards to those who forsake "house, or brethren, or sisters, or father, or mother, or wife, or children, or lands" for His Name's sake, viz. the hundredfold in this life, and in the world to come life everlasting (Matt. 19:29; Mark 10:29, 30).

This temporal "hundredfold" consists partly in spiritual, partly in material advantages. To the spiritual belong first the freedom from temporal cares; the childlike, joyous temperament that religious preserve even in old age; their exemption from the thousand disagreeable vicissitudes of secular and family life; their facility in prayer and the consolation they find in it, for prayer increases in sweetness in proportion as one detaches oneself from exterior things. The material advantages and blessings consist in God's special providence for the temporal wants of those who have made themselves poor for love of Him. This promise of our Saviour has never yet failed, as St. Mark even seems to hint: they will have a hundred times as much in the way of houses, brethren, sisters, mothers, children, and lands, in spite of all persecutions (Mark 10:30). In truth, poverty maintains, feeds and clothes religious, just as she gives them birth in the Orders. Having nothing, they yet possess all things; they are needy and yet enrich many, are sorrowful and yet always rejoicing (II Cor. 6:10). Like the flowers they labor not and spin not, and yet are arrayed in glory (Matt. 6:28, 29); like the birds they sow not and reap not, and yet their Heavenly Father feedeth them (Matt. 6:26). The "dead hand" has become the most powerful and beneficent of any. Our Saviour Himself had nothing, and yet procured Himself money and vassals everywhere; and He does the same now for those who are poor for His Name's sake. This is the fulfilment of His promise.

The second reward consists in eternal life, which is promised, pledged and sealed to religious, if they persevere in their holy vocation till death. Indeed, an exceedingly high degree of glory in heaven will be their reward for not having contented themselves with serving God in an ordinary way here below, but having devoted themselves to Him and His Church in a special manner. For the little they have sacrificed here they will receive in heaven a great and royal treasure (Matt 19:21), and will therefore be numbered among the great ones of the heavenly kingdom; they will sit upon thrones and judge the angels (Matt. 19:28; I Cor. 6:3), and thus be of the nobility of heaven. The fact that, among the four or five hundred servants of God who have been beatified or canonized within the last three or four centuries, no less than about three hundred belong to the religious state, sufficiently proves that our Saviour is faithful to this promise, and that He makes the religious life the school of holiness.

The religious state is one of the institutions established by Christ in His Church, and the masterpiece of His legislative wisdom. It is the expression of His personal holiness, and bears the stamp of His life's perfection; it is the living proof of the power of His grace and His fidelity to His promises, which the single circumstance of the marvelous sprouting and spread of the religious Orders, as soon as ever the Church is free to develop, suffices to show. Lastly, it is a great and important instrument of sanctification and blessing for the Church and the whole world. It provides an outlet for the noblest aspiration of the human heart, enables it to follow its bent for freedom and generosity in the service of God, and fills the earth with the beneficent reflex action of this generosity. Thus the religious state is a great and important part of the after-life of Christ in His Church.

Christ and the Hierarchy

The grandest manifestation of Christ's life and work in the Church is the hierarchy. This hierarchy is the whole body of those who hold and exercise spiritual power, in their various orders and ranks from the Pope downwards; or in other words, the authorities and the government of the Church. Christ continues to live in this hierarchy in three ways: in its authority, its sanctity and its destiny.

1. The Authority of the Hierarchy

The authority of the ecclesiastical hierarchy bears three characteristic marks of similarity to Christ.

The first characteristic feature is the universality and plenitude of its power. Christ possessed for the purpose of His life-work as Redeemer and Mediator of salvation a threefold power: the teaching, the priestly and the pastoral power, because the human race needs truth, grace and external guidance to enable it to attain salvation. And He has left this plentitude of power to the Church, in the persons of the Apostles and their successors in the hierarchy. He gave them the right and the power to teach all truth (Matt. 28:19, 20; John 16:13); He gave them His priestly power to offer sacrifice (Luke 22:19) and dispense the Sacraments (Matt. 28:19; John 20:23); and lastly, He gave them full pastoral power to make laws for the government of the Church and to regulate the use of the means of grace (John 21:15; Matt. 18:18). As far as the needs of man, as far as the dominion and mercy of Christ reach, so far the authority of the hierarchy extends.

The second characteristic is finality and absoluteness. Christ possessed this plentitude of power in its source and absolutely, so that there is no appeal from Him to any other authority. And it is this same power that He has left to the Apostles and the hierarchy. He sends them as His Father sent Him (John 20:21); He makes them His ambassadors and plenipotentiaries (II Cor. 5:20); He makes them the foundation of the Church (Matt. 16:18; Eph. 2:20), makes them the Church herself, so to speak (Matt. 18:17); their decisions are ratified for all eternity (Matt. 18:18); he who refuses to hear them, refuses to hear Christ (Luke 10:16); they are to be the visible head of the Church, as He is her invisible Head (Eph. 1:22; 4:11). All this is literally true, and is fulfilled in the infallible *ex cathedra* decisions of the Pope and the General Councils of the Church. There is no appeal from them; they are absolute and irrevocable for time and eternity. No one is exempt from the authority of the hierarchy of the Church. Her judgments and decisions are made with the whole weight of Christ's plenary power (I Cor. 5:4; II Cor. 2:10; 13:10).

The third characteristic of Christ's power is the beneficial and salutary effect of its exercise. Together with this power Christ has made over to the Church and her hierarchy a fulness of blessing for the entire world. Like Christ she is the light, the life, and the way (John 14:6) of the world to God; and this in three respects. In the first place, by the truth that she constantly preaches. Like Christ she is the sole teacher of the supernatural truth that leads to salvation (Matt. 10:14). All the purely secular educational institutes and universities in the world do not teach as much saving truth as one answer in the Catholic catechism (I Cor. 2:6–13). The Church is the instructress of the whole world and the guardian of even natural truth. Secondly, the Church gives life to the world. One can have everything else outside the Church, but not supernatural life or salvation. The priests and bishops are our true fathers in Christ (I Cor. 4:15). Without the grace of God life is no life at all, but rather death. The third benefit is order and peace in the world. The Catholic hierarchy is the shield of all the conditions of freedom and prosperity. Her laws protect the throne and matrimony, the rights of the monarch and the freedom of the people. She preaches to the poor respect of the rich man's property, and to the rich charity and benevolence towards the poor. Thus the hinges and the poles of human society lie in the hands of the Church. Her hierarchy can do more than all the armies and fortifications in the world. She is immortal, and she never yields. Like Christ she is yesterday, and today, and the same for ever (Hebr. 13:8).

It is certain that no part of the Church represents Christ's power so fully as the hierarchy. In order to make of His Church a perfect society and an organically constructed body (I Cor. 12:14), He did not communicate Himself to all its members equally. Just as He is the Head of the Church and imparts to her all her life and strength, so there were to be members of the Church who should act as her head, as visible images of His personal dignity and activity, and as holders and instruments of His kingly and high-priestly office. These superior members are the bishops, with the Pope at their head. In them the Church is not merely a bride, but a mother; not merely sanctified, but also sanctifying; not merely a hearer, but a teacher; not merely a subject, but a ruler and governor (Eph. 1:22; 4:11; I Cor. 12:17 seq.).

2. THE HOLINESS OF THE HIERARCHY

Christ makes the bishops worthy representatives of His authority (II Cor. 3:6). This takes place first through their holiness, which is a communication and emanation of His own sanctity. He did not give Himself the honor of being a High Priest, but possessed the authorization for His priesthood in His quality of Son of God, that is to say derived it from His Father (Hebr. 5:5); so the bishops in like manner enter upon their office at the call of Christ, and are interiorly sanctified and authorized for it by the Sacrament of Holy Orders, which imparts to them their consecration and official character.

Further, Christ sanctifies His bishops and priests by the virtues that He requires them to practise, according to His own example and model. He has become "a High Priest, holy, innocent, undefiled, separated from sinners and made higher than the heavens; who needeth not daily, as the other priests, to offer sacrifices first for his own sins and then for the people's" (Hebr. 7:26, 27). According to this ideal we may distinguish five priestly virtues. The first is blamelessness and unblemished repute before God and men (II Cor. 4:2; II Tim. 2:15; Titus 2:7, 8), freedom from selfishness, avarice (I Tim. 1:5; 6:8; Titus 1:7) and ambition (I Cor. 2:1, 4). The second is the spirit of sacrifice and renunciation. The priest must be detached and separated not only from sin but also from the world and from flesh and blood; he must be as it were without father or mother (Hebr. 7:3), and serve the Gospel alone (Rom. 1:1). He must be crucified, after the model of his Lord (Gal. 6:14). It is in this self-sacrifice and renunciation that the savor of the apostolic salt lies (Matt. 5:3; Mark 9:49); it is by this that his death produces life in the world (II Cor. 4:12; II Tim. 2:10). The third virtue is prayer. Prayer is an official duty of the priest, after the example of our Saviour, Who "in the days of His flesh with a strong cry and tears offered up prayers and supplications" (Hebr. 5:7). The fourth virtue is labor, the exercise of the preaching office, the administration of the Sacraments, and study (II Cor. 11:23–29). The fifth virtue is the spirit of love and mercy, manifested in compassion for the weaknesses of others, in imitation of our Saviour, Who was so compassionate (Hebr. 5:2; I Cor. 9:22). Even the ordinary degree of these virtues, prayer, continence, and the burden of work which falls to the priesthood, raises the priest far above the ordinary man, and imparts to his life a signal resemblance to the holiness of Jesus (II Cor. 6:4–10).

3. DESTINY OF THE HIERARCHY

The ecclesiastical hierarchy is a continuation of our Saviour's life in this respect also, that on the whole no one experiences more fluctuations of favor and disfavor than its members.

Certainly nothing is of greater importance for the preservation of secular order than the Church and her hierarchy. None do more good, and yet ingratitude is the world's reward for all that they do for her welfare. If the Church upholds her divine and inalienable rights, it is called lust of power; if she requires the submission of the intellect to faith, it is scandalous arrogance; if she petitions for her daily bread, it is greed and avarice; if she holds her priestly virtues in honor, it is only hypocrisy, and people do not believe in her virtue and unselfishness; in spite of all her trouble and labor for the salvation of souls, there is no greater idler in the world; if the hierarchy espouses the cause of the poor and weak and defends their rights, it is sedition and instigation to revolt; if she does good to the poor, it is base ambition and seduction of the people. What a dark cloud of calumny, insult and outrage unceasingly hangs over the Catholic hierarchy throughout the centuries! What a caricature of wickedness and profligacy people have made of her! Even St. Paul already says: "We are made as the refuse of this world, the off-scouring of all" (I Cor. 4:13), and "as sheep for the slaughter" (Rom. 8:36). But with all this she does not forget her task, to bear the sufferings and carry on the redeeming work of the God-Man (Col. 1:24; II Cor. 4:10, 11), Who, when He was reviled, did not revile, but prayed for His tormentors. So she too, when she is reviled, does not cease to work, but blesses when she is persecuted and prays for those who blaspheme her (I Cor. 4:12, 13).

And therefore she is a wondrous spectacle for God, for angels and for men (I Cor. 4:9). God blesses her prayers, labors and sufferings; He glorifies her by bestowing upon them a marvelous fertility, and prepares for her ineffable rewards of power, honor and joy in the kingdom of heaven (Mat. 19:28; Dan. 12:3). Here below she is the refuge and comfort of the world. Who can help and comfort men in terror of the eternity that menaces them, or of the temporal chastisements of God? How often the Church has placed herself between the rebellion of the world and the consuming fire of heaven, staying the destruction wherever she approached with her consecrated incense! (Num. 16:47, 48.) Who can restore order amid the rack and ruin of the social state? Who steps as arbitrator between the clashing weapons of nations and kings, admonishes both sides of their duty and helps each one to his rights? How many a tyrannical oppressor she has struck with terror! Her weapons are "not carnal, but mighty to God unto the pulling down of fortifications . . . and every height that exalteth itself against the knowledge of God" (II Cor. 10:4, 5). Her ban withers the proudest laurels, overturns thrones, and lays armies low in the dust. How many foes she has overcome already, and she is still as intact, her strength as unabated as on the first day of her existence! To the Church and her hierarchy we may fitly apply the words of Balaam with reference to Israel: "How beautiful are thy tabernacles, O Jacob, and thy tents, O Israel! As woody valleys, as watered gardens near the rivers, as tabernacles which the Lord hath pitched, as cedars by the waterside. . . . God hath brought him out of Egypt. . . . They shall devour the nations that are his enemies. . . . Lying down he hath slept as a lion, and as a lioness, whom none shall dare to rouse. He that blesseth thee shall also himself be blessed; he that curseth thee shall be reckoned accursed" (Num. 24:5–9). Such is the Church in her hierarchy; it is her beauty and her strength.

If our Saviour leads a glorious and majestic after-life in the Church, it is certainly in the hierarchy. Here He reveals Himself in the full display of His power, the sanctifying strength of His office, and the glorious destiny of His mortal life. Like Himself, no one does more good to the world, and no one is more hated by some and more loved by others than the Church in her hierarchy.

Christ and the Saints of the Church

We find Saints in all the orders of the Church, and therefore they must be considered specially in their relation to Christ. This relation is threefold, and concerns their virtues, their deeds and their rewards.

1. The Virtues of the Saints

A Saint, in the full sense of the word, is a Christian whose supernatural holiness has been confirmed by miracles and ratified by the Church. But holiness does not consist merely in the possession of sanctifying grace and ordinary virtue, but in a heroic measure of Christian virtues. A Saint must have practised all the important virtues of Christian life, including the more difficult virtues, in an extraordinary manner, with facility and unhesitating assurance, and without consideration for temporal advantages; on the contrary, with evident self-denial. So a Saint must have been a hero and a master in the spiritual life; a hero of Christian virtue, a great and wonderful being, in whom all the grandeur, beauty and magnificence of the spiritual life and of evangelical perfection are revealed.

This leads us as a matter of course to our Saviour, Who is the Author of the spiritual life, the Ideal of holiness, the Master who trains us in virtue and sanctity.

We may distinguish two things in the Saints: first, general features and constituents of their sanctity, and then the peculiar form of holiness that characterizes each Saint in particular. The general characteristics are: first, sanctifying grace, which comes from Christ, its origin and source; and secondly, the principles upon which Christian holiness and perfection are based. These principles of holiness are nothing else than the moral lessons of our Saviour, as contained in the eight beatitudes and the didactic discourses delivered by Him during His public life. The chief of these moral lessons are love of poverty and humility, purity of heart, mercy, mildness, and love of the Cross (Matt. 5:3–12). The Saints have taken to heart these lessons and recommendations of virtue, and have made them the principles of their thoughts, endeavors and actions, and the pillars and groundwork of their lives.

As for the peculiar distinguishing mark of each individual Saint, it consists in the predominance of some one or other of these virtues which is specially suited to his character or his vocation and life-work, which he has chosen out for himself, and in which he has been particularly distinguished. And whence have the Saints derived this peculiar beauty? Who has served them for a model? No other than our Lord and Saviour Himself. He is the true Sun of justice and holiness in the firmament of the Church, and unites in Himself all the light and all the rays of created perfection and goodness. These rays divide and separate as they fall upon the earth and on souls, but are never lost. One ray falls upon this soul, another upon that; each soul reflects the beauty of the ray that has touched it, and it is in this that its peculiar supernatural beauty and holiness consist. The Saints compose as it were a vast and resplendent rainbow, the sublime emblem of our Saviour's beauty and majesty; but each individual Saint, like a single drop of dew or rain, reflects only one ray of the central sun. Thus the vast and glorious beauty of heaven and the Saints is built up in marvelous unity and manifold variety. The unity lies in the central Sun, Christ; the variety is displayed in the different groups of the Saints and in each individual member of these groups. The majesty of the hierarchy, the beauty of the pastoral office shines out in the Apostles; purity in the choir of virgins; holy fortitude in the army of martyrs; but in each Apostle, each virgin, and each martyr there is a peculiar coloring, according as they have received of the beauty of the original light, grace for grace (John 1:16), that our Saviour may be "filled all in all" (Eph. 1:23). That is why He has arranged His life so that all the peculiarities of every calling, every position in life, and every character may have in Him their own proper model. And so the Saints and their virtues are nothing but the living expression of the doctrine, grace and example of our Lord's own life.

2. THE DEEDS OF THE SAINTS

The Saints play an extraordinary part in the great work of the Church. The ordinary and official organs of her activity are the members of the hierarchy. One might call the Saints the extraordinary instruments of God's operation in the Church and through the Church; and this is especially true of such as do not belong to the hierarchy, but occupy another position in life. They have brought virtue to the point of heroism, and virtue is the talent, capital and complete qualification for spiritual work; they have entirely abandoned themselves to the guidance of grace, have filled themselves with its strength and efficacy, and have so become pliable and powerful instruments of this grace of Jesus Christ for the glory of God and the salvation of men (I Cor. 15:10). They are the most fruitful branches of Christ, the Living Vine (John 15:1–3). What cannot faith make of a man? Streams of living water emanate from him for the salvation of the world (John 7:38). And what shall we say of the prayer of faith? Its power with God is little short of magical, and it can obtain whatever it desires (John 15:7; 16:26, 27; Luke 17:6; Matt. 21:21). Our Saviour promises that His faithful followers will do greater works than He Himself performed (John 14:12). Thus we find in the Saints all the conditions of great and efficient work. They are excellent, pliable and durable instruments in the hands of Christ, and are united to Him, Who can and does use them for His work.

History gives us sufficient proof of this. Everything great that has been done in the Church has been done by Saints. They share amongst themselves the various forms of God's operation. What St. Paul says—that grace is given to everyone according to the measure of the giving of Christ . . . to some as Apostles, some as prophets, some as Evangelists, some as pastors and doctors (Eph. 4:7, 11); whilst others have the grace of miracles, of healing, help, government, the gift of tongues and interpretation of speeches (I Cor. 12:28)—is all literally true of the Saints. Some have surrounded the hierarchical body with luster and glory by their holiness and, seated upon their thrones, have guided the Church and the world into quite another path, like St. Gregory the Great and Gregory VII; others have carried the apostolate and its mission-work to the ends of the earth, like St. Francis Xavier; others have organized ecclesiastical science and formed it into a magnificent system, like St. Thomas Aquinas. Others again have created immortal institutions and organizations for works of mercy and charity, like St. Vincent de Paul; others were founders and reformers of the contemplative Orders, like St. Bruno; others of the active and apostolic Orders, like SS. Benedict and Bernard, Ignatius of Loyola, Dominic and Francis. Nay, holiness has rendered also women capable of extraordinary activity and unusual position in the Church, such as for example St. Pulcheria, SS. Catharine of Siena and Theresa. There is not a single Saint who did not do a great work and carry out the gracious intentions of God in his own age and his own sphere. The history of the Saints is the bright side of the Church's history.

3. THE REWARD OF THE SAINTS

The reward of the Saints is threefold. The first reward falls to their lot even in this earthly life. There is scarcely a Saint whose life is not surrounded by the halo of wondrous mystical gifts even here below. This mysticism is the higher Christian life, a marvelous, divine knowledge and work, by the exercise of the gifts of grace upon body and soul, upon oneself and others. The second reward consists in the miracles that God works in answer to their intercession, and which seem to cast a reflection of heavenly radiance around their relics even in this world. And thirdly, their reward is completed by the ecclesiastical beatification and canonization, which gives to the whole Church the assurance that the Saint in question really lives and reigns with God, and gives him a throne of glory and a wider sphere of action here in the Church Militant.

The Author of this glory, as of the holiness and efficacious work of the Saints, is our Saviour. He rewards and consoles the Saints by this gradual glorification, and powerfully promotes their task and vocation of being models of heroic virtue and executing higher commissions from God. He trains and forms them as His instruments. Lastly, these miraculous gifts of the Saints are our Saviour's testimony to the truth and divinity of His promises and His Church. He possessed these miraculous powers Himself, and His Church was to possess them too (Mark 16:17). He has promised it: His servants will be where He is, and His Father will honor them (John 12:26); He Himself will confess them before His

Father and the world (Matt. 10:32). It is precisely in the reward of the Saints that He proves His truth to be eternal, proves that His mercy is confirmed upon His servants and that of His goodness there is no end.

What a wonderful and glorious testimony are the Saints to the life and work of Christ in the Church! They are the living witnesses to the truth and practicability of His doctrine; witnesses to the power of His grace and Sacraments; living witnesses to the grace and power of His example; witnesses to His inexhaustible goodness and generosity towards His faithful servants. How many motives we have here for striving after virtue and perfection! Can there be a nobler, more glorious or more advantageous career than that of the Saints?

Christ and the World

The after-life of Christ in the world and with regard to the world is, like His first life and His earthly life, a conflict.

1. THE WORLD'S WAR AGAINST CHRIST

Christ's adversary is the world. And who is this world? The world is a society that is guided by quite other laws and principles, pursues quite other aims, and employs quite other means than the Church of Christ. Everything in these two bodies is different, opposite and hostile. The world and its spirit as such are not of God (John 15:19; 17:14, 16); the world does not know Christ (John 17:25); it cannot receive His spirit at all (John 14:17); it is wholly "seated in wickedness" (I John 5:19); it is nothing but the lust of the flesh, the lust of the eyes, and the pride of life (I John 2:16), and therefore it hates Christ and His Church (John 7:7; 15:18, 19) and even persecutes Him and His Apostles (John 15:20); whoever is its friend, is God's enemy (James 4:4). And to this world belong, in the truer and wider sense, all who remain in conscious unbelief or heresy; all who reject the moral law of Christ and His Church and resist the appointed order, whether they do so individually or form associations and even States. But all these men who visibly oppose the Church of Christ are only the light troops of the vanguard, who cover the real leader and his forces. This leader is no other than the prince of this world (John 12:31; 14:30; 16:11), and with him the gates of hell (Matt. 16:18). These are the forces that really carry on the warfare. "Our wrestling is not against flesh and blood, but against principalities and powers, against the rulers of the world of this darkness, against the spirits of wickedness in the high places" (Eph. 6:12; Luke 22:53).

The world's method of warfare is the same as that with which it formerly opposed our Saviour Himself. Its aim is always to tarnish and if possible destroy God's honor and rob Him of His praise, by sin and the death and ruin of men in body and soul (Rom. 5:12; 6:23; I Cor. 15:56). Satan and the world seduce men to sin by tempting them with riches, honors and worldly pleasures (Matt. 4:1–10). Sometimes they tempt them singly, sometimes in a body, as a material or intellectual power, e.g. by heathenism, heresies, rationalism, materialism, and social aberrations. If seduction does not attain the desired end, they try the effect of mockery, persecution, proscription, despoiling of property and freedom, and lastly death. Lying, hatred, blasphemy, violence and death—these are the "gates of hell" (Matt. 16:18). And there is one thing especially which runs like a dark thread through the history of conflict and persecution from the first days of the Church (Hebr. 10:32–34) until now, namely the desire of the secular power to enslave the Church, "which is above, which is free, which is our Mother" (Gal. 4:26, 29, 31), the Bride of Christ, and not the slave of the State. To become the slave of a secular power would be the worst thing that could befall her; better a Church on the Cross than a Church with a ring in her nose. This, then, is the war of the world against Christ and His Church. The aim is always the same, and the leader of the battle and the method of warfare also. This method of warfare of the world is called, in flowery speech, policy, or the spirit of the wisdom of the flesh (Rom. 8:6). It is a monster of all wickedness and infamy.

2. CHRIST'S COUNTER-WARFARE IN THE CHURCH

Christ is the real leader in the Church's warfare, since the Church is but the extension of the life and conflict of Christ. And what are His methods? In the first place, if Christ takes up arms, it is not with the intention of destroying the world, but only of saving it (John 3:16, 17; 12:47). His Sacred Heart does not hate it, is not even indifferent to it. He has included it in His compassionate plan of redemption. And though He does not include it directly and unconditionally in His all-powerful mediatory prayer (John 17:9), still He has not forgotten it. He founded the Church on its behalf also. The world is to be brought to the faith by the sight of His devotion even unto death, and by the example of the unity and firmness of the Church (John 14:31; 17:21). For it too He is the Light of life (John 9:5). The Holy Ghost has commissions to execute with regard to it also; in the Church He is constantly convincing it of its sins, of judgment and of justice (John 16:8). He unceasingly inspires people to pray for its conversion (I Tim. 2:1), and His apostles and missionaries traverse the whole earth (Matt. 28:19).

Secondly, our Saviour and His Church do not attack the world's rights; on the contrary, they respect and protect them. The secular State has no stronger prop, no more loyal and powerful protector and shield than the Church. God cannot belie nor contradict Himself. Every rightful authority comes from Him, and He supports it and orders it to be respected within the radius of its prerogative (Rom. 13:1–7; Tit. 3:1). Even when hated and persecuted by secular potentates, the Church has never preached nor excused disobedience to them. What she demands and must demand of the State is freedom in the exercise of the rights she has received from God (Acts 5:29). Both Church and State rest upon the same foundation, and their rights also. The persecutors of the Church really live by the Church.

But thirdly, this respect of the world's rights does not hinder the Church from making a positive use of her spiritual sword and defending her own rights. She is God's representative, and since He will not cede His rights, neither will she. She never ceases to preach the faith and moral law of Christ everywhere, to demand submission from everyone, and to judge, condemn and punish all unbelief and rebellion (II Cor. 10:5). This is the royal power that Christ has conferred upon her; these are the commissions that the Holy Ghost fulfils with regard to the world by means of the Church (John 16:8 seq.). No favor and no violence can ever induce her to renounce this royal power. This has been proved from the words of the Apostles: "We ought to obey God rather than men" (Acts 5:29), down to the *Non possumus* of our days. Thus the scenes of the trial before the Great Council (Luke 22:66) and before Pilate (Luke 23:3) are constantly being renewed: "Art Thou the Messias?" "Art Thou a king?" And Christ always answers, through the voice of the Church: "I am."

Fourthly, it is quite a peculiar and divine method of warfare that our Saviour and the Church pursue, not to oppose violence to violence, but to overcome by patience and temporary defeat.

She has the firm conviction that she will not perish, but that on the contrary it is precisely through suffering, death and defeat that she marches to victory, and that the final triumph and eternity are hers (Matt. 5:10–12; Luke 10:3; I Peter 2:20; 3:14; 4:14; II Cor. 4:17; Hebr. 10:34). This is the new and wonderful method of warfare that Christ introduced and employed, and with which He overcame the enemy, founded His kingdom, and accomplished the Redemption. And it is also the method that His Church employs. These are legitimate, noble, wonderful and divine tactics, so loftly and sublime that the world cannot comprehend them and only feels them in her final defeat.

3. THE FINAL VICTORY OF CHRIST

Under these leaders and with these means of warfare the conflict is constantly being renewed here below, and will be continued to the end of the world. It is a perpetual alternation: venturing and hesitating, rising and sinking, conquest and defeat; and everywhere, as far as the eye can reach in the Church and the world, there is battle and struggle, not merely in the Church as a body, but in every kingdom, every human soul, indeed every good and useful work. Everything must be fought for. There are truces sometimes, to be sure, but peace will never be concluded until the end of time; then, after Christ has won His great, glorious and decisive victory, there will be peace at last.

This victory of Christ in His Church as a body is not merely predicted as a future occurrence, but is already visible at the present time; first, in that the Church never perishes and never can perish, however numerous her foes and however great her losses and apparent defeats may be (Matt. 16:18). One who always rises again will certainly remain master of the field in the long run. Secondly, the Church spreads farther and farther in spite of the injuries done her; ever repulsed, ever returning; ever being extirpated, ever reviving. She founds her patience upon eternal promises (Matt. 16:18; 28:20); she can afford to wait, for time and eternity are hers, and patience must conquer all in the end. She gains everything by patience (Matt. 24:13). Sometimes the victorious power of Christ in the Church flashes out even here in this life, and executes quite a perceptible, palpable judgment upon her enemies and persecutors. Her adversaries do not succeed in all their plans. When their insolence oversteps all bounds, the Lord Himself speaks to them in His anger, and breaks them in pieces like a potter's vessel, with a rod of iron (Ps. 2:5, 9). All the Church's foes pass away, but she stands firm in the joy and beauty of peace, and daily sings: "Why have the Gentiles raged, and the people devised vain things? . . . I am appointed king by Him over Sion His holy mountain, preaching His commandment. . . . Ask of Me, and I will give thee the Gentiles for thy inheritance and the utmost parts of the earth for thy possession" (Ps. 2:1, 6, 8). And at last there will be an end of the conflict, because there will be no foes nor adversaries left, but only victors; and these victors are Christ and His Church. Death will overpower all Christ's foes, as he has overpowered them all hitherto, and finally Death himself will be overpowered by the glorious Resurrection. Then Christ's victory will be complete. That will be the glorious end, when He "shall have brought to naught all principality, and power, and virtue. For He must reign, until He hath put all His enemies under His feet. And the enemy, Death, shall be destroyed last; for He hath put all things under His feet. . . . And then the Son also Himself shall be subject unto Him that put all things under Him, that God may be all in all" (I Cor. 15:24–26, 28).

Such is the final outcome; it is truly marvelous. The foolishness of God has proved wiser than men, and the weakness of God stronger than men; and the word of the Cross has been found to be the power of God (I Cor. 1:18, 25, 27). Death and destruction have brought forth life (II Cor. 4:10). This outcome is full of glory for Christ and His disciples; it is an unalterable and eternal decision, for there will be no more death, nor mourning, nor crying, nor sorrow; all former things have passed away, and everything will be made new (Apoc. 21:4, 5); and lastly, it is sure and unerring. He Who has said: "He that shall overcome, shall possess these things" (Apoc. 21:5, 7), says also: "Have confidence, I have overcome the world" (John 16:33), and helps us likewise to overcome in His strength (I John 5:4). So let us be faithful companions-in-arms of Jesus and His Church. "He that is just, let him be justified still; and he that is holy, let him be sanctified still." Our Leader will "come quickly, and his reward is with him, to render to every man according to his works" (Apoc. 22:11, 12). Christ lives, Christ conquers, Christ reigns!

Concluding Meditation

The whole Life of our Saviour has passed before our gaze. And now what is to be the conclusion? He does not leave us in uncertainty with regard to this either. His recommendations to the Apostles when taking leave of them at the Last Supper shall be the conclusions we draw from the Life of Jesus. And these are simply: Faith, Hope and Charity.

1. FAITH

Faith is the first thing we owe to the Life of Jesus. It is the first fruit we must draw from it, and the most necessary constituent of our relation to Him.

And what is the subject of this faith? What must we believe? All that our Saviour has said, revealed and done. In the first place what He has said and testified of His Person: that He is the true Son of God and true Man like ourselves. We must believe in His divine mission to bring us a new revelation, found a religion, and show us the way to God our last end. We must believe in all the mysteries of His life; in His doctrine, His miracles, and the institutions upon which He based and founded His Church; in His redeeming Death and glorious Resurrection; in His Ascension, His glorious reign upon the throne of glory in heaven, and His continual life and work in the Church, in short, in the whole sum-total of His revelation, as it is laid before us in the Scriptures and proposed to us for belief by the Church.

And what qualities must our faith possess? In the first place, it must be firm and unshakable. Formerly God spoke by the prophets; but now He speaks by His own Son (Hebr. 1:2). "The Only-begotten Son Who is in the bosom of the Father, He hath declared Him" (John 1:18) and borne witness to His revelation by countless miracles. So we must not hesitate an instant, but be ready to give our lives for the Son of God, just as He Himself and innumerable martyrs have sealed their testimony to His Divinity with their lives and their blood. Secondly, our faith must be cheerful and willing, because it is so full of glory for our Saviour. We can bear no more glorious witness to Him than what this faith states and teaches concerning Him. And therefore it must be a heartfelt joy to us every time we make an act of faith in the Divinity and Humanity of Jesus, or in any mystery of His life.

Thirdly, our faith must be lively and practical. It must penetrate, govern and animate our intellect, our will and our whole life. It must become the principle of our thoughts and acts, the aim and end of our intentions and resolves; it must become very deed and life in us, for the just man liveth by faith (Rom. 1:17). We must model our lives on our Saviour's, and make His teaching, principles and views our own; and to this end we must study them unceasingly, imprint them upon our minds and hearts, and put them into practice in daily life. If we are in a difficulty or have any choice or decision to make, we must ask ourselves immediately: "Is there not a mystery, a word, or a deed in the Life of Jesus that tells me what I ought to do or choose now?" Our Saviour will not leave us without an answer; let us abide by it. Our life must be formed by our faith, as a bell is formed out of one cast of metal, or a statue hewn out of one block; and all our thoughts, words and actions must be organically united to it. That is the right sort of faith, the kind that our Lord requires of us and that glorifies Him.

What are the motives for this faith? They result from the consideration of faith from our point of view and from our Saviour's.

On our side there is first the necessity and then the utility of faith. The necessity lies in the fact that belief in our Lord is the first condition of being His disciple, the first step towards following Him, coming to God and being saved (Hebr. 11:6). To believe in Christ is to come to Him (John 6:35, 37). That is why He recommends this faith in Him so highly, praises it, lays stress upon it, and requires this first of all from His followers and Apostles, in all emergencies, and from beginning to end. And that is also the reason why He works so many indubitable miracles of every description to confirm it. Faith is the foundation of the supernatural life, because we cannot grasp the supernatural without faith. For the Jews and Apostles especially a lively faith was most necessary, because it was in itself such an incredible thing that this Man, who behaved and showed Himself in every other respect just like an ordinary human being, should be Very God; and indeed, there were not many who recognized this mystery. But it is necessary for us also, in spite of all the great proofs of Christ's Divinity that we now have, because He is no longer visibly in our midst, and because living by faith is so hard for our nature. So this faith is absolutely necessary for everyone; it is the first demand made upon us by Christ and the first requisite of the supernatural life.

The advantage of faith in Christ lies in this, that it helps us to make Him entirely our own. By faith we participate, first, in the wisdom of Christ. The treasures of His wisdom and knowledge and the whole sum-total of God's commissions to Him on behalf of mankind are deposited in the system of faith, and we make these treasures our own by believing. Through faith we think and judge like Christ, Who thereby shines in our hearts "to give the light of the knowledge of the glory of God" (II Cor. 4:6). The principles upon which our whole life is based are the first and most important item in the supernatural life and Christian perfection. If they are supernatural and perfect, our whole life is supernatural and perfect. And by faith we take the principles and views of our Saviour Himself for our own leading principles. By faith, secondly, we appropriate the strength and efficacious working power of our Saviour. A hearty, vigorous faith can do everything for us and in us and obtain everything from Him. By this means we assure ourselves of His almighty strength and help for ourselves and others and even for the very greatest works (Mark 4:22; John 14:12, 13; Luke 17:6). We see this confirmed in almost all His miracles. In most cases He expressly requires faith as the condition upon which He will work them; many are forcibly wrung from Him, so to speak, by the importunate faith of the petitioners (Matt. 9:21; Mark 7:29); and almost all of them are ascribed by Him to faith. Thirdly, faith ensures us the comfort, light and firmness of Christ in all the trials and emergencies of this life. Whoever believes in Christ, does not walk in darkness (John 8:12; 12:46). Faith accompanies him like a light in a dark place (II Peter 1:19). He contrives to find his way everywhere, and can comfort himself in all afflictions. Everything great that has been done in the Church was done in the strength of faith (Hebr. 11:16–40); by faith the world has been overcome (I John 5:4, 5); to faith heaven itself is promised (John 3:36; 5:24; 6:47). In short, faith effects a union and a spiritual affinity to Christ which He places even before blood-relationship (Matt. 12:48, 49; Luke 11:28). So we have in faith a means of drawing very close to our Saviour and endearing ourselves to Him. He Himself values the faith of His disciples so highly that He speaks of it as the glorious result of His mission, thanks the Father for it (John 17:6, 7), bases His petitions to Him upon it and urges it in support of them (John 17:20), and promises His disciples the love of the Father in return for this faith (John 16:27).

And as regards our Saviour the motive for faith is the glory it procures Him; in the first place, because Christ is the Author of faith (Hebr. 12:2). He brought us the faith, established it by His teaching and life, and sealed it with His blood. In order to preserve and propagate the faith He founded the Church and endowed her with His own power and infallibility. Faith is the first benefit He bestows upon us and the first thing He demands of us. Moreover faith glorifies Christ, because He is not merely the Author but also the object of our faith. Without faith we cannot form a right and fitting idea of Him. On the contrary, the confession of all His divine glory lies in faith, and so this is really the foundation of His kingdom and His glory here below. By our faith we award Him the full measure of His glory as Son of God, as the Father has given it to Him, and with the complete devotion of our intellect and heart. And so faith is a glorious homage that we pay to Christ. We acknowledge Him as the supreme, infallible Truth and our highest Lawgiver. Thirdly, faith is a glorification of our Saviour, because He is "the finisher of faith" (Hebr. 12:2). Faith is "finished" or perfected here below by its victorious power over all passion and sin within us and over all the outward attacks of hell; and in eternity by our glorification and direct vision of God. Both these rewards are the greatest glorification of Jesus in us (John 17:24). Thus faith is something very great and glorious. It glorifies Christ, gives us a share in all His blessings and promises, and forms the foundation of our spiritual intercourse with Him. And therefore we must value faith above all things, must exercise ourselves in it and try to increase and perfect it in ourselves and others. But the most glorious exercise of faith is to disseminate it and contribute to its defence and exaltation by openly confessing it, by taking part in enterprises for the propagation of the faith, and by apostolic work. St. Paul calls his great and glorious life simply a life in the faith of Christ. "And that I live now in the flesh, I live in the faith of the Son of God, Who loved me and delivered Himself for me" (Gal. 2:20).

2. HOPE

The second fruit we must draw from the Life of Jesus is to hope in Him and to exercise ourselves in this hope until death.

Hope is the second theological virtue. By hope we grasp and

embrace God as our Supreme Good, and make vigorous efforts to obtain possession of Him in heaven. The final possession of God in heaven is the principal aim and object of Christian hope. But since this possession is a supernatural good, hard to gain, and only to be obtained by the help of God and our own active cooperation, the object of our hope also includes the means requisite for the attainment of this happy goal. In both these respects our hope is directed towards our Saviour.

The goal of Christian hope is God and the possession of Him in heaven. But our Saviour is our God, and consequently the real object of our hope. He Himself says that He is the way, the truth, and the life (John 14:6); and that this is eternal life, to know the Father and His Son Jesus Christ (John 17:3). Heaven is the true object of the hope of the children of God (Rom. 5:2); their glorious inheritance with Christ and in Christ (John 8:17); the magnificent palace of the Father, with the "many mansions" in which He has prepared a place for us (John 14:2); our heavenly home, where we enjoy the rights of citizens (Phil. 3:20); the glorious kingdom of the love of the Son of God; the sanctuary of God, into which our High Priest has entered (Hebr. 6:19). Heaven is nothing else than the coming and manifestation of the glory of the great God and our Saviour (Tit. 2:13), the eternal, blessed enjoyment of the presence of Jesus (II Cor. 5:8; I Thess. 4:16). Thus we embrace substantially, as the chief object of our hope, our glorious, transfigured Saviour, because He together with the Father and the Holy Ghost is the subject of our final beatitude.

And we embrace Him just as necessarily in the means that are to lead us to this glorious goal. All ways and means, all grace and all merit come to us from our Divine Saviour. Without Him we can do nothing (John 15:2–6); He "of God is made unto us wisdom, and justice, and sanctification, and redemption" (I Cor. 1:30); by Him "we have access through faith into this grace, wherein we stand, and glory in the hope of the glory of the sons of God" (Rom. 5:2); with Him and in Him the Father has given us all things (Rom. 8:32), and in Him we are made rich in all things (I Cor. 1:5). In all positions and emergencies of the Christian life we must look to Him, and may be sure of His help. However great our sins may be and however they oppress and terrify us, we are reconciled to God through Him and by His Death (Rom. 5:10), which expiates the guilt of the whole world (II Cor.

5:19). With Him there is plentiful and infinite ransom for guilt and punishment (Ps. 129:7), and He is the Advocate of all poor sinners (I John 2:2). In all temptations He is our shield and protector, for He too was tempted in all things (Hebr. 15); and He has overcome the world and her prince, so that we can put our trust in Him (John 16:33). In all the difficulties, doubts and perplexities of life He is our light, our way (John 14:6) and our courage. He has so disposed His life that He can be our model, companion, comfort and strength in every situation. And it is especially in all sufferings and persecutions that He is such a faithful companion to us. There is certainly no more effectual consolation than the thought that Christ has suffered the same and still more for the love of us (Hebr. 12:1–3; I Peter 4:1). The Way of the Cross disseminates more true comfort in the world than all the theories and inventions for increasing the people's happiness and prosperity. And lastly, at the moment of our departure from this life, when everything forsakes us, who stays by our side, who comforts us when no one else can do so? Who else, but our Divine Lord with His holy Sacraments and that grace of His that works in the hearts of the dying? No riches, no crowns, no victories, no wisdom, no strength can be of any use then; nothing and no one can help us, only Christ. He it is Whom we have to thank for not being "as others who have no hope" (I Thess. 4:12). In Christ death is gain (Phil. 1:21) through the Resurrection, of which we have the pledge in our faith in Him (John 5:24; 11:25), in the reception of His Sacred Body (John 6:50, 55), and in His own Resurrection (I Cor. 15; I Thess. 4:13–17; Phil. 3:21). So let us not fear even the passage through the shadow of death (Ps. 22:4). Our body rests in the grave with confident hope; Christ will restore our inheritance and fill body and soul with delight by the vision of His glory (Ps. 15:5, 9, 10). Thus the Father has really given us all things with His Beloved Son. Why should we not hope, then, as long as we have Him? And in whom else should we place our hope, but in Him? Who will accuse, and who condemn? "Christ Jesus that died, yea that is risen also again, who is at the right hand of God, who also maketh intercession for us" (Rom. 8:32–34). Through Him we hold fast to the unyielding confession of our hope; for He that has promised is faithful (Rom. 4:21, 23); in Him we are not merely established in hope, but full of joy (Rom. 12:12) and exultant glory (Rom. 5:2). Indeed, we believe in hope even against hope (Rom. 4:18), and there is nothing, nothing whatever, that can rob us of our hope and joy here below, as long as we have our Saviour. In every emergency therefore we must place our hope in Him; and we must exercise ourselves unceasingly in this hope, because this benefits us and elevates our minds, and also greatly glorifies our Saviour, Who is the surety of our testament (Hebr. 7:22).

3. CHARITY

But the principal fruit we must draw from the Life of Jesus is charity, or love. By charity we embrace God as the Supreme Good in Itself. How meet it is that we should love our Saviour, on His account and on our own!

Let us first consider a few motives for this love. The first motive is the amiability of His Nature, which is in every respect calculated to win and satisfy our hearts. What is it that our heart unceasingly seeks and desires? Above all, God. God is our first and inmost want. To Him, the Source and Origin of our existence, preservation and beatitude, our nature turns with an irresistible craving, as the plant to light and water; and nothing can finally satisfy it but God. Now our Saviour *is* our God, Very God of Very God. He has given us sufficient testimony of this. "He that seeth Me, seeth the Father also," He says. "Do you not believe that I am in the Father, and the Father in Me?" (John 10:30, 38; 14:9, 10.) He is God, then, and therefore we are drawn to Him by the whole weight of our obligation to love God with all our hearts, with all our minds, and with all our strength; and also by the fact of our belonging to Him. In Him we have really reached our last end, and if we cannot do without God, we cannot do without Him. "Lord, to whom shall we go? Thou hast the words of eternal life" (John 6:69). "What have I in heaven, and besides Thee what do I desire upon earth? . . . Thou art the God of my heart and the God that is my portion for ever" (Ps. 72:25, 26).

Our nature craves to find its like. After God, man is man's need and joy. And this too we find in our Saviour. He is true Man, just as truly as He is true God. We have in Him a human nature, on the one hand similar to us in everything, suffering and death not excepted; and on the other hand most sublime and glorious, the sum-total of all the glories of nature, grace and glory, and the very essence of all honors and dignities. He is the flower of the universe, its chief beauty; the prototype and primal cause, after which, on account of which, and for which everything has been created. Consequently we belong to Him; He stands infinitely close to us; and this fact of our belonging to Him is the third reason we have for loving Him. Our nature, our life, all our relations in the natural and supernatural order tend towards Him; in Him we take root, so to speak. As Christians we are chosen and called from all eternity in Him (Eph. 1:4; Rom. 6:5), to share in His destiny in life (Rom. 6:4, 5) and reign with Him in heaven (Eph. 2:6). We are not merely vassals and subjects of His great kingdom, the Church, but living images of His Divine Sonship (Rom. 6:5; 8:29; Eph. 1:5), co-heirs of His glory, members of His mystical Body (I Cor. 6:15), and branches grafted on to Him, the Living Vine, that we may bear fruit of eternal life to the glory of His grace (Eph. 1:6) and the complacency of the Heavenly Father (John 15:8).

If we are religious, our very vocation makes us the living expression of the excellence and perfection of His doctrine and His life's example, and as priests we are the holders of His great and glorious powers, for the glory of God and the salvation of men; the representatives of His great office as Prophet, Priest and King; and the government of His kingdom. In whatever state we are, and wherever we are, we are of Him and for Him; we live and derive our sustenance from Him. In His nature and life lies the beautiful significance of our life, all its value and all its glory. He is our Father, Friend, King, High Priest, Light, Shepherd, Way, Goal, Redeemer, God and all. We ought rather to forget ourselves and our life than to forget Him. He is all in all to all of us (Col. 3:11). A further motive for loving Him is the exceeding great love with which He has loved and embraced us all. He loved us with a true and supernatural love, as His creatures, His brethren, co-heirs and friends, and as the children of His Heavenly Father; He loved us with an active, self-sacrificing, unselfish love. His Life and Death, that brought us such untold blessings, indeed all blessings, are a sufficient proof of that. He loved us with a firm, unshakable love, in spite of our past and present unworthiness, ingratitude, faithlessness and callousness. We have no friend who loves us more than Jesus, none more loyal, none more powerful than Jesus. Let us love Him in return.

And what must be the nature of this love? It must be just the same as our love for God; that is to say, in the first place, a love of the highest appreciation, a love above everything, a love as to our Supreme Good and Last End. And therefore we must not compare any creature to Christ. The riches of Christ are unsearchable (Eph. 3:8), and in comparison with them all is poor and perishable, as dung fit to be cast away (Phil. 3:7, 8). Even the most glorious created thing is but a reflection, a shadow of Jesus. So we must not cease to read and meditate and pray, nor rest until we have a high idea of Christ; and we must make use of everything to enhance and perfect it. We must see Christ in all things; in the creations of science, art and nature, as in the destiny of the Church and the course of worldly events. He is reflected everywhere as in a mirror; everything bears the traces of His wisdom, power, beauty and goodness, and everything exists for Him alone. Secondly, this love must be a love of complacency and benevolence. We must never tire of rejoicing over the glories of Jesus Christ, congratulating Him upon them, and thanking God for having chosen Him and made Him so great and glorious. Thirdly, this love must be an active and practical love, such as our Saviour Himself describes. This love keeps the commandments (John 14:15, 21); it will rather lose anything than Christ; it exhausts itself in interior and exterior proofs and manifestations of love; it shares all that it has with Christ. Fourthly, it must be an assimilating love. The intellect must fill itself with His doctrine, His principles and His views; the fancy with pictures of His outward form, His holy life and His mysteries; the will with His virtues and mode of action. In order to complete the resemblance we must make His great aim in life our own: God's glory and the salvation of men in and through the Church.

We must devote our service to His Church, His kingdom, the kingdom of His knowledge and service. It was to found and establish this kingdom that He became Man, preached His doctrine, worked His miracles, and instituted the holy Sacraments and the priesthood; and it was for His Church that He died and ascended into heaven. His entire work as God-Man is nothing but the guidance, defence, propagation and exaltation of His Church. And so it must be our life's aim to work and fight for the Church. And to make the likeness complete we must not only strive after the same end, but also employ the same means as our Saviour, viz. work, prayer, complete detachment, and even the sacrifice of our life. We must seek what He sought, and in the same way as He sought it. That is perfect imitation of Him. Fifthly, this love must be a courageous love, able to stand the test of suffering, sacrifice and adversity. Love of us brought suffering and death upon our Saviour, and helped Him to triumph over it all. In like manner our love for Him must prove itself true by sacrifices and sufferings, and if we can promote the ends of His kingdom at the cost of our lives, we must regard this as the most glorious goal of all our endeavors and the most glorious prize we could gain. These are the noble traits of true love for Jesus. We find living examples of such love as this in the history of the Church, the Apostles and Saints, and especially of St. Paul. He is the noblest expression and the most glorious example of this love, in word and deed, in conflict and suffering, and in labor and death. He was not merely an adherent, disciple and Apostle of Christ; he was thoroughly penetrated, animated, spiritualized by Him, and saw only Christ in himself. His preaching, his journeys, labors and sufferings are a continuation of the preaching (II Cor. 5:20), journeys, labors and sufferings of Jesus (Col. 1:24; II Cor. 11:23–28); his vocation and his very life consisted in giving inward and outward expression to the whole life of Jesus with all its mysteries (Phil. 1:21; II Cor. 4:10), so that it was not so much he who lived, but rather Jesus in him (Gal. 2:20). In his enthusiastic love for our Saviour he breaks out into the glorious words: "Who then shall separate us from the love of Christ? Shall tribulation? or distress? or famine? or nakedness? or danger? or persecution? or the sword? . . . In all these things we overcome because of Him that hath loved us. For I am sure that neither death, nor life, nor angels, nor principalities, nor powers, nor things present, nor things to come, nor might, nor height, nor depth, nor any other creature shall be able to separate us from the love of God, which is in Christ our Lord" (Rom. 8:35 seq.). These words are a very lyric of love, and bear witness to the divine power and invincibility of the love of which God's grace can render a poor fragile human heart capable.

This, then, is the fruit we must draw from the Life of Jesus: Faith, Hope, and Charity. It is the only worthy and complete result of it. There is nothing better nor higher than these three virtues. They are God's most glorious gifts to man (I Cor. 13:13), the loftiest of all virtues, and the exclusive relations of men to God. By them we render divine honor to our Saviour, as to our God. They are the abstract and abridgment of that union with Him that He recommended to us with such touching earnestness on His departure: "Abide in Me" (John 15:4); "believe in Me" (John 14:1); "have confidence" (John 16:33) and "abide in My love" (John 15:9). So "now there remain Faith, Hope, Charity; these three: but the greatest of these is Charity" (I Cor. 13:13). Entire and whole-hearted be our love of Jesus Christ, our Lord and our God, and may He be praised for ever! Amen.

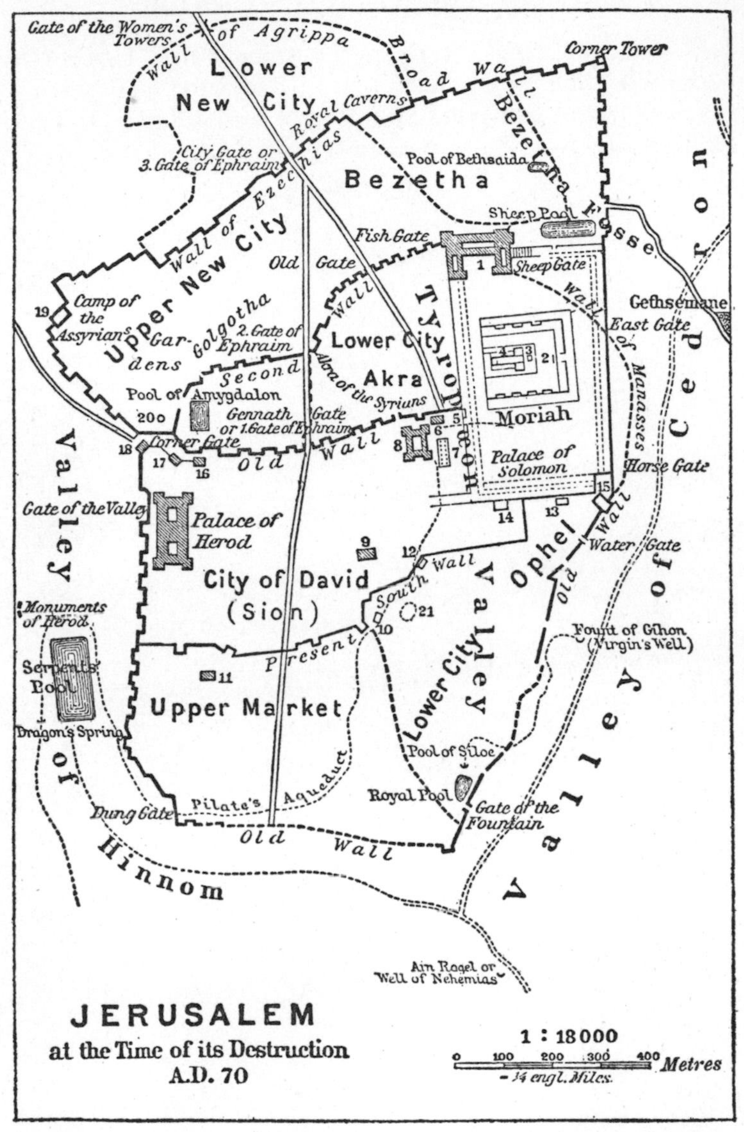

1 Antonia. 2 Court of the Women. 3 Altar of Holocausts. 4 Temple. 5 Tyropoeon Bridge. 6 Council Chamber. 7 Xystus (Gymnasium). 8 Palace of the Hasmonaeans. 9 House of David. 10 David's Tomb. 11 House of Caiphas. 12 Tower of Heroes. 13 House of Eliasib. 14 Armory. 15 The Projecting Tower. 16 Mariamne Tower. 17 Phasael Tower. 18 Hippicus Tower. 19 Psephinus Tower. 20 Tomb of the High Priest John. 21 Cistern.

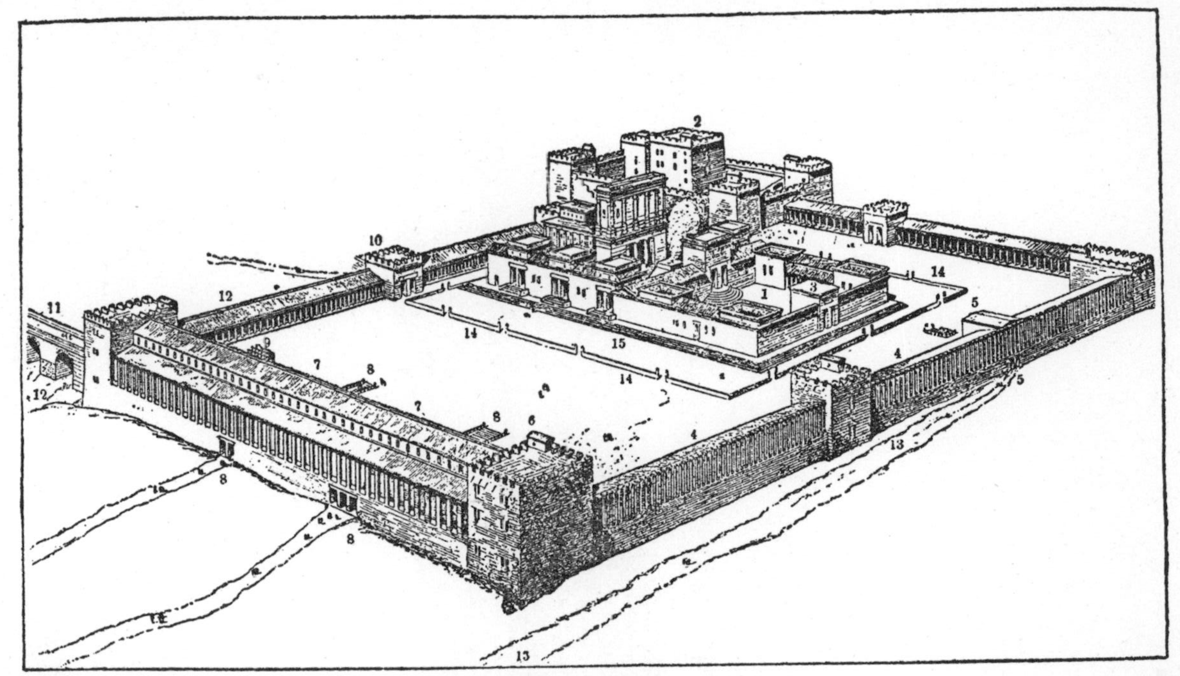

The Temple as restored by Herod.

1 The Temple. 2 Antonia. 3 Nicanor Gate. 4 Solomon's porch. 5 Golden Gate. 6 Pinnacle of the Temple (outside corner). 7 Royal porch. 8 Huldah Gates. 9 Subterranean Passage to the Lower City. 10 Suburb Gates. 11 Bridge leading to the Upper City. 12 Tyropoeon Valley. 13 Valley of Cedron. 14 Soreg (stone partition with inscriptions). 15 Steps leading to the Inner Court.

INDEX OF THE SUNDAY GOSPELS

I Advent . . . . II, 215
II Advent . . . . I, 318
III Advent . . . . I, 181
IV Advent . . . . I, 165
Christmas . . . . I, 110
Sunday after Christmas . I, 123
Circumcision . . . . I, 120
Epiphany . . . . I, 131
I Epiphany . . . . I, 147
II Epiphany . . . . I, 191
III Epiphany . . . . I, 312
IV Epiphany . . . . I, 352
V Epiphany . . . . I, 340
VI Epiphany . . . . II, 44, 46
Septuagesima . . . . II, 139
Sexagesima . . . . I, 335
Quinquagesima . . . . II, 143, 149
I Lent . . . . I, 175
II Lent . . . . I, 430
III Lent . . . . II, 1
IV Lent . . . . I, 380
Passion Sunday . . . . I, 501
Easter Sunday . . . . II, 451
I Easter . . . . II, 466, 469
II Easter . . . . I, 515
III Easter . . . . II, 298
IV Easter . . . . II, 298
V Easter . . . . II, 298
VI Easter . . . . II, 208
Pentecost . . . . II, 300
Trinity Sunday . . . . II, 476
I Pentecost . . . . I, 476
II Pentecost . . . . II, 67
III Pentecost . . . . II, 76
IV Pentecost . . . . I, 238
V Pentecost . . . . I, 298
VI Pentecost . . . . I, 410
VII Pentecost . . . . II, 307
VIII Pentecost . . . . II, 84
IX Pentecost . . . . II, 173
X Pentecost . . . . II, 118
XI Pentecost . . . . I, 407
XII Pentecost . . . . I, 477
XIII Pentecost . . . . II, 110
XIV Pentecost . . . . II, 24
XV Pentecost . . . . I, 315
XVI Pentecost . . . . II, 61
XVII Pentecost . . . . II, 193
XVIII Pentecost . . . . . . I, 245
XIX Pentecost . . . . II, 164
XX Pentecost . . . . I, 222
XXI Pentecost . . . . I, 457
XXII Pentecost . . . . II, 186
XXIII Pentecost . . . . . . I, 365
XXIV Pentecost . . . . . . II, 208
Assumption . . . . I, 482
Christ the King . . . . II, 355
All Saints . . . . I, 279
Immaculate Conception I, 66

INDEX

Note. References are to pages where treatment of the subject begins.

Adultery, woman taken in, I, 497
Advent, keeping of, I, 16
Advent meditation, I, 14
Agony in the Garden, II, 320
Ambition of sons of Zebedee, II, 145
Angel, appearance of: to Mary, I, 67; to Zachary, I, 63
Angel world, I, 34
Angels: birth of Savior proclaimed by, I, 115; after Christ's fast in the desert, I, 180; creation of, I, 34; trial of the, I, 34
Anger, refraining from, I, 298
Annas, Jesus before, II, 335
Annunciation: to Mary, I, 66; to Zachary, I, 61
Apostles
  choice of the, I, 273
  Christ's appearance to the, II, 466, 469
  dispute about precedence, I, 444
  persecutions foretold to, II, 305
  preaching mission of the, I, 372
  sending of the, I, 371
  task of the, I, 292
Apostolic life, calls to the, I, 463
Apostolic poverty, II, 27
Apostolic virtues, II, 92
Arrest of Jesus, II, 329
Ascension, the, II, 482

Baptism: of Jesus, I, 171; by John, I, 168
Baptist; *see* John the Baptist
Barabbas, II, 364
Beatitudes, the, I, 279
Beelzebub, II, 3
Beheading of the Baptist, I, 376
Benedictus, the, I, 99
Bethania, Jesus at, I, 482; II, 94, 159
Bethlehem: Christ's birth at, I, 111; journey to, I, 105; slaughter of the Innocents at, I, 137
Bethsaida, cure of blind man, I, 418
Bethsaida, pool of: cure of infirm man, I, 257
Betrayal by Judas, II, 262
Birth: of Christ, I, 110; of the Baptist, I, 98
Blessed Sacrament; *see* Eucharist
Blessed Virgin; *see* Mary
Blind and dumb man, cure of, II, 1
Blind man of Bethsaida, cure of, I, 418
Blind man of Capharnaum, cure of, I, 370
Blind men of Jericho, cure of, II, 149
Bosom of the Father, Jesus in the, I, 20
Boy, cure of dumb, I, 436
Bread, multiplication of, I, 380, 410
Bread of life, Jesus the, I, 390
Burial of Jesus, II, 431

Caiphas: adjuration by, II, 338; Jesus' trial before, II, 335
Calls to the apostolic life, I, 463
Cana, marriage at, I, 191
Canaanite woman's daughter, cure of, I, 403
Capharnaum
  centurion of, I, 312
  cure of demoniac in synagogue of, I, 232
  cure of Peter's mother-in-law at, I, 235
  Jesus in, I, 228, 235
  Jesus in synagogue of, I, 230, 390
  many cures at, I, 236
  town of Christ's adoption, I, 229

Carrying of the cross, II, 385
Centurion of Capharnaum, I, 312
Changing of water into wine, I, 191
Charity: Christ's, II, 247; law of, 298
Children, Jesus and the, II, 125
Christian people, Christ living in, II, 514
Church, Christ in the, II, 508
Circumcision: of the Baptist, I, 99; of Jesus, I, 120
Cockle, the (parable), I, 340
Coin of the tribute, II, 186
Commandment, the great, II, 193
Conception: of the Baptist, I, 61; of Christ, I, 66
Condemnation of Jesus, II, 381
Confession, fearless, II, 17
Corn, plucking of ears of, I, 266
Correction, fraternal, I, 454
Covetousness, warning against, II, 21
Creation, I, 30: Christ's life before the, I, 20; of man, I, 37
Crippled woman, cure of, II, 41
Cross: carrying of the, II, 385; descent from the, II, 427; doctrine of the, I, 425; erection of the, II, 395; mocking of Jesus on the, II, 401
Crowning with thorns, II, 373
Crucifixion, the, II, 393: events following, II, 419
Cures, miraculous; *see* Miracles

Deaf-mute, cure of, I, 407
Death: of the Baptist, I, 376; of Jesus, II, 416
Debtor, the unjust (parable), I, 457
Decree of the Incarnation, I, 25
Dedication, feast of, II, 49
Demoniac in the synagogue, cure of, I, 232
Demoniacs, cure of blind and dumb, II, 1
Demoniacs of Gerasa, cure of, I, 357
Descent from the cross, II, 427
Desolation of Jesus on the cross, II, 410
Dinner in Pharisee's house, II, 61
Disciples of the Baptist: discussion about fasting, I, 253; dispute with the Jews, I, 208
Disciples of Emmaus, Christ's appearance to, II, 462
Disciples of Jesus: the first, I, 186; Jesus' prayer for His, II, 308; the seventy-two, I, 467
Draught of fishes, miraculous, I, 238; II, 474
Dropsical man, cure of, II, 61
Dumb and blind man, cure of, II, 1
Dumb man, cure of, I, 436

Ecce homo, II, 377
Eclipse of the sun, II, 408
Egypt, the flight into, I, 142
Elect, number of the, II, 54
Elizabeth, visitation by Mary, I, 93
Entry into Jerusalem, II, 164
Epiphany, the, I, 137
Escort of Christ on way to Calvary, II, 389
Espousals of Joseph and Mary, I, 102
Eternity, Jesus in, I, 20
Eucharist: institution of, II, 281; life of Jesus in the, II, 501; promise of the, I, 390
Example of virtue by Jesus, II, 238

Fall of man, I, 37
False prophets, warning against, II, 214
False teachers, warning against, I, 307
Farewell discourse, II, 288
Fasting: Christ's disciples accused of not, I, 253; discussion about, I, 253
Fig-tree (parable), II, 37
Fig-tree cursed, II, 170
Finding of Christ in the Temple, I, 147
Fishes, miraculous draught of, I, 238; II, 474
Fishing-net (parable), I, 343
Flight into Egypt, I, 142
Forgiveness of injuries, I, 457; II, 92
Forgiveness of sins by Christ, I, 324
Fortitude, Christ's, II, 252
Fraternal charity, I, 298
Fraternal correction, I, 454

Gabriel (angel), I, 63, 67
Galilee, Jesus' reception in, I, 220
Garden of Gethsemani, Jesus in, II, 318
Garments divided, Jesus', II, 399
Gentiles seeking Jesus, II, 204
Gerasens, country of the, I, 353
Gethsemani, Garden of: Jesus in, II, 318
God-Man's relations to creation, I, 31
Good Samaritan (parable), I, 477
Good shepherd (parable), I, 515
Good thief, the, II, 403

Great Council; *see* Sanhedrin
Great supper (parable), II, 67
Groat, the lost (parable), II, 76

Hatred, refraining from, I, 301
Heathenism and the Redeemer, I, 47
Herod, King, I, 142
Herod Antipas: attempt to intimidate Christ, II, 57; and Herodias, I, 211; Jesus before, II, 361
Herodians: conspiracy against Jesus, I, 270; leaven of the, I, 414
Herodias, Herod and, I, 376
Hidden life of Jesus, I, 159
Hidden treasure (parable), I, 347
Hierarchy, Christ and the, II, 524
Holy Ghost: operation of, II, 300; promise to send, II, 300
Holy Land; *see* Palestine
Holy women at the crucifixion, II, 405
Humility, practice of, I, 305
Husbandmen, the (parable), II, 179
Hypostatic union; *see* Incarnation

Imprisonment of the Baptist, I, 210
Impurity in thought, I, 304
Incarnation, the, 66
  annunciation of, I, 66
  decree of, I, 25
  effects of, I, 75
  mystery of, I, 73
  revelation of, I, 93
Indissolubility of marriage, II, 121
Infirm man, cure of the, 257
Injuries, forgiveness of, I, 457; II, 92
Innocents, the Holy, I, 142
Israel: and the Messias, I, 42; rejection of, II, 54

Jairus' daughter, raising of, I, 365
Jericho, Jesus in, II, 152
Jerusalem: destruction of, II, 212; entry into, II, 164
Jewish people, moral and religious condition of, I, 9
John (apostle) at the crucifixion, II, 405
John the Baptist
  appearance of, I, 165
  baptism of Christ by, I, 171
  baptism of penance by, I, 168
  beheading of, I, 376
  birth of, I, 98
  Christ's testimony to, I, 321
  circumcision of, I, 99
  conception of, I, 61
John the Baptist (*continued*)
  deputation to, I, 181
  disciples of, I, 206
  disciples' discussion about fasting, I, 253
  disciples' dispute with the Jews, I, 208
  Herod rebuked by, I, 376
  imprisonment of, I, 210
  messengers sent to Christ by, I, 318
  ministry of, I, 168
  preaching of, I, 165
  testimony to Christ, I, 165, 181, 184, 208
  youth of, I, 98
Jonas, sign of, II, 9
Joseph, St., I, 57: espousals of, I, 102; vocation of, I, 57
Joseph of Arimathea, II, 428
Journeys, Christ's: escort during, I, 332
Judas: at arrest of Jesus, II, 329; betrayal by, II, 263; Christ's prediction of betrayal by, II, 273; rebuke of Mary's anointing, II, 161; suicide of, II, 352
Judge, the unjust (parable), II, 116
Judgment, the Last, II, 215
Judgment, rash, I, 302

Kingdom of Christ, for or against, II, 33
Kingdom of God, coming of the, II, 113; *see also* Parables

Laborers in the vineyard (parable), II, 139
Lake Genesareth, appearance of risen Christ at, II, 472
Lamb, preparation of paschal, II, 267
Last Judgment, II, 215
Last Supper, II, 271
Lazarus, raising of, II, 94
Lazarus and rich man (parable), II, 88
Leaven (parable), II, 46
Leaven of Pharisees, I, 414; II, 17
Leper, cure of, I, 241
Lepers, cure of ten, II, 110
Leprosy, I, 242
Levi; *see* Matthew
Levirate marriage, II, 191
"Light of the world," I, 294: Jesus the, I, 501
Loaves, multiplication of, I, 380, 410
Lord's Prayer, the, I, 526
Lost groat (parable), II, 76

Lost sheep (parable), II, 76
Love of neighbor, I, 298
Lunatic boy, cure of, I, 436

Machaerus, castle of, I, 212
Magdalen; *see* Mary Magdalen
Magi, the, I, 137
Man, creation and fall of, I, 37
Man born blind, cure of, I, 508
Marriage: at Cana, I, 191; indissolubility of, II, 121; levirate, II, 191
Marriage feast (parable), II, 182
Martha and Mary, I, 482; II, 159
Mary (Blessed Virgin), I, 52
  espousals of, I, 102
  at Cana, I, 192
  Christ's appearance to her after the Resurrection, II, 449
  at the crucifixion, II, 405
  Jesus in the womb of, I, 89
  journey to Bethlehem, I, 105
  life of, I, 55, 91
  at Nazareth, I, 159
  predestination of, I, 52
  the visitation, I, 93
Mary and Martha, I, 482; II, 159
Mary Magdalen, I, 324: Jesus' appearance to, II, 458
Matthew: call of, I, 249; feast at house of, I, 251
Meditation, method of, I, viii
Meekness, I, 282
Merchants driven from Temple, I, 195; II, 173
Mercy, I, 286
Messianic preaching, I, 228
Messias: Christ asked whether He is the, II, 49; Israel and the, I, 42
Ministry, scenes and times of Christ's, I, 1
Miracles of Jesus, the, II, 233
Miracles of Jesus, list of
  calming of the tempest, I, 352; II, 474
  changing of water into wine, I, 191
  draught of fishes, I, 238
  Jesus walking on the water, I, 386
  multiplication of the loaves, I, 380, 410
  Peter walking on the water, I, 388
  raising of daughter of Jairus, I, 365
  raising of Lazarus, II, 94
  raising of widow's son at Naim, I, 315
  stater in fish's mouth, I, 442
Miracles of Jesus, cures: list of
  blind and dumb demoniac, II, 1
  blind man of Bethsaida, I, 418
  blind men of Capharnaum, I, 370
  blind men of Jericho, II, 149
  Canaanite woman's daughter, I, 403
  at Capharnaum, I, 236
  centurion's servant, I, 312
  crippled woman, II, 41
  deaf-mute, I, 407
  demoniac at Capernaum, I, 232
  demoniacs of Gerasa, I, 357
  dropsical man, II, 61
  dumb man, I, 436
  infirm man, I, 257
  leper, I, 241
  man born blind, I, 508
  man with withered hand, I, 269
  paralytic, I, 245
  paralytic at pool of Bethsaida, I, 257
  ruler's son, I, 222
  St. Peter's mother-in-law, I, 235
  ten lepers, II, 110
  various, I, 235
  woman with issue of blood, I, 362
Miraculous gifts, I, 447
Mocking of Jesus: II, 346, 373; on the cross, II, 401
Mount Olivet, agony on, II, 320
Multiplication of the loaves, I, 380, 410
Mustard-seed (parable), II, 44

Naim, widow's son raised to life, I, 315
Nazareth: hidden life at, I, 154; Jesus in synagogue of, I, 225; Jesus' life threatened at, I, 227; Mary's life at, I, 159
Nicodemus, I, 201; II, 427
Number of the elect, II, 54

Oaths, refraining from, I, 305
Obedience, Christ's, II, 238
Old Law, Jesus' relations to the, I, 295
Opening of Jesus' side, II, 423
Order at a feast (parable), II, 63
Original sin, I, 38
Our Father, the, I, 526

Paganism and the Redeemer, I, 47
Palestine description of, I, 1
Parables, list of
  cockle, I, 340
  fig-tree, II, 37

Parables (*continued*)
fishing net, I, 343
good Samaritan, I, 477
good shepherd, I, 515
great supper, II, 67
hidden treasure, I, 347
husbandmen, II, 179
laborers in the vineyard, II, 139
leaven, II, 46
lost groat, II, 76
lost sheep, II, 76
marriage-feast, II, 182
mustard-seed, II, 44
order at a feast, II, 63
pearl of great price, I, 347
Pharisee and publican, II, 118
porter, II, 224
pounds, II, 156
prodigal son, II, 80
rich man and Lazarus, II, 88
the seed, II, 47
sower and the seed, I, 335
talents, II, 226
ten virgins, II, 225
treasure in the field, I, 345
unjust debtor, I, 457
unjust judge, II, 116
unjust steward, II, 84
Paralytic, cure of, I, 245
Paralytic at pool of Bethsaida, cure of, I, 257
Pasch, first feast of the, I, 195
Paschal lamb, preparation of, II, 267
Paschal meal, II, 271
Passion, the, II, 258: prediction of, I, 425, 440; II, 143, 258
Patience, Christ's, II, 246
Pearl of great price (parable), I, 347
Penance, admonition to do, II, 38
Persecutions, prediction of, II, 208
Peter: confession of, I, 396, 419; walking on the water, I, 388
Peter's denial, II, 341
Peter's mother-in-law, cure of, I, 235
Peter's repentance, II, 344
Pharisee: and publican (parable), II, 118; question about the great commandment, II, 192
Pharisee's house, dinner in, I, 324; II, 61
Pharisees
accusation that Christ's disciples do not fast, I, 253
censured, II, 13, 193, 197
conspiracy against Jesus, I, 270
Pharisees (*continued*)
Jesus attacked by, I, 398; II, 3
leaven of the, I, 414; II, 17
repulse of, II, 193
on violation of the Sabbath, I, 266
Pharisees' attempt to intimidate Christ, II, 57
Piercing of Christ's side, II, 423
Pilate, trial before, II, 355, 364, 377
Pilate's efforts to save Jesus, II, 365
Place at table (parable), II, 63
Porter, the (parable), II, 224
Pounds, the ten (parable), II, 156
Poverty: apostolic, II, 27; Christ's practice of, II, 249; and riches, II, 134; voluntary, II, 134
Prayer: Christ's practice of, II, 242; instruction on, I, 522; perseverance in, II, 116
Preaching: Christ's, I, 230; Messianic, I, 228
Precedence, dispute about, I, 444
Prediction of persecutions, II, 208
Prediction of the Passion, I, 425, 440; II, 143, 258
Presentation of Jesus in the Temple, I, 123
Priesthood, institution of the, II, 284
Primacy promised to Peter, I, 419
Probatica (pond), cures at, I, 257
Prodigal son (parable), II, 80
Prophecies, Jesus in the, I, 37
Providence, divine, II, 24
Public life of Jesus, preparation for, I, 165
Public sinner, the, I, 324
Publicans, I, 250
Purification of Temple, I, 195; II, 173

Rash judgment, I, 302
Redeemer, heathen world and the, I, 47
Rejection of Israel, II, 54
Relatives, Jesus sought by His, I, 349
Religious state, Christ and the, II, 519
Renunciation of self, II, 71
Resurrection of Christ, II, 439: its revelation to His enemies, II, 446
Rich man and Lazarus (parable), II, 88
Rich young man, II, 129
Riches and poverty, II, 134
Risen Christ, appearances of
to the apostles in the cenacle, II, 466
at the Ascension, II, 484

Risen Christ (*continued*)
to disciples of Emmaus, II, 462
at Lake Genesareth, II, 472
to Magdalen, II, 458
to Mary, II, 449
on the mountain, II, 476
to Peter, II, 455
to Thomas, II, 469
Ruler of synagogue and Sabbath observance, II, 41
Ruler's son, cure of, I, 222

Sadducees, repulse of, II, 190
Saints, Christ and the, II, 529
"Salt of the earth," I, 293
Salvete, flores martyrum, I, 141
Samaria, Jesus in, I, 213, 459
Samaritan woman, the, I, 213
Sanhedrin: decision to kill Jesus, II, 105; Jesus before the, II, 335; Jesus condemned by, II, 348; Jesus' arrest ordered by, I, 495; sentence by, II, 348
Savior; *see* Redeemer
Scandal, warning against, I, 450; II, 92
Scourging, the, II, 370
Seed (parable), II, 47
Sellers driven from Temple, I, 195; II, 173
Sepulcher, the, II, 435: holy women at, II, 451; Peter and John at, II, 455
Sermon on the Mount, I, 277
Seventy-two disciples, I, 467
Sheep, the lost (parable), II, 76
Shepherds of Bethlehem, I, 115
Sichar, Jacob's well near, I, 214
Sign of Jonas, II, 9
Simeon, I, 124
Simplicity in speech, I, 304
Sin: original, I, 38; the unforgivable, II, 4
Sins, Christ's forgiveness of, I, 324
Solicitude, excessive, II, 24
Sons of Zebedee, II, 145
Sower and the seed (parable), I, 335
Stater in fish's mouth, I, 442
Steward, the unjust (parable), II, 84
Storm, calming of, I, 352
Sun, eclipse of, II, 408
Superior, office of, II, 30
Swearing, refraining from, I, 305
Synagogue: cure of infirm woman in, II, 41; Jesus in the, I, 225, 230, 269, 390; II, 41
Syrophenician woman, daughter of, I, 403

Tabernacles, Jesus at feast of, I, 459, 487
Talents, the (parable), II, 226
Tax-gatherers, I, 250
Teachers, warning against false, I, 307
Teaching, Jesus', I, 487; II, 228; traits of, I, 329
Tempest, stilling of the, I, 352
Temple: finding of Christ in the, I, 147; presentation of Christ in the, I, 123; purification of the, I, 195; II, 173
Temple tribute, I, 442
Temporal cares, excess of, II, 24
Temptation in the desert, I, 175
Ten lepers, cure of, II, 110
Testimony to Christ, the Baptist's, I, 165, 181, 184, 208
Thief, the good, II, 403
Thirst of Jesus on the cross, II, 414
Thomas (apostle), Christ's appearance to, II, 469
Title over the cross, II, 397
Tradition, dispute concerning, I, 398
Transfiguration, the, I, 430
Treason of Judas, II, 262
Treasure, hidden (parable), I, 345
Trial: before Caiphas, II, 335; before Pilate, II, 355, 364, 377
Tribute: coin of, II, 186; the Temple, I, 442

Unbelief, II, 255
Unforgivable sin, II, 4
Unjust debtor (parable), I, 457
Unjust judge (parable), II, 116
Unjust steward (parable), II, 84

Virginity, II, 121
Virgins, the ten (parable), II, 225
Virtues, apostolic, II, 92
Visitation, the, I, 93

Walking on the water, I, 386, 388
Washing of apostles' feet, II, 277
Widow of Naim, raising of son of, I, 315
Widow's mite, II, 202
Withered hand, cure of man with, I, 269
Woman taken in adultery, I, 497

Woman who called Mary blessed, II, 6
Woman with issue of blood, cure of, I, 362
Women at the sepulcher, II, 451
World, Christ and the, II, 533
Youth of Jesus, I, 66

Zachary, annunciation to, I, 61
Zacheus, II, 152
Zeal, Christ's, II, 240
Zebedee, ambition of sons of, II, 145